ACKNOWLEDGMENTS

I gratefully acknowledge the valuable specialist assistance of (in alphabetical order):

Don Batten, Ph.D. (plant physiology, researcher into the boundaries of the created kind, editor of *The Answers Book*)

John Baumgardner, Ph.D. (geophysicist and leading plate tectonics modeler)

Danny Faulkner, Ph.D. (tenured astronomy professor at the University of South Carolina, Lancaster)

David Graves, M.Th., Ph.D. candidate in Hebrew (Department Fellow in Old Testament, 2003–2005, Trinity Evangelical Divinity School)

Russell Humphreys, Ph.D. (nuclear physicist, author of *Starlight and Time, Evidence for a Young World*)

Doug Kelly, Ph.D. (systematic theologian, author of *Creation and Change*)

Terry Mortenson, Ph.D. (history of geology, thesis on the 19th century scriptural geologists)

Robert Newton, Ph.D. candidate in astrophysics

Mike Oard, M.S. (atmospheric science, author of *An Ice Age Caused by the Genesis Flood* and *Ancient Ice Ages or Gigantic Submarine Landslides?*)

Tas Walker, Ph.D. (engineering, geology, research on the fallacies of radiometric dating)

John Woodmorappe, B.A., M.S. (biologist and geologist, author of *Noah's Ark: A Feasibility Study, Studies in Flood Geology,* and *The Mythology of Modern Dating Methods*); contributor to much of chapter 8

Thanks also to Russell Grigg, M.Sc.; Kym Holwerda; and Carl Wieland, M.B., B.S., for proofreading the manuscript.

REFUTING
COMPROMISE

REFUTING COMPROMISE

A Biblical and Scientific Refutation of
"Progressive Creationism" (Billions of Years)
As Popularized by Astronomer Hugh Ross

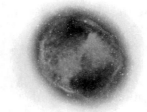

Jonathan Sarfati, Ph.D.,

Author of *Refuting Evolution* & *Refuting Evolution 2*

Master
Books

First printing: March 2004

Copyright © 2004 by Jonathan Sarfati. All rights reserved. No part of this book may be used or reproduced in any manner whatsoever without written permission of the publisher, except in the case of brief quotations in articles and reviews. For information write: Master Books, Inc., P.O. Box 726, Green Forest, AR 72638.

ISBN: 0-89051-411-9
Library of Congress Number: 2003116029

Cover by Farewell Communications

Printed in the United States of America

Please visit our website for other great titles:
www.masterbooks.net

For information regarding author interviews,
please contact the publicity department at (870) 438-5288.

TABLE OF CONTENTS

Foreword 9

Introduction 13

1: The Authority of Scripture 35

2: The Days of Creation 67

3: The History of Interpretation of Genesis 1–11 107

4: The Order of Creation.. 141

5: The Big Bang and Astronomy 147

6: The Origin of Death and Suffering.. 195

7: The Created Kinds 225

8: The Global Flood and Noah's Ark 241

9: The History of Mankind 287

10: "Biblical" Old-Age Arguments.. 321

11: Science and the Young Earth 331

12: Refuting Old-Earth Arguments 367

Conclusion and Summary 389

Subject Index.. 397

Name Index... 401

Scripture Index 405

About the Author 415

In John Bunyan's beloved *Pilgrim's Progress*, there is a wonderful character, "Mr. Valiant for Truth." His heart and zeal for God's truth are like those of Dr. Jonathan Sarfati, whose valor for scriptural truth has never been needed more by the Church than at this hour.

When we consider the foundational importance of Genesis to the whole structure of Christian truth, it is not surprising that the forces of unbelief have generally made their first attacks on this primal doctrine (which shows us who God is, who we are, what our problem is, and God's solution to that problem). As the humanistic theories of the European Enlightenment gained ever more ground after the 1650s, the intellectual classes of Western society were convinced (by the early 1800s) that the world was vastly older than indicated by the Bible. And by the mid-19th century, Charles Darwin, building on this skepticism concerning the plain teaching of Genesis on earth's age, was able to go massively further with his theory of mega-evolution.

Dr. Nigel Cameron has shown how quickly theologians and biblical commentators abandoned the traditional interpretation of Genesis in order to be accepted by the burgeoning "scientific" consensus of the late 19th and early 20th centuries. (Actually, there was far more resistance to an ancient age of the world and to organic evolution from several geologists and scientists than from theologians, but the culture already had its mind made up; empirical arguments were ignored or discounted.)

The reign of evolution/long-age theory was a major factor in turning Western culture from Christianity to naturalistic humanism in the first half of the 20th century. Most of the churches did not really escape this evolutionary world view. "Higher critical" theories of Scripture assumed evolutionary development and negated supernatural revelation, shredding the normal understanding of biblical truth-claims. Because so many ministers and priests were educated in Christian institutions that nearly always (in the event of a conflict) accommodated the Bible to current "scientific" claims, rather than such claims to the Bible, the church was enfeebled. And it was largely unable to offer a viable alternative to the evolutionary humanism which eviscerated traditional Christianity at its Genesis roots. (Part of my own higher education was in one such institution.)

But we have seen substantial changes since the birth of the modern creationist movement in the early 1960s. Hundreds of professional scientists in many different fields have "come on board" over the last 40 years, and the numbers who accept the Genesis paradigm of creation, as opposed to evolution/long ages, show no sign of abatement. Such a scientist is Dr. Jonathan Sarfati, whom I had the pleasure of meeting some years ago in Australia.

Even though evolutionary theory has been wounded far more severely than it likes to admit by the empirical pressure brought against it these last decades, many true Christians are still uneasy over taking a clear stand. Especially is this the case with the conflict between the two paradigms on the age of the earth.

But if we accept parts of Genesis (for example, God is the absolute intelligent Designer), but deny other parts (such as the entrance of struggle, decay, and death through the sin of Adam, as well as the time value of the biblical genealogies), we are like a man trying to stand firm with each foot on different rowboats going down a churning river. And if we go against the plain teaching of the Bible in one area, then how can we seriously ask others to accept the parts that are currently acceptable to us?

This is why I deem Jonathan Sarfati's *Refuting Compromise* to be of such pivotal importance for overcoming the present confusion on Genesis and science among many Christians who wish to expound faithfully and intelligibly the scriptural texts. I think what he has accomplished in this truth-packed (yet understandable) volume is to take us a long step further in supplanting the failed evolutionary/long-age paradigm by the one taught in Scripture.

In order to achieve this, Dr. Sarfati has had to critique fellow Christians, who feel that scientific facts (as on the ancient age of the cosmos) force them to pick and choose from both competing paradigms. This had led some of them to very arcane interpretations of Genesis, whereby the plain meaning as it has always been understood by the Church has been turned upside-down to fit assumptions in the evolutionary paradigm (for instance, they deny that sin brought death to the entire cosmos). Dr. Sarfati does not for a moment wish to deny their sincerity, character, or faith. I join him in the hope that his book ("straight" though it is) will lead to frank but charitable debates over competing interpretations.

Dr. Sarfati calls on Christian scholars to work gladly within a framework that presupposes the truth of God's written Word, to use their reason ministerially, and to know carefully the difference between empirical facts of operational science and the speculative claims of origins science. With all of this in mind, he tackles head-on the remaining differences between creationist scientists and those who feel it necessary to accept major parts of the evolutionary framework, and thereby re-interpret the plain teaching of Scripture accordingly.

Dr. Sarfati's "valor for truth" shines brightly as, with crystal clarity, he works through the often convoluted arguments of those opposed to a plain reading of Genesis in both the scriptural and scientific arenas.

A distinguished professor of Princeton (then Westminster), Dr. Robert Dick Wilson, said (in the context of Old Testament criticism): "I have not avoided the hard questions." This painstaking, luminous, and valiant volume will show that this is also true of Dr. Jonathan Sarfati. His work provides some of the most convincing answers I have so far seen.

Douglas F. Kelly B.A., M.Div., Ph.D. (Edinburgh)
Jordan Professor of Systematic Theology
Reformed Theological Seminary
Charlotte, North Carolina

INTRODUCTION

WHY IS THIS BOOK NEEDED?

Dr. Hugh Norman Ross (b. 1945) is a Canadian astronomer who is now best known for his ostensibly Christian apologetics ministry, Reasons to Believe, which is based in California. This ministrypurports to give Christians scientific evidence to support the Bible and answer anti-Christian arguments by skeptics. This ministry coordinates his many speaking engagements and publishes a newsletter called *Facts and Faith*. Ross has written a number of popular-level books on the Bible, science, and apologetics (see pages 27–28 for abbreviations).

Surely, Christians should support Ross's professed aim to reconcile the Bible and science, shouldn't they? Especially with so much propaganda claiming that science and Christianity are opposed. Ross is even a staunch opponent of Darwinian evolution and proclaims there is irrefutable scientific evidence for a creator. Further, Ross proclaims to believe that Genesis is literal history, not myth or allegory, and that the Bible is the inerrant Word of God. It is not surprising then that many Christian leaders have written glowing endorsements of his ideas, and NavPress has published his books.

Sadly, some people endorsed Ross's books without even reading them thoroughly, but as a favor to friends. This is a most unfortunate, if not irresponsible, use of prestige with the Christian public. Some noted Christian leaders, out of friendship to the editor and also to the pastor of Dr. Ross, recommended his book *Creation and Time* without really having worked through its content. Thus, their stance on creation is not necessarily that of his book. One of them, before January 1998, withdrew his endorsement of it.

Ross was also featured in the June 2003 cover story of the leading Pentecostal magazine *Charisma*, by Andy Butcher, *Charisma*'s senior writer and news director.[1]

---

1. A. Butcher, "He Sees God in the Stars," *Charisma* (June 2003): p. 38–44.
   J. Sarfati "Shame on *Charisma*!" <www.answersingenesis.org/rosspc>, May 29, 2003.

However, when Ross's claims are examined, we find that many times he does not allow Scripture to speak for itself, but, rather, reinterprets Scripture in line with secular "science." So while Ross proclaims he is "anti-evolution," in the sense that he denies that one kind of creature can change into another, he accepts almost every other aspect of evolutionary "science," even when it disagrees with the plain teaching of Genesis. And while Ross professes to believe that Genesis is literal history, this history seems vastly different from the literal text. As shown in the table on the following page, his view is often called "progressive creation," and can be contrasted with the views of Answers in Genesis, which we believe are derived from a careful and hermeneutically consistent reading of the Bible. His own preferred term for himself, "day-age creationist," explicitly reflects the second line in the table. This will be shown in an addendum to this introduction, which is our comment on the differences *as understood by Ross himself.*

Others have written in response to Ross, including Mark Van Bebber's and Paul Taylor's excellent point-by-point rebuttal of *Creation and Time,*[2] but for some reason it hasn't received the attention it deserves. Ross has never answered the main points raised, and still repeats the same errors. The best Reasons to Believe could do was publish a somewhat weak review by a political scientist, which basically attacked the messenger rather than evaluating the message.[3]

Some of Ross's books have been the subject of public reviews,[4] but they also seem to have had minimal effect on Ross's teachings, in the sense that he keeps repeating the same errors. Hence, it was necessary to write a comprehensive book to show that the propositions on the left side of the table on the following page are simply not possible to reconcile with the Bible, and that there is no justification in true science for them either.

Ross Overextends His Areas of Competence

While one can appreciate Dr. Ross's enthusiasm in debate, it unfortunately predisposes him at times to make pronouncements in areas where he lacks expertise. This can have an unhelpful affect on Christians who assume that he is really knowledgeable in all the areas he so willingly addresses.

For instance, in arguing against the young-earth view, Dr. Ross at times resorts to technicalities of the Hebrew language. But this has landed him in trouble more than once, as when he tried to discredit the common biblical creationist identification of

2. M. Van Bebber and P.S. Taylor, *Creation and Time: A Report on the Progressive Creationist Book by Hugh Ross,* Eden Productions, Mesa, AZ, 1994, online at <www.christiananswers.net/paradise/ctb-alt.html>.

3. M. Clark, "A Review of Mark Van Bebber's and Paul S. Taylor's *A Report on the Progressive Creationist Book by Hugh Ross,*" <www.reasons.org/resources/apologetics/review_progcreat.shtml?main>, May 23, 2003.

4. J.D. Sarfati, "Expos of NavPress's New Hugh Ross Book: *The Genesis Question,*" *TJ* 13(2):22–30 (1999); <www.answersingenesis.org/ross_GQ>.

   D. Faulkner, "The Dubious Apologetics of Hugh Ross," *TJ,* 13(2):52–60 (1999); <www.answersingenesis.org/ross_apol>.

HUGH ROSS	ANSWERS IN GENESIS
The earth and universe are billions of years old.	The earth and universe are about 6,000 years old.
The days of creation were really vast ages.	The days of creation were ordinary days.
The sun and stars were created before the earth, and merely "appeared" to a hypothetical observer on earth on the fourth "day."	The sun and stars were created on day 4, after the earth (created on day 1).
The seventh day is still continuing, supported by the alleged "fact" of no new species arising in the last 10,000 years.	The seventh day was also about 24 hours long. Some populations become reproductively isolated (unable to interbreed) today, which, *by definition*, means that a new species is formed.
Animals were eating each other, dying from natural disasters, and suffering from many diseases, for millions of years before mankind existed.	Creation was originally "very good," while death, suffering, and disease ultimately are the result of Adam's sin, which resulted in God's curse upon His creation.
God created almost all species separately.	God created comparatively few "kinds," and many "species" are the results of non-information increasing diversification of the created gene-pools, especially after the Flood.
God created Adam 60,000 to 10,000 years ago [this range incorporates the possibility that Adam post-dates Aboriginals' arrival in Australia, "dated" 40,000 years ago]. Neandertals were not true humans but soulless hominids.	God created Adam about 6,000 years ago. Neandertals, like *Homo erectus*, are fossils of true humans who descended from Adam, and likely lived shortly after Babel.
The order in the fossils is a record of distinct ages with vastly different creatures existing, all the results of separate creative acts by God over periods of time.	Much of the fossil "order" reflects the different stages of burial in a worldwide Flood and subsequent local catastrophes, as well as different ecosystems.
Noah's flood was restricted to the Mesopotamian river valley.	Noah's flood covered the entire globe.
God had to intervene supernaturally to produce the different racial characteristics, to help the people separate *at* Babel.	Adam and Eve had the genetic information to give rise to all the different "races" (people groups) today, allowing for non-information-gaining mutations. The racial characteristics arose after small people groups became separated *after* Babel.

behemoth in Job 40:15 ff. with a sauropod, because he believes the dinosaurs became extinct 65 million years ago. Ross writes (GQ:48): *"The Hebrew word for "behemoth" appears in its plural form, behema. . . ."* However, even beginners in Hebrew know that *"–a"* is often a feminine singular and *"–oth"* is a feminine plural.

So Ross got it back-to-front: *behema* is the singular form, while *behemoth* is grammatically plural. It is a figure of speech known as an *intensive plural* or *plural of majesty*, where "the referent is a singular individual, which is, however, so thoroughly characterized by the qualities of the noun that a plural is used,"[5] "beast of beasts." The context indicates that *behemoth* is the largest beast God made. And Job 40:17 says, *"His tail sways like a cedar,"* which certainly doesn't fit Ross's suggestion of a hippopotamus (unless the reference was to a bonsai cedar, maybe!).

SCOPE OF THIS BOOK

This critique concentrates mostly on Ross's books, rather than his audio recordings and website, since books are an incontrovertible record of his teachings and have presumably been double-checked. Conversely, there is more chance of making a mere slip in speaking, and internet articles are very open to change in content and address.

The main exceptions are:

- Dr. Ross's widely publicized debate with Dr. Kent Hovind on the John Ankerberg Show in October 2000. I critiqued this in detail at <www.answersingenesis.org/ross_hovind>, and some of the points are relevant to this book in several places.

- *Life and Death in Eden, The Biblical and Scientific Evidence for Animal Death before the Fall*, 2001, audio cassette series. This is described as a "round table discussion by Ross and his Reasons to Believe staffers: theologian Kenneth Samples; biologist Fazale Rana; Marj Harman, described as a lay apologist; and Krista Bontrager as moderator and theologian." Chapter 6 shows the flaws in this.

- "RTB Critique of RATE Project," Reasons to Believe radio broadcast, September 18, 2003, 6 to 8 p.m. Pacific time. Moderator: Krista Bontrager; studio participants: Hugh Ross, Fazale Rana, and Marge Harmon; telephone participant: Roger Wiens. Archived at: <www.oneplace.com/ministries/creation_update/Archives.asp> Chapters 11 and 12 deal with the mistakes in this program.

Also, we note the Latin saying *scripta manent*, meaning, "What is written, stands," with the implication, "unless rescinded, equally in writing." Therefore, this book will hold Ross to errors in his books unless retracted in writing. It would be inadequate for him to claim that he has retracted a claim or answered a point in some audio recording somewhere, and demand that his opponents wade through hours of talks by him or his assistants.

---

5. B.K. Waltke and M. O'Connor, *An Introduction to Biblical Hebrew Syntax* (Winona Lake, IN: Eisenbrauns, 1990), p. 122.

Book Outline

The reason this book starts with the topic of the authority of the Bible (chapter 1) is that the most fundamental disagreement between young-earth creationists (YECs) and Ross and his followers (and really all other varieties of theistic evolutionists and old-earth creationists) is *authority*. AiG maintains that God's infallible Word, the Bible, must be our ultimate authority. **This means that Scripture must judge man's fallible theories about the past, not vice versa.** It is our contention that Ross elevates "science" to the level of Scripture, and, in practice, puts science above Scripture by reinterpreting Scripture to fit his idea of science, all the time claiming that his approach is scriptural. So the first chapter explains why Scripture should be authoritative, and why Ross's approach is inconsistent with Scripture. It also documents how evangelicals who disagree with 24-hour creation days acknowledge that the text teaches this, but disagree primarily because they are intimidated by so-called "science," which they believe teaches differently. Science should not be dismissed, but it must be kept in its proper ministerial role as a servant to the Bible, and never placed in a magisterial role over and above the Bible.

Once the Bible is established as foundational, the next step is to determine what it teaches on the areas of contention. Then it's possible to show how true science can illuminate and clarify some teachings. But this can never mean reinterpreting it as the opposite of what it says and how it has always been understood.

Therefore, chapter 2 covers the days of creation, showing that they were 24 hours long. It addresses a number of objections, as well as briefly dealing with other compromise views: the gap theory and framework hypothesis. I also explain the correct meaning and application of "literal" interpretation, showing that Ross is using a very non-literal meaning of "literal"!

Chapter 3 shows how the overwhelming view of the majority of exegetes throughout church history has been that the days were 24 hours long, and that even those who disagreed believed that the earth was less than 6,000 years old at the time of writing. Long-age interpretations of the Bible arose only after these ideas became popular in "science" and conservative exegetes tried to bring Scripture into line. But liberals, with no motivation to defend the authority of Scripture, kept the traditional interpretation, mistakenly believing that it was proof of error in the Bible.

Chapter 4 is a short one, showing that the order of creation in Genesis cannot be reconciled with long-age beliefs. In particular, this deals with the kinds of creatures created on days 3, 5, and 6 (including dinosaurs) and the astronomical objects created on day 4. Then we address Ross's restrictions on the types of creatures created during creation week, and his "order" of creation of creatures and heavenly bodies. Indeed, for an earlier influential day-age advocate, Davis Young, this was a major factor in his repudiation of the day-age view in favor of one that disregards Genesis as historical at all.

Chapter 5 covers the big-bang theory, which has always been foundational to Ross's biblical exegesis. A number of scientific problems for the big bang are analyzed, and evolutionary theories of galaxy, star, and planet formation are found severely wanting. Also, Ross's apologetics with the big-bang and "string theory" are found problematic, as well as unnecessary. In their place, alternative apologetics schemes are provided. Finally, alternative cosmological models are presented that line up with the Bible.

Chapter 6 is about the origin of sin and death. This shows that the Bible teaches that death and suffering began with the Fall. Also, this death must include physical death, not just "spiritual death." Some of the passages explicitly refer only to human death, but even this is a problem because evolutionists "date" fossils of modern humans as earlier than Ross's dates for Adam. But the death of vertebrate animals, classified as *nephesh chayyah* along with humans, also dates from the Fall. This is shown by the original vegetarian diet and the fact that this will be restored. The biblical teaching of sin-death causality is, with pun intended, the death knell for any long-age compromise.

Chapter 7 outlines the biblical creation model in detail, explaining the "created kinds." This also exposes much of the misinformation by both evolutionists and Ross that any variation or "speciation" is evolution. The vital concept of *genetic information* is the key — evolution from goo to you via the zoo requires an *increase* in information, while variation and speciation are the result of *sorting* and *loss* of information. Therefore, this refutes Ross's charge that creationists believe in super-rapid evolution.

Chapter 8 shows that the flood of Genesis was global, and how this is the only possible understanding from Scripture. Ross's ostensibly biblical arguments are refuted, as are supposedly scientific arguments. In fact, the geological record makes more sense if we interpret it as the result of recent catastrophic processes. Ross believes in a local Flood in Mesopotamia, but this is shown to be unworkable because of the nature of the Genesis account, as well as the fact that the Mesopotamian geography cannot support a huge wall of water for a year. The feasibility of the ark's stability and ability to hold all land vertebrate kinds is demonstrated. Ross's arguments about the ark's cargo in a global Flood scenario, mostly identical to those raised in the past by unbelievers, are shown to be straw men. Ross's errors here follow from his errors about the biblical kinds discussed in the previous chapter. This, in turn, arises largely from his belief that the seventh day is still continuing.

Chapter 9 outlines the history of mankind according to the Bible, starting from the creation of Adam and Eve about 6,000 years ago. This date is shown by the genealogies of Genesis 5 and 11, which are shown to have no gaps, and the fact that Jesus said that humans were male and female "from the beginning of creation" (Mark 10:6) shows that this was close to the creation of the universe. Then Adam fell and brought death into the world, and his progeny descended into such depths of evil that they were judged by a worldwide Flood. The Fall and Flood are covered in previous chapters. Noah and his family were saved on the ark, and their descendants disobeyed God's command to fill the earth, so their languages were confused at Babel.

The division of humanity into their separate populations resulted in different "races," or preferably *people groups*, by a natural process of separation of gene pools. However, because of Ross's misunderstanding of variation within a kind, he erroneously believes that God's intervention at Babel included direct creation of different human "racial" characteristics. After Babel, some of these groups became isolated from civilization, so they resorted to living in caves and using stone tools. Some of these isolated populations developed different characteristics and resulted in people we call Neandertals and *Homo erectus*. Ross believes that Neandertals predated Adam and were not true humans but soulless hominids. Ross's faulty dating of Adam would imply that the Australian Aborigines may not have been his descendants, which would make them non-human, under his own criteria.

Chapter 10 is a short one, refuting Ross's supposedly biblical arguments for an age of the earth of billions of years. It also shows how the Bible could have taught vast ages (but didn't), if that were what God had intended to teach.

Chapter 11 explains the philosophy behind "dating" measurements by processes that change over time, contrasted with the superior method of relying on trustworthy eyewitness accounts. Then it is shown that, even given uniformitarian/evolutionary assumptions, there are a number of processes in the earth and solar system that point to an "age" far younger than the billions of years proclaimed by Ross.

Chapter 12 refutes some of the alleged scientific evidence for an old earth. A number of geological objections to recent creation, for example, varves and fossil forests, are shown to make more sense under a framework of recent catastrophism. This chapter also demonstrates that radiometric dating methods rely on assumptions that are questionable. And, indeed, evolutionists question the assumptions frequently, whenever radiometric dating methods give conflicting dates or fail on rocks of known age.

Note: Because this book is written for a wide range of readership, I have put some more technical or peripheral sections in shaded boxes.

Why Write Such a "Negative" Book?

Something more must be said about why the approach in this book is necessary. In one sense, this is written with a heavy heart, and with the overriding emphasis that our intention is not personal attack. Our mandate is to defend the faith and the authority of Scripture. We have long believed that (and explained why) one of the most dangerous attacks on biblical authority in evangelical circles today is not evolution but "progressive creationism," and we aim to prove this conclusively in this book. This widespread compromise with the plain words of Scripture is capable of immense harm, precisely because it is proclaimed as being done in the name of upholding Scripture. The issue is so vital, as it involves the way we handle the very Word of God. Hopefully, the reader will see why this is no mere "side issue" or an example of a "critical spirit" toward someone who just happens to have a different (by implication legitimate) exegetical view. We need to be like the Bereans, commended by Paul in Acts 17:11, checking the Scriptures about all such matters.

Biblical Basis

Rebuke of False Teachers

The problem in exposing fallacious teaching is that it also undermines the credibility of the source of the teaching, and this is perhaps why some have said AiG is being too "personal" in our analyses of Ross's teachings. It might be helpful if such critics were to specify in detail just where they have found the material to be too personal, or how the fallacious teaching of Ross can be decisively exposed without offending feelings. It is a very difficult thing to expose error without hurting the person's feelings, because matters of reputation, pride, and the like are at stake. However, because Dr. Ross has made such fallacious and Bible-undermining arguments in public, our response must also be public. This book will major on Ross's teachings, not his person, concentrating on the issues. However, the following shaded section shows that there is a biblical precedent for far sharper criticism than I or Answers in Genesis will resort to.

Jesus often rebuked His opponents. For example, Matthew 23:27:

Woe to you, scribes and Pharisees, hypocrites! for you are like whitewashed tombs, which outwardly appear beautiful, but within they are full of dead men's bones and all uncleanness.

His chosen Apostles *often* rebuked false teachers — the apostle Paul even opposed the apostle Peter when he was carrying away others with his hypocrisy (Gal. 2:11 ff.). Also, Paul *commanded* Timothy to rebuke error (2 Tim. 4:2), and 2 Corinthians 10:4–5 says, "We demolish arguments and every pretension that sets itself up against the knowledge of God."

Sometimes false beliefs were even mocked, for example, Elijah with the prophets of Baal in 1 Kings 18:27, for the greater good of exposing their destructive influence.

Biblical Word Plays

Some of the word plays in the Bible are deliberate mocking of some person or system that sets itself up against God's revelation. Genesis 11:9 says:

Therefore its name was called Babel, because there the LORD confused the language of all the earth; and from there the LORD scattered them abroad over the face of all the earth.

Some skeptics accuse the Bible of error here, because *Babili* means "gate of the gods"; *balal* means confusion. But, there is no error at all — the word play was *intentional*. While the rebels at Babel pretentiously thought they could make a tower to heaven, God puts their pathetic effort into its true perspective — it would be remembered only for the confusion of languages.

Another possible example is the name Nebuchadnezzar. Some skeptics claim that this is an error, and that the "correct" spelling is –rezzar. Indeed, this is the normal

Hebrew adaptation from the original Akkadian version, *nabu-kudurru-usur*, meaning "Nabu protect(s) the eldest son," after the Babylonian god Nabu. One theory for the difference is that it was normal Hebrew linguistic practice to change the *r* to an *n*.[6] But van Selms proposed another theory, that the OT's *–nezzar* spelling *may* be derived from a snide reference to Nebuchadnezzar's lycanthropy (animal behavior) by Jewish opposition groups. That is, from *nabu-kudanu-usur*, meaning "Nabu protect(s) the mule."[7]

Challenge-riposte paradigm

Some well-meaning Christians claim that any rebuke is "unloving" (see next section), as do some skeptics who try to neutralize Christian opposition! When confronted by the examples in the previous section, these same Christians try to evade the force of these examples by claiming, "Jesus was God, so He had the authority and a moral right to say these things. So did God's Apostles, as well as Elijah when he mocked the prophets of Baal. We do not have either of these."

But this fails to realize the historical context. Modern western culture is engulfed in political correctness with a victim culture, where we simply mustn't offend members of liberal-appointed victim classes. But ancient *public* forums, and some modern ones, were often conducted under a *challenge-riposte paradigm*. In the New Testament cultural milieu, "the game of challenge-riposte is a central phenomenon, and one that must be played out in public."[8]

The object of each party was to try to undermine the honor, or social status, of the other in an exchange that "answers in equal measure or ups the ante (and thereby challenges in return)."[9] Instead of merely defending himself, an honorable man in that culture would counterattack.

We see countless examples in the Gospels where Jesus refuses to defend himself, and instead shifts the debate by a counter-question, and insults if necessary. For example, in Matthew 21:23–27, Mark 11:27–33, and Luke 20:1–8, Jesus entered the temple, and the chief priests and elders confronted Him and demanded to know by what authority He acted. Jesus responded with a counter-question about John the Baptist. When they refused to answer Him, Jesus refused to answer them, which was an insult.

In Matthew 22:15–22, Mark 12:13–17, and Luke 20:20–26, Herodians and Pharisees plotted together to ask Jesus about paying taxes, trying to trap him in a dilemma of either disloyalty to His fellow Jews or sedition against Rome. Jesus again poses a counter-question about the owner of the coin. His famous concluding statement, "Give to Caesar what is Caesar's and to God what is God's" was a further attack on the hypocrisy and disloyalty of his opponents.

---

6. A.R. Millard, "Daniel 1–6 and History," *EQ* 49:67–73 (1977).

7. J.E. Goldingay, *Daniel* (Dallas, TX: Word Books, 1989).

8. R.L. Rohrbaugh and B.J. Malina, "Social Science Commentary on the Synoptics," *Fortress* (June 1993): p. 42.

9. Ibid.

Another example is Matthew 12:5:

> Or have you not read in the Law, how that on the sabbath days the priests in the temple profane the Sabbath, and are blameless?

Most people overlook that Jesus' question "Have you not read. . . ?" was a huge insult to His Pharisaic opponents. Obviously, they had read them, and they were the acknowledged experts in the Bible. So this question undermined their authority in the area they were supposed to know best. It would be just like asking Ross if he understands simple astronomy. It was basically calling them foolish, unable to read what was in front of them, not having done proper study. But once again, in the challenge-riposte paradigm, this was appropriate in the public forum. It was a response to the honor challenge laid down by the Pharisees, who challenged Jesus on the behavior of His disciples. Jesus ups the ante by implying their ignorance of Scripture, attacking them in the very place where they most prided themselves.

There are many other places where Jesus "evidences considerable skill at riposte and thereby reveals himself to be an honorable and authoritative prophet."[10]

"Love your enemies" (Matthew 5:44)

The biblical word "love" in this passage is the verb αγαπαω (agapaō), related to the noun αγαπη (agapē). This word "is not a matter of sentiment and emotion but concrete action and practical concern."[11] The NT in general uses agapē to refer to the "value of group attachment and group bonding," and it "will have little to do with feelings of affection, sentiments of fondness, and warm, glowing affinity."[12]

There is also the issue of needing to love those who are being, and will be, led astray by false teaching. Clearly, from the above, agapē did not preclude discrediting and refuting enemies of the truth as opposed to personal enemies. In some cases, agapē corresponds to today's "tough love."

This is never a simple issue, and the "whole counsel of God" (Acts 20:27) needs to be taken into account. People will find, if the proposed public forum with Dr. Ross comes off (see page 24), that there will be no personal animosity or anything unloving exhibited by AiG personnel. The issue never has been personal, and love (as indicated above) is at the forefront.

Avoid Those Who Cause Divisions?

Romans 16:17 says, "Now I beseech you, brethren, mark those who cause divisions and offenses . . . and avoid them," and some have used this against YECs. But they fail to cite the clause in this passage which defines what Paul meant by causing divisions

---

10. R.L. Rohrbaugh and B.J. Malina, "Social Science Commentary on the Synoptics," *Fortress* (June 1993): p. 42.

11. D. Hill, *Gospel of Matthew* (Grand Rapids, MI: Wm. B. Eerdmans Publishing Co., reprint edition, 1981), p. 130.

12. B.J. Malina, and J.H. Neyrey, *Portraits of Paul: An Archaeology of Ancient Personality* (Louisville, KY: Westminster John Knox Press, 1996).

(*dichostasia*) and offenses (*skandalon*) — it is bringing teachings "*contrary to the doctrine which you have learned.*" As we show, it is those who compromise on a straightforward reading of Genesis that are bringing doctrines contrary to those the Apostles taught, and that the church has understood through most of its 2,000-year history. It's interesting, too, that the Reformers, like Martin Luther, who reasserted the authority of Scripture and salvation by grace through faith alone, were also accused of being "divisive."

Double Standards?

One must also wonder why some people who complain about YEC style never seem to complain when Dr. Ross attacks the "young earth" perspective, which seems to be the whole *raison d'être* of his ministry, Reasons to Believe. Is this not "divisive," too? For example, Ross made an inflammatory comparison of young-earth creationists with some heretics that the apostle Paul anathematized in the Book of Galatians:

> Much as circumcision divided the first-century church, I see the creation date issue dividing the church of this century. As circumcision distorted the gospel and hampered evangelism, so, too, does young-earth creationism (C&T:162).

Ross also resorted to an unworthy attack on the great scholar Archbishop Ussher (see p. 127ff), whose circle of admirers included Sir Isaac Newton.

More recently, *Charisma* cited Ross, with approval, when he claimed that YEC views "encourage a form of Gnosticism."[13] Ross justified this on the grounds that YECs "believe only the Bible is trustworthy, not the physical realm." Regardless, he is comparing YECs to an outright heresy the early Church fought and beat, and *Charisma* applauds it. He had said the same thing earlier, along with Gleason Archer, in his section of the book *The Genesis Debate: Three Views on the Days of Creation.*[14] This was written after the Ross/Archer charge that YEC proponents deny physical reality, forcing a "gnostic-like theology," in their words. It is written under the subtitle, *The Gnostic Factor*.

> Although young-earth/young-universe creationists assume that they truly seek to defend the truth of God's Word and lead people to Jesus Christ, they fail to realize that these theological implications flow from their position. We think that they would repudiate the gnostic notion that "there is no life, truth, or substance in matter," though unfortunately that's the direction in which their view leans. According to Scripture, it's a potentially dangerous direction since God calls all of His creation "good," and since, after the Fall, all of us sin in the physical realm. Even more significantly, the assertion that

---

13. A. Butcher, "He Sees God in the Stars," *Charisma* (June 2003): p. 38–44.
   J. Sarfati "Shame on *Charisma*!" <www.answersingenesis.org/rosspc>, May 29, 2003.
14. D.G. Hagopian, *The Genesis Debate* (Mission Viejo, CA: Crux Press, 2001).
   A.S. Kulikovsky, "Sizing the Day: Review of Hagopian," *TJ* 16(1):41–44 (2002); <www.answersingenesis.org/Gen_Debate>.

matter is devoid of life and truth is then falsified by the fact that our Lord became a man — took on matter as the way, the truth, and the life — to save us from our sin. To deny life, truth, and substance to matter is, at a minimum, to deny the biblical doctrines of creation, sin, Christ, and salvation. Ultimately, this view denies the Bible itself.[15]

This is an even more inflammatory way of implying that the YEC view is tantamount to a denial of the Bible and Christ. Judging by the way that some YEC critics condone such inflammatory comments by Ross yet rail against the slightest firmness in any YEC counter, one must wonder sometimes whether there is one sauce for the goose, and another for the gander.

The charge is absurd anyway:

- First of all, YECs do believe that the physical realm is trustworthy, but not necessarily *man's theories about* the physical realm — especially what happened in it in the past.

- Second, Gnostics believed that matter was evil, so that our realm was created by a demiurge, because God would not sully himself with matter. YECs obviously believe that God created matter. And we don't believe matter is evil; rather we believe that the whole "very good" creation was cursed.

- Third, the word "Gnostic" comes from the Greek *gnosis*, meaning knowledge. They believed in a secret esoteric knowledge that only the initiates possessed. Books like the Bible counted as mere exoteric teaching for the masses. Yet if anyone resembles Gnosticism, it is Ross. After all, he teaches that if we are to understand the Bible, it is not enough to read it with all the tools of grammar and knowledge of its historical context. Rather, we must incorporate the knowledge ("science") of initiates (scientists) that would not have been known to the original readers!

Here are some more questions we have received, and our answers.

- Why don't you set up a debate in an appropriate neutral forum such as the Ankerberg program or James Dobson's program?

Well, if such a rare species as a neutral forum can be found, we hope that it's preserved for posterity. Ankerberg and Dobson are hardly neutral in this matter but strongly pro-Ross. Ankerberg's constant partiality is demonstrated in the analysis[16] of the Ross–Hovind debate on his show that was aired in October 2000 — it was more of a Ross+Ankerberg tag team against Hovind. Dobson has also often hosted Ross on his show, but his producers call Ken Ham "divisive and dogmatic," and

---

15. Archer and Ross in D.G. Hagopian, editor, *The Genesis Debate* (Mission Viejo, CA: Crux Press, 2001), p. 130–131.

16. See in-depth analysis by J. Sarfati, <www.answersingenesis.org/ross_hovind>.

thus will not have him on the program. Neither did Ankerberg bother to contact AiG, although it is one of the leading young-earth creationist organizations in the world.

Anyway, I can't understand the huge attraction of debates. AiG has frequently dealt with Ross's public *statements,* while Ross generally ignores what YECs say and keeps on misrepresenting our arguments. Of importance are the *propositions* taught by both sides, not whether they are made face to face. Debates tend to emphasize personalities more than the issues.

- Why not let God deal with him?

Some have justified this by alluding to Rabban Gamaliel's advice to his fellow non-Christian Jews in dealing with the Jewish Christians in Acts 5:38–39:

> Therefore, in the present case I advise you: Leave these men alone! Let them go! For if their purpose or activity is of human origin, it will fail. But if it is from God, you will not be able to stop these men; you will only find yourselves fighting against God.

However, it's important to remember that not everything *reported* in the Bible is *endorsed* by the Bible. Here, Luke was not *endorsing* this advice, but merely *reporting* it accurately. The *normative* passages are those cited earlier. It should be obvious that Gamaliel's advice is silly if taken as a general rule. To take an extreme example, what if people had argued, "If Hitler is really killing Jews and invading independent countries as suggested, then God will deal with him"? What about cults like the Mormons and Jehovah's Witnesses, which are thriving?

It could also be argued, from the doctrine of the sovereignty of God, that He is *already* dealing with Dr. Ross through AiG's exposure of his errors.

Interestingly, there is a logical problem in that this complaint is *self-refuting* — it backfires on the questioner! That is, if *we* are in error in writing against Ross, then *by their own reasoning*, shouldn't such questioners leave *us* alone and let God deal with us? No, of course not. There is a duty, where a brother in the Lord is apparently erring, to try to correct the error. And this would be particularly the case if you saw the brother leading others into error that leads to apostasy.

Exposing Negatives Shows the Positives in Greater Light

Throughout church history, the great leaders have sought to refute heresies. But in God's sovereign plan, the errors have prompted the orthodox church to clarify key biblical doctrines. One of the most dangerous early heresies was the Arian, which denied that Jesus is God and taught that He was a created being. The great Nicene Creed was written mainly to refute this heresy, and this creed is still widely regarded by all branches of Christendom as one of the clearest statements on the deity of Christ. For example, it states that Jesus was "true God of true God, begotten not made, of one substance with the Father." The teaching of the modern-day Arians, the Jehovah's Witness cult, has been refuted in excellent books such as Ron Rhodes's

Reasoning from the Scriptures with the Jehovah's Witnesses.[17] That book is also an excellent presentation of the biblical basis for vital doctrines such as the deity and bodily resurrection of Christ, the Trinity, and less vital, but still important, doctrines such as eternal conscious punishment for the unsaved.

I hope *Refuting Compromise* will also serve as a strong defense of the authority of Scripture, and of its teachings of a recent creation and global Flood. With this strong foundation in place, the rest of the Bible is likewise firm — in particular, the origin of death through sin, and the gospel as its remedy through the sacrificial death and resurrection of the Last Adam, Jesus Christ.

Can One Believe in Millions of Years and Still Be a Christian?

This is a very important question that must be addressed at the outset. Despite what some opponents have claimed, AiG (like most YECs) has *always* affirmed that one does not need to believe in six-day creation to be saved. The Bible says that salvation is by grace alone through faith alone, not by works (Eph. 2:8), and the *content* of saving faith is belief in the deity of Christ (Rom. 10:9–13, applying a Joel 2:32 reference to YHWH/Jehovah to Christ) and in His death for our sins, His burial, and bodily resurrection from the dead (1 Cor. 15:1–4).

We know that people can be genuine Christians, believing those doctrines, even if they don't accept creation in six 24-hour days. Van Bebber and Taylor's rebuttal to Ross explicitly stated, "We believe that Dr. Ross is saved, and that his expressed desire to live for Christ is genuine."[18] Answers in Genesis has stocked the Bebber and Taylor book for years as the definitive critique of Ross without any disclaimer, which is tacit agreement by AiG that we don't question Ross's salvation.

In fact, the founding chairman of AiG (Australia), Prof. John Rendle-Short, was a saved theistic evolutionist for 40 years (before AiG came into existence). But like so many other people, including his own father Dr. Arthur Rendle Short, an eminent English surgeon and apologist, he struggled with the problem of death and suffering before the Fall,[19] which is the basis for the gospel message (1 Cor. 15:21–22, 45). Fortunately, he wasn't consistent, and, despite the conflict which we demonstrate in chapter 6, held to the foundational message.

Unfortunately, people like Billy Graham's former colleague Charles Templeton, who later apostatized,[20] and the heretical Bishop Spong,[21] *were* consistent, and threw

---

17. R. Rhodes, *Reasoning from the Scriptures with the Jehovah's Witnesses* (Eugene, OR: Harvest House Publishers, 1993).
18. M. Van Bebber and P.S. Taylor, *Creation and Time: A Report on the Progressive Creationist Book by Hugh Ross*, Eden Productions, Mesa, AZ, 1994, online at <www.christiananswers.net/paradise/ctb-alt.html>, p. 9.
19. See his biographical and autobiographical work *Green Eye of the Storm* (Edinburgh, UK: Banner of Truth, 1998). Note that John Rendle-Short hyphenates his surname while his father did not.
20. K. Ham and S. Byers, "The Slippery Slide to Unbelief: A Famous Evangelist Goes from Hope to Hopelessness," *Creation* 22(3):8–13 (June–August 2000); <www.answersingenesis.org/slide>.
21. M. Bott and J. Sarfati, "What's Wrong With Bishop Spong? Laymen Rethink the Scholarship of John Shelby Spong," *Apologia* 4(1)3—27 (1995); <www.answersingenesis.org/spong>.

out the gospel along with the foundations. That's why several AiG articles have concluded that, yes, one can be a Christian and deny a young earth, but it can still have baneful consequences which will be detailed in this book, mainly involving the authority and understandability of Scripture, and sin as the ultimate cause of human and animal death and suffering in the world.[22]

Another Jerusalem Council?

Charisma's June 2003 article on Ross says:

> Ross has advocated a second Jerusalem Council on creation following the model in The Acts of the Apostles, where the early Church leaders held a summit to hammer out an agreement on a contentious issue of whether or not Gentile converts should be required to follow Jewish custom and law. He believes the creation controversy is the biggest issue facing the church, more significant than the question of women's roles, "because of the impact it is having on evangelism."[23]

Such an idea is preposterous, because the Jerusalem Council involved the Apostles (Acts 15:6), thus James's decision in verse 13 ff. had apostolic authority. Jesus gave the power of "binding and loosing" to Peter, then to all His Apostles (Matt. 16:20). In a Jewish frame of reference, these terms had legislative meanings: "to bind" meant to forbid something, and "to loose" meant to permit something. No one today has this level of authority.

A major reason for the need for such authority was that the New Testament was not yet written, so the Church needed to be guided by the Apostles. Now that the Canon of Scripture is closed, and the Apostles are no longer alive, the Church is to be guided by Scripture alone (2 Tim. 3:15–17).

BOOK AND REFERENCE ABBREVIATIONS USED THROUGHOUT THIS BOOK

Ross's Books

- BtC — *Beyond the Cosmos* (Navpress, Colorado Springs, CO, 1996). This explains the mathematical concept of other dimensions — he believes that God is extra-dimensional. This is based on the assumption that the highly

---

22. D. Gish, "Is It Possible to Be a Christian and an Evolutionist? A Leading Creationist Answers an Often-asked Question," *Creation* 11(4):21–23 (September–November 1989); <www.answersingenesis.org/docs/1152.asp>.

K. Ham, "The Big Picture: Being Wrong about the Six Days of Creation Does Not Automatically Mean Someone Is Not a Christian. But If You Think That Makes It Unimportant, Stand Back and Look at the Big Picture," *Creation* 23(2):16–18 (March–May 2001); <http://www.answersingenesis.org/big_picture>.

R. Grigg, "Do I Have to Believe in a Literal Creation to Be a Christian?" *Creation* 23(3):20–22 (June–August 2001); <www.answersingenesis.org/must_believe>. The article concludes, "The short answer is 'No.' The long answer is 'No, but. . . .' "

23. A. Butcher, "He Sees God in the Stars," *Charisma* (June 2003), p. 38–44.

J. Sarfati "Shame on *Charisma*!" <www.answersingenesis.org/rosspc>, May 29, 2003.

speculative "string theory" is correct. Ross believes that this finally enables a solution to theological problems such as the Trinity, hearing millions of prayers simultaneously, and predestination/free will.

- C&C — *The Creator and the Cosmos* (Navpress, Colorado Springs, CO, 1995). This is written as an outreach, supposedly demonstrating how the origin and fine-tuning of the universe point to a God.

- C&T — *Creation and Time* (Navpress, Colorado Springs, CO, 1994). This is aimed at a Christian audience, trying to call a truce between old- and young-earth creationists. Yet, after he waves the white flag of truce in his book, in subsequent chapters he shoots lots of bullets against the young-earth view.

- FoG — *The Fingerprint of God* (Promise Publishing, Orange, CA, 1989, 1991). This is aimed at a general audience; it defends a hot big bang and uses this to prove a creator. This also argues for a day-age view.

- G1 — *Genesis One: A Scientific Perspective* (Wiseman Productions, Sierra Madre, CA, 1983). This is an early book that presents his day-age view.

- GQ — *The Genesis Question* (Navpress, Colorado Springs, CO, 1998, hard-cover). References to this book will generally use the pagination of his second (paperback) edition, 2001. This book is an overview of Genesis 1–11, aimed at Christians, and argues for all his old-earth views and against the young-earth one.

Creationist (YEC) Books and Journals

- AB — Don Batten, editor, Ken Ham, Jonathan Sarfati, and Carl Wieland *The Answers Book* (Master Books, Green Forest, AR; Triune Press, Brisbane, Australia, 1999).

- *Creation* — Formerly *[Creation] Ex Nihilo*. All references to this magazine will be to its current name *Creation*, even for articles published before the name change.

- CRSQ — *Creation Research Society Quarterly*.

- C&C — D.F. Kelly, *Creation and Change: Genesis 1:1–2:4 In the Light of Changing Scientific Paradigms* (Mentor, Christian Focus Publications, Ross-shire, UK, 1997).

- RE — Jonathan Sarfati, *Refuting Evolution* (Master Books, Green Forest, AR; Triune Press, Brisbane, Australia, 1999).

- RE2 — Jonathan Sarfati, *Refuting Evolution* 2 (Master Books, Green Forest, AR; Triune Press, Brisbane, Australia, 2002).

- ST — Russell Humphreys, *Starlight and Time* (Master Books, Green Forest, AR, USA, 1994).

- *TJ* — Formerly *[Creation] Ex Nihilo Technical Journal:* we will always refer to it by its current name *TJ,* even for articles published before the name change.
- VB&T — M. Van Bebber and P.S. Taylor, P.S., *Creation and Time: A Report on the Progressive Creationist Book by Hugh Ross,* Eden Productions, Mesa, AZ, 1994.

Many *Creation* magazine and *TJ* articles are on the Answers in Genesis website, <www.answersingenesis.org/>. Many of the books are available via the online store.

Standard Theological Works

- BDAG — W. Bauer, F.W. Danker, W.F. Arndt, and F.W. Gingrich, *A Greek-English Lexicon of the New Testament and Other Early Christian Literature,* 3rd ed. (Chicago/London: University of Chicago Press, 2000).
- BDB — F. Brown, S.R. Driver, and C.A. Briggs, *A Hebrew and English Lexicon of the Old Testament* (Hendrickson Publishers, UK, 1996).
- EQ — *Evangelical Quarterly.*
- HALOT — K. Koehler and W. Baumgartner, editors, M.E.J. Richardson, translator, *Hebrew-Aramaic Lexicon of the Old Testament,* 2002.
- JETS — *Journal of the Evangelical Theological Society.*
- Keil and Delitzsch — C.F. Keil and F. Delitzsch, *Commentaries on the Old Testament,* n.d., original German in the 19th century, English translation published by Eerdmans, Grand Rapids, MI, the Pentateuch.
- Leupold — H.C. Leupold, *Exposition of Genesis* (Grand Rapids, MI: Baker Book House, 1942).
- TWOT — R.L. Harris, G.L. Archer, and B.K. Waltke, *Theological Wordbook of the Old Testament* (Moody, Chicago, 1980).
- WTJ — *Westminster Theological Journal.*
- And of course OT and NT for Old Testament and New Testament.

Scientific Terms

- Standard SI unit symbols and chemical element symbols will be used throughout.
- Ga = giga-annum or a billion (10^9) years; Ma = mega-annum or a million years; ka = kilo-annum or a thousand years.

ADDENDUM

This is a commentary[24] on a brochure recently sent out by Ross (also posted on his website), giving his own perspective on the differences between "young-earth," or

---

24. Based on J. Sarfati, "Ten Major Differences and Similarities between Calendar-Day and Day-Age Creationists? According to Dr. Hugh Ross," <www.answersingenesis.org/ross_YvO>.

"calendar-day" creationists, like AiG, and "old-earth," or "day-age" creationists, like himself. Since it's his own perspective, we cannot be said to be putting words in his mouth. However, as will be shown, there are many of the same misrepresentations as in his other works. This is only a summary — we indicate where these points are further elaborated in this book.

CDC = Calendar-Day Creationist — i.e., accepts that the days of Genesis 1 were ordinary-length days, for example, Answers in Genesis and Institute for Creation Research; commonly called young-earth creationist (YEC). Note that at times throughout this book, I will simply use the word "creationist(s)" to refer to this position.

DAC = Day-Age Creationist — like Hugh Ross and many other "progressive creationists"; commonly called old-earth creationist (OEC), although that term would also include gap theorists.

Dr. Ross's comments are indented, that is, the lines headed by "CDC" are what Ross **claims** we believe, not necessarily what we **actually** believe.

Ten Major Differences

1. CDC: Natural biological evolution works, producing new species and genera within orders and families.

This is misleading, since we would not describe speciation within a kind as "biological evolution," because *no new* information is produced. However, that new species do arise is indisputable — Ross seems not to understand that producing a new reproductively isolated population is, by definition, a new species. Also, there is no biblical or scientific reason why the created kinds cannot sometimes have enough built-in genetic variation so they can give rise to varieties within the genus or family (a man-made classification after all). This is explained further in chapter 7.

1. DAC: Natural biological evolution fails at all levels except for those species numbering more than about one quadrillion individuals with generation times less than three months and body sizes smaller than one centimeter.

This is an amazing statement — one wonders what this astronomer's source of such biological nonsense could be. This fixity of species view goes well beyond the biblical text and is disproved by *operational* science — see again chapter 7.

2. CDC: Laws of physics were radically different before Adam's sin.
2. DAC: Laws of physics were identical before and after Adam's sin.

One wonders what difference Ross thinks the Fall made, which we cover in chapter 6. However, with the exception that God withdrew some of His sustaining power, we believe that the laws of gravity, thermodynamics, electromagnetism, etc. were operative from creation. AiG is on record denying that the second law of thermodynamics began at the Fall.[25]

---

25. J. Sarfati, "Arguments Creationists Should NOT Use," *Creation* 24(2):20–24 (March–May 2002); <www.answersingenesis.org/dont_use>.

3. CDC: Redeemed humanity will be restored to paradise.

3. DAC: Redeemed humanity will be delivered from paradise to a brand new creation.

This is misleading, and Ross has even made inflammatory accusations that those who believe in "restoration" are "cultic." We are on record as affirming that there will be "a new heaven and a new earth" (Rev. 21:1), and, even now, believers in Christ are new creations (2 Cor. 5:17). We also affirm that the new creation will be even grander than the original paradise, because there will no longer be even the possibility of sin. However, we point out that many references to a future state parallel the pre-Fall world, e.g., vegetarian lions and wolves (Isa. 11:6–9, 65:25), light without the sun like the first three days of creation (Rev. 22:5), and a Tree of Life (Gen. 2:9, 3:22, 24; compare with Rev. 2:7, 22:2,14,19). And although my book doesn't take any eschatological stand, Ross is a premillennialist who believes that the Millennium will have vegetarian animals (GQ:98–99). Premillennialists, such as Charles Ryrie, believe that the Millennium is what is referred to in Acts 3:21, "the period of restoration of all things" (see *Ryrie Study Bible*). And premillennial CDCs would agree with Ross that the Millennium is not the final state, and there will be a brand new creation.

A more accurate way of expressing our difference is that Ross *denies* a pre-Fall deathless paradise altogether. This is shown by his last point of difference, below.

4. CDC: Genesis 1 is the account of physical creation. . . .

Of course. It's not only AiG that believes this, but God himself spoke the Fourth Commandment, giving the reason that He created in six days and rested on the 7th (Exod. 20:8–11).

4. DAC: It is critical to carefully integrate all ten of the major creation accounts in the Bible.

What is Ross talking about? The Bible never contradicts itself, and there is nothing to naysay the plain teaching of Genesis 1 and Exodus 20:8–11 elsewhere in the Bible.

5. CDC: The universe and the stars are eternal.

5. DAC: The universe and the stars are temporal.

Where do we say that the universe or stars are eternal? This statement is without foundation and is totally untrue.

6. CDC: Astronomers are deceiving the public.

6. DAC: Astronomers are telling us the truth.

Which astronomers? Dr. Danny Faulkner, a tenured professor of astronomy who believes in CDC? And we normally point out that secular astronomers are not likely to be consciously deceiving the public, but are looking at the same data as us, only through the wrong "glasses."

7. CDC: The heavens merely reveal the existence of God.

7. DAC: The heavens also reveal God's transcendent qualities and many of His personal attributes.

It's hard to know what Ross is thinking of here. We often quote Romans 1:20. However, what we deny is that creation reveals enough for salvation, and we also deny that the interpretations by fallible humans of the creation should override the propositional revelation of Scripture. See the discussion on general and special revelation on page 59.

8. CDC: There is only one literal interpretation of Genesis 1.

8. DAC: There are several literal interpretations of Genesis 1.

Only if there are several literal interpretations of the word "literal"! The literal meaning of "literal" is: "Taking words in their usual or primary sense and applying the ordinary rules of grammar, without mysticism, allegory or metaphor." The usual and primary meaning of "day" is a single period of earth's rotation, and this is unambiguous when accompanied by a number, evening and/or morning. This is discussed in detail in chapter 2.

9. CDC: Genesis 1 cannot be reconciled with the established record of nature.

9. DAC: Genesis 1 can be reconciled with the established record of nature.

What we *actually* say is: "Genesis 1 cannot be reconciled with the uniformitarian *interpretation* of nature," again discussed in chapter 1.

10. CDC: The pre-Adamic death of the higher animals contradicts the character of God and the doctrine of blood atonement for human sin. The Bible does not attribute the properties of life and death to the plants and lower animals.

Our claim is that plants are never called *nephesh chayyah* (transliteration of the Hebrew in Genesis), meaning that their life and death is qualitatively different. This is shown by the vegetarianism of both humans and animals in both the pre-Fall world (Gen. 1:29–30) and in the restored state (Isa. 11:6–9, 65:25). We cover this in chapter 6.

10. DAC: The pre-Adamic death of higher animals is consistent with a loving, merciful Creator. . . .

Tell that to the animals with their flesh torn apart by predators, and ravaged with disease (often the same sorts of diseases that ravage humanity, too, e.g., cancer), i.e., that it's still a "very good" creation, rather than a sin-cursed world. . . . and in no way impinges upon the doctrine of blood atonement for human sin. The Bible does attribute the properties of life and death to both the plants and the lower animals.

Wrong, as above. See "The God of an Old Earth,"[26] which shows that any billions-of-years compromise entails that death and suffering were always part of God's creation, and how this is inconsistent with the Bible.

Ten Major Similarities

I would agree with all ten. However, I doubt that we understand them the same way as Ross.

1. The Bible must be taken literally unless the context indicates otherwise.

I agree with the sentiment, but it would be preferable to say "plainly," meaning "as the author intended." This incorporates a literal interpretation of a literal context, poetic interpretation of poetic context. Ross would probably have no objection to that, and "literal" is an acceptable way of saying this, but the above should hopefully avoid caricatures by theistic evolutionists. The problem is that Ross has a strange understanding of the word "literal," as shown above.

2. The Bible is inerrant in all disciplines of scholarship.

Definitely. However, while I have no doubt that Ross publicly and sincerely defends the Bible against any error, in practice Ross imposes secular "disciplines of scholarship" over the Bible. The main differences are much the same as one key issue of the Reformation — *Sola Scriptura* — "Scripture alone." That is, the *supreme authority, perspicuity,* and *sufficiency* of Scripture. But Ross claims, "God's revelation is not limited exclusively to God's words. The facts of nature may be likened to a sixty-seventh book of the Bible" (C&T:56). These words alone show that Ross, in effect, teaches *Scriptura et scientia* — Scripture and science. In practice, Ross reinterprets Scripture in an unnatural way to fit in with the alleged "facts of nature" (really evolutionary/uniformitarian interpretations of nature), which is *Scriptura sub scientia* — Scripture below science.

3. The universe was both transcendentally and supernaturally created.

Yes. Alas, Ross believes that God used the alleged big bang, an essentially atheistic notion by which most of its proponents assert the universe created itself. And one in which the order of events contradicts the plain text of the Bible.

4. Naturalism cannot explain the origin of life.

Yes. See Q&A: Origin of Life, <www.answersingenesis.org/origin>.

5. Naturalism cannot entirely explain the history of life, nor can theistic evolution.

No dispute there.

6. Naturalism cannot entirely explain the geophysical history of the earth.

However, Ross concedes much ground to naturalism, because he fails to allow for the devastating global flood of Noah's day, responsible for many of the rock layers and fossils.

---

26. K. Ham, "The God of an Old Earth," *Creation* 21(4)42–45 (September–November 1999); <www. answersingenesis.org/god_oe>.

7. Naturalism cannot explain entirely the astrophysical history of the universe and solar system.

True. But again Ross gives an enormous amount of ground to naturalism, essentially agreeing with the naturalistic big bang and the history of stellar evolution over billions of years.

8. Genesis 1 is both factual and chronological in its context. It describes God's "very good" creation in the space of six days.

I agree with the words, but, as shown above, Ross doesn't think that they mean what they say! Ross's pre-Fall creation is anything but "very good." It has all the horrors of death, struggle, suffering, disease, and carnivory that we see in today's world. And "six days" has a very different meaning for Ross, as will be discussed.

9. Adam and Eve were a literal couple created by God just thousands of years ago.

Yes, we agree that Adam was created out of dust, and Eve from Adam, with no animal ancestry. But by "just thousands," AiG means six thousand, as per a straightforward reading of the chronogenealogies of Genesis 5 and 11. On the other hand, Ross believes it was many times as long ago, which entails inserting huge gaps in the chronologies for which there is no good biblical evidence.

10. All human beings owe their descent to Adam and Eve.

I agree, but we would regard those individuals classified as Neandertals and *Homo erectus* in that category, while Ross regards them as soulless hominids.

Conclusion

Here, as elsewhere, Ross has made misleading accusations against CDC organizations in an attempt to justify his own position. However, we have shown in *many places* that he has frequently misrepresented what we believe, and that his arguments do not hold up against Scripture. It is important not to be sidetracked by Ross's appeal to "scientific consensus," but always to stand on the authoritative Word of God, that is, letting it teach us, rather than imposing outside ideas upon the text.

CHAPTER 1

THE AUTHORITY OF SCRIPTURE

CHAPTER OVERVIEW

The main difference between Hugh Ross and young-earth creationists such as Answers in Genesis is our different authority. AiG believes that the 66 books of the Bible, because it is God's written Word, should be the basis for our thinking in every area on which it touches, including science. The Bible is *propositional revelation*, that is, it uses words to reveal true propositions, or facts about things. Therefore, it can be interpreted according to the rules of grammar and historical context. And because God wrote the Bible to instruct man, starting with the original readers, its propositions would be understandable.

Although many evangelical old-earth believers admit that Scripture seems to *teach* 24-hour days (and a recent creation and global Flood), they do not *believe* it because of "science." Ross explicitly states that "nature" is a 67th book of Scripture. However, nature does not contain propositional revelation, but instead the data must be *interpreted according to a framework*. Ross, in practice, uses long-age interpretations of nature to reinterpret the written Word of God. This also entails that readers of Scripture before the rise of modern science would not have been able to understand what they read.

The Sufficiency of Scripture

The Reformers proclaimed the biblical doctrine of *Sola Scriptura* (Scripture alone). This doctrine says that Scripture is inerrant, authoritative, and sufficient as a guide in matters of doctrine and morality for Christians. Thus, for salvation, no one is obliged to believe anything which is neither taught explicitly by Scripture nor logically deducible from Scripture. Although it is not his intention, the thrust of Hugh Ross's teachings in general is a denial of this vital doctrine.

It is fallacious to limit scriptural authority to only those portions deemed to be about "faith and practice." Doctrine is inextricably linked to history and science, so that whatever Scripture affirms on historical or scientific matters is also true. For example, the key doctrine of the Resurrection is linked to the historical fact that

Jesus' body had vacated the tomb on the third day. This also impinges on science, because naturalistic scientists assert that it is impossible for dead men to rise. And the meaning of Jesus' death and resurrection is tied to the historical accuracy of the event recorded in Genesis (1 Cor. 15:21–22).

Jesus told Nicodemus (John 3:12):

> I have spoken to you of earthly things and you do not believe; how then will you believe if I speak of heavenly things?

If Jesus was wrong about earthly things, such as a recent creation (Mark 10:6 — see chapter 9) and a global Flood (Luke 17:26–27 — see chapter 8), was He also wrong about a heavenly thing like John 3:16? If not, why not? Scripture becomes a restaurant menu, where we choose only the parts that suit us, while we slide down to total unbelief in other passages. Many atheists testify that their rejection of the Bible and Christianity started with compromises on Genesis (see chapter 6).

Sola Scriptura is based on what Paul wrote in 2 Timothy 3:15–17:

> . . . and how from infancy you have known the holy Scriptures, which are able to make you wise for salvation through faith in Christ Jesus. All Scripture is God-breathed and is useful for teaching, rebuking, correcting, and training in righteousness, so that the man of God may be thoroughly equipped for every good work.

- The Greek word for "Scriptures" in verse 15 is γραμματα *(grammata)*, and must refer to the OT alone, as these were the only Scriptures Timothy would have known from his childhood.

- In verse 16, the word is γραφη *(graphē)*, which would include the OT plus all the NT written by then (A.D. 63), i.e., probably all the NT except 2 Peter, Hebrews, Jude, and John's writings. As Paul's writings were divinely inspired, Paul's words would apply even to the latter books not yet written.

- "God-breathed" is indeed a correct translation by the NIV of the Greek word θεοπνευστος *(theopneustos)*. If Scripture is "God-breathed" and God cannot err, it logically follows that Scripture as originally written cannot err.

- Scripture is able to make a man "wise unto salvation" and "thoroughly furnished unto all good works." This implies that Scripture contains all the doctrine and moral law we need.

- 1 Timothy 5:18 cites both Deuteronomy 25:4 and Luke 10:7 as *graphē*; that is, both the Old and New Testaments. This again shows that the NT was already regarded as Scripture even in apostolic times. And Peter affirms that Paul's writings were also Scripture in 2 Peter 3:15–16.

We can also see from the Apostles how important Scripture was:

The brethren immediately sent Paul and Silas away by night to Berea; and when they arrived they went into the Jewish synagogue. Now these Jews were more noble than those in Thessalonica, for they received the word with all eagerness, examining the scriptures daily to see if these things were so (Acts 17:10–11).

Luke commends these Jews as a positive example for his Christian readers because they subjected even Paul's teaching to the test of Scripture. So Christians today should follow that Berean example and test the teachings of any church or person by Scripture.

I would also agree with *The Chicago Statement on Biblical Inerrancy*,[1] a doctrinal statement Reasons To Believe officially adheres to.

Article X

WE AFFIRM that inspiration, strictly speaking, applies only to the autographic text of Scripture, which in the providence of God can be ascertained from available manuscripts with great accuracy. We further affirm that copies and translations of Scripture are the Word of God to the extent that they faithfully represent the original.

WE DENY that any essential element of the Christian faith is affected by the absence of the autographs. We further deny that this absence renders the assertion of biblical inerrancy invalid or irrelevant.

The Perspicuity of Scripture

This word "perspicuity" means that God intended ordinary people (with the help of the Holy Spirit — 1 Corinthians 2:14) to use sound hermeneutical principles to understand the gospel message of Scripture without needing an elite group to interpret it. This follows from the above verses, because the only way the Scriptures can thoroughly equip us is if they are *understandable*. Also, believing fathers were to teach the Scriptures to their children at home (Deut. 6:4–9, Eph. 6:4).

While in Reformation times, the above elite group was the Roman Church Magisterium; nowadays it appears to be "scientists." In other words, the reformers opposed the prevalent church teaching that ordinary people cannot understand Scripture without the guidance of the "infallible" Church of Rome, led by the pope. Now Ross's claim, in effect, is that ordinary people cannot understand Scripture without the insight of modern interpretations of chronology, astronomy, geology, and

---

1.The *Chicago Statement on Biblical Inerrancy* was produced at an international summit conference of evangelical leaders, held at the Hyatt Regency O'Hare in Chicago in the fall of 1978. The International Council on Biblical Inerrancy sponsored this congress. The Chicago Statement was signed by nearly 300 noted evangelical scholars, including James Boice, Norman L. Geisler, John Gerstner, Carl F.H. Henry, Kenneth Kantzer, Harold Lindsell, John Warwick Montgomery, Roger Nicole, J.I. Packer, Robert Preus, Earl Radmacher, Francis Schaeffer, R.C. Sproul, and John Wenham. The statement with exposition can be found at <www.kulikovskyonline.net/hermeneutics/csbe.htm>.

biology from scientists (all of whom, like everyone else, are fallible and have biases, and most of whom are extremely hostile to the Bible and the Christian faith). Both these errors put another mediator between God and man (1 Tim. 2:5), and contrast with the practice of the Bereans in Acts 17:11 (see above).

This would also mean that a man like Timothy would have had no way of understanding the meaning of many passages, despite what Paul told him. Timothy was expected to be able to understand them, and, most importantly, so was the original audience. The only exception is prophecies, which were explicitly stated to become fully understandable when fulfilled some time in the future. Otherwise, the true meaning of Scripture is the meaning the original inspired authors intended to convey to their intended audience.

The perspicuity of Scripture means that a good rule of thumb is, "If the plain sense makes sense, we should seek no other sense, lest we create nonsense." But it must be used with caution. Too many atheist websites attack the Bible by reading it as an English newspaper, and ignore the metaphor, symbolism, and idioms of the language and culture that the original audience would have understood. The *Chicago Statement on Biblical Inerrancy* states more tightly:

Article XIII

WE AFFIRM the propriety of using inerrancy as a theological term with reference to the complete truthfulness of Scripture.

WE DENY that it is proper to evaluate Scripture according to standards of truth and error that are alien to its usage or purpose. We further deny that inerrancy is negated by biblical phenomena such as a lack of modern technical precision, irregularities of grammar or spelling, observational descriptions of nature, the reporting of falsehoods, the use of hyperbole and round numbers, the topical arrangement of material, variant selections of material in parallel accounts, or the use of free citations.

The *Chicago Statement on Biblical Hermeneutics* says:

Article XV

WE AFFIRM the necessity of interpreting the Bible according to its literal, or normal, sense. The literal sense is the grammatical-historical sense. That is, the meaning which the writer expressed. Interpretation according to the literal sense will take account of all figures of speech and literary forms found in the text.

WE DENY the legitimacy of any approach to Scripture that attributes to it meaning which the literal sense does not support.

Analogia Scripturae

An important aspect of *Sola Scriptura* is the principle that Scripture interprets Scripture. The *Chicago Statement on Biblical Hermeneutics* states:

Article XVII

WE AFFIRM the unity, harmony, and consistency of Scripture and declare that it is its own best interpreter.

WE DENY that Scripture may be interpreted in such a way as to suggest that one passage corrects or militates against another. We deny that later writers of Scripture misinterpreted earlier passages of Scripture when quoting from or referring to them.

The perspicuity of Scripture does not mean that all Scripture is equally easy to understand (2 Pet. 3:16). But because Scripture is inerrant and sufficient, if we come to a difficult passage, we should be able to interpret it by referring to a clearer passage, and specific terms should clarify general ones. If we still cannot understand it, we should admit that the fault is in our interpretations and not in the Scriptures!

A large part of this book is devoted to analyzing the chronology of the Genesis creation account by comparison with the rest of Scripture.

The "Timothy Test"

Dr. Russell Humphreys proposed a helpful rule derived from the above Scriptures that should help clarify the perspicuity of Scripture, and avoid those problems.

> To make these points [of a plain meaning of Scripture] a little clearer, imagine a Jewish Christian of the first century who understands Greek, Hebrew, and the Scriptures well. Let's call him "Timothy," since Paul's protégé was called that. But let's also imagine that this Timothy knows nothing of the advanced scientific knowledge of his day, such as Aristotle's works. All that Timothy knows is from either everyday experience or careful study of Scripture, which Paul says is sufficient for wisdom (2 Tim. 3:15). Now if Scripture really is straightforward and sufficient, then the meaning Timothy derives from the words is probably the meaning that God intended for everybody to get.[2]

(Ross supporter Perry Phillips[3] criticized this test by alleging that sometimes the plain meaning could mislead. But both Humphreys[4] and I[5] responded by pointing out that Phillips had misunderstood the Timothy Test, and had instead set up a straw man. Phillips ignored that this "Timothy" had a good understanding of the biblical language and culture.)

---

2. D. Russell Humphreys, *Starlight and Time: Solving the Puzzle of Distant Starlight in a Young Universe* (Green Forest, AR: Master Books, 1994) p. 57. PDF and zipped-PDF files are available at <http://www.trueorigin.org/ca_rh_03.asp>.

3. P.G. Phillips, "D. Russell Humphreys' Cosmology and the 'Timothy Test,'" *TJ* 11(2):189–194, 1997. PDF and zipped-PDF files are available at <http://www.trueorigin.org/ca_rh_03.asp>.

4. D.R. Humphreys, "Timothy Tests Theistic Evolutionism," *TJ* 11(2):199–201 (1997). PDF and zipped-PDF files are available at <http://www.trueorigin.org/ca_rh_03.asp>.

5. J.D. Sarfati, "D. Russell Humphreys" Cosmology and the 'Timothy Test': A Reply," *TJ* 11(2):195–198 (1997).

This is a simplified way of pointing out that the NT was written in what anthropologists call a "high-context" society. That is, its members "presume a broadly shared, well-understood, or 'high' knowledge of the context of anything referred to in conversation or in writing." The authors wrote to intended readers with a certain background and expected them to be able to "fill in the gaps." There was no need to explain things in depth if they all had a shared, background knowledge. Conversely, we in the modern West are a "low-context" society, and expect the context to be spelled out to us: "The obvious problem this creates for reading the biblical writings today is that low-context readers in the United States frequently mistake the biblical writings for low-context documents. They erroneously assume that the author has provided all of the contextual information needed to understand it."[6]

This means that there was nothing to stop Timothy from having a wider knowledge of the context of words used in his day than many 20th century readers would have. For example, Christological passages in the New Testament that support Trinitarian theology and refute cults that deny Christ's deity were written in a background of Jewish wisdom tradition.[7]

For example, this elucidates our understanding of the *logos* (word) in the Johannine Prologue (John 1:1–18). John teaches that the *logos* has all the aspects of contemporary rabbinical concepts of the "word" or *memra*. In this thinking, the *memra* of God was sometimes distinct from God, and sometimes the same as God (see John 1:1). Where the Old Testament says something is done by God, the Targums, Aramaic paraphrases of the Old Testament, often said it was done by the *memra* of God. The rabbis never tried to explain the paradox, because the OT also sometimes describes several personages simultaneously as YHWH who is one (e.g., Gen. 19:24, Isa. 48:16). The *memra* was the agent of creation (John 1:3), salvation (John 1:12), and revelation (John 1:18); the means by which God became visible in theophanies (John 1:14), and by which He made His covenants (John 1:17). The Johannine Prologue identifies Jesus of Nazareth as the embodiment of all aspects of the *memra*.[8]

The Timothy Test also allows Timothy to use archaeological discoveries to clarify the way that some words were used *in that time*, so he could understand the author's intention.

Much of this current book will be applying the "Timothy Test" to Scripture, and analyzing Genesis in its proper grammatical and historical context. For a Christian who believes in *Sola Scriptura*, that should be sufficient. But while Ross also appeals to Scripture, the difference in interpretation is not the main issue — because he doesn't really believe in *Sola Scriptura* but believes there is another source of equal

---

6. B.J. Malina and R.L. Rohrbaugh, *Social-Science Commentary on the Gospel of John* (Minneapolis, MN: Fortress Press, 1998), p. 16 ff.

7. A good summary of scholars such as James Dunn, Richard Longenecker, N.T. Wright is J.P. Holding, "Jesus: God's Wisdom," <www.tektonics.org/JPH_AOA.html>, November 26, 2002.

8. A. Fruchtenbaum, "The Life of Christ from a Jewish Perspective," (audio) Ariel Ministries; <http://icgod.com/Main.htm#1.%20The%20"LOGOS">, July 22, 2003.

authority, despite the above evidence that it is not biblically possible. This is hugely different from using extra-biblical sources merely to find out how the original readers would have understood the words of Scripture. The fact that the Bible is "high context" does not undermine *Sola Scriptura* at all. Rather, it shows the opposite: that bringing "science" to bear on hermeneutics is bringing a completely foreign context to the passages.

The next section will analyze this.

Nature: A 67th Book of Scripture?

While Protestant Christians believe that the Bible contains 66 books, Ross, in practice, does not. In effect, Ross is canonizing nature, as shown by his following statement, which underlies RTB's whole reason of existence, so needs to be analyzed (C&T:56–57):

> God's revelation is not limited exclusively to the Bible's words. The facts of nature may be likened to a sixty-seventh book of the Bible. . . . Some readers might feel that I am implying that God's revelation through nature is somehow on an equal footing with His revelation through the words of the Bible. Let me simply state that truth, by definition, is information that is perfectly free of contradiction and error. Just as it is absurd to speak of some entity as more perfect than another, so also one revelation of God's truth cannot be held as inferior or superior to another.

Ross also says that God's *general revelation* in nature is as important as His *special revelation in* Scripture (see page 59, where these two revelations are explained further).

Facts Versus Interpretations

It sounds very nice to say that God's revelation in Scripture must agree with His revelation in nature. But this overlooks a key difference between nature and the books of the Bible, that is, what constitutes the data in both domains. Ross and AiG would agree that the propositions contained in the 66 canonical books of the Bible are the facts of special revelation, but what are the facts of nature?

Nature is *not* propositional revelation, so it is not subject to objective hermeneutical principles. Rather, in the study of nature (that is, science), propositions must be formulated from the observations by *interpreting* them in a framework or *paradigm*. This framework depends largely on the axioms, or starting assumptions, of the scientist.

It is interesting that many philosophers of science understand this better than most old-earthers and evolutionists. For example, Thomas Kuhn's highly influential book, *The Structure of Scientific Revolutions*,[9] makes it very clear that in many fields the data is interpreted according to the ruling paradigm, and anomalies are explained away. Scientific revolutions occur only when so many anomalies are discovered that

---

9. T.S. Kuhn, *The Structure of Scientific Revolutions*, 3rd edition (Chicago, IL: University of Chicago Press, 1996).

an old paradigm becomes so unwieldy that a new paradigm is developed. Prof. Evelleen Richards, a non-creationist historian of science at the University of NSW, Australia, backed this up when commenting on dogmatism from the establishment, even against a non-Darwinian (neo-Lamarckian) theory:

> Science . . . is not so much concerned with truth as it is with consensus. What counts as "truth" is what scientists can agree to count as truth at any particular moment in time. . . . [Scientists] are not really receptive or not really open-minded to any sorts of criticisms or any sorts of claims that actually are attacking some of the established parts of the research (traditional) paradigm — in this case neo-Darwinism — so it is very difficult for people who are pushing claims that contradict that paradigm to get a hearing. They'll find it hard to [get] research grants; they'll find it hard to get their research published; they'll find it very hard.[10]

Ross plays "bait-and-switch" with the facts of nature and interpretations of these facts. So in reality it is *not* a matter of comparing one revelation of God's truth with another. Ross would have us accept the *interpretations* of the majority of scientists as the "facts" of science or nature, as if truth were decided by majority vote. But new "facts" or interpretations of science are discovered every day, while old "facts" are just as often discarded. The history of science is littered with the wrecks of ideas that were at one time considered to be "true," but have long since fallen out of favor. Elevating this body of knowledge with its changing character to the same level as the Bible should alarm all Christians who are committed to the authority of Scripture.

Ross's Selectivity

Ross is also inconsistent. Throughout his book, he esteems science, and warns Christians against disparaging the conclusions of science and against "sifting" science (GQ:15, 1st ed.). He insists that we use the consensus of the majority of scientists to illuminate the meanings of the Bible. But Ross appeals to majority rule only in matters of age and the sequence of events. If he were consistent, he would prove too much and undermine his own position, because a "majority" of biologists accept organic evolution as a fact, and a majority of origin-of-life researchers accept chemical evolution as fact. Yet Ross rejects both of these views, and rightly so.

Also, Ross is willing to allow for miraculous intervention throughout earth's history (GQ:38):

> Scientists continue to debate the issue of how life originated. More and more questions and problems arise on the naturalistic side while evidence accumulates on the supernaturalistic.

However, conventional (uniformitarian) scientists actually do not have *any* use for any form of divine intervention whatsoever. And, contrary to what Ross's cited

---

10. E. Richards, *Lateline*, ABC (Australian Broadcasting Corporation) TV program, October 9, 1998.

statements suggest, such scientists are *not* attempting in any way to evaluate the possibility of supernatural activity in the origin of plants, or of life itself. They have already made up their minds, in advance, for naturalistic explanations. So why does Ross mislead his readers into thinking that conventional science just might come to accept divine intervention for at least such things as the origin of life and the origin of plants?

All things considered, when it comes to science, it is obvious that Ross wants to have his cake and eat it, too. He holds majority scientific opinion in high esteem, on the one hand. But on the other, Ross goes against conventional science by allowing for the miraculous in earth's past. Were Ross instead to *consistently* listen to the statements of conventional scientists, and adjust his understanding of the Bible accordingly on a consistent (as opposed to selective) basis, he would have to abandon his belief in both God and the Bible.

Science and Bias

For example, it is not generally made plain to the public that evolutionists start with the axiom of *materialism*, that is, matter is all that exists. Professor Richard Lewontin, a geneticist (and self-proclaimed Marxist), is a renowned champion of evolutionary theory (even though he is a critic of extreme neo-Darwinian adaptationism), and certainly one of the world's leaders in evolutionary biology. He recently wrote this very revealing comment (the italics were in the original). It illustrates the implicit philosophical bias against the Genesis account of creation and the flood — regardless of whether or not the facts support it.

> We take the side of science *in spite* of the patent absurdity of some of its constructs, *in spite* of its failure to fulfil many of its extravagant promises of health and life, *in spite* of the tolerance of the scientific community for unsubstantiated just-so stories, because we have a prior commitment, a commitment to materialism. It is not that the methods and institutions of science somehow compel us to accept a material explanation of the phenomenal world, but, on the contrary, that we are forced by our *a priori* adherence to material causes to create an apparatus of investigation and a set of concepts that produce material explanations, no matter how counter-intuitive, no matter how mystifying to the uninitiated. Moreover, that materialism is an absolute, for we cannot allow a Divine Foot in the door [emphases in original].[11]

Dr. Scott Todd, an immunologist at Kansas State University, was more succinct:

> Even if all the data point to an intelligent designer, such a hypothesis is excluded from science because it is not naturalistic.[12]

11. R. Lewontin, "Billions and Billions of Demons," *The New York Review* (January 9, 1997): p. 31.
12. S.C. Todd, correspondence to *Nature* 410(6752):423 (September 30, 1999).

The Fall

As will be covered more completely in chapter 6, because of Adam's sin, the creation is cursed (Gen. 3:17–19, Rom. 8:20–22), man's heart is deceitful (Jer. 17:9) and the thinking of a godless man is "futile" (Rom. 1:21). But although Scripture was penned by fallen humans, these humans were moved by the Holy Spirit, so Scripture itself is "God-breathed" (2 Tim. 3:15–17). Therefore, Scripture is the only source of revelation not tainted by the Fall.

So a biblical Christian should not reinterpret the perfect, unfallen Word of God according to fallible theories of sinful humans about a world we know to be cursed. As the systematic theologian Louis Berkhof approvingly explained about the views of some leading reformed theologians:

> Since the entrance of sin into the world, man can gather true knowledge about God from His general revelation only if he studies it in the light of Scripture, in which the elements of God's original self-revelation, which were obscured and perverted by the blight of sin, are republished, corrected, and interpreted.[13]

Berkhof's own view was:

> Some are inclined to speak of God's general revelation as a second source; but this is hardly correct in view of the fact that nature can come into consideration here only as interpreted in the light of Scripture.[14]

Science Is Fallible and Ever-changing

Indeed, the Bible is not a scientific textbook. And a good thing, too! There would hardly be a textbook in the world that won't be out of date in a few years; and all textbooks have mistakes. Conversely, the Bible has no mistakes and always stays current. If we marry our theology to today's science, we'll be widowed tomorrow. Then we'll have to reinterpret our reinterpretation. A reviewer of C&T expressed this concern:

> I am uneasy with the "but science now understands" language used in support of theistic creationism. The current state of any empirical science is too slender a reed to lean on this way, since tomorrow it may "understand" something much less friendly to theism.[15]

Ross's magisterial approach to science leaves him especially vulnerable, and nowhere more so than in big bang cosmology (see chapter 5).

---

13. L. Berkhof, Introductory Volume to *Systematic Theology* (Grand Rapids, MI: Wm. B. Eerdmans Publishing Co.), p. 60.

14. Ibid., p. 96.

15. S.M. Hutchens, Review of *Creation and Time* by Hugh Ross, *Touchstone* 8:40 (Winter 1995).

Evidentialist Error

It must be noted that some of the more evidentialist young-earth creationist approaches can be equally vulnerable. That is, some YECs have given the impression that the evidence is neutral, that is, it speaks for itself and "proves" the YEC position, or that we try to "prove the Bible with science." However, Answers in Genesis has a presuppositionalist approach. This means that while the biblical framework is non-negotiable, scientific models proposed to elucidate this framework should be held loosely. That's why AiG published the article "Moving Forward: Arguments We Think Creationists Shouldn't Use,"[16] and responded to those who were upset at the idea we were undermining "our" evidences.[17] We published another article explaining more about the important difference between evidence and interpretations of this evidence, and answered the anguished complaint that articles such as this "have taken away 'our' evidence!"[18]

Is Biblical Interpretation Infallible, and Does It Matter?

Some would dismiss the superiority of Scripture over "science" by asserting that while God's Word is infallible, human interpretations are not. From this, they assert that it's not God's Word versus man's fallible interpretations of nature, but man's fallible interpretation of the Bible versus man's fallible interpretation of nature. More colloquially, they might say of a young-earth creationist analysis of Scripture, "That's just your interpretation."

This is fallacious reasoning and borders on postmodernism, where objective truth is denied. One does not need to be an infallible interpreter to be able to interpret the meanings of *most* passages accurately, any more than one needs to be an infallible mathematician to know that $1+1=2$. The accuracy of interpretation of Scripture is determined by how it matches the intended meaning of the author. This is determined by rules of grammar and historical and literary context. Those who wish to deny a particular interpretation of Genesis need to find a basis in the biblical text from the application of these rules; an appeal to general human fallibility is simply not sufficient.

It's also worth noting that such post-modernist claims are self-refuting. When a post-modernist writes "It is impossible to know 100 percent how to correctly interpret a piece of writing," he certainly intends that people correctly interpret *this* particular piece of his own writing. But he has no basis for objecting when an opponent throws his post-modernism back at him and decides to "interpret" that statement as meaning, "A piece of writing has an objective meaning which is usually possible to interpret correctly."

---

16. J. Sarfati, "Moving Forward: Arguments We Think Creationists Shouldn't Use," *Creation* 24(2):20–24 (March–May 2002), <www.answersingenesis.org/dont_use>.

17. C. Wieland, K. Ham, and J. Sarfati, "Maintaining Creationist Integrity," <www.answersingenesis.org/integrity>, December 16, 2002.

18. K. Ham, "Searching for the Magic Bullet," *Creation* 25(2):34–37 (March–May 2003).

Theology Versus Science?

Reasons to Believe has argued:

- Theology is the interpretation of the Bible.
- Science is the interpretation of nature.[19]

However, the historian and theologian Dr. Noel Weeks (who also has an honors science degree in zoology) argues:

> Where there has been some realization of what the Bible actually says about the revelation through the creation, the claims for science have often been modified. It will not be claimed that the findings of science are synonymous with general revelation. Sometimes all that is said is that science studies God's general revelation. It is claimed that, as the study of general revelation, it should be granted as much respect as theology, which studies God's special revelation.
>
> Formally this may be correct, but if it is, there is a consequence which should follow. The first and most basic conclusion of science should be the character of the God who made the world. For we have seen, according to the Bible, the character of the God who made and rules the world is what creation reveals. To avoid the inconvenient fact that science, as we know it, largely ignores God, there are various excuses. The most common is to say that science is concerned with how the cosmos operates, not with how it began or why it operates as it does. . . .
>
> Suppose we had a theology which missed a basic point of the Bible, a theology which, for example, ignored the fact that God "is and that He is a rewarder of those who seek Him" (Heb. 11:6); would we think that theology a valid study of God's special revelation? Of course we would not! How can a science that ignores the existence and attributes of God be called a valid study of God's general revelation? . . .
>
> My concern here is those who want to make science an authority for Christians on the grounds that it is studying God's general revelation. Since science, as we know it today, misses the main point of God's revelation through the creation, it could hardly be said that it should be regarded as an authority by a Christian.
>
> This leaves open the possibility that there could be a very different science which would not ignore the revelation of God himself through his creation. What could that science be expected to learn from creation? . . . Compared with all that the Bible teaches, it offers very little information. Many people have wanted to solve controversial questions like the nature of creation, the

---

19. H. Ross, F. Rana, K. Samples, M. Harman, and K. Bontrager, "Life and Death in Eden, The Biblical and Scientific Evidence for Animal Death Before the Fall," audio cassette set, Reasons to Believe, 2001.

causes of homosexuality, etc. from a study of creation rather than the Bible. Clearly they expect to learn something very certain and definite other than the nature of God. What right have they to expect more definite answers to such questions from a study of creation rather than from the Bible?[20]

"Big Bang" Influenced Ross's Hermeneutics

Ross's testimony is contained in nearly all of his books. The elements are essentially this. Ross was raised in a moral, but not Christian, or even religious, family. As a teenager, he became very interested in science. At the age of 15, he concluded that the big bang must be true (see chapter 5 for refutation), and that the existence of the world demanded that there be a Creator, so he began a study of religions. He decided that the one true religion should be self-consistent and that it should agree with the natural world. He began reading the Bible, starting with Genesis, and he saw that it alone met the requirements of being the one true religion. He found that the Bible contained no errors or contradictions, which led him to salvation through the blood of Jesus.

This story reflects the statements of Romans 1 regarding what is called natural revelation, and we can rejoice in his salvation. But Ross claims that as a teenager he was struck with how well the Genesis account agreed with what he knew that science had revealed about the origin of the world:

> I was a young man of 17. I came at the Bible fresh, without input, and tackled it on my own, and you know, immediately rejected the view that they were six, consecutive 24-hour days. I knew right away those days were not 24 hours.[21]

This shows that he most definitely did not come to the Bible "fresh," but as an impressionable lad already brainwashed into the "facts" of science like the "big bang."

Nearly everyone who reads the Genesis creation account for the first time comes away with the strong impression that the Bible and "science" have serious disagreements about origins. That is why there are so many different ways in which harmonization is attempted. But Ross's testimony makes it very clear that the "fact" of the big bang influenced his hermeneutics. For more on the big bang, see chapter 5.

Much of Ross's harmonization is very similar to that of the late Peter Stoner, who had a popular-level book that enjoyed broad readership about the time that Ross was a teenager.[22] One must wonder whether Stoner influenced Ross. Interestingly, Ross wrote the foreword to the progressive creationist book by Stoner's grandson, which echoes Ross's scientific carelessness, eisegesis, and general *Scriptura sub scientia* approach.[23]

---

20. N. Weeks, *The Sufficiency of Scripture* (Edinburgh, UK: Banner of Truth Trust, 1988), p. 16–17.

21. H. Ross, *Creation Days*, audio tape, 1990.

22. P.W. Stoner, *Science Speaks* (Chicago, IL: Moody Press, 1958).

23. D. Stoner, *A New Look at an Old Earth, Resolving the Conflict between the Bible and Science* (Eugene, OR: Harvest House, 1997). See reviews of the 1992 edition of this book by D. DeYoung, *CRSQ* 31(2):94 (1994); P. Garner, *Origins* 21:17–19 (1996). Most of their criticisms apply equally well to the 1997 edition.

Atheist Recognizes Ross's True Authority!

While Ross (along with many in the Intelligent Design movement) regards the young earth view as a "stumbling block," in practice, both young-earth and old-earth creationists are attacked just as strongly by the materialist establishment. One example is the pretentiously named humanist-founded-and-operated National Center for Science Education, which describes itself as "the only organization entirely devoted to defending the teaching of evolution in the public schools."[24]

One of their contributors is Kenneth Nahigian, whose author's biography listed no scientific qualifications, nor did it reveal his membership (typical of NSCE supporters) in explicitly anti-Christian organizations, presumably lest it upset the NCSE's churchian allies. Nahigian, who critiqued a Ross lecture on progressive creationism, cited Ross as saying, "True science must thus conform to true theological findings."[25] Ross responded to Nahigian (and affirmed his warm support for the atheistic organization NCSE).[26] But he was so eager to appear "science-based" rather than Bible-based that he fell into a trap. He said:

> Not so, incidentally, I do believe (and I said so, though Nahigian must have missed it) that true theology must — and always will — conform to true science.[27]

Nahigian replied in turn:

> Ross's belief that true theology must conform to true science cheers me greatly; somehow I had heard it the other way round. As we know, a shepherd-sheep relationship between religion and science was tried once with poor results [debatable — see page 63]. Now Dr. Ross seems more in league with British evangelicals of the 1830s who wrote that if "sound science appears to contradict the Bible, we may be sure that it is our interpretation of the Bible that is at fault."[28]

Certainly Nahigian gained the impression that in any conflict between "science" and the Bible, Ross would allow "science" to determine the meaning of Scripture. But because of the fallibility of science, and infallibility of the Bible, we should give Scripture the benefit of the doubt and lay on "science" the burden of proof.

---

24. D. Batten, and J. Sarfati, "How Religiously Neutral Are the Anti-Creationist Organisations?" <www.answersingenesis.org/neutral>.

25. K. Nahigian, "Impressions: An Evening with Dr. Hugh Ross," *Reports of the National Center for Science Education* 17(1):27–29 (January/February 1997).

26. H. Ross, reply to Kenneth Nahigian, *Reports of the National Center for Science Education* 17(3):34 (May/June 1997). Ross said, "As a subscriber to NCSE, I applaud your efforts to expose sloppy scholarship and to call for higher academic standards."

27. Ibid.

28. K. Nahigian, Ken Nahigian responds, *Reports of the National Center for Science Education* 17(3):35 (May/June 1997).

MAGISTERIAL VERSUS MINISTERIAL USE OF SCIENCE

So what part can science play? Is it true that creationists reject science, just because we reject the idea that it is the 67th book of the Bible? To answer that, it would be helpful to digress to the role of reason in general. Martin Luther correctly distinguished between the *magisterial* and *ministerial* use of *reason*.[29] Because these terms are already in use, they seem to be well suited to apply to science, because it's at the heart of the dispute.

The *magisterial* use of reason occurs when reason stands over Scripture like a magistrate and judges it. Such "reasoning" is bound to be flawed, because it starts with axioms invented by fallible humans and not revealed by the infallible God. This is the chief characteristic of liberal "Christianity." The great Princeton scholar Gresham Machen showed this in his classic work *Christianity and Liberalism*. This is as pertinent now as it was when it was written 80 years ago. Machen showed that compromise with "science" eviscerated the faith:

> . . . the liberal attempt at reconciling Christianity with modern science has really relinquished everything distinctive of Christianity. . . . In trying to remove from Christianity everything that could possibly be objected to in the name of science, in trying to bribe off the enemy by those concessions which the enemy most desires, the apologist has really abandoned what he started out to defend.[30]

Earlier, he pointed out that compromise with materialism is impossible, for materialists will never be satisfied until all of Christianity is vanquished:

> Modern materialism . . . is not content with occupying the lower quarters of the Christian city, but pushes its way into all the higher reaches of life. . . . Mere concessiveness, therefore, will never succeed in avoiding the intellectual conflict.[31]

The *ministerial* use of reason occurs when reason submits to Scripture. This means that all things necessary for our faith and life are either expressly set down in Scripture or may be deduced by good and necessary consequence from Scripture. Many scriptural passages show that Christians are not supposed to check in their brains at the church door, but to use their God-given minds in subjection to God's Word.[32]

---

29. W.L. Craig, *Apologetics: An Introduction* (Chicago, IL: Moody Press , 1984), chapter 1.

J. Sarfati, "Loving God with All Your Mind: Logic and Creation," *TJ* 12(2):142–151 (1998).

30. J.G. Machen, *Christianity and Liberalism* (New York: The Macmillan Company, 1923), p. 7–8.

31. Ibid., p. 6.

32. A generally first-rate book on the importance of developing a Christ-like mind is J.P. Moreland, *Love Your God With All Your Mind* (Colorado Springs, CO: Navpress, 1997). Its main disadvantage is that Moreland is "sixty-forty in favor of the old-earth position" (p.107), possibly because of a slight overemphasis on extra-biblical revelation.

YECs don't claim that science is of the same order as logic, because valid logical deductions from true premises always lead to true conclusions, while scientific theories come and go. This characteristic of science especially applies to origin science (the study of one-off origins in the past), and some apply this even to operational science (the science of repeatable observations in the present, see page 64)[33] although it's not our main point of debate.

The Chicago Statement on Biblical Inerrancy also opposes the magisterial use of science:

Article XII

WE AFFIRM that Scripture in its entirety is inerrant, being free from all falsehood, fraud, or deceit.

WE DENY that biblical infallibility and inerrancy are limited to spiritual, religious, or redemptive themes, exclusive of assertions in the fields of history and science. We further deny that scientific hypotheses about earth history may properly be used to overturn the teaching of Scripture on creation and the flood.

Ministerial and Magisterial Uses of Science Contrasted

The ministerial use *elaborates* on the clear teachings of the Bible, and may help us decide on equally plausible alternatives consistent with the language. Note that this approach to Scripture does not deny the authority of Scripture, but recognizes that while Scripture is "true truth" it is not exhaustive truth. In contrast, the magisterial use *overrules* the clear teaching of the Bible to come up with a meaning inconsistent with sound hermeneutics. Instead of the Reformation principle of *Sola Scriptura* (Scripture alone), this is *Scriptura sub scientia* (Scripture below science). The following examples can aid our understanding of the differences between the magisterial and ministerial use of science in the interpretation of the Bible:

- Scripture teaches that a year-long global Flood (with various stages) occurred about 1,600 years after creation. Creationist geologists, such as AiG's Dr. Tas Walker, have worked on building a scientific model, based on the types of rock formations predicted in every stage.[34] A magisterial use of science is to claim that uniformitarian science disproves a global Flood, so that Genesis must be reinterpreted to mean a local Flood (as Dr. Ross does), or even dismissed as unhistorical. This is explained in chapter 8.

- The whole tenor of Scripture is that the individual is a human being right from the beginning of biological life; there is nothing to indicate that there is any secondary event of "ensoulment" after the beginning of biological life. In particular, the Psalmist teaches that life begins at conception (Ps. 51:5), that

33. G.H. Clark, *The Philosophy of Science and Belief in God,* 2nd edition (Jefferson, MD: The Trinity Foundation, 1987).
34. Tas Walker, "Biblical Geological Model," <www.uq.net.au/~zztbwalk>.

is, he explicitly states that it was "me" that existed from conception, not some blob of cells that later became "me." Science elaborates on this by showing that the union of sperm and egg (fertilization or conception) is the scientifically irrefutable beginning of the individual's life, so can be equated with the biblical term.

- The Bible teaches (ten times in Gen. 1) that living organisms reproduce "after their kind," and that man was created supernaturally from non-living matter, not from a pre-existing living creature (Gen. 2:7). Since kinds are defined by reproduction, creationists have used hybridization studies to elaborate on the boundaries of the original created kind to elucidate the biblical teaching. For example, the wholphin, a hybrid of a killer whale and a dolphin, shows that they were descendants of the same created kind, despite man's classification of them into different genera. In fact, since the wholphin is fertile, it means that its parents were really members of the same "biological species" by definition (see chapter 7 for more detail). And since the Bible does not specify that the "kind" must equal any modern definition of "species," science can help demonstrate that Ross's equation of these two terms is false.

- A magisterial use of reason is that of theistic evolutionists who claim that all living organisms, including man, have evolved from a simple cell. So if they regard Genesis as remotely historical at all, it must be reinterpreted to be compatible with the idea that one kind has changed into another kind, quite contrary to the plain language of the biblical text.

Geocentrism and the Shape of the Earth

This aspect of ministerial versus magisterial uses of science needs a section of its own. The Bible has some equivocal language on geography and cosmology, that is, language that may have several possible meanings. Science can help us decide on which meaning best fits the facts. For instance, sometimes the Bible describes heaven and earth in a context that has nothing to do with teaching any particular cosmological view. Rather, it is using equivocal language to communicate a point in a way that the original readers would have understood *accurately* with no more detail than necessary.

The best-known example concerns *geocentrism*, the view that the earth is at the absolute center of the universe.[35] Some passages talking about the rising and setting sun (for example, Eccles. 1:5) were describing events in understandable, but *still scientifically valid* terms that even modern people use, so any reader will understand what is meant. In fact, this passage and others in the Psalms are clearly poetic, not historical like Genesis (see chapter 2). Thus, they were never intended to be used as a basis for a cosmological model, such as Ptolemy's geocentric cosmology.

---

35. For a biblical and scientific critique of geocentrism, see D. Faulkner, "Geocentrism and Creation," *TJ* 15(2):110–121 (2001); <www.answersingenesis.org/geocentric>.

Rather, it is the sort of language used even today by non-geocentrists, for example, in weather bulletins and planetaria, simply because it's convenient to use the earth as a *reference frame* for many practical purposes. The language itself cannot determine whether the intent is to teach geocentrism or an earth-referent system.

Modern science helps us to understand these passages as using the earth as a reference frame, and this is a valid understanding and usage even if the original readers wouldn't have known these modern details. But in many matters involving the solar system as a whole, it is more convenient to use the sun as the reference frame, with planets revolving round it in elliptical orbits. This is often called the *heliocentric* (sun-centered) system, but in reality the planets orbit the center of mass of the solar system, which is close enough to the sun for all practical purposes because the sun has such a huge percentage of the mass. Also, the sun itself is in orbit around the galaxy's center of mass. So a more precise term is *"geokineticism"* (moving earth). And as shown on page 84, geokineticism can be used ministerially to provide a possible mechanism for the day/night cycle before the sun was created, that is, directional light and a rotating earth.

The late Sir Fred Hoyle made it clear that using the earth's reference frame was not a scientific error:

> The relation of the two pictures [geocentricity and heliocentricity] is reduced to a mere coordinate transformation and it is the main tenet of the Einstein theory that any two ways of looking at the world which are related to each other by a coordinate transformation are entirely equivalent from a physical point of view. . . . Today, we cannot say that the Copernican theory is "right" and the Ptolemaic theory "wrong" in any meaningful physical sense.[36]

Another passage that has been used as a proof text for geocentrism is Psalm 93:1, "The world is firmly established; it cannot be moved." We should also understand the terms as used by the Psalm's authors. Let's read the next verse: "[God's] throne *is* established of old," where the same word *kûn* is also translated "established." And the same Hebrew word for "moved" (*môt*) is used in Psalm 16:8, "I shall not be moved." Surely, even skeptics wouldn't accuse the Bible of teaching that the Psalmist was rooted to one spot! He meant that he would not stray from the path that God had set for him. So the earth "cannot be moved" can also mean that it will not stray from the precise orbital and rotational pattern God has set ("firmly established") for it.

A ministerial application of science that elaborates on this biblical passage is: life on earth requires that the earth's orbit is at just the right distance from the sun for liquid water to exist. Also, that the earth's rotational axis is at just the right angle from the ecliptic (orbital plane) so that temperature differences are not too extreme.

---

36. F. Hoyle, *Nicolaus Copernicus*, (London: Heinemann Educational Books Ltd., 1973), p. 78.

Galileo

Galileo has become the poster child for the alleged battle between religion and science, and the favorite example of those who believe that religion should be subservient to science. The main propagandists for this cause were the notorious 19th century anti-Christian bigots John William Draper (1811–1882) and Andrew Dickson White (1832–1918). Draper wrote *History of the Conflict between Religion and Science* (1874) as a poorly informed polemic against the Church. White was the founder of Cornell University as the first explicitly secular university in the United States, and published the two-volume work *History of the Warfare of Science with Theology in Christendom* (1896).

However, it was really a matter of *science v. science* not science v. religion. As many historians of science have noticed, the first to oppose Galileo was the scientific establishment. The prevailing "scientific" wisdom of his day was the Aristotelian/Ptolemaic theory. This was an unwieldy geocentric system, with the earth at the center of the universe and other heavenly bodies in highly complex orbits around the earth. And it had its origins in a pagan philosophical system. Conversely, the four leading pioneers of geokineticism — Copernicus, Galileo, Kepler and Newton — were all young-earth creationists!

Dr. Thomas Schirrmacher showed:

> Contrary to legend, Galileo and the Copernican system were well regarded by church officials. Galileo was the victim of his own arrogance, the envy of his colleagues, and the politics of Pope Urban VIII. He was not accused of criticizing the Bible, but disobeying a papal decree.[37]

It is true that the official charge mentioned Scripture, but this should not hide the fact that the church's real beef with Galileo was his disobedience to the church's authority rather than theological error.[38] He had insulted his former friend, Pope Urban, by putting into his mouth the words of the "fool" in his famous Dialogues. Urban was the one who initiated the trial while the inquisitors were apparently indifferent. The final decision lacked three signatures, and two of those who signed did so under protest. Only one cardinal, the pope's brother, zealously pushed the trial ahead.[39] In any case, Galileo was not actually pronounced a heretic — the verdict was "suspicion of heresy."[40]

---

37. T. Schirrmacher, "The Galileo Affair: History or Heroic Hagiography," *TJ* 14(1):91–100 (2000); <www.answersingenesis.org/gal-affair>.

38. Another book with a good discussion on the Galileo affair, as well as many other attacks on Christianity, is V. Carroll and D. Shiflett, *Christianity on Trial: Arguments Against Anti-Religious Bigotry* (San Francisco, CA: Encounter Books, 2001), chapter 3; see my joint review at <www.tektonics.org/chrtrial.html>.

39. T. Schirrmacher, "The Galileo Affair: History or Heroic Hagiography," *TJ* 14(1):91–100 (2000); www.answersingenesis.org/gal-affair, p. 96–97.

40. S. Drake, *Galileo* (Oxford, UK: Oxford University Press, 1980), p. 351.

Science historian John Heilbron provides further evidence in his book *The Sun in the Church*.[41] In this book, favorably reviewed by the secular science journals *New Scientist*[42] and *Science*,[43] he points out:

> Galileo's heresy, according to the standard distinction used by the Holy Office, was "inquisitorial" rather than "theological." This distinction allowed it to proceed against people for disobeying orders or creating scandals, although neither offence violated an article defined and promulgated by a pope or general council. . . . Since, however, the church had never declared that the biblical passages implying a moving sun had to be interpreted in favor of a Ptolemaic universe as an article of faith, optimistic commentators . . . could understand "formally heretical" to mean "provisionally not accepted."[44]

Heilbron supports this simply by documenting the general reactions by Galileo's contemporaries and later astronomers, who:

> . . . appreciated that the reference to heresy in connection with Galileo or Copernicus had no general or theological significance.[45]

This is shown by the fact that far from opposing astronomical research, the church supported astronomers and even allowed the cathedrals *themselves* to be used as solar observatories — hence the subtitle of Heilbron's book, *Cathedrals as Solar Observatories*. These observatories, called *meridiane*, were "reverse sundials," or gigantic pinhole cameras where the sun's image was projected from a hole in a window in the cathedral's lantern onto a meridian line. Analyzing the sun's motion further weakened the Ptolemaic model, yet this research was well supported. And Arthur Koestler documented that only 50 years after Galileo, astronomers of the Jesuit Order, "the intellectual spearhead of the Catholic Church," taught geokinetic astronomy in China.[46]

However, some church authorities became persuaded by the Aristotelians because the latter failed to realize that biblical passages must be understood in terms of what the *author meant to convey*. Instead, they reinterpreted these passages in accordance with the science fashion of their day. Ironically, many people castigate YECs for

---

41. J.L. Heilbron, *The Sun in the Church: Cathedrals as Solar Observatories* (Cambridge, MA: Harvard University Press, 1999).
42. *New Scientist* 164(2214):98 (November 27, 1999).
43. A. van Helden, "Cathedrals as Astronomical Instruments," *Science* 286(5448):2279–80 (December 17, 1999).
44. J.L. Heilbron, *The Sun in the Church: Cathedrals as Solar Observatories* (Cambridge, MA: Harvard University Press, 1999), p. 202–203.
45. J.L. Heilbron, *The Sun in the Church: Cathedrals as Solar Observatories* (Cambridge, MA: Harvard University Press, 1999), p. 203.
46. A. Koestler, *The Sleepwalkers: A History of Man's Changing Vision of the Universe* (London: Hutchinson, 1959), p. 427.

supposedly making the same mistake as the church in Galileo's day. Yet the opposite is true — it's the long-age compromisers and theistic evolutionists who are the true heirs of Galileo's opponents, because both are making the same mistake of using current scientific ideas magisterially over Scripture.[47]

Flat Earth Myth

Some skeptics and even professing Christians have claimed that the Bible teaches a flat earth[48] with a solid dome above.[49] But again, the language is not explicit and simply uses descriptive terms, and even if the readers did not understand modern science, it does not mean that the language in the relevant biblical texts was incorrect, just as an evolutionist would not be charged with scientific ignorance or error when describing a "sunset" to his wife.[50]

Also, the same 19th-century anti-Christians Draper and White promoted the myth that the medieval church universally taught that the earth is flat. This was greatly aided by the fable concocted earlier that century, asserting that Columbus was a great hero flying in the face of almost universal prejudice that the earth was flat. This was started by Washington Irving in his 1828 book *The Life and Voyages of Christopher Columbus*, a self-confessed mixture of fact and fiction. The historian Jeffrey Burton Russell has documented that nearly all Christian scholars who have ever discussed the earth's shape have assented to its roundness.[51]

OLD-EARTH COMPROMISES DUE TO MAGISTERIAL USE OF SCIENCE

If an old earth were really the teaching of Scripture, then one claim is glaringly conspicuous by its absence, that is, any claim in commentaries that the Bible *unambiguously teaches* long ages. Rather, the usual claim is that the biblical text appears on the surface to teach a young earth but *may allow for* an old earth. We never hear something like, "Yes, the decay of the earth's magnetic field and rapid reversals seem to provide irrefutable scientific proof of a young earth. But we mustn't allow even the strongest science to overrule the clear teaching of the Word of God that the earth is billions of years old."

---

47. See R. Grigg, "The Galileo Twist," *Creation* 19(4):30–32 (September–November 1997); <www.answersingenesis.org/gal-twist>.

48. J.P. Holding, "Is the *erets* (earth) Flat? Equivocal Language in the Geography of Genesis 1 and the Old Testament: A Response to Paul H. Seely," *TJ* 14(3):51–54 (2000).

49. J.P. Holding, "Is the *Raqiya'* ('Firmament') a Solid Dome? Equivocal Language in the Cosmology of Genesis 1 and the Old Testament: A Response to Paul H. Seely," *TJ* 13(2):44–51 (1999).

50. P.H. Seely, response to Holding (previous two footnotes), plus reply by Holding, *TJ* 15(2):52–53 (2001).

51. Jeffrey Burton Russell, *Inventing the Flat Earth: Columbus & Modern Historians* (New York: Praeger, 1991). Prof. Russell can find only five obscure writers in the first 1,500 years of the Christian era who denied that the earth was a globe. But he documents a large number of writers, including the Venerable Bede and Thomas Aquinas, who affirmed the earth's sphericity.
See also *Creation* 14(4):21, 16(2):48–9; and the articles under <www.answersingenesis.org/critics#flatearth>.

No, repeatedly we see conservative old-earthers admit that the plainest meaning of the text is young-earth creationism, but since "science" (supposedly) proves an old earth, the text must be reinterpreted. They would also claim to be using science ministerially. But another conspicuous absence is any thought by any respected Christian exegete of "long-age" interpretations until such views became popular in "science" in the early 19th century, as shown in chapter 3. This indicates that such views were not gleaned from Scripture; instead they are novel interpretations diametrically opposed to the text.

It is true that some old-earthers do not even realize they are doing this. For example, some of the signatories to the *Chicago Statement on Biblical Inerrancy* are old-earth creationists. For example, one of the participants at the International Council of Biblical Inerrancy, progressive creationist Dr. Walter Bradley, told AiG's Dr. Terry Mortenson (e-mail, April 20, 2000) that about 90 percent of the ICBI participants (which included at least some who were involved in drafting this statement) rejected the YEC view. So in this case, these old-earth signers were, knowingly or unknowingly, violating Article XII of their own statement. Ross does the same when he cites the Chicago statement with approval. Some might argue that because some signatories were old-earthers, this is therefore allowable by the statement. But we must go by the *words* of this statement, even if some of its signatories were inconsistent (we never claimed they were inspired!).

What follows is a number of admissions by conservative scholars on why they don't accept Genesis. There are a lot of quotes here, and one point is to undermine the common appeal, "but the majority says. . . ." Of course, truth is not decided by democratic vote. But the quotes below demonstrate that the *motivation* for this majority view is faulty:

- Charles Hodge (1797–1878) was a systematic theologian at Princeton seminary who wrote many books and articles defending the truths of Christianity, including biblical inerrancy. But he lapsed by rejecting the plain meaning of Genesis because of alleged geological "facts," which were really uniformitarian *interpretations* of facts: "It is of course admitted that, taking this account [Genesis] by itself, it would be most natural to understand the word [day] in its ordinary sense; but if that sense brings the Mosaic account into conflict with facts [millions of years], and another sense avoids such conflict, then it is obligatory on us to adopt that other."[52]

- J. Barton Payne (1922–1979), a highly regarded Presbyterian Old Testament scholar, admits about a variant of the day-age theory: "[C]onfessedly, it would not have been as readily deduced from the Genesis text had it not been for the evidences advanced by secular science."[53]

---

52. C. Hodge, *Systematic Theology* (Grand Rapids, MI: Wm. B. Eerdmans Publishing Company, 1997), p. 570–571.

53. J.B. Payne, *The Theology of the Older Testament* (Grand Rapids, MI: Zondervan, 1972), p. 136.

- Gleason Archer, Hebrew scholar and staunch defender of biblical inerrancy: "From a superficial reading, the impression received is that the entire creative process took place in six twenty-four hour days. If this was the true intent of the Hebrew author (a questionable deduction, as will be presently shown), this seems to run counter to modern scientific research, which indicated that the planet earth was created several billion years ago . . . the more recently expanded knowledge of nuclear physics has brought into play another type of evidence which seems to confirm the great antiquity of the Earth, that is, the decay of radioactive minerals."[54]

The rest of Archer's section is a rationalization to explain away the clear biblical teaching of six 24-hour days, to fit in with uniformitarian "science," because he (rightly) wants to preserve inerrancy, but (wrongly) reinterprets Scripture rather than the "science."

- Pattle Pun is a biology professor at the ostensibly evangelical Wheaton College. He admits that the plain meaning of Genesis is as YECs say, but rejects it because of the authority of "science": "It is apparent that the most straightforward understanding of Genesis, *without regard to the hermeneutical considerations suggested by science,* is that God created the heavens and the earth in six solar days, that man was created on the sixth day, and that death and chaos entered the world after the fall of Adam and Eve, and that all fossils were the result of the catastrophic deluge that spared only Noah's family and the animals therewith."[55]

- James Montgomery Boice (1938–2000), a staunch defender of biblical inerrancy, admitted much the same: "We have to admit here [concerning those who take the six days of creation as literal days] that the exegetical basis [the arguments from the words of Scripture] of the creationists is strong. . . . In spite of the careful biblical and scientific research that has accumulated in support of the creationists' view, there are problems that make the theory wrong to most (including many evangelical) scientists. . . . Data from various disciplines point to a very old earth and even older universe. . . ."[56]

- Meredith Kline, a leading advocate of the "framework hypothesis" (see page 94), admits that his primary rationale is to avoid a conflict with "science." His abstract states: "To rebut the literalist interpretation of the Genesis creation week propounded by the young-earth theorists is a central concern of this article.

---

54. G.L. Archer, *A Survey of Old Testament Introduction* (Chicago, IL: Moody, 1985), p. 187.

55. P.P.T. Pun, *Journal of the American Scientific Affiliation* 39:14 (1987); emphasis added. Note that creationists would say that *most,* rather than all, fossils were formed during Noah's flood. As shown in chapter 8, creationists acknowledge post-Flood catastrophes.

56. J.M. Boice, *Genesis: An Expositional Commentary* (Grand Rapids, MI: Zondervan Publishing House, Grand Rapids, 1982), 1:57–62.

At the same time, the exegetical evidence adduced also refutes the harmonistic day-age view. The conclusion is that as far as the time frame is concerned, with respect to both the duration and sequence of events, the scientist is left free of biblical constraints in hypothesizing about cosmic origins."[57]

In note 47, Kline says, "In this article I have advocated an interpretation of biblical cosmogony according to which Scripture is open to the current scientific view of a very old universe and, in that respect, does not discountenance the theory of the evolutionary origin of man."

In an unedited draft of this paper, Kline admitted further: "Certainly, Genesis indicates that there were steps or stages. The debate is over the time duration of each step. . . . To be sure, the word *"yôm"* or "day" is almost always used to refer to a 24-hour period so the prima facie indication would be the same in Genesis. . . . My concern here is that the literary structure may indicate something else."

- Henri Blocher, another leading framework proponent, admits: "This hypothesis overcomes a number of problems that plagued the commentators [including] the confrontation with the scientific vision of the most distant past."[58]

- Bruce K. Waltke, leading Hebrew and Old Testament Scholar: "The days of creation may also pose difficulties for a strict historical account. Contemporary scientists almost unanimously discount the possibility of creation in one week, and we cannot summarily discount the evidence of the earth sciences."[59]

A disturbing implication of the above quotes is that sound grammatical principles are not enough to understand Scripture; we need uniformitarian "science." I fail to see the difference, *in principle,* between that view and the claim of the medieval church that we need the Papal Magisterium to understand Scripture.

Scientific Discoveries Supporting Genesis 1–11?

This is the title of Appendix B of Ross's book *The Genesis Question* (GQ). This contains a list of about 50 examples of how modern science confirms Genesis. However, many of Ross's arguments are blatantly circular — that is, they amount to, "Isn't it amazing how modern uniformitarian science backs up what Genesis says?" Hardly surprising, because Ross has reinterpreted Genesis to fit in with uniformitarian science! For example, among these discoveries are the supposed "proof" of millions of years and the alleged "proof" that the Flood would not have left much trace, yet these are meant to "support" Genesis. Why should an absence of any trace be evidence for Ross's version of the Genesis flood, rather than for no flood at all? It's hardly likely

57. M.G. Kline, "Space and Time in the Genesis Cosmogony," *Perspectives on Science and Christian Faith* 48:2 (1996).
58. H. Blocher, *In the Beginning* (Downers Grove, IL: Inter-Varsity Press, 1984), p. 50.
59. B.K. Waltke and C.J. Fredricks, *Genesis: A Commentary* (Grand Rapids, MI: Zondervan, 2001), p. 77.

that unbelievers are going to be convinced by the tenuous connection between this "science" and Genesis. Ross also overstates the case in other respects.

GENERAL AND SPECIAL REVELATION

The Dual Revelation Theory

Ross tries to justify what we call the magisterial use of science by appealing to certain biblical passages. For example, Psalm 19:1–4 and Romans 1:19–20 state that the world around us reveals the existence and some attributes of the Creator. This limited information about God that the physical world impresses upon the minds of men is often called *general revelation*, as opposed to the *special revelation* of the Bible and Jesus Christ. Both reveal information about God, but Ross elevates certain interpretations of the physical world to the level of Scripture itself. This is called the *dual revelation theory*. This is contrasted with his caricature of creationists believing in a *single revelation theory*.

Ross argues that since God is the author of both books, the Bible and the "book" of nature, the two must necessarily agree. As shown, Ross has expanded the dual revelation theory to the point of likening nature to the 67th book of the Bible. In practice, as will be shown, Ross takes gross liberties with the scriptural text, to fit the canonical 66 books into what he calls the "67th book," nature [C&T:56]. There are several problems with this approach.

The Bible Never Makes Such a Claim for Nature

While Psalm 19:1–4 and Romans 1:19–20 state that God's existence and some of His attributes can be inferred from nature, they hardly elevate nature to the level to which Ross insists it must be raised. For one thing, they do not say that we must study the creation *scientifically* to learn God's attributes; rather, they are *already obvious to everyone*, so people are "without excuse." For another, in Romans 1, Paul only says that the witness of creation is sufficient to condemn people for their unbelief and disobedience. There is no hint here or in any other writings of Paul (or any other biblical writer) that he thinks creation should be considered as a book of Scripture.

However, Ross lists a number of biblical passages, including the above, that supposedly support his position on dual revelation (C&T:57). An examination of all of the other verses reveals that they do no such thing; they generally give fewer specifics than Psalm 19 and Romans 1. For example, Ross lists Job 10:8–14, 12:7, 34:14–15, 35:10–12, 37:5–7, 38–41, for which see page 61, "How did Job know?"

The equating of nature to the 67th book of the Bible is an *inference* that Ross has made. Any systematic study of Scripture involves inferences, but those inferences are from actual propositions, and must be continually compared to other passages to check their legitimacy. This is particularly sobering in light of the warning of Revelation 22:18 against adding to the words of the Bible. Such a major expansion of God's revelation should be very carefully scrutinized. As it turns out, Ross has overstated his argument for the dual revelation theory. While he uses many passages to try to make his case, they instead illustrate his attempt to win the reader's support with a blizzard of citations.

General Revelation Is Limited

Ross has given a list of seven such attributes that he claims can be deduced from general revelation [G1:181–182]. The first attribute is God's existence, which comes straight out of Romans 1. The passage also states that God's mighty power may be inferred from nature, which appears to be part of Ross's attribute number two.

Creationists have never denied, but rather have always affirmed, that creation reveals these aspects. Therefore, it is fallacious for Ross to charge that we believe in "single revelation" theology. There is a huge difference between regarding general revelation as *limited* and denying it altogether, as Ross implies we do.

While Romans 1 only mentions these two attributes, Ross continues with four or five more, including such items as God's perfection, justice, love, and mercy. Since neither Romans 1 nor Psalm 19 in any way mentions those attributes in the context of general revelation, Ross must have gleaned them from elsewhere. The most obvious source is the rest of the Book of Romans and the rest of the Bible, which illustrates the gross inadequacy of general revelation. General revelation is sufficient to draw man's mind to the thoughts of a creator; but to really know God and to have a true knowledge of history, one must turn to special revelation.

This inadequacy of general revelation is clearly illustrated by the entire Psalm 19. The first four verses discuss the declaration of God's glory by the heavens, and the next two expand on the sun's role in the heavens. Verse three is translated in the KJV (and similarly in the NIV) as, "*There is* no speech nor language, *where* their voice is not heard," which is sometimes understood to refer to the universality of their message. But three of those words are in italics in the KJV, indicating that they are not in the original Hebrew. It is possible that verse three actually should read, "no speech nor language, their voice is not heard." This is the sense of the translation of the NASB, NJB, and NRSV. In other words, what may be emphasized here is that the message of the heavens is non-verbal and unwritten. Such communication is quite limited, which is why the remainder of the Psalm is so important.

Superiority of Scripture

The final seven verses of Psalm 19 delineate what the Law and the prophets can do. The seventh verse alone states, "The law of the LORD is perfect, converting the soul: the testimony of the LORD is sure, making wise the simple." Notice that this is far more specific and powerful than any claim made for general revelation. That is, the very passage that Ross cites to justify his position underscores the *supremacy* of Scripture — the phrase "the Law and the prophets" encompassed all of Scripture written up to the time of the writing of this Psalm.

The truly important things about God and life that one must know can be found only in Scripture. Ross obviously knows these things from Scripture, and he attempts to imprint them onto general revelation. The Bible does not support this.

Indeed, it appears contrary to the clear teaching of Scripture. If Ross were right, there would be no need for missionary activity, contrary to Romans 10:13 ff (more on this aspect of Ross's thinking below). To state it succinctly from Romans 1 and 10, general revelation is sufficient only to condemn people, *not* to save; for salvation, special revelation is necessary. In his zeal to make a strong case, Ross has grossly overstated this argument. At best, this is sloppy logic and exegesis, and his equation of general and special revelation is seriously flawed.

Misunderstanding "General Revelation"

Not only is the dual revelation theory problematic for the above reasons, but Ross does not even understand the term "general revelation." Ross claims that we must not downplay the significance of general revelation, because knowledge from this source is increasing exponentially.[60] However, in systematic theology, general revelation is defined as knowledge accessible to everyone at any time and in any place.

If "knowledge" is increasing rapidly, then it could not have been known to previous generations, so is not general revelation, by definition. Certainly, as shown in the chapter on the history of biblical interpretation, almost no Christians and few non-Christians before the beginning of the 19th century had any thoughts of the earth being billions of years old. So, this cannot be true general revelation. Rather, general revelation would be knowledge of which the "Timothy" of the Timothy Test (see page 39) would be aware.[61]

How Did Job Know?

Ross reverts to the correct understanding of general revelation when discussing Job, at least insofar as being understandable to people everywhere (FoG:181):

> More than speaking merely of God's existence, the creation, according to Romans 1, also reveals essential truths about God's character, which would include His desire and means to form a relationship with man. As an illustration of the accessibility of that information, the Bible includes an account of an ancient character, Job (Job 7–19), who without the aid of scriptures, discerned all the elements of "the gospel," the good news of how man can find eternal life in God.

But of course, Job didn't have any idea about the big bang or millions of years, which undermines Ross's normal misuse of the term "general revelation." Ross asserts that Job must have gained knowledge through general revelation. However, Job's third reply to Eliphaz indicates that Job was aware of prior divine verbal revelation (Job 23:12):

60. H. Ross and G. Archer, "The Day-Age View," in D.G. Hagopian, *The Genesis Debate* (Mission Viejo, CA: Crux Press, 2001), p. 73.
  A.S. Kulikovsky, "Sizing the Day: Review of Hagopian, *The Genesis Debate*," *TJ* 16(1):41–44 (2002).
61. See also R.L. Thomas, "General Revelation and Biblical Hermeneutics," *The Master's Seminary Journal* 9(1):4–23 (Spring 1998).

I have not departed from the commandment of his lips; I have treasured in my bosom the words of his mouth.

This could even refer to Scripture written up to that time. Job lived not long after the Flood, and there's no reason to believe that he would have not been aware of God's revelation in Genesis 1–11. Orthodox views of inspiration of Genesis regard Moses as the *editor* of pre-existing written accounts.[62]

Job eventually responds in faith to God's *verbal* (that is, involving words) revelation (Job 38–41), albeit via direct oral communication rather than Scripture. But this indicates the *insufficiency* of "general revelation" without God's lecture about its significance.[63]

Job also seemed to know of a future bodily resurrection (Job 19:25–27), which is without parallel in nature. This could be explained either by special direct revelation or by Job's knowledge of the redeemer revealed in the *protevangelion* of Genesis 3:15 or the translation of Enoch (Gen. 5:24).

Ecclesiastes: Reductio ad Absurdum *of General-Revelation–Only*

Many groups, including some cults, like to use Ecclesiastes to justify their teaching of annihilationism or soul sleep because of passages like "the dead know nothing" (Eccles. 9:5). However, they never quote the next clause, "and they have no more reward" which "proves" more than they want. It would entail that there is no heaven for believers to look forward to either!

But most evangelical commentaries point out the frequent phrase "under the sun." Thus, they point out that the writer is deliberately writing from a *humanistic viewpoint*, where the only things that matter are "under the sun," not heavenly things. And the point of the book is to show that all things "under the sun" — human wisdom, material possessions, and relationships — are futile, "vanity of vanities," because everyone dies.

Ecclesiastes pointedly illustrates the misleading character of general revelation, "under the sun," without special revelation to interpret it correctly. From general revelation alone, one might well believe that the dead know nothing, and one would have no reason to believe that they will rise again. Under general revelation, one might assume that there is no ultimate difference between wisdom and foolishness, because both the wise and foolish perish (2:16). What is the benefit of working (3:9)? Is there no judgment for oppressors or relief for the oppressed (4:1)? Why be righteous at all, since some righteous people perish and some wicked prosper (7:15)? Ecclesiastes shows how general revelation in isolation can be misleading, and ends in despair. But the book ends by pointing out that *special revelation* makes sense of all this (Eccles. 12:13):

---

62. R. Grigg, "Did Moses Really Write Genesis?" *Creation* 20(4):43–46 (September–November 1998); <www.answersingenesis.org/genesis#jedp>.

63. M. Maniguet, *The Theological Method of Hugh Ross: An Analysis and Critique*, M.Th. Thesis, Systematic Theology, Baptist Bible Seminary, Clarks Summit, PA, p. 35–38, May 2002.

The end of the matter; all has been heard. Fear God, and keep his commandments; for this is the whole duty of man. For God will bring every deed into judgment, with every secret thing, whether good or evil.

SCIENCE: A RESULT OF CREATIONIST THEOLOGY

Young-earth creationists often point out that science grew out of a Christian world view. In fact, many historians, of a wide number of religious persuasions from Christians to atheists, point out that the basis of modern science depends on the assumption that the universe was made by a rational Creator.[64] An orderly universe makes perfect sense only if it were made by an orderly Creator. But if atheism or polytheism were true, then there would be no way to deduce from these belief systems that the universe is (or should be) orderly. Genesis 1:28 gives us permission (and by implication even commands us) to investigate creation, unlike, say, animism or pantheism, which teach that the creation itself is divine. And since God is sovereign, He was free to create as He pleased. So where the Bible is silent, the only way to find out how His creation works is to *experiment*, not to rely on man-made philosophies, as did the ancient Greeks.

Note that creationists regard "natural laws" as *descriptions* of the way God upholds His creation in a *regular* and *repeatable* way (see Col. 1:15–17), while miracles are God's way of upholding His creation in a special way for special reasons. Because God's work of creation *finished* at the end of day 6 (Gen. 2:1–3), creationists following the Bible would expect that God has since usually worked through "natural laws." The exception would be where He has revealed in the Bible that He used a miracle — and in the case of very rare, localized miracles that God has performed in answer to the prayers of some of His people in a particular place. And since "natural laws" are descriptive, they cannot prescribe what cannot happen; they cannot rule out miracles.

The Christian world view inspired developments essential to the rise of modern scientific method, such as the logical thought patterns of the medieval scholastic philosophers and the little-known but extensive inventiveness and mechanical ingenuity fostered by the monasteries. This does not mean they were right about everything, but the Middle Ages are often falsely dismissed as the "Dark Ages," despite a genuine industrial revolution, including inventions of water and wind power, labor-saving heavy plows, and ingenious architectural devices, such as flying buttresses.[65]

Ross has also argued along the same lines, which is good. Where he falls down is in the next section, which shows how the concept of "science" is hijacked to support false views of history.

64. S. Jaki, *Science and Creation* (Edinburgh and London: Scottish Academic Press, 1974).
   L. Eiseley, *Darwin's Century: Evolution and the Men Who Discovered It* (New York: Doubleday, Anchor, 1961).
65. V. Carroll and D. Shiflett, *Christianity on Trial: Arguments Against Anti-Religious Bigotry* (San Francisco, CA: Encounter Books, 2001), chapter 3.

ORIGIN AND OPERATION SCIENCE

Ross would agree with the previous section. This describes *operation science*, which deals only with repeatable, observable processes in the *present*. This must be distinguished from *origin science* that helps us to make educated guesses about origins in the *past*.[66]

Operation science has indeed been very successful in understanding the world and has led to many improvements in the quality of life, such as putting men on the moon and curing diseases. As explained above, because God *finished* creating at the end of day 6, biblical creationists try to find natural laws for every aspect of operation science, and would not invoke a miracle to explain any repeating event in nature *in the present* (or since the Flood and Tower of Babel, which were the last worldwide disruptions to the normal course of nature). Creationists do not differ too much from evolutionists or long-agers in matters of operation science, despite a common accusation that we are "anti-science."

In contrast, evolution and long-age belief are speculations about the unobservable and unrepeatable *past*. Thus, they come under *origin science,* and that is the main scientific difference between us. Rather than observation, origin science uses the principles of *causality* (everything that has a beginning has a cause; see chapter 5 for some implications concerning the universe and a creator) and *analogy* (for example, we observe that intelligence is needed to generate complex coded information in the present, so we can reasonably assume the same for the past). Operation science also uses these principles, but applies them to actual repeatable observations. And because there was no material intelligent designer for life, it is legitimate to invoke a non-material designer for life. Creationists invoke the miraculous only for origin science and only where there is biblical testimony to God's miraculous activities (such as at the Fall, the Flood, the Tower of Babel, Jesus' ministry), and, as shown, this does *not* mean they will invoke it for operation science.

To explain further, the laws that govern the *operation* of a computer are not those that made the computer in the first place. Much anti-creationist propaganda is like saying that if we concede that a computer had an intelligent designer, then we might not analyze a computer's workings in terms of natural laws of electron motion through semiconductors, and might think there are little intelligent beings pushing electrons around instead. Similarly, believing that the genetic code was originally designed does not preclude us from believing that it works entirely by the laws of chemistry, involving DNA, RNA, proteins, etc. (though creationists, like all Christians, would say that these laws operate under the sustaining power of God). Conversely, the fact that the coding machinery works according to reproducible laws of chemistry does not show that the laws of chemistry were sufficient to build such a system from a primordial soup.

---

66. N.L. Geisler and J.K. Anderson, *Origin Science: A Proposal for the Creation-Evolution Controversy* (Grand Rapids, MI: Baker Books, 1987).

Sir Isaac Newton (1642/3–1727), widely regarded as the greatest scientist of all time, may have been the first to make the distinction between operation and origin science, although not using those terms:

> Where natural causes are at hand God uses them as instruments in his works, but I do not think them sufficient for ye creation.[67]

Were You There?

Some creationist speakers use this phrase as a memorable way to teach laypeople how to deflect arrogant "scientific" pronouncements about the past that conflict with Scripture. It is based on what God told Job: "Where were you when I laid the foundation of the world?" (Job 38:4). This is meant to show that for all the appeal to "science" with its reputation for observation and experimentation, no scientist was there in the beginning. And if the reply is "No, but neither were you," then there is an opportunity to show that the Creator *was* there, and He has given an accurate and understandable eyewitness account.

Ross tries to deflect this argument (C&T:99–100):

> Ken Ham of ICR [true of Ham when Ross wrote] makes these statements: "There were no observers to these long ago events." . . . "No one was there to record these past events. . . . Scientists only have the present — they do not have the past." . . .
>
> Actually, the case is exactly the opposite to what Ham says. Astronomers have only the past — they do not have the present. They cannot record present events. But they can record all manner of past events. For instance, when astronomers observe the sun, they are recording the physics of God's creation as it was eight minutes ago, for that is how long it took for the light of the sun to travel to the astronomers' telescopes. When astronomers observe the Crab Nebula, they are recording the physics of God's creation as it was two thousand years before the birth of Jesus, for the Crab Nebula is 4,000 light years distant.

This last is a mistake. The Crab Nebula is 6,300 light years away. Ross continues:

> In observing the Andromeda Galaxy, astronomers are testing physics as it was two million years ago. In detecting the tiny ripples in cosmic background radiation astronomers are measuring the state of the universe as it was just 300,000 years after the creation event, some 17 billion years ago.
>
> Because of the time it takes for light to travel from the stars, galaxies, and other sources for the astronomers' telescopes, their telescopes operate like time machines into the past. Astronomers can literally measure the heavens to see what God did in the past. In answer to the question, "Were you there?"

---

67. I. Newton, *letter to Thomas Burnett,* 1681.

astronomers can reply, "Yes, we were. We can see what happened back then because the report of it is reaching us today. Have a look for yourself to see how the heavens declare the glory of God."

However, in context, Ham was simply demonstrating the distinction between origin science and operation science. The objection might be resolved by realizing that the distinction can be renamed *inferential* and *observational* science. Any real *observations* by an astronomer would still count as being in the present. This is very different from *inferring* that certain things happened (for example, the sun forming from a collapsing nebula, the "age of reptiles," etc.) that we *cannot* observe. The assumptions made about light travel time are addressed in chapter 5, and this chapter also points out that big-bangers have their own light-travel problem. The point is that the astronomers did *not* see the light travel all those great distances. And they certainly did not see the "big bang," either directly or indirectly. So, Ham's question to big-bang cosmologists still applies.

WHAT DOES OUR AUTHORITY TEACH?

Now that we have established what the authority is, namely, the Bible, we can determine what it teaches. The following is a summary, and the rest of the book elaborates on this.

Genesis contains a number of Hebrew grammatical features, which show that it was intended to teach a straightforward history of the world from its creation. Genesis, backed up by the rest of Scripture, unambiguously teaches that:

- The heavens, earth, and everything in them were created in six consecutive, normal-length days, the same as those of our working week (Exod. 20:8–11).

- The world is about 6,000 years old; Jesus said mankind was there from the "beginning of creation," not billions of years later (Mark 10:6).

- Adam sinned and brought physical death to mankind (Rom. 5:12–19; 1 Cor. 15:21–22).

- Since man was the federal head of creation, the whole creation was cursed (Gen. 3;14–19; Rom. 8:20–22), which included death to animals, with the end of the exclusively vegetarian diet originally mandated for both humans and animals (Gen. 1:29–30, 9:3).

- God judged the world by a globe-covering Flood, which Jesus and Peter compared with the coming judgment at Christ's return (Luke 17:26–27; 2 Pet. 3:3–7). This destroyed all land vertebrate animals and people not on the ocean-liner–sized ark.

- God judged the people again by confusing their language at Babel — after they had refused to spread out and repopulate the earth after the Flood.

CHAPTER 2

THE DAYS OF CREATION

The previous chapter showed that it was vital to establish the primary authority of Scripture over science, and that Ross was wrong to place "science" on the same level or, in practice, at a higher level. After this, we can decide what this authority teaches. So, on the matter of creation days, we should be able to work out the correct meaning from Scripture alone, without trying to make it fit the alleged claims of "science."

This chapter demonstrates, from the grammar of Genesis 1, that the days of creation were 24 hours long. There is much supporting evidence from the way Genesis 1 is interpreted in other parts of the Bible, and from the way the Hebrew word *yôm* ("day") is used throughout the Old Testament in different contexts. In particular, whenever *yôm* is used with a *number* or the words *evening* or *morning*, it can mean only an ordinary day, never a long period of time. And the Fourth Commandment makes sense only if the days of creation week were the same as those of the ordinary working week.

This chapter also refutes many of Ross's fallacious arguments against 24-hour creation days, as well as dealing with other major compromise views, such as the gap theory and the literary framework hypothesis.

Note: The basic arguments for literal days are straightforward, which is why any child can see that this is meant. But some of Ross's explanations invoke alleged technicalities of Hebrew, therefore some of my counterpoints in this chapter must go into some depth to refute his points.

BIBLICAL EVIDENCE FOR LITERAL CREATION DAYS

Semantic Range

The semantic range of a word is all the possible meanings of that word in the given language. For example, in the original Hebrew of Genesis, the word translated "day" is יוֹם (*yôm*). This occurs 2,300 times in the entire Old Testament, with 1,450 in the singular, and 845 in the plural, and five in the dual form (two days). Its semantic range is restricted to only five meanings:

1. a period of light in a day/night cycle;
2. a period of 24 hours;
3. a general or vague concept of time;
4. a specific point of time; and
5. a period of a year.

One rule of thumb is "when the plain sense makes common sense, take no other sense, lest it be nonsense." The normal sense of day and *yôm* is certainly a period of 24 hours,[1] and this is what is normally meant by the word "literal."[2] Significantly, HALOT indicates Genesis 1:5 as a "day of twenty-four hours."

But even more important is analyzing the specific context, because *sometimes* the context justifies other interpretations. Many day-age creationists set up a straw man by claiming that young-earth creationists (YECs) think that *yôm* can only mean a 24-hour day, which is simply not so, as can be seen from our writings. But this explains why old-earth proponents present exceptions to literal days as though it's a knock-down argument and somehow something YECs have never considered. But, as will be shown, old-earthers ignore the precise context.

When Does "Day" Mean "Day"?

Ross appeals to the semantic range of *yôm* to justify his pick of an "age" interpretation of the six creation days of Genesis 1 as millions of years long. He writes (GQ:65):

> In English, the word *day* enjoys flexible usage. We refer to the day of the dinosaurs and the day of the Romans, and no one misunderstands our meaning. But we recognize this usage as figurative, acknowledging just two

---

1. I am perfectly aware that a day is not exactly 24 hours — more like 23 hours and 56 minutes. But the expression "24-hour day" is very well known and understood as meaning a complete day-night cycle. Therefore it's pusillanimous to pedantically attack this phrase and somehow say that this undermines a claim that the Genesis days were not literal, in the sense of a complete rotation of the earth about its axis. So, too, the Genesis days were still "literal" even if the earth's rotation has slowed since then — but they would have been shorter, so it would be the opposite of what old-earthers require!

2. A very thorough study is J. Stambaugh, "The Days of Creation: A Semantic Approach," *CEN Tech. J.* 5(1):70–78 (1991); <www.answersingenesis.org/semantic>. This covers the meanings of the word *yôm* and shows that there were plenty of other words that God could have used if He had wanted to teach long periods of time.

   R. Grigg, "How Long Were the Days in Genesis 1? What Did God Intend to Understand from the Words He Used?" *Creation* 19(1):23–25 (1996); <www.answersingenesis.org/docs/2452.asp>. This is largely based on the above study by Stambaugh.

   A.S. Kulikovsky, "A Summary of Evidence for Literal 24-hr Creation Days in Genesis 1," <www.kulikovskyonline.net/hermeneutics/Gendays.htm>, November 28, 2002, not only summarizes the evidence handily, but refutes a number of objections from Ross's disciple, Don Stoner.

   Another recent scholarly defense of literal days by a professor of Old Testament is R.V. McCabe, "A Defense of Literal Days in the Creation Week," *Detroit Baptist Seminary Journal* 5:97–123 (Fall 2000).

literal definitions: a twenty-four hour period, from midnight to midnight, and the daylight hours (roughly twelve, but varying from one latitude and season to another).

That is, because "day"/*yôm*, in *some contexts,* can have a non-literal meaning, Ross feels justified in assuming that a non-literal meaning is acceptable in the *particular context* of Genesis 1. Ross even claims that "age" is "a literal reading of the Genesis creation chapters" (GQ:86). Since "literal" means the way a word is normally used, apart from certain contexts, this is surely a very non-literal usage of the word "literal"!

But such a justification shows that he could benefit from elementary training in exegesis, for example, that given in the book *Exegetical Fallacies,* by the evangelical New Testament scholar Dr. Don Carson. Ross commits a classic case of a fallacy that Carson called:

> **Unwarranted expansion of an expanded semantic field.** The fallacy in this instance lies in the supposition that the meaning of the word in a specific context is much broader than the context itself allows and may bring with it the word's entire semantic range.[3]

That is, the meaning of a word must be determined by how it is used in the specific context, not by possible meanings in unrelated contexts. Oxford Hebrew scholar James Barr also castigated this sort of word study decades ago.[4] When *yôm* means a period of time, it is heavily modified by other time indicators such as the word for year or month. And even in those cases, it is that other time unit word that gives its length of duration, not the use of *yôm*. Ross's fallacy can be illustrated by the following sentence that has several uses of the word "day."

> In my father's **day**, he would go to bed early Sunday **evening** and rise early in the **morning** of the following **day**, and spend the next six **days** traveling, during the **day**, to cross the whole country.

Of course, "my father's day" is an indefinite period of time. But this doesn't mean that it's legitimate to interpret the "six days traveling" as anything but ordinary days. And the combination of evening and the next morning is another way of showing that his bedtime was contained in one ordinary day, not an indefinite time period. As will be shown, it is significant that Genesis 1 modifies the creation days with *both* "evening and morning" and a number, almost as if God was trying to make it as obvious as possible that they were ordinary days. The phrase "during the day" is also obviously the daylight hours, as per Genesis 1:5.

Also in Genesis 1, we have the heavenly bodies created to be "for signs and for seasons and for *days* and years" (1:14). Once more in the creation account we have

---

3. D.A. Carson, *Exegetical Fallacies,* 2nd edition (Grand Rapids, MI: Baker Book House, 1996), p. 60.
4. J. Barr, *Comparative Philology and the Text of the Old Testament* (Oxford: Clarendon Press, 1968).

"days" used to mean ordinary days — it would be nonsensical to translate this "for signs and for seasons and for *vast geological ages* and years," as we should do if the days of Genesis were really "ages."

Genesis 2:4 — "In the day that the LORD God made the earth and the heavens."

As an example of this fallacy, Ross presents Genesis 2:4 as an exception to the literal days (C&T:52):

> Here the word *day* refers to all six creation days (and the creation of the universe that took place prior to the first creative day). Obviously, then, this is a period longer than 24 hours.

However, this ignores the completely different grammatical context — there is a singular, absolute noun "day" in Genesis 1, but a singular, construct noun "day" in Genesis 2:4. In Genesis 2:4, יוֹם (*yôm*) is prefixed by בְּ (*bᵉ*), thus *bᵉyôm* (בְּיוֹם) — this is often an idiomatic (a more precise word than "figurative") expression for "when."

Dr. Robert McCabe, professor of Old Testament at Detroit Baptist Theological Seminary in Allen Park, Michigan, explains further:

> In Genesis 2:4, "day" appears in a compound grammatical construction.[5] A literal translation of v. 4b will assist in explicating the significance of this construction: "in-the-day-of-making by the LORD God earth and heaven." The five hyphenated words in this translation are what constitute this compound grammatical relationship. These five words involve three closely related words in the Hebrew text: the inseparable preposition בְּ ("in"), immediately attached to the construct, singular noun יוֹם ("day"), and an infinitive construct עֲשׂוֹת ("making").
>
> Thus the "day" in 2:4 is not simply an example of a singular noun but is part of a compound grammatical construction. When the preposition בְּ is prefixed to the construct noun יוֹם and these words are followed by an infinitive construct, this complex construction forms a temporal idiomatic construction.[6] The temporal nature of this construction is reflected in its more than 60 uses

5. McCabe refers to a previous note, "By compound grammatical construction, I am referring to the following types of items: the noun יוֹם being a part of a complex prepositional construction, יוֹם being a part of a longer prepositional construction which has a verbal immediately following it, יוֹם being a part of the multi-word construction known as the construct-genitive relationship, יוֹם being used in a compound construction (יוֹם יוֹם). For a more complete development of this construction, see *TDOT* [*Theological Lexicon of the Old Testament*], s.v. "יוֹם," 6:14–20.

6. E. Kautzsch, editor, *Gesenius' Hebrew Grammar*, rev. A. E. Cowley, 2nd English edition (Oxford: Oxford University Press, 1910), p. 347–348, sec. 114e; and Paul Joüon. *A Grammar of Biblical Hebrew*, 2 vols., trans. and rev. T. Muraoka (Rome: Pontifical Biblical Institute, 1993), 2:471, sec. 129p.

in the Old Testament.[7] When a particular day is in view in a specific context, it may be translated as "on the day when." When the temporal reference is more general, this construction is more generally translated as "when."[8] As a result, rather than translating בְּיוֹם in Genesis 2:4b as "in the day of," a more concise English equivalent would be to render it as "when."[9]

So the NIV is correct to translate this passage as "When the Lord God made the earth and the heavens." The NIV also consistently translates *bᵉyôm* as "when" in Genesis 2:17, 3:5, 5:1, and 5:2. BDB lists numerous examples of *bᵉyôm* meaning "when" (BDB:135). HALOT states that *bᵉyôm* has the meaning "when" in Genesis 21:8 as well. The context of *yôm* in Genesis 2:4 is totally different from Genesis 1, where there are no prepositions with *yôm*.

There is also a parallel passage in Numbers 7:10–84. In verses 10 and 84, *bᵉyôm* is used in relation to the whole 12 days of sacrifice at the dedication of the tabernacle. But in between these, at verses 12, 18, 24, etc., we have *yôm* used with a number to refer to each of the 12 literal days.[10]

Genesis 2:17 — "in the day you eat from it you shall surely die"

John Ankerberg, while supposedly "moderating" a widely publicized debate between Ross and Kent Hovind in October 2000,[11] showed his partiality by making a point for Ross:

> Well, let me bring up the fact here — the fact is, the Bible says that in the day that you eat, you will die. Did he die on that day?

Here, Ankerberg is using this to attack literal days. It's ironic that Ross has a completely different use for this (C&T:61):

> When Adam sinned. He instantly "died" just as God said he would ("In the day that you eat of this, you shall surely die" — Gen. 2:17; NKJV). Yet, he remained alive physically . . . he died spiritually.

Chapter 6 covers the important issue of death. But it's notable that here Ross decides that the day *must* be literal. But here is one case where *yôm* is connected to a preposition, so, as explained above, it is idiomatic. The NIV translated this as, "for when you eat of it you will surely die." Even the long-ager Walter Kaiser agrees:

---

7. TLOT, s.v. "יוֹם," 2:529.

8. TDOT, s.v. "יוֹם," 6:15; see also NIDOTTE [*New International Dictionary of Old Testament Theology and Exegesis*], s.v. "יוֹם," 2:420; Cassuto, *Genesis*, p. 16; Westermann, *Genesis 1–11*, p. 183; and John C. Whitcomb and Donald B. DeYoung, *The Moon* (Grand Rapids, MI: Baker, 1978), p. 77.

9. See BDB, p. 400, and HALOT, 2:401.
   R.V. McCabe, "A Defense of Literal Days in the Creation Week," *Detroit Baptist Seminary Journal* 5:97–123, Fall 2000, p. 117–118.

10. Actually, these verses have *bayôm*, where the "a" represents the definite article, "the," meaning "on the day [xth]," unlike *bᵉyôm*, which lacks the article.

11. See analysis by J. Sarfati, <www.answersingenesis.org/ross_hovind>.

It is just as naïve to insist that the phrase "in the day" means that on that very day death would occur. A little knowledge of the Hebrew idiom will relive the tension here as well. For example, in 1 Kings 2:37, King Solomon warned a seditious Shimei, "The day you leave [Jerusalem] and cross the Kidron Valley [which is immediately outside the walls on the east side of the city], you can be sure you will die." Neither the 1 Kings nor the Genesis text implies *immediacy of action* on that very same day; instead they point to *the certainty of the predicted consequence* that would be set in motion by the act that very day. Alternate wordings include *at the time when, at that time, now when* and *the day [when]* (see Gen. 5:1; Exod. 6:28, 10:28, 32:34) [Emphasis and bracketing in the original.][12]

An alternate translation of Genesis 2:17 is "dying you shall die" — it is a figure of speech where the same word is used twice in a slightly different form (מוֹת תְּמוּת *môt tāmût*). The extra occurrence of the word "die" *(môt)* is in the infinitive absolute, which is used to intensify. As well as the emphasis on the certainty of death, the passage may also be understood in an *ingressive* sense — that is, a verbal form that designates the beginning of an action, state, or event. In other words, the focus is on the beginning of the action of dying, which results in the translation ". . . for when you eat of it you will surely *begin* to die."

Consider this analogy: if a branch is chopped off a tree and it falls onto hard concrete, one can say that it's already dead, cut off from the source of life. But the process of physical death takes some time — the cells in the leaves will continue to photosynthesize for several days at least. Similarly, when Adam sinned, he immediately cut himself off from the source of life, but the dying process took 930 years.[13]

Early church fathers wrestled with this problem. However, they came up with the solution that "one day is like a thousand years," and pointed out that Adam died aged 930, before his "day" was over. As shown in the next chapter, this is one source of claims, by Ross and other long-agers, that they believed that the *creation* days were 1,000 years long. That is not at all what they were talking about.

Now that it has been shown that appeal to semantic range is invalid, it's important to closely examine the specific context by comparison with other Scriptures, to provide the following reasons why the days in Genesis were 24 hours long.

Fourth Commandment

The clearest of all is the Fourth Commandment, which, in both Exodus 20:8–11 and 31:17, has the causal explanation "For in six days the LORD made the heavens and the earth . . . but he rested on the seventh day." The word "for" (Hebrew כִּי *kî,* also having the sense "because") at the beginning of this expression is a causal explanation, showing that the creation week is the very basis of the working week.

---

12. W.L. Kaiser, P. Davids, F.F. Bruce, and Manfred Brauch, *Hard Sayings of the Bible* (Downers Grove, IL: InterVarsity Press, 1996), p. 92.
13. Thanks to Peter Sparrow of Creation Bus fame (Australia) for this illustration.

In these passages, it's explicit that the creation days were the same as those of the human work week. There is no point even trying to understand the Bible if a word in the same passage and same grammatical context can switch meanings, without any hint in the text itself.

Ankerberg again showed his partiality by citing, with approval, a rationalization often advanced by Ross, following old-earth Old Testament scholars Gleason Archer and Bruce Waltke:

> In terms of Exodus 20:8–11, in terms of what the Sabbath is referring back to, he says, "By no means does this demonstrate that twenty-four hour intervals were involved in the first six days any more than the eight-day celebration of the feast of tabernacles proves that the wilderness wanderings under Moses occupied only days." Remember Israel wandered in the wilderness for forty years. So it was a symbolic commemoration of that time is what they're saying.

Ross himself, in the same debate said (much the same as in his books):

> It also ignores the problem of Leviticus chapter 25. There you've got the case of God setting up a work period and a rest period for the agricultural land. It was to be worked six years and rested on the seventh year.

They are referring to Leviticus 25:3–4:

> For six years sow your fields, and for six years prune your vineyards and gather their crops. But in the seventh year the land is to have a sabbath of rest, a sabbath to the LORD. Do not sow your fields or prune your vineyards.

However, this passage does not even mention the working week! Rather, it talks about *years*, **not** days! These were symbolic representations of one time period by a *different* one. So it's comparing apples with oranges. Furthermore, Leviticus is speaking of literal years, not some vaguely defined "period" of time. Also, it lacks the causal connection *kî*. But Exodus 20:8–11 is comparing apples with apples.

Hugh Ross's disciple Don Stoner[14] objects by arguing that sabbath days are merely a "shadow" or *type* of the eternal state, which is the *antitype*. Supposedly this means that we cannot come to a definite conclusion about the length of something by looking at its "shadow." He quotes Colossians 2:16-17 and Hebrews 8:5.

I agree that Stoner is right about a shadow not determining the length of that of which it is the shadow. The Sabbath is a type of the eternal state, and, indeed, one cannot tell how long the latter is. However, since the antitype is the eternal state, we have to wonder why he thinks that has the remotest connection to the days of creation.

Yôm + Number = 24-hour Day or Part Thereof

When modified by a cardinal number (for example, one, two, three . . .) or ordinal number (for example, first, second, third . . .), as used 359 times in the OT outside

---

14. D. Stoner, *A New Look at an Old Earth, Resolving the Conflict between the Bible and Science* (Eugene, OR: Harvest House, 1997), p. 48–50. Ross wrote the foreword.

Genesis 1, *yôm* always means a literal day of about 24 hours, or the light portion of the day-night cycle. This is true in narrative, legal writings, prophecy, wisdom literature, and even poetry. So there must be extraordinary reasons to justify an extraordinary exception, *if* Genesis 1 is indeed an exception. This is clearest of all in numbered series of days, as Genesis 1 is, as in Numbers 7 and 29 — in the Numbers passages there can be no doubt that a literal sequence of days is explicit.

In particular, in 189 occurrences, a cardinal number with day (usually the plural *yāmîm*) denotes a specific duration of time. For example, Genesis 30:36, "Then he put a three-day journey between himself and Jacob." And 162 times, an ordinal is associated with the prepositions "on" or "for" (Hebrew: *be, le*) and "day" (usually in the singular, *yôm*) to show that an action is to take place on a specific *yôm*. For example, Exodus 24:16, "For six days the glory covered the mountain, and on the seventh day the Lord called to Moses from within the cloud." Although the construction in Genesis 1 does not precisely fit this pattern, the phrase "and it was evening, and it was morning" is functioning like a preposition (that is, on the xth day — comprised of an evening and morning), bringing out the semantic significance of a 24-hour day.[15]

Objections

Zechariah 14:7:

> But it shall be one day which shall be known to the LORD, not day, nor night: but it shall come to pass, *that* at evening time it shall be light.

Stoner claims that there is one exception which disproves this rule. He is certainly right that this uses the same expression *yôm echad* for "one day" as Genesis 1:5 (see also next section). But he claims:

> Because of the special context of Zechariah 14:7, we can be certain that the "one day" is longer than 24 hours in length. The theory that a number with the word "day" always forces the 24-hour understanding is simply false.[16]

So let's analyze the context, to see if it supports Stoner. The preceding verses (Zech. 14:1–6) are:

> Behold, the day of the LORD is coming, and your spoil will be divided in your midst. For I will gather all the nations to battle against Jerusalem. . . . And in that day His feet will stand on the Mount of Olives, which faces Jerusalem on the east. And the Mount of Olives shall be split in two, from east to west, making a very large valley; half of the mountain shall move toward the north and half of it toward the south. . . . Thus the LORD my God will come, and all the saints with You. It shall come to pass in that day that there will be no light; the lights will diminish.

15. J. Stambaugh, "The Days of Creation: A Semantic Approach," *TJ* 5(1):70–78 (1991); <www.answersingenesis.org/semantic>.

16. D. Stoner, *A New Look at an Old Earth, Resolving the Conflict between the Bible and Science* (Eugene, OR: Harvest House, 1997), p. 46–48.

The day mentioned in verse 7, cited by Stoner, is obviously the same day mentioned in verses 1, 4, and 6. Verse 5 says that it's a day when the LORD will come. So it's describing a particular *event* on some particular day in the future. How can the Second Coming of the Lord take a long period of time? Rather, it will be *instantaneous*, "in a flash, in the twinkling of an eye" (1 Cor. 15:52; 1 Thess. 4:13 ff.). So it occurs on one moment of an ordinary day, which is certainly not a long period.

Stoner believes it refers to the New Jerusalem, the eternal state. But if the "day" refers to the eternal state — an indefinite period of time — it could hardly be called "unique," or give any justification for a long *finite* period!

Hosea 6:2: "After two days he will revive us; on the third day he will restore us, that we may live in his presence."

The old-earth creationist Alan Hayward, whom Ross praises for "sound theology" despite being a unitarian,[17] so denying the deity of Christ as is clearly taught in the New Testament (for example, John 1:1–14, 5:18; Titus 2:13), claimed that this passage "is at least one exception that shatters the so-called rule."[18] Not surprisingly, Ross accepts and repeats this argument (C&T:47).

However, this verse is set in a very specific sort of poetic synonymous parallelism. It is a common Semitic device, which takes the form X//X+1, that is, one number followed by the next one, but where the numbers are not meant to be taken literally because they refer to the same thing in different ways.[19] Other OT examples that illustrate the synonymity are:

Job 5:19: "From **six** calamities he will rescue you, from **seven** no harm will befall you."

Prov. 6:16: "There are **six** things that the LORD hates, **seven** that are detestable to him:"

Prov. 30:15: "There are **three** things that are never satisfied, **four** that never say, "Enough!""

Prov. 30:18: "There are **three** things that are too amazing for me, **four** that I do not understand."

Amos 1:3: "This is what the LORD says: "For **three** sins of Damascus, even for **four**, I will not turn back my wrath. . . .""

Hosea 6:2 is likewise this specific Semitic figure of speech, so must be interpreted accordingly. So the use of "two days" and "three days" are not intended to give literal

---

17. Hayward admitted this in a letter to creationist David C.C. Watson, who reported it in his review of Hayward's book in *Creation Research Society Quarterly* 22(4):198–199 (1986).

18. Alan Hayward, *Creation and Evolution, The Facts and the Fallacies* (London: Triangle, SPCK, 1985), p. 164.

19. W.M.W. Roth, "The Numerical Saying *x/x* + 1 in the Old Testament," *Vetus Testamentum*, 12:300–311 (1962); "Numerical Sayings in the Old Testament, A Form Critical Study," *Supplements to Vetus Testamentum* 13:6 (Leiden: E.J. Brill, 1965).

numbers, but to communicate that the restoration of Israel mentioned in the previous verse will happen quickly and surely. This applies regardless of eschatological views about when this takes place.

Therefore, these instances must refer to normal days, or maybe even shorter periods, as opposed to long periods, otherwise the device would lose its meaning, that is, the restoration would *not* be quick and sure if the days were long periods of time. So Hayward and Ross are wrong to use this verse with a special grammatical structure to try to overturn the hundreds of crystal-clear examples of *yôm* used with a number.

Ordinals, Cardinals, and Articles

The days of Genesis 1 have an interesting pattern in the Hebrew, which is not often reflected in English translations. The first day has a *cardinal* number (that is, one, two, three . . .), יוֹם אֶחָד (*yôm echad*) day one. The others have *ordinal* numbers (second, third, fourth . . .). Also, days 2–5 lack a *definite article* (ה, *ha*, "the"), while days 6–7 have one on the numeric. So a literal translation of creation week would be day one, a second day, a third day, a fourth day, a fifth day, the sixth day, the seventh day (see interlinear below).

וַיְהִי־עֶרֶב וַיְהִי־בֹקֶר יוֹם אֶחָד	Genesis 1:5
and was eve-ning and was mor-ning day one	
וַיְהִי־עֶרֶב וַיְהִי־בֹקֶר יוֹם שֵׁנִי	Genesis 1:8
and was eve-ning and was mor-ning day second	
וַיְהִי־עֶרֶב וַיְהִי־בֹקֶר יוֹם שְׁלִישִׁי	Genesis 1:13
and was eve-ning and was mor-ning day third	
וַיְהִי־עֶרֶב וַיְהִי־בֹקֶר יוֹם רְבִיעִי	Genesis 1:19
and was eve-ning and was mor-ning day fourth	

וַיְהִי־עֶרֶב וַיְהִי־בֹקֶר יוֹם חֲמִישִׁי	Genesis 1:23
and was eve-ning and was mor-ning day fifth	
וַיְהִי־עֶרֶב וַיְהִי־בֹקֶר יוֹם הַשִּׁשִּׁי	Genesis 1:31
and was eve-ning and was mor-ning day sixth	
וַיְכַל אֱלֹהִים בַּיּוֹם הַשְּׁבִיעִי	Genesis 2:2
And finished God on day the seventh	
מְלַאכְתּוֹ אֲשֶׁר עָשָׂה	
work His which had He made	
וַיִּשְׁבֹּת בַּיּוֹם הַשְּׁבִיעִי	
And He rested on day the seventh	

This pattern is enough to destroy one of Ross's arguments against literal days (C&T:48):

> **The unusual syntax of the sentences enumerating specific creation days.** Looking at the word-for-word translation of the Hebrew text, one finds this phraseology: "and was evening and was morning day X." . . . The word arrangement is clearly a departure from simple and ordinary expression. . . . This syntactic ambiguity does not constitute a proof. However, it does suggest that the "day" here is to be taken in some unusual manner.

As above, Ross is simply wrong about the syntax, so his argument collapses. This is another example of Dr. Ross's misunderstanding of Hebrew. Learned-sounded arguments about Hebrew may sound impressive, but the substance needs to be there.

Rev. Dr. Rowland Ward of Australia has a long history of vexatious opposition to the view that Genesis is straightforward history, even giving credence to the thoroughly scientifically and ethically discredited book *Telling Lies for God* by atheist Ian Plimer.[20] But at least he gets the Hebrew pattern right, unlike Ross. However, like Ross, Ward uses this pattern to argue against a straightforward interpretation of Genesis (he later argues for the framework hypothesis — see page 94):

> These distinctions are not what we would expect if we have emphasis on a mere chronological ordering of events (cf. Num 29:17, 20, 23, 26, 29, 32, 35).[21]

It's worth noting the pejorative word "mere," as if chronology is somehow unworthy, despite its importance in Scripture (see Luke 3:1–2). However, the argument is fallacious. As will be seen, those who *are* specialists in Hebrew, unlike Ross and Ward, contradict them and show that the pattern actually *strengthens* the case for literal days.

Dr. Andrew Steinmann, Associate Professor of Theology and Hebrew at Concordia University in Illinois, has analyzed the pattern in Genesis in detail. Far from being an exception to the *yôm*+numeric = literal day rule, he argued that the pattern was strong *support* for 24-hour days in Genesis:

> If אחד [*echad*] is used as a cardinal number, what is the force of Genesis 1:5? [Quote in Hebrew and English]
>
> The answer may lie in the use of the terms "night," "day," "evening," and "morning." Genesis 1:5 begins the cycle of the day. With the creation of light it is now possible to have a cycle of light and darkness, which God labels "day" and "night." Evening is the transition from light/day to darkness/night. Morning is the transition from darkness/night to light/day. **Having an evening and a morning amounts to having one full day**. Hence, the following equation is what Genesis 1:5 expresses: **Evening + morning = one day**.
>
> Therefore, by using a most unusual grammatical construction, Genesis 1 is defining what a day is. This is especially needed in this verse, since "day" is used in two senses in this one verse. Its first appearance means the time during a daily cycle that is illuminated by daylight (as opposed to night). The second use means something different, a time period that encompasses both the time of daylight and the time of darkness.
>
> It would appear as if the text is very carefully crafted so an alert reader *cannot* read it as "the first day." Instead, by omission of the article it must be read as "one day," thereby **defining a day as something akin to a twenty-four hour solar period** with light and darkness and transitions between day and night, even though there is no sun until the fourth day. This would explain the lack of definite articles on the second through fifth days. Another evening

---

20. For thorough refutation, see <www.answersingenesis.org/plimer>.
21. R.S. Ward, *Foundations in Genesis: Genesis 1–11 Today* (Melbourne, Australia: New Melbourne Press, 1999), p. 45.

and morning constituted "a" (not "the") second day. Another evening and morning made a third day, and so forth. On the sixth day, the article finally appears. But even here, the grammar is strange, since there is no article on יוֹם as would be expected. This would indicate that the **sixth day was a regular solar day**, but that it was also *the culminating day of creation*. Likewise, the seventh day is referred to as יוֹם הַשְׁבִיעִי (Gen. 2:3), with lack of an article on יוֹם. This, also, the author is implying, was a **regular solar day**. Yet it was a special day, because God had finished his work of creation."[22]

Note that the last section on the seventh day is enough to refute Ross's claim that the seventh day is still continuing. (See page 82 for more discussion on this fallacy.)

Steinmann concluded (while also pointing out the fallacy of interpreting a word by its whole semantic range, rather than the specific context) that the Hebrew clearly teaches 24-hour days.

יוֹם, like the English word "day," can take on a variety of meanings. It does not in and of itself mean a twenty-four hour day. . . . This alone has made the length of days in Genesis 1 a controversial subject. . . . However, the use of יוֹם in Gen 1:5 and the following unique uses of the ordinal numbers on the other days demonstrates that **the text itself indicates these as regular solar days.**[23]

Creation Is the One Exception?

Long-agers Bradley and Olsen claim that all exegetical bets such as the number/day connection are off, because creation is the *one* exception to the rule:

There is no other place in the Old Testament where the intent is to describe events that involve multiple and/or sequential, indefinite periods of time. If the intent of Genesis 1 is to describe creation as occurring in six, indefinite time periods, it is a unique Old Testament event being recorded. Other descriptions where *yôm* refers to an indefinite time period are all for a single time period. Thus, the absence of the use of *yāmîm* for other than regular days and the use of ordinals only before regular days elsewhere in the Old Testament cannot be given an unequivocal exegetical significance in view of the uniqueness of the events being described in Genesis 1 (i.e., sequential, indefinite time periods).[24]

---

22. A. Steinmann, "אֶחָד as an Ordinal Number and the Meaning of Genesis 1:5," *JETS* 45(4):577–584 (December 2002); quote from p. 583–584; *italics* in original, bold added.

23. Ibid., p. 584, bold added. He has a footnote, "Whether or not one believes in the veracity of the Genesis account of creation in six solar days is another matter altogether." As the JETS accepts biblical inerrancy, we can presume that the author himself doesn't intend to advocate error in Genesis. Rather, he is pointing out that it is more honest to say that Genesis teaches 24-hour days but is wrong, than pretending that it's right but teaches something else.

24. W.L. Bradley and R.L. Olsen, "The Trustworthiness of Scripture in Areas Relating to Natural Science," in E.D. Radmacher and R. Preus, *Hermeneutics, Inerrancy, and the Bible* (Grand Rapids, MI: Zondervan, 1984).

This is classic question-begging — they *assume* that the authors' intent was to describe sequential indefinite periods of time, yet this is what needs to be *demonstrated*. And claims of exceptions require exceptionally strong reasoning! Secondly, as we have pointed out, we are perfectly aware that there are some occasions where *yôm* can mean an indefinite period of time. This is so only when it is modified by a preposition such as *b* (for example, as we have shown with Genesis 2:4). However, none of the instances in Genesis 1 are modified in this way.

Furthermore, Daniel 4:23 (4:22 in Hebrew) and 7:25 are examples where multiple and/or sequential, indefinite periods of times much longer than a day are mentioned, using a different time word (עִדָּן *'iddān*), which is an Aramaic word. A similar indefinite time word used with a number is the Hebrew word מוֹעֵד (*mô'ēd*, Daniel 12:7). See also chapter 10.

Another example of the same question-begging comes from J. Oliver Buswell Jr.:

> It may be true that this is the only case in which the word "day" is used figuratively when preceded by any numeral, but the reason is that this is the only case in Scripture in which any indefinitely long periods of time are enumerated. The words *aion* in the Greek and *'ôlām* in Hebrew are literal words for "age," but we do not happen to have any case in which God has said "first age," "second age," "third age," etc. The attempt to make a grammatical rule to the effect that the numeral preceding the word "day" makes it literal, breaks down on the simple fact that this is the only case in all the Scriptures, and in all Hebrew language, I think, in which ages are enumerated one after the other. There is no such rule in anybody's Hebrew grammar anywhere. The author of this objection, or the one from whom he has attempted to quote, has simply put forth with a sound of authority a grammatical rule which does not exist.[25]

It's hard to imagine a more blatant example of *presuming* that this is a unique example of numbered days being ages, then using this as "evidence" against the straightforward 24-hour interpretation.

Days of Christ in the Tomb: An Exception to Literal Days?

Some people argue that an exception to the rule about *yôm*+number being a 24-hour day is the time that Christ was in the tomb. After all, in Matthew 12:40, Christ said that He would be "three days and three nights" in the tomb, but if Jesus was crucified on Good Friday and rose on Sunday, it couldn't have been three full 24-hour periods.

Others, overlooking the qualification that "day" with a number can mean a part of the earth-rotation cycle, suggest that the crucifixion occurred on a Wednesday or a Thursday. But this is hard to fit in with the other evidence from Scripture. The Bible

---

25. J.O. Buswell, Appendix: "The Length of the Creative Days," in P.P.T. Pun, *Evolution: Nature and Scripture in Conflict?* (Grand Rapids, MI: Zondervan, 1982), p. 269.

claims that Christ rose on the "first day of the week" (Mark 16:9), which was "on the third day" (1 Cor. 15:4), as Christ predicted (Luke 24:7). Many biblioskeptics even claim that the Bible contradicts itself here. But if we believe in the inspiration and authority of Scripture, this is not an option. The solution lies in a correct understanding of Jewish idiom, which explains the need for the qualification.

The critics overlook the fact that for Jews, the phrases "on the third day" and "three days and three nights" were synonymous. Jews distinguished the word "day" in the sense of daylight hours from "day" as a 24-hour cycle, by referring to the latter as "night and a day." Further, in Jewish counting, a part of a day was counted as a whole day (a figure of speech known as *synecdoche*), for example, 1 Samuel 30:12, where "he had not eaten bread or drunk water for three days and nights" is equated in verse 13 with *hayyôm shelosha* (three days ago), which could only mean the day before yesterday. Another example is 1 Kings 20:29 (NIV):

> For seven days they camped opposite each other, and on the seventh day the battle was joined.

In English counting, if they started fighting on the 7th day, it means they were only camping for six whole days. But in Jewish reckoning, the partial days are counted as wholes, so the text says they were camping for seven days. See also Genesis 42:17–18. Another proof is Matthew 27:63–64:

> "Sir," they said, "we remember that while he was still alive that deceiver said, '**After three days** I will rise again.' So give the order for the tomb to be made secure **until the third day**. Otherwise, his disciples may come and steal the body and tell the people that he has been raised from the dead. This last deception will be worse than the first."

Note that even His enemies understood that "after three days" meant that they only had to secure the tomb "until the third day." If three full 24-hour periods were meant, then they would want to secure the tomb until the fourth day to make sure.

Note that the above analysis was based on the principle that Scripture is its own best interpreter. A comparison with other Scriptures shows that sometimes a part of a day could be counted as a whole day. But this is not denying that the days are ordinary days, whether parts or wholes, so cannot remotely be used as a justification for the day-age interpretation of Genesis — it's the wrong direction! It is ludicrous to claim that "three days and three nights" could mean that Christ was buried for 3,000 or three billion years!

So, to conclude this excursus into the day of the Crucifixion, the best explanation is that Christ was buried before about 6 p.m. Good Friday (Luke 23:54). Since the Jewish day started at sunset, the late afternoon of Good Friday was the first day; Friday sunset to Saturday sunset was the 2nd day; the 3rd day began on Saturday at sunset, and Jesus had risen from the dead by early Sunday morning.

Evening and Morning ('*ereb* and *boqer*) Plus *yôm* = 24-hour Day

The two words, "evening" (*'ereb* ערב) and "morning" (*boqer* בקר), are combined with *yôm* 19 times each outside of Genesis 1 (three times these words share the same reference — Num. 9:15; Deut. 16:4; and Dan. 8:26). Every time, they clearly mean that particular literal part of a 24-hour day, regardless of the literary genre or context. Also, even when "morning" and "evening" occur together without *yôm* (38 times outside of Genesis 1, including 25 in historical narrative), it always, without exception, designates a 24-hour day. All the instances of *yôm* in the Genesis 1 account are qualified by the statement ויהי ערב ויהי בקר (*wayehî 'ereb wayehi boqer*) — "and there was evening, and there was morning," which by comparing with other Scripture, must denote a 24-hour day.

Ross claimed that the use of "morning" is metaphorical (C&T:46). But *boqer* is used 205 times in the OT, and there is no obvious example of metaphor. Even Ross's source, TWOT 1:125, doesn't support him:

> *Boqer may* denote "early" or "promptly" as in "God will help her right early" (lit. "at the turning of morning . . .") *but the case cannot be proved.*

An example cited is Psalm 46:5. Notice that the literal translation of the Hebrew shows that "morning" is being used literally. The KJV reading given here is not as literal as the NAS "when morning dawns."

In GQ:65–66, Ross turns the evidence on its head:

> Likewise, many English Bible readers failed to note that twenty-four hours in biblical Hebrew are bracketed by evening to morning, less frequently by morning to evening, but not by evening was and morning was. Moreover, the Hebrew words for evening and morning (*'ereb* and *boqer*) also carry the literal definitions "ending of the day" and "beginning of the day" respectively. The repeated use of "evening was and morning was" for the first six creation days indicates that they were not twenty-four hour days but rather time periods with definite start-and-stop epochs.

As shown, the reverse is true — the use of evening and morning *reinforces* the fact of literal days. His claim about the particular phrase "evening was and morning was" is nonsense. He relies on one Paul Elbert, whom he called a "Hebrew scholar." But he is not — he is a physicist and a visiting professor (that is, part-time lecturer) of "theology and science" at a college and would hardly be labeled as even an Old Testament scholar in the normal sense of the word.[26]

But the claim would be news to just about every *actual* Hebrew scholar who has written on this topic. The church fathers, Luther and Calvin, certainly did not think this way, and neither do commentaries by many evangelical and liberal scholars including Archer, Waltke, Sailhamer, Hamilton, Barr, Leupold, Wenham, Kidner,

---

26. According to his paper, "The Globalization of Pentecostalism: A Review Article," <www.pneuma-foundation.com/resources/articles/review.guest0002.pdf>.

Arnold, Speiser, Young, and Davis. These are all outstanding Hebraists, yet none argue in this way. In fact, most (even those who believe in billions of years) admit that the presence of the evening and morning clauses is strong evidence for taking the days as literal.

Daniel 8 — An Exception?

On the Ankerberg show, Ross alluded to Daniel 8 as an exception, relying on an article by an engineer, Dr. Otto Helweg. Both this article and refutations by Hebrew scholars Drs. David Shackelford and David Fouts were published in *TJ* 11(3):299–308, 1997.

Helweg's case was built on Daniel 8:26: "The vision of evenings and mornings . . ." supposedly not referring to literal days, because the original Hebrew words *'ereb* and *boqer* are in the singular yet the time frame is longer than 24 hours.

However, the OT never uses plural form (*'ereb* does occur in the dual [meaning "two evenings"] 11 times, and in every case is rendered as "twilight")! The English translators correctly render them as plurals when they are modified by a numerical adjective. The context should make this clear. What vision? Obviously, the one referred to most recently, Daniel 8:1–14, which concludes with "It will take 2,300 evenings and mornings; then the sanctuary will be reconsecrated." Here, also, the singulars are used, but must obviously be plural in function because there are 2,300 of them — 2,300 is definitely a numerical adjective! And these must be literal days, so this reinforces our point. None other than Ross's debate partner Gleason Archer says they must be either 2,300 24-hr days, or the 2,300 comprises 1,150 evenings and 1,150 mornings, meaning only 1,150 days, but not long ages![27]

Day with Night

The word for night (ליל *layil* or לילה *layla*) is combined with *yôm* 53 times in the Old Testament outside of Genesis 1. Whether in the historical (26 times), poetic (16 times), or prophetic (11 times), it unambiguously means the dark portion of a 24-hour cycle. Because of the day-night cycle, this use of *yôm* as the opposite of *layla* as a literal 24-hour cycle of light and dark is the core meaning.

OTHER OBJECTIONS

Does the Seventh Day Continue?

Ross claims (C&T:48–49):

> Of the first six creation days Moses wrote: "There was evening, and there was morning, the Xth day [not exactly so, as shown on page 76]." This wording indicates that each of the first six creation days had a beginning and an ending. However, no such wording is attached to the seventh creation day, neither in Genesis 1–2 nor anywhere else in the Bible. Given

---

27. G.L. Archer in: *Expositor's Bible Commentary* 7:102–3, 1985.

the parallel structure marking this distinct change in form for the seventh day strongly suggests that this day has (or had) not yet ended.

However, the evening and morning mark the *beginning* and end of a day respectively. So if Ross thinks the absence of *both* means the seventh day has not ended, then to be consistent, it would follow that the seventh day had not *begun* either![28]

In any case, from his above tenuous thread, Ross hangs the conclusion that the other creation days could be long ages. However, systematic theologian Dr. Doug Kelly responded to Ross's argument as follows (C&C:111):

> To say the least, this places a great deal of theological weight on a very narrow and thin exegetical bridge! Is it not more concordant with the patent sense of the context of Genesis 2 (and Exodus 20) to infer that because the Sabbath differed in quality (though not — from anything we can learn out of the text itself — in quantity), a slightly different concluding formula was appended to indicate a qualitative difference (six days involved work; one day involved rest)? The formula employed to show the termination of that first sabbath: "And on the seventh day God ended His work which He had made; and He rested on the seventh day from all His work which He had made" (Gen. 2:2) seems just as definite as that of "and the evening and the morning were the first day."

Another possible reason for leaving off the refrain about evening and morning was to further emphasize that God's *creation* work was completed, as Genesis 2:1–3 says so clearly. Certainly, John 5:17 says, "But Jesus answered them, 'My *Father* is *working* still, and I am *working*.' " But in context, Jesus is referring to God's *providential* and *redemptive* work, not creative work. The Father still works, but He is not creating, in the Genesis 1 sense of the word. He is resting from all that He made.

Ross also argues that Hebrews 4:1–11 teaches "that the seventh creation day began after the creation of Adam and Eve, continues through the present, and extends into the future" (GQ:64). However, again Ross repeats an argument rebutted in VB&T: 69–73. Hebrews 4 never says that the *seventh day of creation* is continuing to the present; it merely says that God's *rest* is continuing. If someone says on Monday that he rested on Saturday and is still resting, it in no way implies that Saturday lasted until Monday.[29] Kulikovsky carefully analyzes the grammar of Hebrews 4 and concludes:

> The "rest" of Hebrews 4 clearly refers to the Kingdom of God. This type of rest was aluded to right back at the time of creation, as well as at the time of the Exodus. Nowhere in the text is it equated with the seventh day

28. M. Maniguet, *The Theological Method of Hugh Ross: An analysis and Critique*, M.Th. Thesis, Systematic Theology, Baptist Bible Seminary, Clarks Summit, PA, May 2002, p. 22.

29. Anon (based on research by Mike Kruger), "Is the Seventh Day an Eternal Day?" *Creation* 21(3):44–45 (1999).

of creation, nor is there any grammatical or contextual data suggesting any such equation. Thus, the progressive creationists' claim that the seventh day of creation is still continuing is without any exegetical foundation whatsoever, making it a worthless argument for non-literal creation days.[30]

Days and Nights before the Sun Was Created

The argument is that days 1–3 could not have been literal because the sun wasn't made till day 4. Supposedly, the sun is necessary for the day-night cycle. From this, critics of the calendar-day view claim that none of the creation days are literal.

This old argument is often put forward as though creationists have never thought of it.[31] Some historical research would have shown that this "problem" was answered centuries ago. Christians have long realized that God can create light without a secondary source, and the Bible tells us clearly that God created *light*, as well as the earth, on the first day. We are told that in the heavenly city there will be no need for sun or moon, because God's glory will illuminate it, and the Lamb will be its lamp (Rev. 21:23). In Genesis, God even defines a day and a night in terms of light or its absence.

For example, Reformer Calvin (1509–1564) had no problem, for he taught:

- The day-night cycle was instituted from day 1 — before the sun was created [commenting on "Let there be light" (Gen. 1:3)]: "Therefore the Lord, by the very order of the creation, bears witness that he holds in his hand the light, which he is able to impart to us without the sun and the moon. Further, it is certain, from the context, that the light was so created as to be interchanged with the darkness . . . there is, however, no doubt that the order of their succession was alternate. . . ."[32]

- The sun, moon, and stars were created on day 4 — after the earth — and took over the role as light dispensers to the earth [commenting on "let there be lights . . ." (Gen. 1:14)]: "God had before created the light, but he now institutes a new order in nature, that the sun should be the dispenser of diurnal light, and the moon and the stars should shine by night. And he assigns them to this office, to teach us that all creatures are subject to his will, and execute what he enjoins upon them. For Moses relates nothing else than that God ordained certain instruments to diffuse through the earth, by reciprocal changes, that light which had been previously created. The only difference is this, that the light was before dispersed, but now proceeds from lucid bodies; which, in serving this purpose, obey the commands of God."[33]

---

30. A.S. Kulikovsky, "God's Rest in Hebrews 4:1–11," *TJ* 13(2): 61–62 (1999).
31. For modern answers, see R. Grigg, "Light, Life and the Glory of God," *Creation* 24(1):38–39 (2001); J. Sarfati, "How Could the Days of Genesis 1 Be Literal If the Sun Wasn't Created Until the Fourth Day?" <www.answersingenesis.org/docs/1203.asp>.
32. J. Calvin, *Genesis*, 1554; (Edinburgh, UK: Banner of Truth, 1984), p. 76–77.
33. Ibid., p. 83.

The Father of the Reformation, Martin Luther (1483–1546), was similarly clear and emphatic about the sun, moon, and stars being created on day 4.[34] The founder of Methodism, John Wesley (1701–1791), agreed.[35]

Earlier still, many ancient Rabbinic interpreters taught that God created a primordial light not dependent on the sun, which came into existence at God's command but was later withdrawn and stored up for the righteous in the messianic future.[36] This is feasible, and in line with John's teaching in Revelation. Also, the Jewish commentator from medieval Spain, Abraham Ibn Ezra (c. 1089–1164), wrote:

> One day refers to the movement of the celestial sphere. . . .
> The heavenly sphere made one revolution. The sun was not yet seen in the firmament; neither was there a firmament.[37]

These great exegetes were right not to see this as a problem for the God of the Bible. But modern geokinetic astronomy makes the solution even easier. All it takes to have a day-night cycle is a rotating earth and light coming from one direction. Thus, we can deduce that the earth was already rotating in space relative to the light created on day 1.

This unusual, counter-intuitive order of creation (light before sun) actually adds a hallmark of authenticity. If the Bible had been the product of later "editors," as alleged by the Wellhausen school ("Documentary Hypothesis"),[38] they would surely have modified this to fit with their own understanding. Having "day" without the sun would have been generally inconceivable to the ancients.

Having the sun appear after the light would have been very significant to pagan world views which tended to worship the sun as the source of all life. God seems to be making it pointedly clear that the sun is secondary to himself as the source of everything. He doesn't "need" the sun in order to create life, in contrast to old-earth beliefs.

In fact, early church writers used the literal fourth day creation of the sun as a polemic against paganism. For example, in the second century, Theophilus, bishop of Antioch, wrote in an apologetic work to the learned pagan magistrate Autolycus:

> On the fourth day the luminaries came into existence. Since God has foreknowledge, he understood the nonsense of the foolish philosophers who were going to say that the things produced on earth come from the stars, so that they might set God aside. In order therefore that the truth might

---

34. Martin Luther, *Luther's Works*, Vol. I: Commentary on Genesis 1–5, J. Pelikan, editor (St. Louis, MO: Concordia, 1958); see his comments on verses 1:5-6 and 1:14ff.

35. J. Wesley, "God's Approbation of His Work," 1872, available from <gbgm-umc.org/umhistory/wesley/sermons/serm-056.stm>.

36. J.P. Lewis, "The Days of Creation: An Historical Survey," *JETS* 32:449 (1989).

37. Ibn Ezra, *Commentary on the Pentateuch, Genesis (Bereshit)*, translated and edited by H.N. Strickman and A.M. Silver (New York, NY: Menorah Publishing Co., 1999), p. 33 and footnote.

38. R. Grigg, "Did Moses Really Write Genesis?" *Creation* 20(4):43–46 (September-November 1998).

be demonstrated, plants and seeds came into existence before the stars. For what comes into existence later cannot cause what is prior to it.[39]

In the 4th century, Basil the Great (see page 112) commented on the same passage:

> Heaven and earth were the first; after them was created light; the day had been distinguished from the night, then had appeared the firmament and the dry element. The water had been gathered into the reservoir assigned to it, the earth displayed its productions, it had caused many kinds of herbs to germinate and it was adorned with all kinds of plants. However, the sun and the moon did not yet exist, in order that those who live in ignorance of God may not consider the sun as the origin and the father of light, or as the maker of all that grows out of the earth. That is why there was a fourth day, and then God said: "Let there be lights in the firmament of the heaven."[40]

2 Peter 3:8 — "One day is like a thousand years."

> But do not forget this one thing, dear friends: With the Lord a day is like a thousand years, and a thousand years are like a day. The Lord is not slow in keeping his promise, as some understand slowness. He is patient with you, not wanting anyone to perish, but everyone to come to repentance (2 Pet. 3:8–9).

The first thing to note is that the context has *nothing to do* with the days of creation. Also, it is not defining a day because it doesn't say "a day **is** a thousand years." The correct understanding, as always, is derived from the context — the apostle Peter's readers should not lose heart because God seems slow at fulfilling His promises about the second coming of Christ. Rather they are to remember that He is patient, and also because He is not bound by time as we are.

The text says "one day is *like* [or *as*] a thousand years" — the word "like" (or "as") shows that it is a figure of speech, called a *simile*, to teach that God is outside of time (because He is the Creator of time itself). In fact, the figure of speech is so effective in its intended aim precisely because the day is *literal* and contrasts so vividly with 1,000 years — to the eternal Creator of time, a short period of time and a long period of time may as well be the same.

The fact that the passage is actually contrasting a short and long period can be shown by the fact that Peter is likely referring to Psalm 90:4 (Peter's statement "do not forget" implies that his readers were expected to recall something, and this passage has this very teaching). This reads:

> For a thousand years in your sight are like a day that has just gone by,
> *or like a watch in the night.*

---

39. Theophilus, *To Autolycus* 2:15, A.D. 181, *Ante-Nicene Fathers* 2:100.
40. Basil, *Hexaëmeron* 6:2; <www.newadvent.org/fathers/32016.htm>.

This is *synonymous parallelism*, where a long period of a thousand years is contrasted with two short periods: a day, and a night watch. But those who try to use this verse to teach that the days of Genesis might be 1,000 years long forget the additional part in **bold**. For if they were consistent, they would have to say that a watch in the night here *also* means 1,000 years. It's difficult to imagine that the same Psalmist is thinking on his bed for thousands of years (Ps. 63:6), or that his eyes stay open for thousands of years (Ps. 119:148).

The immediate context of the psalm is the frailty of mere mortal man in comparison to God. This verse amplifies the teaching, saying that no matter how long a time interval is from man's time-bound perspective, it is like a twinkling of an eye from God's eternal perspective.

The Days Were "God's Days," Not "Man's Days"

Some critics claim that the days of creation week were "God's days," and chide creationists for thinking that they are the same length as "man's days." So, despite the overwhelming evidence from the rest of Scripture that the context of Genesis 1 indicates ordinary-length days, they still assert that creation days are a special case, and so don't have the normal meaning. Ross himself has made such a claim, which also impinges on the previous section (C&T:45):

> The same author of Genesis (Moses) wrote in Psalm 90:4, "For a thousand years in your sight are like a day that has just gone by, or like a watch [4 hours] in the night." Moses seems to state that just as God's ways are not our ways (Isaiah 55:9), God's days are not our days.

But as pointed out in chapter 1, God wrote the Bible to teach (2 Tim. 3:15–17), so He wrote to be understood. Scripture would have no ability to communicate if words didn't mean the same to God and man. A *reductio ad absurdum* of this idea is to consider any other word in Scripture. Perhaps what God meant by "steal" or "murder" in the Decalogue isn't what man means either? After all, this was a "special case" where God wrote with His own finger. And since Jesus is God and He was in the grave for three days, were these days not literal either? This whole approach is existentialist nonsense.

Also, as mentioned, the point of Psalm 90:4 is that God is outside of time, so He doesn't experience time as we do. So what is "God's day" supposed to mean? To take another example, 1 Kings 2:11:

> And the time that David reigned over Israel was forty years; he reigned seven years in Hebron, and thirty-three years in Jerusalem.

Did God experience the 7 and 33 years in the same way David did? No! Were those still ordinary years? Yes! Therefore, when He said "day," in the context of Genesis, He meant day from our perspective, since we are the creatures in the created space-time dimension who experience time. He even told us that they were ordinary days by the comparison in Exodus 20:8–11 in the same Decalogue.

Too Little Time for All the Tasks of Day 6?

Ross claims (FoG:149–150):

> **The events of the sixth day cover more than 24 hours.** Genesis 1 tells us that all the land mammals and *both* Adam and Eve were created on the sixth day. Genesis 2 provides further amplification, listing events between the creation of Adam and the creation of Eve. First, God planted a garden, making "all kinds of tree to grow out of the garden." Then Adam worked and cared for the garden of Eden. After that, he carried out his assignment from God to name all the animals. In the process Adam discovered that none of these creatures was a suitable helper for him. Next, God put Adam in a deep sleep, performed an operation, awakened Adam, and introduced him to the newly created Eve. Adam's expression upon seeing Eve was *happa'am*. This expression is usually translated "now at length" (see Gen. 29:34–35, 30:30 and 46:30 and Judges 15:3), roughly equivalent to our English expression, "at last." Finally, Adam and Eve received instructions from God concerning their responsibilities in managing the plants, animals, and resources of the earth. Many weeks', months', or even years' worth of activities took place in this latter portion of the sixth day.

Here, Ross makes several claims, and it's worth analyzing them individually.

Time for Tree Growth?

Genesis 2:9 says:

> And the LORD God made all kinds of trees grow out of the ground — trees that were pleasing to the eye and good for food.

This doesn't say that the trees needed time to grow. God is capable of making trees grow at the same rate as He turned water into wine and multiplied the loaves and fishes — instantaneously. A number of the church fathers believed that God caused *instantaneous* growth, for example, Basil the Great (see page 112):

> "Let the earth bring forth grass." In a moment earth began by germination to obey the laws of the Creator, completed every stage of growth, and brought germs to perfection. . . .
>
> At this command every copse was thickly planted; all the trees, fir, cedar, cypress, pine, rose to their greatest height, the shrubs were straightway clothed with thick foliage. The plants called crown-plants, roses, myrtles, laurels, did not exist; in one moment they came into being, each one with its distinctive peculiarities. Most marked differences separated them from other plants, and each one was distinguished by a character of its own. . . .
>
> "Let the earth bring forth." This short command was in a moment a vast nature, an elaborate system. Swifter than thought it produced the countless qualities of plants. It is this command which, still at this day,

is imposed on the earth, and in the course of each year displays all the strength of its power to produce herbs, seeds, and trees. Like tops, which after the first impulse, continue their evolutions, turning upon themselves when once fixed in their center; thus nature, receiving the impulse of this first command, follows without interruption the course of ages, until the consummation of all things.[41]

Actually there is nothing to suggest that the Hebrew can't simply mean that the trees were created *as* growing, as long as they were still mature enough to produce seeds.

Adam Worked for a Long Time?

Genesis 2:15 actually states the *purpose* of Adam in the garden, not that he actually worked for a long time before the other events. Rather, the passage indicates that as soon as Adam was given instructions about eating, God paraded the land vertebrates He *had* formed (see page 90) for Adam to name.

Naming All the Animals?

Ross claims that the only creationist answer is that the pre-Fall Adam was physically and mentally perfect, so he could name the animals at superhuman speed. But this is hardly the main factor. Genesis 2:19 clearly states that God brought the animals to Adam. Therefore, "carrying out his assignment" would not require tracking or capturing the animals. As will be shown in chapters 7 and 8, the number of kinds was much smaller than the number of today's species.[42]

Scripture explicitly states that Adam named all the "livestock" (בהמה *behemah*), the "birds of the air" (עוֹף הֹשמים *ôph hashamayim*), and all the "beasts of the field" (חיה הֹשׂדה *chayyah hassadeh*). There is no indication that Adam named the fish in the sea, or any other marine organisms, nor any of the insects, beetles, or arachnids. So, like the ark's obligate passengers, there was only a tiny fraction of all the kinds of animals. Furthermore, the animals Adam had to name were even fewer — Genesis 2:20 omits "creeping things" (רמֹש *remes*, reptile), and the "beasts of the field" are a subset of the "beasts of the earth" of Genesis 1:24.

Combining both facts — that "kinds" are broader than species, and that there was only a small subset of all kinds — there are probably only a few thousand animals involved at most. Interestingly, Ross's ally Archer estimated that only "many hundreds of species must have been involved."[43] Even if we assume that Adam had to name as many as 2,500 kinds of animals, if he took five seconds per kind, and took a five-minute break every hour, he could have completed the task in well under four

---

41. Basil, *Hexaëmeron* 5:5,6,10, A.D. 370, <www.newadvent.org/fathers/32015.htm>.

42. G. Wenham, *Genesis*, Word Biblical Commentary, 1:47, notes that the Samaritan Pentateuch and LXX insert "still, again" (dw[*evti*) harmonizing with 1:21, 25, but Westermann in his commentary notes how this is superfluous.

43. G.L. Archer, in E.D. Radmacher and R. Preus, *Hermeneutics, Inerrancy, and the Bible* (Grand Rapids, MI: Zondervan, 1984), p. 326.

hours.[44] This hardly seems onerous even for people today, and with Adam's pre-Fall stamina and memory recall abilities, the problem disappears totally. But Ross even claims that Adam's abilities would slow him down (FoG:150):

> Adam in his perfect state would be all-the-more meticulous in performing his God-assigned tasks.

But this seems to be an *ad hoc* attempt to stretch out the days, without the slightest basis in Scripture or even common sense. Perhaps Ross is making the same erroneous assumption that Archer makes in his similar argument about the sixth day — that Adam was giving double Latin scientific names based on long and careful study of each creature, as the great creationist taxonomist Carl Linnaeus (1707–1778) did. The text neither states nor implies any such thing. And greater abilities would give Adam greater speed at accomplishing his tasks.

One of God's purposes in parading all the animals before Adam was to reinforce Adam's delegated authority (Gen. 1:28), since the act of naming someone or something was an assertion of authority. But another purpose was to reinforce the fact that he was different in kind from the rest of creation, so that none of these animals could ever serve as a physical, emotional, intellectual, or spiritual companion. The passage indicates that God would not have kept Adam lonely ("not good," Gen. 2:18) for the years that Ross proposes.

Happa'am = "at last"?

Happa'am (הפעם) is merely *pa'am* (פעם) with the definite article added, so the "p" is doubled. Although Ross claims this is "usually translated as 'now at length,' " this is simply not supported by major translations such as the KJV, NKJV, NIV, or NASB. Nor is it supported by other parts of the Bible. Rather, the lexicons show that while *pa'am* has a variety of meanings, and is most often translated "time," with the definite article it means "this time."[45] This is illustrated by passages Ross conveniently omits:

- Judges 6:39 — Gideon says to God, "May I speak once more . . . let me make a test once more." Both times, "once more" is the NASB translation of *happa'am*, but the second test is only 24 hours after his first test. The KJV has "but this once."

---

44. A. Kulikovsky, "How Could Adam Have Named All the Animals in a Single Day?" <www.answersingenesis.org/naming_animal>.

R. Grigg, "Naming the Animals: All in a Day's Work for Adam," *Creation* 18(4):46–49 (September–November 1996); <www.answersingenesis.org/animalnames>.

45. E. Kautzch, *Gesenius' Hebrew Grammar*, 2nd edition, translated by A.E. Cowley (Oxford: Oxford University Press, 1910), p. 404. Also compare HALOT: 5. time (often with a numeral): — הפעם; once, finally Gn 2:23; אך הפעם; just once more Gn 18:32 = אך הפעם הזה; Ju 16:28; רק הפעם; just one time more Ju 639; עתה הפעם; but on this occasion Gn 29:34; הפעם; once again Gn 29:35 (6 occurrences).

- Genesis 18:32 — Abraham said to God, "I shall speak only this once" (NASB); "I will speak yet but this once" (KJV). Here, *happa'am* is translated "this once," and it is used at the end of a short dialogue about the coming destruction of Sodom.

There is no basis for saying that this word carries with it the idea of a long period of time in Genesis 2.

Toledoth *(Generations) Indicates a Long Time Span?*

Ross claims (C&T:52):

> Hebrew lexicons verify that the word for generation (*toledah*) refers to the time between a person's birth and parenthood or to an arbitrarily longer time period. . . . In Genesis 2:4 the plural form, generations, is used, indicating that multiple generations have passed.

However, the very lexicon Ross cited as a reference, TWOT:378–380, says:

> The common translation as "generations" does not convey the meaning of the word to modern readers. . . . As used in the OT, *toledot* refers to what is produced or brought into being by someone, or follows therefrom.

Therefore, it has nothing to do with "the time between a person's birth and parenthood," despite Ross's claim. Note that there is a very good reason that the lexicon refers to the word in the plural:

> It (*toledot*) occurs only in the plural, and only in the construct state or with a pronominal suffix.

Ross's argument for long ages, because the word is plural in Genesis, falls flat, since according to his own lexicon, the word always occurs in the plural in the OT!

The lexicon further states about the very passage in question:

> It is reasonable to translate Genesis 2:4, "these are the *toledot* of the heaven and earth," as meaning, not the coming of heaven and earth into existence, but the events that followed the establishment of heaven and earth.

Toledot תלדות is used in Genesis as a literary marker to designate a new narrative section of the book. It is generally combined with אלה (*eleh*) and a proper noun, and the NIV renders the phrase "This is the account of. . . ." The ten uses of אלה תלדות in Genesis are: 2:4, 5:1, 6:9, 10:1, 11:10, 11:27, 25:12, 25:19, 26:1, 37:2.

Once more, Ross's appeal to lexicons, instead of establishing his position, undercuts it. In fact, one has to wonder whether Ross's fallacious use of the lexicon is a reflection of incompetence or intention.

Genesis 2:19: Contradiction?

Some compromisers (*not* including Ross) use the alleged contradiction in Genesis 2:19 as "proof" that Genesis is not chronological. However, Hebrew verbs don't correspond neatly to English grammatical rules. The tense must be decided by context. If there are several possible translations, it makes sense to choose the one that doesn't lead to a contradiction. In this passage, it is grammatically possible to translate it into the pluperfect tense as "God *had* formed the animals"; the "contradiction" then disappears.

The verb "to form" is a *waw* consecutive or *wayyiqtol*. Normally, this is used to indicate a sequence of events. But within the context of sequential narrative, the *waw* consecutive may be used to indicate a time previous to the time of the main narrative. In such cases, it may have the effect of recapitulation or the equivalent of a pluperfect in English. Joüon points out that, because of its frequent use in narrative, at times it loses its idea of sequence and may express simultaneous acts (Jer. 22:15; Ruth 2:3) or logically anterior (previous) circumstances (Judg. 16:23; 1 Sam. 18:11).[46]

In discussing this passage, Hebrew grammarians Waltke and O'Connor say:

Moreover, *wayyqtl* in the received text, the object of our grammatical investigation, must be understood to represent the pluperfect.[47]

They demonstrate two examples of this usage from the Pentateuch (Num. 1:47–49; Exod. 4:11–12, 18). There are a number of other places throughout the Pentateuchal narrative where Moses uses the *waw* consecutive for logically anterior acts or as a pluperfect throughout Pentateuchal narrative. For example, in Exodus 11:1, Moses inserts a *waw* consecutive as a pluperfect into a sequential narrative in order to introduce a revelation previously given to Moses: "Now the Lord said to Moses, 'One more plague I will bring on Pharaoh and on Egypt. . . .' " This section begins with the *waw* consecutive, but Moses introduces it in the middle of his last interview with Pharaoh (Exod. 10:24–11:8). So Exodus 11:1–3 actually provides the prior background of God's command before Moses' interview with Pharaoh. The NIV translates Exodus 11:1 with a pluperfect, too, as with Genesis 2:19, "Now the Lord had said to Moses. . . ." For the sake of emphasis, Moses used the *waw* consecutive as a pluperfect, and then resumed the chronological sequence of his narrative.

---

46. P. Joüon and T. Muraoka, *A Grammar of Biblical Hebrew: Part Three: Syntax* (Rome: Pontifical Biblical Institute, 1991), p. 390.

47. B.K. Waltke and M. O'Connor, *Introduction to Biblical Hebrew Syntax* (Winona Lake, IN: Eisenbrauns, 1990), p. 552.

Compare C.H.J. van der Merwe, J.A. Naud, and J.H. Kroeze, *A Biblical Hebrew Reference Grammar,* Biblical Langauges: Hebrew 3 (Sheffield: Sheffield Academic Press, 1999), p. 141 notes: In contrast to English, the tense system of other languages may be much simpler, as is the case with Afrikaans that has no grammatical means of differentiating between the *simple past,* the *present perfect* and the *pluperfect.* (Emphasis in the original. Note that van der Merwe is South African hence the reference to Afrikaans.)

Leupold made the point well about the pluperfect in Genesis 2:19:

> Without any emphasis on the sequence of acts the account here records the making of the various creatures and the bringing of them to man. That in reality they had been made prior to the creation of man is so entirely apparent from chapter one as not to require explanation. But the reminder that God had "molded" them makes obvious His power to bring them to man and so is quite appropriately mentioned here. It would not, in our estimation, be wrong to translate *yatsar* as a pluperfect in this instance: "He had molded." The insistence of the critics upon a plain past is partly the result of the attempt to make chapters one and two clash at as many points as possible.

Keil and Delitzsch justified this translation as follows (*Pentateuch* 1:87):

> The circumstance that in ver. 19 the formation of the beasts and birds is connected with the creation of Adam by the *imperf. c. waw consec.*, constitutes no objection to the plan of creation given in chap. i. The arrangement may be explained on the supposition that the writer, who was about to describe the relation of man to the beasts, went back to the creation, in the simple method of early Semitic historians, and placed this first instead of making it subordinate; so that our modern style of expressing the same thought would be "God brought to Adam the beast which He had formed."[Footnote to following paragraph.]
>
> A striking example of this style of narrative we find in 1 Kings vii.13. First of all, the building and completion of the temple are noticed several times in chapter vi, and the last time in connection with the year and month (chap. vi. 9, 14, 37, 38); after that, the fact is stated, that the royal palace was thirteen years in building; and then the writer proceeds thus: "And Solomon sent and fetched Hiram from Tyre . . . and he came to king Solomon, and did all his work; and made the two pillars," etc. Now, if we are to understand the historical preterite with *consec.* here, as giving the order of the sequence, Solomon would be made to send for the Tyrian artist, thirteen years after the temple was finished, to come and prepare the pillars for the porch, and all the vessels needed for the temple. But the writer merely expressed in Semitic style the simple thought, that "Hiram, whom Solomon fetched from Tyre, made the vessels," etc. Another instance we find in Judg. ii. 6.

OTHER VIEWS OF GENESIS

While this book is specifically aimed at refuting Ross's day-age theory, as the subtitle indicates, we also want to proclaim the biblical truth in the face of other errors of compromise. So this section will briefly address other deviant views of Genesis. As chapter 3 shows, these views weren't dreamt of till the rise of long-age "science."

Framework Hypothesis

This view arose in the 20th century from capitulation to "science," but also because of dissatisfaction with the poor exegesis required to read millions of years into Genesis. Therefore, this seems to be an increasingly popular compromise in evangelical seminaries today.

The framework hypothesis dispenses with Genesis as history, and instead treats it as a literary device. In other words, Genesis 1 is not a record of what actually happened, but the literary framework within which God teaches us about himself and His creation.

It is claimed that one aim of this framework is to teach the theology of six days of work plus the Sabbath. This is back to front — Exodus 20:8–11 makes it clear that the Sabbath was based on the *historical* events of Genesis, not vice versa.

Is Genesis Poetry?

The defining characteristic of Hebrew poetry is not rhyme or meter, but parallelism. That is, the statements in two or more consecutive lines are related in some way. For example, in synonymous parallelism there is one statement, then it is immediately followed by another statement saying the same thing in different words. Psalm 19:1–2 nicely illustrates this:

> The heavens are telling the glory of God;
> > and the firmament proclaims his handiwork.
> Day to day pours forth speech,
> > and night to night declares knowledge.

In *antithetical* parallelism, the first statement is followed by a statement of the opposite, as in Proverbs 28:1 and 7:

> The wicked flee when no one pursues,
> > but the righteous are bold as a lion.
> He who keeps the law is a wise son,
> > but a companion of gluttons shames his father.

In *synthetic* or *constructive parallelism*, the first statement is extended by the next one, as in Psalm 24:3–4:

> Who shall ascend the hill of the LORD?
> > And who shall stand in his holy place?
> He who has clean hands and a pure heart,
> > who does not lift up his soul to what is false,
> > and does not swear deceitfully.

However, parallelism is absent from Genesis, except where people are quoted, for example, Genesis 4:23–24. But they stand out from the rest of Genesis — if Genesis were truly poetic, it would use parallelisms throughout.[48] In fact, the Bible has a poetic celebration of God's creative work of Genesis — Psalm 104 — so if we want to see what a poetic account of creation looks like, that's where to look. For example, Psalm 104:7, 11 illustrates parallelism perfectly:

> At your rebuke they fled;
>> at the voice of Thy thunder they hastened away.
> They give drink to every beast of the field;
>> the wild asses quench their thirst.

Indeed, the historian Dr. Noel Weeks (with a Th.M. from Westminster Theological Seminary) argues that Genesis 1 is *structured prose* with a recurring theme, and *definitely* not poetry.[49]

Triads of Days?

One of the supposed major "evidences" for a poetic structure is the alleged two triads of days. In this view, Moses arranges the days in a very stylized framework with days 4–6 paralleling days 1–3. Leading framework advocate Meredith Kline suggests that days 1–3 refer to the Kingdom, and days 4–6 to the Rulers, as per the following table:[50]

Days of Kingdom	Days of Rulers
Day 1: Light and darkness separated	Day 4: Sun, moon, and stars (luminaries)
Day 2: Sky and waters separated	Day 5: Fish and birds
Day 3: Dry land and seas separated, plants and trees	Day 6: Animals and man

But even if this were true, it would not rule out a historical sequence — surely God is capable of creating in a certain order to teach certain truths. Dr. Weeks argues that the structure is *covenantal*.[51] That is, it outlines several covenants between a suzerain and vassal — God is the Lord, and we are His servants; in turn, man is to rule over creation. So, he argues, that ruler/rulee covenant is built into the very creation itself. Dr. Weeks pointed out that when one covenant is broken, as when we sin against our Lord, the other covenant is also broken — the creation rebels against man.[52]

---

48. W.C. Kaiser Jr., "The Literary Form of Genesis 1–11" in J.B. Payne, *New Perspectives on the Old Testament* (Waco, TX: Word Inc., 1970), p. 59–60.

49. N. Weeks lecture *Futile Compromises: Let the Bible Speak*, AiG conference, Sydney, Australia, 2001 (available on video, and audio file is <www.answersingenesis.org/AnswersMedia/play.asp?mediaID=010123_special07>).

50. M.G. Kline, "Space and Time in the Genesis Cosmogony," *Perspectives on Science and Christian Faith* 48:2–15 (1996).

51. See footnote 48 above.

52. Ibid.

Also, other theologians argue that the "literary devices" are more in the imagination of the proponents than the text. For example, the parallels of these two trios of days is vastly overdrawn. Systematic theologian Dr. Wayne Grudem summarizes:

> First, the proposed correspondence between the days of creation is not nearly as exact as its advocates have supposed. The sun, moon, and stars created on the fourth day as "lights in the firmament of the heavens" (Gen.1:14) are placed not in any space created on day 1 but in the "firmament" . . . that was created on the second day. In fact, the correspondence in language is quite explicit: this "firmament" is not mentioned at all on day 1 but five times on day 2 (Gen.1:6–8) and three times on day 4 (Gen.1:14–19). Of course day 4 also has correspondences with day 1 (in terms of day and night, light and darkness), but if we say that the second three days show the creation of things to fill the forms or spaces created on the first three days (or to rule the kingdoms as Kline says), then day 4 overlaps at least as much with day 2 as it does with day 1.
>
> Moreover, the parallel between days 2 and 5 is not exact, because in some ways the preparation of a space for the fish and birds of day 5 does not come in day 2 but in day 3. It is not until day 3 that God gathers the waters together and calls them "seas" (Gen.1:10), and on day 5 the fish are commanded to "fill the waters in the seas" (Gen.1:22). Again in verses 26 and 28 the fish are called "fish of the sea," giving repeated emphasis to the fact that the sphere the fish inhabit was specifically formed on day 3. Thus, the fish formed on day 5 seem to belong much more to the place prepared for them on day 3 than to the widely dispersed waters below the firmament on day 2. Establishing a parallel between day 2 and day 5 faces further difficulties in that nothing is created on day 5 to inhabit the "waters above the firmament," and the flying things created on this day (the Hebrew word would include flying insects as well as birds) not only fly in the sky created on day 2, but also live and multiply on the "earth" or "dry land" created on day 3. (Note God's command on day 5: "Let birds multiply on the earth" [Gen.1:22].)
>
> Finally, the parallel between days 3 and 6 is not precise, for nothing is created on day 6 to fill the seas that were gathered together on day 3. With all of these points of imprecise correspondence and overlapping between places and things created to fill them, the supposed literary "framework," while having an initial appearance of neatness, turns out to be less and less convincing upon closer reading of the text.[53]

Is Genesis Just a Polemic?

One common argument by framework proponents is that Genesis 1 was written as a polemic against paganism. Supposedly, its purpose was to refute pagan beliefs

---

53. W. Grudem, *Systematic Theology* (Grand Rapids, MI: Zondervan, 1994), p. 302.

involving worship of the sun or other luminaries. In other words, Genesis is allegedly teaching us not to worship the sun but our true God who made the sun.

However, even if true, this doesn't mean that it can't be history. As shown on pages 85 and 86, Theophilus of Antioch and Basil the Great thought that God had deliberately made the sun on day 4 to refute pagan ideas. So the truth will automatically be a polemic against falsehood. Conversely, it would be useless to argue against a pagan using Genesis if it were just a story — one must show that the pagan is contradicted by what God *actually* did.

Also, most framework proponents have a naive view of paganism. Real pagans didn't just worship the physical object, but a god behind it (see 1 Cor. 10:19–20). For example, the Babylonian Shamash, the sun god, was sometimes personified as the sun itself, but at other times was clearly distinct from the sun. So if the Israelites said to the Babylonians, "The sun isn't a god; our God made the sun," a sophisticated pagan would reply, "I believe my god created the sun, too — maybe they are the same."[54]

Therefore, it's actually no wonder that Genesis 1 has no disclaimer that it's only a polemic, and nor do later biblical writers use it as a polemic. Real anti-pagan polemics which recognize the god behind the object are found in Isaiah 37:18–20 and 45:12–20.

Another problem with the pagan polemic idea is the likelihood that Genesis was the original and the pagan myths were the result of distortions of that original account. There is archaeological evidence consistent with the biblical teaching that mankind was originally monotheistic, and only later degenerated into idolatrous pantheism.[55]

It is most likely that Moses was the *editor* of Genesis, using pre-existing tablets that long predated pagan myths. Under this theory, the tablets were originally written by the patriarchs, who appended their signature, "This is the *toledoth* of. . . ." This theory was first proposed by Air Commodore P.J. Wiseman, and his son, Professor of Assyriology D.J. Wiseman, has updated and revised his father's work.[56] (See table on following page.)

The view that *toledot* marks the closure of a narrative is admittedly a minority view. Most conservative commentators see it as starting a new narrative section of the book (see page 91).

The antiquity of Genesis is shown by many editorial comments (see Gen. 26:33, 32:32), where Moses explains some points for his Israelite readers living many years after the events. But, tellingly, sometimes the ancient tablets were left alone, for

54. N. Weeks lecture *Futile Compromises: Let the Bible Speak*, AiG conference, Sydney, Australia, 2001 (available on video, and audio file is <www.answersingenesis.org/AnswersMedia/play. asp?mediaID=010123_special07>).

55. W. Schmidt, *The Origin and Growth of Religion* (New York: Cooper Square, 1971).

56. P.J. Wiseman, *Ancient Records and the Structure of Genesis* (Nashville, TN: Thomas Nelson Inc., 1985).

Tablet	Starting Verse	Ending Verse	Owner or Writer
1	Genesis 1:1	Genesis 2:4a	God himself (?)
2	Genesis 2:4b	Genesis 5:1a	Adam
3	Genesis 5:1b	Genesis 6:9a	Noah
4	Genesis 6:9b	Genesis 10:1a	Shem, Ham & Japheth
5	Genesis 10:1b	Genesis 11:10a	Shem
6	Genesis 11:10b	Genesis 11:27a	Terah
7	Genesis 11:27b	Genesis 25:19a	Isaac
8	Genesis 25:12	Genesis 25:18	Ishmael, through Isaac
9	Genesis 25:19b	Genesis 37:2a	Jacob
10	Genesis 36:1	Genesis 36:43	Esau, through Jacob
11	Genesis 37:2b	Exodus 1:6	Jacob's 12 sons

Table 2.1 Proposed Tablets That Were Edited into Genesis[57]

example, 10:19, where directions are matter-of-factly given to Sodom and the other cities of the plain, long destroyed and under the Dead Sea by Moses' time. This shows that this tablet dates from the time of Abraham or even earlier, when these cities were still standing as landmarks.

Genesis 2:5 Teaches That Normal Providence Was Used?

Kline has made a very tenuous argument based on Genesis 2:5.[58] He rightly states that God did not make plants before the earth had rain or a man (although this is talking about cultivated plants). So, Kline asks, what's to stop God making them anyway because He could miraculously sustain them? The answer, according to Kline, is that God was working by ordinary providence:

> The unargued presupposition of Genesus 2:5 is clearly that the divine providence was operating during the creation period through processes which any reader would recognize as normal in the natural world of his day.[59]

Note that Kline admits that this alleged presupposition is *not* argued in the text. This would explain why no exegete saw this for thousands of years. Then he makes another amazing leap to say that there was ordinary providence operating throughout creation week:

> Embedded in Genesis 2:5 ff. is the principle that the *modus operandi* of the divine providence was the same during the creation period as that of ordinary providence at the present time.[60]

---

57. C. Sewell, "The Tablet Theory of Genesis Authorship," *Bible and Spade* 7(1) (Winter 1994); updated <www.trueorigin.org/tablet.asp>, March 2002.
58. M.G. Kline, "Because It Had Not Rained," *WTJ* 20:146–157 (1958).
59. Ibid., p. 150.
60. Ibid., p. 151.

But this is desperation. Even if normal providence were operating, it would not follow that miracles were *not*. In fact, there is no miracle in the Bible that does *not* operate in the midst of normal providence. Michael Horton points out that those who reject God acting in the normal course of events do it from a philosophical *a priori* and not from anything in the text.[61]

A miracle is properly understood not as a "violation" of providence but an *addition*. So when Jesus turned water into wine (John 2), the other aspects of "providence" were still operating. Perhaps Jesus created the dazzling variety of organic compounds in the water to make the wine, but gravity still held the liquid in the barrels, taste buds were still working in the guests, their hearts pumped blood without skipping a beat, etc.

Aside from this logical error, the very next verse contradicts Kline. Noel Weeks observes that:

> [O]ne of the emphases of the narrative is that God prepares the environment for the creature. It is natural to see 2:5 as part of this emphasis. All that is needed for vegetation was not present. Hence God set about providing it. There is nothing which clearly indicates that normal providence was functioning during the creation period. Whereas rain is mentioned as the normal way in which vegetation is watered, in 2:6 the earth is watered by the going up of a mist. We cannot infer from 2:5 that there had been a long period prior to the situation reported in that verse during which the earth had become dry. Rather it fits into the framework of God first providing the environmental necessity (water) and then making the plants. Certainly springs do continue as one of the ways in which the earth has been watered since creation but the concern of the verse is the way it first began. The actual beginning does not assume the operation of normal providence.[62]

Kline also argues:

> Hence the twenty-four-hour day theorist must think of the almighty as hesitant to put in the plants on "Tuesday" morning because it would not rain until later in the day! (It must of course be supposed that it did rain, or at least that some supply of water was provided, before "Tuesday" was over, for by the end of the day the earth was abounding with that vegetation which according to Genesis 2:5 had hitherto been lacking for want of water.)[63]

But aside from the caricature of "the twenty-four-hour day theorist," Kline mistakenly applies Genesis 2:5 to day 3 of creation week ("Tuesday") when God created vegetation. Genesis 2:5 describes these plants and herbs as "of the *field*," whereas

---

61. M.S. Horton, *Covenant and Eschatology: The Divine Drama* (Louisville, KY: Westminster John Knox Press, 2002).
62. N. Weeks, *The Sufficiency of Scripture* (Edinburgh, UK: Banner of Truth Trust, 1988), p. 16–17.
63. M.G. Kline, "Because It Had Not Rained," *WTJ* 20:146–157 (1958): p. 152.

Genesis 1:12 describes plants of the earth as a whole. And the Genesis 2:5 plants needed a man to tend them, so they are clearly *cultivated* plants, not just plants in general. Genesis 2:4b ff is focusing on the creation of man, and the preparation of Eden for him.

So, in conclusion, Kline presupposes normal providence as God's **sole** *modus operandi* for Genesis 2:5, wildly extrapolates it to the entire creation week, and further presumes that normal providence excludes miracles. This error is compounded by failing to note the narrow focus of Genesis 2 on man.

Hebrew Grammar Affirms That Genesis Is Historical Narrative

Most importantly, the Hebrew grammar of Genesis shows that Genesis 1–11 has the same literary style as Genesis 12–50, which no one doubts is historical narrative. For example, the early chapters of Genesis frequently use the construction called the "*waw* consecutive" (or *wayyiqtol*), a singular mark of sequential narrative, as Hebrew grammars consistently point out.[64] Genesis 1–11 also has several other trademarks of historical narrative, such as "accusative particles" (את *'eth*) that mark the objects of verbs, and many terms that are carefully defined.[65]

And the Hebrew verbs of Genesis 1 have a particular feature that is exactly what would be expected if it were representing a series of past events. *Gesenius' Hebrew Grammar* states:

> One of the most striking peculiarities in the Hebrew *consecution* of tenses is the phenomenon that, in representing a series of past events, only the first verb stands in the perfect, and the narration is continued in the imperfect.[66]

Joüon and Muraoka concur:

> This form is very common in narratives. Usually a narrative begins with a *qatal* (historic perfect) and continues with a *wayyiqtol* (*waw* consecutive), which is followed, if need be, by other *wayyiqtols*. . . ."[67]

In Genesis 1, the first verb is ברא (*bara'*, create), which is perfect, while the subsequent verbs that move the narrative forward are a series of imperfects, including ויאמר (*wayyômer*, "And . . . said," v. 3) and ויהי (*wayehi*, "and there was," v. 3).

---

64. P. Joüon and T. Muraoka, *A Grammar of Biblical Hebrew: Part Three: Syntax* (Rome: Pontifical Biblical Institute, 1991), p. 389–393.

J. Weingreen, *A Practical Grammar for Classical Hebrew* (Oxford: Clarendon Press, 1967), p. 90–92.

B.K. Waltke and M. O'Connor, *Introduction to Biblical Hebrew Syntax* (Winona Lake, IN: Eisenbrauns, 1990), p. 543–553.

65. W.C. Kaiser Jr., "The Literary Form of Genesis 1–11" in J.B. Payne, *New Perspectives on the Old Testament* (Waco, TX: Word Inc., 1970).

66. *Gesenius' Hebrew Grammar*, 2nd ed., trans. A.E. Cowley (Oxford: Oxford University Press, 1910), p. 132–133.

67. P. Joüon and T. Muraoka, *A Grammar of Biblical Hebrew: Part Three: Syntax* (Rome: Pontifical Biblical Institute, 1991), p. 390.

The New Testament Interprets Genesis as History

Finally, the New Testament writers cite Genesis as history, not merely literature, or even parable. For example, Paul teaches about the role of women in church by appealing to the historical order of creation and the fact that Eve was deceived and Adam was not (1 Tim. 2:11–14). There is not the slightest hint that they were symbols that needed to be explained. By contrast, in the Bible, a parable is always stated to be so, and the symbols are always explained. For example, in the Parable of the Sower (Luke 8), "The seed is the word of God"; "Those on the rock are the ones who receive the word with joy when they hear it, but they have no root"; "The seed on good soil stands for those with a noble and good heart." Also, in Luke 8:10, Jesus explained that He spoke in parables to hide the truth from the masses, while to His disciples He spoke plainly.

Luke 3 and Hebrews 11 have an extensive list of people from both Genesis 1–11 and later chapters of the OT. There is no hint that the characters from Genesis 1–11 are symbolic, with historicity only beginning after that. Jesus treats both Genesis 1 and 2 as straightforward history in Matthew 19:3–6 and Mark 10:6–9, when he cites both Genesis 1:27 and 2:24.

Thus, the framework hypothesis is without the slightest exegetical merit, despite its wide popularity in some evangelical circles.[68]

Gap Theory

This aims to fit the alleged millions of years into a gap between Genesis 1:1 and 1:2. God originally created a perfect world, but then, in this gap, the anointed cherub fell to become Satan (meaning "adversary"), and God judged the world by a catastrophe, which formed most of the fossils. Thus, gappists translate Genesis 1:2 as "the earth *became* formless and void." Then the six days of creation are said to be a re-creation of this fallen world. But this fails on several grounds:[69]

---

68. J.A. Pipa, "From Chaos to Cosmos: A Critique of the Framework Hypothesis," <http://capo.org/cpc/pipa.htm> January 13, 1998.

    A. Kulikovsky, "A Critique of the Literary Framework View of the Days of Creation," *CRSQ* 37(4): 237–244 (March 2001); <www.kulikovskyonline.net/hermeneutics/Framework.pdf>.

69. R. Grigg, "From the Beginning of Creation: Does Genesis Have a Gap?" 19(2):35–38 (March–May 1997); <www.answersingenesis.org/gap>.

    The definitive critique of the Gap Theory is W.W. Fields, *Unformed and Unfilled* (Collinsville, IL: Burgener Enterprises, 1976). In chapter 8, Fields devastates the day-age view as well, saying (p. 165–66): "However, it also shares one disadvantage with the Gap Theory in this particular — indeed, it outdoes the gap theory in this particular: it rests on very scanty exegetical evidence. The lexical exility on which it is based is almost unbelievable; consequently, we must conclude that it springs from presupposition — a fact transparent even to the casual reader. Its defenders, even to a greater extent than gap theorists, have been bullied into abandoning the prima facie meaning of the creation account for a more scientifically palatable (at least in their thinking) interpretation." Fields' book, written well before Ross, answers many of the same fallacious arguments that Ross puts forward, demonstrating that Ross is merely repeating the discredited arguments of older compromisers.

- Although the gap theory originated out of a desire to accommodate the millions of years of supposed geological time, only the most naive would think it does. Uniformitarian geologists reject the idea of any global flood, whether the biblical Noah's flood, or the imagined "Lucifer's flood" of the gap theory.

- It postulates the fall of Satan and death in a world God declared "very good" in Genesis 1:31 (see chapter 6).

- It contradicts the Sabbath command of Exodus 20:8–11, which is based on the creation of the "heavens, earth, sea and everything in them" in six ordinary days. In the Old Testament Hebrew, whenever the words "heaven(s) and earth" are conjoined, it is a figure of speech called a *merism*, in which two opposites are combined into an all-encompassing single concept.[70] Throughout the Bible (for example, Gen. 14:19, 22; 2 Kings 19:15; Ps. 121:2), this means the totality of creation, not just the earth and its atmosphere, or our solar system alone. It is used because Hebrew has no word for "the universe" and can at best say "the all."[71]

- "*Waw*" is the name of the Hebrew letter ו which is used as a conjunction. It can mean "and," "but," "now," "then" and several other things depending upon the context and type of *waw* involved. It occurs at the beginning of Genesis 1:2 and is translated in the KJV, "And [*waw*] the earth was without form, and void." Gappists use this translation to support the gap theory. However,

---

70. An English example is "open day and night." This doesn't simply mean during sunlight and darkness but not dusk; rather, "day and night" means the whole 24-hour day-night cycle. Other examples are "far and near" and "hill and vale."

One old-earther named John Holzmann who runs an ostensibly Christian home school book supply business has tried to refute this argument: "In 2 Samuel 18:9 we find Absalom riding a mule. He rides under an oak tree and gets his hair tangled in the branches. The mule keeps going while Absalom finds himself, according to the Hebrew, "lifted up between the heavens [*hashamayim*] and the earth [*haerets*]." I hope you can appreciate my attempt at humour when I suggest, "That must have been one tall tree to lift Absalom somewhere into outer space where he found himself in the middle of [between] 'the totality of creation, not just the earth and its atmosphere, [n]or our solar system alone!' " John Holzmann, "Young- and Old-Earth Creationists: Can We Even Talk Together?" <www.sonlight.com/articles/young-or-old-earth.html>, December 4, 2002.

But for all his "humour," Holzmann seems unaware of what the Hebrew structure should have taught him. The Hebrew grammar is completely different: **both** *hashamayim* and *haerets* have the preposition *beyn* (between). So this has no bearing on what we said above, where it is simply the conjunction of heaven and earth *without any preposition* that is the merism for "universe." The extra prepositions mean there is no merism in 2 Samuel 18:9. This error is not really surprising, since he's also previously swallowed arguments that show that *yôm* (day) can sometimes mean an age — but again with prepositions, not in the *specific context* of Genesis 1. He's not open to reason about this either, it seems.

71. See Leupold 1:41, who cites similar usage in Jeremiah 10:16; Isaiah 44:24; Psalm 103:19, 119:91; and Ecclesiastes 11:5.

the most straightforward reading of the text sees verse 1 of Genesis 1 as the principal subject-and-verb clause, with verse 2 containing three "circumstantial clauses." Hebrew grammarian Gesenius called this a *"waw explicativum,"* and compares it to the English "to wit." Other terms are called *waw copulative* or *waw disjunctive* or explanatory *waw*.

Such a *waw* disjunctive is easy to tell from the Hebrew, because it is formed by *waw* followed by a non-verb. It introduces a parenthetic statement; that is, it's alerting the reader to put the passage following in brackets, as it were — a descriptive phrase about the previous noun. It does *not* indicate something following in a time sequence — this would have been indicated by a different Hebrew construction called the *waw consecutive*, where *waw* is followed by a verb. (The *waw consecutive* is in fact used at the beginning of every day of creation — indeed, the beginning of every sentence. In in some cases it is used in the middle of a sentence — from Genesis 1:3 through 2:3 — which is strong evidence that it is historical narrative — see page 100.) While it is true that *w+x+qatal*, where x = the subject, normally denotes a pause or a turning point in a text, in the beginning of a text it would just show that the next *wayyiqtol* will begin the forward movement of the narrative.

- It is simply grammatically impossible to translate the verb היה (*hayah*) as "became" when it is combined with a waw disjunctive — in the rest of the Old Testament, *waw* + a noun + היה (*qal* perfect, 3rd person) is always translated, "was" or "came," but never "became." Moreover the *qal* form of היה does not normally mean "became," especially in the beginning of a text, where it usually gives the setting.[72]

- Also, the correct Hebrew idiom for "become" is to attach the verb "to be," for example, "was," to the preposition "to" (Hebrew *le*). The verb "to be" does NOT mean "become" without this preposition. Since Genesis 1:2 lacks the preposition, it *cannot* mean "became."

- The Hebrew words *tohu* and *bohu*, translated "without form" and "void" in Genesis 1:2, are claimed by gap theorists to indicate a judgmental destruction rather than something in the process of being built. But *tohu* occurs several times in the Bible in which it is used in a morally neutral fashion, describing something which is unfinished, and confused, but not necessarily evil! Hebrew scholars and the church have for centuries taken the view that Genesis 1:2 is not a scene of judgment or an evil state created by the fall of angels, but a description of the original undeveloped state of the universe. The plain and simple meaning of what Moses says is that on the first day there was a mass

---

72. A.F. den Exter Blokland, *In Search of Text Syntax: Towards a Syntactic Text Segmentation Model for Biblical Hebrew*, Applicatio, 14 (Amsterdam: VU University Press, 1995), p. 52.

covered by water, with no dry land involving features (*tohu* = "unformed"), and no inhabitants yet (*bohu* = "unfilled").

- Some have attempted to use Jeremiah 4:23 to teach the gap theory, because it uses the same phrase *tohu va bohu* to describe the results of a judgment. Leading gap theorists like Arthur Custance used this fact to assert that "without form and void" must mean "laid waste by a judgment." But this is fallacious — there is nothing in the Hebrew words *tohu va bohu* themselves to suggest that. The only reason they refer to being "laid waste" is due to the context in which the phrase is found. The words simply mean "unformed and unfilled." This state can be due either to nothing else having been created, or some created things having been removed. The context of Jeremiah 4 is a prophecy of the Babylonian sacking of Jerusalem, not creation. In fact, Jeremiah 4:23 is known as a *literary allusion* to Genesis 1:2 — the judgment would be so severe that it would leave the final state as empty as the earth before God created anything.

  An analogy might help here. When I open my word processor, my document screen is blank. But if I delete an entire document the screen would likewise be blank. So "blank" means "free from any text." In some contexts, the lack of text is because I haven't written anything, in others it is due to a deletion of text. You would need to know the context to tell which — you couldn't tell from the word "blank" itself. However, a gappist-type analysis of the word might conclude, "blank" can refer to a screen with all the text deleted, so the word "blank" itself signifies a text deletion event, even when none is stated.

  This is in line with the common biblical principle where a judgment is a *reversal of creation*. Jeremiah 4:23 is taking the land back to its unformed state, unfit for man to live in. Similarly, the Flood took the world back to its condition on day 2, before the land and water had separated.

  Furthermore, the gap theory violates the principle of God's progressive revelation in Scripture. Later texts presuppose the prior revelation of earlier texts, not vice versa. Therefore, Jeremiah 4:23 cannot be used to interpret Genesis 1:2 as a judgment — that would be completely back-to-front, because an allusion works only one way.

- The English word "replenish" in the KJV translation of Genesis 1:28 (". . . and God said unto them, Be fruitful and multiply and replenish the earth") does not support the gap theory as claimed. Linguist Dr. Charles Taylor writes, "As translated in 1611, it ("replenish") was merely a parallel to "fill," and the prefix "re-" didn't mean "again," but "completely."[73] The same Hebrew word *mālē'* is used in Genesis 1:22, and is there translated "fill (the seas)," so there was no need to translate it differently in verse 28."

---

73. C. Taylor, "What Does 'Replenish the Earth' Mean?" *Creation* 18(2):44–45 (March–May 1996); <www.answersingenesis.org/replenish>.

CONCLUSION

In Genesis, the word day (*yôm*) has certain grammatical contexts, any of which alone point strongly to 24-hour days:

1. with a numeric
2. with evening and morning
3. associated with night

Yet Genesis 1 has all three features, so this becomes overwhelming evidence that the days are ordinary-length days. In fact, one must ask: just suppose that God really did mean to communicate creation in six ordinary days, how could He have done so more clearly? Or conversely, if God really did create over millions of years, how could He have been more misleading (compare chapter 10)?

While Ross points to other meanings of *yôm*, no creationist disputes that. Rather, we point out that *yôm* means a longer period of time only in a context completely different from Genesis 1, for example, with a preposition *bᵉ* (in). Other objections to literal days are mere rationalizations that do not stand up under careful attention to the text.

Other views of Genesis besides Ross's day-age view include the gap theory and framework hypothesis. Likewise, they are reactions to perceived conflicts with "science" and have not the slightest basis in the Hebrew of Genesis.

CHAPTER 3

THE HISTORY OF INTERPRETATION OF GENESIS 1–11

G enesis has been analyzed by theologians since the beginnings of the church. Ross often claims that they back his day-age interpretation, while few ever thought the days were 24 hours long. The opposite is true. Most believed that the days were 24 hours long, and the minority who dissented believed they were instantaneous, not long. Belief in a "young" earth was unanimous among those who commented. Ideas such as the day-age and gap theories arose in the early 19th century only in response to old-age "science."

WHY IS CHURCH HISTORY RELEVANT?

Some may argue, "Isn't the Bible all we need? Don't you realize that interpreters can err?" Indeed, the correct view must be obtained from the Bible alone. But then, modern exegetes are not the first who have known about the original languages and cultures of the Bible. The onus is on those proposing a novel interpretation to prove their case.

There are two more reasons why it is instructive to analyze the history, which will be explained in detail in this chapter:

1. Generally: If long-age interpretations had always been popular, then a case could be made for assuming that the Bible hints at this. But if they were absent until long ages became popular in "science," it's more likely that such interpretations were motivated by trying to reconcile the Bible with "science."

2. Specifically for Ross: he often claims that interpreters throughout history have allowed for long creation days. Since this is a book on his claims, it's important to address evidence that he uses to overcome the charge that he's motivated by "science" and not the biblical text.

Caution

"Traditional" churches such as Eastern Orthodox and Roman Catholic churches hold that the combined testimony of the church fathers is on a par with Scripture itself. A common argument is that they were closer to the Apostles than we, so they know better.

However, this doesn't necessarily follow. Paul's letters were written largely to correct error in churches founded by the Apostles themselves. Furthermore, as the church became primarily Gentile, knowledge of Hebrew diminished, so that even some of the leading church fathers knew no Hebrew at all, including the highly influential Augustine (see also page 118). Still, many of the fathers had tremendous wisdom, which showed in the battles against anti-Trinitarian heresies.

The main point of this chapter is to address Ross's claims, and show that even by his own reasoning, we should accept 24-hour creation days.

Ross's Claims

For example, in C&T, chapter 2, Ross claimed:

> A majority of those who wrote on the subject rejected the interpretation of the Genesis creation days as six consecutive 24-hour periods.

He listed 14 "church fathers": Philo, Josephus, Justin Martyr, Irenaeus, Hippolytus, Ambrose, Clement of Alexandria, Origen, Lactantius, Victorinus of Pettau, Methodius of Olympus, Augustine, Eusebius, and Basil the Great.

For another example, Ross claims (in GQ:66–67):

> Ante-Nicene[1] scholars devoted some two thousand pages of commentary to the "hexaëmeron," that part of Genesis 1 describing the six days of creation. No other portion of the Bible received nearly as much of their attention. Yet in all their pages of commentary only about two pages addressed the meaning of "day" or the time of creation [cited his own book C&T]. Their comments on the subject remained tentative, with the majority favoring the "long day" (typically a thousand year period) — apart from the influence of science. Not one explicitly endorsed the twenty-four hour interpretation.

And on the RTB website, he asserts:

> Many of the early church fathers and other biblical scholars interpreted the creation days of Genesis 1 as long periods of time. The list of such proponents includes the Jewish historian Josephus (1st century); Irenaeus, bishop of Lyons, apologist, and martyr (2nd century); Origen, who rebutted heathen

---

1. This refers to people before the First Ecumenical Council of the Catholic (universal) Church at Nicaea in Bithynia (now Isnik, Turkey) in A.D. 325. It was called by the Roman Emperor Constantine and attended by over 300 bishops. It resulted in the condemnation of the Arian heresy that taught, as do modern Jehovah's Witnesses, that Jesus was a created being, and led to the Nicene Creed, a summary of true Christian doctrine accepted by Roman Catholicism, Eastern Orthodoxy and Protestantism.

attacks on Christian doctrine (3rd century); Basil (4th century); Augustine (5th century); and, later, Aquinas (13th century), to name a few.[2]

Another Ross claim is in C&T:24:

> Perhaps most significant is that nearly all the key figures acknowledged that the length of creation days presented a challenge to their understanding and interpretation. Those that did not implied the same in their studious avoidance of any specific comment on the subject.

While the first sentence more or less summarizes the other claims, the second sentence betrays a methodological flaw in the way Ross and certain others use church history. It's one thing to claim certain people supported his view, but another to claim support from those who never commented! This is obviously the fallacy of arguing from silence. A related error is misinterpreting a non-specific statement about creation as claiming that they didn't have a position on the days and time frame. It's worse when clear statements about the creation days and time frame are ignored in favor of non-specific ones. The correct practice is to interpret the non-specific passages by the specific ones.

Note that, by the same methodology, someone hundreds of years in the future could find articles by me or other AiG scientists that are not specific on days or the time frame and, by ignoring our clear statements elsewhere, claim that we don't have any position on the issues!

The only way to settle this is by quoting the people in question in their proper context, to analyze what they *actually* say instead of what people *claim* they say. Ross rarely provides quotations himself, evidently expecting his readers simply to take his word for it. It's a shame that too many people have accepted Ross's word for it instead of checking them out. Sadly, we really must wonder if Ross has actually read the people he quotes, because the quotes below do not support his claims; rather, they contradict them. Therefore, I will cite a number of the authorities Ross invokes on both the days of creation and the age of the earth.

Van Bebber and Taylor have already quoted and documented the evidence that refutes Ross's claims in their response to Ross's book *Creation and Time* [VB&T:93–104]. An obvious point is that Philo and Josephus were non-Christian Jews, not church fathers. If Ross was so careless in his historical research on this point, we should wonder about the rest of his statements, even before we investigate the Christians he claims in support. For a careful, thorough, and reliable survey of historical views on the days of creation, see the treatments by J.P. Lewis.[3] One of the most thorough and extensive analyses of church fathers on Genesis is in a book by

---

2. "Biblical Evidence for Long Creation Days," <www.reasons.org/resources/apologetics/longdays.html>, December 1, 2002.

3. J.P. Lewis, "The Days of Creation: An Historical Survey of Interpretation," *JETS* 32(4):433–455 (December 1989).

the Eastern Orthodox scholar Fr. Seraphim Rose.[4] Also, J.L. Duncan and D. Hall make a strong case in their defense of literal Genesis in a book where Ross himself defends the day-age view and had a chance to interact with them.[5] But Ross still keeps making the same claims.

Yet another contrary source is the well-known long-ager Davis Young (see chapter 2). Because he is a *hostile* (to YECs) *witness*, his testimony is even more powerful. And because he wrote before Ross, Ross has even less excuse for his false claims. Young writes:

> The virtually unanimous opinion among the early Christians until the time of Augustine was that human history had lasted approximately fifty-five hundred years.[6] It is also very probable that the age of the world was regarded as the same number of years, for the writings of the church fathers generally do not reveal any sharp distinctions between the initial creation and the creation of man. . . .
>
> It is also generally necessary that the days of creation (Gen. 1) be regarded as ordinary days if one were to hold that the earth was only fifty-five hundred years old. We find absolutely no one arguing that the world is tens of thousands of years old on the grounds that the days are used figuratively for long periods of time. . . .
>
> Many of the church fathers plainly regarded the six days as ordinary days.[7]

So let us turn now to examine the men that Ross uses in support of his views.

Flavius Josephus (A.D. 37–c. 101)

Josephus came from a distinguished priestly family and became a Pharisee, then became a general in the Jewish revolt against Rome (A.D. 66–73). But he barely escaped the massacre of his garrison in A.D. 67, and was captured and taken to the Roman general Vespasian. Josephus shrewdly prophesied that Vespasian would become emperor. When this came to pass in A.D. 69, he freed Josephus. Then he tried,

---

4. S. Rose, *Genesis, Creation and Early Man* (Platina, CA: St. Herman of Alaska Brotherhood, 2000).
   T. Mortenson, "Orthodoxy and Genesis: What the Fathers *Really* Taught," [review of Rose, entry above], *TJ* 16(3):48–53 (2002); <www.answersingenesis.org/seraphim>.
5. J.L. Duncan and D. Hall, "The 24-Hour View," in D.G. Hagopian, *The Genesis Debate: Three Views on the Days of Creation* (Mission Viejo, CA: Crux Press, 2001), p. 21–66, 95–119.
   A.S. Kulikovsky, "Sizing the Day: Review of Hagopian," *TJ* 16(1):41–44 (2002); <www.answersingenesis.org/Gen_Debate>.
6. This figure comes from the Septuagint (LXX), the Greek translation of the OT, c. 250 B.C. However, this is demonstrably inflated, and contains the obvious error that Methuselah survived the Flood by 17 years. For a defense of the primacy of the Masoretic text versus the Septuagint (LXX) and Samaritan Pentateuch, see P. Williams, "Some Remarks Preliminary to a Biblical Chronology," *TJ* 12(1):98–106 (1998); <www.answersingenesis.org/chronology>.
7. D.A. Young, *Christianity and the Age of the Earth* (Grand Rapids, MI: Zondervan, 1982), p. 19, 22.

at personal risk, to persuade the Jews to surrender Jerusalem, so was regarded as a traitor. But his efforts were in vain, and Jerusalem was captured violently in A.D. 70. Afterward, Josephus enjoyed the imperial patronage of Vespasian and his sons, Titus and the cruel Domitian, and he wrote some valuable works. The one most relevant to this book is *Ioudaike Archaiologia* (*Jewish Antiquities* a.k.a. *The Antiquities of the Jews*), comprising 20 books on the whole history of the Jews from the creation to the outbreak of the revolt in A.D. 66.

Ross claims (C&T:17):

> Josephus, in writing a survey of the Genesis creation days, noted the need to explain the meaning of the expression "one day" and promised to offer an explanation, but he never fulfilled his promise. His comments suggest that he did not find this expression either easy or straightforward to interpret.

However, here is what Josephus said:

> In the beginning God created the heaven and the earth. But when the earth did not come into sight, but was covered with thick darkness, and a wind moved upon its surface, God commanded that there should be light: and when that was made, he considered the whole mass, and separated the light and the darkness; and the name he gave to one was *Night,* and the other he called *day:* and he named the beginning of light, and the time of rest, *The Evening* and *The Morning,* and this was indeed the first day. But Moses said it was one day; the cause of which I am able to give even now; but because I have promised to give such reasons for all things in a treatise by itself, I shall put off its exposition till that time. After this, on the second day, he placed the heaven over the whole world, and separated it from the other parts, and he determined it should stand by itself. He also placed a crystalline [firmament] round it, and put it together in a manner agreeable to the earth, and fitted it for giving moisture and rain, and for affording the advantage of dews. On the third day he appointed the dry land to appear, with the sea itself round about it; and on the very same day he made the plants and the seeds to spring out of the earth. On the fourth day he adorned the heaven with the sun, the moon, and the other stars, and appointed them their motions and courses, that the vicissitudes of the seasons might be clearly signified. And on the fifth day he produced the living creatures, both those that swim, and those that fly; the former in the sea, the latter in the air: he also sorted them as to society and mixture, for procreation, and that their kinds might increase and multiply. On the sixth day he created the four-footed beasts, and made them male and female: on the same day he also formed man. Accordingly Moses says, that in just six days the world, and all that is therein, was made. And that the seventh day was a rest, and a release from the labor of such operations; whence it is

that we celebrate a rest from our labors on that day, and call it the Sabbath, which word denotes *rest* in the Hebrew tongue."[8]

This passage, as a whole, provides no hint that the days were anything but 24 hours long. Josephus compares them with the Sabbath command, says that the heavenly bodies were created on the fourth day, and that the seventh day is an ordinary day which has ended; both contrary to Ross. Furthermore, the heading of the book was:

Containing the interval of three thousand eight hundred and thirty-three years From the Creation to the death of Isaac.

As explained in chapter 9, Josephus used the Septuagint for his claims about the age of the patriarchs at the birth of their sons, but his chronology rules out any long creation days.

So Ross is grasping at straws to claim that Josephus' enigmatic comment is proof of long creation days. Rather, it was a reference to the fact that day 1 has a cardinal number, "day one"; while the others have ordinals, "a second day," "a third day," as explained in chapter 2. This is actually *reinforcement* of the 24-hour view, as shown, and Basil the Great (next section) *does* explain what Josephus forgot to.

Basil the Great (A.D. 329–379)

Basil is one of Ross's alleged authorities for his day/age interpretation. His Christian credentials are excellent. He was bishop of Caesarea Mazaca, Cappadocia, from A.D. 370–379. He argued strongly against various heresies of the church of that day. In particular, he defended the vital biblical doctrine of the Trinity against the Arian heresy which denied the Deity of Christ, and later against the Sabellian (modalist) heresy which denied the distinctness of the three persons. Basil's classic Trinitarian formula, that God is three persons (*hypostases*) in one substance (*ousia*), is still one of the best summaries of the biblical doctrine, and is accepted by all branches of orthodox Christianity.

This is all very well, but did Basil teach what Ross claimed? We can find out, because some of his sermon collections have been preserved, including the *Hexaëmeron* (= "six days"), nine Lenten sermons on the days of creation in Genesis 1. The following quotation from this shows that Basil believed that the creation days were ordinary days about 24 hours long:

"And there was evening and there was morning: one day." And the evening and the morning were one day. Why does Scripture say "one day" not "the first day"? Before speaking to us of the second, the third, and the fourth days, would it not have been more natural to call that one the first

---

8. Josephus, *Antiquities of the Jews* 1(1):1, in W. Whiston, tr., *The Works of Josephus* (Edinburgh: William P. Nimmo, n.d.), p. 25; numbers rendered in numerals; <http://www.ccel.org/j/josephus/works/ant-1.htm>.

which began the series? If it therefore says "one day," it is from a wish to determine the measure of day and night, and to combine the time that they contain. Now *twenty-four hours fill up the space of one day* — we mean of a day and of a night; and if, at the time of the solstices, they have not both an equal length, the time marked by Scripture does not the less circumscribe their duration. It is as though it said: *twenty-four hours measure the space of a day*, or that, in reality a day is the time that the heavens starting from one point take to return there. Thus, every time that, in the revolution of the sun, evening and morning occupy the world, their periodical succession never exceeds the space of one day.[9]

Ross even quotes part of this in C&T:21–22, but somehow omits the clear references to 24-hour creation days, again strong evidence of careless historical research. Hebrew scholar Steinmann concurred that the Genesis expression "day one" with the context of dark/light and evening/morning was defining the creation days as 24 hours,[10] as we showed in the previous chapter.

Neither can Davis Young help but admit that "Basil explicitly spoke of days as a twenty-four-hour period."[11] So much for Ross's claim that "not one explicitly endorsed the twenty-four hour interpretation" (GQ:67)! Furthermore, a detailed study of the *Hexaëmeron* shows that Basil had practically identical beliefs as AiG about Genesis.[12]

Ambrose of Milan (339–397)

Ambrose was a gifted orator and popular bishop of Milan who staunchly defended orthodoxy, and was partly responsible for the conversion of Augustine, whom he baptized on Easter A.D. 386. He's another one claimed as an ally of Ross's day-age view, and some have claimed support with the following quote:

> Scripture established a law that twenty-four hours, including both day and night, should be given the name of day only, as if one were to say the length of one day is twenty-four hours in extent. . . . The nights in this reckoning are considered to be component parts of the days that are counted. Therefore, just as there is a single revolution of time, so there is but one day. There are many who call even a week one day, because it returns to itself, just as one day does, and one might say seven times revolves back on itself. Hence, Scripture appeals at times of an age of the world.[13]

---

9. Basil, *Hexaëmeron* 2:8, A.D. 370, <www.newadvent.org/fathers/32012.htm>.

10. A. Steinmann, "אחד as an Ordinal Number and the Meaning of Genesis 1:5," *JETS* 45(4):577–584 (December 2002).

11. D.A. Young, *Christianity and the Age of the Earth* (Grand Rapids, MI: Zondervan, 1982), p. 22.

12. D. Batten, "Genesis Means What It Says According to Great Church Father, Basil of Caesarea (A.D. 329–379)," *Creation* 16(4):23, <www.answersingenesis.org/basil>.

13. Ambrose, *Hexaëmeron*, A.D. 393; as cited by the Roman Catholic website <www.catholic.com/library/Creation_and_Genesis.asp>.

But those who cite this (including Ross in C&T:22), especially the last sentence, as proof that Ambrose believed the day-age theory did not read attentively.[14] Ambrose clearly states that the "law" established by Scripture was 24-hour days, and he's referring to the creation week in Genesis 1. The other meanings are clearly stated to be *secondary*. The nearest Ross gets to admitting this is his grudging admission, "He appears to imply, though, that the creation days are twenty-four hour periods." Furthermore, Ambrose said, in the same context:

> God commanded that the heavens should come into existence, and it was done; He determined that the earth should be created *in a moment*, and it was created. . . . These things were made *in a moment*.[15]

Days as *Types* for Millennia

As shown on page 86, many people today use 2 Peter 3:8 and Psalm 90:4, "one day is like a thousand years," to argue for non-literal days. We noted there that this passage is teaching that God is outside time, not defining the length of creation days. But many early church writers cited this passage frequently, and this misunderstanding might explain how Ross and other detractors of a literal Genesis have asserted that they believed in thousand-year *creation* days.[16]

However, the detractors seriously err by failing to realize that the fathers used this passage to teach that the days of creation were *types* for *the whole of world history*. They believed the world would only last for six thousand years from creation before the return of Christ and the Millennium. In other words, each day of creation *corresponded to* (but was not equal to) one thousand years of subsequent earth history, which culminated in the Millennium (the thousand-year reign of Christ) that paralleled the seventh day (of rest), and the world as we know it would last no longer than seven thousand years. Long-ager Davis Young affirms:

> But the interesting feature of this patristic view is that the equation of days and millennia was not applied to the creation week but rather to subsequent history. They did not believe that the creation had taken place over six millennia but that the totality of human *history* would occupy six thousand years, a millennium of history for each of the six days of creation.[17]

---

14. The webmaster of the site in the previous footnote, much like Ross, claims this and other patristic quotes as proof that "There was wide variation of opinion on how long creation took. Some said only a few days; others argued for a much longer, indefinite period." However, they do nothing of the kind, as shown here. This webmaster makes it clear that a major motivation is to avoid conflicts with "modern cosmology."

15. Ambrose, *Hexaëmeron* 1.10.3–7, *The Nicene and Post-Nicene Fathers* 10:187–188.

16. R. Forster and P. Marston, *Reason, Science and Faith* (Crowborough, East Sussex: Monarch Books, 1999).
   A.S. Kulikovsky, "Fostering Fallacy: Review of Forster and Marston," review of subject of previous footnote, *TJ* 16(2):31–36 (2002).

17. D.A. Young, *Christianity and the Age of the Earth* (Grand Rapids, MI: Zondervan, 1982), p. 20.

It's possible that they based this on the fact that five verses before 2 Peter 3:8, the Apostle refers to both "His coming" and "from the beginning of creation," so they made the connection between six literal creation days and six millennia from the beginning of time till the second coming.

Many rabbis had the same general idea, believing that the Messiah would come at the end of six thousand years; for example, the Talmud states:

> Six thousand years shall the world exist, and (one thousand, the seventh), it shall be desolate, as it is written, "And the Lord alone shall be exalted in that day. . . ." It is also said, "For a thousand years in thy sight are but as yesterday when it is past."[18]

Since the Fathers didn't believe the days were thousands of years long after all, it's totally illegitimate to claim that they would have regarded billions of years as supported by Scripture. What they actually said is shown by the following quotes.

Lactantius (240–c. 320)

One of the clearest teachings of this typological view was the Roman apologist Lactantius:

> Therefore let the philosophers, who enumerate thousands of ages from the beginning of the world, know that the six-thousandth year is not yet complete. . . . Therefore, since all the works of God were completed in six days, the world must continue in its present state through six ages, that is, six thousand years. For the great day of God is limited by a circle of a thousand years, as the prophet shows, who says, "In thy sight, O Lord, a thousand years are as one day [Ps. 90:4]"[19]

Not only is the typology crystal clear, but it boggles the mind how Ross can cite Lactantius in support (C&T, chapter 2) when he stated so plainly "the six-thousandth year is not yet complete." This can only mean that he believed the world was less than 6,000 years old, and he said that it would last for only 6,000 years. This is a clear indication of young-earth creationism! And, obviously, if Lactantius really believed that the *creation* days were 1,000 years long, then he wouldn't have said that the world was less than 6,000 years old, would he? He would have had to say at least 10,000 to take into account the alleged 6,000-year-long creation week plus the 4,000 years from creation to Christ. Actually, Lactantius relied on the inflated LXX chronology[20] that would place the creation date over 5000 B.C., meaning that he saw the present age coming to a close fairly soon, and Christ ushering in the new Millennium.

---

18. *Talmud*, Sanhedrin 97a and 97b.

19. Lactantius, *Divine Institutes* 7:14.

20. Williams, P., Some remarks preliminary to a Biblical chronology, *TJ* 12(1):98–106 (1998); <www.answersingenesis.org/chronology>. This shows that the Masoretic text is likely to be the original.

Irenaeus (125–202)

Irenaeus was a disciple of Polycarp, who in turn was a disciple of the apostle John. Irenaeus became bishop of Lyons, and was an early apologist for the faith who became a martyr. He was also a clear exponent of the days-as-types-of-millennia interpretation, and also clearly believed that the world was less than 6,000 years old when he wrote:

> For in six days as the world was made, in so many thousand years shall it be concluded. . . . For that day of the Lord is a thousand years; and in six days created things were completed: it is evident, therefore, that they will come to an end at the sixth thousand year.[21]

This must be considered when analyzing another passage, where Irenaeus analyzes Genesis 2:17:

> And there are some again, who relegate the death of Adam to the thousandth year; for since "a day of the Lord is as a thousand years," he did not overstep the thousand years, but died within them, thus bearing out the sentence of his sin. Whether, therefore, with respect to disobedience, which is death; whether [we consider] that, on account of that, they were delivered over to death, and made debtors to it; whether with respect to [the fact that on] one and the same day on which they ate they also died (for it is one day of the creation); whether [we regard this point] that with respect to this cycle of days, they died on the day in which they did also eat, that is, the day of the preparation, which is termed "the pure supper," that is, the sixth day of the feast, which the Lord also exhibited when He suffered on that day; or whether [we reflect] that he (Adam) did not overstep the thousand years, but died within their limit. . . .[22]

Thus, Irenaeus was not applying the thousand years to the *creation* days, but to another occurrence of *yôm* in a totally different context, with the preposition *b'*, in an attempt to solve a problem. This was a typical view of Jewish literature around that time. For example:

> And at the close of the Nineteenth Jubilee, in the seventh week in the sixth year thereof Adam died, and all his sons buried him in the land of his creation, and he was the first to be buried on the earth. And he lacked seventy years of one thousand years; of one thousand years are as one day in the testimony of the heavens and therefore was it written concerning the tree of knowledge: "On the day ye eat thereof ye shall die." For this reason he did not complete the years of this day; for he died during it.[23]

(The correct solution for the "problem" of "or in the day that you eat from it you will surely die" is given on page 69.)

---

21. Irenaeus, *Heresies* 5.28.3 (*Ante-Nicene Fathers* 1:557).
22. Ibid., 1:551–552).
23. *Book of Jubilees* (c. 105–153 B.C.) 4:29.

Justin Martyr (c. 100–c. 165)

Justin converted from paganism in about 130, and became an early apologist and debater, wrote prolifically on the faith, and was martyred, hence the usual name. He applied similar reasoning above to Adam's life span, and again, *not* to creation days:

> Now we have understood that the expression used among these words, "According to the days of the tree [of life] shall be the days of my people; the works of their toil shall abound," obscurely predicts a thousand years. For as Adam was told that in the day he ate of the tree he would die, we know that he did not complete a thousand years. We have perceived, moreover, that the expression, "The day of the Lord is as a thousand years," is connected with this subject.[24]

So we see that none of these witnesses brought forward by Ross support his case.

The Alexandrian School

Ross continues on his internet article:

> The significance of this list lies not only in the prominence of these individuals as biblical scholars, defenders of the faith, and pillars of the early church (except Josephus), but also in that their scriptural views cannot be said to have been shaped to accommodate secular opinion. Astronomical, paleontological and geological evidences for the antiquity of the universe, of the earth, and of life did not come forth until the nineteenth century.[25]

This is simply not true. Philo was a Hellenistic Jew in Alexandria, heavily influenced by Greek philosophy. He resorted to "an extensive allegorical interpretation of Scripture that made Jewish law consonant with the ideals of Stoic, Pythagorean, and especially Platonic thought."[26] Philo was clearly more concerned with harmonizing the Old Testament with Greek philosophy than with careful exegesis. Furthermore, his philosophical ideas and allegorical method had a direct impact on Christian theology through the "Alexandrian school." This was founded by Clement of Alexandria, and was continued by Origen and Augustine.

It's significant that the only exceptions to literal-day views are from the Alexandrian school. But an appeal to them proves far too much, because they allegorized almost everything in Scripture — far more than Ross or his conservative constituency would like!

Origen (182–251)

Origen was an outstanding thinker and textual scholar, and was one of the first to try to work out the doctrine of the Trinity from the Bible. But his tendency to

---

24. Justin Martyr, *Dialogue with the Jew Trypho*, 81 (*Ante-Nicene Fathers* 1:239–240).
25. "Biblical Evidence for Long Creation Days," <www.reasons.org/resources/apologetics/longdays. html>, December 1, 2002.
26. Philo, in Paul J. Achtemeier, editor, *Harper's Bible Dictionary* (San Francisco, CA: Harper and Row, 1985).

allegorize the Bible led him into views bordering on heresy, though he unambiguously affirmed a "young earth," as in this passage from his famous refutation of the anti-Christian writer Celsus:

> After these statements, Celsus, from a secret desire to cast discredit upon the Mosaic account of the creation, which teaches that the world is not yet ten thousand years old, but very much under that, while concealing his wish, intimates his agreement with those who hold that the world is uncreated. For, maintaining that there have been, from all eternity, many conflagrations and many deluges, and that the flood which lately took place in the time of Deucalion is comparatively modern, he clearly demonstrates to those who are able to understand him, that, in his opinion, the world was uncreated. But let this assailant of the Christian faith tell us by what arguments he was compelled to accept the statement that there have been many conflagrations and many cataclysms, and that the flood which occurred in the time of Deucalion, and the conflagration in that of Phaethon, were more recent than any others.[27]

Augustine (354–430)

Augustine was certainly one of the outstanding theologians of the early church. However, he was not an expert in the biblical languages by any stretch of the imagination. The Western (Roman Catholic) church at his time was using Latin. When Augustine started working on his Genesis commentary in 401, his knowledge of Greek was almost non-existent. Although he attained a modest ability to read Greek by the time he was an old man, he knew no Hebrew. His Latin Bible was a translation of the Septuagint (the Greek translation of the OT), not the Hebrew Bible.[28]

In any case, he cannot remotely be used in support of old-earth beliefs. The reason is that he tried to compress the days into an *instant*, which is *diametrically opposite* to what long-agers claim! Because of Augustine's lack of Hebrew knowledge, he may not have been aware that there was a perfectly good word available for "moment" or "instant" (רגע, *rega'*), if that's what God had intended to communicate, and it could have been combined with "time" or "day." It is used of God's activity four times in the Old Testament: Exodus 33:5, Numbers 16:21, 16:45 and Ezra 9:8.

Not only was Augustine's error the opposite to Ross's, he also *explicitly* taught what would now be called a "young" earth. In his most famous work, *City of God*, he has a whole chapter, "Of the Falseness of the History Which Allots Many Thousand Years to the World's Past," where he says:

> Let us, then, omit the conjectures of men who know not what they say, when they speak of the nature and origin of the human race. . . . They are deceived, too, by those highly mendacious documents which profess to

---

27. Origen, *Contra Celsum* (*Against Celsus*) 1.19, *Ante-Nicene Fathers* 4:404.
28. See J.H. Taylor's introduction to St. Augustine, *The Literal Meaning of Genesis*, J.H. Taylor, transl. (New York: Newman Press, 1982), 1:5.

give the history of many thousand years, though, reckoning by the sacred writings, we find that not 6,000 years have yet passed.[29]

Since he believed creation was in an instant, then in Augustine's thinking, the time from Adam to the present was also the time from the beginning of creation to the present, which was less than 6,000 years. Furthermore, contrary to Ross's assertion, Augustine wrote against a backdrop of evolutionary thinking in his time.[30] He summarizes various proto-catastrophist and proto-uniformitarian theories this way:

> There are others who think that our present world is not everlasting. Of these, some hold that, besides this one, there are a number of other worlds. The remainder, who admit only one world, claim that over and over again, it periodically disintegrates and begins again. In either theory, they are forced to conclude that the human race arose without human procreation, since there is no room here for the hypothesis that a few men would always remain each time the world perished, as was the case in the previous theory where floods and fires did not affect the whole world but left a few survivors to repeople it. For they hold that, just as the world is reborn out of its previous matter, so a new human race would arise from the elements of nature and only thereafter would a progeny of mortals spring from parents. And the same would be true of the rest of the animals.
>
> There are some people who complain when we claim that man was created so late [i.e., recently]. They say that he must have been created countless and infinite ages ago, and not, as is recorded in Scripture, less than 6,000 years ago. . . .
>
> It was this controversy [over the beginning of the things of time] that led the natural philosophers to believe that the only way they could or should solve it was by a theory of periodic cycles of time according to which there always has been and will be a continual renewal and repetition in the order of nature, because the coming and passing ages revolve as on a wheel. These philosophers were not sure whether a single permanent world passes through these revolutions or whether, at fixed intervals, the world itself dissolves and evolves anew, repeating the same pattern of what has already taken place and will again take place. . . .[31]

Once again we see that Ross has not done his historical homework.

---

29. Augustine, *De Civitate Dei (The City of God)*, 12(10).

30. The early 20th century evolutionist director of the American Museum of Natural History, Henry Fairfield Osborn, showed in his book *From the Greeks to Darwin* (New York: Charles Scribner's Sons, 1929) that all the essential ideas of Darwin's theory can be found in the writings of the ancient Greeks long before Augustine or even Christ.

31. Augustine, *The City of God*, Books VIII–XVI, translated by G.G. Walsh and G. Monahan (Washington, DC: Catholic University of America Press, 1952), p. 265, 267.

Was Augustine a Flat-earther?

Long agers such as the Christadelphian Alan Hayward have tried to paint Augustine as a flat-earther,[32] glibly parroting 19th century humanists Draper and White (see page 53). However, as the historian Jeffrey Burton Russell showed, he never disputed the roundness of the earth. Here is what he actually said:

> As to the fable that there are Antipodes, that is to say, men on the opposite side of the earth, where the sun rises when it sets on us, men who walk with their feet opposite ours, there is no reason for believing it. Those who affirm it do not claim to possess any actual information; they merely conjecture that, since the earth is suspended within the concavity of the heavens, and there is as much room on the one side of it as on the other, therefore the part which is beneath cannot be void of human inhabitants. They fail to notice that, even should it be believed or demonstrated that the world is round or spherical in form, it does not follow that the part of the earth opposite to us is not completely covered with water, or that any conjectured dry land there should be inhabited by men. For Scripture, which confirms the truth of its historical statements by the accomplishment of its prophecies, teaches not falsehood; and it is too absurd to say that some men might have set sail from this side and, traversing the immense expanse of ocean, have propagated there a race of human beings descended from that one first man.[33]

This shows that Augustine disputed a totally different concept, that of the *Antipodes*, although wrongly. But this is not the same as disputing the round earth, as opposed to something that doesn't necessarily follow from this. As Russell explains:

> Christian doctrine affirmed that all humans must be of one origin, descended from Adam and Eve and redeemable by Christ, "the Second [*sic* 1 Cor. 15:45 says "last"] Adam." The Bible was silent as to whether antipodeans existed, but natural philosophy had demonstrated that if they did, they could have no connection with the known part of the globe, either because the sea was too wide to sail across or because the equatorial zones were too hot to sail through. There could be no genetic connection between the antipodeans and us. Therefore, any alleged antipodeans could not be descended from Adam and therefore could not exist.[34]

It's especially inexcusable for Hayward to quote this passage and not even realize that it says nothing against a round earth. In fact, in another place, Augustine explicitly called the earth a "globe."[35]

---

32. Alan Hayward, *Creation and Evolution: The Facts and the Fallacies* (London: Triangle, SPCK, 1985), p. 70.

33. Augustine, *The City of God* 14:9.

34. J.B. Russell, *Inventing the Flat Earth: Columbus & Modern Historians* (New York: Praeger, 1991).

35. Augustine, *The Literal Meaning of Genesis*, J.H. Taylor, transl. (New York: Newman Press, 1982), 2.13.27.

SUMMARY: THE LENGTH OF THE DAYS OF CREATION ACCORDING TO PATRISTIC WRITERS

The following table[36] shows that the majority of those who commented on the days believed they were ordinary days.

Writer	Date	24 hours	Figurative	Unclear	Reference
Table 3.1: Specific Statements Made by the Writers in the Early Church Age Concerning the Days of Creation					
Philo	c 20 B.C.– c A.D. 50		X		*Creation* 13
Josephus	A.D. 37/38 –c 100			X	*Antiquities* 1.1.1 (1.27-33)
Justin Martyr	c 100–c 165			X	
Tatian	110–180			X	
Theophilus of Antioch	c 180	X			*Autolycus* 2.11-12
Irenaeus of Lyons	c 115–202			X	
Clement of Alexandria	c 150–c 215		X		*Miscellanies* 6.16
Tertullian	c 160–c 225			X	
Julius Africanus	c 160–240			X	
Hippolytus of Rome	170–236			X	*Genesis*, 1.5
Origen	185–253		X		*Celsus* 6.50, 60
Methodius	d. 311	X			*Chastity* 5.7
Lactantius	240–320	X			*Institutes* 7.14
Victorinus of Pettau	d. c 304	X			*Creation*
Eusebius of Caesarea	263–339			X	
Ephrem the Syrian	306–373	X			*Commentary on Genesis* 1.1
Epiphanius of Salamis	315–403	X			*Panarion* 1.1.1
Basil of Caesarea	329–379	X			*Hexaëmeron* 2.8
Gregory of Nyssa	330–394			X	
Gregory of Nazianzus	330–390			X	
Cyril of Jerusalem	d. 387	X			*Catechetical Lectures* 12.5
Ambrose of Milan	339–397	X			*Hexaëmeron* 1.10.3-7
John Chrysostom	374–407			X	
Jerome	347–419/420			X	
Augustine of Hippo	354–430		X		*Literal*, 4.22.39

36. From Robert Bradshaw's in-depth study, *Genesis, Creationism and the Early Church*, chapter 3; <www.robibrad.demon.co.uk/Chapter3.htm>, August 13, 2003.

However, as shown on page 116, Irenaeus really did teach literal days. And despite putting "unclear" in this table, Bradshaw agrees:

> So Irenaeus seems to have seen no contradiction here. For him the days of Genesis were 24 hours long and served as a pattern for the history of the world.[37]

About the other "unclear" ones, Bradshaw says:

> We cannot be sure of the views of most writers for a variety of reasons already mentioned above. My own view based upon the style of exegesis of other passages of Scripture would lead me to think that the vast majority of those listed as having an unclear view would opt for 24 hours had they discussed the subject. The shortage of references does not mean that they thought the issue of the age of the earth was unimportant. On the contrary it was clearly a contentious issue in the early church, because the Greeks believed that the world was extremely ancient.[38]

Table 3.2: Specific Statements Made by Writers of the Early Church Age Concerning the Age of the Earth[39]			
Writer	Date	Date of Creation of Adam (B.C.)	Reference
Clement of Alexandria	c. 150–c. 215	5,592	*Miscellanies* 1.21
Julius Africanus	c. 160–240	5,500	*Chronology*, Fragment 1
Hippolytus of Rome	170–236	5,500	*Daniel* 4
Origen	185–253	< 10,000	*Against Celsus* 1.20
Eusebius of Caesarea	263–339	5,228	*Chronicle*
Augustine of Hippo	354–430	< 5,600	*City* 12.11

THE REFORMATION

Ross claims [C&T:25]:

> Throughout the Dark and Middle Ages, church scholars maintained the tolerant attitude of their forefathers toward differing views and interpretations of the creation time scale.

Ross fails to back up this bald assertion. In any case, any non-literal views of the "forefathers" (if such actually existed) were vestiges of the Alexandrian school. This changed with the Reformation, which rejected their allegorizing tendency

---

37. Robert Bradshaw, *Genesis, Creationism and the Early Church,* chapter 3; <www.robibrad.demon. co.uk/Chapter3.htm>, August 13, 2003.
38. Ibid.
39. Ibid.

and returned to the grammatical-historical approach. This can be shown by its leading figures.

Martin Luther (1483–1546)

Luther is credited with launching the Protestant Reformation, when he nailed his famous "95 Theses" on the door of the church in Wittenberg, Germany, in 1517. Not only did he rediscover the biblical doctrines of Scripture alone and salvation by grace through faith alone, he also returned to the plain meaning of many scriptural passages as opposed to allegorization. This applied to Genesis as well, where he clearly reveals himself to be a staunch young-earth creationist:

> He [Moses] calls "a spade a spade," i.e., he employs the terms "day" and "evening" without Allegory, just as we customarily do . . . we assert that Moses spoke in the literal sense, not allegorically or figuratively, i.e., that the world, with all its creatures, was created within six days, as the words read. If we do not comprehend the reason for this, let us remain pupils and leave the job of teacher to the Holy Spirit.[40]

> The "days" of creation were ordinary days in length. We must understand that these days were actual days [his Latin text reads, *veros dies*], contrary to the opinion of the holy fathers. Whenever we observe that the opinions of the fathers disagree with Scripture, we reverently bear with them and acknowledge them to be our elders. Nevertheless, we do not depart from the authority of Scripture for their sakes.[41]

Luther also affirmed that the world was "young":

> We know from Moses that the world was not in existence before 6,000 years ago.[42]

Was Luther a Geocentrist?

Some try to dismiss Luther's powerful testimony on the days of creation by dismissing him as a geocentrist. For example, Hayward irresponsibly resorts to a secondary citation from *History of the Warfare of Science with Theology in Christendom* (1896) by the strident anti-Christian polemicist Andrew Dickson White (see page 53).[43] However, White misleadingly failed to mention that, far from a sustained strong opposition, Luther's only recorded comment on the issues is a single off-hand remark (hardly a concerted campaign), during a "table talk" in 1539 (four years before the publication

---

40. Martin Luther in J. Pelikan, editor, *Luther's Works, Lectures on Genesis* (St. Louis, MO: Concordia Publishing House, 1958), chapters 1–5, 1:6.
41. E.M. Plass, *What Martin Luther Says: A Practical In-Home Anthology for the Active Christian* (St. Louis, MO: Concordia Publishing House, 1959).
42. Martin Luther in J. Pelikan, editor, *Luther's Works, Lectures on Genesis* (St. Louis, MO: Concordia Publishing House, 1958), p. 3.
43. Alan Hayward, *Creation and Evolution: The Facts and the Fallacies* (London: Triangle, SPCK, 1985), p. 71, 213(n).

of Copernicus' book). The *Table Talk* was based on notes taken by Luther's students, which were later compiled and published in 1566 — 20 years after Luther's death. Luther actually said:

> *Whoever wants to be clever must agree with nothing that others esteem. He must do something of his own.* This is what that fellow does who wishes to turn the whole of astronomy upside down. Even in these things that are thrown into disorder I believe the Holy Scriptures, for Joshua commanded the sun to stand still and not the earth [Josh. 10:12].

Hayward failed to cite the parts I have italicized. These show that a major reason for Luther's objection was Copernicus's challenging the establishment and common sense *for its own sake* (as Luther saw it). At the time, there was no hard evidence for geokineticism. And Kepler, a devout Lutheran, saw no conflict between the Bible and Lutheran theology. He showed how Joshua 10:12 could be explained as phenomenological language, using Luther's own principles of biblical interpretation! See page 51 for more on geocentrism.

John Calvin (1509–1564)

Calvin was a French lawyer and theologian, and one of the most influential of the Reformers. He became leader of Geneva (Switzerland), which became a refuge for 6,000 Protestants. Calvin founded the University of Geneva in 1559, which attracted many foreign scholars, and still does today. His monumental *Institutes of the Christian Religion* (1559) proclaimed the grace of God and salvation in Jesus Christ. He was also a skilled commentator on books of the Bible, including Genesis. His teachings influenced many confessions, catechisms, preachers, leaders of modern Christian revivals, and were brought to America by the Pilgrim Fathers.[44]

It's very interesting that on every point on which AiG disagrees with much of modern Christendom, Calvin took our side.[45] For example, Calvin believed that God created in six consecutive normal days:

> Here the error of those is manifestly refuted, who maintain that the world was made in a moment. For it is too violent a cavil to contend that Moses distributes the work which God perfected at once into six days, for the mere purpose of conveying instruction. Let us rather conclude that God himself took the space of six days, for the purpose of accommodating his works to the capacity of men.[46]

> I have said above that six days were employed in the formation of the world; not that God, to whom one moment is as a thousand years, had need

---

44. J.I. Packer, "John Calvin and Reformed Europe" in *Great Leaders of the Christian Church*, J.D. Woodbridge, editor (Chicago, IL: Moody Press, 1988), p. 206–215.

45. J. Sarfati, "Calvin Says: Genesis Means What It Says," *Creation* 22(4)44–45 (September–November 2000); <www.answersingenesis.org/calvin>.

46. J. Calvin, *Genesis* 1554 (Edinburgh, UK: Banner of Truth, 1984), p. 78.

of this succession of time, but that he might engage us in the contemplation of his works.[47]

> For it is not without significance that he divided the making of the universe into six days, even though it would have been no more difficult for him to have completed in one moment the whole work together in all its details than to arrive at its completion gradually by a progression of this sort.[48]

Calvin, like Luther, also believed in a "young" earth, and was steadfast although he knew it could come in for ridicule:

> They will not refrain from guffaws when they are informed that but little more than five thousand years have passed since the creation of the universe.[49]

Haak Bible (1637)

The Haak Bible[50] was produced by the Dutch Staten Vertaling with a commentary written by Reformed theologians of the Netherlands in the 1600s. Their comments on Genesis in the heyday of the Reformation showed that the leading Reformed scholars maintained the literal meaning of Genesis 1, that the days were 24 hours. The comment on Genesis 1:5, translated into English, reads:

> AND GOD CALLED THE LIGHT DAY, AND THE DARKNESS HE CALLED NIGHT; THEN IT HAD BEEN EVENING, AND IT HAD BEEN MORNING THE FIRST DAY. (Heb. ONE DAY. But it is very usual with the Hebrews to put ONE for FIRST, as Genesis 8:5, Numbers 29:1, Matthew 29:1, 1 Corinthians 16:2. The meaning of these words is that night and day had made up one natural day together, which with the Hebrews began with the evening {the darkness having been before the light} and ended with the approach of the next evening, comprehending twenty four hours.)

The Westminster Confession of Faith (1646)

After the Bible itself, this is one of the major statements of faith for many Presbyterian and Reformed churches. Statement 4:1 is unambiguous:

> It pleased God the Father, Son, and Holy Ghost, for the manifestation of the glory of his eternal power, wisdom, and goodness, in the beginning, to create or make of nothing the world, and all things therein, whether visible or invisible, in the space of six days, and all very good.

47. Ibid., p. 105.
48. J. Calvin, *Institutes of the Christian Religion*, J. T. McNeill, editor (Philadelphia, PA: Westminster Press, 1960), 1.14.22.
49. Ibid., 2:925.
50. Thanks to Rev. Chris Coleborn of Victoria, Australia, for bringing this to my attention.

However, there are certain revisionists, including Ross, who claim (in the face of all the evidence) that when the Reformed Confessions were written, the church did not consider the length of the days, but only that God created. That is, because the text did not explicitly state that the days were 24 hours, they were allowing for the possibility of long days.

However, the Westminster Confession's statement clearly follows the language of Calvin (above), saying "*in the space of six days.*" There is no room in the language of either Calvin or the WCF for anything other than normal-length days. There was no need to state the obvious — an employee asking his boss for six days vacation doesn't have to explain that they are 24-hour days and not long periods of time! Calvin, the Haak Bible, and the WCF reflect the normal orthodox view of the Reformed faith.

Even more importantly, we have more explicit statements from the WCF's framers themselves! The *Westminster Annotations* is a five-volume set of annotations on the Scriptures, first printed in 1645 — right in the middle of the sitting of the Westminster Assembly. The *New Schaff-Herzog Encyclopedia* explains the later editions of the *Westminster Annotations* (emphasis added):

> In 1657 there was published *Annotations upon All the Books of the Old and New Testament. . . .* Wherein the text is explained, doubts resolved, Scriptures paralleled, and various readings observed by the labor of certain learned divines thereunto appointed and therein employed, as is expressed in the preface, 2 vols., London, 1657. This work is usually called the "Assembly's Annotations," from the circumstances of its having been composed by members of the Westminster Assembly.[51]

In particular, they commented specifically on Genesis 1:5, explicitly teaching that the creation days were 24 hours long:

> V. 5. God called (Or, decreed it to be so called: for contrary things must be called by contrary names, Isai. 5:20, the light, day) The word day, in the former part of the verse, noteth the day artificial from morning till night, Exod. 16:12, 13, which is the time of light, measured out to twelve hours, John 11:9. Matt. 20:3, 6, which were not more nor fewer, but longer or shorter according to the different proportion of the days in Summer and Winter: the first began with the Sun-rising, and the last ended with the Sun-setting; which division was in use, not only with the Jews, but with the Romans, *Cal. Rohdig. Lib. 2. Antiq. Lection*, chap. 9, but in the latter part of the verse, the word day, is taken for the day natural, consisting of twenty four houres, which is measured most usually from the Sun-rising to the Sun-rising; or, from the Sun-setting to the Sun-setting: for the use of the word day in this sense, compare Exod. 12:29 with Num. 3:13 & 8:17 the first day.

---

51. "Bibles, Annotations, and Bible Summaries," *New Schaff-Herzog Encyclopedia* 2.

In the Hebrew, it is one day in number, not expressly the first in order; the like expression we find in Gen 8:5, Numb. 29:1 and it is followed in the Greek, Matth. 28:1, Joh. 20:1, I Cor. 16:2.

This first day consisting of twenty four hours had (as some think) for the first half of it the precedent darknesse, and for the other the light newly created: the night they take to be meant by evening a part of it, and the day by the morning, which is a part of it also: and according to this the Sabbath, (being as large a day as any of the rest, and *so containing twenty four hours*) is measured from even to even, Levit. 23:32, the Romans, and other Western Nations, reckon the twenty four hours from mid-night to mid-night; the Egyptians contrariwise from mid-day to mid-day.

Yet it may be with good probability, thought that at the first (according to the Chaldean account, which is quite contrary to the Jewes fore-cited, measuring the day from Sun-rising to Sun-rising) the day natural began with the light: for Even is the declining light of the fore-going day; and the Morning may as well be called the end of the night past, as the beginning of the day following: and so divers of the Learned by the Evening understand the day, as the end thereof, and by Morning the night, at which time it is at an end: for denominations are many times taken from the end, because thereby the thing is made complete; for the whole week is called by the name, Sabbath, Levit. 23:15 and Luke 18:12. because with it the week is made up and fully finished.

James Ussher (1581–1656)

Ussher was archbishop of Armagh, the highest position in the Irish Anglican Church, a product of the Reformation in England. He was also a noted historian and Hebrew scholar. In 1650, he published his *magnum opus*, *The Annals of the World*,[52] a 1,600-page tome in Latin on a history of the world covering every major event from the time of creation to A.D. 70. In this, he calculated the date of creation at October 23, 4004 B.C., and this is what he is best known for today.[53] But John Lightfoot (1602–1675), vice-chancellor of the University of Cambridge, was the one responsible for the more precise claim that Adam was created at 9:00 a.m. on October 23. Today, Ussher is widely scoffed at, including by Ross (C&T:26–27):

---

52. Actually, this title, by which it is best known, was of a posthumous English edition, published in 1658. Volume 1, published in 1650, was entitled *Annales veteris testamenti a prima mundi origine deducti* (*The Annals of the Old Testament, Deduced from the First Origin of the World*). Volume 2 was published in 1654, two years before he died. Larry and Marion Pierce have published Ussher's work in modern English (Green Forest, AR: Master Books 2003).

53. See L. Pierce, "The Forgotten Archbishop," *Creation* 20(2):42–43 (March–May 1998); <www.answersingenesis.org/ussher>, for a summary of Ussher's method and an outline of the life of this brilliant scholar; and "Archbishop's Achievement: Jonathan Sarfati Interviews Larry and Marion Pierce about Their New Ussher Translation," *Creation* 26(1):24–27 (December 2003 – February 2004).

Both Lightfoot and Ussher ignored Hebrew scholarship and assumed that no generations were omitted from mention in the biblical genealogies. They also assumed, based on the wording of the King James Version, that the numbered days of the Genesis creation account could only be six consecutive 24-hour periods.

Ross was even more inflammatory in a RTB comic book he co-authored for kids.[54] This disrespectfully portrayed the godly bishop as a fool with dunce-cap-like headgear (see cartoons, below).

However, Ussher's date was in the typical ballpark for calculations of his day. He even had good reasons for the October 23rd date,[55] although creation hardly stands or falls on such precision. (Note that Ross couldn't even get that date right on the cartoon, saying October 3.)

And as we have seen, it was the almost universal view of Christendom that the world was only a few thousand years old, the days 24 hours long, and there were tight chronologies in Genesis 5 and 11. So it's historically absurd to blame this belief on the KJV wording in Genesis, which is followed by nearly all other English translations today. In any case,

Much of the confusion about the earth being created in six 24-hour days can be traced back to this guy ... James Ussher, the Anglican Archbishop of Ireland in 1650.

Ussher figured that the earth was created on October 3rd, 4004 B.C. Since he was a big wheel in the church, hardly anyone questioned his "date," at least not for a long while.

One ... Two ... Three ...

---

54. H. Ross and R. Bundschuh, *Destination: Creation*, Reasons to Believe Comix, 1997, p. 5.

55. L. Pierce, "The Forgotten Archbishop," *Creation* 20(2):42–43 (March–May 1998); <www.answersingenesis.org/ussher>.

both these scholars wrote exclusively in Latin! (Besides, the translators of the KJV were no amateurs when it came to the proper translation and interpretation of Genesis, either. They too were convinced young-earth creationists.)

It's also highly improper for Ross to claim that they ignored Hebrew. Lightfoot was an expert in Hebrew, including the Old Testament, and later Jewish writings called the Talmud and the Midrash, as well as being skilled in Latin and Greek. Ussher was recognized as one of the greatest scholars of his time, being an expert on Semitic languages and ancient history. He was one of only six theologians allowed to address Parliament and the king. In 1628, King James I of England (James VI of Scotland) appointed him to his Privy Council in Ireland. Ussher was critical of Oliver Cromwell's rebellion against James's son and successor, Charles I. However, Cromwell also held Ussher in great esteem. When Ussher died in 1656, Cromwell held a magnificent funeral for him and had him buried in Westminster Abbey.

It's a well-kept secret that some great scientists also calculated creation dates very close to Ussher's. For example, Johannes Kepler (1571–1630), who formulated the laws of planetary motion, calculated a creation date of 3992 B.C. (See page 131.) Also, Sir Isaac Newton (1643–1727), widely regarded as the greatest scientist of all time, developed the laws of motion, gravity, and calculus. But he wrote more on biblical history than science, and he, too, vigorously defended a creation date of about 4000 B.C. According to Cambridge archaeologist and historian Colin Renfrew, as far as Newton was concerned:

> For an educated man in the seventeenth or even eighteenth century, any suggestion that the human past extended back further than 6,000 years was a vain and foolish speculation.[56]

By contrast to Ross's derogatory treatment of Ussher, famous evolutionist Stephen Jay Gould (1941–2002) treated Ussher very fairly.[57] While obviously Gould thought that "Ussher could hardly have been more wrong about 4004 B.C.," he argued, "his work was both honorable and interesting — therefore instructive for us today," and showed that Ussher used the best scholarship available in his day:

> I shall be defending Ussher's chronology as an honorable effort for its time and arguing that our usual ridicule only records a lamentable small-mindedness based on mistaken use of present criteria to judge a distant and different past. . . .
>
> Ussher represented the best of scholarship in his time. He was part of a substantial research tradition, a large community of intellectuals working toward a common goal under an accepted methodology. . . .
>
> I close with a final plea for judging people by their own criteria, not by later standards that they couldn't possibly know or assess."[58]

---

56. I. Newton, *The Chronology of Ancient Kingdoms Amended,* published posthumously, 1728, cited in C. Renfrew, *Before Civilization* (UK: Penguin Books, 1976), p. 22–23.

57. S.J. Gould, "Fall in the House of Ussher," *Natural History* 12(11):12–21 (1991).

58. Ibid., p. 14, 16, 21.

It's a sad indictment on an ostensibly Christian ministry like RTB that an atheist treated Ussher with the respect he deserves, instead of mockery. One must wonder if we can also look forward to a new comic from Ross, portraying Kepler and Newton as dunces, since they agreed with a creation in about 4000 B.C.!

LATER CONSERVATIVE EXEGETES

John Wesley (1701–1791)

This great evangelist and founder of Methodism never wrote extensively on creation or the Flood, but he explicitly stated his belief that the various rock strata were "doubtless formed by the general Deluge"[59] and that the account of creation, which was about 4,000 years before Christ, was, along with the rest of the Scriptures, "void of any material error." In several published sermons, he repeatedly emphasized that the original creation was perfect, without any moral or physical evil (such as earthquakes,[60] volcanoes, diseases,[61] weeds or animal death), which both came into the world after man sinned.

Many other conservative commentators, right up till the time of the rise of old-earth "science," also supported a straightforward understanding of Genesis. Dr. Terry Mortenson, in his Ph.D. thesis on the history of geology,[62] documents the young-earth views of a number of commentaries in use in the early 19th century.[63]

Young's Concordance

This is a well-regarded 19th-century concordance and Bible dictionary. In the entry on creation,[64] Young cites a study by Dr. Hales,[65] which is tabulated on the following page, on the creation dates calculated by a number of authorities.[66] As can be seen, they are all around a few thousand years B.C., with no hint of millions or billions of years. The differences within biblically based calculations are mainly due to the Old Testament texts and the date assigned to Abraham.

59. J. Wesley, *The Works of the Rev. John Wesley (1829–1831)* IV:54–65, 1829–1831.

60. Ibid., VII:386–399 (The cause and cure of earthquakes).

61. J. Wesley, "On the Fall of Man," 1872, available from <gbgm-umc.org/umhistory/wesley/sermons/serm-057.stm>.

62. T.J. Mortenson, *British Scriptural Geologists in the First Half of the Nineteenth Century,* Ph.D. thesis, Coventry University, England, 1996. This is available from the British Library Thesis Service either on microfilm for loan or on paper for purchase at <www.bl.uk/services/document/brittheses.html>. Chapters of this work are also available at <www.answersingenesis.org/tmortenson>. An edited version of the thesis has been accepted for publication.

63. T. Mortenson, "Commentaries in the Early Nineteenth Century," <www.answersingenesis.org/commentaries>.

64. R. Young, *Analytical Concordance to the Holy Bible,* 1879, 8th ed. (London: Lutterworth Press, 1939), p. 210.

65. Hales, *A New Analysis of Chronology and Geography, History and Prophecy* 1:210, 1830.

66. D. Batten, "Which Is the Recent Aberration? Old-Earth or Young-Earth Belief?" *Creation* 24(1)24–27 (December 2001–February 2002).

Source of Creation Date	Authority	Date B.C.
Alfonso X (Spain, 1200s)	Muller	6984
Alfonso X (Spain, 1200s)	Strauchius, Gyles[67] 1632–1682	6484
India	Gentil, French astronomer c. 1760	6204
India	Arab records	6174
Babylonia	Bailly, John Silvain (French astronomer, 1736–1793)	6158
China	Bailly	6157
Diogenes Laertius (Greece 3rd Cent.)	Playfair	6138
Egypt	Bailly	6081
Septuagint (LXX)	Albufaragi	5586
Josephus (1st Century Jew)	Playfair	5555
Septuagint, Alexandrine	Scaliger, Joseph (French classical scholar, 1540–1609)	5508
Persia	Bailly	5507
Chronicle of Axum, Abyssinian	Bruce (1700s)	5500
Josephus	Jackson	5481
Jackson		5426
Hales		5411
Josephus	Hales	5402
India	Megasthenes,[68] Greek historian (c. 340–282 B.C.)	5369
Talmudists	Petrus Alliacens	5344
Septuagint, Vatican		5270
Bede (673–735)	Strauchius	5199
Josephus	Univ. Hist.	4698
Samaritan computation	Scaliger	4427
Samaritan text	Univ. Hist.	4305
Hebrew (Masoretic) text		4161
Playfair and Walker		4008
Ussher, Spanheim, Calmet, Blair, etc.	4004	
Kepler (Astronomer, 1571–1630)	Playfair	3993
Petavius (France, 1583–1652)		3984
Melanchthon (Reformer, 1500s)	Playfair	3964
Luther (Reformer, 1500s)		3961
Lightfoot		3960
Cornelius a Lapide	Univ. Hist.	3951
Scaliger, Isaacson		3950
Strauchius		3949
Vulgar Jewish computation	Strauchius	3760
Rabbi Lipman (1579–1654)	Univ. Hist.	3616

---

67. *Brevarium Chronologicum* Book IV, 3rd edition, 1699, in English.

68. A Greek historian from Iona, he was Ambassador to India for King Seleucus I. He published *Indika* in four books.

How Interpreters Responded to the Long-Age Challenge

It is very instructive to note how various theologians responded to the challenge to Genesis, first by theories of long ages, then by evolution. As shown, before the rise of these ideas, long ages were not even thought of by conservative exegetes. This is strong evidence that they are not in the text at all.

But when long-age ideas became popular, there were three broad types of responses:

1. Challenging the "Science"

There has always been a remnant who stood firm on Genesis and challenged the long-age conjectures. These included the 19th-century scriptural geologists. They have been largely forgotten, but knowledge of these important figures has been revived by Dr. Terry Mortenson's Ph.D. thesis.[69]

The Scriptural Geologists

Dr. Mortenson identified about 30 scriptural geologists, mainly in Great Britain, but there was never a formal group. They included clergymen and highly trained scientists, and they raised some formidable biblical and geological arguments against long ages. Most of their biblical arguments are still cogent today, and if they had been heeded, much of the church's capitulation towards Darwinism and liberalism would have been avoided.

According to Dr. Mortenson, four of the most geologically competent scriptural geologists were the Scotsmen George Young, George Fairholme, John Murray and William Rhind. Their writings show that they were up to date with the scientific (especially geological) literature of their day, and they extensively investigated in the field as well.

George Young (1777–1848)

After his training in science and theology, he faithfully served for 42 years as pastor of a Presbyterian church in Whitby, Yorkshire (England), where a great percentage of the so-called "geological column" was exposed in the mines and on the sea coast. He helped found the Whitby museum and was the coastal representative of the Yorkshire Philosophical Society (which focused on natural science), collecting rock and fossil samples. He gave the most thorough analysis of the geological record of any scriptural geologist. Three of his 21 books dealt with geology: *Geological Survey of the Yorkshire Coast*, Whitby, 1822, with expanded 2nd edition in 1828; *Scriptural Geology*, London, 1838; and *Appendix to Scriptural Geology*, London, 1840. He also published geological articles in scientific journals.

George Fairholme (1789–1846)

He was a self-educated wealthy landowner who traveled extensively in Britain and Europe studying geology, geography, fossils, and living creatures. He wrote two large books on the subject of geology: *General View of the Geology of Scripture* (1833) and

---

69. See <www.answersingenesis.org/mortenson>.

New and Conclusive Physical Demonstrations of the Mosaic Deluge (1837), and several science journal articles. These were based on reading, experimentation, and field investigations, and showed him to be a careful observer and thoughtful interpreter of nature. His study of the valley systems of England and Europe along with the erosion of sea coasts and some major waterfalls in Germany and America led to his conclusion that Noah's flood had occurred about 5,000 years ago. See also page 257.

John Murray (1786?–1851)

Murray attained M.A. and Ph.D. degrees in science, becoming well known and highly regarded throughout Great Britain as a traveling lecturer on physics and chemistry. He developed an impressive breadth of knowledge in many subject areas of both science and literature, but he contributed much to chemistry and mining in particular. He had nearly 20 scientific inventions (including a miner's safety lamp) which came into practical use. His 28 books and 60 science journal articles addressed subjects in chemistry, physics, medicine, geology, natural history, and manufacturing. He was also a prominent anti-slavery activist, writing a pamphlet strongly arguing for the end of slavery in the colonies. He wrote two books which directly related to geology and the Bible, *The Truth of Revelation* (1831, expanded edition 1840) and *Portrait of Geology*, London, 1838.

William Rhind (1797–1874)

Rhind originally trained to be a surgeon and practiced medicine for several years before devoting the rest of his life (most of it spent in Edinburgh) to scientific research, lecturing and writing, primarily in the areas of botany, zoology, and geology. He published six scientific journal articles in the areas of biology, medicine, and geology. Many of his books reflected his strong commitment to seeing good science textbooks made available for the education of children aged 10–18 years. His *magnum opus* discussing living and fossil plants was his 700–page *History of the Vegetable Kingdom* (1841), which went through eight editions up to 1877. Three of his adult-level books dealt with geology. Two were purely descriptive and praised by geologists for their accuracy. *The Age of the Earth* (1838) presented his biblical and geological reasons for rejecting the old-earth theories.

Leupold

Another who stood firmly on Scripture was Dr. Herbert Carl Leupold, who lived long after the scriptural geologists. He was a Hebrew scholar and professor of Old Testament theology at Evangelical Lutheran Theological Seminary at Capital University in Columbus, Ohio. He refused to be intimidated, recognizing the biases behind uniformitarian geology. In his two-volume commentary on Genesis (1942), he wrote about Genesis 1:5, and rejected the day-age theory. It's notable that Leupold countered arguments which were hardly any different from what Ross uses today. This was instructive in noting how the lexical support for the day-age theory has always been non-existent. However, this doesn't stop long-age compromisers from raising the same tired old canards as if no young-earth creationist had ever addressed them. Leupold wrote:

There ought to be no need of refuting the idea that *yôm* means period. Reputable dictionaries like Buhl,[70] BDB, or K.W.[71] know nothing of this notion. Hebrew dictionaries are our primary source of reliable information concerning Hebrew words. Commentators with critical leanings utter statements that are very decided in this instance. Says Skinner: "The interpretation of *yôm* as *aeon*, a favorite resource of harmonists of science and revelation, is opposed to the plain sense of the passage and has no warrant in Hebrew usage." Dillmann remarks: "The reasons advanced by ancient and modern writers for construing these days to be longer periods of time are inadequate." There is one other meaning of the word "day" which some misapprehend by failing to think through its exact bearing: *yôm* may mean "time" in a very general way, as in 2:4 *beyôm*, or Isa. 11:16; cf. BDB p. 399, No. 6, for numerous illustrations. But that use cannot substantiate so utterly different an idea as "period." These two conceptions lie far apart. References to expressions like "the day of the Lord" fail to invalidate our contentions above. For "the day of the Lord" as BDB rightly defines, p. 399, No. 3, is regarded "chiefly as the time of His coming in judgment, involving often blessedness for the righteous.

Other arguments to the contrary carry very little weight. If it be claimed that some works can, with difficulty, be compressed within twenty-four hours, like those of the third day or the sixth, that claim may well be described as a purely subjective opinion. He that desires to reason it out as possible can assemble fully as many arguments as he who holds the opposite opinion. Or if it be claimed that "the duration of the seventh day determines the rest," let it be noted that nothing is stated about the duration of the seventh. This happens to be an argument from silence, and therefore it is exceptionally weak. Or again, if it be claimed that "the argument of the fourth (our third) commandment confirms this probability," we find in this commandment even stronger confirmation of our contention: six twenty-four hour days followed by one such day of rest alone can furnish a proper analogy for our laboring six days and resting on the seventh day; periods furnish a poor analogy for days.

Finally, the contention that our conception "contradicts geology" is inaccurate. It merely contradicts one school of thought in the field of geology, a school of thought of which we are convinced that it is hopelessly entangled in misconceptions which grow out of attempts to co-ordinate the actual findings of geology with an evolutionistic conception of what geology should be, and so is for the present thrown into a complete misreading of the available

---

70. F. Buhl, *Gesenius' Hebräisches und Aramäisches Handwörterbuch über das Alte Testament* (Leipzig, Germany: Vogel, F.C.W., 1905).

71. E. Koenig, *Wörterbuch zum Alten Testament*, 2nd and 3rd edition (Leipzig, Germany: Dieterich, 1922).

evidence, even as history, anthropology, Old Testament studies and many other sciences have been derailed and mired by the same attempt.[72]

2. Conservative Capitulation

Nigel Cameron[73] and Doug Kelly (C&C) have documented how most conservative commentators were intimidated by "science." It is only after the rise of science that we see the invention of ways to add millions of years to the Bible. The conservative exegetes were trying to preserve Scripture this way, but in adopting these hermeneutics, they were in effect placing science in authority over the Bible. On page 55, we showed this to be true also for modern conservatives who oppose literal days.

In this category, there are two main views, *concordism* and *discordism*. Concordism tries to preserve Genesis as history and reinterprets certain passages. Discordant views regard Genesis as non-historical, and tend towards full-blown theistic evolution.

Concordism

The following are the two most widespread compromise concordist views. They have already been discussed in more detail on page 93 ff. This chapter is giving the historical perspective, to show that they are aberrations of church history.

Gap Theory

The idea of a gap of millions of years between Genesis 1:1 and 1:2 was virtually unknown until Thomas Chalmers (1780–1847), founder of the Free Church of Scotland and popular evangelical preacher, started promoting it. As a very young pastor in 1804 (seven years before he became an evangelical), he startled his congregation by telling them that millions of years was compatible with Scripture. In response to Cuvier's catastrophist theory in 1813, Chalmers began to argue against the day-age view and for the gap theory and persuaded many Christians.[74] The idea of a gap was "canonized" for some Christians when C.I. Scofield included it in the footnotes of the *Scofield Reference Bible* in 1909. But many gap theorists admit explicitly that their motivation (as it was for Chalmers) is to find a place in the Bible to fit millions of years.

Day-Age

This is Ross's view, which makes him a concordist. As we have seen, his attempts to find this view in early church fathers fall flat. In fact, a respected evangelical Anglican theologian in the 1820s, George Stanley Faber, was the first theologian to use this interpretation of Genesis 1 to harmonize the Bible with the supposed millions of

---

72. See H.C. Leupold, *Exposition of Genesis* (Grand Rapids, MI: Baker Book House, 1942), 1:57–58.

73. N.M.deS. Cameron, *Evolution and the Authority of the Bible* (Exeter, Devon, UK: Paternoster, 1983).

74. Compare "Chalmers, Thomas, D.D. (1780–1847)," *Dictionary of National Biography* (Oxford: Oxford University Press, 1917), Leslie Stephen and Sidney Lee, eds., III:1358 and Francis C. Haber, *The Age of the World: Moses to Darwin* (Baltimore, MD: John Hopkins Press, 1959), p. 201–203.

years of geological ages.[75] This view was not widely accepted in the church (the gap theory was preferred by most compromisers) until the Scottish geologist and professing evangelical, Hugh Miller (1802–1856), abandoned the gap theory and started promoting the day-age view in his book *Testimony of the Rocks*. This was published in the year after his untimely death (by suicide). He speculated that the days were really long ages. Miller held that Noah's flood was a local flood and that the rock layers were laid down over long periods of time.

Discordism

There is one main view in this camp if one wants to maintain any semblance of conservative Christianity (the alternative is liberalism, which denies the authority of Scripture completely):

Literary Framework Hypothesis

This view is popular among compromising evangelical academics who can see the futility of day-age and gap theory compromises. But it's strange, if it were the true meaning of the text, that no one interpreted Genesis this way until Arie Noordtzij in 1924. Actually, it's not so strange, because the leading framework exponents, Meredith Kline and Henri Blocher, admitted that their rationale for a bizarre, novel interpretation was a desperation to fit the Bible into the alleged "facts" of science (see chapter 1, "Authority").

Liberal Theologians

In contrast to conservatives, the liberals saw no need to try to preserve biblical authority. So the liberals saw no need for the conservative rationalizations. Rather, it suited their purpose that the "facts of science" undermined biblical authority. But they gave not the slightest credence to the compromise views, because they could see that such views didn't line up with the grammar of Scripture. They could also point out that the compromise views were novelties and not thought of before the rise of long-age "science." Here are two exemplars, one from the 19th century and one from the 20th.

Marcus Dods (1834–1909)

Dods was a Scottish theologian and author, who became professor of New Testament exegesis and then principal of New College, Edinburgh. He wrote:

---

75. See, for example, chapter 3 in volume 1 of his *Treatise on the Genius and Object of the Patriarchal, the Levitical, and the Christian Dispensations* (1823). William Whiston was a young-earth creationist and successor to Newton's chair of mathematics at Cambridge, but he argued that each day was one year long in his *A New Theory of the Earth* (1697). The French scientist Comte de Buffon (probably a deist or secret atheist) suggested a day-age interpretation in his *Epochs of Nature* (1779) but was forced to recant under pressure from Catholic authorities. André DeLuc, a Swiss Calvinist geologist, wrote *An Elementary Treatise on Geology* in 1809. He was troubled by and opposed the vast antiquity of the earth advocated by James Hutton, but he also suggested a figurative day-age interpretation.

If, for example, the word "day" in these chapters does not mean a period of twenty-four hours, the interpretation of scripture is hopeless."[76]

James Barr

James Barr was a leading Hebrew scholar, and Oriel professor of the interpretation of Holy Scripture, Oxford University, England. His studies on Hebrew word meanings were a milestone, overthrowing the faulty methodology of trying to derive meaning from etymology (derivation), or the "root fallacy." While he would be on the liberal side of any liberal/conservative divide, he would be more properly regarded as a neo-Orthodox interpreter. So he does not believe Genesis, but he understood what the Hebrew so clearly teaches:

> . . . probably, so far as I know, there is no professor of Hebrew or Old Testament at any world-class university who does not believe that the writer(s) of Genesis 1–11 intended to convey to their readers the ideas that:
> (a) creation took place in a series of six days which were the same as the days of 24 hours we now experience,
> (b) the figures contained in the Genesis genealogies provided by simple addition a chronology from the beginning of the world up to later stages in the biblical story,
> (c) Noah's flood was understood to be worldwide and extinguish all human and animal life except for those in the ark.[77]

Some try to avoid the force of Barr's argument by pointing out that Barr was an avowed enemy of inerrancy, but they miss the whole point. That is, he is a hostile witness, which of course makes the case even more strongly. He knows what Genesis really *means*, even though he doesn't *believe* it.

Another counter is to try to claim that by "world-class university" he means one where the faculty accepts the same rationalistic view as Barr. There are genuine Hebrew scholars, such as Walter Kaiser, Gleason Archer, C. Laird Harris, and Bruce Waltke, who disagree. But they make it clear that they agree that the plain meaning is as Barr says, and they disagree because of so-called "science." And Barr was talking about leading Hebrew scholars at universities widely recognized as leading, such as Oxford, Cambridge, Harvard, Yale, etc.

Interpreters Bible

This is a standard commentary for liberal "scholarship," and it continued the liberal tradition of accepting the way that "day" has been understood throughout church history:

> There can be no question that by day the author meant just what we mean — the time required for one revolution of the earth on its axis.[78]

---

76. Marcus Dods, *The Book of Genesis*, Armstrong, NY, 1907, p. 4.
77. J. Barr, letter to David C.C. Watson, April 23, 1984.
78. *Interpreters Bible* (New York: Abingdon-Cokesbury Press, 1952), p. 471.

Response to Such Evidence by a Ross Disciple

Don Stoner is a B.S. (B.Sc.) physicist who, likewise, places "science" above the Bible and defends an old earth. Hugh Ross wrote the foreword to his book *A New Look at an Old Earth*. But Stoner tacitly acknowledged, unlike Ross, that long-age interpretations were almost absent until the last two centuries. He explained this away by, astonishingly, invoking passages stating that God sometimes hides the truth.[79] For example, he noted that Matthew 11:25 says:

> At that time Jesus answered and said, "I thank you, O Father, Lord of Heaven and earth, because you have hidden these things from the wise and prudent, and have revealed them unto babes."

But as the Reformed Baptist theologian John Gill (1697–1771) pointed out in his extensive commentary:

> . . . *because thou hast hid these things from the wise and prudent.* The "things" he means are the doctrines of the Gospel; such as respect himself, his person, as God, and the Son of God; his office, as Messiah, Redeemer, and Saviour; and the blessings of grace, righteousness, and salvation by him. . . .
>
> The persons from whom these things were hid, are "the wise and prudent"; in things worldly, natural, and civil; men of great parts and learning, of a large compass of knowledge, having a considerable share of sagacity, penetration, and wisdom; or, at least, who were wise and prudent in their own conceits, as were the Scribes and Pharisees . . . who thus applaud themselves at the eating of the passover every year, and say . . . "we are all wise, we are all prudent, we all understand the law."
>
> . . . babes; foolish ones, comparatively speaking, who have not those natural parts, learning, and knowledge others have, that wisdom and prudence in worldly and civil things; and are so in their own account, and in the esteem of the world; and who are as babes, helpless, defenseless, and impotent of themselves, to do or say anything that is spiritually good, and are sensible of the same: now to such souls God reveals the covenant of his grace, Christ, and all the blessings of grace in him, the mysteries of the Gospel, and the unseen glories of another world.[80]

Therefore, Stoner completely misconstrues this passage — the "wise" were those proud of their own worldly wisdom, while the "babes" were those humble enough to rely on God's grace. The application to a later age would mean that the "wise" were those who despise biblical revelation in favor of human "reason," while the "babes" were those who allow themselves to be instructed by biblical truth. However, it is

---

79. Don Stoner, *A New Look at an Old Earth* (Eugene, OR: Harvest House Publishers, 1997), p. 37–41.
80. *John Gill's Exposition of the Bible*, Online Bible; available from <www.onlinebible.net>.

the former who invented long-age ideas, while it was never dreamt of by those who relied on the Bible alone. A logical implication of Stoner's argument, and probably the most disturbing aspect of his book, is that God deliberately hid the alleged "truth" of long ages from the most devout and knowledgeable exegetes in Christian history. Instead, God revealed that supposed truth to deists, agnostics, and atheists — who then used this "truth" to mock the Bible! How any professing Christian can think this way about God and truth is mystifying.

Conclusion

Despite Ross's attempts to claim that his day-age view has been held by exegetes throughout the ages, this claim backfires on him. Rather, the vast majority of exegetes, from the early church fathers through the Reformers and up to the early 19th century, believed that the creation days were 24 hours long. Even those that did not accept literal days erred in the opposite direction from Ross, by allegorizing the six days into an instant. Furthermore, those who commented on the age of the earth, whether taking the six days allegorically or literally, affirmed that the earth was less than 10,000 years old at the time they wrote — most said it was less than 6,000 years.

Analyzing the reactions of commentators to billions of years and evolution is instructive. The liberals, not caring about biblical authority, were and are happy to affirm that it meant what people had always thought it had meant and that it was simply wrong because "science" is always right. However, conservative commentators have tried to preserve biblical inerrancy by reinterpreting Genesis to fit with long-age "science." The fact that these views were unknown before the rise of uniformitarian "science" is strong evidence that these views are not grounded in the biblical *text* itself but are a (misguided) *reaction* to this "science."

CHAPTER 4

THE ORDER OF CREATION

Many Christians have the mistaken impression that the order of events accepted by long-agers matches the general order given in Genesis. However, there are irreconcilable differences. Ross makes serious errors in exegesis in his attempt to try to make the Bible fit the evolutionary order.

One of Hugh Ross's main aims is to show that Genesis can be fitted into uniformitarian astronomy and paleontology. However, there are major contradictions between a straightforward reading of Scripture and the order claimed by uniformitarian/evolutionary "science," as shown in the following table:[1]

Order of Appearance (long-age)	Order of Appearance (Bible)
1. Sun/stars existed before earth	1. Earth created before sun/stars
2. Sun is earth's first light	2. Light on earth before sun
3. First life = marine organisms	3. First life = land plants
4. Reptiles predate birds	4. Birds predate land reptiles
5. Land mammals predate whales	5. Whales predate land mammals
6. Disease/death precede man	6. Disease/death result from man's sin

FANCIFUL EISEGESIS[2] ABOUT CREATED ANIMALS

To avoid the plain teaching of Genesis — that land dinosaurs were created with man and after whales — Ross also claims (GQ:53–54):

> The list [of creatures created on day 6] does not purport to include all the land mammals God made. . . . Though remes refers occasionally in

---

1. From D. Manthei, "Two World-views in Conflict," *Creation* 20(4):26–27 (September–November 1998).
2. *Exegesis* means reading *out* of the text (that is, letting the text teach you); *eisegesis* means reading one's own ideas *into* the text. See K. Ham, "Eisegesis — A Genesis Virus," *Creation* 24(3):16–19 (September–November 2002).

Hebrew literature to reptiles, the opening phrase of Genesis 1:25 makes it clear that these are mammals. . . . Both behema and chayyah refer to long-legged land quadrupeds. The former group encompasses those that easily can be tamed or domesticated for agricultural purposes, and the latter, those that are difficult to tame but have the potential to become excellent pets. Remes refers to short-legged land mammals, such as rodents, hares, and armadillos.

However, this is typical of Ross's imaginative eisegesis. Genesis 1:25 teaches nothing so restrictive. And his analysis of Hebrew terms has no basis — *Ross's own source*, TWOT, doesn't support him. *Chayyah* is simply a generic word for a living creature, although it *can* often refer to wild animals (TWOT 1:281) — the phrase *nephesh chayyah* is used of sea creatures in Genesis 1:20, and of man in Genesis 2:7 (see also chapter 6). *Behema* refers to *both* wild beast *and* domesticated animal (TWOT 1:92). *Remes* describes small creeping animals "especially reptiles" (TWOT 2:850). The TWOT shows that Ross is "over-defining" these terms. Van Bebber and Taylor (VB&T:86–91) pointed out the same errors in Ross's earlier book, C&T, but he keeps repeating the same tired arguments time after time.

Note that even if we were to grant Ross's contention that *remes* means "short-legged land mammals," it *still* wouldn't match the uniformitarian order in the fossil record. Such creatures are alleged to have appeared millions of years before whales, which Ross identifies as created on the millions-of-years-long "day 5." And mesony-chids and artiodactyls, both of which have been touted as predecessors of whales, were certainly "long-legged mammalian quadrupeds," so would fit even Ross's descriptions of 6th-day creatures.

Those who promote Ross's material as sound science should thus think again. It is doubtful that secular people will be impressed by Ross's claim that the order of Genesis matches "science." When they point out exceptions, Ross redefines terms so that Genesis 6 doesn't really refer to any creature that appeared before whales. And when all else fails, he claims that the "days" overlapped (G1:12).

Fourth-day Creation of Sun Undermines Day-Age Views

We have already dealt with the argument that the first three days were not literal before the sun was created. Further, we showed how early Christian writers used this to refute pagan cosmologies. However, the creation of the sun after the earth also fatally undermines progressive creationists' attempts to harmonize the Bible with billions of years. This is because they believe the big-bang theory, which has the sun and stars existing before the earth.

So they must explain this teaching away. Some assert that what really happened on this fourth "day" was that the sun and other heavenly bodies "appeared" when a dense cloud layer dissipated after millions of years. This is not only fanciful science but bad exegesis of Hebrew. The word *'asah* means "make" throughout Genesis 1, and is sometimes used interchangeably with "create" (*bara*) — for example, in

Genesis 1:26–27. It is pure desperation to apply a *different meaning* to the *same word* in the *same grammatical construction* in the *same passage*, just to fit in with atheistic evolutionary ideas like the big bang. If God had *meant* "appeared," then He presumably would have *used* the Hebrew word for appear (*ra'ah*), as He did when He said that the dry land "appeared" as the waters gathered in one place on day 3 (Gen. 1:9). We have checked over 20 major translations, and all clearly teach that the sun, moon, and stars were *made* on the fourth day.

John Ankerberg again betrayed his moderator's role during the Hovind debate of October 2000[3] by teaming up on this issue, and again making a clear error:

> **Moderator:** All right, we're gonna, we got to get to that too, but we've got to get through these seven days here. Can I move down to day four, because this gets us into the light again [reads Genesis 1:14–19]. Question: Did God make the sun, did God make the stars on day four? Hugh?

> **Ross:** I'd say no, it's in the *qal*-perfect form. . . .

Here again, Ross says that the verb in Genesis 1:16 translated "made" is *qal*-perfect, when it's actually *qal*-imperfect. (See page 254 for more on Ross's poor grasp of Hebrew.)

> **Ross:** . . . which means that they were formed either on the fourth day, the third day, the second day, the first day, or in the beginning. I go back to Genesis 1:1, "In the beginning God created the *shamayim wa ha-arets.*" That includes all the matter, energy, space, and time, stars, and galaxies. So that's when the light was, that's when the stars existed, and what you see there in the text is that these are to serve for signs for the animals that are gonna be created on the fifth and sixth days. You'll note that all the animals mentioned on the fifth and sixth days are sufficiently complex. They need at least the occasional visibility of the sun, moon, and stars to regulate their biological clocks.

> **Moderator:** This is one I actually looked it up, and the Hebrew verb is *wayya'as* [the *waw*-consecutive form of *'asah*] in verse 16 and according to Archer again, God had made the two great luminaries. This would be, Hebrew had no special form for the pluperfect tense, but uses the perfect tense, or the conversive imperfect here to express either the English past or the English perfect. So what he's saying is God had made two great lights. So that seems to open the door that the sun and so on were already there, but it does say, He also made the stars. Did He make stars on day four or did he make them at the beginning?

There is no basis from the biblical text (as opposed to outside "scientific" influences) for using the pluperfect here, because the reader reading the *waw* consecutive would connect the making (note: *not* appearing) of the lights with the "Let there be

---

3. See in-depth analysis by J. Sarfati, <www.answersingenesis.org/ross_hovind>.

lights" of the previous verse. This is different from Genesis 2:19, where the pluperfect makes sense, because the reader would think of the prior creation of animals in Genesis 1. For further explanation of the pluperfect in Genesis 2:19, see page 91.

Note that the Ankerberg/Archer explanation, "had made," contradicts Ross's explanation that the sun, moon, and stars really "appeared," which is not possible from the text. Furthermore, Meredith Kline, a leading promoter of the "Framework Hypothesis," demonstrates that the Ross–Ankerberg eisegesis about the pluperfect is untenable:

> Also entailed in the minimalist interpretation of day four is the pluperfect rendering of the verbs expressing the making of the luminaries in the fulfillment section (v. 16, 17), introduced by "and it was so" (v. 15b). If adopted, the pluperfect could not be restricted to these verbs. For consistently in Genesis 1, what immediately follows the fiat and the "and it was so" formula that answers to the fiat is a detailing of what God proceeded to bring into being in execution of the fiat. In day four then the verbs of fulfillment in verses 16, 17 cannot be pluperfect with respect to the fiat of verses. Temporally they follow the fiat, which means the fiat would have to be put in the same pluperfect tense as its subsequent fulfillment, yielding the translation "And God had said." That is, day four as a whole would have to be cast in the pluperfect, and that with reference to the time of the events in the preceding days. Ironically, such a translation would make explicit the non-chronological sequence of the narrative, the very thing the pluperfect proposal was trying to avoid.[4]

As shown in chapter 1, Kline is so intimidated by evolution and billions of years that he rejects a literal interpretation. But as shown above, he also realizes the futility of attempts to preserve Genesis as some sort of historical narrative while accepting the uniformitarian time scale and order of events. Kline's only recourse is to reject Genesis as history, when he should be questioning evolution/long ages instead.

LEADING DAY-AGER CONCEDES DEFEAT

One of the most influential defenders of the day-age theory was the geologist Davis Young. He was the son of the orthodox Old Testament scholar, Edward J. Young, but early on decided to accept the secular geological theories over God's Word. But, for a time, he rejected evolution as unscriptural, and tried to maintain a semblance of belief in scriptural authority by claiming the days were long ages. That is, his beliefs and even his eisegetical contortions were very similar to those now advocated by Ross.

But eventually Young came to realize that the harmonizations were futile, because there was no satisfactory way to reconcile the order of events in Genesis with

---

4. M.G. Kline, "Space and Time in the Genesis Cosmogony," *Perspectives on Science and Christian Faith* 48:2–15, 1996.

those claimed by secular theories. He became embarrassed by the biblical gymnastics required. So he repudiated the day-age theory. He explains why in a lecture at a Christian university that for years has accepted evolution,[5] and readers can see how Ross's Scripture-twisting has already been tried and rejected before:

> The day-age hypothesis insisted with at least a semblance of textual plausibility that the days of creation were long periods of time of indeterminate length, although the immediate context implies that the term *yôm* for "day" really means "day." Having devised a means for allowing Genesis 1 to be in harmony with an ancient planet, day-age advocates needed to demonstrate that the sequence of creative activities of Genesis chapter 1 matched the sequence of events deciphered by the astronomers and geologists. Well, day-agers outdid themselves in constructing impressive correlations. Of course, these correlations . . . all differed from each other. While a fairly convincing case could be made for a general concord . . . specifics of these correlations were a bit more murky.
>
> There were some textual obstacles the day-agers developed an amazing agility in surmounting. The biblical text, for example, has vegetation appearing on the third day and animals on the fifth day. Geology, however, had long realized that invertebrate animals were swarming in the seas long before vegetation gained a foothold on the land. This obvious point of conflict, however, failed to dissuade well-intentioned Christians, my earlier self included, from nudging the text to mean something different from what it says. In my case, I suggested that the days were overlapping days. Having publicly repented of that textual mutilation a few years ago, I will move on without further embarrassing myself.
>
> Worse yet, the text states that on the fourth day God made the heavenly bodies after the earth was already in existence. Here is a blatant confrontation with science. Astronomy insists that the sun is older than the earth. How do day-agers worm out of this? The usual subterfuge involves the suggestion that the light originally visible on earth was sunlight that was obscured and diffused by the thick atmosphere that began to dissipate with the separation of the waters on the second day. Not until the fourth day, however, had the mists thinned to the point where the sun became visible from the earth. . . .
>
> Ingenious as all these schemes may be, one is struck by the forced nature of them all. While the exegetical gymnastic maneuvers have displayed remarkable flexibility, I suspect that they have resulted in temporary damage to the theological musculature.

---

5. D.A. Young, *The Harmonization of Scripture and Science*, science symposium at Wheaton College, March 23, 1990.

This shows that what finally convinced Young of the futility of the day-age theory was the order of creation in Genesis. Alas, instead of repenting of trusting "science" over God's Word, Young departed even further from Scripture. Now Young is open to theistic evolution and regards Genesis as non-historical. This shows that the day-age theory is an unstable position, and a continued trust in secular science will lead to further sliding down the slippery slope away from belief in the Bible as real history.

SUMMARY

The order of creation revealed by Genesis cannot be reconciled with the order claimed by secular astronomers and geologists. All attempts at harmonization are blatantly forced and not the result of sound exegesis. One leading day-ager, Davis Young, eventually saw through the fanciful Scripture-twisting he and other day-agers resorted to, and repudiated the theory. But he refused to abandon "science" as his ultimate authority, and departed even further from biblical creation into overt theistic evolutionism. This is good evidence for the futility of the day-age compromise.

CHAPTER 5

THE BIG BANG AND ASTRONOMY

Ross's eisegesis of Genesis is hugely motivated by his dogmatic acceptance of the big-bang theory. He fails to realize that it is based on several non-biblical philosophical *assumptions* — these include naturalism, and that the universe has no center. Citing its so-called predictive success fails to recognize that many theories can predict the same observations, and that the big bang's alleged predictive success is based on circular reasoning. There are also many scientific problems with the big bang, as well as with auxiliary theories such as the nebular hypothesis origin of the solar system. Ross rightly appreciates the causality argument for God from the beginning of the universe. But to use this argument does not require the big bang. More importantly, perceived apologetic usefulness should never override scriptural teachings.

WHAT IS THE BIG-BANG THEORY?

The most widely held cosmogony, or model of the universe's beginning and development, is called the *big-bang theory*. Here, the universe is supposed to have "exploded" from a "cosmic egg," sometimes called the *ylem*. The *Encyclopædia Britannica* states that the big bang is a:

> . . . widely held theory of the evolution of the universe. Its essential feature is the emergence of the universe from a state of extremely high temperature and density — the so-called big bang that occurred at least 10,000,000,000 years ago. . . .
>
> The big bang is based on two assumptions. The first is that Einstein's general theory of relativity describes the gravitational attraction of all matter. The second assumption, called the cosmological principle, states that the observer's point of view of the universe depends neither on the direction in which he looks nor on his location. This principle applies only to the large scale properties of the universe, but it does imply that the universe has no edge, so that the big bang occurred not at a particular point in space but rather throughout space at the same time. These two assumptions make it possible to calculate the history of the cosmos after a certain epoch called

the Planck time. Scientists have yet to determine what prevailed before Planck time.[1]

Philosophical Assumption: The Cosmological Principle

It is important to note that while the first assumption is scientific, and one which creationists should have no quarrel with, the second (sometimes misnamed the "Copernican Principle") is completely *philosophical.* This is illustrated by none other than the famous lawyer-turned-cosmologist Edwin Hubble (1889–1953), who discovered that distant objects had red shifts approximately proportional to distance from us (see page 151), which he interpreted as evidence of an expanding universe. He made a revealing admission in 1937:

> Such a condition [these red shifts] would imply that we occupy a unique position in the universe. . . . But the unwelcome supposition of a favored location must be avoided at all costs . . . is intolerable . . . moreover, it represents a discrepancy with the theory because the theory postulates homogeneity.[2]

This is from his book titled *The Observational Approach to Cosmology,* ironic because this statement has nothing to do with observation! But there is no scientific or biblical reason why Christians should accept this assumption. The popular view of the big bang, which Ross seems to foster, pictures everything exploding from a central point in a universe bounded by an edge. As shown by Hubble and the *Encyclopedia Britannica,* this is a totally misleading picture — the big bang posits a universe without a center and without an edge (unbounded).

Another famous physicist, Richard Feynman (1918–1988), who won a third share of the 1965 Nobel Prize in physics for his work on quantum electrodynamics, also admitted that the cosmological principle is based on "prejudice":

> . . . I suspect that the assumption of uniformity of the universe reflects a prejudice born of a sequence of overthrows of geocentric ideas. . . . It would be embarrassing to find, after stating that we live in an ordinary planet about an ordinary star in an ordinary galaxy, that our place in the universe is extraordinary. . . . To avoid embarrassment we cling to the hypothesis of uniformity.[3]

George Francis Rayner Ellis is a high profile cosmologist who has co-authored papers with big bang guru Stephen Hawking (b. 1942). In a profile in *Scientific American,* he honestly admitted the role of philosophical assumptions:

1. "Big Bang Model," *The New Encyclopaedia Britannica,* 15th edition, 2:205, 1992.
2. E.P. Hubble, *The Observational Approach to Cosmology* (Oxford: Clarendon, 1937), p. 50–51.
3. R.P. Feynman, F.B. Morinigo, and W.G. Wagner, *Feynman Lectures on Gravitation* (London: Penguin Books, 1999).

"People need to be aware that there is a range of models that could explain the observations," Ellis argues. "For instance, I can construct you a spherically symmetrical universe with earth at its center, and you cannot disprove it based on observations." Ellis has published a paper on this. "You can only exclude it on philosophical grounds. In my view there is absolutely nothing wrong in that. What I want to bring into the open is the fact that we are using philosophical criteria in choosing our models. A lot of cosmology tries to hide that."[4]

Another Unstated Assumption: Naturalism

Another assumption the *Britannica* failed to mention, one which should ring alarm bells for Christians, is naturalism — that is, the universe today is the result of entirely natural processes — though some people (like Ross) assert "God started it," unlike most big-bang theorists. The big bang model posits that all the cosmic structure, stars, galaxies, and planets evolved by natural processes, and were not (at least directly) created by God. So the big bang is definitely an evolutionary cosmogony. This also means that attempts to use the big bang as evidence for a creator are misplaced, especially because mainstream big bang cosmologists reject a creator (see page 181).

ALLEGED EVIDENCE FOR THE BIG BANG

As shown in chapter 1, Ross was convinced of the big bang before he read Genesis. This, not any special study of Hebrew, led him to reject that creation occurred in six 24-hour days. In his book *The Fingerprint of God*, he presents alleged scientific evidence for the big bang, and why rival secular theories, such as steady state and oscillating universe, don't work.

There are three main lines of evidence that are alleged to support the big bang: expansion of the universe, cosmic microwave background radiation, and elemental abundances. To look at each in turn, we find that they are far from conclusive, while there are other problems overlooked. But there is an important logical point to consider before analyzing specifics.

Fallacy of Verified Prediction

While it is common to cite verified predictions as "proof" of a scientific law, this commits a basic logical fallacy called *affirming the consequent*.[5] That can be seen if we analyze it ($\therefore$ = therefore):

1) Theory T predicts observation O;
2) O is observed;
$\therefore$ T is true.

---

4. W. Wayt Gibbs, "Profile: George F.R. Ellis; Thinking Globally, Acting Universally," *Scientific American* 273(4):28, 29, 1995.

5. J. Sarfati, "Loving God with All Your Mind: Logic and Creation," *TJ* 12(2):142–151, 1998; <www.answersingenesis.org/logic>.

G.H. Clark, *The Philosophy of Science and Belief in God*, 2nd edition (Jefferson, MD: The Trinity Foundation, 1987).

To see why this does not follow, consider:

1) If I had just eaten a whole pizza, I would feel very full;
2) I feel very full;
∴ I have just eaten a whole pizza.

But I could feel very full for many different reasons, for example, eating lots of another type of food. Similarly, there are many possible theories that could predict a given observation.

On the other hand, the famous falsification criterion for a scientific theory devised by the Austrian-British philosopher of science Sir Karl Popper (1902–1994)[6] is based on the valid form of argument known as *denying the consequent*:[7]

1) Theory T predicts O will not be observed;
2) O is observed;
∴ T is false.

However, some philosophers of science regard Popper as somewhat simplistic. The American historian of science Thomas Kuhn (1922–1996) pointed out that, in reality, in periods of "normal science," scientists do not throw out the ruling paradigm readily, but tolerate a large number of "anomalies." It takes many anomalies to build up before there is a scientific revolution.[8]

The theory of the Hungarian-Jewish philosopher Imre Lakatos (1922–1974) has sometimes been regarded as a synthesis of Popper and Kuhn. He retained the falsification criterion in one sense, but also took into account that scientists in practice do not follow this strictly. But instead of Kuhn's sociological treatment, Lakatos put this in a logical perspective. He pointed out that core theories are not tested in isolation, but are "protected" by auxiliary hypotheses. Denying the consequent only shows that one of the premises needs to be false, and it need not be the core theory. So the auxiliary hypotheses are modified instead.[9] In schematic form, the valid argument is as follows:

1) Theory T and auxiliary hypothesis A predict that O will not be observed;
2) O is observed;
∴ Either T or A is false.

For example, Newton's theory predicted certain motions of Uranus, provided there were no other massive objects interfering. When Uranus didn't move as predicted,

6. K. Popper, *The Logic of Scientific Discovery* (New York: Basic Books, 1959); Routledge Classics 2002; translated from his *Logik der Forschung*, 1934.
7. J. Sarfati, "Loving God with All Your Mind: Logic and Creation," *TJ* 12(2):142–151 (1998); <www.answersingenesis.org/logic>.
8. T. Kuhn, *The Structure of Scientific Revolutions* (Chicago, IL: University of Chicago Press, 1970).
9. I. Lakatos, "Falsification and the Methodology of Scientific Research Programmes," in I. Lakatos and A. Musgrave, editors, *Criticism and the Growth of Knowledge*, <www.philosophy.ru/edu/ref/sci/lakatos.html>.

either Newton's theory was falsified or there was another massive object perturbing the orbit — this turned out to be the planet Neptune.[10]

These considerations are important in analyzing the alleged support for the big bang. There are three main alleged evidences for the big bang: cosmic expansion, the cosmic microwave background radiation, and the abundance of light elements. Let's discuss each of these three in detail.

1) Cosmic Expansion

Red Shift

The fact that distant galaxies are receding was shown by Hubble's red shift analysis. One way to produce a red shift is by the Doppler effect on light. This is named after the Austrian physicist Christian Doppler (1803–1853), who analyzed sound waves from moving sources in 1842. The effect is well known — as a train moves toward you, more sound wave crests can reach the ear in a given time, so you hear a greater frequency, or higher pitch. The reverse happens after the train passes you and recedes from you. Then fewer wave crests per unit time reach you, so you hear a lower frequency. So you hear a sudden drop in pitch as the train passes, which remains low as it moves away.

This effect applies to all waves, but it is hard to observe for light because familiar objects move at negligible speed compared with light. So Doppler didn't have equipment precise enough to measure it. But only six years later, French physicist Armand Fizeau (1819–1896) measured the lines in spectra of moving objects, and showed that they were Doppler shifted. When the source is moving away, the lines are shifted towards the lower frequency (red) end of the spectrum, hence the term *red shift*. And when the source is moving closer, the lines are shifted towards the higher frequency (blue) end of the spectrum — a *blue shift*. (The next year, Fizeau became the first to reliably measure the speed of light on earth.) The Doppler effect applies to all electromagnetic radiation, not just light. For many people, the best-known application is radar speed traps.

Hubble's Contribution

Hubble was the first to realize that many "nebulae" were not inside our galaxy, but were actually galaxies themselves. Therefore, the universe was far bigger than was thought up till that time.

Hubble found that most galaxies had red shifts. He interpreted the shifts as caused by the Doppler effect of receding objects, produced entirely by the velocity, v, of the light source with respect to the earth. Red shifts are often expressed as the ratio, z, of the change of wavelength and the wavelength itself, and this, in turn, is approximately equal to the ratio of the object's velocity, v, to the speed of light, c:

---

10. For extensive discussion of the views of Popper and Lakatos, and other attempts to define science, see W.R. Bird, *The Origin of Species Revisited* (New York: Philosophical Library, 1991), Vol. II, chapters 9–10.

$$z = {}^{\Delta\lambda}/_\lambda \approx {}^{v}/_c$$

Hubble found that the red shifts were proportional to distance, now called the *Hubble law*. He interpreted this as, the further away the object, the faster it was receding, that is:

$$v = Hr$$

where v is the recession velocity, r the distance, and H a constant, now named after Hubble.

However, the modern view is that the greater component of a red shift is "cosmological," caused by expansion of *space* itself (called Hubble flow), not the Doppler effect. But there is no observational way to distinguish them. Therefore, astronomers still find it convenient to describe red shifts with "equivalent velocities," as if they were caused by a Doppler effect on real recessions. But it's important to note that the modern view is *not* expansion of objects *through* space, but expansion of space, which carries the objects along with it. However, the objects usually have some proper motion through space, which *does* have a Doppler shift component, so the observed red shifts are a combination of the two. The further away the object, the more the cosmological portion of the red shift dominates.

What Big Bang Theorists Really Believe

Note that this is combined with the no-center assumption to illustrate how most cosmologists picture the big bang. Space itself can be represented in two dimensions as the surface of a balloon as it inflates, with a number of small cardboard disks glued on it to represent galaxies. As the balloon inflates, the disks don't move *per se*, but they appear to move apart because they are carried by the balloon's expanding surface. Also, a tiny observer on *any* disk will see the others move away — *no* disk has any unique central location on this 2-D surface. Scaling back up one dimension, it is a complete misapprehension to think that big bang theorists believe any observer is in a spot corresponding to the 3-D center of an inflating balloon.

Two Rival Theories: Big Bang Versus Steady State

Historically, there were two main evolutionary theories to explain the expansion of the universe: the big-bang and steady state theories.

Big Bang

One theory was that an "explosion" of highly dense matter was the beginning of all space and time. Big-bang cosmologists don't conceive of this as an explosion in the usual sense, but as a rapid expansion of space itself from a point of infinite density. (Note that this comes from the unproven assumption that since the universe is expanding, it started from zero size. There is no observational evidence against the idea that the universe was created with some finite, perhaps very large, size.)

In his 1950 BBC radio series, *The Nature of the Universe*, Sir Fred Hoyle (1915–2001),[11] mockingly called this idea the big bang, considering it preposterous. Hoyle never wavered from this opinion. In 1994 he wrote, "Big-Bang cosmology refers to an epoch that cannot be reached by any form of astronomy, and, in more than two decades, it has not produced a single successful prediction."[12] And in 2000, he co-authored the book *A Different Approach to Cosmology*, slamming the big bang and advocating the quasi-steady-state-creation (QSSC) model.[13] Yet the big-bang theory — and the derisive term — have become mainstream, not only in astronomy but in society as well.

Steady State

In the 1940s, Hoyle, along with Hermann Bondi and Thomas Gold, proposed a rival theory. This was the "steady state" theory, a belief that the universe had no beginning or end, but always existed and would continue to exist. This came from their strong humanist bias. They therefore rejected any theory that seemed to teach a beginning for the universe, because that would point to a Beginner.[14] Their philosophical assumption was even elevated to become the overarching perfect cosmological principle. Not only is the universe assumed to look the same (on a large scale) in any place and from any direction, but also at any *time*. (This underlying philosophical principle was once widely held, and yet today it is almost universally rejected. So can we trust today's equally baseless cosmological principle, and hence the big-bang theory that depends on it?)

But this led to a problem in an expanding universe. So they posited a continual spontaneous appearance of hydrogen atoms from nothing. This shows how a humanistic bias can cause people to violate one of the most fundamental laws of science — the law of conservation of mass/energy, which states that mass/energy in the universe can neither be created nor destroyed. Of course, this fundamental law is consistent with Genesis — God's creation of the space-time universe was finished after six days.

Big Bang Proven by Its "Prediction" of Cosmic Expansion?

It is historically inaccurate to claim that the big bang predicts the expansion of the universe. It is the other way round — the expansion of the universe was discovered first, and the big bang was developed to explain it. But so was the steady state

11. See Hoyle's obituary, G. Demme and J. Sarfati, " 'Big-bang' Critic Dies," *TJ* 15(3):6–7 (2001), <www.answersingenesis.org/hoyle>.

12. F. Hoyle, *Home Is Where the Wind Blows* (Mill Valley, CA: University Science Books, 1994), p. 414; as reported in *The Skeptic* 16(1):52.

13. F. Hoyle, G. Burbidge, and J.V. Narlikar, *A Different Approach to Cosmology* (UK: Cambridge University Press, 2000).
   J.G. Hartnett, "Different but Still the Same" (review of the Hoyle book mentioned in the previous footnote), *TJ* 16(1):29–35 (2002).

14. J. Sarfati, "If God Created the Universe, Then Who Created God?" *TJ* 12(1):20–22 (1998); <www.answersingenesis.org/docs/3791.asp>.

theory. So by the same reasoning as that employed by many big bang advocates, one could claim that the steady state predicted the expansion. But hardly anyone today would claim that expansion proves the steady state.

2. Cosmic Microwave Background Radiation (CMB)

Probably the most important prediction claimed by big bang proponents, and that credited for destroying the steady state model, was cosmic microwave background radiation. In 1946, the Russian-American physicist Georgi Antonovich Gamow, a.k.a. George Gamow (1904–1968), predicted that the "hot" big bang would have an "afterglow" of radiation that would be highly red shifted.[15] (Gamow also formulated the standard theory of radioactive alpha-decay by quantum mechanical tunneling, and was also the first to propose the idea of the *genetic code*, that is, that the nucleotide sequence of DNA was *coded information* for the synthesis of proteins.)

In 1948, his students Ralph Alpher and Bob Herman predicted that the radiation would correspond to that emitted by a body of a temperature of 5 K (degrees above absolute zero).[16] In 1964, Russian cosmologists Doroshkevich and Novikov predicted that this would have a spectrum matching that of a *black body*[17] (a black body is a theoretical perfect absorber and emitter of radiation, so is in perfect thermal equilibrium with its surroundings).

The "triumph" came in 1965 when Arno Penzias and Robert Wilson, two radio-astronomers at the Bell Labs in New Jersey, made a chance discovery. Their radio-telescope, tuned to a wavelength of 7.35 cm, detected a signal that came from everywhere in the sky at the same intensity. It turned out that the radiation had a spectrum matching that of a black body. The corresponding temperature of this radiation was 2.726 K. This discovery was regarded as a vindication of the big bang. They won the Nobel prize in 1978.[18]

Nowadays, this is not regarded as light from the big bang *per se*. Rather, the light is supposed to come from the time the universe cooled down to 3,000°C (5,400°F), about 300,000 years after the big bang. This is cool enough for atoms to form from the plasma of charged subatomic particles. Since light is electromagnetic radiation, plasma is opaque, while once neutral atoms formed, the universe became transparent.

15. G. Gamow, "Expanding Universe and the Origin of the Elements," *Physical Review* 70:572–573 (1946); *Nature* 162:680 (1948); cited in R.W. Wilson, "The Cosmic Microwave Background Radiation," *Nobel Lecture* (December 8, 1978); <www.nobel.se/physics/laureates/1978/wilson-lecture.pdf>.

16. R. Alpher and R.C. Herman, "Evolution of the Universe," *Nature* 162:774–775 (1948); *Physical Review* 75:1089 (1949); cited in R.W. Wilson, "The Cosmic Microwave Background Radiation," *Nobel Lecture* (December 8, 1978); <www.nobel.se/physics/laureates/1978/wilson-lecture.pdf>.

17. A.G. Doroshkevich and I.D. Novikov, *Dokl. Akad. Navk. SSR* 154:809 (1964); *Sov. Phys. Dokl.* 9:111 (1964); cited in R.W. Wilson, "The Cosmic Microwave Background Radiation," *Nobel Lecture* (December 8, 1978); <www.nobel.se/physics/laureates/1978/wilson-lecture.pdf>.

18. R.W. Wilson, "The Cosmic Microwave Background Radiation," *Nobel Lecture* (December 8, 1978); <www.nobel.se/physics/laureates/1978/wilson-lecture.pdf>.

However, this nice story is undermined by the fact that later in the 1950s, Gamow and his students made a number of estimates of the background temperature ranging from 3 to 50 K.

More importantly, spectral analysis before Gamow had already found a 2.3 K background temperature, so it was no more a "prediction" of the big bang than expansion of the universe, as per the previous section.

Starting in 1937, Adams and Dunham had found some absorption lines, which were later identified with the interstellar molecules CH, CH⁺, and CN.[19] The CN (cyanide) molecule also had an absorption line from what is called the first rotationally excited state. Rotational quantum states have energy spacings corresponding to microwave radiation.[20] Also, the higher the temperature, the more highly the higher energy states are populated.[21] So, in 1940–41, the Canadian astrophysicist and spectroscopist Andrew McKellar (1910–1960) could analyze the data. From the observed ratios of the populations of these energy states, he calculated that the CN molecules were in thermal equilibrium with a temperature of about 2.3 K.[22] The source of this temperature was taken to be black body radiation. The transition between the two rotational states can emit or absorb microwave radiation at 2.64 mm wavelength, near the peak of a 3 K black body spectrum.

3. Light Element Abundances

Modern cosmologists claim that the big bang produced only light elements, that is, hydrogen, helium — only the first two elements in the periodic table. The big bang was incapable of forming "metals" (in stellar astronomy, this means all elements heavier than helium), with the possible exception of a tiny amount of lithium. Metals up to iron are attributed to nuclear fusion in stars, while elements above iron require supernovae (exploding stars) to form them.

The observed abundance of helium is supposed to be a major triumph of big-bang cosmology. However, this "prediction" was achieved only by making *ad hoc* assumptions about the baryoni[23] density in their models to make sure the observed

---

19. T. Dunham Jr. and W.S. Adams, *Publ. Am. Astron. Soc.* 9:5 (1937); cited in R.W. Wilson, "The Cosmic Microwave Background Radiation," *Nobel Lecture* (December 8, 1978); <www.nobel.se/physics/laureates/1978/wilson-lecture.pdf>.

20. From the equation $E = h\nu = \frac{hc}{\lambda}$, where E is energy, h is Planck's constant, ν = frequency, c = speed of light and λ = wavelength.

21. From the Boltzmann distribution, where for a Kelvin temperature T, the ratio of the population of two states with an energy difference ΔE is given by $N_2/N_1 = \exp(-\Delta E/kT)$, where k is Boltzmann's constant.

22. A. McKellar, *Proc. Ast. Soc. Pac.* 52:187 (1940); *Publ. Dominion Astrophysical Observatory Victoria B.C.* 7(15):251 (1941); cited in R.W. Wilson, "The Cosmic Microwave Background Radiation," *Nobel Lecture* (December 8, 1978); <www.nobel.se/physics/laureates/1978/wilson-lecture.pdf>.

23. A baryon (from Greek βαρυς *barys/barus* = heavy) is a particle comprising three quarks and which participates in the strong nuclear force. Protons and neutrons are the lightest baryons.

abundance would arise. Under such conditions, it would be a surprise if they did *not* fulfill such adjustable "predictions"!

Scientific Problems with the Big Bang

The current big bang model has a number of scientific problems, which are generally glossed over.

Quantized Red Shifts Point to Galactocentric Universe

As Hubble admitted, the observed cosmic expansions could equally well be explained by the fact that we really are near the center of the universe. In fact, features of the red shift are consistent with this but are a problem if the earth is not unique.

William Tifft at the Steward Observatory in Tucson, Arizona, analyzed a number of red shifts. He performed standard statistical techniques, and the red shifts were clustered around discrete intervals or quantized. He observed clusters at z intervals of 0.00024, or 0.024 percent, or equivalent velocity intervals of 72 m/s, and other clustering at 36 m/s. Tifft published his observations in the major astrophysical journals over more than 20 years.[24]

Tifft's observations are a puzzle if the earth is not in a unique position. A non-unique position can explain observed recession, but would predict z in a continuous range not in discrete intervals. But Tifft's data make sense if our galaxy (not necessarily the earth itself) was at or very near the center of the universe and surrounded by concentric spherical shells of stars.[25]

This fatally undermines one of the key assumptions behind the big bang, that is, the part of the cosmological principle that there is no preferred location or center in the universe.

CMB Patterns Indicate a Rotating Cosmos

Dr. Max Tegmark, of the University of Pennsylvania, has analyzed WMAP CMB data and reported:

> We found something very bizarre; there is some extra, so far unexplained structure in the CMB.
>
> We had expected that the microwave background would be truly isotropic, with no preferred direction in space but that may not be the case.[26]

Instead, he found certain symmetry patterns:

24. W.G. Tifft, "Discrete States of Redshift and Galaxy Dynamics," in "Internal Motions in Single Galaxies," *Astrophysical J.* 206:38–56 (1976).
W.G. Tifft and W.J. Cocke, "Global Redshift Quantization," *Astrophysical J.* 287:492–502 (1984).
W.G. Tifft, "Redshift Quantization in the Cosmic Background Rest Frame," *J. Astrophysics and Astronomy* 18(4):415–433 (1997).
25. R. Humphreys, "Our Galaxy Is the Center of the Universe, 'Quantized' Redshifts Show," *TJ* 16(2):96–104 (2002).
26. M. Tegmark, cited in D. Whitehouse, "Map Reveals Strange Cosmos," *BBC News,* <http://news.bbc.co.uk/1/hi/sci/tech/2814947.stm>, March 3, 2003.

The octopole and quadrupole components are arranged in a straight line across the sky, along a kind of cosmic equator.[27]

This corroborates the journal *Science*, which said, "But the CMB is not perfectly isotropic."[28] A preferred direction undermines the part of the cosmological principle that there is no preferred direction in space. But the data are consistent with a slow general rotation of the matter in the cosmos (with respect to an inertial frame or the "fabric" of space), because this would produce a quadrupole moment and possibly an octopole moment in the CMB, and would explain the "cosmic equator."

This would be consistent with earlier data, showing "systematic rotation of the plane of polarization of electromagnetic radiation propagating over cosmological distances." The discoverers proposed an *ad hoc* explanation that the vacuum itself could twist the polarization of radio waves to a degree depending on their direction of travel.[29] But the data would also be explained by a rotating cosmos.[30] It remains to be seen if this earlier implicit indication of a rotation axis turns out to be perpendicular to this equatorial plane indicated by the new WMAP data.

Dr. Tegmark also made another very revealing comment:

The entire observable universe is inside this sphere, with us at the center of it.[31]

This comment confirms that the actual data are certainly consistent with a center to the universe. So, although Tegmark probably believes the no-center view of the cosmological principle (judging by his strong advocacy of the multiverse idea — see page 187), it is an *assumption* taken on faith, *despite* the data, not because of them.

The Horizon Problem

The cosmic microwave radiation indicates that space is the same temperature everywhere, to within 1 part in 100,000.[32] However, the initial conditions of the big bang would have produced wide fluctuations in temperatures between different regions. So to produce the observed temperature uniformity, there must have been a

27. Ibid.

28. A Gangui, "A Preposterous Universe," *Science* 299(5611):1333–1334 (February 28, 2003).

29. B. Nodland and J.P. Ralston, "Indication of Anisotropy in Electromagnetic Propagation Over Cosmological Distances," *Physical Review Letters* 78:3043 (1997); <http://publish.aps.org/eprint/gateway/eplist/aps1997apr20_001>.

   J.P. Ralston and B. Nodland, "An Update on Cosmological Anisotropy in Electromagnetic Propagation," *Proceedings of the 7th International Conference on the Intersections of Particle and Nuclear Physics*, Big Sky, Montana, 1997, T.W. Donnelly, editor (Woodbury, NY: American Institute of Physics, 1997); <xxx.lanl.gov/abs/astro-ph/9708114>.

30. R. Humphreys, "New Evidence for a Rotating Cosmos," <www.answersingenesis.org/docs/509.asp>, April 29, 1997.

31. M. Tegmark, cited in D. Whitehouse, "Map Reveals Strange Cosmos," *BBC News,* <http://news.bbc.co.uk/1/hi/sci/tech/2814947.stm>, March 3, 2003.

32. P.J.E. Peebles, *Principles of Physical Cosmology* (Princeton, NJ: Princeton University Press, 1993), p. 404.

common influence, that is, all parts of space must have once been in thermal equilibrium. The fastest way for regions to come into equilibrium would be for electromagnetic radiation to carry heat from one region to another. However, some of these regions are too distant for light to have traversed between them, even in the assumed time since the alleged big bang. The finite speed of light is a "horizon" which can't be crossed, hence the term "horizon problem." Even when the CMB was emitted, supposedly 300,000 years after the big bang (see page 154), it already had a uniform temperature over a range at least ten times larger than this horizon.[33]

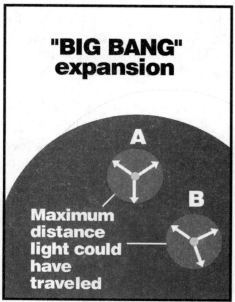

One of the most common attacks on the YEC model by old-earthers such as Ross is that light would supposedly not have had enough time to reach earth from distant stars (see page 189 for some creationist ideas and proposals on this issue). But the horizon problem is the big bangers' own "light travel probem." How can old earthers so freely criticize YEC on the very problem that they have not yet solved from their own perspective?[34]

As an *ad hoc* solution to the horizon problem, Alan Guth (b. 1947) proposed in 1980 that the universe once underwent a period of very rapid growth, called "inflation."[35] Guth, then a particle physicist at the Stanford Linear Accelerator Center in

33. P. Coles and F. Lucchin, *Cosmology: The Origin and Evolution of Cosmic Structure* (Chichester, England: John Wiley & Sons Ltd., 1996), p. 136.

34. R. Newton, "Light Travel-time: A Problem for the Big Bang," *Creation* 25(4):48–49 (September–November 2003).

35. A.H. Guth, "Inflationary Universe: A Possible Solution to the Horizon and Flatness Problems," *Physical Review D* 23(2):347–356 (January 15, 1981).

California, proposed that 10^{-35} seconds after the big bang, the universe expanded by a factor of 10^{25} in 10^{-30} seconds. Twenty-five orders of magnitude is mind-boggling — it is like going from smaller than a pea to the size of our galaxy, an expansion rate much faster than the speed of light. Guth's proposal starts with the universe tinier than a subatomic particle, so the different regions of space were so close that they could come to the same temperature before inflation occurred.

It's important to note that it's space itself that is expanding, so inflation doesn't violate relativity, which prohibits only mass/energy from moving *through* space faster than light. But, despite that, now it seems that even this may have its own horizon problem. So some physicists have proposed that the speed of light was much faster in the past, which would allow the "horizon" to be much farther away and thus accommodate the universe's thermal equilibrium.[36]

This is ironic, because creationists have been disparaged for suggesting the speed of light may have been faster in the past, with accusations that they don't understand relativity. Apparently, it is now acceptable to promote a "scientific heresy" if used to support evolutionary scenarios;[37] and for that matter, to explain fine structure constant changes.[38]

It's also notable that Guth's original hypothesis was proven false,[39] and modern inflationary cosmologies have since modified his original proposal. Also, there is no satisfactory *physical mechanism* for starting inflation, as opposed to playing with mathematical equations. Nor is there a mechanism for halting the inflation, which is known as the "graceful exit problem."[40]

Missing Antimatter

Antimatter was first predicted by the English physicist and Nobel laureate Paul Dirac (1902–1984), who conceived of it in terms of a negative energy hole. When a subatomic particle meets its corresponding antiparticle, they annihilate each other with a huge release of energy, again as per $E=mc^2$.

Whenever matter is generated from energy, as per Einstein's $E=mc^2$, there is always an equal quantity of antimatter produced. This follows from very well-attested physical laws about conservation of elementary particles. These are the law

36. S. Adams, "The Speed of Light," *Inside Science* 147:4, *New Scientist* 173(2326) (January 19, 2002).
37. J. Barrow, "Is Nothing Sacred?" *New Scientist* 163(2196)29–32 (July 24, 1999).
    C. Wieland and J. Sarfati, "God and the Electron: Interview with Physicist Keith Wanser," *Creation* 21(4):38–41 (September–November 1999).
38. P.C.W. Davies, T.M Davis, and C.H. Lineweaver, "Black Holes Constrain Varying Constants," *Nature* 418(6898):602–603 (August 8, 2002).
    C. Wieland, "Speed of Light Slowing Down after All?" *TJ* 16(3):7–10 (2002); <www.answersin-genesis.org/cdk>.
39. P. Coles and F. Lucchin, *Cosmology: The Origin and Evolution of Cosmic Structure* (Chichester, England: John Wiley & Sons Ltd., 1996), p. 151.
40. G.V. Kraniotis, "String Cosmology," *International Journal of Modern Physics A* 15(12):1707–1756 (2000).

of conservation of baryon number and the law of conservation of lepton[41] number, applying to types of heavy and light particles respectively. Ordinary particles are assigned a value of +1, and antiparticles are assigned a value of -1, and the sum has never been observed to change. So if there is no matter to start with, and energy is converted to matter, the number of pluses must balance the number of minuses. But our universe is almost entirely matter.

That is a mystery for big bang theorists. But the paradigm is more important than physical laws. So they have proposed a way to break the symmetry by postulating the existence of a particle called the Higgs boson,[42] sometimes pretentiously called "The God Particle." However, these theories also predict that the proton would be unstable, and decay into a pion plus a positron (anti-electron). The best estimate for the mass of the Higgs boson leads to a proton life span of only 500,000 years. Yet experiments show that the life span of a proton must be over 5×10^{32} years, 30,000 billion billion times greater than even the assumed evolutionary age of the universe, 1.5×10^{10} years.[43]

Galaxy Formation

The big-bang model posits that large clouds of gas millions of light-years across began to form early in the universe. These clouds slowly collapsed to form galaxies. However, a perfectly homogeneous big bang could not have produced any of the irregularities needed for gas to "clump" into clouds instead of spreading out perfectly smoothly. Big bang cosmologists therefore hypothesize that the early universe contained small inhomogeneities, and these then acted as gravitational seeds to cause the initial clumping that produced the structure in the universe that we see today. But small intrinsic variations of the order of over one part in 10^4 would be required for gravity to be able to coalesce galaxies in the alleged time since the big bang.[44] And recent infrared data from the European Space Agency shows that the need for substantial unevenness (inhomogeneity) is even more acute, since galactic clustering at even the allegedly early stages of the big bang is greater than previously thought:

> Rather than being randomly distributed in space, these red galaxies are also found to prefer company, i.e., **they tend to cluster close to each other** [bold in original].[45]

---

41. The word *lepton* was originally the name of a small Greek coin. But now it refers to the truly elementary particles which, as far as we know, are not divisible into smaller particles such as quarks, i.e., the electron, muon and tauon and their corresponding neutrinos. Leptons participate in the weak nuclear force.

42. A boson is an elementary particle with integral spin quantum number. The opposite is a fermion, with half-integral spin.

43. M. Matthews, "Rock Solid," *New Scientist* 162(2187):48–52 (May 22, 1999).

44. M. Rowan-Robinson, "Dark Doubts for Cosmology," *New Scientist* 129:24–28 (1991).

45. "Deepest Infrared View of the Universe: VLT Images Progenitors of Today's Large Galaxies," ESO press release 23/02, December 11, 2002; <www.eso.org/outreach/press-rel/pr-2002/pr-23-02.html>.

COBE and WMAP Satellite Data

COBE stands for the **Co**smic **B**ackground **E**xplorer satellite which NASA launched on November 18, 1989, the operations of which were terminated on December 23, 1993. Its function was to search for these inhomogeneities as temperature variations in the background radiation. COBE did detect some variation, so naturally NASA announced, with fanfare, how they were looking right back into the beginning of the universe. However, these minute and dubious variations were only one part in 10^5, actually ≤70 mK,[46] far less than what would have been required for galaxy formation.[47]

COBE was succeeded by WMAP (Wilkinson Microwave Anisotropy Probe), launched on June 30, 2001. It was originally just MAP, but was rechristened WMAP in February 2003 after David Wilkinson, a pioneer in physics and cosmology, who died in September 2002. These satellites had/have sensitive equipment to monitor the CMB.

The media have often trumpeted claims that they have mapped the universe as it was seen 380,000 years after the big bang.[48] And in the popular reports, the detected anisotropies are treated as if they are proof of the big-bang model, whereas it is more circular reasoning. That is, the evidence (anisotropies) is interpreted *assuming* the truth of the big-bang paradigm, then it is used as support of this paradigm.

Galaxy Formation Problems Acknowledged

Dr. James Trefil, professor of physics at George Mason University, Virginia, accepts the big-bang model, but he agrees that there are fundamental problems about galaxy formation:

> "There shouldn't be galaxies out there at all, and even if there are galaxies, they shouldn't be grouped together the way they are." He later continues: "The problem of explaining the existence of galaxies has proved to be one of the thorniest in cosmology. By all rights, they just shouldn't be there, yet there they sit. It's hard to convey the depth of the frustration that this simple fact induces among scientists."[49]

46. P. de Bernardis et al., "A Flat Universe from High-resolution Maps of the Cosmic Microwave Background Radiation," *Nature* 404:955–959 (2000).
    S.S. McGaugh, "Boomerang Data Suggest a Purely Baryonic Universe," *Astrophys. J.* 541:L33–L36 (2000).
47. J.G. Hartnett, "Recent Cosmic Microwave Background Data Supports Creationist Cosmologies," *TJ* 15(1):8–12 (2001).
48. A recent example is A.M. MacRobert, "Mapping the Big Bang," *Sky and Telescope* (February 11, 2003); <http://skyandtelescope.com/news/current/article_877_1.asp>.
49. J. Trefil, *The Dark Side of the Universe* (New York: Charles Scribner's Sons, Macmillan Publishing Company, 1988), p. 3 and 55.
    See also W. Gitt, "What About the 'Big Bang'?" *Creation* 20(3):42–44 (June–August 1998).

The famous Stephen Hawking said much the same:

> This [big bang] picture of the universe . . . is in agreement with all the observational evidence that we have today. . . . Nevertheless, it leaves a number of important questions unanswered . . . (the origin of the stars and galaxies).[50]

The creationist cosmologist Dr. John Rankin also showed mathematically in his Ph.D. thesis that galaxies would not form from the big bang.[51]

Galaxies and Stars Out of "Date" Order

In late 2002, the European Space Agency released the deepest-ever infrared pictures of galaxy fields.[52] However, even with this alleged look back right at the beginning of time, there seems no sign of galaxies in the process of forming. For one thing, even the earliest galaxies seem to have already formed their stars:[53]

> [I]n contrast to the galaxies at similar redshifts (and hence, at this early epoch) found most commonly in surveys at optical wavelengths, **most of the "infrared-selected" galaxies show relatively little visible star-forming activity**. They appear in fact to have *already formed most of their stars* and in quantities sufficient to account for at least half the total luminous mass of the universe at that time. Given the time to reach this state they must clearly have formed even earlier in the life of the universe and are thus **probably amongst the "oldest" galaxies now known.** [italics added; bold in original][54]

Furthermore, recent data from WMAP, even interpreted under a big-bang paradigm, defied previous predictions:

> The first stars formed when the universe was only 100 to 400 million years old (between redshift 30 and 11), generally earlier than astronomers once expected. WMAP discovered this by measuring polarization patterns in the microwave background. These yielded the date of the "reionization era," when the first starlight began ionizing the cold hydrogen that filled the universe during the "dark age" after the big bang cooled.[54]

---

50. S. Hawking, *A Brief History of Time,* 10th edition, (New York: Bantam Doubleday Dell Pub, 1998).

51. J. Rankin, *Protogalaxy Formation from Inhomogeneities in Cosmological Models*, Ph.D. thesis, Adelaide University, May/June 1977.

52. "Deepest Infrared View of the Universe: VLT Images Progenitors of Today's Large Galaxies," ESO press release 23/02, December 11, 2002; <www.eso.org/outreach/press-rel/pr-2002/pr-23-02.html>.

53. See also A. McIntosh and C. Wieland, " 'Early' Galaxies Don't Fit!" *Creation* 25(3):28–30 (June–August 2003).

54. A.M. MacRobert, "Mapping the Big Bang," *Sky and Telescope* (February 11, 2003); <http://sky-andtelescope.com/news/current/article_877_1.asp>.

However, despite this claim of stars at z = 11–30, *no* galaxies have been discovered at that distance.

Galaxies Spiraling Out of Control

The famous spiral structure of many galaxies, including our own, is meant to be caused by differential rotation. The farther away from the center, the slower the rotation. Supposedly, this transforms an original bar structure into the spiral arms. So, since one galactic rotation period is hundreds of millions of years, several rotations would take a long time. Ross uses this as evidence for vast age (C&T:113):

> Because only 6 percent of the galaxies near our own are spirals, the universe cannot be any younger than about 12 billion years.

However, the European Space Agency infrared data have shown that even the very distant (and thus very "early") galaxies, already have a spiral structure, although they should not have had time to evolve them, and this is an anomaly:

> [A] **few of them are clearly rather large and show spiral structure similar to that seen in very nearby galaxies**, cf. **PR Photo 28d/02**. It is not obvious that current theoretical models can easily account for such galaxies having evolved to this stage so early in the life of the Universe.[55] [bold in original]

Also, after a few rotations, galaxies will "wind themselves up" and destroy the spiral structure.[56] This puts an upper limit on their age, of much less than a billion years.[57]

Ross cites some outdated (1971) attempts by Kevin Prendergast to explain this problem by claiming that star formation would stabilize the spiral structure (C&T:112–114). However, modern evolutionists still recognize the problem, and instead postulate a complex theory of *spiral density waves* as a solution.[58] But this is an *ad hoc* solution, that is, there is no evidence for it; it is an arbitrary assumption merely concocted to solve the problem, and requires much fine-tuning.

A biblical solution is that the spiral galaxies did not evolve, but were created that way. God could easily have created galaxies with different degrees of spiraling, bars, and ellipticals, and the variety would have declared "the glory of God" (Ps. 19:1).[59]

---

55. "Deepest Infrared View of the Universe: VLT Images Progenitors of Today's Large Galaxies," ESO press release 23/02, December 11, 2002; <www.eso.org/outreach/press-rel/pr-2002/pr-23-02.html>.

56. H. Scheffler and H. Elsasser, *Physics of the Galaxy and Interstellar Matter* (Berlin: Springer-Verlag, 1987), p. 352–353, 401–413.

57. This is compatible with Russell Humphreys's white hole cosmology, discussed later in this chapter, as he explains at <www.answersingenesis.org/spiral>.

58. See footnote 56 above.

59. A. McIntosh and C. Wieland, " 'Early' Galaxies Don't Fit!" *Creation* 25(3):28–30 (June–August 2003).

Star Formation

It's vital for any cosmological theory to explain the origin of stars. But there are two major problems in this area. The first is the lack of observational evidence of the stars that should have formed first after the big bang, and the second is the mechanics of clouds collapsing to form these first stars.

Missing Population III Stars

During WWII, the German-American Walter Baade (1893–1960) classified stars into two major groups: population I and population II. Population I are "young," so comprise all spectral classes, including the very hot blue ones which burn quickly. Population II are "old" and lack the fast-burning stars. Population III is a category added after Baade, and are meant to be the first stars formed after the big bang. Since the big bang produced almost no metals, these stars should have spectra lacking any metal absorption lines. Such distinctive spectra should enable easy detection, if they exist. Standard theories demand that because they formed so early, some should exist at enormous red shifts, with z>10, and even as high as 20–30.[60]

However, there is no observational evidence, even in our own galaxy, that population III stars exist or have ever existed.[61] Evolutionists now claim that they were all hot and massive, therefore "fast-burning" stars. However, this is *ad hoc*, and contradicts the earlier papers that argued that population III stars could have masses from 0.1 to 100 times the mass of our sun (M_{sol}). The lower mass (red) stars should have a long enough life span to be still burning today. Indeed, 90 percent of the stars observed today are "main sequence" (not white dwarfs, giants, or supergiants), and more than 70 percent of these have masses less than 0.8 M_{sol}. So, if stars all formed naturalistically, one should expect a large number of low-mass population III stars to have been formed, as allegedly happened for population II stars. The total absence of these stars counts as a falsified prediction of big-bang cosmology.

Collapse of Gas Clouds

Stars are supposed to form when a gas cloud condenses under its own gravity. This would compress the interior so it becomes hot enough for nuclear fusion to start. However, gas clouds have a tendency to expand rather than contract.

The British mathematician and astrophysicist James Jeans (1877–1946) studied the problem of cloud collapse. The only way such cloud collapse could happen is if gravity can overcome the tendency for gas to expand. According to the *virial theorem*, this means the gravitational (potential) energy must be over twice the thermal (kinetic) energy of the gas particles (ignoring the tendency of the cloud to fragment due to turbulence). Half the gravitational energy heats the gas cloud, while the other half is radiated into space as heat. The mathematics leads to the Jeans Mass (M_J), the minimum required for collapse:

60. J.P. Ostriker and N.Y. Gnedin, "Reheating of the Universe and Population III," *Astrophysical Journal Letters* 472:L63 (1996).

61. R. Bernitt, "Stellar Evolution and the Problem of 'First' Stars," *TJ* 16(1):12–14 (2002).

$$M_J = K\, r^{-1/2} T^{3/2}.$$

Here, K is a constant, r is the density, and T is the temperature. The main points are that high density and low temperature favor collapse. Astronomers often express this quantitatively as:

$$M_J \approx 45 M_{sol}\, n^{-1/2} T^{3/2}.$$

Where M_{sol} is the solar mass, n is the density of atoms per cm^3, and T is the temperature in Kelvins. According to the big bang, at the time the universe became transparent and the CMB was generated, $T \approx 3{,}000$ and $n \approx 6{,}000$, therefore $M_J \approx 10^5\, M_{sol}$. This is the size of a globular cluster, therefore nothing smaller than this could have formed. So the theory is that the mass of the universe first broke into clumps the size of clusters, then, somehow, these contracting chunks of gas must have broken further to produce the population III stars.

To try to solve the problem, there are two basic ways of reducing the Jeans Mass: increasing the density and lowering the temperature. As for the first, the creationist astronomer Dr. Danny Faulkner pointed out:

> Stars supposedly condensed out of vast clouds of gas, and it has long been recognized that the clouds don't spontaneously collapse and form stars, they need to be pushed somehow to be started. There have been a number of suggestions to get the process started, and almost all of them require having stars to start with [e.g., a shock wave from an exploding star causing compression of a nearby gas cloud]. This is the old chicken-and-egg problem; it can't account for the origin of stars in the first place.[62]

The other way would be to cool a gas cloud enough. But this requires molecules to radiate the heat away. However, the big bang would produce mainly hydrogen and helium, unsuitable for making the molecules apart from H_2, which would be destroyed rapidly under the ultraviolet light present. Further, H_2 usually needs dust grains for its formation — and dust grains require "metals," which are precisely what's missing for population III stars. The heavier elements, according to the theory, require *pre-existing* stars. Again, there is a chicken-and-egg problem of needing stars to produce stars.

Another idea is that gas clouds were four to five times denser than clouds observed today, so they could generate enough H_2 from collisions of H atoms. There are more esoteric ways of increasing density, for example, "dark matter," which by its very nature is speculative. A number of candidates for the identity of this dark matter have disappointed its proponents.[63]

---

62. "He Made the Stars Also" — interview with creationist astronomer Danny Faulkner, *Creation* 19(4):42–44 (September–November 1997).
63. M. Oard and J. Sarfati, "No Dark Matter Found in the Milky Way Galaxy," *TJ* 13(1):3–4 (1999).

Abraham Loeb, of Harvard's Center for Astrophysics, says, "The truth is that we don't understand star formation at a fundamental level."[64] A more recent article, which purported to show that cosmologists all agree about the big bang, had to affirm this problem, " 'It's a huge mystery exactly how stars form,' said Dr. Richard Bond of the Canadian Institute for Theoretical Astrophysics."[65]

Rapid "Stellar Evolution"

Creationists don't necessarily disagree with "stellar" evolution, because, unlike biological evolution, it requires no naturalistic process to generate new information. But we would not agree with most of the theories of stellar *origins*, or the *time scales*. In fact, there is much observational evidence that stars can change very quickly.

Sakurai's Object: This was discovered in the constellation of Sagittarius by the Japanese amateur astronomer Yukio Sakurai, in February 1996.[66]

In 1994, this star was most likely a white dwarf in the center of a planetary nebula, with a diameter about the same as earth's, though enormously denser. But a team of astronomers, including Bengt Gustafsson at McDonald Observatory in Texas and Martin Asplund of the Uppsala Observatory in Sweden, have observed it change to a bright yellow giant. This was about 70 million km in diameter, 80 times wider than the sun. This means the diameter has increased by a factor of 8,000, and the volume by a factor of over 500,000 million. The astronomers expressed great surprise at the rapidity at which this change had occurred.[67]

But this wasn't the end of it. In 1998, it had expanded even further, to a red supergiant with a diameter of 210 million km, 150 times that of the sun. But as fast as it grew, it shrank, releasing much debris. By 2002, the star itself was invisible even to the most powerful optical telescopes, although it is detectable in the infrared, which shines through the dust.[68]

Sakurai's Object is an example of what evolutionary astronomers call a "born-again" star. They presume that all white dwarfs are collapsed remnants of stars that have burnt (by nuclear fusion) nearly all their hydrogen and helium fuel. But when first formed, they should have an outer layer of hydrogen unused by fusion, although this is sometimes not observed. So one model proposes that instabilities might reignite fusion of unused helium. These would be so violent that the resulting convection would drag hydrogen into the core. In turn, already-existing metals would be dredged up from the core, and more would be generated from the intense nuclear reactions.[69]

---

64. Quoted by Marcus Chown, "Let There Be Light," *New Scientist* 157(2120):26–30 (February 7, 1998). See also, "Stars Could Not Have Come from the 'Big Bang,' " sidebar, *Creation* 20(3):42–43 (June–August 1998).

65. D. Overbye, "In the Beginning . . .," *NYTimes.com* (July 23, 2002).

66. H. Muir, "Back from the Dead," *New Scientist* 177(2384):28–31 (March 1, 2003).

67. *New Scientist* 154(2085):17 (June 7, 1997); referring to *Astronomy & Astrophysics* 321:L17 (1997).

68. See footnote 66 above.

69. Ibid.

This seems to broadly explain Sakurai's Object. Astronomers analyzing the star's spectrum could see only the surface, and they observed the hydrogen drop by 80 percent, and heavy elements such as lithium, zinc, strontium, and yttrium appear.[70]

However, the speed was 50 times greater than what the theory predicted in the 1980s, as Asplund says:

> There were predictions that born-again giants would evolve quickly, but most people thought the timescale would be 10 to 100 years, not a mere few months.[71]

Don Pollaco, an astronomer at Queen's University, Belfast, agreed:

> The time scales are just crazy.[72]

This is a good lesson that there is still much to learn about stellar evolution. Astronomers have not observed stars changing over millions of years, but now they have observed them changing over months!

FG Sagittae: This star has changed from being a blue star (with a temperature of 12,000 K) to a yellow star (temperature 5,000 K) in only 36 years of observation.[73]

Are Stars Forming Today?

Ross claimed in a debate with YEC Duane Gish, hosted by the strong Ross supporter James Dobson of *Focus on the Family*:

> . . . we see star formation in real time. You can take your pair of binoculars out tonight and watch it. It's actually happening.[74]

But no other astronomer would agree. The most they would say is that one could see *regions* in space where stars are *thought* to be forming now, which is vastly different from what Ross said.

There are claims that the Hubble Space Telescope (HST) has taken some spectacular pictures of stars forming. Creationist astronomer Dr. Ronald Samec comments as follows, clearly showing the difference between what is claimed and what is actually seen:

> As a former planetarium director and a current professor of astronomy, I have shown slides of the "Eagle Nebula" and other similar gas complexes such as the "Horse-Head Nebula" in Orion. These two regions are favorites since they show more than one type of nebula.

---

70. Ibid.
71. Ibid., p. 31.
72. Ibid.
73. *New Scientist*, p. 28–41 (September 14, 1991).
74. Text of the *Focus on the Family* radio broadcast on August 12, 1992. The transcript (apparently heavily edited by *Focus on the Family* to remove Dr. Gish's strongest points) may be found at: <www.talkorigins.org/faqs/gish-ross-debate.html> (on a pro-evolution, and mainly atheistic, website).

These regions are called *dark, reflection,* and *emission* nebulae.

- Dark nebulae are made mostly of dust.
- Emission nebulae are fluorescent regions of gas glowing in the presence of embedded stars.
- Reflection nebulae are cold, un-ionized gas.

When dark nebulae collide with emission nebulae, features like those noted in the HST image result. The dust pushes its way through the hot gas. Gas along the front edge of the collision compresses and glows hotter. This results in the whitish appearing areas at the edges of the dark "fingers" of dust.

I presume that the temperatures of these areas are near 10,000 K so that they glow like the surfaces of stars of similar temperature, that is, *white.* Gas at such temperatures will quickly disperse and there *is no chance of it forming stars.* We should not be convinced that embedded stars exist within the "finger tips" of these dust regions unless they are actually imaged.[75]

SOLAR SYSTEM FORMATION: NEBULAR HYPOTHESIS PROBLEMS

Evolutionary cosmologies of all types, including the big bang, must explain the origin of the solar system. The usual explanation is the *nebular hypothesis.* This proposes that the sun, the earth, and the rest of the solar system formed from a *nebula,* or cloud of dust and gas. This hypothesis was first proposed in 1734 by the Swedish mining engineer and mystic Emanuel Swedenborg (1688–1772).[76] He seriously proclaimed that this was revealed in seances by men from Jupiter and Saturn.

However, better known for advocating this idea, 21 years later, is the German agnostic philosopher Immanual Kant (1724–1804),[77] who was influenced by Swedenborg. He proposed that the sun had ejected a tail, or a filament, of material that cooled and collected, and thus formed the planets. Finally, the French atheistic mathematician Pièrre-Simon Laplace (1749–1827) elaborated on Kant's idea, proposing that a contracting gas cloud would throw off rings, which would condense into planets.[78]

However, all variants of the nebular hypothesis have many problems. One authority summarized: "The clouds are too hot, too magnetic, and they rotate too rapidly."[79] Some more problems are as follows.

Angular Momentum

One major problem can be shown by accomplished skaters spinning on ice. As skaters pull their arms in, they spin faster. This effect is due to what physicists call

---

75. R.G. Samec, "Are Stars Forming Today?" *Creation* 19(1):5 (December 1996–February 1997); <www.answersingenesis.org/docs/438.asp>.
76. E. Swedenborg, *Philosophiae Retiocinantis de Infinito et Cause Creationis, 1734.*
77. I. Kant, *General History of Nature and Theory of the Heavens, 1755.*
78. P.S. Laplace, *Exposition of the System of the World, 1796.*
79. H. Reeves, "The Origin of the Solar System," in S.F. Dermott, editor, *The Origin of the Solar System* (New York: John Wiley & Sons, 1978), p. 9.

the *law of conservation of angular momentum*. Angular momentum = mass x velocity x distance from the center of mass, and always stays constant in an isolated system. When the skaters pull their arms in, the distance from the center decreases, so they spin faster or else angular momentum would not stay constant. In the formation of our sun from a nebula in space, the same effect would have occurred as the gases allegedly contracted into the center to form the sun. This would have caused the sun to spin very rapidly. Actually, our sun spins very slowly, while the planets move very rapidly around the sun. In fact, although the sun has over 99 percent of the mass of the solar system, it has only 2 percent of the angular momentum. This pattern is directly opposite to the pattern predicted for the nebular hypothesis. Evolutionists have tried to solve this problem, but a well-known solar system scientist, Dr. Stuart Ross Taylor, has said in a recent book, "The ultimate origin of the solar system's angular momentum remains obscure."[80]

The Sun

T-Tauri Phase

As the gas from the collapsing nebula would pull together into the planets, the young sun would pass through what is called the *T-Tauri phase*. In this phase, the sun would give off an intense solar wind, far more intense than at present. This solar wind would have driven excess gas and dust out of the still-forming solar system and thus there would no longer be enough of the light gases left to form Jupiter and the other three giant gas planets. This would leave these four gas planets smaller than we find them today.[81]

Faint Young Sun Paradox

The sun's known energy source should make the sun shine ever more brightly over time. But this means that if billions of years were true, the sun would have been much fainter in the past. However, there is no evidence that the sun was any fainter at any time in the earth's history. Astronomers call this the "faint young sun paradox," but it is no paradox at all if the sun is only as old as the Bible says — about 6,000 years.

The sun and other stars are now known to obtain their energy from a process called nuclear fusion, where small, extremely-fast–moving atomic nuclei join to form a larger one (the nucleus, plural nuclei, is the tiny positively charged part of the atom that has nearly all the mass). Some mass is lost and converted into a huge amount of energy as per Einstein's famous formula, $E = mc^2$. In the sun, 4 million tons of matter are converted into energy every second — this is huge, but negligible compared to the sun's enormous total mass of 1.99×10^{27} (1,990,000,000,000,000,000,000,000,000) tons.

---

80. S.R. Taylor, *Solar System Evolution: A New Perspective* (Cambridge, England; New York: Cambridge University Press, 1992), p. 53.

81. See W. Spencer, "Revelations in the Solar System," *Creation* 19(3):26–29 (June–August 1997); <www.answersingenesis.org/docs/214.asp>.

Most fusion in stars combines four hydrogen nuclei into one helium nucleus.[82] Thus, the sun is like a huge hydrogen bomb.[83] Fusion produces a vast number of ghostly and extremely low-mass particles called neutrinos,[84] which are now known to switch between "flavors" (types).[85]

A large heavy nucleus takes up much less room than four small nuclei, so there is a lot more mass in a given volume, i.e., greater density. So, as the sun "burns" hydrogen in the core, the core will contract. The higher temperature and pressure then make fusion easier, so the core will heat further. Therefore, the sun should become brighter as it ages.

Evolutionists and long-agers believe that life appeared on the earth about 3.8 billion years ago. But if that were true, the sun would be 25 percent brighter today than it was back then. This implies that the earth would have been frozen at an average temperature of 3°C. However, most paleontologists believe that, if anything, the earth was warmer in the past.[86]

The only way around this is to make *ad hoc* and unrealistic assumptions of a far greater greenhouse effect at that time than today.[87] This would require a concentration of CO_2 about 1,000 times PAL (present atmospheric level). However, analyses of acritarchs (eukaryotic algal microfossils) dated to 1.4 Ga, when the sun would have been only 88 percent as bright as today, provide evidence for only 10–200 times PAL. Still, the researchers optimistically hope that this would have compensated for the fainter sun.[88]

The evidence is consistent with the sun having the age that we would expect from a straightforward reading of the Bible. With a time scale of 6,000 years or so, there would have been no significant increase in energy output from the sun. It is a problem only for old-age ideas.

---

82. Four hydrogen atoms (mass = 1.008) convert to helium (mass 4.0039) losing 0.0281 atomic mass units (1 AMU = 1.66×10^{-27} kg), releasing 4.2×10^{-12} joules of energy.

83. Man-made hydrogen bombs use the heavy hydrogen isotopes deuterium and tritium, plus some lithium. The sun uses mainly ordinary hydrogen, which is much harder to fuse, which is a good thing because it means the sun burns steadily. Deuterium is a hard-to-form intermediate step and thus controls the fusion rate.

84. The complete fusion reaction is $4\ ^1H \longrightarrow\ ^4He + 2e^+ + 2\nu_e$, where e^+ is a positron or anti-electron, and ν_e is an electron-neutrino.

85. Before this neutrino oscillation was demonstrated, this was a huge problem for the fusion theory and thus for billions of years. Theoretical physicists taught that neutrinos had precisely zero rest-mass, which would make oscillation impossible. But in 2001, oscillation was detected, so the theorists were proved wrong. See R. Newton, "Missing Neutrinos Found! No Longer an 'Age' Indicator," *TJ* 16(3):123–125 (2002).

86. D. Faulkner, "The Young Faint Sun Paradox and the Age of the Solar System," *TJ* 15(2):3–4 (2001); <www.answersingenesis.org/faint_sun>.

87. Ross himself does so in "The Faint Sun Paradox," *Facts for Faith* 10 (2002).

88. A. Kaufman and S. Xiao, "High CO_2 Levels in the Proterozoic Atmosphere Estimated from Analyses of Individual Microfossils," *Nature* 425(6955):279–282 (September 16, 2003); comment by S.J. Mojzsis, "Probing Early Atmospheres," same issue, p. 249–251.

Evolutionists assume that the sun's core has 4.5 billion years worth of helium, but this has not been directly observed. In any case, even if there was a large amount of helium, the record shows that the sun was never faint. Rather, if the core contained lots of helium it would be a design feature so that the sun would be hot enough. It may also be responsible for the sun's exceptional stability.[89] Actually, long-agers don't directly measure the age of the sun at all. Rather, they infer it from the radiometric dating of meteorites, and radiometric dating has its own problems, as shown in chapter 12.

Also, some argue for long ages on the basis that the calculated time for a photon to travel from the core to the surface (actually by absorption and reradiation) exceeds the biblical time scale. But this is explained if the main purpose of fusion is *stability* — producing enough energy to balance that lost from the surface, that is, the sun was created in a *steady state condition*, with the outward pressure generated by fusion matching the inward gravitational pressure, maintaining a constant temperature profile.[90] This means that it could immediately fulfill its function as the "greater light," and keep shining at a constant rate. It is no different from believing that God created Adam with oxygen in his bloodstream in his extremities, even though it now takes some time for oxygen to diffuse through the alveoli in the lungs, then be transported by the blood.

Sun's Axial Tilt

If the sun were formed by a collapsing nebula, then it should be spinning in the same plane as the planets. However, its axis is tilted 7.167° away from the ecliptic. But the ecliptic is defined by Earth's orbit. A better comparison would be Jupiter's orbital plane, since that has most of the mass and angular momentum of the solar system. Jupiter's orbital inclination is 1.308° from the ecliptic, so this leaves almost 6° difference. The planets' tilts are usually explained by collisions, but this would not apply to the sun.[91]

Rocky Planets in General

Evolutionary astronomers believe:

> Astronomers agree that the planets and moons of our solar system formed in a swirling disc of dust and gas around the sun. In the outer regions, cold, slushy gases condensed into the giants Jupiter, Saturn, Uranus, and Neptune. And in the inner regions, dusty particles melted and stuck together, forming hot blobs of rock that cooled and merged to make Mercury, Venus, Earth, and Mars.[92]

89. J. Sarfati, "The Sun: Our Special Star," *Creation* 22(1)27–30 (1999); <www.answersingenesis. org/sun>.
90. R. Newton, reply to R. Bernitt on the sun's energy source, *TJ* 17(1):64–65 (2003).
91. B. Worraker, *TJ* (in press).
92. H. Muir, "Earth Was a Freak," *New Scientist* 177(2388):24 (March 29, 2003).

But recent research shows that there was no reason for the rock to melt — what would heat it? If anything, as shown above, the sun would have been cooler than today, so only a small and very close planet like Mercury could conceivably become hot enough. Farther from the sun:

> While asteroid-sized rocks would have aggregated in the inner solar system, they would not have melted and clumped together to form planets. . . . the solid rocks would just zoom past each other or collide and recoil like snooker balls.

Evolutionary astronomers propose that a supernova within 50 light-years exploded and supplied the nebula with radioactive aluminium-26, which provided heat as it decayed. But the chances of a supernova exploding that close to a forming solar system are minute. So the astronomer Thomas Clarke, of the University of Central Florida in Orlando, thought that the chance of finding rocky extrasolar planets was very small. And once more, he illustrated his philosophical bias towards the cosmological principle:

> It's a bit depressing to think that earth-like planets are too special.[93]

Venus

The nebular hypothesis predicts that as the nebula spiraled inward, all the resulting planets would rotate in the same direction (*prograde*). But Venus rotates in the opposite direction, called *retrograde*. Evolutionists once tried to explain this away by proposing that Venus rotated prograde at first, but it had a bulge on which gravitational tidal forces on Earth could act and turn the rotation around. Aside from the weakness of tidal forces, which decrease with the *cube* of the distance, it is now known that Venus is even rounder than Earth so there is no bulge on which to act.

Venus's chemistry is also very different from Earth's. For example, the ratio of the isotopes of the inert gas argon (used to fill light bulbs), that is, ^{36}Ar to ^{40}Ar, is 300 times greater than on Earth. If the nebular hypothesis were correct, then it would mean a vastly different composition in the region of Venus, and such differences are implausible in a relatively small region of a nebula.

Another problem for evolutionary theories about the planets is their magnetic fields. As will be shown in chapter 11, Earth's magnetic field is a good example of design, and the field's decay (as well as the evidence for rapid magnetic field reversals) is excellent evidence for a young Earth. But no spacecraft has detected any magnetic field on Venus, and the sensitivity of the instruments places an upper limit on any magnetic field of 25,000 times weaker than Earth's.

Evolutionists believe that planetary magnetic fields are explained by self-sustaining dynamos, so they explain Venus's weak field by its much slower rotation (243 Earth days for one rotation). But Mercury also rotates slowly (58.82 days), yet its

93. H. Muir, "Earth Was a Freak," *New Scientist* 177(2388):24 (March 29, 2003).

field is about five times stronger than Venus's, while Mars rotates almost as fast as Earth (1.03 days), yet its field is less than 1/10,000 of Earth's.

However, the theory of the creationist physicist Dr. Russell Humphreys explains all the data.[94] He proposed that when all the planets' cores were formed, they started off with a magnetic field produced by a decaying electrical current. The smaller the core and the poorer its electrical conductivity, the faster the field would decay. It is thought that Venus has a smaller and less conductive core than Earth, so the field is now very weak, just as the Humphreys model suggests.

Venus provides yet another problem for billions-of-years beliefs: its surface, as shown from radar images from the Magellan satellite, seems very fresh. There are high mountains, including Mount Maxwell (11,000 m or 36,000 ft. above the mean surface level), rift valleys, including one 9,000 km (5,600 miles) long, shield volcanoes, steep slopes, large rocks, and smooth plains. There is no evidence for millions of years of erosion, although the thick atmosphere and extreme atmospheric temperature differences would be expected to whip up huge sand and dust storms.

There are also circular structures thought to be impact craters, but the mystery is that there are many fewer — only 935 — than predicted by evolutionary theories. They are also fairly uniformly distributed. So evolutionists propose that the whole surface was recycled due to volcanic and tectonic activity. They claim that the resurfacing ceased 800–300 million years ago, yet 84 percent of the craters show no sign of modification.[95] Rather, the evidence seems best explained by recent cratering episodes during creation week or the Flood, as proposed by creationist astronomers Dr. Danny Faulkner and Wayne Spencer.[96]

Saturn's Rings

Saturn's spectacular rings around its equator were first discovered by Galileo in 1610. However, it took till 1659 for Christiaan Huygens to work out their correct shape. The rings span a radius of more than 66,900 to ~480,000 km, which compares with a 60,268 km equatorial radius of Saturn itself (about 9.449 times Earth's).[97] They are only 200 meters thick, except the A-ring (~50 m) and the C-ring (~10 m). The rings are composed of particles, mainly of water ice, ranging from microns to meters in size.

The traditional uniformitarian belief is that Saturn's spectacular rings were formed when a body about 200 km across shattered. The following evidence indicates that it happened relatively recently:

94. D.R. Humphreys, "The Creation of Planetary Magnetic Fields," *CRSQ* 21(3):140–149 (1984); <www.creationresearch.org/crsq/articles/21/21_3/21_3.html>.

95. Face of Venus website: 3.0 Impact Craters, <www.eps.mcgill.ca/~bud/craters/venus_impact.html>, March 30, 2001.

96. See the exchange between Danny Faulkner and Wayne Spencer in *TJ* 14(1):46–49 (2000), for similarities and differences in their proposals, and the references to their papers therein.

97. "Saturnian Rings Fact Sheet," <http://nssdc.gsfc.nasa.gov/planetary/factsheet/satringfact.html>.

Now Renée Prangé of the Institute of Space Astrophysics in Orsay, France, and colleagues in the US, France, and Canada, have shown that the ring is losing water relatively rapidly. The water is disappearing so fast, the team believes, that it would all have gone already if the ring is more than about 30 million years old.[98]

These "very young"[99] (by uniformitarian standards) rings do not "prove" that the entire solar system is young. But they are just what we would expect to find in a biblical framework, and are explained by solar-system–wide catastrophism during the year of the Flood.[100]

Ice Giants

The planets Uranus and Neptune are called "Ice Giants" as opposed to the ordinary gas giants Jupiter and Saturn. Uranus and Neptune are very similar, and even have strong magnetic fields where the axis is off-center — and the strengths turned out to be in line with creationist predictions but totally different from evolutionary ones.[101] But there are significant differences, hard to explain if they formed from the same region of the nebula in the same way. For example, Uranus rotates on its side, while Neptune is a net *generator* of heat, unlike Uranus,[102] radiating twice as much energy as it receives from the sun.[103] It also has the strongest winds in the solar system, up to 2,200 km/h (1,300 mph). But the hardest problem of all is forming this pair in the first place:

> Pssst . . . astronomers who model the formation of the solar system have kept a dirty little secret: Uranus and Neptune don't exist. Or at least computer simulations have never explained how planets as big as the two gas giants could form so far from the sun. Bodies orbited so slowly in the outer parts of the solar system that the slow process of gravitational accretion would need more time than the age of the solar system to form bodies with 14.5 and 17.1 times the mass of Earth.[104]

---

98. J. Hecht, "Water 'Rains' on the Ringed Planet," *New Scientist* 152(2053):18 (October 26, 1996).
99. Ibid.
100. See the exchange between Danny Faulkner and Wayne Spencer in *TJ* 14(1):46–49 (2000), for similarities and differences in their proposals, and the references to their papers therein.
101. Dr. Humphreys had predicted field strengths of the order of 10^{24} J/T — *CRSQ* 27(1):15–17 (1990). See also his article, "Beyond Neptune: Voyager II Supports Creation," *Impact* 203 (May 1990); <http://www.icr.org/pubs/imp/imp-203.htm>. The fields of Uranus and Neptune are hugely off-centered (0.3 and 0.4 of the planets' radii) and at a large angle from the planets' spin axis (60° and 50°). This is a big puzzle for dynamo theorists, but explainable by a catastrophe which seems to have affected the whole solar system. See W. Spencer, "The Existence and Origin of Extrasolar Planets," *TJ* 15(1):17–25 (2001).
102. S. Psarris, "Uranus — The Strange Planet," *Creation* 24(3):38–40 (June–August 2002); J. Henry, "The Energy Balance of Uranus: Implications for Special Creation," *TJ* 15(3):85–91 (2001).
103. S. Psarris, "Neptune: Monument to Creation," *Creation* 25(1):22–24 (December 2002–February 2003).
104. R. Naeye, "Birth of Uranus and Neptune," *Astronomy* 28(4):30 (2000).

The Moon

Mystery of the Moon's Origin

It has long been a puzzle to evolutionists how the moon could have formed. They have come up with several theories, but they all have serious holes, as many evolutionists themselves admit. For example, the solar system theorist Stuart Ross Taylor said, "The best models of lunar origin are the testable ones, but the testable models for lunar origin are wrong."[105] Another astronomer, Irwin Shapiro, said, half-jokingly, that there were no good (naturalistic) explanations, so the best explanation is that the moon is an illusion![106]

One of the earliest theories comes from Charles Darwin's son, the astronomer George. He proposed the *fission theory* — that the earth spun so fast that a chunk broke off. But this theory is universally discarded today. The earth could never have spun fast enough to throw a moon into orbit, and the escaping moon would have been shattered while within the Roche limit. This is as close as a massive satellite can get to the body it's orbiting before shattering because of tidal forces (i.e., the result of different gravitational forces on different parts of the moon). For earth, this is 11,500 miles (18,400 km).

The currently fashionable idea is the *Giant Impact Hypothesis* (GIH), so naturally that's what Ross believes (see page 176). This proposes that the earth was hit by the glancing impact of another object, one the size of a planet. The earth absorbed most of the impactor's material, while the remaining debris was blasted into orbit to eventually coalesce into the moon. A related hypothesis, the *Impact-triggered Fission Hypothesis*, propounds that the moon formed from the debris of multiple impacts of smaller planetesimals rather than a single giant body. However, some leading researchers have questioned whether the popularity of impact hypotheses is due to their merits or a process of elimination of even weaker evolutionary models:

> This [GIH] has arisen not so much because of the merits of [its] theory as because of the apparent dynamical or geochemical short-comings of other theories. . . .[107]

Calculations show that to get enough material to form the moon, the impacting object would need to have been twice as massive as Mars. Then there is the unsolved problem of losing the excess angular momentum.[108] There is also some

---

105. S.R. Taylor, paraphrased by geophysicist Sean Solomon, at Kona, Hawaii, Conference on Lunar Origin, 1984; cited in Wm. K. Hartmann, *The History of Earth* (Broadway, NY: Workman Publishing Co. Inc., 1991), p. 44.

106. I. Shapiro, in a university astronomy class about 20 years ago, cited by J.J. Lissauer, "It's Not Easy to Make the Moon," *Nature* 389(6649):327–328.

107. A. Ruzicka, G.A. Snyder, and L.A. Taylor, "Giant Impact and Fission Hypotheses for the Origin of the Moon: A Critical Review of Some Geochemical Evidence," *International Geology Review* 40:851–864, 1998.

108. Shigeru Ida et al., "Lunar Accretion from an Impact Generated Disk," *Nature* 389(6649):353–357 (September 25, 1997).

skepticism about whether the computer modeling that's supposed to support this theory is valid:

> However, Jay Melosh (University of Arizona) argued that we do not know the equations of state well enough to calculate the energy of such an impact and that we may have grossly underestimated them, to the point that specific dynamic models are currently unjustified.[109]

Furthermore, while geochemistry is supposed to provide support for the GIH, researchers analyzed the amounts of key elements Ni, Co, Cr, V, and Mn in the moon and meteorites. They concluded:

> . . . that there is no strong geochemical support for either the Giant Impact or Impact-triggered Fission hypotheses.[110]

Ross, despite accepting the GIH (of which there is no hint in Scripture) cheerfully, actually manages to garble the idea. He claims that it was a "nearly head-on hit" [GQ:30]. But this is wrong, according to the model — a head-on collision is one where the paths of the centers of mass of both bodies intersect, that is, the direction of impact is perpendicular to the surface. However, as mentioned above, the impact in the GIH was a *glancing* one. Only this has any hope of ejecting enough material with the proper trajectory to form the moon. So one must wonder whether he didn't really understand the GIH, or merely didn't understand the basic mechanics term "head-on."

Transient Lunar Phenomena

Because the moon has a mass of only 0.0123 times earth's, any heat should have dissipated; therefore, any geological activity should have ceased. One astronomy text says:

> There is no evidence that the interior of the moon contains significant heat. . . . The moon is now a cold, geologically inactive world.[111]

In fact, based on models of the solar system's formation and lunar rock samples, lunar geological activity is claimed to have ceased 3 billion years ago.

However, there are a number of observations of lunar surface changes that must be due to internal activity, not outside meteorite impacts. These are called "transient lunar phenomena" (TLPs). Since people first started observing the moon through telescopes in the 1600s, nearly 1,500 TLPs have been reported and catalogued by

---

109. A.N. Halliday and M.J. Drake, "Colliding Theories," *Science* 283:1861–1863 (1999).

110. A. Ruzicka, G.A. Snyder, and L.A. Taylor, "Giant Impact and Fission Hypotheses for the Origin of the Moon: A Critical Review of Some Geochemical Evidence," *International Geology Review* 40:851–864 (1998).

111. M. Seeds, *Foundations of Astronomy* (Albany, NY: Wadsworth, 1997), p. 453.

NASA.[112] Astronomer William Herschel reported several apparent volcanic eruptions between 1783 and 1787.[113]

TLPs indicate that the moon is still geologically active, and this implies that the moon has not had time for its interior to cool. TLPs are also consistent with the *observed* high heat flow measurements from the Apollo missions. Both these observations are consistent with the biblical timescale.[114]

Also, Peter Schultz, of Brown University in Rhode Island, argues that the fresh surface of Ina, a 25-km-across region in the moon's northern hemisphere, indicates that the surface formed only a few million years ago, far younger than the alleged billions of years interpreted from radiometric "dating." Further, according to a *New Scientist* article, he argues that Ina may still have "vents funneling volcanic gas and material up to the surface," and says, "These could be the moon's last gasps." The article's first sentence was, "Far from being a dead lump of rock, the moon may still be alive."[115]

Lunar "Ghost" Craters

A "ghost crater" is "the bare hint which remains of a lunar feature that has been practically destroyed by some later action."[116] These are not well known, but are a huge problem for evolutionary theories of lunar cratering.

When we observe the moon, we notice light and dark regions. The light ones are the highlands, made of the low-density, light-colored granite rocks, and are heavily cratered. The dark regions are the *maria* (singular, *mare*), the Latin word for "seas," the name given by Galileo. The dark color is caused by the higher-density volcanic rock basalt, and therefore they are thought to be lava flows.

Craters are thought to have formed from leftovers in the accretion process that formed the planets and moons. The impact rate would have dropped off exponentially as this material was used up. This intense bombardment would have left the highlands highly cratered, but on the *maria*, lava covered up many of the craters. Ghost craters result from incomplete coverage. The evolutionary theory of crater bombardment is that the impacts happened over the course of half a billion years and were followed by the last huge lava flows that formed the *maria*.

But why didn't the lava flow all over the moon? Astronomers believe that the roughly circular shape of the *maria* points to very large impacts forming "impact basins." These had so much energy that they caused lava to erupt, either by melting the rock or by fracturing the crust deeply enough to let magma escape from the interior.

112. *NASA Technical Report R-277*, <www.mufor.org/tlp/lunar.html>, July 1968, catalogues 579 TLPs, and a revision now totals 1,468 TLPs.
113. W. Lea, *Ranger to the Moon* (NY: The New American Library, 1965), p. 71.
114. D. DeYoung, "Transient Lunar Phenomena: A Permanent Problem for Evolutionary Models of Moon Formation," *TJ* 17(1):5–6 (2003).
115. E. Samuel, "Dying Gasps of a Tempestuous Moon," *New Scientist* 170(2294):13, June 9, 2001.
116. D. Alter, *Pictorial Guide to the Moon*, 3rd ed. (New York, NY: Thomas Y. Crowell Company, 1973).

They would also have obliterated any previous lesser craters. Therefore, any ghost craters must have formed after the impact, but before the lava flowed over them.

The problem for the long-agers is: astronomers believe that the impact clearly stimulated the lava to flow. But this means there can't be a time gap of 500 million years between the basin-causing impact and the lava flow, but surely much less than a year. So this is a very narrow window of time for the impacts that formed the ghost craters. But after the lava had hardened, there were comparatively few impacts.

This points to an intense bombardment, thousands of times heavier than evolutionists thought, but over a very short time span. Astronomer Dr. Danny Faulkner proposes that the impact basins were formed by a narrow, intense swarm of meteoroids, traveling on parallel paths, that hit the moon during the year of the Flood on earth. Actually, since 11 of the 12 maria are in one quadrant, it seems that the major impacts occurred before the moon had even moved far enough in one orbit (month) to show a different face to the swarm. This contrasts with the smaller craters on the highlands which probably occurred after the Fall or possibly during creation week.[117]

Extrasolar Planets

In the last few years there have been many claims of extrasolar planets. However, even a proponent of extrasolar planets, Paul Kalas, has pointed out that there are many examples of "crying wolf" and wishful thinking.[118] After Kalas wrote, an alleged Jupiter-sized extrasolar planet orbiting the star HD192262 turned out to be a giant sunspot on the star's surface.[119] There is also the evolutionary bias related to the cosmological principle. Since the earth is nothing special, then because a solar system formed here, such must have formed around other stars, too.

However, some creationists believe that there is very strong evidence for some extrasolar planets.[120] There is nothing in the Bible to rule them out, and they would be among the heavenly objects created on day 4. But far from providing support for evolutionary hopes that solar systems form readily, they present problems of their own.

For example, the best-established claims are of gas giants bigger than Jupiter but orbiting their star closer than Mercury does our sun. At this distance, ice would evaporate, whereas it is thought that ice is essential in order for a growing planetoid to become massive enough to attract gas. And, as above, the T-Tauri phase is a problem even for the alleged evolutionary formation of the huge planets in our own system many times farther from the sun than Earth, so how much more would it be a problem for these alleged extrasolar gas giants? So speculative theories are proposed in which giant planets migrate millions of miles inward after formation.

Also, the cosmological principle not only drives evolutionists to look for other stellar systems, but predicts that they would resemble ours since we are nothing

---

117. D. Faulkner, "A Biblically-based Cratering Theory," *TJ* 13(1):100–104 (1999).
118. P. Kalas, "Dusty Disks and Planet Mania," *Science* 281(5374):182–183, July 10, 1998.
119. *New Scientist* 175(2360):24, September 14, 2002.
120. W. Spencer, "The Existence and Origin of Extrasolar Planets," *TJ* 15(1):17–25, 2001.

special in their view. But nearly all the systems we have discovered so far are very different from our own. This flies in the face of the cosmological principle and came as quite a surprise to the evolutionists. Stellar systems are an example of God's creativity.[121]

Big Bang "Apologetics"

The big bang has become a huge plank in the apologetics of Ross and others. However, the perceived apologetic usefulness of an idea should never override scriptural considerations. In any case, the main apologetic argument that incorporates the big bang actually predates it by centuries, and its leading proponents use other evidence as well. So I have no objection to Ross using the argument per se (especially as I have also used it),[122] just to the way he connects the big bang to it. Therefore, I will show how it can be defended without the big bang, which undercuts his claim about how anti–big-bangers are undermining allegedly vital apologetics.

The *Kalām* Cosmological Argument

This is a very important argument, and Christians should understand it. It undercuts a common atheistic objection, "If God created the universe, then who created God?" It goes back to the church theologian Bonaventure (1221–1274),[123] and was also advocated by medieval Arabic philosophers. The word *kalām* is the Arabic word for "speech," but its broader semantic range includes "philosophical theism" or "natural theology." The *kalām* argument's most prominent modern defender is the philosopher and apologist Dr. William Lane Craig.[124] The logical argument is formulated as follows:

1. Everything **which has a beginning** has a cause.[125]
2. The universe has a beginning.
3. ∴ the universe has a cause.

The words in bold are important, showing that the critic has misread the Christian claim. It is not everything that has a cause, but only everything which begins to exist. The universe requires a cause because it had a beginning, as will be shown below. God, unlike the universe, had no beginning, so doesn't need a cause. In addition, Einstein's general relativity, which has much experimental support, shows that time is linked to

121. R. Newton, "New Planet Challenges Evolutionary Models," *TJ* 17(3):9 (2003); <www.answers-ingenesis.org/newplanet>.

122. J. Sarfati, "If God Created the Universe, Then Who Created God?" *TJ* 12(1):20–22 (1998); <www.answersingenesis.org/docs/3791.asp>.

123. F.C. Copleston, *A History of Medieval Philosophy* (Garden City, NY: Image Books, 1993), chapter 11. This was the second volume of a nine-part series on the history of philosophy by a Jesuit priest and philosopher, who also defended the existence of God in a famous BBC radio debate against agnostic philosopher Bertrand Russell in 1948.

124. W.L. Craig, *The Kalām Cosmological Argument* (New York: Barnes & Noble, 1979).

125. Actually, the word "cause" has several different meanings in philosophy. But in this section, I am referring to the *efficient cause*, the chief agent causing something to be made.

matter and space. So time itself would have begun along with matter and space, an insight first pointed out by Augustine. Since God, by definition, is the Creator of the whole universe, He is the Creator of time. Therefore, He is not limited by the time dimension He created, so has no beginning in time — God is "the high and lofty One that inhabits eternity" (Isa. 57:15). Therefore, He doesn't have a cause.

Cause and Effect

It is a metaphysical principle that things which begin have a cause, but it is also self-evident — no-one really denies it in his heart. Even the Scottish antitheistic philosopher David Hume admitted that it was crazy to deny it even though it could not be demonstrated:

> But allow me to tell you that I never asserted so absurd a Proposition as that anything might arise without a cause: I only maintain'd, that our Certainty of the Falsehood of that Proposition proceeded neither from Intuition nor Demonstration; but from another Source.[126]

All science and history would collapse if this law of cause and effect were denied. So would all law enforcement, if the police didn't think they needed to find a cause for a stabbed body or a burgled house. Also, the universe cannot be self-caused — nothing can create itself, because until it exists, it is not in a position to cause itself.

Evidence 1: Impossibility of an Infinite Series of Concrete Events

Bonaventure argued that the universe must have begun in time. Otherwise, there would exist an actual infinite set of events in time — and, while an infinite set is possible mathematically, an infinite set of *concrete* things, as opposed to abstractions such as numbers, makes no sense (except the actual things an omniscient being knows). Also, while it is possible to break up any time interval into an infinite number of infinitesimally small time units (as in the famous Zeno Paradox), an infinity of concrete time units would be impossible.[127]

Also, it would be impossible to traverse an actual infinite set, so the universe could not be eternal. Otherwise, one could never reach the present moment. For no matter how many finite time intervals pass, one will never pass an infinite set of moments. However, an eternal universe entails an infinite set of moments in the past. Therefore, the present moment would never have arrived, so one could not possibly reach it. But as we know, we have reached the present moment; the series of time intervals cannot have been infinite, but must have had a beginning.[128]

Evidence 2: The Laws of Thermodynamics

Modern science has provided strong support to Bonaventure's argument, which doesn't depend on the big bang. These are the *laws of thermodynamics,* the most fundamental laws of the physical sciences.

---

126. D. Hume, letter to John Stuart, 1754.
127. F.C. Copleston, *A History of Medieval Philosophy* (Garden City, NY: Image Books, 1993).
128. Ibid.

- 1st law: The **total** amount of mass-energy in the universe is **constant**.

- 2nd law: The amount of energy **available for work** is running out, or *entropy* is increasing to a maximum.

If the total amount of mass-energy is limited, and the amount of usable energy is decreasing, then the universe cannot have existed forever; otherwise, it would already have exhausted all usable energy — the "heat death" of the universe. For example, all radioactive atoms would have decayed, every part of the universe would be the same temperature, and no further work would be possible. So the obvious corollary is that the universe began a finite time ago with a lot of usable energy, and is now running down.

Other Evidence: Infeasibility of Many Alternatives

Ross spends much time demolishing ideas such as eternal oscillation, hesitation, and steady state, and I have no quarrel with this.

Objections

From reading Ross, one would think that the big bang cosmologists are all Christians, or at least theists. Craig, too, wrote:

> When I was at the 16th World Congress on Philosophy in Düsseldorf in 1978, I found that the only scientists who opposed the big-bang theory were Marxists from communist nations.[129]

This may well be true, and indeed the steady state theory was motivated by antitheistic bias. But Craig's implication that the big bang is somehow theistic fails miserably — by the same reasoning, one could argue that Darwinism must be theistic because the only opposition at an evolution conference came from the Stalinist biologists led by Lysenko, the neo-Lamarckian! Indeed, most big bang theorists are likewise atheists, although some are agnostic or possibly pantheistic.

Denial of Cause and Effect

Most big bang theorists do not postulate God as any cause for the universe's beginning. For example, Alan Guth, the inventor of the inflationary model, has stated:

> In the context of inflationary cosmology, it is fair to say that the universe is the ultimate free lunch.[130]

In *Scientific American*, Guth and another leading big bang cosmologist, Paul Steinhardt, wrote:

> From a historical point of view probably the most revolutionary aspect of the inflationary model is the notion that all the matter and energy in the observable universe may have emerged from almost nothing. . . . The

129. W.L. Craig, *Apologetics: an Introduction* (Chicago, IL: Moody Press, 1984), p. 91.
130. A.H. Guth, *The Inflationary Universe* (Reading, MA: Addison-Wesley, 1997).

inflationary model of the universe provides a possible mechanism by which the observed universe could have evolved from an infinitesimal region. It is then tempting to go one step further and speculate that the entire universe evolved from literally nothing.[131]

A *Discover* article, appropriately titled "Guth's Grand Guess," summarized his views as:

> The universe burst into something from absolutely nothing — zero, nada. And as it got bigger, it became filled with even more stuff that came from absolutely nowhere. How is that possible? Ask Alan Guth. His theory of inflation helps explain everything.[132]

The most common dodge is to explain the universe as a result of quantum fluctuations, claiming that quantum mechanics violates this cause/effect principle and can produce something from nothing. For instance, Paul Davies writes:

> . . . spacetime could appear out of nothingness as a result of a quantum transition. . . . Particles can appear out of nowhere without specific causation . . . the world of quantum mechanics routinely produces something out of nothing.[133]

But this is a gross misapplication of quantum mechanics. I have plenty of theoretical and practical experience at quantum mechanics (QM) from my doctoral thesis work.[134] Quantum mechanics never produces something out of nothing. All this is a smokescreen for nothing but a naturalistic "miracle," but lacking a sufficient cause for any such miracle. Davies himself admitted on the previous page that his scenario "should not be taken too seriously."

Theories that the universe is a quantum fluctuation must presuppose that there was something to fluctuate — their "quantum vacuum" is a lot of matter-antimatter potential — not "nothing." For example, Raman spectroscopy is a QM phenomenon, but from the wavenumber and intensity of the spectral bands, we can work out the masses of the atoms and force constants of the bonds causing the bands. To help the atheist position that the universe came into existence without a cause, one would need to find Raman bands appearing without being caused by transitions in vibrational quantum states, or alpha particles appearing without pre-existing nuclei, etc. If QM was as acausal as some people think, then we should not assume that these phenomena have a cause. Then I may as well burn my Ph.D. thesis, and all the spectroscopy journals should quit, as should any nuclear physics research.

---

131. A. Guth and P. Steinhardt, "The Inflationary Universe," *Scientific American,* 250(5):128 (May 1984).
132. "Guth's Grand Guess," *Discover* (April 2002).
133. P. Davies, *God and the New Physics* (New York: Simon & Schuster, 1983), p. 215.
134. J. Sarfati, *A Spectroscopic Study of some Chalcogenide Ring and Cage Molecules,* Ph.D. Thesis, Victoria University of Wellington (New Zealand), 1994.

Also, if there is no cause, there is no explanation as to why *this particular universe* appeared at a *particular time,* nor why it was a universe and not, say, a banana or cat which appeared. This universe can't have any properties to explain its preferential coming into existence, because it wouldn't have *any* properties until it actually came into existence.

Is Creation by God Rational?

A last, desperate tactic by skeptics to avoid a theistic conclusion from the evidence for the universe's beginning is to assert that creation in time is incoherent. Davies correctly points out that time itself began with the beginning of the universe, which is true for biblical creation and is also what big-bangers believe. Therefore, it is meaningless to talk about what happened "before" the universe began. But then he makes an unwarranted metaphysical claim that causes must precede their effects. So, if nothing happened "before" the universe began, then (according to Davies) it is meaningless to discuss the cause of the universe's beginning.

But Craig, in a useful critique of Davies,[135] pointed out that Davies is deficient in philosophical knowledge. First, since the *Kalām* cosmological argument on page 179 is logically valid, if the premises are accepted as true, the conclusion (the universe has a cause) *must* be true. Therefore, it is futile to argue against it.

Second, his argument fails to demonstrate any problem with the conclusion, anyway, because philosophers have long discussed the notion of *simultaneous causation.* Kant gave the example of a weight resting on a cushion simultaneously causing a depression in it. Many philosophers actually argue that *all* causation is simultaneous on a subatomic level! Craig argues that the first moment of time is the moment of God's creative act and of creation's simultaneous coming to be.

Assessment

The *Kalām* argument can withstand all the arguments thrown against it, but does not need the big bang at all. It was proposed well before the big bang, and the evidence from the logic about infinity and the science of thermodynamics is strong enough. It can survive long after the big bang is discredited. However, even if the *Kalām* argument required the big bang to survive, Christianity does not require the *Kalām* argument to survive! Therefore, there is no excuse to twist Scripture to support the big bang.

Multi-dimensional Deity?

String Theory in the Bible?

In Ross's book *Beyond the Cosmos,*[136] he uses a very current idea called string theory to explain a number of theological problems. This posits that there are six dimensions of space in addition to the normal three dimensions. We can't observe these extra six dimensions today — *the extra dimensions are now "rolled up" or compressed into loops tinier than a proton* — but they supposedly affect the interaction

135. W.L. Craig, "God, Creation and Mr. Davies," *Brit. J. Phil. Sci.* 37:163–175 (1986).

of elementary particles and the structure of the universe. The theory was devised to explain some features of the universe. But this is speculative and controversial, and lacks experimental support. And the recent measurement of the speed of gravity severely limits these alleged extra dimensions:

> Our result . . . restricts how many extra dimensions there may be, and their size. The more compact these extra dimensions, the less able gravity is to take a short cut through them, and the closer the speed of gravity must be to the speed of light.[137]

In fact, the measurement supported Einstein's prediction that gravity travels at exactly the speed of light (c), within the experimental uncertainty (speed of gravity = 1.06±0.21c).[138] But Ross makes theological pronouncements based on the alleged "fact" of these extra dimensions. In particular, Ross proclaims that God must work in these. He further argues that there must be one or more extra time dimensions in which God works, hence there are at least 11 dimensions in total at God's disposal. This extra-dimensionality becomes the thesis of *Beyond the Cosmos*. Indeed, Ross claims that these dimensions are found in the Bible.

Although Ross proclaims that his work is effective apologetics, unbelievers are more likely to be bemused. For example, the atheist Kenneth Nahigian wrote about attending one of Ross's lectures, and he claimed that Ross said, "The Bible teaches that God moves in six dimensions."

Nahigian commented:

> My curiosity is killing me. Where?
> But of course no theologian or Bible scholar said such a thing until String Theory came along. It would have astonished Aquinas! And if String Theory had postulated fifteen dimensions, I suspect somehow Dr. Ross would have found verses proving God moves in eleven.
> Theological retrofitting, it's called.[139]

But Ross puts string theory to other uses. Since God is working in extra dimensions, and especially the extra time dimension, God has an infinite amount of time during each instant to accomplish His many tasks. This supposedly enables God to hear the prayers of millions of believers simultaneously and for Jesus to have suffered for each person individually during His crucifixion. Ross also claims that this extra-dimensionality explains other difficult topics such as the Trinity, omnipresence, and predestination.

---

136. See also D.R. Faulkner, book review of *Beyond the Cosmos*, by Hugh Ross, *CRSQ* 34:242–243 (1988).

137. E. Fomalont, "How Fast Is Gravity?" *New Scientist* 177(2377):23–35.

138. Ibid.

139. K. Nahigian, "Impressions: An Evening with Dr. Hugh Ross," reports of the *National Center for Science Education* 17(1):27–29 (January/February 1997).

First, it is folly to base theology on such a speculative theory. Second, it is highly presumptuous to suggest that only in the latter 20th century have we learned enough to finally grasp some of the theological issues raised and supposedly answered by Ross. So much for "general revelation" if most of the church could not answer these problems because they had no idea about string theory.

Ross argues that Augustine erred in claiming that God operates *outside* of space and time. Of course, most of the Church agreed with Augustine, and this seems perfectly adequate to explain the "problems" Ross thinks he's solving for the first time. Instead, Ross insists that God must operate *within* space and time, which necessitates the additional dimensions. But this implies that God is somehow limited by space and time, which Augustine taught were created dimensions (see below). But God is NOT so limited.

The philosopher/apologist William Lane Craig has severely criticized Ross's teachings on this. This criticism is even more significant because Craig is a self-proclaimed Ross supporter (Craig even calls Ross *"evangelicalism's most important scientific apologist,"* which, as shown throughout my book, does not reflect well on Craig's own scientific competence):

> . . . I have been mystified by evangelicals' apparently uncritical acquiescence to some of the positions advocated in this book [BtC].
> . . . I find his attempt to construe God as existing in hyperdimensions of time and space and to interpret Christian doctrines in that light to be both philosophically and theologically unacceptable.[140]

Good Applications of Extra-dimensional Analysis

There is no harm in applications of mathematics to apologetics, but dogmatism is out of place. Analogies are just that! However, here are two examples of helpful analogies. And they were invented by young-earth creationists, refuting any idea that an old earth is necessary for this sort of apologetics (or any other sort, for that matter).

Augustine and the Tower

Augustine taught the idea that space and time are created entities, so God is not subject to them. Augustine presented the analogy of a person in a tower overlooking a curvy path on which other people are walking. The people on the path can't see too far ahead of them, but the person on the tower can, so knows exactly what obstacles the people are going to encounter. The path represents time, and we can't see the future. But the person in the tower represents God, who is outside of time and can thus see the whole "path" or time-line, as it exists to Him. In a sense, that is a "good" extra-dimensional analogy.

---

140. W.L. Craig, "Hugh Ross's Extra-dimensional Deity: A Review Article," *JETS* 42(2):293–304 (1999); quotes on p. 193, 304; <www.ldolphin.org/craig/index.html>.

Creationists and Flatland

Another analogy has been used by creationists such as the British triple-doctorate Dr. A.E. Wilder-Smith (1915–1985).[141] He borrowed from the novel *Flatland*,[142] where a three-dimensional "creature" (a sphere) came across a world where everything was confined to only two dimensions, including some intelligent "creatures" such as a square. So the sphere could appear and disappear from locked rooms, and even touch the square on his inside.

Wilder-Smith posited that Jesus might have had access to another spatial dimension after His resurrection. Therefore, He, like the sphere, could, at will, appear in, and disappear from, locked rooms.[143]

ALTERNATIVE COSMOLOGIES TO THE BIG BANG

Secular Cosmologies

As pointed out on page 153, the late Sir Fred Hoyle was a life-long opponent of the big bang. He proposed the quasi-steady-state-creation (QSSC) model.[144] But his is not the only alternative the secularists have proposed.

Ekpyrotic Model

Even within the big-bang paradigm, another totally non-theistic alternative to the inflationary model, called the ekpyrotic theory, has recently been proposed.[145]

This comes from the Greek word *ekpyrosis*, meaning "conflagration" (disastrous fire or conflict). It posits that our current universe is a four-dimensional membrane ("brane") embedded in a five-dimensional "bulk" space, and is analogous to a sheet of paper in ordinary three-dimensional space. The trigger for the universe's expansion was another brane's colliding with ours, releasing energy and heat.

Its proponents admit, "Our proposal is based on unproven ideas in string theory and is brand new."[146] But they hope to solve the so-far intractable difficulties of standard big-bang theory, including the horizon problem (see page 157) and the lack of observed monopoles, which the standard model predicts in abundance.

---

141. A.E. Wilder-Smith, *The Scientific Alternative to Neo-Darwinian Evolutionary Theory* (Costa Mesa, CA: Word for Today Publishers, 1987), p. 159–191.

142. E. Abbot, *Flatland: A Romance of Many Dimensions*, 1884: <www.geom.uiuc.edu/~banchoff/Flatland/>.

143. R. Grigg, "The Gospel in Time and Space," *Creation* 21(2):50–53 (March–May 1999).

144. F. Hoyle, G. Burbidge, and J.V. Narlikar, *A Different Approach to Cosmology* (UK: Cambridge University Press, 2000).

145. J. Khouri, B.A. Ovrut, P.J. Steinhardt, and N. Turok, "The Ekpyrotic Universe: Colliding Branes and the Origin of the Hot Big Bang," *Physical Review* D64:123522 (2001); <xxx.lanl.gov/PS_cache/hep-th/pdf/0103/0103239.pdf>.

  P. Steinhardt, N. Turok, "A Cyclic Model of the Universe," *Science* 296(5572):1436–1439 (2002).

146. " 'Brane-Storm' Challenges Part of Big Bang Theory," <www.space.com/scienceastronomy/astronomy/bigbang_alternative_010413-3.html>, February 28, 2003.

Multiverse: Parallel Universes

This "multiverse" idea proposes that our universe is not the only one, but that space is filled with an infinite number of "parallel universes." This is popular in science fiction, and now a number of astronomers are seriously promoting this idea. For example, Sir Martin Rees, who holds the honorary title of Astronomer Royal, is a strong advocate of multiverse cosmology,[147] and more recently Dr. Max Tegmard's article on parallel universes was the cover story in *Scientific American*. Tegmark explains the idea:

> Is there a copy of you reading this article? A person who is not you but who lives on a planet called Earth, with misty mountains, fertile fields and sprawling cities, in a solar system with eight other planets? The life of this person has been identical to yours in every respect. But perhaps he or she now decides to put down this article without finishing it, while you read on.
>
> The idea of such an alter ego seems strange and implausible, but it looks as if we will just have to live with it, because it is supported by astronomical observations. The simplest and most popular cosmological model today predicts that you have a twin in a galaxy about 10 to the 10^{28} meters from here. This distance is so large that it is beyond astronomical, but that does not make your doppelgänger any less real.[148]

The number 10 to the 10^{28} is one followed by 10^{28} zeros. To illustrate how huge this number is, even to write it down in paper and ink would require a pile of paperback books over 50 light-years high! The huge number comes from an assumption of an infinite number of universes, each able to hold about 10^{118} protons. Since a proton may or may not be present, there are 2 to the 10^{118} possible quantum states. So if there were an infinite number of universes, there could only be at most this number before they started repeating identically. Tegmark argues that a universe with someone exactly like us would be a lot closer than this maximum distance.

In any case, universes beyond our own are not observable even in principle, therefore they are not scientific, by most definitions. However, Tegmark confidently proclaims that they are genuine, and that there are several levels of these multiverses, but appears oblivious to his own assumptions:

> Although we cannot interact with other Level II parallel universes, cosmologists can infer their presence indirectly, because their existence can account for unexplained coincidences in our universe. To give an analogy, suppose you check into a hotel, are assigned room 1967 and note that this is the year you were born. What a coincidence, you say. After a moment of reflection, however, you conclude that this is not so surprising after all.

147. M. Rees, "Exploring Our Universe and Others," *Scientific American* 281(6):44–49 (December 1999).

148. M. Tegmark, "Parallel Universes: Not Just a Staple of Science Fiction, Other Universes Are a Direct Implication of Cosmological Observations," *Scientific American* 288(5):30–41 (May 2003).

The hotel has hundreds of rooms, and you would not have been having these thoughts in the first place if you had been assigned one with a number that meant nothing to you. The lesson is that even if you knew nothing about hotels, you could infer the existence of other hotel rooms to explain the coincidence.

As a more pertinent example, consider the mass of the sun. The mass of a star determines its luminosity, and using basic physics, one can compute that life as we know it on Earth is possible only if the sun's mass falls into the narrow range between 1.6×10^{30} and 2.4×10^{30} kilograms. Otherwise Earth's climate would be colder than that of present-day Mars or hotter than that of present-day Venus. The measured solar mass is 2.0×10^{30} kilograms. At first glance, this apparent coincidence of the habitable and observed mass values appears to be a wild stroke of luck. Stellar masses run from 10^{29} to 10^{32} kilograms, so if the sun acquired its mass at random, it had only a small chance of falling into the habitable range. But just as in the hotel example, one can explain this apparent coincidence by postulating an ensemble (in this case, a number of planetary systems) and a selection effect (the fact that we must find ourselves living on a habitable planet). Such observer-related selection effects are referred to as "anthropic," and although the "A-word" is notorious for triggering controversy, physicists broadly agree that these selection effects cannot be neglected when testing fundamental theories.

What applies to hotel rooms and planetary systems applies to parallel universes. Most, if not all, of the attributes set by symmetry breaking appear to be fine-tuned. Changing their values by modest amounts would have resulted in a qualitatively different universe — one in which we probably would not exist. If protons were 0.2 percent heavier, they could decay into neutrons, destabilizing atoms. If the electromagnetic force were 4 percent weaker, there would be no hydrogen and no normal stars. If the weak interaction were much weaker, hydrogen would not exist; if it were much stronger, supernovae would fail to seed interstellar space with heavy elements. If the cosmological constant were much larger, the universe would have blown itself apart before galaxies could form.

Although the degree of fine-tuning is still debated, these examples suggest the existence of parallel universes with other values of the physical constants [see footnote 147]. The Level II multiverse theory predicts that physicists will never be able to determine the values of these constants from first principles. They will merely compute probability distributions for what they should expect to find, taking selection effects into account. The result should be as generic as is consistent with our existence.

It's notable that there is another possible explanation for both the hotel room and fine-tuning of the universe — they are the result of *intelligence*. For example, if I were the hotel guest, I could assume that the hotel manager had perhaps found out the year of my birth and deliberately assigned that room to me. Similarly with the fine-tuning — this is precisely what we would expect if the universe had been intelligently created so that life could exist in it.

Tegmark has made a *philosophical* decision, not a scientific one, to exclude this option *a priori*, and then declare that parallel universes are virtually a proven fact. It's ironic that many materialists exclude God as an explanation for the complexity of the universe because He cannot be observed by science; but they are happy to postulate the existence of other universes which are also unobservable, even in principle.

This demonstrates that the exclusion of a designer has nothing to do with any criteria for what counts as "science," but is really the result of materialistic *presuppositions*. So on the grounds of "science," there is really no difference. But a multiverse explanation has no hope of improving the amount of knowledge about them, while when it comes to God, we have another means to obtain knowledge apart from scientific observation — *revelation*.

On a pragmatic level, the design explanation makes more sense in another way. Consider if we found a pattern of markings on a beach which spelled your name. Naturally you would conclude that an intelligence had written it. This is more plausible than thinking that wind and wave erosion eroded that pattern by chance, *even though there is a definite but extremely tiny probability of this happening*.

But under Tegmark's multiverse reasoning, there are an infinite number of parallel universes containing every possible quantum state, "In infinite space, even the most unlikely events must take place somewhere."[149] So if a person had an *a priori* bias that no one could have written your name, he could argue that we just happen to be in one of the tiny fraction of universes where this improbable erosion pattern arose naturally. If this sounds totally unreasonable, then by the same logic, so is the preference of Rees and Tegmark for an infinite number of universes over a creator.

Implications for Ross's Apologetics

What would happen to Ross's big bang apologetic if these alternative materialist ideas were to become vogue? He would no longer be able to appeal to an alleged consensus view of modern cosmologists, which even now doesn't support theistic interpretations.

What about the Distant Starlight?

Fallacious Distant Starlight Solution: "Light Created in Transit"

After presenting an alternative cosmology that provides a plausible solution to the "distant starlight" problem, it is worth showing why another idea is unsound. Some older creationist works proposed that God may have created the light in transit, and Ross harps on at this as if it is still mainstream creationist thinking (for example, C&T:96–97). But AiG long ago pointed out the problems with this idea.

---

149. M. Tegmark, "Parallel Universes: Not Just a Staple of Science Fiction, Other Universes Are a Direct Implication of Cosmological Observations," *Scientific American* 288(5):30–41 (May 2003).

It would entail that we would be seeing light from heavenly bodies that don't really exist; and even light that seems to indicate precise sequences of events predictable by the laws of physics, but which never actually happened. This, in effect, suggests that God is a deceiver.

This is very different from creating Adam as fully grown, looking like a 20-year-old, say, although he was really only a few minutes old. Ross himself claims that Adam would have shown none of the usual signs of aging, for example, "liver spots on the skin, scar tissue, muscle and skin tone, visual acuity, blood and bone chemistry . . ." (C&T:54). Any test would certainly regard Adam as looking like a 20-year-old (although incredibly youthful looking) and not a newborn. The real point here, though, is that there is no deception, because God has *told* us that He created Adam from the dust, not by growing from an infant. But God has also told us that the stars are real, and that they are signs (Gen. 1:14), not just apparitions from light waves.

Possible Valid Solutions

There are several ways in which the distant starlight problem might be solved. Some creationists have proposed that the speed of light may have been different in the past. It could have traveled greater distances before slowing down to today's rate. Evolutionists have also proposed a higher c in the past to solve their light-travel–time problem — see page 157.

Or, time-dilation might provide a solution. The well-tested science of relativity shows that time can proceed at different rates for different velocity or gravitational reference frames. Dr. Russ Humphreys, while working as a physicist at Sandia National Laboratories in Albuquerque, New Mexico, pointed out that time-dilation might solve the distant starlight problem by allowing light to traverse billions of light-years while only a few days pass on earth.[150] This is covered in the next section.

Each of these ideas has difficulties in the details, so we should not be dogmatic.[151] But, as stated on page 157, distant starlight cannot be used as an argument for Ross's ideas since the big bang also has a light-travel–time problem.

White Hole Relativistic Cosmology

Humphreys rejects the key assumption of the cosmological principle, but keeps the other assumption, that of general relativity (GR). This predicts that *gravity slows time*.

Black Holes

GR predicts that there could be some objects so dense that even light can't escape, now called *black holes*. Black holes are a point of matter at infinite density, called a *singularity*. This is surrounded by an *event horizon*, an imaginary surface where the

---

150. R. Humphreys, *Starlight and Time* (Green Forest, AR: Master Books, 1994).

151. See also, "How Can We See Distant Stars in a Young Universe?" *The Answers Book,* chapter 5; <www.answersingenesis.org/docs/405.asp>.

escape velocity is equal to the speed of light. The size of the event horizon is proportional to the mass and is given by the Schwarzchild radius $R_S = 2GM/c^2$. This means that it expands as the black hole gobble up matter. At the event horizon, time stops, while close to it, time slows down. Black holes can be formed after a collapse of a very massive star.

The book *Einstein's Universe*, although pro–big-bang, provides a fascinating illustration of what an astronaut might experience near a black hole, depending on the size of the black hole and how close he might be.[152] If he could orbit close enough, he might even get into a time zone where his "clocks" run a thousand times slower. Outside observers would see his signals enormously redshifted. They would need a week to record his daily ten-minute report, but it would arrive only once every three years. When checking his heart, they would hear it beat once every 20 minutes.

However, and this is the important thing, the astronomer would notice nothing different *in his own space ship*. But he would see strange things from his friends far from the black hole — everything would appear in super fast-forward. Their signals would be blueshifted, a daily news bulletin would arrive every 90 seconds, a U.S. president would be elected five times a week. If he listened to their heartbeats, they would just be a high-pitched hum. But not for long — after a few weeks of the astronaut's time, all his friends might be dead. After ten years of orbiting, he would return to the earth and finds that 10,000 years have passed and his "own" time is relegated to a few lines in an ancient history book.

Einstein's Universe points out that it would be impossible to orbit a black hole with the mass of a star because of dangerous forces that would rip the craft apart. But it points out that around a very large black hole, these forces would not be a danger.[153] So they should be no problem near a huge galaxy-mass hole.

White Holes

One feature of GR is that its equations are *time-symmetric*. This means that any solution has a mathematically valid "mirror" solution where the time flows backward rather than forward. Therefore, if a black hole is a valid solution, *and it is*, then so is a *white hole*. Whereas a black hole sucks in matter and its event horizon expands, a white hole expels matter and its event horizon shrinks. There seems no naturalistic way to produce a white hole, but if God created the universe this way, it would work the way Dr. Humphreys says.

---

152. Nigel Calder, *Einstein's Universe* (London: BBC, 1979), chapter 13: "Methuselah in a Space-ship."

153. The main danger to an astronaut near a black hole is *tidal forces*, caused by the fact that gravity is stronger on the parts of the body closer to the hole than on the parts away from the hole. The tidal forces near a black hole with a mass of a star are intense enough to stretch a spacecraft and astronaut into tiny pieces. However, while gravitational attraction decreases with the *square* of the distance ($1/r^2$), the tidal effect decreases with the *cube* of the distance ($1/r^3$). So the safest black holes to be near are the biggest ones.

In place of the cosmological principle, Humphreys makes a more biblical assumption, consistent with the quantized red shift data. That is, the universe has a boundary; it has a center (roughly where our galaxy is) and an edge — that if you were to travel off into space, you would eventually come to a place beyond which there was no more matter.

He also uses many of the same biblical passages as Ross which talk about the expansion of the universe. But Humphreys believes that the universe began as a white hole. Note that the Humphreys model proposes a universe-mass white hole, so again the dangerous stresses at the event horizon would be negligible. However, when the event horizon passes through the earth, then (relative to a point far away from it) all clocks would have been virtually frozen in time. An observer on earth would not in any way "feel different." "Billions of years" would be available (in the frame of reference within which it is traveling in deep space) for light to reach the earth, for stars to age, etc. — while less than one ordinary day is passing on earth. The observer on earth would be just like the astronaut orbiting close to a giant black hole's event horizon. This massive gravitational time dilation would seem to be a scientific inevitability if a bounded universe expanded significantly.

This results in a cosmology which allows for the formation of the universe in the biblical time frame, as well as the traveling of light to earth from stars billions of light years distant. This plausible solution to a commonly raised skeptical problem works because general relativity shows that time is different in different reference frames with different gravitational fields. So the universe could have been made in six ordinary days in earth's reference frame, but the light had ample time to travel in an extraterrestrial reference frame. However, as with all scientific theories, we should not be too dogmatic about this model, although it seems very good.

Criticisms Refuted

Ross and various supporters have attempted to criticize Humphreys's model, but Humphreys has, to date, answered all Ross's objections.[154] Many of the critics have missed the point that all the mathematical equations of general relativity require certain boundary conditions, which are based on the *assumptions* chosen.

The viability of Humphreys's model has been further strengthened in late 2003. Two secular cosmologists, Joel Smoller and Blake Temple, have published a white whole cosmogony in the Proceedings of the National Academy of Sciences.[155]

Smoller and Temple, like Humphreys, reject the Copernican principle, and propose that the matter started its expansion in a white hole. But they choose a different metric from Humphreys, and postulate that the event horizon is still "out there," even beyond the range of the Hubble Space Telescope. They also invoke shock waves in the expanding ball of gas. Humphreys's earliest model omitted these

---

154. The criticisms and responses are all available at <www.trueorigin.org/ca_rh_03.asp>.
155. J. Smoller and B. Temple, "Shock-wave Cosmology Inside a Black Hole," *PNAS* 100(20):11216-11218 (September 30, 2003).

for simplicity, but his later work invoked shock waves to explain the concentric-shell arrangement of galaxies around our own galaxy, as suggested by quantized red shifts (see page 156).[156]

Rotating Cosmos

Another possible creationist alternative is the rotating cosmos of Robert Gentry,[157] elaborated upon by J.K. West.[158] This would be consistent with the suggestions of a rotating cosmos already discussed (see page 156). According to Humphreys, there is nothing in his model that is incompatible with the cosmic rotation,[159] so the best model may be a combination of his model and Gentry's.

156. R. Humphreys, "Prestigious Journal Endorses Basics of Creationist Cosmology," <www.icr.org/headlines/whiteholecosmology.html>, October 2003.

157. R.V. Gentry, "A New Redshift Interpretation," *Modern Physics Letters A* 12(37):2919–2925 (1997); <www.creationists.org/Downloads/9806280.pdf>.

158. J.K. West, "Polytropic Model of the Universe," *Creation Research Society Quarterly* 31(2):78–88 (September 1994).

159. R. Humphreys, "New Evidence for a Rotating Cosmos," <www.answersingenesis.org/docs/509.asp>, April 29, 1997.

CHAPTER 6

THE ORIGIN OF DEATH AND SUFFERING

P robably the most serious problem with all compromise views of Genesis is the origin of death and suffering. A straightforward interpretation of Genesis shows that death of humans and vertebrate animals (Hebrew *nephesh chayyah*, "living creature") is the result of Adam's fall. But if long ages are true, then the fossil record must predate Adam by millions of years. Therefore, Ross must try to reinterpret the Scriptures that talk about death in order to deny that the Fall was responsible. Adam's death is relegated to merely spiritual; animal death is apparently still "very good," and animal suffering is no big deal because plants suffer, too.

This chapter also analyzes other parts of Scripture to show where death is regarded as an evil. The original vegetarian diets of both humans and animals are good supporting evidence for a lack of animal death in the beginning. The origin of carnivory from originally vegetarian animals is explained from a biblical perspective, and the end of carnivory in the Restoration is further argument that it was not present in the beginning. The importance for apologetics is demonstrated with case studies of Charles Darwin and Charles Templeton.

Creation Was "Very Good"

One important teaching of Genesis is that the completed creation was "very good" (Gen. 1:31). The Hebrew for "good" is טוֹב *tov*, and "very good" is טוֹב מְאֹד *tov me'od*. As will be shown, this is a strong indicator, especially with more explicit teachings, that the world originally had no death or disease. This is enough to refute ideas of millions of years, because such views put the fossil record in this "very good" world. This would entail that cancer and gout are "very good." The next major heading explains how death is the penalty for Adam's sin, so would not have been part of the original creation.

Ross and his staff argue that "very good" really means only that it was perfect for what it was intended for, but not that there was no death or disease.[1] Their outline

---

1. H. Ross, F. Rana, K. Samples, M. Harman, and K. Bontrager, "Life and Death in Eden, The Biblical and Scientific Evidence for Animal Death Before the Fall," audio cassette set, Reasons to Believe, 2001.

gives some other examples of the phrase, and I've added the context of what it was describing in square brackets:

> **God's very good creation does not mean that it is "perfect."** Most occurrences of this phrase (*me'od tov*) are translated as "very beautiful" or "very wonderful" — Genesis 24:16 [Rebekah's beauty], Numbers 14:7 [the promised land], Judges 18:9 [land of Laish/Dan], 2 Samuel 11:2 [Bathsheba's beauty], 1 Kings 1:6 [Adonijah's handsomeness], Jeremiah 24:2–3 [figs].[2]

But here again we have Ross's propensity for unwarranted expansion of the semantic field. Certainly, the phrase *can* be used of people and things in a fallen world.[3] But the specific context of Genesis 1 shows what God meant by *me'od tov*. The "very good" was the culmination of creation week, where God had already pronounced things "good" six times. This is a clear indication of no principle of actual evil in what God had made.

There is a Hebrew word תמים (*tamim*) that's usually translated "perfect" or "without blemish." Ross makes a lot of the fact that this is not used to describe creation, and he correctly points out that it is used of Noah. But this actually undercuts Ross, because it demonstrates that even *tamim* is used of fallen people, including one who later got drunk (Gen. 9:21). Rather, John Gill comments on Genesis 6:9:

> . . . **and perfect in his generations**; not that he was perfectly holy, or free from sin, but was a partaker of the true grace of God; was sincere and upright in heart and life; lived an unblemished life and conversation, untainted with the gross corruptions of that age he lived in, which he escaped through the knowledge, grace, and fear of God; and therefore it is added, that he was holy, upright, and blameless "in his generations": among the men of the several generations he lived in, as in the generation before the flood, which was very corrupt indeed, and which corruption was the cause of that; and in the generation after the flood: or "in his ages," in the several stages of his life, in youth and in old age; he was throughout the whole course of his life a holy good man.[4]

The related word תם (*tam*) is also used of Job, who was likewise not sinless. But the words refer to completeness and moral integrity, not sinless perfection (BDB). So there is no reason that *tamim* would have been used instead of *me'od tov* to describe a sinless creation. Rather, *tov me'od*, as the culmination of many occurrences of *tov*,

---

2. H. Ross, F. Rana, K. Samples, M. Harman, and K. Bontrager, "Life and Death in Eden, The Biblical and Scientific Evidence for Animal Death Before the Fall," audio cassette set, Reasons to Believe, 2001.

3. At least Ross isn't as bad as some anticreationists, who claim, on the "authority" of the ancient anti-Christian Kabbalist Nachmanides, that *me'od tov* really means "mostly good." As this hasn't even a smidgen of lexical support, and even Ross doesn't make such an absurd claim, it need detain us no further.

4. *John Gill's Exposition of the Bible*, Online Bible; <www.onlinebible.net>.

makes more sense when used to describe the goodness of God's creation and the physical perfection of its completion.

No *Actual* Evil in the Finished Creation

When God created moral beings, there was no actual evil. In fact, evil is not a "thing" *in itself*, even though it is real. Rather, evil is the *privation* of some good that something ought to have, as Augustine pointed out (endorsed by RTB staffer Kenneth Samples[5]). Murder is the removal of a good human life. Adultery is a privation of a good marriage. Good is fundamental and can exist in itself; evil cannot exist in itself. It is always a parasite on good. For example, a wound cannot exist without a body, and the very idea of a wound presupposes the concept of a healthy body. Blindness in a human is a physical evil, because humans are supposed to see (but oysters are not, so blindness is not an evil for oysters). Also, evil actions are done to achieve things like wealth, power, and sexual gratification, which the evildoer finds "good" (meaning "pleasing"). Evil things are not done as ends in themselves, but good things are. Now, since evil is not a thing, God did not create evil [although He does create *calamity* as He has a right to do, and this is the correct understanding of Isaiah 45:7].

The Power of Contrary Choice

God created both Adam and Eve, as well as the angels, with the *power of contrary choice*. This means that they had the power to make a choice contrary to their own nature. Even God does not have this power, for He *cannot* sin and go against His perfectly holy nature (Hab. 1:13, 1 John 1:5).

The power of contrary choice was good, with no *actual* evil, but it meant that there was the *possibility* of evil. But evidently God saw that a greater good would come from it, in that the result would be creatures who genuinely love God *freely*. Actually, real love must be free — if I programmed my computer to flash "I love you" on the screen, it would hardly be genuine love. But Adam's misuse of this good resulted in actual evil befalling him and the rest of the material creation, over which he had dominion (Gen. 1:28).

Satan's Fall

Many commentators regard Ezekiel 28:11–19 as referring to the fall of the being we now call Satan (Hebrew for "adversary").[6] Evidently, Satan had also misused his power of contrary choice before Adam's fall, because he could control the snake as the instrument of temptation (Rev. 12:9). One possible interpretation of Revelation 12:4 is that a third of the angels joined in the rebellion[7] — they would have become

---

5. H. Ross, F. Rana, K. Samples, M. Harman, and K. Bontrager, "Life and Death in Eden, The Biblical and Scientific Evidence for Animal Death Before the Fall," audio cassette set, Reasons to Believe, 2001.

6. J. MacArthur, *The Battle for the Beginning* (Nashville, TN: W Publishing Group, 2001), p. 199–204.

7. Ibid., p. 203.

the demons referred to in Scripture. But the fall of Satan and the demons was clearly not during the "very good" creation week; it must have been some time after that, but in time to be able to instigate the fall of mankind.

Mankind's Fall

Eve was deceived by the serpent's temptation, and in turn gave the forbidden fruit to Adam, who was *not* deceived, but still ate (1 Tim. 2:13–14).

As a result of his sin, Adam and his descendants acquired a sin nature (Rom. 5:12 ff.), and lost the power of contrary choice. But in this case, it now meant that they could no longer go against their sin nature (Ps. 51:5; Jer. 17:9; Rom. 7:15–25). So people today don't get their sin natures by sinning; they sin because of their sin nature.

The potentiality of evil, but not the actuality, is also illustrated by the Tree of the Knowledge of Good and Evil. In the original creation, God knew evil in the same way as an oncologist knows about cancer — not by personal experience but by knowledge about it (in God's case, by foreknowledge). But after Adam and Eve sinned, they knew evil in the same way as a cancer sufferer knows cancer — by sad personal experience.[8]

In the eternal state, redeemed humanity will no longer have the potential for sin. So in this sense, the eternal state, with the new creation of the new heavens and new earth, will be even better than Eden.

In summary, following Augustine:

- Adam and Eve were created with the ability not to sin.
- After the Fall, humans had no ability not to sin.
- In the eternal state, redeemed humans will have no ability to sin.

History of Interpretation of Genesis 1:31

It is folly to claim that the view that creation was lacking any evil is something unheard of in church doctrine, and was just a novelty that AiG has recently invented. Rather, it has been the view of the Christian church consistently. Here are some esteemed commentators who understood the repetition of "good" culminating in "very good," enabling them to teach an absence of any principle of evil or death in the original creation.

Calvin

As shown, Calvin affirmed that creation was in six 24-hour days less than 6,000 years ago. But he also affirmed the following about the meaning of "very good" in the context of creation. He agreed with AiG and disagreed with Ross. Commenting on Genesis 1:31:

> On each of the days, simple approbation was given. But now, after the workmanship of the world was complete in all its parts, and had received,

---

8. J. MacArthur, *The Battle for the Beginning* (Nashville, TN: W Publishing Group, 2001), p. 211.

if I may so speak, the last finishing touch, he pronounces it perfectly good; that we may know that there is in the symmetry of God's works the highest perfection, to which nothing can be added.[9]

John Wesley

Wesley (1703–91) was a great evangelist and founded the Methodist Church. In his sermons on Genesis 1:31, he explicitly pointed out that "very good" entailed no death or chaos:

> When God created the heavens and the earth, and all that is therein, at the conclusion of each day's work it is said, "And God saw that it was good." Whatever was created was good in its kind; suited to the end for which it was designed; adapted to promote the good of the whole and the glory of the great Creator. This sentence it pleased God to pass with regard to each particular creature. But there is a remarkable variation of the expression, with regard to all the parts of the universe, taken in connection with each other, and constituting one system: "And God saw everything that he had made, and, behold, it was very good." . . .
>
> But, however this was, we are sure all things were disposed therein with the most perfect order and harmony. Hence there were no agitations within the bowels of the globe, no violent convulsions, no concussions of the earth, no earthquakes; but all was unmoved as the pillars of heaven! . . .
>
> For as the human body, though not liable to death or pain, yet needed continual sustenance by food; so, although it was not liable to weariness, yet it needed continual reparation by sleep. By this the springs of the animal machine were wound up from time to time, and kept always fit for the pleasing labor for which man was designed by his Creator. Accordingly, "the evening and the morning were the first day," before sin or pain was in the world. The first natural day had one part dark for a season of repose; one part light for a season of labor. And even in paradise "Adam slept," (Gen. 2:21) before he sinned: Sleep, therefore, belonged to innocent human nature. Yet I do not apprehend it can be inferred from hence, that there is either darkness or sleep in heaven. Surely there is no darkness in that city of God. Is it not expressly said (Rev. 22:5), "There shall be no night there"? Indeed they have no light from the sun; but "the Lord giveth them light." So it is all day in heaven, as it is all night in hell! On earth we have a mixture of both. Day and night succeed each other, till earth shall be turned to heaven.[10]

Keil and Delitzsch

C.F. ("Johann") Keil (1807–1888) and Franz Delitzsch (1813–1890) were 19th-century Lutherans who were experts on the Hebrew language and biblical culture.

---

9. J. Calvin, *Genesis*, 1554 (Edinburgh, UK: Banner of Truth, 1984), p. 100.

10. J. Wesley, "God's Approbation of His Work," Sermon 56 (Gen. 1:31), 1872; <http://gbgm-umc. org/UMhistory/Wesley/sermons/serm-056.stm>.

Their commentary series on the Old Testament is still often regarded as unequaled. Delitzsch was also a Hebrew Christian, and his translation of the New Testament into Hebrew is still the translation used in Israel today. They comment on Genesis 1:31 as follows (Pentateuch, 1:67):

> God saw his work, and *behold it was all very good;* i.e., everything was perfect in its kind, so that every creature might reach the goal appointed by the Creator, and accomplish the purpose of its existence. By the application of the term "good" to everything God had made, and the repetition of the word with the emphasis "very" at the close of the whole creation, the existence of anything evil in the creation of God is absolutely denied, and the hypothesis entirely refuted, that the six days' work merely subdued and fettered an ungodly, evil principle, which had already forced its way into it.[11]

Leupold

Leupold wrote about Genesis 1:31:

> The writer says, with emphasis, that no imperfection inhered in the work God had wrought up till this point: for after all preceding statements to the effect that individual works were good comes this stronger statement to the effect that it was "very good," making a total of seven times that the word is used — seven being the mark of divine operation. The thought that God might be the author of evil and imperfection must be guarded against most strenuously (Strack[12]). The "behold" moves the expression "very good" prominently into the foreground (K.S. 341V).

Death Caused by Sin

The biggest problem of non-literal interpretations of Genesis is that there would then have been billions of years of death, struggle and suffering before man's fall. But Scripture teaches that human death is the result of Adam's fall (Rom. 5:12–19), and 1 Corinthians 15:21–22 states:

> For since death came through a man, the resurrection of the dead comes also through a man. For as in Adam all die, so also in Christ shall all be made alive.

Adam's Sin Is the Defining Point

After the Fall, God cursed all three participants, in the order in which they sinned: the serpent, the woman, and the man (Gen. 3:14–19). However, this is the reverse of the order in which God first interviewed them. In Genesis 3:9–13, God first asks

---

11. C.F. Keil and F. Delitzsch, *Commentaries on the Old Testament,* n.d. original German in the 19th century, English translation published by Eerdmans, Grand Rapids, MI, The Pentateuch, 1:67.
12. H.L. Strack, C.H. Zöckler, and C.H. Beck, editors, *Kurzgefasster Kommentar (Genesis),* München, Germany, 1905.

the man, who blamed the woman, who in turn blamed the serpent. After that, God pronounces judgment, starting with the serpent.

It was only when God addressed Adam that the death sentence was pronounced (Gen. 3:19), and, as shown below, it was physical death. The rest of the Bible attributes death to *Adam*, not Eve or Satan (Rom. 5:12–19, 1 Cor. 15:21–22). There is no biblical connection of the angelic fall with physical death or suffering in the material world, contrary to what Ross claims.[13]

The Bible Says That Death Is an "Enemy" and a Thing of Sadness

Paul then calls death "the last enemy" (1 Cor. 15:26). All (mis-)interpretations of Genesis which deny its plain meaning, and so involve death before sin, must assert that the "last enemy" was part of God's "very good" creation.

Jesus made clear his thoughts on human physical death in the shortest verse in the Bible (in response to the death of his close friend Lazarus), "Jesus wept" (John 11:35). Especially since Jesus knew that He would soon resurrect Lazarus, this points very strongly to His knowing that death was an unmitigated tragedy, and hardly something He would call "very good."

Finally, in the eternal state, there will once again be no death or suffering of any sort, as Revelation 21:4 says:

> He [God] will wipe away every tear from their eyes, and death shall be no more, neither shall there be mourning nor crying nor pain any more, for the former things have passed away.

The reason for this is given in the next chapter, "there shall be no more curse" (Rev. 22:3). So, from the first book of the Bible to the last, there is the clear connection of death and suffering with the Curse.

Adam's Sin Just Brought Spiritual Death?

However, Ross dismisses the above argument by claiming that the death referred to was "spiritual death," not physical (C&T:60–61, bold in original):

> **"Death through sin" is not equivalent to physical death.** Romans 5:12 addresses neither physical nor soulish death. It addresses spiritual death. . . . He died spiritually. He broke his harmonious fellowship with God and introduced the inclination to place one's way above God's.
>
> In the same manner, it has been established that 1 Corinthians 15:21 ("since death came through a man") also must refer to spiritual death rather than to physical death. As the following two verses explain, "For as in Adam all die, so in Christ all will be made alive. But each in his own turn: Christ, the firstfruits; then when he comes, those who belong to him" (verses 22–23).

---

13. H. Ross, F. Rana, K. Samples, M. Harman, and K. Bontrager, "Life and Death in Eden, The Biblical and Scientific Evidence for Animal Death Before the Fall," audio cassette set, Reasons to Believe, 2001.

But this is amazing, since the whole of 1 Corinthians 15 is about the bodily (*physical*) resurrection of Christ, who was *physically* dead. In fact, Ross, in the quote above, neglected to quote the second half of 1 Corinthians 15:21. This makes it very clear that the death Adam brought was contrasted with the bodily resurrection brought by the Last Adam, "For since death came through a man, **the resurrection of the dead comes also through a man**." If Adam died only spiritually, then, logically, Jesus must only have needed to rise spiritually. This goes against the whole tenor of Paul's chapter, and a non-bodily resurrection would have been nonsense to Jews.

The Actual Curse

Even Genesis itself shows that Adam's punishment could not just have been spiritual death. In Genesis 3:19, God pronounces judgment on Adam:

> In the sweat of your face you shall eat bread till you return to the ground,
> for out of it you were taken; you are dust, and to dust you shall return.

Returning to the dust can mean only physical death, and there would be no point to this punishment unless there was no physical death before. Otherwise, Adam could have said, "So what? That was gonna happen to me, anyway!"

Actually, in one sense, the Curse of physical death has a benefit to man, in that it prevents an even worse evil: living forever in a state of sin. And it provides the means of redemption, via the physical death of the God-man Jesus Christ on the cross.

Was Immortality Part of Adam's Original State?

God prevented Adam from eating from the Tree of Life after the Fall, lest he live forever in sin (Gen. 3:22). From this, some argue that Adam was not created immortal. However, this does not follow, because God ordains both the *means* and the *end*. RTB theologian Kenneth Samples is a Calvinist, so would argue that God predestines who will be saved (the end) as well as the means (preaching the gospel). Similarly, in the original creation, the end is that Adam would be without death, and part of the means could have been the Tree of Life. I won't argue for or against Calvinism, which is outside the scope of this book, but it shows that a RTB staffer can have no problems in principle with my explanation. In the eternal state, where death and the Curse will be no more, the Tree of Life will once more flourish (Rev. 22:2).

In this view, God had ordained the Tree of Life as providing eternal continuance of life. Since God's will cannot be thwarted, even by the Fall (which He foreknew), the tree's property would need to be true even after the Fall. Since Adam and Eve would not be allowed to live forever in sin, they could not be allowed to eat any of this fruit. If they had, God would have been forced by His own perfect truthfulness to keep them alive forever. So the Tree of Life was not to become accessible till the eternal state, when we will no longer have even the possibility of sin.

Another argument is made in 1 Timothy 6:16, quoted as God "who alone has immortality." But here the Greek text is saying that God alone *possesses* (Greek εχω *echō*) everlasting undyingness (Greek αθανασια *athanasia*). So in God's case, immortality is part of His *essence*, while *creaturely* immortality is based on God's moment-by-moment sustaining power (Col. 1:16–17). This passage has nothing to do with teaching that Adam would have died without sin.

What Did the Fall Change?

Ross would have us believe (C&T:69):

> While the sin we humans commit causes us all to react negatively to decay, work, physical death, pain and suffering . . . there is nothing in Scripture that compels us to conclude that none of these entities existed before Adam's first act of rebellion against God.

To Ross, all the Fall did was to make bad things worse. However, this is far from the teachings of Scripture. In his audio series, Ross and his collaborators elaborate on this.[14]

For example, they believe that there was hard work in the garden. They even go as far as to say that the term "subdue" in Genesis 1:28 has "harsh negative connotations" of "coercion," and that the earth would "fight back" with "hostility," citing a compromising commentary by Victor Hamilton.

But the word for subdue is כבש (*kabash*). This *can* have negative connotations, but this is caused by the *context*, not the word itself. For example, it can have the sense of crushing, like grapes in a wine press, but it can also mean reigning over something, controlling it. Control or reign can of course be benevolent, as well as destructive. For example, Micah 7:19, in which to subdue (*kabash*) our sins is a sign of God's compassion.

The same goes for dominion רדה (*radah*). Certain anti-Christian environmentalists blame Genesis for the abuse of the environment, conveniently overlooking both the environmental problems revealed in countries which had been under atheistic communism and the implications of believing that we evolved by survival of the fittest, that is, ruthless extermination of the weak.

Leviticus 25:43 ff. condemns *ruthless* dominion (*radah*). In contrast, 1 Kings 4:24–25 says that Solomon's dominion (*radah*) resulted in peace, safety, and "each man under his own vine and fig tree." So the type of *radah* must be decided by *context*. Since these words were spoken by God into an Edenic situation, before the Fall, it is especially hard to imagine any sort of destructive or ruthless implication to them.

The work in Eden was light tending of the garden, but after the Fall it was sweaty, hard toil (Gen. 3:17–19). The Curse on the ground loses all its force if it hardly made a difference to the work.

---

14. H. Ross, F. Rana, K. Samples, M. Harman, and K. Bontrager, "Life and Death in Eden, The Biblical and Scientific Evidence for Animal Death before the Fall," audio cassette set, Reasons to Believe, 2001.

Ross also argues (C&T:67–68):

> If we turn back to the passage recounting God's response to Adam and Eve's sin, we see evidence that physical pain — closely connected with decay — must have existed before the Fall. In Genesis 3:16, God says to Eve, "I will greatly increase [or multiply] your pains in childbearing." He does not say "introduce." He says "increase" or "multiply," implying there would have been pain in any case.

First of all, it would be an "increase" even if Eve would have suffered no pain in childbirth had she not fallen before conceiving any children. After all, zero pain to some pain is an increase! But even if we grant Ross's argument that Eve would have had childbirth pains before the Fall, it would not prove his case. A pain is just an intense sensation, and isn't always perceived as bad. Many bodybuilders *want* to have some slight muscular pain a day after training. But the implication, even granting that Ross is right, is that childbirth before the Fall would have involved bearable, and not necessarily unpleasant, pain, rather than excruciating pain. Perhaps, while below some threshold, it might even have had a pleasurable component.

Commentators on Sin-Death Causality

That death was not part of the original creation is hardly a novel view of the Bible, as shown by commentators before the rise of long-age "science."

Calvin agreed that physical human death is the result of sin:

> And therefore some understand what was before said, "Thou shalt die," in a spiritual sense; thinking that, even if Adam had not sinned, his body must still have been separated from his soul. But since the declaration of Paul is clear, that "all die in Adam, as they shall rise again in Christ" (1 Cor. 15:22), this wound was inflicted by sin. . . . Truly the first man would have passed to a better life, had he remained upright; but there would have been no separation of the soul from the body, no corruption, no kind of destruction, and, in short, no violent change.[15]

Wesley answered the "problem of pain" explicitly by man's sin, in particular the fall of Genesis 3:

> Why is there *pain* in the world; seeing God is "loving to every man, and his mercy is over all his works?" Because there is sin: Had there been no sin, there would have been no pain. But pain (supposing God to be just) is the necessary effect of sin. But why is there sin in the world? Because man was created in the image of God: Because he is not mere matter, a clod of earth, a lump of clay, without sense or understanding; but a spirit like his Creator, a being endued not only with sense and understanding, but also with a will exerting itself in various affections. To crown all the rest, he was endued

---

15. J. Calvin, *Genesis*, 1554 (Edinburgh, UK: Banner of Truth, 1984), p. 180.

with liberty; a power of directing his own affections and actions; a capacity of determining himself, or of choosing good or evil. Indeed, had not man been endued with this, all the rest would have been of no use: Had he not been a free as well as an intelligent being, his understanding would have been as incapable of holiness, or any kind of virtue, as a tree or a block of marble. And having this power, a power of choosing good or evil, he chose the latter: He chose evil. Thus, "sin entered into the world," and pain of every kind, preparatory to death."[16]

What Was Subject to Death?

Since the Bible says that death was introduced with Adam's sin, we must understand the context to work out the extent of death. Verses such as Genesis 2:17, Genesis 3:17–19, Romans 5:12, 1 Corinthians 15:21–22 are very clear on the sin-death connection. While these verses refer explicitly to human death, Genesis 3 is clear that Adam's sin had further unpleasant effects because Adam was the federal head of creation.

This is supported by Paul's teaching of Romans 8:20–22, that God subjected the *whole creation* (πασα 'η κτισις, *pasa hē ktisis*) to futility, and many commentators believe Paul was alluding to Genesis 3. For example, Calvin commented on Genesis 3:19:

> Therefore, we may know, that whatever unwholesome things may be produced, are not natural fruits of the earth, but are corruptions which originate from sin.[17]

Creationists have often pointed out that the creatures affected were those the Bible calls נפש חיה (*nephesh chayyah*). When it refers to man, it is often translated "living soul," but, of other creatures, including fish, it is often translated "living creature." However, it is never applied to plants or invertebrates. Therefore, there is a qualitative difference between the deaths of the (vertebrate) animals called *nephesh chayyah* and plant death. This is further supported by the account of the Flood and ark. The living creatures (*nephesh chayyah*) rescued on the ark did not include plants (or invertebrates).

Wesley also related the groaning and travailing in pain of Romans 8:20–22 to Adam's fall, contrasting it with the "paradise" of the original creation:

> We may inquire, in the First place, What was the original state of the brute creation? And may we not learn this, even from the place which was assigned them; namely, the garden of God? All the beasts of the field, and all the fowls of the air, were with Adam in paradise. And there is no question but their state was suited to their place: It was paradisiacal; perfectly happy.

---

16. J. Wesley, "On the Fall of Man," Sermon 57 (Genesis 3:19), 1872; <http://gbgm-umc.org/UMhistory/Wesley/sermons/serm-057.stm>.
17. J. Calvin, *Genesis*, 1554 (Edinburgh, UK: Banner of Truth, 1984), p. 180.

Undoubtedly it bore a near resemblance to the state of man himself. By taking, therefore, a short view of the one, we may conceive the other. . . .

How true then is that word, "God saw everything that he had made: and behold it was very good!" But how far is this from being the present case! In what a condition is the whole lower world! — to say nothing of inanimate nature, wherein all the elements seem to be out of course, and by turns to fight against man. Since man rebelled against his Maker, in what a state is all animated nature! Well might the Apostle say of this: "The whole creation groaneth and travaileth together in pain until now." This directly refers to the brute creation in what state this is at present we are now to consider.[18]

However, none of these [animals] then attempted to devour, or in anyway hurt, one another. All were peaceful and quiet, as were the watery fields wherein they ranged at pleasure. . . .

It seems the insect kinds were at least one degree above the inhabitants of the waters. Almost all these too devour one another, and every other creature which they can conquer. Indeed, such is the miserably disordered state of the world at present, that innumerable creatures can not otherwise preserve their own lives than by destroying others. But in the beginning it was not so. The paradisiacal earth afforded a sufficiency of food for all its inhabitants; so that none of them had any need or temptation to prey upon the other. The spider was then as harmless as the fly, and did not then lie in wait for blood. The weakest of them crept securely over the earth, or spread their gilded wings in the air, that wavered in the breeze, and glittered in the sun, without any to make them afraid. Meantime, the reptiles of every kind were equally harmless. . . .

But . . . there were no birds or beasts of prey; none that destroyed or molested another; but all the creatures breathed, in their several kinds, the benevolence of their great Creator.[19]

Vegetarian Diets in the Creation

Probably the best support for the position that no animals died before the Fall comes from the original diets in Genesis 1:29–30:

> And God said, "Behold, I have given you every plant yielding seed which is upon the face of all the earth, and every tree with seed in its fruit; you shall have them for food. And to every beast of the earth, and to every bird of the air, and to everything that creeps on the earth, everything that has the breath of life, I have given every green plant for food." And it was so.

18. J. Wesley, "The General Deliverance," Sermon 60 (Romans 8:19–22), 1872; <http://gbgm-umc.org/UMhistory/Wesley/sermons/serm-060.stm>.

19. J. Wesley, "God's Approbation of His Work," Sermon 56 (Gen. 1:31), 1872; <http://gbgm-umc.org/UMhistory/Wesley/sermons/serm-056.stm>.

This teaches that vegetarianism was a worldwide phenomenon, not just restricted to Eden. Even after the Fall, after Adam and Eve were expelled from Eden, their diet was vegetarian, as Genesis 3:17–19 says:

> To Adam he said, "Because you listened to your wife and ate from the tree about which I commanded you, "You must not eat of it, Cursed is the ground because of you; through painful toil you will eat of it all the days of your life. It will produce thorns and thistles for you, and you will eat the plants of the field. By the sweat of your brow you will eat your food until you return to the ground, since from it you were taken; for dust you are and to dust you will return."

Ross himself provides inadvertent support by his "analysis" of Genesis 1:29. He agrees that this teaches that humans originally had a vegetarian diet, not "merely an indication that all food resources derive from plants" (GQ:71). Otherwise, God's statement to Noah after the Flood in Genesis 9:3 makes no sense:

> Every moving thing that lives shall be food for you; and as I gave you the green plants, I give you everything.

If Noah was already eating animals that ate plants, this would make no sense. However, this verse is stating only that *human* carnivory was permitted after the Flood. The Fall is the big discontinuity of earth history, and that's where animal carnivory began (see page 211). It's possible that rebellious humans also ate meat before the Flood.

However, Ross has contradicted what he said about original human vegetarianism in his analysis of verse 30. Here, he claims that this verse **was** merely teaching that all animals benefit either directly or indirectly from plants.[20] But he "explains" the original vegetarian diet of humans (GQ:71):

> Vegetarianism perfectly suits the potential longevity of the first humans. Animal tissue contains between ten and ten thousand times the concentration of heavy elements that plant material contains. This difference sounds drastic, but it poses an insignificant health risk for people living only 120 years (the limit God imposed at the time of the Flood). However, the difference is by no means trivial for people living nearly a thousand years.

Ross provides no documentation. And how could he know what dangers would face long-living people without any to test? This statement is falsified by the life spans, greatly exceeding 120 years, after people were permitted to eat meat. And his statement is hopelessly imprecise: *which* plants and animals? Some plants take up heavy elements so readily that they are used to clean up waterways. Soy and

---

20. H. Ross, F. Rana, K. Samples, M. Harman, and K. Bontrager, "Life and Death in Eden, The Biblical and Scientific Evidence for Animal Death before the Fall," audio cassette set, Reasons to Believe, 2001.

tea plants are known to take up aluminium readily. Conversely, many animals can excrete such elements. And accumulation is more of a problem in animals higher in the food chain, for example, sharks with mercury, as well as filter-feeders. This might be a reason for God's injunctions in the Mosaic laws against eating carnivores and shellfish.

But even leaving aside the inadequacy of Ross's explanation, Ross undercuts one of his key claims, that animals were eating each other for millions of years. That is, Ross agrees that Genesis 1:29 teaches original vegetarianism for humans, but then surely *by his own reasoning*, the next verse must teach original vegetarianism in land animals and birds. But Ross denies this without realizing the contradiction, because he believes that carnivore fossils predate Adam.

In the Restoration

Also, the Restoration of creation (Acts 3:21–22) will have many features of the pre-Fall paradise. But since all the creation that "was subjected to frustration" is eventually to be restored (Rom. 8:20–22, Acts 3:21–22), then in a long-age scenario, one must ponder: "Restored to what? Billions of years of death and suffering?"

Isaiah 11:6–9 and 65:25 state that there will be a time in the future with no bloodshed in the animal kingdom. These are famous passages about a lion and calf, wolf and lamb, and a vegetarian lion and a non-harmful viper. Significantly, both passages close with indications that this reflects a more ideal world and the current world does not: "They shall not hurt or destroy. . . ." "They shall do no evil or harm. . . ." These indicate that hurting, harming, and destroying animal life would not have been part of a "very good" creation.

Ross himself takes this passage straightforwardly (GQ:98–99):

> Some time in the future, when Jesus reigns for a time on earth and His followers serve alongside Him in managing the planet, carnivores will no longer eat herbivores, according to Isaiah 65:25. This change most likely results from Christ's bringing peace and harmony among all humans and between humans and animals so that under God's authority we can provide the carnivores with all the processed, nutritionally adequate food they need. During this time, referred to as the Millennium by many Bible scholars, God will remove all human excuses for sin — including our carnivorous activity — to demonstrate, once and for all, that our weakness lies within us, not in our external environment (see Jer. 17:9–10).

The above is all very reasonable, and I will neither support nor dispute his eschatology, since that topic is outside the scope of this book and AiG. The main point is that Ross correctly sees that carnivory is opposed to "peace and harmony." But he is inconsistent and fails to see that "peace and harmony" must have likewise prevailed in the pre-Fall Eden, entailing a lack of carnivory — as Genesis 1:29–30 says! Likewise, if it will be possible in the Millennium for man to provide the nutritional requirements for all animals without killing other animals, then how much more would it have been possible for God to do the same in Eden?

Premillennialists like Ross and many creationists, such as Whitcomb and Morris, all agree that this is a literal Millennium, lasting for 1,000 years, followed by a creation of the new heavens and new earth. Actually, orthodox Christians, regardless of their view of the Millennium or creation week, believe in the second coming of Christ, which is connected in various ways to this "brand new creation." So Ross is wrong to accuse creationists of denying the latter.

The Bible on Predation in the Current Era

God uses images from predation to portray violent judgment on Israel (Hos. 13.8). This gives an indication that predation is a violent intruder into our world. However, there are several passages that indicate that, in this cursed creation, predation is part of God's provision for some animals, for example, Psalm 104:21, Job 38:39–41, 39:27–30. These passages are the only plausible supports for Ross's view that carnivory is part of the original created order, and indeed he makes much of them.[21]

Psalm 104 is the most widely cited passage used as an excuse for this eisegesis. But it is poor hermeneutics to interpret Scripture against Scripture. Indeed, this psalm is a poetic version of Genesis. It is in part a hymn to God's acts in the past — note the past tense of the verbs from verses 5–9. But it is also a hymn of praise for God's provisions in the present, as shown by the present tense of the verbs afterwards. So Psalm 104:21 deals with the present day, not the original creation. Therefore, it cannot be used to override the clear teaching that animals were originally vegetarian, and will once again be vegetarian.

Furthermore, there are a number of provisions for a fallen world which even Ross would not claim were necessary pre-Fall. One is the death penalty for murder (Gen. 9:6), yet Ross would not believe there was murder before the Fall.

Plant Death

Ross says (GQ:100):

> Eating, which makes animal life possible, requires the death of some other living thing. For example, when herbivores eat, plants or other plant parts die.

Again, he persistently misrepresents what creationists *actually teach*, as above. We have *never* taught that *plants* didn't die before the Fall, but only *nephesh chayyah*. The Bible is clear: it should be obvious from Genesis 1:29–30, which regards plants as the main food source, that plants do **not** have life in the sense of *nephesh*, while animals do. This also means that biblical passages about plants withering etc. are irrelevant to the discussion.

---

21. H. Ross, F. Rana, K. Samples, M. Harman, and K. Bontrager, "Life and Death in Eden, the Biblical and Scientific Evidence for Animal Death Before the Fall," audio cassette set, Reasons to Believe, 2001.

Plant Suffering?

Ross claims (C&T:63):

> But even plants suffer when they are eaten. They experience bleeding, bruising, scarring, and death. Why is the suffering of plants acceptable and not that of animals?

It's hard to believe Ross is serious. Plants don't have a brain to interpret tissue damage as pain.

Cell Death

Of late, Ross is using a new word, *apoptosis*, in his newsletters. This is usually explained as "programmed cell death," so naturally Ross loves this as supposed proof of the goodness of death. Apoptosis has been the subject of much research, and its peak was probably when Sydney Brenner, Bob Horvitz, and John Sulston won the 2002 Nobel Prize in physiology and medicine for their research on apoptosis in a nematode worm, *Caenorhabditis elegans*.

However, cells are hardly *nephesh chayyah*. (We humans shed millions of "dead" skin cells all the time, but none of these were ever "living creatures" in their own right.) So what we call death of cells has no relation to the death brought about by sin. Also, the use of the word "death" to describe this process is highly anthropomorphic. Apoptosis is a very orderly, programmed process, where the cells shrink, fragment, and are removed without trace by macrophages, "professional 'undertaker' cells," as Dr. David Hume of the University of Queensland put it.[22] Apoptosis is an important aspect of God's original created design.[23]

For example, apoptosis is responsible for the development of digits in amniotes (all land vertebrates apart from amphibians). The amniote embryo develops a thickening on the limb tip called the AER (apical ectodermal ridge), then apoptosis divides the AER into five regions that then develop into digits (fingers and toes).[24]

By contrast, in frogs, the digits grow outwards from buds as cells divide (see diagram, right).[25] This huge difference refutes one of the most commonly argued "proofs" of evolution,

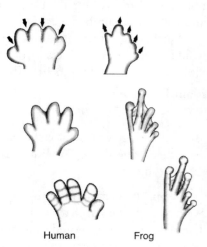

Human   Frog

---

22. D. Hume, "Gobbling Up Cells," letter to *New Scientist* 177(2388):29 (March 29, 2003).
23. P. Bell, "Apoptosis: Programmed Cell 'Death' Reveals Creation," *TJ* 16(1):90–102 (2002).
24. T.W. Sadler, editor, *Langman's Medical Embryology*, 7th ed. (Baltimore, MD: Williams and Wilkins, 1995), p. 154–157.
25. M.J. Tyler, *Australian Frogs: A Natural History* (Sydney, Australia: Reed New Holland, 1999), p. 80.

the pentadactyl limb pattern, that is, the five-digit limbs found in amphibians, reptiles, birds, and mammals. Under evolution, it's *genes* that are inherited, not structures per se. So one would expect the similarities, if they were the result of evolutionary common ancestry, to be produced by a common genetic program (whereas this may or may not be the case for common design). However, they develop in a completely different manner in amphibians and the other groups, as per the two previous notes. This is a strong argument for a common Designer who planned a similar end result but used two different programs to achieve this. See RE2, chapter 6.

Apoptosis is totally different from *necrosis*, another mode of cell death where the term "death" is more apt. Here, the process is unprogrammed, disorderly, and leaves behind remnants that produce an inflammatory response.[26] Recent research has suggested that even necrosis is often not as chaotic as previously thought, and the researchers have argued that its distinction from apoptosis may not be clear cut in some cases.[27] However, Dr. Hume criticized that article, saying:

> One key difference between apoptosis and necrosis is the failure in the latter case of a process that would normally permit the orderly removal of the corpses of the dead.[28]

Indeed, necrosis is often seen in cancerous tumors, basically because cells become starved of adequate blood supply. Conversely, *failure* of apoptosis is what causes many tumor cells in the first place; that is, cells that "hang around" beyond their use-by ("die-by"?!) date.[29] There is every reason to believe that necrosis, at least the truly disorderly sort, occurred only after the Fall, while apoptosis was programmed to occur from creation.

CARNIVORY AND DISEASE

The Bible doesn't specifically explain how carnivory originated, but since creation was finished after day 6 (Gen. 2:1–3), there is no possibility that God later created new carnivorous animals. Instead, creationists have three explanations in general, although the specific explanation depends on the particular case.[30]

1. The Bible appears not to regard insects and other invertebrates as "living," in the same sense as humans and vertebrate animals — the Hebrew never refers to them as *nephesh chayyah* ("living soul/creature"), unlike humans and even fish (Gen. 1:20, 2:7). Also, insects don't have the same sort of "blood" that vertebrates do, yet "the life of the flesh is in the blood" (Lev. 17:11). Therefore, the pre-Fall diet of animals did not necessarily exclude invertebrates.

---

26. P. Bell, "Apoptosis: Programmed Cell 'Death' Reveals Creation," *TJ* 16(1):90–102 (2002).
27. N. Tavernarakis, "Death by Misadventure," *New Scientist* 177(2382):30–33 (February 15, 2003).
28. D. Hume, "Gobbling Up Cells," letter to *New Scientist* 177(2388):29 (March 29, 2003).
29. P. Bell, "Apoptosis: Programmed Cell 'Death' Reveals Creation," *TJ* 16(1):90–102 (2002).
30. This topic is covered more fully in AB, chapter 6.

2. Before the Fall, many attack/defense structures could have been used in a vegetarian lifestyle. For example, even today, some baby spiders use their webs to trap pollen for food,[31] and there was the case of a lion that wouldn't eat meat.[32] Even many poisons actually have beneficial purposes in small amounts.[33] Microbes help prime the immune system, and many allergies might be due to a society that's too clean. Note that the immune system would be important even before the Fall to distinguish between "self" and "non-self."

3. God foreknew the Fall, so He programmed creatures with the information for attack and defense features, which they would need in a cursed world. This information was "switched on" at the Fall.

Pathogens and Creation

Some people wonder where disease germs fit into the biblical framework, if God created everything "very good." Under this framework, obviously the Fall was responsible for disease, but how, if God had finished creating at the end of creation week? Ross's biologist, Fuz Rana, believes that disease is the inevitable result of germs being present. He also believes that non-pathogenic diseases such as gout and cancer are just results of the laws of physics.[34]

However, even something usually known as a deadly germ can have a mild variant that causes no illness. Presumably, something like this was created during creation week — even today, *Vibrio cholerae*, the germ that causes cholera, has a non-virulent form. It also has a role in the ecosystems of brackish waters and estuaries, and the original may have had a role living symbiotically with some people. Even its toxin probably has a beneficial function in small amounts, like most poisons. The virulence arose after the Fall, by natural selection of varieties producing more and more toxin as contaminated water became more plentiful. No new information would be needed for this process. Also, recent evidence shows that the *loss* of *chemotaxis* — the ability to move in response to changes in chemical concentrations — will "markedly increase infectivity in an infant mouse model of cholera."[35]

Another likely example of virulence arising by information loss is the *mycoplasmas*, the smallest known self-reproducing organisms (parasitic bacteria with no cell walls and fewer than 1,000 genes, found in the respiratory system and urogenital tracts of humans). Loss of genetic information, for example, for amino acid synthesis, could

31. See "Pollen-Eating Spiders," *Creation* 22(3):8 (June–August 2000); *Nature Australia* (Summer 1999–2000): p. 5.

32. D. Catchpoole, "The Lion That Wouldn't Eat Meat," *Creation* 22(2):22–23 (March–May 2000).

33. See J. Bergman, "Understanding Poisons from a Creationist Perspective," *TJ* 11(3):353–360 (1997); <www.answersingenesis.org/poison>.

34. H. Ross, F. Rana, K. Samples, M. Harman, and K. Bontrager, "Life and Death in Eden, The Biblical and Scientific Evidence for Animal Death Before the Fall," audio cassette set, Reasons to Believe, 2001.

35. D.S. Merrell et al., "Host-induced Epidemic Spread of the Cholera Bacterium," *Nature* 417(6889):642–644 (June 6, 2002).

have resulted in the mycoplasmas' becoming increasingly dependent on their hosts for survival.[36]

Some clues to possible benign pre-Fall roles for viruses can be gleaned from functions they have even today. Viruses are non-living entities, because they can't reproduce on their own, but need the copying machinery of more complex cells. But they have a number of useful functions, including transporting genes among plants and animals, keeping soil fertile, keeping water clean, and regulating gases in the atmosphere.[37] So, once again, some alleged evidence for evolution actually provides support for the creation/Fall model.

Thermodynamics and the Fall

The second law of thermodynamics is one of the most fundamental laws of nature. It can be stated in many different ways. For example:

- that the *entropy* of the universe tends towards a maximum (in simple terms, entropy is a measure of disorder)
- usable energy is running out
- information tends to get scrambled
- order tends towards disorder
- a random jumble won't organize itself

Some older creationist literature claims that the second law of themodynamics began at the Fall. However, the second law is responsible for a number of good things which involve increases in entropy, so are "decay" processes in the thermodynamic sense, but maybe not what most people would imagine are decay:

- solar heating of the earth (heat transfer from a hot object to a cold one is the classical case of the second law in action)
- walking (requires the highly entropic phenomenon of friction, otherwise Adam and Eve would have slipped as they walked with God in Eden!)
- breathing (based on air moving from high pressure to low pressure, producing a more disordered equalized concentration of molecules)
- digestion (breaking down large, complex food molecules into their simple building blocks)
- baking a cake (mixing the ingredients produces a lot of disorder), etc.

Thus, it is a mistake to equate anthropomorphic conceptions of "running down" with thermodynamic entropy increase. It is more likely that God withdrew some of

---

36. T.C. Wood, "Genome Decay in the Mycoplasmas," *Impact* 340, October 2001; <http://www.icr.org/pubs/imp/imp-340.htm>.

   C. Wieland, "Diseases on the Ark (Answering the Critics)," *TJ* 8(1):16–18, 1994, explains important related concepts.

37. J. Bergman, "Did God Make Pathogenic Viruses?" *TJ* 13(1):115–125, 1999.

His sustaining power at the Fall. He still sustains the universe (Col. 1:17); otherwise, it would cease to exist. Most of the time He doesn't sustain it in the way that He prevented the Israelites' shoes and clothes from wearing out during the 40 years in the wilderness (Deut. 29:5). But this special case may have been the rule rather than the exception in the brief period before the Fall.

Ross independently came up with similar arguments against this older creationist view. But I must question whether he really understands it. He claims that the Romans 8:20–22 reference of "bondage to decay" is evidence that the second law began at creation.

Ross amazingly says (C&T:63):

> Considering how creatures convert chemical energy into kinetic energy, we can say that carnivorous activity results from the laws of thermodynamics, not from sin.

However, there is not the slightest thing in the laws of thermodynamics that mandates carnivory. Ross's statement is equivalent to "A completely herbivorous ecosystem would violate the laws of thermodynamics," and this is physico-chemical nonsense.

Redemption

One of the major themes of the Bible is God's plan to redeem fallen humanity. This will eventually result in a Restoration, then finally a brand new creation (which Ross accuses creationists of denying).[38] Note, the intention here is not to take any particular stance, and neither will we quarrel with Ross's premillennial view. Rather, for the purposes of the book, I will grant that his general scheme is correct, and show that even then it makes far more sense in a YEC framework.

To reconcile God and man, God provided a mediator who is both God and man, Jesus Christ (1 Tim. 2:5). God the Son, the second person of the Trinity, took on a human nature in addition to His full divinity, becoming a perfect God-man — Jesus Christ. Also, God's perfect justice requires that sin must be atoned for, either by the sinner or one of the same nature. The Book of Hebrews amplifies how Jesus took upon himself the nature of a man to save mankind (Heb. 2:11–18).

In His humanity, Jesus was a descendant of Adam (through Noah, Abraham, and David). He thus became our relation! He is called "the last Adam" (1 Cor. 15:45), because He took the place of the first Adam. He became the new head and, because He was sinless, He was able to pay the penalty for sin. We are *all* related (Acts 17:26). The gospel makes sense only on the basis that all humans alive, and all who have ever lived, are descendants of the first man, Adam.[39] Only descendants

---

38. H. Ross, F. Rana, K. Samples, M. Harman, and K. Bontrager, "Life and Death in Eden, The Biblical and Scientific Evidence for Animal Death Before the Fall," audio cassette set, Reasons to Believe, 2001.

39. Eve, in a sense, was also a "descendant" of Adam in that she was made from his flesh and thus had a biological connection to him (Gen. 2:21–23).

of Adam can be saved, because Isaiah spoke of the coming Messiah as literally the "Kinsman-Redeemer," that is, one who is related by blood to those he redeems (Isa. 59:20, which uses the same Hebrew word גּוֹאֵל (gôēl) as is used to describe Boaz in relation to Ruth).

Christ suffered death (the penalty for sin) on the cross, shedding His blood, so that those who repent of their sin of rebellion and put their trust in His work on the cross can be reconciled to God. This works because of the teaching "without shedding of blood is no forgiveness" (Heb. 9:22), which is based on Leviticus 17:11, "For the life of the flesh is in the blood, and I have given it to you on the altar to make atonement for your souls; for it is the blood by reason of the life that makes atonement." And this, in turn, was prefigured back in Genesis, where God killed one or more animals to make coats of skins for Adam and Eve (Gen. 3:21) to replace the fig leaves they had sewn together (Gen. 3:7). Further support in Genesis comes from God's acceptance of Abel's animal sacrifice and rejection of Cain's vegetable offering (Gen. 4:3–5).

On the Cross, our sins were imputed (credited) to His account (Isa. 53:6). And His perfect righteousness was imputed to believers in Him (2 Cor. 5:21). We are saved by what He has done for us, not by any of our own righteous acts, even those He works in us, for salvation is by grace through faith, not by works (Eph. 2:8–9).

This is an outline of the essential biblical teaching of the substitutionary atonement, where Jesus shed His blood for our sins.

Link to Sin-Death Causality

The Book of Hebrews draws a clear connection between the animal sacrifices of the Levitical laws and the death of the Messiah. RTB theologian Kenneth Samples tried to undermine this by claiming that only Christ's blood atones, while animal blood is just a reminder, and based this on Hebrews 9 and 10.[40] He's not wrong that it is only Christ's blood that takes away sins (Heb. 9:21), which is what is often meant by atonement. That's why Jesus' sacrifice is "once for all" (Heb. 7:27 and 9:28).

He is also right that the blood of animals could not take away sins (Heb. 10:4). However, he is wrong to dismiss the connection with atonement. The Jewish festival of *Yôm Kippur,* or Day of Atonement, was based on animal sacrifices. But the word translated "atone" in the Old Testament is *kaphar* (*Kippur* is a form of this word), and means to *cover*. The Book of Hebrews stresses the importance of this teaching "without shedding of blood is no forgiveness" (Heb. 9:22), and links this with Christ's sacrifice. But the point was that the animal sacrifices were only a temporary covering, and had to be offered year after year. And the priest had to offer sacrifices for his own sins (Heb. 7:27), but Christ was sinless. So the animal sacrifices of the Levitical priesthood were *inadequate*, but were a *type* of Christ's perfect sacrifice. They looked

---

40. H. Ross, F. Rana, K. Samples, M. Harman, and K. Bontrager, "Life and Death in Eden, The Biblical and Scientific Evidence for Animal Death Before the Fall," audio cassette set, Reasons to Believe, 2001.

forward to the time when Christ would sacrifice himself to take away sin, while we look backward to that event.

The *Bible Science Association* (BSA) pointed out:

> Ross's version of earth history rejects the connection that Scripture established between sin, death, and Christ's atonement.[41]

I agree that the whole philosophy of the Atonement is undermined by teaching that there were millions of years of bloodshed before sin. However, Ross claimed that the BSA falsely accused him, "claiming that I reject Christ's atonement" (C&T:83).

However, as shown, this is not at all what BSA said. I would also affirm that Ross and Samples have an orthodox view of the Atonement. However, BSA and I would point out that they have isolated it from the rest of the Bible, and ruined the Atonement's basis by divorcing sin from death. But people can have saving faith despite other beliefs that would logically undermine it. Because of "blessed inconsistency," they fail to make that connection.

Were Adam and Eve Saved?

The Bible does not say specifically that Adam and Eve are now in heaven, so we can't be dogmatic. But there are certain principles that may apply, leading us to believe that the answer to the question is probably yes.

Hebrews 11:1–2 reads, "Now faith is the assurance of things hoped for, the conviction of things not seen. For by it the men of old gained approval." Although Adam and Eve are not named in this chapter, their actions after their disobedience indicate they did have faith in the promises of God.

The Protevangelium of Genesis 3:15

The first promise of God was to Eve in Genesis 3:15:

> And I will put enmity between you and the woman, and between your offspring and hers; he will crush your head, and you will strike his heel.

Many have interpreted the seed in this verse as the Messiah, including the Jewish Targums,[42] hence the Talmudic expression "heels of the Messiah."[43] This verse hints at the virginal conception prophesied in Isaiah 7:14, as the Messiah is called the seed of the woman, contrary to the normal biblical practice of naming the father rather than the mother of a child (see Genesis chapters 5 and 11; 1 Chronicles chapters 1–9).

When Eve bore Cain, she said, literally, "I have gotten a man: YHWH," or "I have received a man, namely Jehovah," as Martin Luther put it.[44] The Hebrew Christian

---

41. Pulse, editorial, *Bible Science News* 30(8):12 (1992).

42. Aramaic paraphrases of the OT originating in the last few centuries B.C., and committed to writing about A.D. 500. See F.F. Bruce, *The Books and the Parchments,* Revelation Ed. (Westwood, NJ: Fleming H. Revell Co., 1963), p. 133.

43. A.G. Fruchtenbaum, *Apologia* 2(3):54–58 (1993).

44. Luther, cited in V.P. Hamilton, *The Book of Genesis: Chapters 1–17,* in R.K. Harrison, Genesis ed., *New International Commentary on the Old Testament* (Grand Rapids, MI: Eerdmans, 1990), p. 221.

scholar Dr. Arnold G. Fruchtenbaum supports this interpretation by pointing out that the word YHWH is preceded by the untranslated accusative particle את (*et*), which marks the object of the verb, in this case "gotten."[45] Genesis 4:1 reads, "And Adam knew Eve his wife; and she conceived, and bare Cain, and said, I have gotten a man: the LORD (YHWH/Yahweh/Jehovah)." Compare the last few words of this, and the Hebrew, with the account of Abel's birth in the next verse:

. . . and said, I have gotten a man: the LORD

וַתֹּאמֶר קָנִיתִי אִישׁ אֶת־יְהוָה

And she again bare his brother: Abel.

וַתֹּסֶף לָלֶדֶת אֶת־אָחִיו אֶת־הָבֶל

The *Midrash Rabbah* also cites Rabbi Akiba, admitting that the Hebrew construction would seem to imply that Eve thought she was begetting YHWH, which created interpretive difficulties for them, so the translation "with the help of the LORD" is required[46] — as the NASB also renders it.

The *Jerusalem Targum* reads: "I have gotten a man: the angel of Jehovah," while the *Targum Pseudo-Jonathan* says: I have gotten for a man the angel of Jehovah."[47] The Targums[48] often substituted "Angel of God" or "Word of God" for "God."

Fruchtenbaum believes that Eve's actual statement shows that she understood that the seed would be both God and man, but she was grossly mistaken in believing that Cain was the seed in question.[49]

Teaching Their Offspring

Cain and Abel were both aware that God had to be approached only through the correct form of sacrifice, that is, a spotless blood sacrifice (Gen. 4:3–5). This knowledge would have come from their parents, Adam and Eve, who had witnessed God himself make the first sacrifice by killing an animal to clothe them. They also, presumably, passed on this instruction to Seth, who in turn taught Enosh, setting an example for people to call upon the Lord (Gen. 4:26).

Just as the faith in God's promises of the people listed in Hebrews 11 was credited to them as righteousness, it's likely that the apparent faith of Adam and Eve was credited to them as righteousness, thus enabling them to spend eternity with God in heaven.

---

45. A.G. Fruchtenbaum, *Messianic Christology* (Tustin, CA: Ariel Ministries, 1998), p. 15–16.

46. Ibid., p. 16.

47. Ibid., p. 15.

48. F.F. Bruce, *The Books and the Parchments*, Revelation Ed. (Westwood, NJ: Fleming H. Revell Co., 1963).

49. See J. Sarfati, "The Virginal Conception of Christ," *Apologia* 3(2):4–11 (1994); <www.answersingenesis.org/virgin>.
See also Walter Kaiser Jr., *Toward an Old Testament Theology* (Grand Rapids, MI: Zondervan, 1978), p. 37.

Importance for Apologetics

The origin of death and suffering is vitally important in defending Christianity. Many people use the present suffering and death as an excuse not to believe. So it is vital to have an answer — such a justification of God's goodness in the face of evil is known as a theodicy (from Greek *theós* (God) and *dikē*, order, right, just).

The big picture is that Adam's sin is the reason for all the death in the world. However, while the Bible teaches that *individual* suffering is part of this "big picture," it is *not* always correlated with a *particular* sin by that individual.[50] For example, Job suffered intensely although he was the most righteous man on earth. A man was born blind, and Jesus refuted the idea that it was due to his own sin or his parents'; rather, it was to demonstrate the power of God (when Jesus healed the man — John 9). Jesus explicitly said that the victims of one of Pilate's purges and those of the collapse of the Tower of Siloam were not more evil than the rest (Luke 13:1–4).

But if a Christian teaches that suffering existed before there was any sin to warrant it, how then can he give a good apologetic answer to questions such as "Why would God allow mass murders such as the terrorist attack on New York?" A consistent biblical answer points out that death is an intruder, so it is not part of God's original creation, but is ultimately due to man's sin. However, according to long-age theology, death has always been with us, and theistic evolution even says that God used this "last enemy" as His *means* of producing His "very good" creation!

To illustrate the problems with the compromise view, here are two case studies, Charles Darwin and Charles Templeton, plus some other quotes from prominent evolutionary propagandists.

Death of Darwin's Daughter and the Problem of Evil

The PBS television series *Evolution*, episode 1, dramatized a turning point in the spiritual life of Charles Darwin (1809–1882) — the sickness and death of his beloved daughter Annie (1841–1851). Although the series does not spell it out, Darwin's biographer, James Moore, makes it clear that this tragedy destroyed the truth of Christianity in Darwin's mind. How could there be a good God if He allowed this to happen? Instead, Darwin decided that Annie was an unfortunate victim of the laws of nature, that is, she lost the struggle for existence.

Annie's death raised, for Darwin, serious questions about God's goodness, but the prevailing view of his day — that the earth was old and had long been filled with death and violence — provided no adequate answers.

Alas, the prevailing church view was a "long age" of the earth, which placed fossils millions of years *before* Adam. This view entails that death and suffering were

---

50. K. Ham and J. Sarfati, *Why Is There Death and Suffering?* (Florence, KY, USA; Brisbane, Australia: Answers in Genesis, 2001).

Ken Ham and Carl Wieland, *Walking through Shadows* (Green Forest, AR: Master Books, 2002).

around for millions of years before Adam, and yet God called His acts of creation "very good." Such a view of God evidently didn't appeal to Darwin.[51]

However, a consistent biblical view, that death is an intruder, provides a coherent solution. But this is impossible unless the fossil record was formed after Adam's sin, which rules out billions of years.

It's sad to see Ross promoting the same view as Darwin's clerical contemporaries. He claims that this long-age view is *more* acceptable to unbelievers than the literal Genesis view, failing to realize that this approach had already been tried and failed miserably in Darwin's day.

The Apostasy of Charles Templeton (1915–2001)

Templeton was once a colleague of Billy Graham, and at least as famous an evangelist. But, eventually, he apostatized, left the ministry, and wrote the book *Farewell to God*, explaining why he had publicly rejected Christianity.[52] Therefore, one would surely have reason to strongly question whether he had genuine saving faith to begin with (1 John 2:19). His own writings indicate that he had an emotional experience rather than a true conversion to faith in Jesus' dying for his sins and rising from the dead:

> Slowly, a weight began to lift, a weight as heavy as I. . . . An ineffable warmth began to suffuse through my body. It seemed that a light had turned on in my chest and that it had cleansed me. . . . Later, in bed, I lay quietly at the center of a radiant, overwhelming, all-pervasive happiness.[53]

But many of his reasons for leaving the faith were questions that could have been easily answered by anyone familiar with elementary creationist rebuttals.[54] And even many of his non-creation-related objections were merely "arguments from outrage," chronological snobbery and dogmatic rejection of miracles.[55] Romans 1:18 ff. suggests that Templeton's objections are ultimately pseudo-intellectual smokescreens for a willing rejection of God.

The crime journalist and popular-level Christian apologist Lee Strobel interviewed Templeton shortly before his death (after a long battle with Alzheimer's). In his book *The Case for Faith*,[56] Strobel interviewed scholarly apologists about responses to the strongest objections to Christianity. Strobel based these objections largely on Templeton's book and interview notes. Strobel and some of his

51. J.M. Brentnall and R.M. Grigg, "Darwin's Slippery Slide into Unbelief," *Creation* 18(1):34–37, 1995; <www.answersingenesis.org/docs/1314.asp>.

52. C. Templeton, *Farewell to God* (Toronto: McLelland and Stewart, 1996).

53. Ibid., p. 3.

54. See K. Ham and S. Byers, "Slippery Slide to Unbelief: A Famous Evangelist Goes from Hope to Hopelessness," *Creation* 22(3):8–13 (June–August 2000); <www.answersingenesis.org/slide>.

55. J.P. Holding, review of *Farewell to God*, <www.tektonics.org\CT.FTG_0771085087.html>, January 9, 2003.

56. L. Strobel, *The Case for Faith* (Grand Rapids, MI: Zondervan, 2000).

interviewees are old-earth creationists, but it's notable how the question of animal suffering is addressed.

Animal Suffering

Templeton wrote:

> The grim and inescapable reality is that *all life is predicated on death*. Every carnivorous creature *must* kill and devour another creature. It has no option. How could a loving and omnipotent God create such horrors? . . . Surely it would not be beyond the competence of an omniscient deity to create an animal world that could be sustained and perpetuated without suffering and death.[57]

Strobel put this to Norman Geisler, a leading evidentialist apologist, and strong supporter of old-earth creationism, although he has helped young-earth creationists in court.[58] Geisler responded:

> [Y]es, God can create those kind [*sic*] of animals. And the fact is, He did. The original paradise had those kind [*sic*] of animals and the paradise to come — the paradise restored — is going to have those kind [*sic*] of animals. In fact, we are told that God originally created animals and human beings to be herbivorous. [Reads from Genesis 1:29–30, then continues] . . . God did not create animals to be eaten in paradise, and animals weren't eating each other. The prophet Isaiah said someday God will "create a new heavens and a new earth" where "the wolf and the lamb will feed together and the lion will eat straw like an ox." In other words, there's not going to be the same kind of killing that goes on now.
>
> In sum, everything God created was good. What changed things was the Fall. When God was told, in effect, to shove off, he partially did. Romans 8 says all creation was affected — that includes plant life, human beings, animals, everything. There were fundamental genetic changes; we see, for instance, how life spans rapidly decreased after the Fall [*sic*]. God's plan was not designed to be this way; it's only this way because of sin. Ultimately it will be remedied.[59]

This is significant, because Geisler is a hostile witness, yet his response is essentially identical to that of young-earth creationists! This shows how a leading apologist realizes that the only way to answer the objections of Templeton and others is with the biblical teaching that death and suffering resulted from sin. However, he fails to realize that this totally contradicts his old-earth belief. Ross is more consistent — he

---

57. C. Templeton, *Farewell to God* (Toronto: McLelland and Stewart, 1996), p. 197–199.

58. N.L. Geisler A.F. with Brookes and M.J. Keough, *The Creator in the Courtroom — "Scopes II": The 1981 Arkansas Creation-Evolution Trial* (New York: Fromm Intl., 1982).

59. Geisler; cited in L. Strobel, *The Case for Faith* (Grand Rapids, MI: Zondervan, 2000), p. 176–177.

wants to keep billions of years at all costs, so rejects teaching like Geisler's, above. However, Geisler wrote the following endorsement for C&T (back cover):

> *Creation and Time* is the best book on the topic in print. It is a must for anyone interested in the conflict between science and Scripture. Dr. Ross's pleas to overzealous "young earthers" not to make the age of the earth a test of orthodoxy is long overdue.

However, as we often point out, the "young earth" is not, per se, the test of orthodoxy. Rather, it is a *deduction* from other beliefs which *are* orthodox, including the sin-death causality *accepted by Geisler himself,* as shown above! Since Ross's book *explicitly* contradicts the apologetic arguments Geisler explicitly stated, one must wonder how carefully Geisler read the book before endorsing it.

It also shows that many old-earth apologists, for example, Geisler and Strobel, have not carefully thought through the issues and don't realize the contradictions in their views. (This should be remembered when Ross appeals to people like Geisler and others in support. It's notable that Ross is aware of that book, since his audio series[60] mentioned it — but of course there was no mention of Geisler's answer!) Conversely, those who have thought through the issues and still desire to hang on to billions of years, such as Ross, must necessarily hold to unscriptural views on death as well as the age of the earth.

Sir David Attenborough (b. 1926)

Attenborough is famous for his decades of spectacular TV programs about nature, where he never fails to push evolution. A number of Christians have written to him asking, "Why don't you give credit to Almighty God?" Attenborough has explained:

> When creationists talk about God creating every individual species as a separate act, they always instance hummingbirds, or orchids, sunflowers and beautiful things. But I tend to think instead of a parasitic worm that is boring through the eye of a boy sitting on the bank of a river in West Africa, [a worm] that's going to make him blind.
>
> And [I ask them], "Are you telling me that the God you believe in, who you also say is an all-merciful God, who cares for each one of us individually, are you saying that God created this worm that can live in no other way than in an innocent child's eyeball? Because that doesn't seem to me to coincide with a God who's full of mercy."[61]

Of course, this is explained by the Fall, but Ross can't use this explanation, since he is forced by his billions-of-years presuppositions to believe that parasites (which are found in the fossil record) have been part of creation long before man.

---

60. H. Ross, F. Rana, K. Samples, M. Harman, and K. Bontrager, "Life and Death in Eden, The Biblical and Scientific Evidence for Animal Death Before the Fall," audio cassette set, Reasons to Believe, 2001.

61. M. Buchanan, "Wild, Wild Life," *Sydney Morning Herald*, The Guide (March 24, 2003): p. 6.

Carl Sagan (1934–1996)

Sagan was an atheistic astronomer who ardently promoted evolution and the search for extraterrestrial intelligence (SETI), and wrote best-selling books such as *Cosmos*, which was made into a TV series. In this book, he wrote:

> If God is omnipotent and omniscient, why didn't he start the universe out in the first place so it would come out the way he wants? Why is he constantly repairing and complaining? No, there's one thing the Bible makes clear: The biblical God is a sloppy manufacturer. He's not good at design, he's not good at execution. He'd be out of business if there was any competition.[62]

Again, we see a leading atheist thinking so, because once we allow that the fossil record is a sequence of long ages, design arguments are futile. *Sagan realized that any long-age view must interpret the history of life as a series of false starts, extinctions, and generally constant brutality for millions of years — in short, a sloppy "god."*

BIZARRE ARGUMENTS

Ross tried to explain certain fossil transitional series as follows, during the Hovind debate on the John Ankerberg Show in October 2000:[63]

> I mean, when you look at the fossil record, where do you see the evidence for the so-called transitional forms? It's creatures like whales and horses. And these are creatures of population levels so small, generation times so long, body sizes so huge, they have a zero probability for evolutionary advance, they're even lower for our probability for evolutionary advance. Yet we see these, all these transitions. My explanation for that, God loves horses and whales. He knows because of their huge size and small populations, they're gonna go extinct rapidly. When they do, He makes new ones.

Yes, right. God loves horses and whales so much that He lets many of them become extinct! Note that in Ross's theology, these extinctions are before Adam's sin, which was the real originator of death. So even the British evolutionist (and communist) J.B.S. Haldane (1892–1964) made more sense in his (possibly apocryphal) quip that God "must have an inordinate fondness for beetles" — at least in this case it was because there are so many *living* species (about one-fifth of all known species are beetles — 350,000 known).

Actually, the horses and whales are very different cases. The evolutionary horse "series" is constructed from what appears to be a non-horse called *Hyracotherium* on the bottom, while the rest consist of nothing but different varieties of horses, little different in many respects from the range of sizes, toe numbers, etc. seen in horses

---

62. C. Sagan, *Contact* (New York: Pocket Books, Simon & Schuster, Inc., 1985).
63. See in-depth analysis by J. Sarfati, <www.answersingenesis.org/ross_hovind>.

living today.[64] However, as shown in RE, chapter 5, the alleged transitional series of whales from land mammals is nothing of the kind. Some of the creatures are postulated from just a few fragments of bones, and others, like *Basilosaurus,* were totally aquatic and also totally unrelated to modern whales.

Would Adam Have Understood Death without Seeing a Dead Animal?

RTB theologian Kenneth Samples raised the common canard that Adam would not have known what death was unless he had seen a dead animal.[65] But this ignores the fact that God would have programmed Adam with language, as He did the clans of Babel. The only difference is that with Babel, the people would already have personal experience of using grammar and vocabulary, and it was merely changed; in Adam's case, the programming would have included these concepts so he was already able to communicate with God.

It's preposterous to argue that Adam would need to see something to comprehend it. Adam was instructed NOT to eat a fruit — did Adam see a "NOT"? Did Adam have to visualize a logical relationship between propositions such as "eat fruit" and "die"?

In any case, death is really not an entity in itself, but the negation of life. Even Ken Samples must agree that Adam could comprehend life and negation. In fact, this would be very similar to Augustine's argument that evil is not a thing, but a privation of good, with which Samples and I both agree (see page 197).

Finally, this claim is a tacit admission that **physical** death was in view, contrary to Ross (see page 201), since Adam could not have seen any **spiritual** death!

---

64. J. Sarfati, "The Non-evolution of the Horse," *Creation* 21(3):28–31 (June–August 1999); <www.answersingenesis.org/horse>.

65. H. Ross, F. Rana, K. Samples, M. Harman, and K. Bontrager, "Life and Death in Eden, The Biblical and Scientific Evidence for Animal Death Before the Fall," audio cassette set, Reasons to Believe, 2001.

CHAPTER 7

THE CREATED KINDS

This chapter explains the concept of the created kinds, and how they gave rise to modern species. The all-important concept of information is explained. This refutes claims by both evolutionists and Ross that any change is "evolution," because evolution requires an *increase* of information. Ross argues that because God has stopped creating, speciation has ceased. This is falsified by proof of new species arising.

KINDS AND SPECIES

Creationists, starting from the Bible, believe that God created different *kinds* of organisms, which reproduced "after their kinds" (Gen. 1:11, 12, 21, 24, 25). There is another term, *biological species*, which means a population of organisms that can interbreed to produce fertile offspring but that cannot so breed with other biological species.

Each biblical kind would therefore have *originally* been a distinct biological species. But creationists point out that the biblical "kind" is often larger than one of *today's* "species."

The creationist founder of modern classification, Carl Linnaeus, originally defined "species" in much the same way as modern creationists define "kind." However, most organisms today have been classified without any consideration of their ability to interbreed. There has been a proliferation of species and even genus names far beyond the created kinds.

Each of the original kinds was created with a vast amount of information. God made sure that the original creatures had enough variety in their genetic information so that their descendants could adapt to a wide variety of environments.

WHAT IS EVOLUTION?

It is vitally important that words such as "evolution" be used accurately and consistently. The theory of "evolution" that creationists oppose is the idea that particles turned into people over time, without any need for an intelligent designer. The evolutionist Kerkut accurately defined this "General Theory of Evolution" (GTE) as "the theory that all the living forms in the world have arisen from a single source which itself came from an inorganic form." He continued, ". . . the evidence which supports this is not sufficiently strong to allow us to consider it as anything more than a working hypothesis."[1]

Equivocation

However, many evolutionary propagandists are guilty of the practice of *equivocation*; that is, switching the meaning of a single word (evolution) part way through an argument. A common tactic, "bait-and-switch," is simply to produce examples of change over time, call this "evolution," then imply that the GTE is thereby proven or even essential, and creation disproved. As will be shown, Ross also uses this fallacy when attacking YECs.

Natural Selection

Natural selection is where a creature has some inheritable trait that gives it a better chance of passing on this trait to the next generation. Creatures without this trait are less likely to survive, so they don't pass on their genes. Therefore, this trait will become established in the population.

However, natural selection cannot create anything new, therefore demonstrating that because natural selection occurs does not prove that goo-to-you evolution occurs. Rather, it works by *removing* genes from the population. It has long been recognized as a conservative force, removing unfit organisms and thus hindering the effects of the Curse. A creationist, the chemist/zoologist Edward Blyth (1810–1873), wrote thus about natural selection in 1835–37, and as Stephen Jay Gould pointed out, "Natural selection ranked as a standard item in biological discourse."[2] William Paley's famous *Natural Theology* had also recognized the role of natural selection, although not by that name.[3]

Modern creationists also recognize natural selection as a way of producing many varieties from comparatively few created kinds. Therefore, it is an important part of the creation/Fall/Flood/dispersion model.

According to Gould, Darwin's contribution was not natural selection per se, but *natural selection as a creative force*. In this, he may have been anticipated by the Scottish fruit grower Patrick Matthew (in 1831) and the Scottish-American physician William Charles Wells (in 1813, published in 1818).[4]

Furthermore, Professor Paul Pearson of the University of Cardiff (Wales) discovered that James Hutton, better known as "the father of modern (uniformitarian) geology" (see page 245), anticipated the concept of natural selection.[5] In 1794, Hutton wrote a little known work, *Elements of Agriculture*, and Pearson says, "Although he

---

1. G.A. Kerkut, *Implications of Evolution* (Oxford, UK: Pergamon, 1960), p. 157.
2. S.J. Gould, *The Structure of Evolutionary Theory* (Cambridge, MA: Harvard University Press, 2002), p. 137–141.
3. Ibid.
4. Ibid.
5. P.N. Pearson, "In Retrospect," *Nature* 425(6959):665, Oct. 16, 2003.

never used the term, Hutton clearly articulated the principle of evolution by natural selection."[6] Hutton argued that natural selection was creative in producing new traits, but he took it only as far as adapting species to new environments, not transforming them into other species.

Wells, Matthew, and Darwin were all educated in Hutton's home town of Edinburgh, a place famous for its scientific clubs and societies, so they could all have been influenced by him. Pearson discounts the idea of Darwin stealing from Hutton:

> There is no question of Darwin knowingly stealing Hutton's idea. But it is possible that an old half-forgotten concept from his student days later resurfaced, as he struggled to explain his many observations on species and varieties made voyaging around the world in HMS *Beagle*.

> Darwin rightly gets the credit for applying the principle to the transformation of species and assembling the evidence that convinced the scientific world.[7]

Information — The Real Problem with Evolution

The main scientific objection to the GTE is *not* that changes occur through time, and neither is it about the *size* of the change (so use of the terms "micro-" and "macro-evolution" should be discouraged). It isn't even about whether natural selection happens. The key issue is the *type* of change required — to change microbes into men requires changes that *increase the genetic information content*. The three billion DNA "letters" stored in each human cell nucleus convey a great deal more information (known as "specified complexity") than the half a million DNA "letters" of the "simplest" self-reproducing organism. The DNA sequences in a "higher" organism, such as a human being or a horse, for instance, code for structures and functions unknown in the sort of "primitive first cell" from which all other organisms are said to have evolved.

All (sexually reproducing) organisms contain their genetic information in *paired* form. Each offspring inherits half its genetic information from its mother, and half from its father. So there are two genes at a given position (*locus*, plural *loci*) coding for a particular characteristic. An organism can be heterozygous at a given locus, meaning it carries different forms (*alleles*) of this gene. For example, one allele can code for blue eyes, while the other one can code for brown eyes; or one can code for the **A** blood type and the other for the **B** type. Sometimes two alleles have a combined effect, while at other times only one allele (called *dominant*) has any effect on the organism, while the other does not (*recessive*).

With humans, both the mother's and father's halves have 35,000 genes. The information in our DNA is equivalent to a thousand 500-page books (3 billion base pairs). The ardent neo-Darwinist Francisco Ayala points out that humans today

---

6. "Hutton's Other Unconformity," *Geological Society News* (UK), October 16, 2003; <www.geolsoc.org.uk/template.cfm?name=Hutton>.

7. Ibid.

have an "average heterozygosity of 6.7 percent."[8] This means that for every thousand gene pairs coding for any trait, 67 of the pairs have different alleles, meaning 6,700 heterozygous loci overall. Thus, any single human could produce a vast number of different possible sperm or egg cells — 2^{6700} or 10^{2017}. The number of atoms in the whole known universe is "only" 10^{80}, extremely tiny by comparison. So there is no problem for creationists explaining that the original created kinds could each give rise to many different varieties. In fact, the original created kinds would have had much more heterozygosity than their modern, more specialized descendants. No wonder Ayala pointed out that most of the variation in populations arises from reshuffling of previously existing genes, not from mutations. Many varieties can arise simply by two previously hidden recessive alleles coming together. However, Ayala believes the genetic information came ultimately from mutations, not creation. His belief is contrary to information theory.

None of the alleged proofs of "evolution in action" to date provide a *single* example of functional new information being added to genes. Rather, they all involve sorting and/or loss of information. To claim that mere change proves that such information-*increasing* change will occur is like saying that because a merchant can sell goods, he will sell them for a profit. The origin of information is an insurmountable problem for the GTE.[9]

Information theory is a whole new branch of science that has effectively destroyed the last underpinnings of evolution — explained fully in the monumental work *In the Beginning Was Information* by Dr. Werner Gitt, recently retired professor and head of the Department of Information Technology at the German Federal Institute of Physics and Technology.[10] There is even a specialized branch called bio-informatics, the study of biological information.

Can Beneficial Mutations Drive Evolution?

Informed creationists do not deny that some copying mistakes (mutations) can be beneficial, by the normal definition that they help the organism. But in all known cases, they still add no new information.

The best known is sickle-cell anemia, a common blood disorder in which a mutation causes the sufferer's hemoglobin to form the wrong shape and fail to carry oxygen. People who carry two copies of the sickle-cell gene (homozygous) develop fatal anemia. But this misshapen hemoglobin also resists the malaria parasite (*Plasmodium*). So humans who are heterozygous (have both a normal and abnormal gene) have some

---

8. F.J. Ayala, "The Mechanisms of Evolution," *Scientific American* 239(3):48–61 (September 1978); quoted on p. 55.

9. C. Wieland, "Beetle Bloopers," *Creation* 19(3):30 (June–August 1997); <www.answersingenesis.org/beetle>.

K. Ham, "How Would You Answer?" *Creation* 20(3):32–34 (June–August 1998).

R. Grigg, "Information: A Modern Scientific Design Argument," *Creation* 22(2):50–53 (March–May 2000); RE, RE2.

10. W. Gitt, *In the Beginning Was Information* (Bielefeld, Germany: CLV, 1997).

advantage in areas where malaria is prevalent, even though half their hemoglobin is less effective at its job of carrying oxygen.

There are other examples, such as wingless beetles that survive on windy islands because they can't fly, so won't be blown into the sea,[11] and animals in dark caves with shriveled eyes that are less prone to damage.[12] And one way that the *Staphylococcus* bacterium becomes resistant to penicillin is *via* a mutation that disables a control gene for production of penicillinase, an enzyme that destroys penicillin. When it has this mutation, the bacterium *over*-produces this enzyme, which means it is resistant to even huge amounts of penicillin. But in the wild, this mutant bacterium is less fit, because it squanders resources by producing unnecessary penicillinase.

Still another example is a cattle breed called the *Belgian Blue*. This is very valuable to beef farmers because it has 20–30 percent more muscle than average cattle, and its meat is lower in fat and very tender. Normally, muscle growth is regulated by a number of proteins, such as *myostatin*. However, Belgian Blues have a mutation that *deactivates* the myostatin gene, so the muscles grow uncontrolled and become very large. This mutation has a cost, in reduced fertility.[13] A different mutation of the same gene is also responsible for the very muscular Piedmontese cattle. In all these cases, a mutation causes information *loss,* even though it is "beneficial." Therefore, it is in the *opposite* direction required for particles-to-people evolution, which requires the generation of *new* information.

Ross's Attempt to Undermine the Information Criterion

On a radio broadcast, "Information Theory and the Young-Earth Speciation Model" (October 1, 2002), Ross and RTB's resident biologist, Dr. Fazale ("Fuz") Rana, tried to undermine this definition. About three-quarters of the way through the broadcast, they finally got to the point. Rana tried what can only be called a "snow-job" about different kinds of information, but just talked past what YECs say about information as specified complexity. This is also the definition used by intelligent design (ID) theorists such as William Dembski[14] and biophysicist Dr. Lee Spetner of the Jewish faith.[15] It is related to probability.

Instead, Rana used another way of describing information, the pragmatic level, that is, he defined an increase in information as one that gives the animal an advantage (information theorist Dr. Werner Gitt was of course ignored although he pointed out several levels of information).[16]

11. C. Wieland, "Beetle Bloopers," *Creation* 19(3):30 (June–August 1997); <www.answersingenesis. org/beetle>.

12. C. Wieland, "New Eyes for Blind Cave Fish?" <www.answersingenesis.org/cave_fish>.

13. J. Travis, "Muscle-bound Cattle Reveal Meaty Mutation," *Science News* 152(21):325 (November 22, 1997).

14. Wm. B. Dembski, *The Design Inference: Eliminating Chance Through Small Probabilities* (UK: Cambridge University Press, 1998).

15. L.M. Spetner, *Not By Chance* (Brooklyn, NY: The Judaica Press, 1996, 1997).

16. W. Gitt, "Information, Science, and Biology," *TJ* 10(2):181–187 (1996).

But this is no different from what was said about beneficial mutations (see page 228), just dressed up in different terminology. For example, Rana doesn't seem to deny that the sickle-cell gene is a change in the direction of loss of specificity which can confer immunity to malaria. Creationists using the same definition of information as the ID movement would say this is an information loss that's beneficial.

So why is this, also, not "evolution" in the Ross/Rana definition? The problem for Rana and Ross is that they have no reasonable criterion for saying evolution can't occur. How much change counts as "micro" and how much counts as "macro"? Biblical creationists have a consistent criterion — "goo-to-you" evolution requires changes that increase information, therefore not simply any old change is evolution. Further, so far, all observed change is always in the direction of lower specificity. And even if the occasional information-increasing change were found, it would not confirm that goo-to-you evolution has a viable mechanism, since this would predict *many* such changes to be observed. So while there are beneficial changes, none have increased information in the sense of specificity, as evolution requires.

Judging by their radio broadcast, Rana and Ross have no problem actually believing in changes that increase information, so there is no reason, in principle, why they shouldn't believe in the notion of goo-to-you evolution, assuming enough time, and they do believe in billions of years!

What Are the Kinds?

Anticreationist physicist Lawrence Lerner is typical of many anticreationists, and mocks the idea of "kind" by claiming:

> In creationist literature, however, the breadth of a kind can vary from a species to a phylum, including everything in between.[17]

Hybridization Criterion

One must wonder what creationist literature Lerner has actually studied. Based on the biblical criterion for kinds, creationists have extended the criterion used to assign "biological species" to apply to the definition of kinds. That is, while members of the biological species can hybridize to produce fertile offspring, creationists deduce that as long as two modern creatures can hybridize with true fertilization, the two creatures are descended from the same kind.[18] This was first proposed in 1941 by Dr. Frank Marsh, who explained:

> True fertilization is necessary because in hybridization the union of the gametes may result in an embryo which does not live beyond the gastrula stage; or the fetus may die at full period; or the hybrid may be a healthy individual in every way except that it is sterile; or the hybrid may be a completely normal, fertile individual. The requirement of *true* fertilization

17. L.S. Lerner, "Good Science, Bad Science: Teaching Evolution in the States," Thomas B. Fordham Foundation, September 26, 2000.
18. F.L. Marsh, *Variation and Fixity in Nature* (Mountain View, CA: Pacific Press, 1976), p. 37.

is met when the chromosome groups of *both parents* take part in formation of the early blastomeres of the embryo. This is a distinguishing requirement for a true hybrid because offspring may be produced where the germ cells of the male take no other part in the development of a new individual than to stimulate an artificial parthenogenesis whereby the egg will proceed with its development into an embryo.

The microbiologist Dr. Siegfried Scherer of the University of Munich, Germany, extended Marsh's criteria logically. He argued that, if two creatures can hybridize with the same third creature, they are all members of the same kind.[19] He also elaborated on Marsh's explanation of true fertilization:

> Two individuals belong to the same basic type if embryogenesis of a hybrid continues beyond the maternal phase, including subsequent co-ordinated expression of both maternal and paternal morphogenetic genes.[20]

It's notable that this definition was published by a YEC in a major work of the ID movement,[21] so we are hardly out of step. This is ironic since Ross tries to curry favor with the IDM, many of whom also disagree with the YECs' emphasis on biblical chronology. Furthermore, he was a contributor to the very same publication in which Scherer's above-quoted analysis appeared, so Ross can hardly claim to have no knowledge of these matters.

The implication is one-way — hybridization can inform us that two creatures *are* the same kind. But it does *not* necessarily follow that if hybridization *cannot* occur then they are *not* members of the same kind (failure to hybridize could be due to degenerative mutations). After all, there are couples who can't have children, and we don't classify them as a different species, let alone a different kind.

Some atheistic skeptics have demanded that creationists should *list* every single "kind." Of course, to even begin to do so, it would be necessary to perform hybridization experiments on all sexually reproducing organisms, so this is unreasonable. No evolutionist has ever listed all biological species, anyway, as opposed to a list of organisms classified into arbitrary man-made groupings classified as species. And the skeptic's demand for a list of every single kind overlooks the fact that a *denotative definition* (i.e., exhaustive list) is not the only kind of definition. The hybridization criterion is a more reasonable *operational definition*, which could *in principle* enable researchers to list all the kinds.

Discontinuity Systematics

Hybridization is *additive evidence* — it can enable us to *add* to the list of the members of a particular kind. For *subtractive evidence*, that is, *removing* creatures

19. S. Scherer, "Basic Types of Life," in Wm. A. Dembski, *Mere Creation: Science, Faith, and Intelligent Design* (Downers Grove, IL: InterVarsity Press, 1998), p. 197.

20. Ibid.

21. See C. Wieland, "AiG's Views on the Intelligent Design Movement," <www.answersingenesis.org/IDM>, August 30, 2002.

from consideration as members of a kind, there are biblical criteria. For example, whales and birds do not share ancestry with land creatures (Gen. 1:20–25), and mankind does not share ancestry with other animals (Gen. 1:26–27). Further refinements are more difficult but creationist systematists work with features of discontinuity.[22]

Kind Boundaries: *Baramin*

The boundaries of the "kind" do not always correspond to any given man-made classification such as "species," genus, or family. But this is not the fault of the biblical term "kind"; it is actually due to inconsistencies in the man-made classification system. That is, several organisms classified as different "species," and even different genera or higher groupings, can produce fertile offspring. This means that they are really the same *biological* species that has several varieties, hence a *polytypic* (many-type) species. A good example is Kekaimalu, the wholphin, a fertile hybrid of two different so-called *genera*, the false killer whale and bottlenose dolphin.[23] There are more examples in *Variation and Fixity in Nature* by F.L. Marsh.[24]

Because of the inadequacies of man-made classification systems, creationists have devised a biblically based system called baraminology. This is based on Marsh's term "baramin" for "created kinds,"[25] from Hebrew *bara* = create and *min* = kind, which he also called "basic types," characterized by the hybridization criterion (page 230).

Do Creationists Believe in "Evolution Above the Species Level"?

On November 25, 2000, Ross's assistant, Fuz Rana, claimed:

> I mean in the case of the wholphin, what you're looking at is evolution happening at the family level, which is two levels in the biological classification hierarchy above speciation, so this is no longer speciation. This is evolution happening at the family level, which is quite extensive evolutionary type of transformations.

But here, he has missed the point completely; that is, the so-called "family" is just an arbitrary man-made classification, which in this case is really a single biological species. Just before this, he had said:

> I'm sitting here listening to young earth creationists attacking us for taking an anti-evolutionary stance, and that's highly ironic because we're ac-

---

22. T.C. Wood, "A Baraminology Tutorial with Examples from the Grasses (Poaceae)," *TJ* 16(1):15–25 (2002).

W.J. ReMine, "Discontinuity Systematics: A New Method of Biosystematics Relevant to the Creation Model," in R.E. Walsh and C.L. Brooks, editors, *Proceedings of the Second International Conference on Creationism* (Pittsburgh, PA: Creation Science Fellowship, 1990), p. 207–213.

23. D. Batten, "Ligers and Wholphins? What Next?" *Creation* 22(3):28–33, June–August 2000; <www.answersingenesis.org/liger>.

24. F.L. Marsh, *Variation and Fixity in Nature* (Mountain View, CA: Pacific Press, 1976), p. 37.

25. Ibid.

cused, at least Hugh's accused, of being a theistic evolutionist, and of being a compromiser, yet who's the camp that's siding with the evolutionists? It's not us, and we're being attacked for taking a supernatural stance with respect to the creation of life.

The key issue is not how much "change" we are willing to accept — we are not interested in playing "more-antitransformist-than-thou" to their untenable extent of denying speciation. Rather, the issue is the authority of Scripture — including recent creation, global Flood, and animals reproducing "after their kind."

Wolves and Dogs: A Case Study

Creationists have often pointed out that Noah didn't need to take wolves, foxes, coyotes, dingoes, chihuahuas, great danes, spaniels, dachshunds, etc. on the ark, because it was sufficient to take a pair of wolf-like creatures with all the potential for diversifying into different varieties. And evolutionists now concede that domestic dogs came from wolves only a few thousand years ago, and are not really very different, although they insist on calling this "evolution."[26]

For example, the original dog/wolf kind probably had the information for a wide variety of fur lengths. The first animals probably had medium-length fur. In the simplified example illustrated here,[27] a single gene pair is shown under each dog as coming in two possible forms. One form of the gene (L) carries instructions for long fur, the other (S) for short fur. In this simplified example for illustration, a single gene pair is shown under each dog as coming in two possible forms. One form of the gene (L) carries instructions for long fur, the other (S) for short fur.

In row 1, we start with medium-furred animals (LS) interbreeding. Each of the offspring of these dogs can get one of either gene from each parent to make up their two genes. In row 2, we see that the resultant offspring can have either short (SS), medium (LS)

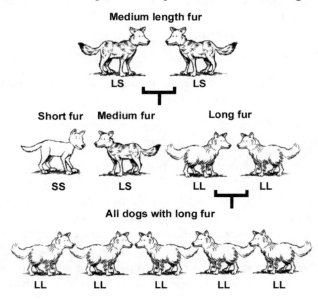

Medium length fur

LS   LS

Short fur   **Medium fur**   **Long fur**

SS   LS   LL   LL

All dogs with long fur

LL   LL   LL   LL   LL

---

26. K. Lange, "Evolution of Dogs: Wolf to Woof," *National Geographic* (January 2001): p. 5.

27. Based on P. Weston and C. Wieland, "Bears Across the World" *Creation* 20(4):31 (September–November 1998).

or long (LL) fur. Now imagine the climate cooling drastically (as in the post-Flood ice age). Only those with long fur survive to give rise to the next generation (line 3). So from then on, all the dogs will be a new, long-furred variety. Note that:

- They are now *adapted* to their environment.

- They are now more *specialized* than their ancestors on row 1.

- This has occurred through *natural selection.*

- There have been *no new genes* added.

- In fact, genes have been lost from the population — i.e., there has been *a loss of genetic information*, the opposite of what microbe-to-man evolution needs in order to be credible.

- Now the population is *less* able to adapt to future environmental changes — were the climate to become hot, there is no genetic information for short fur, so the dogs would probably overheat.

This possibility has been supported by experiment. In Berlin, a female wolf and (large!) male poodle were mated. The pups looked fairly similar to each other and nothing special, with genetic information from both parents. But the inbred "grand-pups" were very different from each other: one was like its grandmother wolf in appearance and killer instincts, while another looked clearly "poodle" and still others were mixtures.[28]

This shows that:

- The poodle and wolf are the same kind, and even the same biological species.

- The first generation of pups had enough genetic variety to produce a wide variety of descendants.

- Therefore, it would have been possible in principle to have a single pair on the ark with similar variation.

Note that one of the poodle's most famous traits, the long hair, is caused by an information-losing mutation — loss of ability to shed hair at the right length.

Another example involved a Russian research group breeding a husky and jackal to produce a "jacksy." This takes advantage of the domestication of the husky and the sharp sense of smell of the wild jackal, sharper than that of any domestic dog. The jacksy is thus the "ultimate" drug sniffer dog.[29] This also shows that the process which produced the husky from its original canine ancestor resulted in a loss of genetic information, such as reduction in smell sensitivity.

28. R. Junker and S. Scherer, *Evolution: Ein kritisches Lehrbuch*, 4th edition (Giefsen, Germany: Weyel Lehrmittelverlag, 1998), p. 39.
29. "A Dog Called Jacksy," *New Scientist* 174(2343):19 (May 18, 2002).

Ross's "Theology of Speciation" and Its Implications

Ross effectively treats *fixity of species* as "gospel truth." In fact, he goes as far as constructing an entire theology on his belief that no species have arisen in the last tens of thousands of years. Specifically, Hugh Ross would have us believe that the seventh day of creation week is still going on (see page 82), and the alleged fact that there are no recently originated species corroborates the fact that God is resting from His creative activities (GQ:64–65,155).

As evidence, Ross cites (GQ:64) the claim by Paul and Ann Ehrlich that the birth of a new species has yet to be documented in nature.[30] This is an incorrect statement. And the Ehrlichs are in any case hardly the most reliable source of information. Paul (b. 1932), a butterfly specialist, is most famous for advocating fanatical population control ideas, and for the falsified prophecies of doom by mass starvation and resource depletion made in his 1968 book *The Population Bomb*. But he and his wife still promote their radical ideas, including radical pro-abortion policies.

In his debate with Dr. Kent Hovind on the John Ankerberg Show in October 2000,[31] Ross claims (essentially repeating what he had written in C&T:79–80):

> Well, just by scientific modeling, we can determine that there is no possibility for a species changing into a distinctly different species unless it exceeds one quadrillion individuals with a body size less than one centimeter and a generation time less than three months. Which means it's gonna work for viruses and bacteria, but it's gonna have no capacity to explain the existence of new species of birds, mammals, or any of the creatures we see from the Cambrian explosion onward.

I know of no biologist who says the things Ross says, and Ross is not qualified in the subject. What has body size to do with anything? As shown on page 237, there are proven examples of new species arising that don't meet Ross's criteria.

The Biblical Model Predicts *Rapid* Speciation

The biblical creation/Fall/Flood/dispersion model would also predict *rapid* formation of new varieties and even species. This is because all the modern varieties of land vertebrates must have descended from comparatively few animals that disembarked from the ark only 4,500 years ago. In contrast, Darwin thought that such a process would surely take eons. It turns out that the very evidence claimed by evolutionists to support their theory supports the biblical model.

In fact, the prominent view of Darwin's opponents was that God created organisms in their present locations. In his arguments against creation and for evolution, Darwin wondered why God would create not-quite-identical finches on almost identical islands.

---

30. P. R. Ehrlich and A.H. Ehrlich, *Extinction* (New York: Ballantine, 1981), p. 26.
31. See in-depth analysis by J. Sarfati, <www.answersingenesis.org/ross_hovind>.

In this case, Darwin rightly thought that the island animals were descended from mainland ones. But this is what biblical creationists would believe, too, with a global Flood and subsequent migration from Ararat via continents to islands. So Darwin's arguments only work against a compromised creationist view, not the biblical view.

Present-day "progressive creationists" such as Ross hold essentially the same view as Darwin's opponents, so they are trying to fight a battle that was lost 150 years ago — but the battle would have had the correct focus, and could have been won, if Christians had not compromised on the earth's age and the global Flood.

The simple fact is this: there are *numerous* species which are now known to have arisen not only within the last few thousand years, but also within historic times, as will be shown in the next section.[32] This is true of individual species as well as large clusters of them, especially in the tropics. But again, it's important to stress that speciation has nothing to do with *real* evolution, because it involves *sorting* and *loss* of existing genetic information, rather than formation of *new* information.

All of this evidence of speciation emphatically falsifies Ross's belief that God has been "resting" in the recent past (that is, in the contrived manner with which Ross defines the seventh day). Therefore, those Christians relying on Ross for apologetic information could be easily shot down by skeptics. What happens when a Christian, armed only with Ross's assurance that speciation can't happen today, is confronted with that evidence, and indoctrinated with Ross's repetition of the atheistic claim that agreeing to speciation is agreeing to evolution?

But Ross, in his November 25, 2000, broadcast, tried to brazen it out against examples of proven rapid speciation that AiG had pointed out:

> Well, we have the research papers right here, and all these papers are claiming is evidence for reproductive isolation. That's not the same as speciation.

But this does not follow, for reproductive isolation is the very definition of biological speciation! Ross has even acknowledged elsewhere that a common definition of species is "a class of creatures that can mate and produce fertile offspring" (C&T:78). (It is also worth noting the looseness of using the word "class" when defining taxonomic categories, since it has a definite meaning as a group above "order" and below "phylum.")

If Ross does not mean this when he talks about speciation, then it's up to *him* to provide an alternative definition, and to explain why we should accept that. But we have on good authority that both he and his biologist Fuz Rana have been repeatedly challenged to explain what precisely they mean, but have failed to meet this challenge. Their fuzziness about species definitions is counter-productive, because

---

32. J. Woodmorappe, *Noah's Ark: A Feasibility Study* (El Cajon, CA: Institute for Creation Research, 1996), p. 181.

the other definitions are actually looser — so there would be even *more* examples of speciation by these alternative criteria.

Examples and Mechanisms of Speciation

Small Populations

For one species to split into two, some differences must arise, for example, losing different amounts of information such that they are no longer capable of interbreeding. This is most likely to happen in small, isolated populations. There is a bigger chance of a mutation being fixed in a small population simply by chance, and a greater chance of losing certain genes (genetic drift). In a larger population, it's harder to fix a mutation into the population, because of the cost of substitution — the creatures lacking the gene must die off.[33] Also, it's harder to lose genes, because even if one individual doesn't pass on a particular gene or genes, there is a good chance that others will.

Allopatric Speciation

Many varieties can arise rapidly from an initial population with large genetic variety. If this population splits into isolated small populations, each subgroup may carry a fraction of the total genetic information and/or different mutations. If these populations become subjected to different selective pressures, then they might become separate species. This is known as allopatric speciation, a term coined by Ernst Mayr (b. 1904), from Greek *allos* (other) and *patris* (homeland).

Biologists have identified several instances of rapid adaptation, including guppies on Trinidad, lizards in the Bahamas, daisies on the islands of British Columbia, and house mice on Madeira.[34] Another good example is a new "species" of mosquito, that can't interbreed with the parent population, arising in the London underground train system (the "Tube") in only 100 years. The rapid change has "astonished" evolutionists, but *should* delight *informed* creationists.[35]

The following is an example of artificial "allopatric" speciation, where the isolation was provided by the researcher:

> William R. Rice of the University of New Mexico and George W. Salt of the University of California at Davis demonstrated that if they sorted a group of fruit flies by their preference for certain environments and bred those flies separately over 35 generations, the resulting flies would refuse to breed with those from a very different environment."[36]

---

33. W.J. ReMine, *The Biotic Message* (St. Paul, MN: St. Paul Science, 1993), chapter 8.
34. D. Catchpoole and C. Wieland, "Speedy Species Surprise," *Creation* 23(2):13–15 (March–May 2001).
35. See C. Wieland, "Brisk Biters," *Creation* 21(2):41 (March–May 1999).
36. John Rennie, editor, "15 Answers to Creationist Nonsense," *Scientific American* 287(1):82–83. See refutation at <www.answersingenesis.org/sciam> and RE2.

Sympatric Speciation

Not as well known is *sympatric speciation,* where reproductive isolation occurs without geographical isolation (Greek *syn–/sym–* with, same). But there are other factors that can cause division. For example, changes in song or color might result in birds that no longer recognize a mate, so they no longer interbreed.

A major scientific conference on speciation held in Asilomar, California, in May 1996, shows that sympatric speciation is more widespread than Mayr thought.[37] For example, certain types of fruit-eating insects use the fruits of their host plant for courtship displays and mating. If one group decides to try a new type of fruit, then they will mate only with others which also choose the same plant. This results in reproductive isolation (speciation) even within the same geographical area.

As a further example, fish living in the same lake may become reproductively isolated because of genetically determined variation in food choices, and natural selection will favor the fittest size, and, thus, different mate choices. This could explain the hundreds of cichlid species in Lake Victoria. The following is a more recent description of the 300 species of cichlid fishes which have originated in only the last several thousand years:

> Despite its young age, Lake Victoria has hundreds of endemic species and six endemic genera. The presumption is that all of the fishes evolved *in situ* within this very brief time.[38]

Indeed, the creationist zoologist Dr. Arthur Jones studied cichlid speciation for his Ph.D. thesis, and affirmed that starting from the biblical creation/Flood/dispersion model provided him with important research insights.[39]

Genetic Rearrangements

Biologists have identified several ways that a loss of genetic information through mutations (copying mistakes) can lead to new species. For example, the loss of a protein's ability to recognize "imprinting" marks can result in the inability to mate successfully.[40] A chromosomal rearrangement can result in mutual infertility, as can "jumping genes" (where the already existing gene moves around), but this is reshuffling already existing information, not forming any new information. A polyploid organism, that is, containing one or more extra sets of chromosomes, will sometimes be unable to interbreed with the parent population. This is usually viable only in plants, not animals.

---

37. A. Gibbons, "On the Many Origins of Species," *Science* 273:1496–1499 (1996).
   V. Morell, "Starting Species with Third Parties and Sex Wars," *Science* 273:1499–1502 (1996).
   C. Wieland, "Speciation Conference Brings Good News for Creationists," *TJ* 11(2):135–136 (1997); <www.answersingenesis.org/docs/459.asp>.
38. L.S. Kaufman et al., "Evolution in Fast Forward," *Endeavour* 21(1):23, (1997).
39. J. Ashton, editor, *In Six Days: Why 50 [Ph.D.] Scientists Choose to Believe in Creation* (Green Forest, AR: Master Books, 2001).
40. P. Cohen, "The Great Divide," *New Scientist* 160(2164):16 (1998).
   P. Jerlström, "Genomic Imprinting," *TJ* 13(2):6–8 (1999).

However, polyploidy is the result of repetitious doubling of the *same* information, not generating new information (a brave student might try handing in two copies of the same assignment to see if he gets extra marks!).

Post-Flood Speciation

Hand in hand with his other misconceptions about speciation, Ross reflexively repeats other common arguments about speciation after the Flood. He tells us that there was not enough time for the animals released from the ark to have given rise to new species (GQ:155). The fact is, some of the just-discussed recently originated species developed in as little as one generation,[41] in a similar way to the offspring of the wolf and poodle discussed on page 234. There are also numerous examples of spectacularly different life forms arising within a few generations, albeit without necessarily speciating.[42]

Indeed, creationists point out that Mayr's allopatric model would explain the origin of many different animal varieties after they migrated out from Ararat.[43] The mountainous topography and the different migration routes would provide ideal conditions for geographical isolation of small populations. Also, it explains the origins of the different people groups ("races") after the confusion of languages at Babel induced small population groups to spread out all over the earth, as creationists have often shown (AB chapter 18). Of course, the modern people groups are *not* reproductively isolated and are still a single biological species. Knowing this would have saved Ross from potentially serious mistakes (see page 302).

Hugh Ross also claims that if species were forming rapidly, biologists should see large numbers of new ones forming today (GQ:155). In making this statement, Ross further displays his ignorance about the processes of speciation. There is no mystery at all about the fact that speciation seldom occurs today — although, as we showed, it does happen, despite Ross's claims. It is widely recognized that new species seldom form when the ecological niches are already filled by pre-existing forms of life, but are much more likely to form when the niches are largely vacant.[44] Obviously, niches were largely vacant immediately after the Flood, and numerous new species arose in a short time. But in doing so, they have largely filled the ecological niches available, thus reducing the opportunities for further speciation down to a trickle.

Do Creationists Believe in "Ultra-rapid Evolution"?

Finally, Ross repeats the fallacious argument that, because creationists advocate the rapid speciation of life forms released from the ark, creationists are ironically embracing evolutionism more intensively than are the evolutionists themselves (GQ:91–92). In actuality, speciation, in itself, is not the origin of a totally new life

---

41. J. Woodmorappe, *Noah's Ark: A Feasibility Study* (El Cajon, CA: Institute for Creation Research, 1996), p. 181.
42. Ibid., p. 180.
43. Ibid., p. 165.
44. Ibid., p. 179–182.

form at all. The new species is merely a minor variant (generally a subset) of the parent species.

As we pointed out, there is no evolution because there is no new information. More informed evolutionists themselves acknowledge that the origin of a new species is simply an ecological adaptation of a life form that exhibits the same or lower grade of complexity (i.e., information content) as the parent species.

By contrast, the origin of higher taxonomic categories, the "meat and potatoes" of evolutionism, is quite different. In terms of biological novelty, speciation itself does not qualify as evolution, and hence creationists are not advocating rapid evolution when they speak of rapid speciation.

Of course, not a few evolutionists have tried to confuse the issue by insisting that an acknowledgement of new species forming (or even of variety existing within a species) is tantamount to acceptance of molecules-to-man evolution. It is unfortunate that Ross has evidently fallen for this sophistry (equivocation, see page 226).

Also, a fellow progressive creationist of Ross's, Walter Bradley, agrees that variation is not evolution:

> God created the major types of animals and plant life and then used process to develop the tremendous variety of life forms we observe today.[45]

So if creationists believe in "rapid evolution," then so do some progressive creationists. This shows that Ross's "fixity of species" view is not universally held within the mainstream of his own belief system. His advocacy of this untenable view unfortunately serves to bolster the efforts of atheists in denouncing all creationists.

CONCLUSION

The biblical creation/Flood/dispersion model entails that God created a number of created kinds with immense genetic variety. After the Flood, representatives of all the kinds of vertebrate animals migrated out from Ararat and diversified, adapting to different environmental niches. The isolated small populations were ideal for producing new species.

Furthermore, the complete failure of what I, here, call "Ross's theology of speciation" provides an excellent example of the danger inherent in attempting to construct a non-conventional interpretation of Scripture around some presumed fact of science. Once the presumed fact is shown to be false (in this case, Ross's belief that there has been no speciation in the most recent thousands of years) the theological construct (in this case, Ross's belief that the seventh day still continues, as God is ostensibly not creating anything today) goes down with it. Ross is in no position to object, since his broader theology is based on subjugating Scripture to "science."

---

45. W.L. Bradley and R.L. Olsen, "The Trustworthiness of Scripture in Areas Relating to Natural Science," in E.D. Radmacher and R. Preus, *Hermeneutics, Inerrancy, and the Bible* (Grand Rapids, MI: Zondervan, 1984), p. 290.

CHAPTER 8

THE GLOBAL FLOOD AND NOAH'S ARK

This chapter demonstrates that the Bible teaches a global Flood that occurred about 4,500 years ago, in contrast to Ross, who believes in a local flood that occurred in Mesopotamia "between twenty thousand and thirty thousand years ago" (GQ:177). Scientific evidence for a global Flood is presented, as well as a plausible mechanism in catastrophic plate tectonics. It also refutes many of Ross's geological arguments against a global Flood, and answers skeptical attacks on Noah's ark.

BIBLICAL EVIDENCE THAT NOAH'S FLOOD WAS GLOBAL

Genesis 6–9 emphasizes the global extent of the flood in Noah's day. A straightforward reading of the Genesis chronologies (see next chapter) clearly suggests that it occurred about 4,500 years ago.

Emphasis of Universal Words

In the Flood account, the frequency of the word כֹּל (*kol* = all, every) indicates that God is going out of his way to emphasize the universality of the Flood.[1] Genesis 7:19–23 reads:

> They rose greatly on the earth, and **all** the high mountains under the **entire** heavens were covered. . . . **Every** living thing that moved on the earth perished — birds, livestock, wild animals, **all** the creatures that swarm over the earth, and **all** mankind. **Everything** on dry land that had the breath of life in its nostrils died. **Every** living thing on the face of the earth was wiped out; men and animals and the creatures that move along the ground and the birds of the air were wiped from the earth. **Only** Noah was left, and those with him in the ark.

Leupold comments on Genesis 7:19:

> A measure of the waters is now made by comparison with the only available standard for such waters — the mountains. They are said to have

---

1. M. Kruger, "Genesis 6–9: Does 'All' Always Mean All?" *TJ* 10(2):214–218 (1996).

been "covered." Not a few merely but "all the high mountains under all the heavens." One of these expressions alone would almost necessitate the impression that the author intends to convey the idea of the absolute universality of the Flood, e.g., "all the high mountains." Yet since "all" is known to be used in a relative sense, the writer removes all possible ambiguity by adding the phrase "under all the heavens." A double "all" (*kol*) cannot allow for so relative a sense. It almost constitutes a Hebrew superlative. So we believe that the text disposes of the question of the universality of the Flood.

By way of objection to this interpretation, those who believe in a limited flood, which extended perhaps as far as mankind may have penetrated at that time, urge the fact that *kol* is used in a relative sense, as is clearly the case in passages such as Genesis 41:57; Exodus 9:25, 10:15; Deuteronomy 2:25; and 1 Kings 10:24. However, we still insist that this fact could overthrow a single *kol*, never a double *kol*, as our verse has it.

A question could be asked of Ross: "Just suppose, for the sake of the argument, that God had wanted to teach a global Flood — how could He have said it more clearly than in Genesis 7?"

Ross's Ally Gleason Archer Rejects a Local Flood

Strong support for a global Flood comes from an ironic source, Gleason Archer. He is undisputably a top Hebrew scholar, but now often finds himself in the company of Hugh Ross, who is by no stretch of the imagination a Hebrew scholar (see pages 14 and 254). For example, they teamed up to comprise the "day-age" side in *The Genesis Debate*.[2] But Archer completely rejected a local Flood in his best known book, the outstanding *Encyclopedia of Bible Difficulties*:

> The biblical record in Genesis 7–8 describes no local inundation confined to the Mesopotamian Valley (as some scholars have suggested) but a water level that surpassed the summits of the highest mountains.
> Genesis 7:19 states "And the waters prevailed more and more upon the earth, so that *all* the high mountains *everywhere* under the heavens [lit. 'which were under all the heavens' or 'under the whole sky'] were covered."
> Now the most elementary knowledge of physical law leads to the observation that water seeks its own level . . . the episode here described lasted more than a year; and there is therefore far more involved here than a temporary surge."[3]

Other Biblical Reasons Why the Flood Must Be Global

Here are some more reasons why the Flood makes sense only as a global one.[4] If the Flood was local:

2. D.G. Hagopian, *The Genesis Debate* (Mission Viejo, CA: Crux Press, 2001).
3. G.L. Archer Jr., *Encyclopedia of Bible Difficulties* (Grand Rapids, MI: Zondervan, 1982), p. 82–84.
4. Anon., *Creation* 21(3):49 (June–August 1999).

- Why did Noah have to build an ark? He could have walked to the other side of the mountains and avoided it.

- Why did God send every kind of animal to the ark so they would escape extinction? There would have been other animals to reproduce that kind if these particular ones had died.

- Why was the ark big enough to hold all the kinds of land vertebrate animals that have ever existed? If only Mesopotamian animals were aboard, the ark could have been much smaller.

- Why would birds have been sent on board? These could simply have winged across to a nearby mountain range.

- How could the waters rise to 15 cubits (8 meters) above the mountains (Gen. 7:20)? Water seeks its own level. It couldn't have risen to cover the local mountains while leaving the rest of the world untouched. Nor would a local flood take a whole year to subside.

- People who did not happen to be living in the vicinity would not have been affected by it. They would have escaped God's judgment on sin. If this happened, what did Christ mean when He likened the coming judgment of all men to the judgment of "all" men (Matt. 24:37–39; 2 Pet. 3:3–7) in the days of Noah? A partial judgment in Noah's day would mean a partial judgment to come.

- God would have repeatedly broken His promise (Gen. 9:11–16) never to send such a flood again, because there have been many *local* floods since then.

- The Bible uses special words for Noah's flood: Hebrew מבול (*mabbûl*) and Greek κατακλυσμο *kataklusmos* (verb κατακλυζω *katakluzō*). Compare the words used to describe ordinary localized floods, for example, Hebrew שטף (*sheteph*), נהר (*nahar*) נחל (*nachal*), זרם (*zaram*); Greek πλημμυρα (*plēmmura*).

HISTORY OF INTERPRETATION ABOUT THE FLOOD

One of many inconsistencies on Ross's part involves the selective citing of church fathers. As shown in the chapter "History of Interpretation," Ross alleges that most of the church fathers believed that the days in Genesis 1 were long periods of time. I showed that Ross's claim is false. So let us see if he is any better on the church fathers' attitudes towards a local flood — a position which Ross completely endorses (GQ chs. 17–18). It turns out that most of the church fathers, notably Tertullian, Pseudo-Eustatius, and Procopius, as well as those in the table below, accepted a *global* Flood.[5] Many of them reacted strongly against local flood ideas held by all the Greek

---

5. J. Woodmorappe, *Noah's Ark: A Feasibility Study* (El Cajon, CA: Institute for Creation Research, 1996), p. xi.

philosophers (including Plato), except for Xenophon. Only Pseudo-Justin seems to have supported a local flood.

Table 8.1: The Opinion of Ancient Writers Concerning the Extent of Noah's Flood[6]				
Writer	Date	Extent of Flood		Reference
		Local	Global	
Philo	c.20 B.C.–C.A.D. 50		X	*Abraham*, 41–44
Josephus	A.D. 37/38–100		X	*Antiquities*, 1.3.4 (1.89)
Justin Martyr	c.100–c.165		X	*Dialogue*, 138
Theophilus of Antioch	Wrote c.180		X	*Autolycus*, 3.18–19
Tertullian	c.160–c.225		X	*Pallium*, 2; *Women*, 3
Gregory of Nazianzus	330–390		X	*2nd Theol. Orat.* 18
John Chrysostom	374–407		X	*Genesis*, 25.10
Augustine of Hippo	354–430		X	*City* 15.27

So if Ross were to be consistent in his use of church fathers as authority figures, he, too, would feel obligated to support a global Flood.

Calvin[7] is another who supported a global Flood:

> *And the flood was forty days, etc.* Moses copiously insists on this fact, in order to show that the whole world was immersed in the waters.[8]

Ross (GQ chapter 11) emulates anticreationists such as the apostate Ron Numbers,[9] in claiming that flood geology is a recent aberration invented by George McCready Price (1870–1963). Price was a Seventh-Day Adventist who wrote a number of books in the 1910s and '20s criticizing evolution and long ages and defending a global Flood. Ross criticizes Whitcomb and Morris[10] for ostensibly not giving sufficient credit to Price for his ideas on flood geology (GQ:89), despite the fact that he is mentioned a number of times in their text. Ross goes even further, attributing biblical creationism and flood geology to "the visions of an Adventist prophetess [Ellen White]" via George McCready Price.

---

6. From Robert Bradshaw's in depth study, *Genesis Creationism and the Early Church*, chapter 6; <www.robibrad.demon.co.uk/Chapter6.htm>, August 13, 2003.

7. J. Sarfati, "Calvin Says: Genesis Means What It Says," *Creation* 22(4)44–45 (September–November 2000); <www.answersingenesis.org/calvin>.

8. J. Calvin, *Genesis*, 1554 (Edinburgh, UK: Banner of Truth, 1984), p. 272.

9. See the review of Numbers's historically unreliable (perhaps due to his anticreationist bias) book *The Creationists*, by E. Andrews, *Origins* 8(20):21–23 (1995). Numbers was raised in a SDA home but now regards himself as agnostic.

10. J.C. Whitcomb and H.M. Morris, *The Genesis Flood* (Grand Rapids, MI: Baker Book House, 1961).

Ken Ham pointed out that he had never even heard of Price at the time he helped found CSF/AiG, and that he adopted six-day creation and a global Flood (and hence Flood geology) because of the biblical teaching.[11] But as Dr. Terry Mortenson demonstrated in his Ph.D. thesis, the early 19th-century scriptural geologists presented such ideas well before Price (see page 132). Furthermore, Price and White were simply taking Genesis 1–11 as literal history just as the scriptural geologists and virtually all earlier Christians had done. So even if Ross were right about Price, he is wrong to think that discrediting Price would be enough to refute creationism — this is a classic case of the genetic fallacy.

With such serious logical fallacies in Ross's book, it is astonishing that it was endorsed by Christian philosopher J.P. Moreland, who is usually very astute at spotting such fallacies. (One might wonder whether he actually read it. As pointed out on page 13, he wouldn't be the first to have endorsed one of Ross's books without reading it.[12])

Hugh Ross also appears to have different expectations of other authors, as opposed to himself, when it comes to giving proper bibliographic credit for predecessors' ideas. When Ross discusses the alleged evidences (GQ chapter 18) for a local flood in his own book, the reader is given the impression that the ideas originated with Ross himself. No mention at all is made of the fact that all, or virtually all, of the arguments advanced by Ross could have been copied from 19th-century local-flood advocates.

One of the most influential was the evangelical Congregationalist theologian John Pye Smith (1774–1851). In the late 1830s, he wrote two books advocating that the Flood was restricted to the Mesopotamian Valley (essentially modern-day Iraq).[13] Evangelicals rightly decried this at first, but eventually yesterday's heresy became today's orthodoxy, an all-too-familiar story in Church history. Local flood advocates have repeated Pye Smith's arguments without much refinement to this day.

James Hutton (1726–97)

The Scotsman James Hutton is often called "the Founder of Modern Geology." He was the originator of the doctrine of slow and gradual changes over vast eons of time. He was actually not trained as a geologist, but in medicine. He turned to farming for many years before eventually becoming interested in geology. In his *Theory of the Earth* (1795), he proposed that the continents were gradually and continually being eroded into the ocean basins. These sediments were then gradually hardened and raised by the internal heat of the earth to form new continents, which would

---

11. K. Ham, "Demolishing 'Straw men,' " *Creation* 19(4):13–15 (1997).
12. See also K. Ham, C. Wieland, and T. Mortenson, "Are (Biblical) Creationists 'Cornered'? — A Response to Dr. J.P. Moreland: The Bible Talks of 'The Four Corners of the Earth.' Does This Mean the Days of Creation Could be Non-literal, Too?" *TJ* 17(3):43–50 (2003); <www.answersingenesis.org/moreland>.
13. J.P. Smith, *Mosaic Account of Creation and the Deluge illustrated by Science* (London, 1837).
J.P. Smith, *On the Relation Between the Holy Scriptures and Some Parts of Geological Science* (London, 1839).

be gradually eroded into the ocean again. With this slow cyclical process in mind, Hutton said that he could see "no vestige of a beginning" to the earth.

Hutton's bias was clear. In 1785, *before examining the evidence* he proclaimed:

> The past history of our globe *must be explained* by what can be seen to be happening now. . . . No powers are to be employed that are not natural to the globe, *no action to be admitted* except those of which we know the principle (emphasis added).[14]

Hutton's principle for interpreting the rocks is a not a refutation of the biblical teaching of creation and the Flood, but a dogmatic refusal even to consider them as possible explanations.

Charles Lyell (1797–1875)

Hutton's view became geological dogma through the work of the lawyer Charles Lyell in the 1830s, due to his three-volume *Principles of Geology* in 1830. Lyell built on Hutton's ideas, and insisted that the geological features of the earth can, and indeed must, be explained by slow gradual processes of erosion, sedimentation, earthquakes, and volcanism operating at essentially the same rate and power as we observe today. He rejected any notion of regional or global catastrophism. He assumed that earthquakes, volcanoes, and floods in the past were no more frequent or powerful on average compared to those in the present. By the 1840s his view became the ruling paradigm in geology.

Even some modern evolutionists acknowledge that Lyell was biased and unscientific, driven by anti-biblical philosophical assumptions, whereas the "catastrophists" of his day (who believed in a Flood catastrophe) were more empirically based followers of the scientific method (though most of them did not believe that the global Flood was responsible for most of the sedimentary rock layers and did also believe in an earth much older than the Bible teaches). Stephen Jay Gould (1941–2002), himself a leading evolutionist, wrote:

> Charles Lyell was a lawyer by profession, and his book is one of the most brilliant briefs published by an advocate. . . . Lyell relied upon true bits of cunning to establish his uniformitarian views as the only true geology. First, he set up a straw man to demolish. In fact, the catastrophists were much more empirically minded than Lyell. The geologic record does seem to require catastrophes: rocks are fractured and contorted; whole faunas are wiped out. To circumvent this literal appearance, Lyell imposed his imagination upon the evidence. The geologic record, he argued, is extremely imperfect and we must interpolate into it what we can reasonably infer but cannot see. The

---

14. J. Hutton, "Theory of the Earth," a paper (with the same title as his 1795 book) communicated to the Royal Society of Edinburgh, and published in *Transactions of the Royal Society of Edinburgh*, 1785; cited with approval in A. Holmes, *Principles of Physical Geology*, 2nd edition (London: Thomas Nelson and Sons Ltd., 1965), p. 43–44.

catastrophists were the hard-nosed empiricists of their day, not the blinded theological apologists.[15]

The biblically faithful, early 19th century "scriptural geologists" were even more empirical than the old-earth catastrophists (see page 132). But being an atheist, Gould did not care to mention them or was perhaps even ignorant of their existence.

One infamous example of Lyell's bias was his decision to ignore eyewitness accounts of the rate of erosion of Niagara Falls, and publish a different figure to suit his purpose.[16]

The label "uniformitarianism," to describe Lyell's approach, was coined by the great historian and philosopher of science William Whewell (1794–1866), who also invented the term "catastrophism," the old-earth theory dominant just prior to Lyell.

Uniformitarian Bias Prophesied by the Apostle Peter

The *a priori* rejection of global catastrophes is just what the apostle Peter prophesied would happen in 2 Peter 3:3–7:

> First of all, you must understand that in the last days scoffers will come, scoffing and following their own evil desires. They will say, "Where is this 'coming' he promised? Ever since our fathers died, everything goes on as it has since the beginning of creation." But they deliberately forget that long ago by God's word the heavens existed and the earth was formed out of water and with water. By water also the world of that time was deluged and destroyed. By the same word the present heavens and earth are reserved for fire, being kept for the day of judgment and destruction of ungodly men.

Hutton was probably a deist,[17] that is, he believed that there was a god who created, but then never intervened later in his creation in any miraculous ways. His god was much like a watchmaker who makes a watch, winds it up and then lets it run according to the way that he made it to operate. As a reviewer of two recent Hutton biographies wrote:

> The Scottish 18th-century natural philosopher James Hutton was a deist whose theology allowed his mind "to grow giddy looking so far into the abyss of time."

So, consistent with Peter's prophecy, Hutton didn't deny a creation,[18] but said that things had been going on at a constant rate since a creation in the unknowable past. Hutton's decree fulfilled Peter's prophecy of the scoffers who "deliberately forget" about the past judgment by water.

---

15. S. Gould, *Natural History* (February 1975): p. 16.

16. L. Pierce, "Niagara Falls and the Bible," *Creation* 22(4):8–13 (September–November 2000).

17. D. Palmer, "Old Father Time," *New Scientist* 179(2402):50, (July 5, 2003).

18. Some of his contemporaries suspected that he was really an atheist, largely because of his "no vestige of a beginning" claim. But it was not culturally acceptable to be an atheist in Britain at that time. So, if he was an atheist, he may have disguised the fact with occasional allusions to a creator.

Some Ross supporters like Dr. James Dobson, of *Focus on the Family*, evidently believe the overwhelming biblical evidence for a global Flood, but fail to see the inconsistency of this position with billions of years. A global Flood would have laid down a vast thickness of fossil-bearing sedimentary rock in a year, which would nullify much geological "evidence" for billions of years. This is precisely what Hutton and his followers were trying to avoid, and the millions of years was a corollary of denying the Flood. Therefore, accepting that the fossil record was formed over billions of years eliminates any evidence for the Flood. Ross is more consistent, and believes the Flood was restricted to Mesopotamia.

EVOLUTIONARY GEOLOGY INSPIRED EVOLUTIONARY BIOLOGY

In order to better understand why Hugh Ross denies the global nature of the Noachian deluge, for ostensibly scientific reasons, it's important to examine his thought process when it comes to the earth's past. Too often, misguided believers focus only on organic evolution and fail to appreciate how conventionally accepted geologic evolution thwarts the Scriptures just as much. In fact, old-earth geology provided the foundation for Darwin's theory.

Darwin and Uniformitarian Geology

One of the greatest influences on Darwin, for example, was a book he took on the *Beagle* voyage, *Principles of Geology*, by Charles Lyell, which pushed the idea of slow and gradual geological processes occurring over millions of years, and denied the global Noachian flood.

But Lyell convinced Darwin, who eventually linked slow and gradual geological processes with slow and gradual biological processes. For example, he said that mountains were the products of thousands of small rises. The PBS television series *Evolution*, episode 1, portrays Darwin saying, "Time, unimaginable tracts of time, is the key," and arguing that if small changes over ages can throw up mountains, so small changes accumulating over ages in animals can produce new structures.

Since Hutton was the inspiration for Lyell, Darwin was thus indirectly influenced by him as well. Also, as shown on page 226, Hutton probably had a more direct influence on Darwin's biology as well, by anticipating the idea of natural selection as a creative force.

Not only Darwin, but also many prevailing churchmen of his day, such as John Pye Smith (above), had capitulated to uniformitarian ideas. Even some leading "anti-evolutionists" had capitulated to long ages, for example, Adam Sedgwick (1785–1873), professor of geology at Cambridge and Darwin's mentor, and William Buckland (1784–1856), his counterpart at Oxford. It was worse that they were ordained clergymen, so the public tended to trust these men who betrayed their confidence.

Evolutionary Geology Influences Ross

It soon becomes obvious that Ross openly cites the conclusions of conventional evolutionary geology as "evidences" against a global Flood (GQ chapter 18). Throughout *The Genesis Question*, Hugh Ross lists the conventional isotopic dates used by geologists as if they were gospel truth, and then constructs his theological speculations around them. The unsuspecting reader does not even get a glimpse of the countless flaws, contradictions, selective usage,[19] etc., involved on a widespread scale[20] whenever these dating methods are applied in practice (see also chapter 12).

In chapter 1, I noted how Ross wants to eat his scientific cake and have it, too. That is, he argues against YECs by appealing to majority opinion about "science" when it comes to vast ages in astronomy, but he contradicts majority opinion among biologists about biological evolution. This also applies to Ross's acceptance of conventional evolutionary historical geology. While claiming to reject the transformation of one life form into another (evolutionary biology), Ross clearly accepts the evolutionary interpretation that the fossil sequence represents a succession of life forms appearing over millions of years. Then he attempts to weave the events of Genesis 1 around it. In doing so, Ross ends up, ironically, performing the very thing which he condemns (GQ:16):

> But, because the Bible does have the capacity to communicate to all generations of humanity, many Bible interpreters are tempted to read into the text far too much of the science of their time.

Note, from the ensuing quotations, that Ross unquestionably believes in a slowly evolving earth, a sequential appearance of life forms on earth over long periods of time, and sequential disappearance (extinction) of the same:

> The erosion rate changes as the land masses increase and earth's rotation rate decreases (rotation has slowed as a consequence of tidal interactions between the earth and the sun and the moon by a factor of about three during the past four billion years) (GQ:27).

> Earth's geology testifies that marine life did indeed arise before all other life forms (GQ:29).

In this respect, Ross's position is no different from that of the standard evolutionist. And when it comes to origin-of-life theories, only the rather vague "God-was-behind-it" concept otherwise separates his view from that of the standard atheistic evolutionist:

> Between 3.5 and 3.86 billion years ago, dozens of life-exterminating bombardment events took place (for example, collisions with enormous asteroids). Apparently, life originated and reoriginated as many as fifty times within the 360-million-year time span (GQ:40).

---

19. J. Woodmorappe, *Studies in Flood Geology*, second edition (El Cajon, CA: Institute for Creation Research, 1999). See pages 147–175 for scientific reasons why no one should take the dates seriously.

20. J. Woodmorappe, *The Mythology of Modern Dating Methods* (El Cajon, CA: Institute for Creation Research, 1999). This book demonstrates, among other things, that, contrary to the claims of apologists for isotopic dating, discrepant dates are the rule, not the exception, and that there are no truly reliable means of distinguishing ostensibly "good" from "bad" dates.

Clearly, the position held by Ross is a hybrid of what is usually considered theistic evolution and progressive creation.

Considering his acceptance of evolutionary geology as unassailable truth, Ross ends up actually mixing interpretations with facts, as I pointed out on page 41. The reader of Ross's book gets only one side of the story. Nowhere does the reader get even an inkling of the amount of interpretation that goes into the construction of fossil sequences in conventional evolutionary geology.

The reader is not told, for instance, that only a fraction of the superposed fossils can be found at any one location on earth,[21] or that, in terms of "time," fossils tend to overlap more than one geologic period.[22] And even this does not include the many fossils found in "wrong" strata[23] — which must be explained away as redeposited (whether justified by independent evidence or not). In chapter 12, I show how much other alleged old-earth "proof" fits best under a biblical creation/Fall/Flood model.[24]

Ross asserts that fossiliferous marine deposits predate the Noachian deluge by many millions of years (GQ:154). This is the very crux of the matter! Ross must necessarily try to relegate the Flood to a local or regional event because of the fact that his acceptance of evolutionary geology, and its time scale, prevents him from admitting that the Flood could have been a major cause of the fossiliferous deposits that are underneath our feet in most parts of the world!

No doubt, Ross believes that the local-Flood position makes the Bible more credible to scientists and other intellectuals. He has also resorted to guilt by association — Ross complains that a TV documentary about the alleged discovery of the "ark" gave the skeptics an easy target (GQ:165–167). The obvious implication is that it's all the fault of global Flood proponents, although the major global Flood organizations have repudiated such claimed discoveries.[25] Many global Flood proponents even agree with Ross that the ark is unlikely to be found because its timber would probably have been used for construction. So this is not an insight unique to local-flood proponents.

Trying to make the Bible teach a local flood, far from making it more credible to unbelievers, draws their contempt. They are prone to see it an evasion of the plain meaning of the biblical text to try to make the Bible rationally acceptable to skeptics.[26] And as stated, the compromises failed in Darwin's day, so there is no reason to expect a better fate today.

---

21. J. Woodmorappe, *Noah's Ark: A Feasibility Study* (El Cajon, CA: Institute for Creation Research, 1996), p. 46–47.

22. Ibid., p. 25–28.

23. J. Woodmorappe, *Studies in Flood Geology*, second edition (El Cajon, CA: Institute for Creation Research, 1999), p. 87–94.

24. See also J. Morris, *The Young Earth* (Green Forest, AR: Master Books, 1994).

25. A.A. Snelling, "Amazing 'Ark' Exposé," *Creation* 14(4):26–28 (1992); <www.answersingenesis.org/arkfraud>.

26. J. Woodmorappe, *Noah's Ark: A Feasibility Study* (El Cajon, CA: Institute for Creation Research, 1996), p. xii.

Ross's Pseudo-biblical Arguments for a Geographically Local, but Anthropologically Universal Flood

Ross's main motivation for denying the global Flood is to keep billions of years, because of his desire to fit the Bible into "science." But as with the creation days, he ignores or manipulates Scripture to fit his conception of "science." But he still claims to believe in a "universal" Flood, because he believes that all humanity (except for Noah's family) was wiped out, since people were not spread out over the whole globe but, according to him (GQ:148), "humanity had settled in only one geographical region," Mesopotamia.

"All" Doesn't Always Mean "All"?

In reply to the obvious teaching of the Bible that the whole globe was covered with water (see page 241), Ross uses verses such as Genesis 41:56 and 1 Kings 10:24, where global terms are used in a geographically regional sense, to argue that the same could be true of the global terms associated with the Flood (GQ:146–147). Only a little reflection will show this to be fallacious reasoning, which when applied elsewhere makes a mockery of Scripture. It would mean that, wherever Scripture mentions God being the Creator of all the world, it could really be saying that God is the Creator of only the Middle East.

One must also wonder about the apostle Peter's comparison of the Flood with the coming judgment of the world by fire (2 Pet. 3). Does this mean that only part of the world will be affected by Christ's second coming? By Ross's reasoning, could people escape the coming judgment merely by staying away from Baghdad? Surely not. The fact that "all" does not literally mean "all" in some biblical texts does not mean that this is the case everywhere. Literally all have sinned and fallen short of the glory of God (Rom. 3:23), except the God-man Jesus Christ. Jesus knows what is in the heart of literally all people (John 2:24–25) and literally all authority has been given to Him in heaven and on earth (Matt. 28:18).

So, once again, Ross is guilty of unwarranted expansion of an already-expanded semantic field.[27] As shown on page 241, it's not just the use of the word "all," but its repetition that matters, and it is reinforced by the use of other universal terms (such as "everywhere under the heavens" and "in whose nostrils is the breath of life"). In Hebrew, as in any other language, repetition is a way of emphasizing the literalness of the meaning of "all" in this Flood account.

The Census of "All the World"

Luke 2:1 reads:

> In those days a decree went out from Caesar Augustus that all the world should be enrolled.

---

27. D.A. Carson, *Exegetical Fallacies,* 2nd edition (Grand Rapids, MI: Baker Book House, 1996), p. 60.

From this, some local flood advocates argue that since the whole world wasn't enrolled, the flooding of the whole world need not have involved the whole world either.

First, once again, this ignores the fact that Genesis 6–9 has such *emphasis* on the word "all," unlike the above verse and the passages that Ross cites. Second, even in Luke 2:1 there is no need to believe that "all" is limited; rather it is "world" that is limited. The Greek in this verse is πασαν την οικουμενην (*pasan tēn oikoumenēn*), and it's the Greek that counts. The basic word translated "world" is οικουμενη (*oikoumenē*), from which we derive the word "ecumenical." Greek scholars recognize that in the New Testament as well as secular Greek literature at the time, *oikoumenē* was often used to refer to the "Roman empire" only.[28] So Caesar Augustus really *did* initiate a census of *all* the *oikoumenē*, that is, all the Roman Empire.

Noah Had Limited Perspective?

I have already demonstrated the fallacy of trying to downplay the repeated emphasis on "all" and "every" in the Genesis Flood account. But Ross also argues (GQ:146) that it would be sufficient fulfilment of everything being covered with water (Gen. 7:19) if it were merely everything *in Noah's field of view*.

In fact, the biblical description of the Flood covering the mountains is from a *God's-eye view* and not from a Noah's-eye view. God, not Noah, is the One who needs to see all the mountains covered with water, to accomplish His goal of destroying all creatures on the land. And God is not limited by such things as distance, clouds, heavy rain, fog, or the curvature of the earth.[29]

The text reveals information that could not possibly have been known by Noah simply by looking out the window of the ark, e.g., that "all the high mountains everywhere under the heavens were covered" (Gen. 7:19) and that all birds and other land creatures had died (Gen. 7:21–22). Nor could Noah have known by observation that the fountains of the deep were closed (Gen. 8:2). This information describes what God saw and would only have been knowable to Noah by divine revelation.

Pre-Flood Distribution of People

Hugh Ross supposes that all pre-Flood humans, the descendants of Adam and Eve, had been confined to the Middle East (GQ:147–148). Therefore, a regional flood was supposed to destroy them all — save for Noah's family. But this has problems with the distribution of people, as shown in the next chapter.

"The Boundaries of God's Wrath"

This heading is the title of GQ chapter 6. Ross asserts that the defilements of sin reach only as far as a person's progeny, his "soulish animals," material goods, and then finally his inhabited land (GQ:140).

28. BDAG, οικουμενη, definition 2, listing the examples Acts. 17:6 and Acts 24:5.

29. J.C. Whitcomb, *The World That Perished* (Grand Rapids, MI: Baker Book House, 1973), p. 48–64.

Ross cites the conquest of Canaan in support of this claim, but gives no specific texts. The only passages that Ross mentions explicitly are Exodus 21:28–29 (which refers to a man's ox killing someone) and Leviticus 20:15–16 (which refers to human sex with animals).

Neither passage justifies Ross's generalization. He concludes the paragraph on the conquest of Canaan by saying that "no amount of sin affects the behavior of insects and bacteria for example." But this cannot be justified from the account of the conquest of Canaan. It is unlikely that absolutely no insects or worms or bacteria died (certainly an effect on their behavior) when all the animals were slaughtered in a city and especially when everything was killed and then the city was burned to the ground, as in Ai and Hazor (Josh. 8:19, 28 and 11:11).

Ross's doctrine of sin is an invention of his own mind, not the teaching of Scripture. Farther down the same page he does acknowledge that insects, plants, viruses, bacteria, etc. have died in God's judgments, but then he makes the biblically unsupported and illogical claim that "though they were untainted by reprobation, to save them was neither practical nor necessary." Since Almighty God could easily save them if He wanted, these creatures' deaths must be part of His judgment and reprobation of sinners.

If (as Ross supposes) Adam's progeny never spread further than the Mesopotamian valley, his sin would not have defiled the other parts of the earth. For example, since humans never reached Antarctica, they would not have defiled the emperor penguins. So there was no need to flood this area (GQ:144). But this ignores the fact that Adam had dominion over all creation (Gen. 1:28). Hence, when he sinned, the effects were cosmic, so that the "whole creation" was subjected to futility (Rom. 8:20–22). Therefore, it was appropriate for God to flood the whole earth.

Does "Covered" Really Mean "Covered"?

Genesis 7:19–20 stresses the global coverage of the Flood:

> And the waters rose greatly on the earth, and all the high mountains under all the heavens were covered. The waters rose above the mountains, covering them fifteen cubits deep.

However, Ross argues (GQ:149):

> The Hebrew verb translated "covered" is *kasah*. This "covering" can be defined in any of three ways: "residing upon," "running over" or "falling upon." The distinctions among these definitions are important. *Kasah* can be interpreted to mean that more than twenty feet of water stood, that is, remained, over the high hills or mountains; or it could mean that this quantity of water either ran over them as in a flash flood or fell upon them as rainfall. The context gives no clear indication which of the three meanings to choose. Not that the choice is significant for understanding the effects of such "covering." Any of the three scenarios would guarantee total destruction, no survivors.

However, once again he is making an unwarranted expansion of the semantic field. Indeed, *kasah* (כסה) can have the meanings Ross says. But in the Pentateuch, it overwhelmingly means only "cover" or "conceal," not the other meanings. And in the Flood account, it is combined with another verb, גבר (*gabar*), which is translated "prevailed" or "rose."

The meaning of *kasah* in this context can only be "covered." It makes no sense for it to have any of the other meanings when combined with "rose." The verbs for "rose" and "covered" are in the *waw* consecutive forms, so they move the narrative along. So the waters rose then covered the earth. Also, the verb *gabar* (rose) is qualified with the adverb מלמעלה *milma'lâ* (upward), which is further indication that the waters rose up and *covered* the earth (BDB:751–752) rather than Ross's alternatives of "running over" or "falling upon."[30]

Is the Word "High" Missing from the Hebrew Originals?

A few years ago, RTB stocked a tape by Ross on the Flood.[31] This included commentary on Genesis 7:19, which reads:

> And the waters prevailed exceedingly upon the earth; and all the high hills that were under the whole heaven were covered.

Ross made this definitive pronouncement:

> If you want to get at the scientific details, you must read it in the Hebrew. Let's do that. As you go through the Hebrew, "the waters rose greatly on the earth, and all the high mountains" — the word "high" is not in the original. It's not there. Now, it comes up in almost every English translation. But in translations into other languages, it's not always there, and it's not in the Hebrew. So you can take your Bible and cross out the word "high." It's not there. I don't recommend you do that all the time as you go through your Bible, but in this case there is a good basis for it: it's simply not there in the original Hebrew.

So Ross claimed *six times* that the word "high" is not in the Hebrew of Genesis 7:19. Surely, no one would make such a claim unless he was sure of his facts. He is, however, completely wrong. The standard Hebrew text, *Biblia Hebraica Stuttgartensia*, reads (right to left):

אֲשֶׁר	הַגְּבֹהִים	כָּל־הֶהָרִים	וַיְכֻסּוּ
ʰsher	*hag'vōhîm*	*kol hᵉhārîm*	*wayᵉkussû*
which are	high	all the mountains	and were covered

---

30. M. Maniguet, *The Theological Method of Hugh Ross: An Analysis and Critique*, M.Th. Thesis, Systematic Theology, Baptist Bible Seminary, Clarks Summit, PA (May 2002): p. 85–86.

31. H. Ross, *The Flood,* Reasons to Believe tape A8712, Part 1, 1990 (transcript available from James Stambaugh, librarian at Michigan Theological Seminary).

Here, it's crystal clear that the word *hagᵉvōhîm* (the masculine plural form of גבה *gavoah* prefixed by the definite article ה; *ha*) is most definitely in the text. The translators of all Bible versions were and are absolutely correct to insert this word, and Ross, who does not know the Hebrew language (nor probably any of the other languages he refers to in this statement), is absolutely wrong and has misled Christians to cut out a word from (i.e., mutilate) the inspired Word of God.

Ross subsequently withdrew this tape after being confronted with this error. Such are the perils in trying to deny that the text means what it says!

Ross has a section on "high mountains" in GQ:148–51. Here, he does admit that the word "high" is there, but still tries to downplay the height of a "high mountain." And he asserts that the ark landed in the foothills of Ararat. However, this fails to note that it took 70 days for Noah to see any mountains after the ark landed. The text ties this to the recession of the waters (Gen. 8:4–5).

Names of Pre-Flood Geographical Features

In GQ:148, Ross is also incorrect in insisting that the major features of the pre-Flood geography of the world had been identical to the post-Flood Middle East (and that, by implication, the flood had been local). Ross is, at best, using an argument from silence. Also, a careful analysis of the place-names of the antediluvian world demonstrates that they were highly non-specific as to location, and therefore cannot legitimately be used to argue that the identical places had existed before and after the Flood, let alone in the Middle East.

For example, many people are confused by the rivers Tigris (חדקל *Chiddeqel*) and Euphrates (פרת *pᵉrath*) mentioned in Genesis 2:14, and think that they are the modern rivers with those names. This would explain why Ross and many others think that Eden was in Mesopotamia. However, the whole passage from Genesis 2:10 describes one river splitting into four. Also, the river Gihon (Gen 2:13) could not possibly flow from modern-day Mesopotamia and encompass modern-day Ethiopia (כוש Cush).

This shows that the topography of Eden was different from Mesopotamia today. We would expect that a global Flood would totally rearrange the earth's topography. Martin Luther recognized this (though underestimating its magnitude):

> Therefore one must not imagine that the source of these rivers is the same today as it was at that time; but the situation is the same today as in the case of the earth, which now exists and brings forth trees, herbs, etc. If you compare these with the uncorrupted creation, they are like wretched remnants of that wealth which the earth had when it was created. Thus these rivers remain like ruins, but, to be sure, not in the same place; much less do they have the same sources.[32]

---

32. M. Luther, *Luther's Works*, Vol. I: Commentary on Genesis 1–5, J. Pelikan, editor (St Louis, MO: Concordia, 1958), p. 99.

Augustine also seems to have recognized the likelihood of a changed geography. He posed a rhetorical question about what happened to the spring of water that watered the whole earth (Gen. 2:6), and answered that the world has changed since the time of creation.[33]

The simple explanation for the similar geographical names of the pre-Flood world is:

> In recent history, we have seen that new towns established by British settlers in North America, Australia, and New Zealand were frequently assigned names that were familiar place-names in the land they had left; e.g., Liverpool, Hamilton, Oxford, Sheffield, and Brighton. Similarly, features in the post-Flood world were given names familiar to those who survived the Flood.[34]

Extra-biblical Flood Traditions

Ross also makes a variety of other dubious statements in trying to defend his idea of a local flood. One claim is that extra-biblical traditions of the Flood become progressively more unlike the biblical account the farther one goes from Bible lands (GQ:171). Ross provides no documentation to substantiate his assertion, and also fails to show how it would differentiate between a global and local flood view. Global flood proponents accept the biblical teaching that the descendants of the ark survivors migrated only as far as Babel before God confused the languages. So Babel would be the central point, and it might seem reasonable to suppose that the farther away a people group is from Babel, the more divergent the ark stories would be expected to be from Genesis.

However, there appears to be no such pattern. Rather, the contrary view can in fact be documented. It is thus simplistic to believe that geographic distance from the place of origin is the only factor in divergence of stories. Nelson[35] has tabulated flood traditions from all over the world, and rated them according to their correspondence with 12 essential points of the biblical Flood narrative. Now, if Ross were correct, then fewer and fewer of the 12 essential points should be held by local traditions the farther one proceeds to the other side of the world from the Middle East. Instead, with the exception of the Assyrio-Babylonian account, one does not see such a pattern at all. Often it is almost the opposite. Thus, for instance, the versions from nearby Syria, Persia, and Asia Minor coincide with the biblical account in only 3–6 of the 12 major points. By contrast, the ones from distant India, Canada (Cree Indian),

---

33. Augustine, Augustine, *The Literal Meaning of Genesis*, 5.7.20, (Taylor, No. 41, 158).

34. J.R. Hughes, "An Examination of the Assumptions of 'Eden's Geography Erodes Flood Geology,' " *CRSQ* 34(3):154–161 (1997). The names used in the early chapters of Genesis are "generic." Furthermore, the same geographic place-names of the pre-Flood world could have been reused after the Flood. In fact, duplicate usage of names commonly occurs elsewhere throughout Scripture.

35. B. Nelson, *The Deluge Story in Stone* (Minneapolis, MN: Bethany Fellowship, 1931, 1968), p. 169.

the Leeward Islands, and the Hawaiian Islands share 6–7 of the 12 major points of the biblical account.

Purpose of the Ark

Finally, Ross tells us that, although the ark would technically not have been needed in a (supposed) local flood, it was built so that Noah would have a platform from which to preach (GQ:164–165):

> First, when God pours out judgment, He gives ample warning ahead of time. He sends a spokesperson, a prophet, and gives that prophet a kind of platform from which to be heard. For the antediluvians, Noah was that prophet and the scaffolding around the ark was his platform.

This is highly imaginative, to say the least! I wonder why *none* of the prophets in the Bible, of whatever epoch, were deemed to have needed some sort of special platform from which to preach, let alone one requiring such a huge expenditure of labor? Of course, the Bible gives the real purpose of the ark — to save land vertebrates and Noah's family from being wiped out by the Flood (Gen. 6:18–22, 7:23, 8:1)!

Scientific Evidence for a Global Flood

The evidence for the Flood is in two parts: first, features in thick rock layers consistent with rapid deposition; second, features showing that there was little time between these layers.

The scriptural geologist George Fairholme pointed out the many dry valleys that must have been scooped out by much larger volumes of water than are seen today, and the network of the valleys was evidence that they were formed around the same time. He also looked at erosion of cliffs, coasts, and Niagara Falls and concluded that the erosion commenced only about 5,000 years ago.

Fairholme also pointed out what are now commonly called polystrate fossil trees (see picture on following page), indicating that the layers were laid down quickly. He also noted the lack of erosion features and presence of ephemeral markings such as ripple marks, indicating there was very little time between layers. This refuted both Lyell's uniformitarianism and Cuvier's view of multiple catastrophism, both of which contradicted the Bible.

This is one good example of how the concept of Flood geology is much older than George McCready Price, despite the claims of Ross and others to the contrary.

Huge Sandstone Deposits

The Grand Canyon's Coconino sandstone has an average thickness of 315 feet (96 meters) and, with equivalent sandstones to the east, covers an area of about 200,000 square miles (518,000 square kilometers), thus a total volume of at least 10,000 cubic miles (41,700 cubic kilometers).[36]

---

36. D.L. Baars, "Permian System of the Colorado Plateau," *American Association of Petroleum Geologists Bulletin*, vol. 46 (1962): p. 200–201.

Photo by Andrew Snelling

Figure 8.1: Polystrate tree trunk.

This was once thought to have formed by wind, originally as desert sand dunes. One evidence for this was thought to be the slanting patterns, called crossbeds. However, the angles are determined by the angle of repose, that is, the maximum slope a pile of granular substance can sustain. And it turns out the angle matches that for sand under water, not under air.

As shown in Figure 8.2, flowing water can make the sand form dunes under water. The water moves the grains of sand up the back of each sand wave until they reach the top. Then they roll down the front of the sand wave. As the sand wave moves forward, it buries the previous downhill slope, but these slopes are preserved in the crossbedding pattern. The orientation of the sand waves indicates the direction of flow. Some of the beds in the Coconino sandstone are as much as 30 feet (9 meters) thick.[37] To form these, calculations show that the sand waves must be at least 60 feet (18 meters) high and in water about 300 feet (between 90 and 95 meters) deep. And the flow rate would have to be 3–5.5 feet (0.95–1.65 m) per second, or 2–4 mph. Considering the huge extent of the sandstone formation, the amount of fast-flowing water required must have been staggering — just what the Flood would provide![38] And the lack of erosion channels above and below indicates that it was deposited not long after the previous layer, and it was in turn overlain very quickly.

In Australia, there is also a well-known, huge sandstone formation in the area of its largest city Sydney, the Hawkesbury Sandstone. It is a 330 feet to 660 feet (100 m to 200 m) thick and 160 mile (250-km) wide system, and extends 1,200 miles (2,000 km) north. And again, there are enormous crossbeds. Dr. Patrick Conaghan, senior lecturer at the School of Earth Sciences at Macquarie University, proposed that they

37. S. Gould, *Natural History* (February 1975).

38. A. Snelling and S. Austin, "Grand Canyon: Startling Evidence for Noah's Flood!" *Creation* 15(1):46-50 (December 1992).

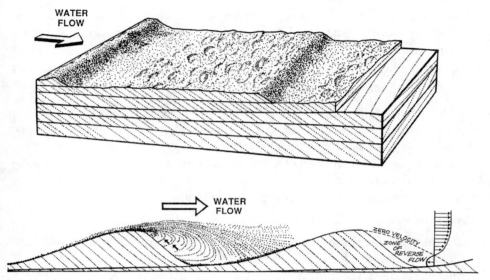

Figure 8.2: Schematic diagram showing the formation of cross beds during sand deposition by migration of underwater sand waves due to sustained water flow.[39]

were formed by a wall of water up to 65 feet (20 m) high and 150 miles (250 km) wide coming down from the north at enormous speed, depositing tons of sand.[40] This is some wave! Once more, the enormously wide, thick layers are explained best by a catastrophic Flood.[41]

Possible Mechanism for the Flood

Plate Tectonics

Most geologists believe that the earth once contained one land mass, which broke up. The large fragments separated to form today's continents. This is supported by the following lines of evidence (and as will be shown next section, this need not be an evolutionary/uniformitarian theory):[42]

- The fit of the continents (taking into account the continental shelves).

- Correlation of fossil types across ocean basins.

39. S. Austin, editor, *Grand Canyon: Monument to Catastrophe* (Santee, CA: ICR, 1994), p. 34–35.
40. J. Woodford, "Rock Doctor Catches Up with Our Prehistoric Surf," *The Sydney Morning Herald* (April 30, 1994): p. 2. For more detail, see P.J. Conaghan, "The Hawkesbury Sandstone: Gross Characteristics and Depositional Environment," *Bulletin, Geological Survey of New South Wales* 26:188–253, (1980).
41. T. Walker, "Three Sisters: Evidence for Noah's Flood, *Creation* 25(2):38–42 (March–May 2003).
42. This section is based on AB chapter 11; J. Baumgardner, "Catastrophic Plate Tectonics: The Physics Behind the Genesis Flood, in R.L. Ivey Jr., editor, *Fifth International Conference on Creationism*, Creation Science Fellowship, Pittsburgh, Pennsylvania, (August 2003): p. 113–126; <www.globalflood.org/papers/2003ICCcpt.html>.

- A zebra-striped pattern of magnetic reversals parallel to mid-ocean floor rifts, in the volcanic rock formed along the rifts, implying seafloor spreading along the rifts.

- Seismic observations interpreted as slabs of former ocean floor now located inside the earth.

Most geologists explain these observations by the theory of plate tectonics. This may be stated as follows (AB; chapter 11). The earth's surface consists of a mosaic of rigid plates, each moving relative to adjacent plates. Deformation occurs at the edges of the plates by three types of horizontal motion: extension (or rifting, moving apart), transform faulting (horizontal slipping along a fault line), and compression, mostly by subduction (one plate plunging beneath another):

1. Extension occurs as the sea floor pulls apart at rifts, or splits.

2. Transform faulting occurs where one plate slips horizontally past another (e.g., the San Andreas Fault of California).

3. Compression deformation occurs when one plate subducts beneath another, e.g., the Pacific Plate beneath Japan and the Cocos Plate beneath Central America, or when two continental plates collide to produce a mountain range, e.g., the Indian-Australian Plate colliding with the Eurasian Plate to form the Himalayan Mountains. Volcanoes often occur in regions of subduction.

Catastrophic Plate Tectonics

Uniformitarian geologists believe that the plate movements happened over millions of years, but this contradicts the biblical time scale. Ross also supports slow and gradual continental drift (GQ:35–37). Conversely, some creationist geologists have argued against the whole concept of plate tectonics. But other creationists argue that a better idea is *catastrophic plate tectonics* (CPT), which argues that this plate movement happened very rapidly in the past. Pro and against have been debated in depth in *TJ*.[43] Having more than one possible model is a strength, not a weakness.

In my view, the pro-CPT case is far stronger than the anti. Indeed, it was a creationist, Antonio Snider, who first proposed in 1859 that horizontal movement of continents took place catastrophically during the Genesis flood.[44] The statements in Genesis 1:9–10 about the gathering together of the seas in one place, which implies there was one landmass, influenced his thinking.

Dr. John Baumgardner, working at the Los Alamos National Laboratories (New Mexico), has used supercomputers to model processes in the earth's mantle to show that tectonic plate movement could have occurred very rapidly, and spontaneously.[45]

---

43. See forum on catastrophic plate tectonics, *TJ* 16(1):57 (2002); <www.answersingenesis.org/cpt_forum>.

44. A. Snider, *Le Création et ses Mystères Devoilés* (Paris: Franck and Dentu, 1859).

45. See Dr. Baumgardner's technical papers at <www.answersingenesis.org/tectonics>

He is acknowledged as having developed the world's best 3-D supercomputer model of plate tectonics.[46]

Baumgardner's model begins with a pre-Flood super-continent. While uniformitarian models assume that the ocean crust has always had mostly hot rock and very little cold rock, Baumgardner started with cold rock. This meant it was denser than the mantle below. At the start of the Flood year, this began to sink into the softer, less dense mantle beneath. Without any warm crust to resist, it could sink much more quickly than today.

The friction from this movement generates heat, especially around the edges. The mantle minerals are known to soften markedly under heat, so the friction would reduce, making it less resistant to further sinking. So the crust sinks faster, generating more heat, which further softens the mantle, which makes the crust sink still faster.

Eventually it would sink at several km/h, billions of times faster than is happening today. This is called *runaway subduction.*

The sinking ocean floor would drag the rest of the ocean floor along, in conveyor belt fashion, and would displace mantle material, starting large-scale movement throughout the entire mantle. However, as the ocean floor sank and rapidly subducted adjacent to the pre-Flood super-continent's margins, elsewhere the earth's crust would be under such tensional stress that it would be torn apart (rifted), breaking up both the pre-Flood super-continent and the ocean floor.

Thus, crustal spreading zones would rapidly extend along cracks in the ocean floor for some 6,000 miles where the splitting was occurring. Hot mantle material displaced by the subducting slabs would well up, rising to the surface along these spreading zones. On the ocean floor, this hot mantle material would vaporize copious amounts of ocean water, producing a linear geyser of superheated steam along the whole length of the spreading centers. This could be what the "fountains of the great deep" means (Gen. 7:11; 8:2).

This steam would disperse, condensing in the atmosphere to fall as intense global rain ("and the flood-gates of heaven were opened" Gen. 7:11). This could account for the rain persisting for 40 days and 40 nights (Gen. 7:12).

Baumgardner's catastrophic plate tectonics global flood model for earth history is able to explain more geological data than the conventional plate tectonics model with its many millions of years. For example, rapid subduction of the pre-Flood ocean floor into the mantle results in new ocean floor that is dramatically hotter, especially in its upper 60 miles, not just at spreading ridges, but everywhere. Being hotter, the new ocean floor is of lower density and therefore rises 3,000 to 6,000 feet higher than before, causing a dramatic rise in global sea level.

This higher sea level floods the continental surfaces and makes possible the deposition of large areas of sedimentary deposits on top of the normally high-standing continents. The Grand Canyon provides a spectacular window into the amazing

---

46. J. Beard, "How a Supercontinent Went to Pieces," *New Scientist* 137:19 (January 16, 1993).

layer-cake character of these sediment deposits that in many cases continue uninter-rupted for more than 600 miles. Uniformitarian ("slow and gradual") plate tectonics simply cannot account for such thick continental sediment sequences of such vast horizontal extent.

Moreover, the rapid subduction of the cooler pre-Flood ocean floor into the mantle would have resulted in increased circulation of viscous fluid (note: plastic, not molten) rock within the mantle. This mantle-flow (that is, "stirring" within the mantle) suddenly altered the temperatures at the core-mantle boundary, as the mantle near the core would now be significantly cooler than the adjacent core, and thus con-vection and heat loss from the core would be greatly accelerated. The model suggests that under these conditions of accelerated convection in the core, rapid geomagnetic reversals would have occurred. These in turn would be expressed on the earth's surface and recorded in the so-called magnetic stripes. However, these would be erratic and locally patchy, laterally and at depth, just as the data indicate.

This model provides a mechanism that explains how the plates could move relatively quickly (in a matter of a few months) over the mantle and subduct. And it predicts that little or no movement would be measurable between plates today, because the movement would have come almost to a standstill when the entire pre-Flood ocean floor was subducted. From this we would also expect the trenches adjacent to subduction zones today to be filled with undisturbed late-Flood and post-Flood sediments, just as we observe.

Aspects of Baumgardner's mantle modelling have been independently duplicated and thus verified by others. Furthermore, Baumgardner's modeling predicts that because this thermal runaway subduction of cold ocean floor crystal slabs occurred relatively recently, during the Flood (about 5,000 or so years ago), then those slabs would not have had sufficient time since to be fully assimilated into the surrounding mantle. So, evidence of the slabs above the mantle-core boundary (to which they sank) should still be found today. Indeed, evidence for such unassimilated relatively cold slabs has been found in seismic studies.[47]

Plate collisions would have pushed up mountains, while cooling of the new ocean floor would have increased its density, causing it to sink and thus deepen the new ocean basins to receive the retreating Flood waters. It may be significant, therefore, that the "mountains of Ararat" (Gen. 8:4), the resting place of the ark after the 150th day of the flood, are in a tectonically active region at what is believed to be the junc-tion of three crustal plates.

If an inch (2.54 centimeters) or so per year of inferred movement today is ex-trapolated back into the past as uniformitarians do, then their conventional plate tectonics model has limited exploratory power. For example, even at a rate of four

---

47. S.P. Grand, "Mantle Shear Structure Beneath the Americas and Surrounding Oceans," *Journal of Geophysical Research*, 99:11591–11621 (1994); J.E. Vidale, "A Snapshot of Whole Mantle Flow," *Nature*, 370:16–17 (1994); S. Vogel, "Anti-matters," *Earth: The Science of Our Planet* (August 1995): p. 43–49.

inches (10.16 centimeters) per year, it is questionable whether the forces of the collision between the Indian-Australian and Eurasian Plates could have been sufficient to push up the Himalayas. On the other hand, catastrophic plate tectonics in the context of the Flood can explain how the plates overcame the viscous drag of the earth's mantle for a short time due to the enormous catastrophic forces at work, followed by a rapid slowing down to present rates.

Solving the Heat Problem

Baumgardner has also shown that these geysers would be capable of removing the enormous heat generated in the runaway subduction. He shows that the interaction of seawater with molten rock in such zones of plate divergence actually results in supersonic steam jets that readily penetrate the layer of ocean water, and in the process, entrain large quantities of liquid water that falls back to the earth as rain. It appears that the steam jets which form as a curtain above the zone where two ocean plates are diverging achieve velocities which are not only supersonic but may exceed the earth's escape velocity, as water that circulates through the cooling rock and into this V-shaped zone is converted into supercritical steam. Steam with a velocity of 14 km/s, for example, carries away enough energy (about 10^8 J/kg) to cool 140 times its mass of crustal rock by 1,000 K, assuming a specific heat for the rock of 700 J/kg-K. A layer of water 500 meters thick, converted to such high velocity steam, removes enough heat to cool a layer of rock about 20 km thick by 1,000 K. The energy in these jets is transported through the layer of ocean water and the atmosphere with relatively little heat transfer to these layers. This water that falls as rain remains in the liquid phase and does not require any loss of latent heat to condense from vapor to liquid. Most of the specific energy in the steam is kinetic (as opposed to thermal), and this kinetic energy is converted to gravitational potential energy as the steam moves upward through the earth's gravity field.

Ross's Pseudo-Scientific Arguments against the Global Flood

The Local Flood According to Ross

Ross believes in a local flood that he estimates would require at least six billion acre-feet of water (GQ:159). Ross errs right from the start in his belief of how much water would be necessary to cover the hills where the ark would later land. At the location where he places the landing of the ark, he informs us that "the Ararat hills [are] just a few hundred feet above sea level. . . ." (GQ:166). However, a check of the actual topography of the relevant area shows that it actually varies between 1,640 feet and 6,560 feet (500–2,000 meters).[48] And this applies to the *least* elevated southern portion of the entire Ararat region.

The researcher who recognizes the reality of a past global Flood looks for the evidences for it in the sedimentary strata, and not in the present-day topography. Present-day topography is largely the product of the receding floodwaters modified

---

48. Anon., *Atlas of the Arab World and the Middle East* (London: Macmillan and Co., 1960), p. 31, 39.

by relatively minor weathering in the post-Flood period. A local-flood advocate, by contrast, must assume the essential consistency of pre-Flood and post-Flood topography. A major cornerstone of Hugh Ross's belief in a local Flood, and the resulting "reconciliation with science," is his supposition (wishful thinking?) that such a flood would leave behind no evidence of its past occurrence (GQ:159, 208).

"Straw Man" Arguments Against Covering the Highest Mountains

Ross often misrepresents what YECs believe and have clearly stated. For example (GQ:152):

> Some global flood proponents who acknowledge the problem of a grossly inadequate water supply propose that earth's surface was "smoothed," or flattened, by the Flood, thus reducing the water requirement. More specifically, they claim that during the forty days and nights when the floodwaters rose, earth's mountains radically eroded from their lofty heights of ten, fifteen and even twenty thousand feet to just one or two thousand feet, perhaps less.

This is inexcusable, because Ken Ham had responded to a similar Ross misrepresentation (which was even then hard to excuse), well before *The Genesis Question* was published, as follows:

> In my 20 years of involvement in creation ministry, I have never known of any material from any biblical creationists indicating that God "eroded the mountains from a height of 30,000 feet down to sea level during the forty days"! . . . Biblical creationists believe that most mountains today did not exist before the Flood, but were raised up (and ocean basins sank) towards the end of the Flood, thus causing the water to run off to where it is today.[49]

It's also important to note that there is plenty of water available to cover the whole earth. If the earth's topography was totally smoothed out, so that the mountains were flattened and the sea bottoms raised, the amount of water would be enough to cover the whole globe to a depth of nearly 3 km.

It is even more inexcusable that Ross doesn't correct this in the second edition, published after I pointed out this error in my book review of his first (hardcover) edition.[50] (We have strong indications that RTB regularly monitors AiG's website, so he can hardly claim to have been unaware of it.)

The "Rossian Flood": Geologically Insignificant?

Ross labors under the belief that short floods cannot do much geologic work (GQ:159):

> The Flood, though massive, lasted but one year and ten days. A flood of such brief duration typically does not leave a deposit substantial enough to be positively identified thousands of years later.

---

49. K. Ham, "Demolishing 'Straw Men,'" *Creation* 19(4):13–15 (1997).

50. J. Sarfati, "Exposé of NavPress's New Hugh Ross Book: *The Genesis Question*," *TJ* 13(2):22–30, (1999); <www.answersingenesis.org/ross_GQ>.

Oh, no? Consider the fact that the ancient Bonneville flood of Utah is believed to have lasted, in its most active phase, as little as eight weeks.[51] Yet it certainly left behind many deposits. Clearly, then, the fact that the Noachian deluge lasted "only a year" is not the slightest ground for supposing (as Ross would have us believe) that it would leave no geologic effects to observe today! Furthermore, a year-long flood is "brief" and "typical"!? Are any of Ross's followers reading carefully what he writes?

How Does 2 Peter 3:3–6 Fit In?

I discussed this passage on page 247, but it has another application. The relevant sections are:

> Scoffers will . . . deliberately ignore this fact . . . the world that then existed was deluged with water and perished.

However, Ross argues that the Flood left no traces. So how can the scoffers be held culpable for "deliberately ignoring" the fact of the Flood if there is no evidence?

By similar reasoning, Romans 1:18–22 is a good argument against theistic evolution. Verse 20 says:

> Ever since the creation of the world his invisible nature, namely, his eternal power and deity, has been clearly perceived in the things that have been made. So they are without excuse.

This passage clearly teaches that unbelievers don't have the slightest excuse for unbelief, because God's power and deity can be "clearly seen" from nature. This seems to be a strong support for the argument from design. However, according to Gould, one of Darwin's main motivations was to counteract the argument from design.[52] So if evolution were true, where is the clear evidence for God's power from what has been made? Far from being evidence for a divine hand, evolution, according to Gould, gives "evidence" that "there's nothing else going on out there — just organisms struggling to pass their genes on to the next generation. That's it." So once again, if evolution were true, there is no evidence for a God from what has been made, but evidence only for ruthless struggle for existence. So why would unbelievers be "without excuse" if evolution were true?

Ross would probably not disagree with the Romans 1:20 connection to design and biological evolution. However, that is a blind spot because the same applies to the geological evolution he accepts contrary to the Bible, and which likewise would entail that the scoffers would not, in those circumstances, be "without excuse."

Intensity Scaling Laws

Hugh Ross also shows a complete lack of understanding of the rules of scaling that apply to differing intensities of flood events. He cites a California flood leaving

---

51. R.D. Jarrett and H.E. Malde, "Paleodischarge of the Late Pleistocene Bonneville Flood, *Geological Society of America Bulletin* 99:134, (1987).

52. C. Wieland, "Darwin's Real Message: Have You Missed It?" *Creation* 14(4)16–19 (September–November 1992); <www.answersingenesis.org/docs/1347.asp>.

no lasting traces after covering an area with 3–4 feet of water, and, from that, makes a leap to the claim that his suggested flood of 200–300-foot depth would also fail to leave behind any lasting geomorphic evidence (GQ:159)!

Yet it is precisely such a difference in depth which plays a major role in the power of the flood, and whether or not it will leave behind a substantial geomorphic imprint. Equating the erosional/depositional intensity of a 3–4-foot flood with one that is 200–300 feet deep is a lot like equating the thermal intensity of a match flame with that of a blast furnace, and suggesting that because a match won't soften an iron bar at all, then a blast furnace couldn't possibly melt it. How can anyone take such illogical reasoning seriously?

The Rossian Flood Versus the Spokane (Lake Missoula) Flood

What about the area covered by Ross's proposed flood? Is it conceivable that such a local flood left its deposits over such a small geographic area that they have not been found yet? Hardly. Let us first compare the areas of the "Rossian flood" with that of the Spokane flood. This occurred when ancient Lake Missoula in Montana burst a natural ice dam, the toe of a massive Canadian glacier, in Idaho. This resulted in 2,000 km³ (500 cubic miles) of water — the equivalent of Lake Erie and Lake Ontario combined — pouring westward at express-train speed. Most of the Spokane flood was concentrated in an area of approximately 100 x 100 miles (160 x 160 km),[53] in eastern Washington. The most geologically active part of the Spokane flood lasted only a few *hours*, and left *plenty* of evidences of its occurrence. It eroded 50 cubic miles (200 km³) of sediment and bedrock, carving the elaborate Channeled Scablands in eastern Washington.[54] This includes the Grand Coulee, a 50-mile-long trench (80-km), one to six miles wide, with steep walls up to 900 feet (275 m) high, chiseled through hard basalt and granite.[55]

The amount of erosion and sedimentation accomplished by this local flood, in comparison with tens of thousands of years of inferred uniformitarian processes, is nothing short of staggering:

> Power multiplied by time gives potential work. For the Missoula flood, with power per unit area of 10^8 ergs/cm²-sec applied for about 3 hours (10^4 seconds), the potential work is 10^{14} ergs/cm². By comparison, the same potential work would require 10^{14} seconds (3×10^5 years) of continual glacial action at a power per unit area of 1 erg/cm²-sec. Even a major river in flood, such as the Mississippi, only generates about 10^4 ergs/cm²-sec. The river would have to be in continuous flood for 10^{10} seconds (300 years) to produce equivalent work. However, the river probably achieves this power

53. V.R. Baker et. al., "Columbia and Snake River Plains," *Geological Society of America Centennial Special* 2: 415 (1987).
54. S. Austin, editor, *Grand Canyon: Monument to Catastrophe* (Santee, CA: ICR, 1994), p. 94–95.
55. Ibid.

only 1 percent or less of the time, so its required time would be at least 3 x 10⁴ years.[56]

The story of the interpretation of the Channeled Scablands illustrate the baneful controlling power of the paradigm. When J Harlan Bretz[57] proposed a catastrophic explanation in 1923,[58] it was rejected out of hand because of the anticatastrophist bias in the geological community. One exception was Joseph T. Pardee, who wrote to Bretz (June 3, 1925) suggesting (correctly) a possible source of water, which Bretz did not have in his theory at first, asking "whether you have considered the possibility of the sudden draining of a glacial lake." Bretz wasn't vindicated till almost 40 years later.[59] There is evidence for an Ice Age (that is, after the biblical flood) catastrophe on a similar scale in Siberia.[60]

Ross's inferred flood, by contrast, would have been much larger. At the suggested six billion acre-feet (GQ:155), at 200–300 feet (61–92 meters) depth, the area covered would have ranged from 177 x 177 miles to 217 x 217 miles (110 x 110 km to 135 x 135 km). It would also be difficult, if not impossible, for Ross to make his flood appreciably smaller, if only because of the constraints imposed by the birds released from the ark (Gen. 8:7 and 8:9–12).

Littoral (seashore) birds typically stray 20–25 miles from land.[61] This means that the waters of the Flood must have had a diameter of at least 40–50 miles, and thus still covered an area which is a large proportion of the one covered by the Spokane flood. And this was applicable to the *latter* stages of Ross's flood. At its height, the allegedly local flood would have had to cover a considerably larger area. Even this estimate is conservative. The southern cape pigeon, a close relative of the dove released from the ark (Gen. 8:9–12), may be encountered far from land.[62] This implies that the ark's dove may also have strayed at considerable distances from the ark before encountering land, and then returning with the olive leaf.

Other factors in the "Rossian flood" point to intensities greater than the Spokane flood, and make Ross's suggestion that such a flood left no traces all the more absurd. Let us first turn our attention to the gradient of the flow. The intensity of a flood is proportional to the gradient over which the water flows. Let us apply this to the Spokane flood:

56. V.R. Baker et. al., "Columbia and Snake River Plains," *Geological Society of America Centennial Special* 2: 415 (1987): p. 428.
57. Gould says that Bretz's wrath would fall on anyone who used a full stop after his initial. See S.J. Gould, "The Great Scablands Debate," *Natural History* 87(7):12–18, (1978).
58. J.H. Bretz, "The Channeled Scablands of the Columbia Plateau," *Journal of Geology* 31:617–649 (1923); "Glacial Drainage on the Columbia Plateau," *Geological Soc. Amer. Bull.* 34:573–608 (1923).
59. S. Austin, editor, *Grand Canyon: Monument to Catastrophe* (Santee, CA: ICR, 1994), p. 46–47.
60. See C. Wieland, "Tackling the Big Freeze: An Interview with Creationism's 'Mr. Ice Age' — Weather Scientist Michael Oard," *Creation* 19(1):42–43 (1996).
61. J. Hornell, "The Role of Birds in Early Navigation," *Antiquity* 20(79):147 (1946).
62. H. Gatty, *Nature Is Your Guide* (Harmondsworth, UK: Penguin Books, 1958), p. 214.

However, Missoula flood flows were exceptionally deep (60 to 120 m). The steep water surface gradients (2 to 12 m km^{-1}) resulted in the exceptionally high mean flow velocities.[63]

To begin with, it can be seen that the depth of the Spokane flood was, on average, less than Ross's flood. In addition, the gradient of the Spokane flood had been 0.002 to 0.012. Let us compare this gradient with that of Ross's local Noachian deluge.

To compute the gradients, we need to first examine the geographic extent of the "Rossian flood" and the topography of the Mesopotamian-Ararat region.[64] To roughly center this flood, we need to return to the fact that Ross places the landing of the ark in the southern Ararat region (GQ:166), some 20 to 50 miles north of Nineveh. In terms of geographic coordinates, the ark lands at approximately 36.2N, 43.5E. This means that, at minimum, the "Rossian flood" must have covered the surrounding areas. Also, the other mountains became visible after 2.5 months.

Let us start with the northern Mesopotamian plain, at the present-day city of Shara, and work our way northward some 40 miles (64 kilometers) to the southernmost point where Ross would place the landing of the ark. Over this transect, the elevation increases some 300 meters over the 64 kilometers, thus amounting to a gradient of 0.0047. This is the *most favorable* (that is, the *least* steep) gradient available to a hypothetical flood that is supposed to leave no lasting traces.

Unfortunately for Ross's ideas, even this value already falls within the aforementioned range of the Spokane flood: 0.002–0.012, which did leave considerable traces of its occurrence — putting it mildly.

Of course, the 0.0047 value is an average. In some places across the 40-mile transect, the topography is less steep, and, in others, more steep. But even this irregularity favors, in comparison with a monotonously sloping area with a uniform gradient of 0.0047, the accumulation of locally thick flood deposits (which, by virtue of this fact, are all the more likely to persist with time). This is not only due to the fact that the power of a flood increases linearly with increasing gradient, but also because highly channelized flood flow is much more powerful than an equivalent depth of less-channelized flood flow.[65] In addition, there is an especially destructive process called *cavitation*, where tiny vacuum "bubbles" form in very fast-moving water and explode with enough force to pulverize even hard rock. For example, in 1983, cavitation was responsible for huge damage in the steel-reinforced concrete and surrounding sandstone bedrock at the Glen Canyon Dam, a hole 32 x 40 x 150 feet (10 m x 13 m x 45 m).[66]

---

63. V.R. Baker et. al., "Columbia and Snake River Plains," *Geological Society of America Centennial Special* 2:415 (1987): p. 425.

64. *Atlas of the Arab World and the Middle East* (London: MacMillan & Co., 1960), p. 31, 39.

65. V.R. Baker et. al., "Columbia and Snake River Plains," *Geological Society of America Centennial Special* 2:415 (1987): p. 424.

66. E. Holroyd, "Cavitation Processes During Catastrophic Floods," in R.E. Walsh and C.L. Brooks, editors, *Proceedings of the Second International Conference on Creationism* (Pittsburgh, PA: Creation Science Fellowship, 1990), 2:101–113.

When more northerly areas, indisputably affected by the "Rossian flood," are considered, the "no-traces-left" scenario becomes all the more untenable. Thus, within the 30-mile zone where Ross believes the ark landed, the gradient is computed at 0.016. Proceeding north, it rapidly increases to around 0.03. These gradients dwarf the 0.002–0.012 gradient of the Spokane flood, and the power of the water flowing across such a gradient is even hard to imagine. In fact, a modest increase in floodwater-flow velocity implies a very large increase in its sediment-carrying capacity.[67]

It is obvious that a large flood having no lasting effects is sheer fantasy. It would have taken a miracle for Ross's proposed local Noachian deluge to have left no geologic traces of its past work. Now, if Ross is willing to accept that, then why not accept the biblical teachings of a global Flood — with or without miracles?

Mesopotamian Flood Versus Geology

As usual, compromise views not only commit hermeneutical assault and battery, they raise more problems than they solve. One major problem is that the geography of Mesopotamia is a half-bowl *open to the south*. Since the Rossian flood requires a wall of water 200–300 feet high (GQ:159–160), what would hold it up for a year, and stop it flowing out to the Indian Ocean?

Even at ordinary river-drainage speeds of 3–5 mph (5–8 km/h), such a flood would drain in well under a year. Furthermore, a 300-foot-high wall of water would have far more potential energy than ordinary rivers. And, as pointed out in the previous section, its least-steep gradient is far greater than that of the Spokane flood, which carved the Channeled Scablands.

Ross realizes the problem about covering Mount Ararat, so he argues that the "mountains of Ararat" include the foothills. He has a map (GQ:170) showing a 600-foot contour line to indicate where the ark could have landed (GQ:151). However, it is implausible to claim that the ark landed in the foothills of Ararat, because Noah would have seen the mountains behind the foothills. Yet the Bible says the mountains were covered. So it is futile to try to limit the extent of the Flood by an appeal to Noah's perspective, because even that doesn't work.

Furthermore, Ross fails to explain how a 300-foot-high flood could have levitated the ark another 300 feet! Since the water flow direction would be toward the south, the ark would be carried this way till it landed on a beach in Arabia.

Some anti-creationists have pointed out these fallacies in Mesopotamian flood theories in general and Ross's book GQ in particular. But there is nothing original in these criticisms. Over 40 years ago, Whitcomb and Morris pointed out the fallacy of John Pye Smith's Mesopotamian flood compromise on essentially the same grounds, for example, "appealing to the supernatural power of God, as an invisible wall, to hold the Flood within the Near East."[68] They also point out that the earlier proponent of

---

67. D. Allen, "Sediment Transport and the Genesis Flood," *TJ* 10(3):361 (1996).
68. J.C. Whitcomb and H.M. Morris, *The Genesis Flood* (Grand Rapids, MI: Baker Book House, 1961), p. 60–62.

the "day-age" theory, Hugh Miller (1802–1856), realized this problem. But Miller proposed the desperate solution that the Near East sank as fast as the waters arose, so that the Flood could have covered Ararat and still have been local. He proposed that the Near East sank 400 feet per day, so 16,000 feet in 40 days, and the ocean poured into the resulting basin, covering the mountains inside.[69] Then, somehow, the water drained out of this basin again. The ludicrous lengths to which people will go in order to evade the plain teaching of Scripture are truly breath-taking.

Ross Repeats Irresponsible Skeptics' Arguments About a Global Flood

Misrepresentations of Noah's Ark Itself

Perhaps the most disappointing aspect of Ross's thinking is his willingness to not only embrace, but also to actively disseminate the arguments of Bible-mocking apostates. It is difficult to understand why Ross (GQ:163, 227) would even dignify the very poorly reasoned article of Moore[70] by repeating its claims, when Moore used this as an excuse to apostatize from the Christian faith in which he was raised. Sadly, Ross often relies heavily on biblioskeptics in his crusade against the biblical creation/Fall/Flood model. Also, virtually all of Moore's intellectual-sounding arguments have been thoroughly refuted.[71] How many people have been and will be misled by Ross's implicit endorsement of Moore's sophistry?

A Global Flood Would Destroy the Ark?

For a start, Ross repeats the yarn about the ark's destruction being a certainty in a global Flood (GQ:149, 156). That oft-repeated assertion is not supported by a shred of evidence. Keeping in mind that a day is 86,400 times longer than a second, one also wonders how he arrives at the conclusion that G-forces would shatter the ark (GQ:153), as a result of tectonic movements of 200 feet *per day* and erosional ones of 700 feet *per day*, when the value of G, in Imperial units, is 32 feet *per second* (9.8 m/s^2).

Ross repeats the following common mythology about the construction of giant wooden ships (GQ:165):

> Some skepticism about Noah's ability to construct the ark comes from the observation that until the late nineteenth century A.D., no nation had ever built such a huge vessel. No nation to this day has succeeded in constructing one from wood. The largest wooden vessels ever assembled were the clipper ships of the last century, a little more than three hundred feet long. When New England shipyards attempted to build longer vessels, they discovered that they could not make them seaworthy. Their oak beams lacked the necessary tensile strength.

---

69. H. Miller, *The Testimony of the Rocks* (New York: Robert Carver and Brothers, 1875), p. 358.

70. R.A. Moore, "The Impossible Voyage of Noah's Ark," *Creation/Evolution* XI:3–36, (1983).

71. See J. Woodmorappe, *Noah's Ark: A Feasibility Study* (El Cajon, CA: Institute for Creation Research, 1996).

To begin with, Ross and the skeptical sources he accepts uncritically commit a fallacy of *argumentum ad ignorantiam* or appeal to ignorance. What does it matter what could be achieved by 19th-century technology? All it would prove is that *they* could not build big wooden ships, not that it was impossible. By the same "reasoning," one could argue that since nobody in the 19th century could build a heavier-than-air flying machine, clearly it's impossible for something as big as a Boeing 747 to fly, or that since no moderns have built stone structures equivalent to the pyramids of Egypt, they were not built by humans.

Also, Ross and his misotheistic sources are ignorant of classical literature of huge wooden ships of a comparable size to the ark.[72] But we must wonder about the creative imagination of Ross and his skeptical sources, because there is no record of New England shipyards ever attempting to build ships substantially longer than about 330 feet, let alone about them failing in the sea — it is pure fiction. Nor is it at all true that the excessive bending (and leaking) of large wooden ships had *anything* to do with the engineering limitations of wood itself.

Instead, as Woodmorappe has pointed out and documented,[73] the excessive flexibility of large wooden hulls had been caused by the fact that the standard plank-to-frame point connections lacked rigidity. The ark would have been much more rigid and leaking would have been eliminated if it had been constructed as a *monocoque* (French for "single shell") — a construction technique where the external skin provides the structural support, as opposed to using an internal framework that is then covered with a non-structural skinning. Alternatively, Woodmorappe has suggested logs connected to each other laterally and vertically.

Rod Walsh, who has extensively modeled the ark,[74] has pointed out that the ancients used the technique of *mortice and tenon* joints. This is where one piece of wood has fairly thick projections, *tenons*, that fit into matching sockets drilled into another piece of wood, *mortices*, forming a very strong joint. However, this is labor-intensive, so later ship-builders largely abandoned it. But Noah had about 100 years (Gen. 6:3) to build the ark, and had no need to spare expenses on hiring workmen (and Ross acknowledges this, partly (GQ:165–166)). So Noah could have built the strongest structure possible without worrying about other considerations.

It's also important to note that the ark did not have to be streamlined because it didn't have to travel. Rather, it was designed for floating. The ark also did not have masts, which were the main hazard of wooden ships, because they provide a long lever for the force of the wind to generate large torques. Ross, to his credit, points out that the "gopher" wood could have been far stronger than oak, for example,

72. L. Pierce, "The Large Ships of Antiquity," *Creation* 22(3):46–48 (June–August 2000).
73. J. Woodmorappe, *Noah's Ark: A Feasibility Study* (El Cajon, CA: Institute for Creation Research, 1996), p. 50–51.
74. D. Batten, "Modeling the Size of Noah's Ark," *Creation* 21(1):12–14 (December 1998–February 1999).

tropical hardwoods, and Woodmorappe has pointed out that the ancients knew about wood-hardening methods.

Furthermore, Korean naval architects have confirmed that a barge with the ark's dimensions would have optimal stability. They concluded that if the wood were only 30 cm thick, it could have navigated sea conditions with waves higher than 30 m.[75] Compare this with a tsunami ("tidal wave"), which is typically only about 10 m high. Also, they are dangerous only near the shore — out at sea, they are hardly noticeable.

Pitching the Ark?

Ross repeats another discredited argument from skeptics: that it would be impossible to "pitch" the ark without millions of years for petroleum products to accumulate (GQ:158). Ross is unwilling to admit to his readers that biblical creationists have already addressed most of his arguments long ago. Dr. Tas Walker had pointed out 15 years before GQ was published that pitch need not be made from petroleum at all — the pitch-making industries in Europe made pitch from pine resin for centuries.[76] The *Encyclopædia Britannica* says, about naval pitch: "Oleoresin, *also called gum or pitch* . . . is extracted from the pine. . . ."[77]

But even assuming that a petroleum-based sealant was necessarily meant by Scripture (as opposed to a wood-based resinous sealant, as above), Ross needs to be informed of the fact that at least some petroleum deposits are reportedly inorganic in origin,[78] and so would have been available before the worldwide Flood.

Misrepresentations of Noah's Ark's Cargo

Polar Animals?

Ross complains about skeptics laughing at a worldwide Flood, because, they say, it would require polar bears to have entered the ark (GQ:159). The joke is on the biblioskeptic and on Ross himself. Polar bears and other forms of presently cold-adapted life can, and do, easily acclimatize to warm temperatures — they live in many warm temperate zoos.[79] Also, polar bears probably did not, as such, exist until after post-Flood radiation of animals. They are clearly part of the bear kind, as shown by their ability to hybridize with brown and grizzly bears.[80] But they could have arisen by separating

75. S.W. Hong et al., "Safety Investigation of Noah's Ark in a Seaway," *TJ* 8(1):26–36 (1994); <www.answersingenesis.org/arksafety>. All the co-authors are on the staff of the Korea Research Institute of Ships and Ocean Engineering, in Daejeon.

76. T.B. Walker, "The Pitch for Noah's Ark," *Creation* 7(1):20 (1984).

77. "Naval Stores," *Encyclopædia Britannica*, 8:564–565, 15th ed. (1992); emphasis added.

78. J. Woodmorappe, *Noah's Ark: A Feasibility Study* (El Cajon, CA: Institute for Creation Research, 1996), p. 51.

79. J. Woodmorappe, *Noah's Ark: A Feasibility Study* (El Cajon, CA: Institute for Creation Research, 1996), p. 120–123.

80. D.J. Tyler, "Adaptations with the Bear Family: A Contribution to the Debate about Limits of Variation," *Creation Matters* 2(5):1–4 (1997).

out already existing genetic information from the bear kind that came off the ark, and experiencing two losses of genetic information (see previous chapter):[81]

1. Whiteness: a mutation causing loss of fur pigment. In an arctic environment, this would be an advantage by camouflaging it against the snow, so its prey would be less likely to see them.

2. Webbed feet: As explained in chapter 6, mammalian digits are formed in the embryo by developing a ridge, then apoptosis, dissolving the tissue in between. A polar bear has a mutation preventing the toes from dividing properly during its embryonic development. This defect would give it an advantage in swimming, which would make it easier to survive as a hunter of seals among ice floes.

Ross's associate Dr. Fuz Rana, in their November 25, 2000, broadcast, reinforced his boss's claim that AiG is teaching biological evolution, and showed that he also had not grasped the information issue, just like most atheistic evolutionary propagandists (and, as shown in the previous chapter, he hadn't grasped the point two years later):

> Okay, what they basically are trying to do is to dance around the whole idea that they don't embrace biological evolution by somehow claiming that when changes happen in nature it's not producing new information, that God was responsible for putting all the information in place and it doesn't really change, no new information is added. . . .
>
> And to kind of point out that they are holding to an evolutionary perspective, and that they are arguing even though they are asserting that no new information is created, they do actually indirectly argue for new information being created in an evolutionary process. Here's a paper I have from their website, it's called Bears across the world, it's written by Paula Weston and Carl Wieland, and this was published in *Creation Ex Nihilo*, and they talk about the bears on the planet today being descended from a single bear kind, and with respect to the origin of polar bears, they say that polar bears' partly webbed feet may have come from a mutation which prevented the toes from dividing properly during its embryonic development, and this defect would give it an advantage in swimming, which would make it easier to survive as a hunter of seals among ice floes. Thus bears carrying this defect would be more likely to pass it on to their offspring, but only in that environment.
>
> So what they're talking about here is that mutations, according to their model, are generating new information that allows bears to have webbed feet and survive in its environment specifically.

How plain do we have to make it? We said that the webbed feet were the result of a *loss* of genetic information so that the toes didn't divide completely, but Rana

---

81. P. Weston and C. Wieland, "Bears Across the World," *Creation* 20(4):28–31 (November 1998); <www.answersingenesis.org/bears>.

uses this to "prove" that we accept information-*gaining* mutations. As explained in the previous chapter, we have many examples of information-losing changes being advantageous, for example, wingless beetles on a windswept island and animals with shriveled eyes in dark caves.

Fitting All the Animals on Board

Whenever the global Flood is attacked, we invariably hear about the impossibility of putting all those animals on the ark. For example, anticreationist physicist Lawrence Lerner is typical of many anti-creationists, and mocks the idea of "kind" by claiming:

> In order to avoid overcrowding Noah's ark, some creationists adhere to the biblical term "kinds" rather than species as the limiting barrier to evolution.[82]

As shown in the previous chapter, the creationist concept of kind does not come from trying to fit things on the ark. Rather, it is based on careful attention to the text and sound biblical exegesis aided by scientific concepts such as hybridization. In reality, the converse is true — skeptics hate the creationist analysis of "kinds" partly because it neutralizes skeptical attacks on the ark that try to pack it full of millions of "species" — including many of which are marine, invertebrate, or plant, so could have survived off the ark.

Alas, Ross has swallowed the whole skeptic claim. Ironically, when promoting his local flood idea, he supposes that only birds and mammals were on the ark (GQ:166–168). In reality, the passengers consisted of mammals, birds, reptiles, and possibly some of the more terrestrial amphibia.[83] But when criticizing modern creationists and their global Flood, Ross performs an about-face and has his readers believe that the ark would have been required to carry marine creatures such as trilobites, which were also invertebrates (GQ:91). Actually, since Ross, in the same paragraph, claims that creationists believe there were 30,000 pairs of land animals on board (he got the "land" part right, at least), we must wonder whether he even knows what a trilobite is!

Ross also parades an argument that is seemingly obligatory for skeptics — the "every species on the ark" argument. As for speciation after the Flood, Ross would have us believe that there would not be enough time for this (GQ:154–155). This is a patently specious argument, and my previous chapter was devoted to it. But in summary, there would have needed to have been only 8,000 pairs of land vertebrate animals at the most, representing pairs corresponding to every genus that has ever lived. There would be even fewer animals if the kind corresponded mainly to today's families (see page 230).

---

82. L.S. Lerner, *Good Science, Bad Science: Teaching Evolution in the States*, Thomas B. Fordham Foundation (September 26, 2000).

83. J. Woodmorappe, *Noah's Ark: A Feasibility Study* (El Cajon, CA: Institute for Creation Research, 1996), p. 3–5.

The ark measured 300 x 50 x 30 cubits (Gen. 6:15), which is about 450 x 75 x 45 feet, or 140 x 23 x 13.5 meters, so its volume was 43,500 m³ (cubic meters) or 1.54 million cubic feet. To put this in perspective, this is the equivalent volume of 522 standard American railroad stock cars, each of which can hold 240 sheep. Most vertebrates are actually rather small (rodents, lizards, birds), and the median size would have been that of a rat.

If the animals were kept in cages with an average size as large as 1 cubic meter, the 16,000 animals would only have occupied 16,000 m³, a little over one entire deck.

Even if a million insect species had to be on board, it would not be a problem, because they require little space. If each pair was kept in cages of four inches (10 cm) per side, or 1,000 cm³, all the insect species would occupy a total volume of only another 1,000 m³, a small fraction of a deck. This would leave a massive amount of room for food, Noah's family, and "range" for the animals. However, Noah probably would not have taken insects on board as obligate passengers, anyway. Insects are not included in the meaning of *behemah* or *remes* in Genesis 6:19–20. Also, the Flood wiped out all land animals which breathed *through nostrils* except those on the ark (Gen. 7:22). Insects do not breathe through nostrils but through tiny tubes in their exterior skeleton. Many insects and other invertebrates were small enough to have survived on floating mats of vegetation and pumice.

In fact, Darwin himself performed experiments that inadvertently support the validity of the biblical Flood/ark account. By floating snails on saltwater for prolonged periods, Darwin convinced himself that, on rare occasions, snails might have "floated in chunks of drifted timber across moderately wide arms of the sea."

Other experiments by Darwin showed that garden seeds could still sprout after 42 days' immersion in saltwater, so they could have travelled 1,400 miles (2,240 km) on a typical ocean current.[84] This shows how plants could have survived without being on the ark — again by floating on driftwood, pumice, or vegetation rafts — even if they were often soaked.

Caring for the Cargo

Virtually every attack on the workability of Noah's ark also includes a section on the "assured impossibility" of eight people having cared for, fed, and cleaned up after thousands of animals, and Ross's criticism is no exception (GQ:163). It is unfortunate that these critics have never spent the time actually studying how long it takes to care for animals. But YECs have. Based on actual *applied* (as opposed to theoretical) manpower studies cited,[85] it is definitely possible for eight people to have cared for, fed, watered, and removed daily waste from 16,000 animals — and still had time left over in the workday for other tasks. And all this is under low-tech, non-miraculous conditions.

---

84. Cited in J. Weiner, *The Beak of the Finch: Evolution in Real Time* (London: Random House, 1994), p. 136.
85. J. Woodmorappe, *Noah's Ark: A Feasibility Study* (El Cajon, CA: Institute for Creation Research, 1996), p. 71–81.

Furthermore, in this scenario it is not necessary for the animals to hibernate.[86] But hibernation is a possibility which would reduce these requirements even more. It is true that the Bible does not mention it, but it does not rule it out either. Some creationists suggest that God created the hibernation instinct for the animals on the ark, but we should not be dogmatic either way.

Some skeptics argue that food taken on board rules out hibernation, but this is not so. Hibernating animals do not sleep all winter, despite popular portrayals, so they would still need food occasionally.

For example, the ark would probably have carried compressed and dried food-stuffs, and probably a lot of concentrated food. Perhaps Noah fed the cattle mainly on grain, plus some hay for fiber. The volume of foodstuffs would have been only about 15 percent of the ark's total volume. Drinking water would only have taken up 9.4 percent of the volume. This volume would be reduced further if rainwater was collected and piped into troughs. It doesn't require high technology to store dried food in airtight containers, and refill feeding troughs via chutes every week or so.

It's notable that Ross himself acknowledges, to his credit (GQ: 169):

> Given their hundred-year building, planning, and preparation time, Noah and his family could have adapted and installed many labor-saving devices. Dumb waiters, carts, chutes, rails, and simple plumbing could have greatly streamlined their efforts.

Indeed so, but Ross underestimates their capacity, and invokes these scenarios in the context of his greatly reduced cargo.

Ross paraphrases a biblioskeptic (GQ:163):

> How could eight people possibly care for all the ark's animals? Even equipped with large shovels (if they had them), how could they possibly ever clean up after the ark's animals?[87]

Ross "answers" this by emasculating the numbers of the ark's cargo (GQ:169):

> The image of Noah drowning in the excrement of the ark's animals is based on a faulty understanding of how many animals were on board.

However, taking care of the waste products of all 8,000 pairs of land vertebrate genera would also be well within the capacity of Noah and his family. Possibly, they had sloped floors or slatted cages, where the manure could fall away from the animals and be flushed away (plenty of water around!) or destroyed by vermicomposting (composting by worms), which would also provide earthworms as a food source. Very deep bedding can sometimes last for a year without needing a change. Absorbent material (for example, sawdust, softwood shavings, and especially peat moss) could have reduced the moisture content and hence the odor.

---

86. Ibid., p. 127–135.
87. R.A. Moore, "The Impossible Voyage of Noah's Ark," *Creation/Evolution* XI:3–36, (1983).

MISCONCEPTIONS ABOUT THE PRE-FLOOD WORLD

For quite some time, biblioskeptics have been making up a whole series of intellectual-sounding arguments against a global Flood. Most of them obviously have little if any understanding of what they are alleging. It is disappointing to read Hugh Ross repeat the most baseless of these canards as scientific fact. (For answers to some other claims by Ross and other anti-creationists, see chapter 12 — as pointed out there, billions of years are intimately linked to denial of the global Flood.)

Limit to the Earth's Biomass?

To begin with, this is what Ross says about the earth's past life (GQ:157):

> We see no indications of a radically larger biomass in the Flood's time frame, and we can calculate from the laws of physics that earth, right now, carries a biomass close to its upper limit. The total mass of all life on earth is limited, of course, by the flow of solar energy to earth.

Anyone with the slightest background in ecology knows the error of Ross's assertion. Without a doubt, deserts and tundra have only a tiny fraction of the productivity of the earth's tropical forests. Are the laws of physics different in the tropics than they are in the deserts and tundra regions of the world? Of course not. The simple fact of the matter is this: The earth's productivity is primarily governed by temperature (including length of growing season) and available moisture (including the provision for rainfall not to run off). The amount of solar radiation falling on an area assumes only minimal significance for primary productivity.

> As farming communities based on modern irrigation schemes can testify, utilizing water from a dammed river or piped in from elsewhere can immediately increase the desert biomass per unit area by more than a hundredfold. This graphically demonstrates that the earth's productivity could readily be increased to a level significantly higher than at present.[88]

In addition, if the world's pre-Flood temperate and polar regions were warmer, frost-free, and with more precipitation (e.g., no deserts), the earth's productivity could well have been many times higher than at present.

As for Ross's assertion about a lack of past high-quantity biomass, he is clearly begging the question by assuming the correctness of what he believes as part of his argumentation. Thus, Ross denies that the world's coal deposits could have been caused by the Flood, and then completes the circle of reasoning by telling us that there is no indicator of higher biomass in a time frame compatible with the Flood. Such circular reasoning is, of course, a consequence of Ross's uncritical acceptance of the conventional evolutionary-geologic timescale, a fact discussed earlier in some length. When, in contrast to Ross, we free ourselves of the shackles of conventional

---

88. L. Rodin et al., "Productivity of the World's Main Ecosystems," in *Productivity of World Ecosystems* (Seattle, WA: National Academy of Sciences, 1975), p. 19–21.

uniformitarian geology and its time frame, we find evidences of very considerable amounts of past biomass — but *not* so much as to be unaccountable in a young-earth context.

Global Flood Too Violent?

In repeating old arguments which his unsuspecting readers may accept as fact, Ross shows a consistent tendency to be surprisingly ignorant of creationist research. Thus, he would have his readers believe that an olive tree would need to survive "tens of thousands of feet of erosion, tectonics, and vulcanism . . ." (GQ:152–154). Never mind the fact that this old chestnut has been answered long ago,[89] and also, in greater detail, more recently.[90]

Ross asserts that all the volcanic dust emitted in a global Flood would make the earth too cold for photosynthesis to occur for many years thereafter (GQ:153). His assertion speaks volumes about his lack of knowledge of up-to-date research. The fact of the matter is this: we now know that the atmospheric effects of volcanoes are self-limiting.[91] That is, beyond a certain level of aerosol loading, the stratosphere becomes "saturated." The global cooling effects are neither intensified nor prolonged as more and more volcanoes erupt and spew their gases and dust into the stratosphere. Instead, the stratospheric aerosol particles simply coagulate and are removed faster than before.

Vapor Canopy

Ross goes on to criticize the vapor canopy as an impossibility (GQ:153). While the canopy theory is not favored by most creationists, he would be unjustified and unscientific to call it an impossibility (either by natural or supernatural causation). Even if correct, his argument would be vacuous, because a canopy is not necessary for there to have existed a markedly warmer and more biologically productive ante-diluvian world than the present one.[92] In any case, most YECs have warned against treating the canopy notion too dogmatically, and most don't agree with it now (AB chapter 12).

Earth Would Still Be Ringing?

Still other comments made by Ross cannot be evaluated, because he provides no evidence to back them up, so the reader cannot even contemplate how Ross arrived at his conclusions. For instance, Ross claims that the planet Earth should still be "ringing" from a global Flood if a worldwide catastrophe had occurred thousands of years ago (GQ:149, 1st ed.).

89. J.C. Whitcomb and H.M. Morris, *The Genesis Flood* (Grand Rapids, MI: Baker Book House, 1961), p. 104–106.

90. J. Woodmorappe, *Noah's Ark: A Feasibility Study* (El Cajon, CA: Institute for Creation Research, 1996), p. 161–162.

91. J. Woodmorappe, "Hypercanes as a Cause of the 40-day Global Flood Rainfall," in R.E. Walsh, editor, *Proceedings of the Fourth International Conference on Creationism* (Pittsburgh, PA: International Conference on Creationism, 1998), p. 645–658.

92. Ibid., p. 648.

However, a check of the references he cites does not include any sort of claim that seismic phenomena that occurred thousands of years ago should still be measurable. Nor do the cited sources even provide a basis for deducing how long it would take the "ringing" to die out after a global Flood and its associated tectonism.

Rather, the cited articles are speaking of very low amplitude *atmospherically induced* seismic sound, maintained by *continued input* of atmospheric energy. Without this, the sound would dissipate rapidly because of energy losses due to friction, absorption, reflection, and other means.

Even some anti-creationists were embarrassed by such a weak argument against the Flood, and it seems that Ross withdrew it for the second edition.

Fossil Species Numbers Exaggerated by Orders of Magnitude

Continuing his practice of embracing the evolutionary geologic system, Hugh Ross goes on to make the following statements about the fossil record (GQ:155,161):

> According to the fossil record, at least a half-billion to a billion new species of life arose between the Cambrian explosion (circa 543 million years ago) and the arrival of human beings (circa 30,000 to 50,000 years ago). . . . . Earth cannot possibly support at one time the half-billion or more species of life the fossil record documents, which would be required according to the global Flood theory.

One wonders what planet Ross is referring to, because it certainly cannot be the earth. As a reality check, we should point out that the actual number of fossil species recovered is about 200,000. This includes just over 190,000 marine-invertebrate species,[93] and about 10,000 species of fossil vertebrates.[94] If we correct for sampling bias, and even accommodate some uniformitarian assumptions about past diversity of life, we project the existence of perhaps 1.2 million fossil species.[95] However, recent evidence shows that many fossils that have been identified as different species are really the same species. This means that the number of fossil species has been inflated by an estimated 32–44 percent.[96] We can see that Hugh Ross exaggerates the number of fossil species in the earth's crust by a factor of at least 400!

The source of Ross's astronomically inflated numbers (GQ:91) is the husband and wife partnership Paul and Ann Ehrlich,[97] who cite an antiquated (1952) number mentioned by George Gaylord Simpson. The latter had casually ventured a guess at the number of species that had ever lived. However, this was influenced

---

93. D.M. Raup, "Species Diversity in the Phanerozoic," *Paleobiology* 2:279–288 (1976).

94. K. Padian and W.A. Clemens, "Terrestrial Vertebrate Diversity," in J.W. Valentine, editor, *Phanerozoic Diversity Patterns* (Princeton, NJ: Princeton University Press, 1985), p. 43.

95. Ibid., p. 146, P.W. Signor, "Real and Apparent Trends in Species Richness through Time."

96. E. Sohn, "The Fossil Files," *New Scientist* 179(2409):32–35 (2003).

97. P.R. Ehrlich and A.H. Ehrlich, *Extinction* (New York: Ballantine, 1981), p. 26.

by evolutionary bias. For evolution to be true, there would have to have been innumerable transitional forms between different types of creature. Therefore, for every known fossil species, many more must have existed to connect it to its ancestors and descendents. This is yet another example of evolutionary conclusions coming before the evidence. Really, the claim is an implicit admission by evolutionists that large numbers of transitional forms are predicted, which heightens the difficulty for evolutionists, given how few there are that even they could begin to claim were candidates.

Ross's use of evolutionary *conjectures* (about how many species *may* once have lived) to attack the global Flood is ironic. This is because using these numbers involves an implicit (if unwitting) acceptance of the very evolutionary transformism which Ross spends so much time denying and attacking elsewhere. He cannot have his cake and eat it, too.

The Ehrlichs acknowledge that their guesstimate is "a ballpark guess" (if it even deserves to be dignified as such), and as shown in chapter 7, they are notoriously unreliable. It is unfortunate that Ross has accepted this totally conjectured number from this credibility-lacking source as gospel truth, and presented it to his readers as such. Even worse, he has also failed to accurately inform himself and his readers of the small actual number of fossil species that have been discovered.

How Many Species Are There Today?

There is a further irony to Ross's assertion about all those (imagined) "half-billion to billion fossil species that could not all be alive at the same time on the earth." The simple truth of the matter is this: we have no clear idea of how many species there are on the earth, let alone how many species the earth could simultaneously support! Consider the following sobering points:[98]

> At the purely factual level, we do not know to within an order of magnitude how many species of plants and animals we share the globe with: fewer than 2 million are currently classified, and estimates of the total number range from under 5 million to more than 50 million. At the theoretical level, things are even worse: we cannot explain from first principles why the global total is of the general order of 10^7 rather than 10^4 or 10^{10}.

As if all of the foregoing were not enough, we also know that the tropics support a much higher diversity of species than do other areas of the earth.[99] Let us consider another implication of the previously discussed warmer antediluvian earth (which, as noted, does *not* require a canopy). If the earth were warmer and wetter in the mid and high latitudes, it could support several times the number of species than it can at present.

---

98. R.M. May, "How Many Species Are There on Earth?" *Science* 241:1441 (1988).
99. E.G. Leigh, Introduction: "Why Are There So Many Kinds of Tropical Trees?" in *The Ecology of a Tropical Forest,* Leigh et al., editors (Washington, DC: Smithsonian Institution, 1982), p. 63.

Dinosaurs on the Ark?

Multiplying Names

It's likely that many so-called fossil species and even genera within a family were merely varieties of a single polytypic "biological species," and therefore of the same created kind. This helps to reduce the number of animals required on board the ark even further. This is especially important for the huge dinosaurs, created on day 6 — the same day as Adam and Eve. For example, the dinosaur name *Antrodemus* purports to refer to a distinct genus — but all they found was a partial tail vertebra, and even this was probably just from an *Allosaurus*.

Diplodocus and *Apatosaurus* have virtually identical skulls, so it's possible that the former was a very long and slender variant and the latter, a shorter, but much more massive, variety. Note that *Brontosaurus* is an invalid taxon, because it is the result of placing the wrong (camarasaurid-like) head onto an *Apatosaurus* skeleton instead of the correct diplodocid head. Furthermore, according to the pro-evolution *Walking with Dinosaurs* website:

> A huge animal called *Seismosaurus* was found in New Mexico and many palaeontologists believe it is really an old *Diplodocus*. It weighed 30 tons and was 45 meters long.[100]

Therefore, it's likely that all the Diplodocidae family were one created kind.

Although there are an estimated 668 dinosaur "species," it's more likely that there were only about 55 kinds. Consider the sauropods, which were the largest dinosaurs — the group of huge plant-eaters like the diplodocids (above) as well as *Brachiosaurus,* etc. There are 87 sauropod genera commonly cited, but only 12 are "firmly established" and another 12 are considered "fairly well established."[101]

How Could Huge Dinosaurs Fit?

All dinosaurs started life in eggs no bigger than footballs — a dinosaur egg cannot be any bigger, otherwise the shell would need to be so thick to support the weight that oxygen could not get through. Also, as the above quote about *Seismosaurus* acknowledges, dinosaurs were probably like some modern reptiles and kept growing throughout their lifetimes. According to the *Encyclopedia Britannica* CD:

> The significant difference between growth in reptiles and that in mammals is that *a reptile has the potential of growing throughout its life*, whereas a mammal reaches a terminal size and grows no more, even though it may subsequently live many years in ideal conditions [italics added].

However, new studies on dinosaur bones actually help creationists further. They show that dinosaurs had a type of adolescent growth spurt — the pattern is

100. <www.abc.net.au/dinosaurs/fact_files/scrub/diplodocus.htm>, November 28, 2002.
101. J.S. McIntosh, "Sauropoda," in D.B. Wieshampel et al., *The Dinosauria* (Berkeley, CA: University of California Press, 1992), p. 345.

called *sigmoidal,* or s–shaped. For example, in the huge *Apatosaurus,* the spurt started at the age of about five years and the growth leveled off at the age of 12–13 (see graph).[102] It means that God, who brought the animals to Noah (Gen. 6:20), could well have chosen specimens He knew would undergo their growth spurt as soon as they left the ark. This would solve the common skeptical problem of feeding huge dinosaurs on the ark, by showing

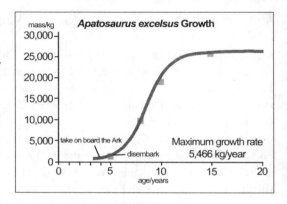

that they weren't actually that huge while they were on board. The growth spurt just after their ark sojourn would also mean that they could quickly outgrow predators.

Ross's Bait-and-Switch about Ark Animals

Ross claims, about "creation scientists (also known as Flood geologists)" (GQ:91–92):

> Shortly after the Flood, they say a large proportion of the thirty thousand species on board — the dinosaurs, trilobites, and so on — went extinct; the remaining few thousand species must have evolved by rapid and efficient natural processes alone into seven million or more species.

We can quickly dismiss Ross's blunder of implying that the trilobite was a land animal (and a nostril-breather, i.e., vertebrate). It's also clearly evident that he's just made up the number seven million, given that only two million are actually classified. What's worse is that he has conflated (old) creationist estimates of the number of *land vertebrate* species (a few thousand) with numbers of *total* species (millions), a dishonest straw man. Obviously, creationists don't think that the land vertebrates gave rise to all species, including the non-vertebrates!

In fact, only about 2 percent of the two million known extant species are vertebrates.[103] This number is further reduced when the 25,000 marine vertebrates (mainly fish)[104] and most of the four thousand amphibians[105] are discounted, since God told Noah to take on board only land animals — marine creatures don't need preservation from a flood! So it is hardly startling to believe that 8,000 kinds of land vertebrates represented on board the ark could give rise to the 11,000 living species, even if some of the ark kinds have become extinct.

---

102. G.M. Erickson et al., "Dinosaurian Growth Patterns and Rapid Avian Growth Rates," *Nature* 412(6845):429–433, Fig. 2 (July 26, 2001).

103. D. Burnie, "Animal," Microsoft® Encarta *Online Encyclopedia* 2002, <http://encarta.msn.com>.

104. J.W. Orr, "Fish," Microsoft® Encarta *Online Encyclopedia* 2002, <http://encarta.msn.com>.

105. D. Burnie, "Vertebrate," Microsoft® Encarta *Online Encyclopedia* 2002, <http://encarta.msn.com>.

The Ice Age

There is strong evidence that, following the Flood, for a time ice and snow covered much of Canada and northern USA, northwestern Eurasia, Greenland, and Antarctica. Evolutionists and long-agers believe there were many ice ages, but it's more likely that the "later" ones at least were advance/retreat cycles of a *single* Ice Age. And it is increasingly likely that alleged evidence of earlier ice ages really points to such non-ice phenomena as underwater debris flows.[106]

Evolutionists find the cause of an Ice Age a mystery. Obviously, the climate would need to be colder. But global cooling by itself is not enough, because then there would be less evaporation, so less snow. How is it possible to have both a cold climate and lots of evaporation?

The creationist meteorologist Michael Oard proposed that the Ice Age [possibly referred to in Job 37:10 and 38:22] was an aftermath of Noah's Flood.[107] When "all the fountains of the great deep" broke up, much hot water and lava would have poured directly into the oceans. This would have warmed the oceans, possibly to as warm as 30°C (86°F), increasing evaporation in the years after the Flood. At the same time, much volcanic ash in the air after the Flood would have blocked out much sunlight, cooling the land.

So the Flood would have produced the necessary conditions for lots of evaporation from the warmed oceans and cool continental climate from the volcanic ash "sunblock." This would have resulted in increased snowfall over the continents. With the snow falling faster than it melted, ice sheets would have built up.

The End of the Ice Age

This ice buildup would probably have lasted several centuries, perhaps as long as 500 years. Eventually, the seas gradually cooled, so evaporation would decrease, therefore the snow supply for the continents would also decrease. And as the ash settled out of the atmosphere, it would allow sunlight through. So the ice sheets began to melt, possibly over a period of 200 years.

Sometimes the melting would have been rapid enough for the rivers that drained these ice sheets to have flooded. Other times ice dams would have failed suddenly. These catastrophes would have happened for about 700 years after the Flood. An example was the Spokane flood, explained on page 266.

Ice Sheets

Hugh Ross glibly informs us that the Antarctic ice sheet is too thick to have formed in even tens of thousands of years (GQ: 146). In fact, with the warmer ocean

---

106. M. Oard, *Ancient Ice Ages or Submarine Landslides?* (Chino Valley, AR: Creation Research Soc., 1997).

107. Oard explains this in his technical book, *An Ice Age Caused by the Genesis Flood* (El Cajon, CA: ICR, El Cajon, 1990). He also wrote *Life in the Great Ice Age* (co-authored with Beverley Oard (Green Forest, AR: Master Books, 1993), which combines a colorful children's novel with a simplified scientific explanation.

See also D. Batten, editor, *The Answers Book* (Green Forest, AR: Master Books, 1999), chapter 16.

after the Flood, it could have formed in a few centuries.[108] Even in modern times, rapid buildup of ice was dramatically illustrated with the burial of WWII fighter planes in Greenland to a depth of 250 feet (75 m) in only about 50 years.[109]

CONCLUSION

Ross concludes *The Genesis Question* by encouraging readers to test everything that they hear or read (GQ:192). I have taken up Ross's own suggestion and have applied it to his book. Ross's claims fail almost every test of both theology and science. As charitable as one might want to be, the following conclusion is inescapable: Hugh Ross plays fast and loose with the facts and makes seriously unsound arguments. In fact, much of what he says has been conjectured, with little thought, by others, and was also shown to be incorrect a long time ago. It is unfortunate that so many unsuspecting and sincere Christians take Ross's teachings seriously. They may think that Ross's rather contrived synthesis of the Book of Genesis and conventional evolutionary geology has actually effected reconciliation between science and the Bible. As we have seen (and much more could be said about this), it has done no such thing. Far from it. Conventional scientific opinion has no use for *any* divine involvement in earth's past. And trying to make the Book of Genesis support long ages of time and a local flood is completely contrary to both the Bible and science, not to mention self-contradictory and self-defeating.

Clearly, then, Ross builds his understanding of the Bible on an uncritical reading of conventional evolutionary geology. And, unfortunately, it gets even worse when he attempts to understand the function of Noah's ark. It is sad to watch him borrow the most widely refuted arguments of skeptics. How many unsuspecting readers will be misled by all this?

This may be a bitter pill for some to swallow, but we must face the fact that the Bible, on one hand, and the evolutionary system of biology *and* geology, on the other, are completely and everlastingly incompatible. In fact, two more diametrically opposed systems of thought could hardly be imagined. The mere rejection of organic evolution is not enough. No reconciliation of science and the Book of Genesis can succeed which denies the global nature of the Flood and which buys into the standard geologic time scale. Thus, *both* organic evolution and geologic evolution must necessarily be uprooted before the creation and Flood are properly understood. Fortunately, many believers already see though the artificiality of trying to make the days of Genesis out to be long periods of time, and of trying to make the Noachian deluge a local one.

---

108. M. Oard, "An Ice Age within the Biblical Timeframe," in R.E. Walsh et al., editors, *Proceedings of the First International Conference on Creationism* II:157–163 (1986); <www.answersingenesis.org/iceage>.

109. C. Wieland, "The Lost Squadron: Deeply Buried Missing Planes Challenge 'Slow and Gradual' Preconceptions," *Creation* 19(3)10–14 (June–August 1997); <www.answersingenesis.org/docs/233.asp>.

Hugh Ross complains that creationists are "sifting science" and that "not much real science gets through." Ironically, Ross's approach of attempting to marry the Book of Genesis with large parts of the evolutionary-uniformitarian paradigm sifts both science and theology into an incoherent mess, which ends up satisfying neither science nor Scripture.

Intelligent believers have, to a considerable extent, come to appreciate the efforts of creationist scientists — unlike Ross, who denigrates them (GQ:11). It is these very scientists who work tirelessly to free *all* of science from the rationalistic shackles which have held it for the last two centuries, and to erect a brand-new paradigm which will be faithful both to Scripture and to the actual empirical scientific evidence.

THE HISTORY OF MANKIND

A straightforward reading of the biblical genealogies according to the reliable Masoretic text shows that Adam was created about 4,000 B.C., and this was on the 6th day of creation. And Jesus said, "But from the beginning of the creation God made them male and female" (Mark 10:6), not billions of years later. But Ross accepts the evolutionary dates of 4.5 billion years for the earth, and only tens of thousands of years for Adam. Since he also accepts the "earlier" evolutionary "dates" for other hominids, Ross concludes that they have no relationship to man, although they buried their dead, made tools and musical instruments, painted pictures, etc. A baneful implication of Ross's dating is that it opens the possibility that Australian Aborigines were not descendants of Adam, and therefore not human even by his own theology. Ross's faulty understanding of biological variation also leads him to conclude that God supernaturally introduced racial characteristics at Babel.

BIBLICAL HISTORY OUTLINE

- The heavens, earth, and everything in them were created in six consecutive normal days, the same as those of our working week (Exod. 20:8–11) — chapter 2.

- Adam sinned and brought physical death to mankind (Rom. 5:12–19; 1 Cor. 15:21–22) — chapter 6.

- Since man was the federal head of creation, the whole creation was cursed (Rom. 8:20–22), which included death to animals, with the end of the original vegetarian diet for both humans and animals (Gen. 1:29–30) — chapter 6.

- God judged the world by a globe-covering Flood (which Jesus and Peter compared with the coming judgment — Luke 17:26–27; 2 Pet. 3:3–7). This destroyed all land vertebrate animals and people not on the ocean-liner–sized ark — chapter 8.

- God then judged the people by confusing their language at Babel — after they had refused to spread out and repopulate the earth after the Flood. See page 301.

So when did this happen? In fact, the Bible provides an accurate time-line for all these events. The following sections on the biblical genealogies and statements by Christ are important evidence for the existence of mankind for almost as long as the earth has existed.

BIBLICAL GENEALOGIES

Which Text Should Be Used?

There are three main ancient texts of the Old Testament:

- The Masoretic Text which is used by modern Hebrew Bibles and is the basis behind most English Old Testaments. It is named after specialist copiers of the Bible called Masoretes ("transmitters"), who standardized the text and added vowel points to aid pronunciation to the text, which previously had only consonants. The Masoretes did not standardize the vowel points until the 7th or 8th century AD.[1]

- The Septuagint (LXX) was a Greek translation of the OT. The name comes from the Latin *septuaginta* (70), because, according to legend, 72 rabbis (6 from each of the 12 tribes) were responsible for the translation, in Alexandria in c. 250 B.C. In reality, it was composed over decades beginning in the 3rd century B.C. The multiple translators mean that it is uneven in accuracy, although mostly good on the Pentateuch. The LXX was in widespread use by Jews outside Israel in NT times. This explains why it was commonly (but far from exclusively) cited in the New Testament — if not, then people like the noble Bereans of Acts 17:11 might have checked the Apostles' teachings by the OT and said, "That's not how we find it in our Bible."[2] But it's important not to overstate the LXX's influence on the OT. Jesus clearly cites the OT 64 times in the Synoptics — Matthew, Mark and Luke (there are many more allusions, of course). Of these:

  - More than half (32+) *agree* with *both* the LXX and the MT (simply because the LXX is a *good* translation of the MT in those cases).

  - One-fifth of the 64 *differ* from *both* the LXX and the MT.

  - One-fifth of the 64 *agree* with the MT against the LXX.

  - The rest agree with the LXX *against* the MT (but we have a couple of verses where we see different versions of the LXX itself! (For example, Mark 13:25 versus Mark 9:48).[3]

- The Samaritan Pentateuch is a Hebrew version dating from the 1st century B.C. After the Assyrians deported many of the inhabitants of the Northern Kingdom of Israel, they imported colonists to the area centered around Samaria. The

---

1. G.L. Archer Jr., *Encyclopedia of Bible Difficulties* (Grand Rapids, MI: Zondervan, 1982), p. 40.
2. Ibid. Gleason Archer makes this point.
3. From G. Miller, "Septuagint," <www.christian-thinktank.com/alxx.html>, January 30, 1995.

Samaritans were mixed descendants of these colonists and Jews. They had their own system of worship centered at Mount Gerizim (John 4:20–21), and based only on the Law of Moses, or Pentateuch, which was slightly different from the one used by the mainstream Jews. The SP differs from the Masoretic text in about 6,000 places. In about 2,000 of these cases, it agrees with the LXX against the MT.

As shown in the table on the following page, these three have different ages for the patriarchs at the birth of the next one in line and their deaths, but they all agree that the creation is only thousands of years old, not millions or billions of years. However, a biblical chronology should be based on the Masoretic Text, because the other texts show evidence of editing.[4] For example, the Septuagint chronologies are demonstrably inflated, such as, they contain the (obvious) error that Methuselah lived 17 years after the Flood.

Date of Creation

We can define the year of the creation of the world as A.M. 1 (A.M. = *Anno Mundi* = year of the world). Then Adam died in A.M. 930, Noah was born in A.M. 1056, the Flood occurred 600 years later, therefore in A.M. 1656. Abraham was born when Terah was 130, 352 years after the Flood, in A.M. 2008. This narrows down the possible range for the date of creation. The only reason for the uncertainty is the dating of Abraham, and that depends on the dates of the sojourn in Egypt and the date of the Israelite monarchy. Once this is known, the other dates follow mathematically.

The late Dr. Gerhard Hasel, who was professor of Old Testament and Biblical Theology at Andrews University, calculated from the Masoretic Text that Abraham was born in about 2170 B.C. Thus, the Flood occurred at 2522 B.C. and creation at 4178 B.C.[5] Dr. Hasel rightly assumed that there were no gaps in the genealogies, as will be justified below.

Do the Genealogies Have Gaps?

James Barr, then Regius Professor of Hebrew at Oxford University, wrote in 1984:

> . . . probably, so far as I know, there is no professor of Hebrew or Old Testament at any world-class university who does not believe that the writer(s) of Genesis 1–11 intended to convey to their readers the ideas that: . . . the figures contained in the Genesis genealogies provided by simple addition a chronology from the beginning of the world up to later stages in the biblical story.[6]

---

4. For a defense of the Masoretic text versus the altered Septuagint (LXX), see P. Williams, "Some Remarks Preliminary to a Biblical Chronology," *TJ* 12(1):98–106 (1998); <www.answersin-genesis.org/chronology>.

5. G.F. Hasel, "The Meaning of the Chronogenealogies of Genesis 5 and 11," *Origins* 7(2):53–70, (1980); <www.grisda.org/origins/07053.htm>.

6. J. Barr, letter to David C.C. Watson, 1984.

Table 9.1 Chronogenealogies of the Patriarchs According to Different Texts						
NAME	**Age at begetting next in line**			**Remaining years of life**		
	LXX	*Masoretic Text*	*Samaritan Pentateuch*	*LXX*	*Masoretic Text*	*Samaritan Pentateuch*
Adam	230	130	130	700	800	800
Seth	205	105	105	707	807	807
Enosh	190	90	90	715	815	815
Cainan	170	70	70	740	840	840
Mahalaleel	165	65	65	730	830	830
Jared	162	162	62	800	800	785
Enoch	165	65	65	200	300	300
Methuselah	167	187	67	802	782	653
Lamech	188	182	53	565	595	600
Noah	500	500	500	450	450	450
Total Adam to Flood	2242	1656	1307			
Shem	100	100	100	500	500	500
Arphaxad	135	35	135	430	403	303
[Cainan]	[130]	–	–	[330]	–	–
Shelah	130	30	130	330	403	303
Eber	134	34	134	370	430	270
Peleg	130	30	130	209	209	109
Reu	132	32	132	207	207	107
Serug	130	30	130	200	200	100
Nahor	79	29	79	129	119	69
Terah[7]	70	70	70	135	135	75
Total Flood to Abraham	1070	290	940			

Barr, consistent with his neo-orthodox/liberal views, does not *believe* Genesis, but he understood what the Hebrew so clearly *taught*. It was only the perceived need to harmonize with the alleged age of the earth which led later conservative commentators to think anything different — it was nothing to do with the text itself.

Long-ager Davis Young points out:

> The church fathers also suggested that the world was less than six thousand years old at the time of Christ because of the chronology of

---

7. Note that Abraham was not Terah's firstborn. Gen. 12:4 says Abraham was 75 when he left Haran, and this was soon after Terah died at 205 (Gen. 11:32), and the difference (205–75) means Terah was actually 130 years old when Abraham was born, not 70 (Ussher seems to have been the first modern chronologist to have noticed this point). The latter figure refers to Terah's age when the oldest of the three sons mentioned was born, probably Haran.

the genealogical accounts of Genesis 5 and 11 and other chronological information in Scripture.[8]

The Jewish historian Flavius Josephus (A.D. 37/38 – c. 100), in his *Antiquities of the Jews,* also presents a chronology that has no hint of any gaps. This is significant since this indicates that the Jews of his time never saw any. The names and ages show that Josephus mostly used the LXX.[9]

This calamity [Flood] began in the 600th year of Noah's government [age]. . . . Now he [Moses] says that this flood began on the 27th [17th] day of the forementioned month [Nisan]; and this was 2,656 [1,656] years from Adam, the first man; and the time is written down in our sacred books, those who then lived having noted down, with great accuracy, both the births and dates of illustrious men.

For indeed Seth was born when Adam was in his 230th year, who lived 930 years. Seth begat Enos in his 205th year, who, when he had lived 912 years, delivered the government to Cainan his son, whom he had in his 190th year; he lived 905 years. Cainan, when he lived 910 years, had his son Malaleel, who was born in his 170th year. This Malaleel, having lived 895 years, died, leaving his son Jared, whom he begat when he was in his 165th year. He lived 962 years; and then his son Enoch succeeded him, who was born when his father was 162 years old. Now he, when he had lived 365 years, departed, and went to God; whence it is that they have not written down his death. Now Methuselah, the son of Enoch, who was born to him when he was 165 years old, had Lamech for his son when he was 187 years of age, to whom he delivered the government, which he had retained for 969 years. Now Lamech, when he had governed 777 years, appointed Noah his son to be ruler of the people, who was born to Lamech when he was 182 years old, and retained the government for 950 years. These years collected together make up the sum before set down; but let no one enquire into the deaths of these men, for they extended their lives along together with their children and grandchildren, but let him have regard for their births only. . . .[10]

I will now treat of the Hebrews. The son of Phaleg, whose father was Heber, was Ragau, whose son was Serug, to whom was born Nahor; his son was Terah, who was the father of Abraham, who accordingly was the tenth from Noah, and was born in the 290th year after the Deluge; for Terah begat

8. D.A. Young, *Christianity and the Age of the Earth* (Grand Rapids, MI: Zondervan, 1982), p. 19.

9. Josephus, *Jewish Antiquities,* Books I–IV (Cambridge, MA: Harvard Press, 1930, p. 73, Loeb Classical Library No. 242.

   R. Young, *Analytical Concordance to the Holy Bible,* 1879; 8th edition (London: Lutterworth Press, 1939), p. 210. Josephus calculated the creation date at 5555 B.C., because he used mainly the inflated figures of the LXX (5508 or 5586 B.C.).

10. Josephus, *Antiquities of the Jews* 1(3):3–4, <www.ccel.org/j/josephus/works/ant-1.htm>.

Abram in his 70th year.[11] Nahor begat Haran [*sic* — Terah?] when he was 120 years old; Nahor was born to Serug in his 132nd year; Ragau had Serug at 130; at the same age also Phaleg had Ragau; Heber begat Phaleg in his 134th year; he himself being begotten by Sala when he was 130 years old whom Arphaxad had for his son at the 135th year of his age, Arphaxad was the son of Shem, and born 12 years after the Deluge.[12]

Also, this comes from "Book 1, containing the interval of 3833 years: From the creation to the death of Isaac." Once more, this rules out any gaps or long creation days.

To demonstrate that the quotes of Barr and Josephus are not merely the fallacy of *argumentum ad verecundiam* (appeal to authority), here is some exegetical evidence for the tightness of the chronology.

Grammar

Ross points to some biblical genealogies that do have gaps to claim that the Genesis 5 and 11 genealogies are largely incomplete (GQ:108–109). He also claims (GQ:109):

> The words translated into English say this: "When X had lived Y years, he became the father of Z." Someone reading the same passage in Hebrew would see a second possibility: "When X had lived Y years, he became the father of a family line that included or culminated in Z."

However, none of his examples of gaps in genealogies (Matt. 1:8–9 versus 1 Chron. 3:10–12) mention the age of the father at the birth of the next name in the line, so are irrelevant to the issue of the *Genesis* genealogies, which do. Also, Matthew's genealogy was clearly *intended* to be incomplete, expressly stated to be three groups of 14 names (Matt. 1:17). This is in turn probably due to the fact that the Hebrew letters for the name David add up to 14. In Genesis 5 and 11, there is no such intention. So the Genesis 5 and 11 lists are sometimes correctly called *chronogenealogies*, because they include both time and personal information. Hasel explained the difference:

> As far as the genealogy in Matthew is concerned, the schematization is apparent and can be supported by comparison with genealogical data in the OT. Can the same be demonstrated for Genesis 5 and 11? Is there a ten-plus-ten scheme in Genesis 5 and 11? A simple counting of patriarchs in Genesis 5 and 11 reveals that there is no schematic ten-ten sequence. In Genesis 5 there is a line of ten patriarchs from Adam to Noah who had three sons, but in Genesis 11:26 the line of patriarchs consists of only nine members from Shem to Terah who "became the father of Abram, Nahor and Haran"

---

11. But see footnote 7.
12. Josephus, *Antiquities* 1(6):5.

(Gen. 11:26;NASB). If Abraham is to be counted as the tenth patriarch in Genesis 11, then consistency requires that Shem is counted as the eleventh patriarch in Genesis 5, because each genealogy concludes with a patriarch for whom three sons are mentioned. It appears that a comparison of Genesis 5:32 and 11:26 reveals that there are no grounds to count one of the three sons in one instance and not in the other, when in fact the formula is the same. Thus, if one counts in Genesis 5 ten patriarchs, consistency demands the counting of nine patriarchs in Genesis 11, or, vice versa, if one counts eleven in Genesis 5, then one needs to count ten in Genesis 11. The figures 10/9 to 11/10 respectively can hardly qualify as an intentional arrangement or a symmetry. In short, the alleged "symmetry of ten generations before the Flood and ten generations after the Flood" [Refs.] is non-existent in the Hebrew text. Thus the analogy with the three series of fourteen generations in Matthew 1:1–17 is a *non sequitur* [it does not follow].[13]

Ross also points out that the Hebrew word *'ab* (father) can mean grandfather or ancestor, while *ben* (son) can mean grandson or descendant (GQ:109). But Ross again errs by *unwarranted expansion of an expanded semantic field*.[14] That is, the fact that these words *can* have these meanings in *some* contexts does *not* mean they can have these meanings in *any* context. The Genesis 5 and 11 genealogies say that X "begat sons and daughters," implying that Z is likewise a son of X *in this specific context*.

And even if we grant that Z is a descendant of X, Z is always preceded by the accusative particle אֵת (*'et*), which is not translated but marks Z as the direct object of the verb "begat" (וַיּוֹלֶד- *wayyôled*). This means that the begetting of Z by X still occurred when X was Y years old, *regardless* of whether Z was a son or a more distant descendant. The Hebrew grammar provides further support — *wayyoled* is the *hiphil* waw-consecutive imperfect form of the Hebrew verb *yalad* — the *hiphil* stem communicates the *subject participating in action that causes an event,* for example, Seth as the begetter of Enosh. Hasel pointed out:

> The repeated phrase "and he fathered PN [personal name]" (*wayyôled 'et*-PN) appears fifteen times in the OT — all of them in Genesis 5 and 11. In two additional instances the names of three sons are provided (Genesis 5:32; 11:26). The same verbal form as in this phrase (i.e., *wayyôled*) is employed another sixteen times in the phrase "and he fathered (other) sons and daughters" (Genesis 5:4, 7, 10, etc.; 11:11, 13, 17, etc.). Remaining usages of this verbal form in the Hiphil in the Book of Genesis reveal that the expression "and he fathered" (*wayyôled*) is used in the sense of a direct

---

13. G.F. Hasel, "The Meaning of the Chronogenealogies of Genesis 5 and 11," *Origins* 7(2):53–70, (1980); <www.grisda.org/origins/07053.htm>.

14. D.A. Carson, *Exegetical Fallacies,* 2nd edition (Grand Rapids, MI: Baker Book House, 1996), p. 60.

physical offspring (Genesis 5:3; 6:10). A direct physical offspring is evident in each of the remaining usages of the Hiphil of *wayyôled*, "and he fathered," in the OT (Judges 11:1; 1 Chronicles 8:9; 14:3; 2 Chronicles 11:21; 13:21; 24:3). The same expression reappears twice in the genealogies in 1 Chronicles where the wording "and Abraham fathered Isaac" (1 Chronicles 1:34; cf. 5:37 [6:11]) rules out that the named son is but a distant descendant of the patriarch instead of a direct physical offspring. Thus, the phrase "and he fathered PN" in Genesis 5 and 11 cannot mean Adam "begat an ancestor of Seth." The view that Seth and any named son in Genesis 5 and 11 is but a distant descendant falters in view of the evidence of the Hebrew language used.[15]

Where Can the "Gaps" Be Inserted?

- Seth: Seth is definitely a direct son of Adam and Eve, and seen as a replacement for Abel, killed by Cain (Gen. 4:25).

- Enosh: must be a son of Seth, because Seth named him (Gen. 4:25).

- Enoch: Jude 14 says Enoch was seventh from Adam, which indicates straightforward father-son relationships from Adam to Enoch.

- Noah: Lamech named him, so Lamech must be his father, not just an ancestor (Gen. 5:29).

- Shem, Ham and Japheth were definitely ordinary sons of Noah, since they accompanied him on the ark.

- Arphaxad was plainly a son of Shem, because he was born two years after the Flood (Gen. 11:10).

- Abram, Haran, and Nahor were Terah's ordinary sons, since they journeyed together from Ur of the Chaldees (Gen. 11:31).

- Methuselah: Enoch, a pre-Flood prophet (Jude 14), gave his son a name meaning "when he dies it shall be sent," and the Masoretic chronology without any gaps would place his death in the year of the Flood.

Some commentaries claim that the name means "man of the spear," but the Hebrew Christian scholar Dr. Arnold Fruchtenbaum argues:

[T]he name Methuselah could mean one of two things. Therefore, it will either mean "man of the spear" or "when he dies it shall be sent." The debate is not over the second part of the word which, in Hebrew, is *shalach;* and *shalach* means "to send." While the concept of sending is the primary meaning of *shalach*, it has a secondary meaning of being thrown or cast forth in a context where the sending is with heavy force or speed. On that basis, some would conclude that *shalach* would mean either "missile" or "dart" or

15. G.F. Hasel, "The Meaning of the Chronogenealogies of Genesis 5 and 11," *Origins* 7(2):53–70, (1980); <www.grisda.org/origins/07053.htm>.

"spear." However, that is a derived meaning because the primary meaning of *shalach* is "to send," as any lexicon shows.

Ultimately, how one deals with *shalach* depends on how you deal with the first part of the word, which has the two Hebrew letters spelling *mat*. Based upon the root, then the meaning would indeed be "man." Hence, commentaries conclude that it means "man of the spear" or "man of the dart." However, the use of the term "spear" or "dart" is not the meaning of *shalach* in any lexicon that I know of. It is simply a derived meaning going from sending to throwing to trying to make a specific object. If *mat* was intended to mean man, if one was to keep it strictly literal, it would not mean "man of the spear" or "man of the dart," but "a man — sent."

The second option for *mat* is that it comes from the root that means "to die." Furthermore, the letter "*vav*" between *mat* and *shalach* gives it a verbal force. That is why I prefer to take it strictly literally, using the root "to die" and literally it would mean "he dies it shall be sent."

I prefer that translation of the name, "when he dies it shall be sent," for two reasons. The first reason is that I find it fitting the Hebrew parsing of the name much better. Secondly, it is better in the wider context since, if we follow the chronology of Genesis, the same year he died was the year of the flood. I do not think this was purely coincidental.[16]

The Number of Missing Generations Would Need to Be Huge

It's important to note that Ross needs more than just a few missing names. Normally, people want to push the Flood right back, and since the Genesis 11 chronologies are the ones that link the Flood to Abraham, these are the ones that must be "expanded." Ross "dates" the Flood to "between twenty thousand and thirty thousand years ago" (GQ:177). But since the Genesis 11 people had sons at age 35 or less, to add even 10,000 years would take over 250 missing generations! One must wonder how a genealogy could miss out all these without any trace. And since many of the names that *are* mentioned include no trace of any deeds or sayings by them, why would the writer bother to mention these when so many others had been omitted?

Is Cainan a Gap?

Ross also points out that Luke 3:36 has the extra name Cainan, which is not mentioned in Genesis 11:12 (GQ:109). He uses this to claim, in effect, here's one proven gap, so there's nothing to prevent unlimited multiplication of gaps.

This appears in most Greek manuscripts of Luke and the LXX of Genesis 11.[17] But the name was probably not in the original autographs, as shown by the textual evidence of both:

---

16. A.G. Fruchtenbaum, personal communication, November 7, 2000.
17. J. Sarfati, "Cainan: How Do You Explain the Difference Between Luke 3:36 and Genesis 11:12?" <www.answersingenesis.org/cainan>.

- The extra Cainan in Genesis 11 is found only in manuscripts of the LXX that were written long after Luke's gospel. The oldest LXX manuscripts do not have this extra Cainan.

- The earliest known extant copy of Luke omits the extra Cainan. This is the 102-page (originally 144) papyrus codex of the Bodmer Collection labeled P[75] (dated between A.D. 175 and 225).[18]

- Josephus used the LXX as his source, but did not mention the second Cainan (see page 291).

- Julius Africanus (c. A.D. 180 – c. 250) was "the first Christian historian known to have produced a universal chronology." In his chronology, written in c. A.D. 220, he also followed the LXX ages but once again omitted this mysterious Cainan.

Now that the extra Cainan is shown not to have been in the original manuscripts, it is helpful to try to plausibly reconstruct how the error crept into the copies.

Note that the Greek New Testament was originally written without punctuation or spaces between words. So Luke 3:35–38 would have been originally written as below. In this manuscript, TOYKAINAN (*the son* of Cainan) could have been on the end of the third line:

ΤΟΥΣΑΡΟΥΧΤΟΥΡΑΓΑΥΤΟΥΦΑΛΕΓΤΟΥΕΒΕΡΤΟΥΣΑΛΑ
ΤΟΥΑΡΦΑΞΑΔΤΟΥΣΗΜΤΟΥΝΩΕΤΟΥΛΑΜΕΧ
ΤΟΥΜΑΘΟΥΣΑΛΑΤΟΥΕΝΩΧΤΟΥΙΑΡΕΔΤΟΥΜΑΛΕΛΕΗΛΤΟΥΚΑΙΝΑΝ
ΤΟΥΕΝΩΣΤΟΥΣΗΘΤΟΥΑΔΑΜΤΟΥΘΕΟΥ

But suppose an early copyist of Luke's gospel was copying the first line, but his eyes glanced at the end of the third line at TOYKAINAN. Then he would have written it on the first line as well:

ΤΟΥΣΑΡΟΥΧΤΟΥΡΑΓΑΥΤΟΥΦΑΛΕΓΤΟΥΕΒΕΡΤΟΥΣΑΛΑΤΟΥΚΑΙΝΑΝ
ΤΟΥΑΡΦΑΞΑΔΤΟΥΣΗΜΤΟΥΝΩΕΤΟΥΛΑΜΕΧ
ΤΟΥΜΑΘΟΥΣΑΛΑΤΟΥΕΝΩΧΤΟΥΙΑΡΕΔΤΟΥΜΑΛΕΛΕΗΛΤΟΥΚΑΙΝΑΝ
ΤΟΥΕΝΩΣΤΟΥΣΗΘΤΟΥΑΔΑΜΤΟΥΘΕΟΥ

In English, keeping the same line formatting, and with italics indicating words added by the translators which were understood in the Greek, the passage makes sense:

the son of Serug, *the son* of Reu, *the son* of Peleg, *the son* of Eber, *the son* of Shelah, ***the son* of Cainan**,
the son of Arphaxad, *the son* of Shem, *the son* of Noah, *the son* of Lamech,
the son of Methuselah, *the son* of Enoch, *the son* of Jared, *the son* of Mahalaleel, ***the son* of Cainan**,
the son of Enosh, *the son* of Seth, *the son* of Adam, *the son* of God.

---

18. N.L. Geisler and Wm. E. Nix, *A General Introduction to the Bible*, revised and expanded (Chicago, IL: Moody Press, 1986), p. 390–391.

So if a copyist of Luke's gospel is responsible for the error, why is it in the LXX as well? As shown, it is not in the earlier copies, so must have been added later, by a copyist who wanted to bring it in line with Luke. And further supporting evidence comes from the fact that the ages of "Cainan" at the birth of his son and at his death are identical to the dates of Shelah, the next one in line. This is not surprising — the copyist is confronted with the extra name in Luke, but this provides no ages. So all the copyist can do to maintain the pattern is to repeat the ages of the next patriarch.

The doctrine of biblical inerrancy is not affected in the least by the Cainan difference. As shown, it is not an error in the original autographs of Scripture, but one of the extremely few copyist's errors in the manuscripts available today. The Chicago Statement on Biblical Inerrancy, which Ross says he agrees with, states in Article X:

> WE AFFIRM that inspiration, strictly speaking, applies only to the autographic text of Scripture, which in the providence of God can be ascertained from available manuscripts with great accuracy. We further affirm that copies and translations of Scripture are the Word of God to the extent that they faithfully represent the original.

> WE DENY that any essential element of the Christian faith is affected by the absence of the autographs. We further deny that this absence renders the assertion of biblical inerrancy invalid or irrelevant.

SECULAR HISTORY

Ross also uncritically claims that missionaries teaching a literal Genesis were discredited by:

> Chinese historical accounts placing Chinese national origins earlier than 4004 B.C. . . . The same reaction comes today from . . . Australian Aborigines, who date back to 25,000 B.C. . . . All are firmly established dates (GQ:108).

However, the *Encyclopædia Britannica* says on China: "The first dynasty for which there is definite historical material is the Shang, or Yin (18th–12th century BC)."[19] Also, studies of the earliest Chinese writings on oracle bones show that they were based on events recorded in Genesis.[20]

The Australian Aborigines were an oral culture, without writing, so their "dates" are not based on historical records but on "dating methods." However, some of these methods claim that Aborigines existed before even Ross's oldest "date" for Adam. What will happen to his apologetics if such dates become widely accepted?

Jesus and the Age of the World

The "secular timeline," from an alleged big bang to now, is the basis for Ross's chronology. However, this puts people at the "end" of creation, almost as an afterthought. One illustration was by Neil Shubin, an evolutionary paleontologist from

---

19. "China," *Encyclopædia Britannica* 3:230, 15th ed. (1992).
20. E.R. Nelson, R.E. Broadberry, and G.T. Chock, *God's Promise to the Chinese* (Saint Louis, MO: Concordia, 1997).

the University of Chicago, on episode 2 of the PBS *Evolution* series. Like Ross, he proclaimed that the earth is 4.5 billion years old, and to show how insignificant humans are, he scaled this time to one hour. Then, he claimed, animals existed only in the last ten minutes, while humans appeared only in the last one hundredth of a second. Ross himself used a similar analogy (FoG:178):

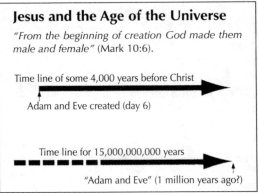

Jesus and the Age of the Universe

"From the beginning of creation God made them male and female" (Mark 10:6).

Time line of some 4,000 years before Christ

Adam and Eve created (day 6)

Time line for 15,000,000,000 years

"Adam and Eve" (1 million years ago?)

> If the time since the creation of the universe were scaled down to a single year, the whole of human history would be less than one minute.

This is one of many examples of the contradiction of evolution/billions of years with Christ's teachings. In several places in the Bible, the Lord Jesus Christ, the second person of the triune godhead made flesh (John 1:1–14), makes it plain that this is wrong — people were there from the beginning of creation. This means that the world cannot be billions of years old.

For example, explaining that the doctrine of marriage is founded upon the creation of marriage, Jesus quotes from Genesis 1:27 and 2:25 (Matt. 19:3–6, Mark 10:6–9). In particular, Jesus says in Mark 10:6:

> But *from the beginning of creation*, God made them male and female (emphasis added).

This makes sense only if Jesus affirmed that Genesis was intended to be interpreted straightforwardly. That is, where the earth was created about 4,000 years before He spoke those words, and Adam and Eve were created on day 6, which, on the scale of 4,000 years, is almost indistinguishable from the beginning (0.0004 percent away on that number line). This contrasts with the usual evolutionary view that we swung down from the trees a few million years ago, and even more with Ross's view that Adam and Eve were created 10–60 thousand years ago.[21]

Some would wishfully claim that it simply means "from the beginning of 'their' creation." But this makes little sense — of course they were male and female from the beginning of their own creation. What else would they have been — hermaphrodites? No, the context is clear that Jesus is pointing out God's plan right from the beginning of the creation. The Greek also supports the reading "from beginning of creation" (απο δε αρχης κτισεως, *apo de archēs ktiseōs*). This is supported by other passages where this phrase is clearly used of the whole creation.

21. H. Ross, "Genesis One, Dinosaurs and Cavemen," Reasons to Believe, <http://reasons.org/kidsspace/dinocave.shtml?main>, accessed March 15, 2003.

Mark 13:19: "For in those days there will be such tribulation as has not been from the beginning of the creation which God created until now, and never will be."

2 Peter 3:4: "[Scoffers say] 'Where is the promise of His coming? For since the fathers fell asleep, all things continue as they were from the beginning of the creation.' "

These two passages have the Greek phrase απ αρχης κτισεως *(apo de archēs ktiseōs)*, which is identical to that in Mark 10:6 — it makes no difference to the point that these lack the preposition *de* (which is a new topic marker, or sometimes "but") and have the *ap* instead of *apo*, since the former is used before a vowel *(archēs)* and the latter before a consonant *(de)*. Further, both these passages reinforce the teaching that mankind has been around about as long as creation itself.

There are other passages that also show how matter-of-factly Jesus and the Apostles accepted that mankind was there from the beginning.

In Luke 11:50–51, Jesus says: "That the blood of all the prophets, which was shed from the foundation of the world, may be required of this generation; From the blood of Abel to the blood of Zacharias. . . ." That is, prophets have been slain for almost as long as the world has existed. Since Seth was a replacement for Abel and was born when Adam was 130 (Gen. 4:25, 5:3), this makes sense because Abel's death would have occurred only 3 percent of the way into that time-line.

Paul, in Romans 1:20, makes it plain that people can clearly see God's power by looking at the "things that are made," and that people have been able to see this "from the creation of the world." Again, this rules out mankind being created billions of years after creation.

Timing of the Fall

When did the Fall happen? We can logically deduce from Scripture that it couldn't have been during creation week, because God called everything "very good" (Gen. 1:31). Nor is there any indication that it happened on the 7th day, because God blessed this, and there was no hint of any sin or curse on this day. Therefore, the Fall must have occurred after creation week.

However, the Fall can't have been too long afterward, because of the history of their immediate descendants. Adam and Eve were commanded to "fill the earth"; they would have obeyed in their unfallen state, and their physically perfect bodies would have been capable of conceiving immediately, at least within the first menstrual cycle. But the first child they conceived (Cain) was indisputably sinful.

Therefore, their Fall must have occurred a very short time, perhaps three to four weeks at most, after creation week. Therefore, we can also narrow down Satan's fall to the narrow window between the blessed 7th day and the fall of mankind.

Human Longevity

Ross does accept the biblical long life spans, and rejects any redefinition of the word "year" (a pity he isn't so careful with the word "day"). But, in GQ chapter 15,

Ross interprets the 120 years of Genesis 6:3 as shortening individual life spans. This is clearly fallacious because it contradicts other Scriptures showing that many people lived for hundreds of years well after the Flood. The best understanding is that the 120 years was the time left for mankind *as a whole* before the Flood would destroy it, with only a remnant surviving on the ark.

Ross's explanation for shortening human life spans is that God supernaturally increased the rate of apoptosis (programmed cell death) to "protect" us from increasing risk of cancer in the aftermath of a radiation burst from the Vela supernova. He claims that this was the closest supernova to erupt since mankind arose, occurring 1,300 light-years away and supposedly "18,000 ± 9,000 or 31,000 ± 6,000 years ago" (GQ:121–123). But it's bizarre to talk about "protecting" people from cancer at 500 or 900 by making sure they become decrepit and die before 120! What next, "protecting" people from Alzheimer's disease at 80 by causing fatal heart attacks at 60?

In any case, the Vela hypothesis makes no sense for another reason. About 700 years ago, the earth experienced the supernova RXJ0852.0-4622 from 600 light-years away. This is far closer than Vela, yet we see no evidence of another sharp, *permanent* drop in life spans in about A.D. 1300!

A Possible Scientific Explanation for Longevity

A sensible physical explanation for the drop in longevity is loss of "longevity genes" by genetic drift because of the sharp population decrease at the Flood, and the splitting of the gene pool after Babel as well, but Ross's book ignores creationist literature and evidence from gene studies.[22] (If a large fraction of a population or species is killed or otherwise prevented from reproducing, and the population is reduced by 50 percent or more, it is known as a *bottleneck*. This name comes from the graph of this change resembling the neck of a bottle, from wide to narrow; hence the name. Bottlenecks are well known for increasing the effects of genetic drift and natural selection.)

One explanation of longevity involves the role of *telomeres*, lengths of repetitive DNA on the ends of chromosomes, which serve to protect the genetic information stored. Each cell division results in shorter telomeres, and once they are lost the information can be corrupted and the cell dies. An enzyme called *telomerase* elongates the telomeres, and was discovered in 1980 by the winner of the 1998 Australia Prize, Professor Elizabeth Blackburn. Transfecting telomerase genes into cultured human cells can give them an unlimited capacity for cell divisions.[23] Telomerase is active in the reproductive cells, which means that the information passed on to the offspring is still fairly "fresh." One feature of Dolly the cloned sheep was that she inherited "aged" telomeres, which probably caused her premature aging.

---

22. C. Wieland, "Living for 900 Years," *Creation* 20(4):10–13, (1998); <www.answersingenesis.org/900>.

     C. Wieland, "Decreased Lifespans: Have We Been Looking in the Right Place?" *TJ* 8(2):138-141, (1994); <www.answersingenesis.org/lifespan>.

23. Bodnar et al., *Science* 279:349–352, (1998).

Unfortunately, telomerase is often active in cancer cells, too, so they divide uncontrollably. A famous illustration is the case of Henrietta Lacks, a 31-year-old Baltimore, Maryland, African-American mother of five who had cells removed from a malignant cervical tumor. Unfortunately, Henrietta died of this cancer in 1951, only eight months after it was discovered. But those cells have been dividing for over 50 years after her death, so this HeLa cell line (from the first two letters of each of her names) is effectively immortal. HeLa cells have supplied medical labs for decades, and have been instrumental in developing the polio vaccine and other medical advances.

In the second edition (GQ:124–125), Ross dropped the apoptosis explanation, realizing, according to his website, that he may have overstated the case.[24] Instead, he latched on to telomeres. But now he claims that God lowered telomerase activity, again to "protect" us from cancer by lowering our lifespans!

Premature Aging — Progeria

Support for a genetic cause of longevity comes from the opposite direction — the premature aging disease *progeria* (like gerontology, from the Greek word for old age, γερας *geras*). The technical name is Hutchinson-Gilford progeria syndrome (HGPS), and affects one in 8 million children. Sufferers age 5–10 times faster than usual, with typical geriatric symptoms of baldness, cataracts, and osteoporosis, dying by the age of about 13, usually from heart attack or stroke. The National Human Genome Research Institute discovered that progeria is caused by a mutation changing only one of the 25,000 base pairs in the lamin A (*LMNA*) gene.[25] If a single change from cytosine to thymine can cause a tenfold drop in life spans, perhaps a similar mutation caused a life span drop by a similar factor after the Flood.

ORIGIN OF RACES

Babel Division and the "Days of Peleg" (Genesis 10:25)

One important event recorded in the Bible is the confusion of languages at Babel (Gen. 11). This occurred in the "days of Peleg" (Gen. 10:25). Commentators well before Lyell and Darwin (including Josephus,[26] Calvin,[27] Keil, and Delitzsch[28]), as well

24. <www.reasons.org/resources/faf/98q1faf/98q1corr.shtml?main>, December 5, 2002.
25. M. Eriksson et al., "Recurrent *de novo* Point Mutations in Lamin A Cause Hutchinson–Gilford Progeria Syndrome," *Nature* 423(6937):293–298, (May 15, 2003).
26. Josephus, *Antiquities* 1(6):4: Heber begat Joctan and Phaleg: he was called Phaleg, because he was born at the dispersion of the nations to their several countries; for Phaleg among the Hebrews signifies *division*.
27. J. Calvin, *Genesis*, 1554 (Edinburgh, UK: Banner of Truth, 1984, p. 324: "For after he [Moses] has mentioned Arphaxad as the third of the sons of Shem, he then names Peleg, his great grandson, in whose days the languages were divided."
28. Also C.F. Keil and F. Delitzsch, *Commentaries on the Old Testament*, n.d., original German in the 19th century, English translation published by Eerdmans, Grand Rapids, MI. The Pentateuch, 1:171: "Among the descendants of Arphaxad, Eber's eldest son received the name of Peleg, because in his days the earth, i.e. the population of the earth, was divided, in consequence of the building of the tower of Babel."

as after (such as Leupold[29]) are almost unanimous that this passage refers to linguistic division at Babel and subsequent territorial division. Some creationists theorize that it refers to a supposed post-Flood division of continents, but that would have been as catastrophic as the Flood itself!

We should always interpret Scripture with Scripture, and there's nothing else in Scripture to indicate that this referred to continental division. But only eight verses on (note that chapter and verse divisions were *not* inspired), the Bible states, "Now the whole earth had one language and one speech" (Gen. 11:1), and as a result of their disobedience, "the LORD confused the language of all the earth" (Gen. 11:9). This conclusively proves that the "earth" that was divided was the same earth that spoke only one language, that is, "earth" refers *in this context* to the people of the earth, not Planet Earth.

From Table 9.1 on page 290 we can calculate that Peleg was born 101 years after the Flood. Given the long life spans and large numbers of sons mentioned, there could have been 3,000 people by this time. And if Eber named Peleg prophetically, as with Methuselah, then Babel could have occurred late in Peleg's lifetime, allowing even more time for the population to increase.[30]

Effects of Babel

The obvious effect was to produce the major language families, from which modern languages have developed. But the division of people according to their newly created language groups had other effects, too.

Babel resulted in the isolation of small people groups, each containing a fraction of the total gene pool. This helped to fix certain characteristics and produced the different people groups ("races") we see today. Natural selection and sexual selection would also have acted on these to "fine-tune" the results.

Ross also believes that the Babel division was significant for the origin of "races," but makes a critical error in denying its sufficiency. He says (GQ:181–182):

> The origin of humanity's different racial groups remains a mystery. Neither the Bible nor extrabiblical literature nor modern scientific research offers a direct explanation. One fact we can derive from Scripture: racial diversity existed from the time of the Exodus. . . .
>
> This question cries out for an answer: How did the human species develop such distinct skin colors and other more subtle differences in the relatively brief time from the days of Noah to the days of Moses? The usual answer that it happened in response to natural selection seems inadequate. . . .

29. H.C. Leupold, *Exposition of Genesis* (Grand Rapids, MI: Baker Book House, 1942), 1:378, "Peleg means 'division,' for he lived at the time when the earth was divided (niphlegah) and the name given to the man is in memory of this event. The event referred to must be the one under consideration — the Confusion of Tongues."

30. D. Batten, "Where Are All the People?" *Creation* 23(3):52–55, (June–August 2001); <www.answersingenesis.org/people>.

Sun sensitivity works poorly as a selection effect. . . . Evidence of how weakly natural selection favors one skin color over another comes from the observation that dark-skinned Eskimos live in the Arctic and fair-skinned Greeks on the Mediterranean isles.

These findings imply that natural selection cannot explain the development of racial diversity over just a few tens of thousands of years. At the risk of adopting a "God-of-the-gaps" approach, I can suggest an alternative explanation.

Given that Genesis 1 so explicitly describes God's personal intervention in breaking up destructive unity and in motivating people to spread through earth's habitable land masses, God may have done more than diversify language at the time. He possibly may have introduced also some external changes — those we recognize as racial distinctives — to facilitate the peoples' separation.

. . . God might have intervened . . . by miraculously introducing something new, in this case new genetic material that would generate racial distinctives.

However, some simple genetics can easily explain the origin of racial features. Rapid production of "varieties" can be shown in humans. It is well known that a marriage between two mulattos (the offspring of a union between, say, an African-American and an Anglo-American, who thus have a wide variety of "racial" traits) can produce children with a large variety of skin colors. Of course it couldn't happen quickly by *evolutionary* means, because they must rely on random mutations to generate *new genes*, and slow substitution over many generations to establish them in the population.[31]

This is why both Eskimos and native equatorial South Americans have mid-brown skins instead of having developed very light or very dark skins — the relevant genetic information is simply not present. Such "people groups" today are highly specialized, with less genetic variation than mulattos (and Adam and Eve), which is why they produce offspring of limited variety.

But Ross postulates direct divine intervention at Babel to introduce "racial" traits into separate populations. The Bible doesn't even hint at this. Ross admits that it's a "God of the gaps" explanation. This would be unnecessary if he had understood basic creationist literature.

But the most disturbing is Ross's claim that the different "racial" characteristics were designed to aid man's dispersal. Ross makes it clear (and I accept) that he is not intentionally endorsing any form of racial supremacy at all, because he says:

This should not be taken as an indication that there is anything wrong in different people cooperating and mixing, as in trade or marriage.

---

31. W.J. ReMine, *The Biotic Message* (St. Paul, MN: St. Paul Science, 1993).

But his ideas do in fact bring to mind 19th-century racism. During that time, some individuals refused to recognize the equality of all humans, especially when it pertained to intellectual and spiritual matters. These racists believed that not all races of humans had descended from Adam and Eve. Only members of their race were thus blessed, and they considered it futile to send missionaries to soul-less dark-skinned people.

Ross's idea, that God directly intervened in the biological line of inheritance from Adam so as to ensure that certain groups of people should be different from others, certainly smacks of such discredited notions. It also virtually implies that God designed racial prejudice, in order, as Ross suggests, "to facilitate the peoples" separation."

Finally, his postulate of "extra genetic material" seems to reinforce the prejudicial notion that there are in fact substantial genetic differences, differences in kind, between people groups. But virtually all modern geneticists acknowledge — due to biological fact, not "political correctness" — that the genetic differences are so trivial as to make the whole concept of "race," when applied to humanity, biologically meaningless.

Does Ross's Chronology Allow Aborigines to Be Non-Human?

Date Range for Adam and Eve

On his website, Ross claimed in 1997:

> In time, all these bipedal primates went extinct. Then, about 10 to 25 thousand years ago, God replaced them with Adam and Eve. From Adam and Eve came all the people that live on the earth today.[32]

Constraints

Ross has thus provided a range. In chronological studies, there are two terms for the absolute upper and lower limits of a time range. The *terminus a quo* (Latin for "limit from which") is the earliest limiting point, and the *terminus ad quem* (Latin, "limit to which") is the final limiting point in time. These points are the *constraints* on the range.

Aboriginal "dates"

Ross agrees with AiG that the Aborigines are human and that they therefore must be descendants of Adam and Eve. And as shown in the previous chapter, Ross agrees that since even his local flood wiped out humanity except for Noah's family, they must be descendants of Noah.

Therefore, any ostensibly "fixed" date for the Aborigines must be a *terminus ad quem* for the dating of the Flood. That is, any date of the Flood *must* be before this fixed date. And certainly the creation of Adam and Eve must, in turn, be before the Flood.

---

32. H. Ross, "Genesis One, Dinosaurs and Cavemen,"'Reasons to Believe, <http://reasons.org/ kidsspace/dinocave.shtml?main>, accessed May 20, 1998.

Ross uncritically accepts radiometric dating, but this leads to a grave problem for his anthropology. The ostensibly reliable Accelerator Mass Spectrometry (AMS) ^{14}C method "dates" Aborigines in Australia to 41,000 B.P. (before present).[33] Less reliable thermoluminescence methods date the Aborigines to about 60,000 years B.P.[34]

Since Ross trusts these dates, at least the AMS one, he couldn't have the Aborigines before the entire range of Adam and Eve's dates. This is because only descendants of Adam can be human, according to both RTB and AiG, yet the supposedly "fixed" date of 41,000 years places them older than all of Ross's possible dates for Adam. So by 2002, Ross had changed the middle sentence in the quote to:

> Then about 10 to 60 thousand years ago, God replaced them with Adam and Eve.[35]

Of course, there was no new Hebrew scholarship to justify this change. Rather, this change was solely brought about by so-called "science," showing once more how this overrides everything else.

However, Ross fails to realize that this doesn't solve the problem. He provides a range for the creation of Adam of 10,000–60,000 B.P. Note that a range means that Adam's date can be anything from 10,000 to 60,000 years B.P. But this still *allows for the possibility* that the Aborigines are non-human. If Ross believes that the Aborigines are 60,000 years old, this should have been the *terminus ad quem* of his date range, so it should be more than 60,000 years ago, but he has mistakenly used the Aboriginal date as the *terminus a quo*, which is the opposite of what it should be.

It's even worse, because Ross dates his anthropologically universal local flood to "between twenty thousand and thirty thousand years ago" (GQ:177). But Ross also refers to "Australian Aborigines, who date back to 25,000 B.C." (GQ: 108). Once again, because according to both RTB and AiG, all of today's people groups are descended from Noah, so must be younger, there is the possibility that Aborigines aren't human. And this is independent of the reliability of any dating methods — his own book has the incongruity because of his own estimated dates.

"APEMEN"

Creationist View of Cavemen and Neandertals

We have noted the importance of the Babel dispersion in separating the human gene pool and resulting in different "people groups." Also, some people groups would be isolated from civilization. Consider even the typical small extended family group today, if suddenly isolated from civilization, for example, on a desert island. Many such groups would not have the ability to smelt metals or build houses. Therefore,

---

33. S. O'Connor, "Carpenter's Gap Rockshelter 1: 40,000 Years of Aboriginal Occupation in the Napier Ranges, Kimberley, WA," *Australian Archaeology* 40 (June 1995).

34. J. Allen, "A Matter of Time," *Nature Australia* 26(10):60–60 (Spring 2000).

35. H. Ross, "Genesis One, Dinosaurs and Cavemen," Reasons to Believe, <http://reasons.org/kidsspace/dinocave.shtml?main>, accessed March 15, 2003.

they would have to use the hardest material available (stone) and make use of already-existing structures (caves). Different family groups would also have different levels of artistic ability.

Therefore, based on the biblical timeline, creationists regard Neandertals and most likely *Homo erectus* to be real humans, post-Babel descendants of Adam and Eve. They were probably post-Babel humans who became isolated from major cities, and developed certain physical characteristics because certain genes became fixed, due to the small population and selective factors. The notion of a "stone age" is fallacious — rather, it's a cave/stone technology stage of different people groups. Some people even today have this level of technology, but they live at the same time as us, and are just as human, for example, the Dani people of Irian Jaya.

Spirit Expression

But Ross states his basic view about all such claimed "apemen" specimens:

> Starting about 2–4 million years ago God began creating man-like mammals or "hominids." These creatures stood on two feet, had large brains, and used tools. Some even buried their dead and painted on cave walls. However, they were very different from us. They had no spirit. They did not have a conscience like we do. They did not worship God or have religious practices. In time, all these man-like creatures went extinct. In time, all these bipedal primates went extinct. Then, about 10 to 60 thousand years ago, God replaced them with Adam and Eve. From Adam and Eve came all the people that live on the earth today.[36]

Ross commits several errors when he points to a supposed first appearance of "spirit expression," all based on the (presumed) first known objects of religious expression dating to only 24,000 years ago (GQ:110). Some of these will be discussed further with Neandertal man, and the relevant points become even more fatal for Ross's notions when we shift our discussion to undoubted members of the human race.

First: as noted earlier, there is not the slightest evidence that archaic *Homo sapiens*, conventionally "dated" at pre-60,000 years ago, is in any way cognitively different from modern man. To the extent that religion is a cognitive process (for example, awareness of one's own mortality, ability to form abstract concepts of right and wrong, desire to worship powerful entities, etc.), Ross's attempt to divide *Homo sapiens* groups according to "spirit expression" and "non-spirit expression," or "capable of worshiping" and "non-worshiping," has no substantive basis in fact. It is entirely *ad hoc*.

Second: Ross is once again engaging in argumentation from silence. In fact, Hayden specifically warns against mistaking absence of evidence for evidence of absence. For instance, the apparent recent origins of paintings on cave walls may be, in reality, nothing more than a relatively recent shift from painting on external surfaces

---

36. H. Ross, "Genesis One, Dinosaurs and Cavemen," Reasons to Believe, <http://reasons.org/kidspace/dinocave.shtml?main>, accessed March 15, 2003.

(wherein the painting gets easily washed away) to painting in deep caves (where the painting is likely to be preserved for long periods of time).[37]

What if, for instance, we subsequently discover the remains of altars or other religious relics that are "dated" at more than 60,000 years ago? Will Ross then say that these objects are only part of a *seeming* religious worship, by some soulless pre-Adamite, the way the clearly human remains said to be over 60,000 years old only *seem* to be human, but are actually of soulless pre-Adamites? And why not? Such is the *reductio ad absurdum* of his position.

Third: Hugh Ross creates an artificial dichotomy between worship and other forms of religious expression. Simply because some animals, according to Ross, superficially bury their dead, and do so without apparent religious worship, does not mean that ancient hominids who buried their dead with artifacts were also essentially acting in a pre-spirit, animal-like manner. At least there is not the slightest evidence to support Ross's suggestion that they were. Instead, we can see the transparency of Ross's attempt to deny the existence of spirituality in members of *Homo* "dated" at pre-60,000 B.P.

Fourth: Ross commits another error in insisting that actual remains of altars or other religious relics are the *sine qua non* of religious activity, and even of worshipful spiritual capabilities.

What about all of the modern tribal religions that do not employ altars or religious relics during worship? Are these people lacking in what Ross would call "spirit expression" or "ability to worship"? Hardly.

More importantly, the true God of the Bible was one who forbade any idol worship (Exod. 20:4) or an altar made of hewn stone (Exod. 20:25). This part of the Mosaic Law was consistent with all His dealings with His people. And the evidence is consistent with the biblical teaching that mankind was originally monotheistic, and only later degenerated into idolatrous pantheism.[38] Therefore, in the true biblical view of history, we would not expect any lasting trace of religion in the form of idols and hewn altars in these early descendants of Noah.

And how can Ross know that the much earlier-found artifacts (stone tools, etc.) did not also double as religious paraphernalia — including objects of worship? For instance, Hayden points out that rock piles used by Neandertals show geometric patterns that point to their ritualistic significance.[39] This is comparable to the rock piles used in symbolic or religious behaviors of some modern tribes of humans. Even if we allow for his contrived dichotomy between "non-worshipful ritual" and "worshipful ritual," we can only wonder how Ross knows that these did not include worship-containing behaviors.

---

37. B. Hayden, "The Cultural Capacities of Neandertals: A Review and Re-evaluation," *Journal of Human Evolution* 24, (1993), p. 124–125.

38. W. Schmidt, *The Origin and Growth of Religion* (New York: Cooper Square, 1971).

39. B. Hayden, "The Cultural Capacities of Neandertals: A Review and Re-evaluation," *Journal of Human Evolution* 24, (1993), p. 121.

All of the foregoing evidence completely falsifies Ross's belief that we can derive some sort of creation of Adam and Eve 7,000 to 60,000 years ago. It also completely refutes Ross's claim that the descendants of Adam and Eve were once all confined to the Middle East, wherein a local Noachian flood could be "universal" in the sense of destroying them all, except for Noah and his family. (In any case, given mankind's known territorial and migratory impulses, the notion that, for thousands of years, none had ventured outside of a very narrow geographical area seems to fall within the extreme range of special pleading to salvage an apologetic scheme.)

Instead, the evidence indicates the presence of modern humans, distributed over most of the continents, over the last 100,000 years (according to current dating methods and the evolutionary geology that Ross accepts). That is, *according to the fossil evidence interpreted according to long-age assumptions, at no time* was there a sudden human origin, and *at no time* were modern humans confined to the Middle East!

Instead, Ross asserts that these fossils are merely of *apparent* human beings. That is, despite appearing human because of their skeletal anatomy, apparent communicative capabilities, artifacts, art, etc., they are actually subhuman beings who are incapable of religious worship. So, while Ross wants to preserve the uniqueness of our species, in fact he undermines it by attributing many of our characteristics to beings that he claims were not human.

Hugh Ross's rather contrived division of ancient human remains into "soulless pre-Adamites" and "fully human descendants of Adam and Eve" is no less arbitrary than, and just as baseless as, that of the 19th-century racist's division of contemporary peoples into the two comparable categories.

Hominid Fossil Record

While Ross agrees with us that humans are distinct creations, he disagrees about what should be classified as human. Certainly, the fossil record, even granted the evolutionary "dating" methods, indicates that the clear-cut progression shown in many textbooks exists only in the minds of evolutionary popularists. Marvin Lubenow shows that the various alleged "apemen" do not form a smooth sequence in evolutionary "ages," but overlap considerably.[40] For example, the time span of *Homo sapiens* fossils contains the time span of the fossils of *Homo erectus,* supposedly our ancestor.

Fragmentary Evidence: Case Study, Ardipithecus ramidus kadabba

Claims of intermediate fossils, both "apemen" and other creatures, are often based on fragmentary fossil remains. For example, *Time* magazine reported on a specimen called *Ardipithecus ramidus kadabba* (from the local Afar language: *ardi* = ground or floor; *ramid* = root; *kadabba* = basal family ancestor), "dated" between 5.6 and 5.8 million years old.[41] *Time* claimed that this new specimen was already walking upright, at (what they claim was) the dawn of human evolution:

---

40. M. Lubenow, *Bones of Contention* (Grand Rapids, MI: Baker Books, 1992).
41. M.D. Lemonick and A. Dorfman, "One Giant Step for Mankind," *Time* magazine cover story (July 23, 2001).

But unlike a chimp or any of the other modern apes that amble along on four limbs, *kadabba* almost certainly walked upright much of the time. The inch-long toe bone makes that clear.

But how clear is this really? *Time* reports the opinion of the discoverer of "Lucy," Donald Johanson:

> Beyond that, he's dubious about categorizing the 5.2 million-year-old toe bone with the rest of the fossils: not only is it separated in time by several hundred thousand years, but it was also found some 10 miles away from the rest.

Note that this toe was the major "evidence" for uprightness, yet, at ten miles distance, it boggles the mind how it could be regarded as part of the same specimen![42] As one researcher put it, "Fossils are fickle. Bones will sing any song you want to hear."[43] When the various fossils are analyzed in depth, they turn out not to be transitional or even mosaic.

Humans Are Distinct

This is shown when there is enough fossil evidence to analyze carefully. Humans are distinct from ape-like creatures such as the australopithecines, as Ross and I agree. But the details show that Ross is wrong about many of the other so-called ape-men. The analysis of a number of characteristics[44] indicates that *Homo ergaster, H. erectus, H. neanderthalensis* as well as *H. heidelbergensis*, were most likely "racial" variants of modern man. This is contrary to the claims of Ross, who relegates all these to spiritless hominids. Conversely, many specimens classified as *H. habilis* and another specimen called *H. rudolfensis* were just types of australopithecines (extinct apes).[45]

Table 9.2: Summary of the results of analyses of characteristics of fossil *Homo* species.[46] 1) body size, 2) body shape, 3) locomotion, 4) jaws and teeth, 5) development, and 6) brain size. H = like modern humans, A = australopith-like, I = intermediate, ? = data unavailable.

Species name	1	2	3	4	5	6
H. rudolfensis	?	?	?	A	A	A
H. habilis	A	A	A	A	A	A
H. ergaster	H	H	H	H	H	A
H. erectus	H	?	H	H	?	I
H. heidelbergensis	H	?	H	H	?	A
H neanderthalensis	H	H	H	H	H	H

---

42. For example, see J. Sarfati, "*Time's* Alleged 'Ape-man' Trips Up (Again)" *TJ* 15(3):7–9 (2001); <www.answersingenesis.org/kadabba>.
43. J. Shreeve, "Argument Over a Woman," *Discover* 11(8):58 (1990).
44. B. Wood and M. Collard, "The Human Genus," *Science* 284(5411):65–71 (1999).
45. J. Woodmorappe, "The Non-transitions in 'Human Evolution' — on Evolutionists' Terms," *TJ* 13(2):10–13 (1999); <www.answersingenesis.org/non-transitions>.
46. Table is from footnote 44.

For some years now, many evolutionist specialists have agreed that *H. habilis* was probably always a phantom taxon, with a bag of fossils belonging to either *H. erectus/ergaster* or to australopithecines thrown into this "taxonomic wastebin." This expression was used in an interview with Dr. Fred Spoor, a Dutch-born paleoanthropologist in the UK, and joint editor of the *Journal of Human Evolution*.[47]

The assignments by the evolutionists Wood and Collard (see Table 9.2) match those of the slightly earlier ones by creationist paleoanthropologist Dr. Sigrid Hartwig-Scherer, research fellow at the Institute for Anthropology and Human Genetics, Ludwig-Maximilian University, Munich. She concluded that *H. erectus/ergaster*, Neandertals and *H. sapiens* were members of the same basic type (created kind — see chapter 7) Homininae. But she assigned to another basic type, Australopithecinae, the fossils called *Australopithecus afarensis, A. anamensis, A. africanus, A. robustus, A. aethiopithecus, A. boisei* and possibly *Ardipithecus ramidus*.[48]

Ross was a contributor to the very same book in which Hartwig-Scherer's assignments appeared (*Mere Creation*), so Ross has little excuse for relegating *Homo erectus* and Neandertals to sub-human status.

Two Rival Evolutionary Views

There are two major evolutionary views of the origin of modern man. One major theory is called the "Out of Africa" or single-origin model, or even the "Noah's ark model." This states that modern humans came out of Africa and replaced less evolved hominids that had emerged from Africa much earlier. But there is another evolutionary idea, called the "multi-regional" or "regional-continuity" model, or even the "Noah's Sons" model. This proposes that the hominids that allegedly emerged from Africa two million years ago evolved into modern humans in many parts of the world.

This is one of the most vitriolic debates among paleoanthropologists — the acrimony between the proponents of these rival theories is due, according to the anthropologist Peter Underhill, of Stanford University, to: "Egos, egos, egos. Scientists are human." Ross and I agree that *both* sides are right — in their criticisms of each other — because humans did not evolve at all![49]

Dr. Hartwig-Scherer has proposed a single-origin model that fits in with a human basic type, and is consistent with human migration patterns after Babel:

> Three migration waves may have occurred originating from the Afro-Arabian shield. During the first migration, a population with unknown

47. See video, *The Image of God*, Keziah Productions.

48. S. Hartwig-Scherer, "Apes or Ancestors?" chapter 9 of Wm. A. Dembski, *Mere Creation: Science, Faith and Intelligent Design* (Downers Grove, IL: InterVarsity Press, 1998).

49. For an explanation of both the out of Africa and regional-continuity ideas and a biblical alternative, see C. Wieland, "No Bones about Eve," *Creation* 13(4):20–23 (September–November 1991); <www.answersingenesis.org/eve2>; and S. Hartwig-Scherer, "Apes or Ancestors?" chapter 9 of Wm. A. Dembski, *Mere Creation: Science, Faith and Intelligent Design* (Downers Grove, IL: InterVarsity Press, 1998).

morphology spread into different directions and developed the typical *ergaster* morphology in Africa and *erectus* traits in Southeast Asia. A second migration wave produced the Neanderthal morphology in the comparatively isolated Europe. Finally, a third migration wave filled the world with modern *Homo sapiens*. The mosaic features, a combination of Pleistocene forms, may be considered the consequence of either hybridization between members of the different migration waves or the expression of hidden traits in the (polyvalent?) ancestral gene pool or a mixture of both.[50]

Undoubted Homo Sapiens *"Dated" Before Ross's "Date" for Adam?*

Hugh Ross also completely misses the mark about fossils of undoubted *Homo sapiens*. Even if we were to grant, just for the sake of argument, his belief that Neandertals were "soulless pre-Adamites," Ross's ideas would collapse solely in the face of the evidences available from remains of modern man. To begin with, any sort of indicator pointing to a unique appearance of humans sometime in the interval between 7,000 years B.P. and 60,000 years B.P., is completely lacking. Worse yet for Ross's position, anatomically modern humans predate even his 60,000 years figure — *according to dating methods he defends:*

> "The fossils from this site [Klasies River Mouth, South Africa] are *totally modern in all observable respects*," comments Richard Klein of the University of Chicago, "including the presence of a strongly developed chin." The dating of 100,000 years is strongly supported [emphasis added].[51]

> . . . a basic cranial *bauplan* was maintained for at least 100,000 years.[52]

All lines of evidence considered, there is no indication that conventionally dated "early humans" were, in any sense, cognitively inferior to their modern counterparts:

> Specifically, there are no data suggesting any major qualitative changes in language abilities corresponding with the 200,000–100,000 B.P. dates for modern *Homo sapiens* origins proposed by single origin models or the 40,000–30,000 B.P. period proposed as the time for the appearance of modern *Homo sapiens* in Western Europe. Instead, there appears to be archaeological and paleontological evidence for complex language capabilities beginning much earlier, with the evolution of the genus *Homo*.[53]

Homo sapiens idàltu

The recent discoveries of *Homo sapiens* fossils in Ethiopia "dated" to 160,000 and 154,000 years ago have provided further evidence against Ross's anthropology.

50. Ibid., p. 229–230.
51. R. Lewin, *Human Evolution* (Cambridge: Blackwell Scientific Publications, 1993), p. 153.
52. W.A. Neves et al., "Modern Human Origins as Seen from the Peripheries," *Journal of Human Evolution* 37:132 (1999).
53. L.A. Schepartz, "Language and Modern Human Origins," *Yearbook of Physical Anthropology* 36:91–126 (1993).

Dr. Tim White of the University of California, Berkeley, discovered them in 1997 near Herto, a village 230 km northeast of Addis Ababa. It was on the cover of the prestigious journal *Nature* (June 12, 2003), and this issue contains articles about this discovery by leading evolutionary paleoanthropologists. White and colleagues reported on the fossils,[54] and another paper reported on dates, derived via the latest radio-isotope methods, and on the evidence for fully human behavior.[55] Another leading evolutionary paleoanthropologist, Dr. Chris Stringer, of the Human Origins Group at the Natural History Museum, London, commented on the article in depth.[56] He claimed that this was further support for the "out of Africa" model of human origins and against the rival evolutionary multi-regional model (see page 310).

These Ethiopian skeletal remains are not totally dissociated anatomically from "earlier" type human bones, that is, despite being clearly *Homo sapiens*, they show some features reminiscent of "archaic" human anatomy. Hence the suggestion that they be given the fuller name *Homo sapiens idāltu*, indicating that they are a subspecies (i.e., subgroup) of our species. This means that not only are they clearly modern-type humans, they indicate a genetic connection with the types of skulls that Rossists have been trying to sideline as being not in the human family at all, including the Neandertals (see page 313).

There is no way to escape that these are *Homo sapiens* and not a primitive non-human. They actually had *larger* braincases than the average modern human. Some evolutionary experts were quoted in *The Age*, the leading newspaper in Melbourne, Australia:[57]

> Skulls of the *oldest modern humans* have been uncovered in Herto, Ethiopia, showing that people looking remarkably like us were roaming the African plains 160,000 years ago. . . .
>
> Professor [Tim] White [co-leader of the excavation team] said the early *humans* at Herto lived on a shallow lake alongside hippos, crocodiles, catfish, and buffalo. Over 600 stone artifacts, including axes, were also found. . . .
>
> Australian anthropologists expressed surprise at how *modern* the skulls looked. "It's quite extraordinarily modern-looking really," said Stephen Collier, a lecturer in archaeology at the University of New England. "You wouldn't have expected this 10 years ago, anything this modern."
>
> Geologist Jim Bowler, who discovered Australia's oldest human remains, the allegedly 40,000-year-old Mungo man in 1974, said the skulls looked

---

54. T. White et al., "Pleistocene *Homo sapiens* from Middle Awash, Ethiopia," *Nature* 423(6941):742–747 (June 12, 2003).
55. D. Clark et al., "Stratigraphic, Chronological and Behavioral Contexts of Pleistocene *Homo sapiens* from Middle Awash, Ethiopia," *Nature* 423(6941):747–752 (June 12, 2003).
56. C. Stringer, "Human Evolution: Out of Ethiopia," *Nature* 423(6941):692–695 (June 12, 2003).
57. S. Cauchi, "Fossils Find Writes New Chapter in Our Narrative," *The Age* (June 12, 2003): p. 1 (emphases added).

THE HISTORY OF MANKIND · 313

remarkably like modern people. *"If you put this fellow in a grey charcoal suit, they wouldn't look out of place on Collins Street."*

"*Homo sapiens sapiens* is a very slippery concept," said Colin Groves, of the Australian National University's anthropology department. "The new specimen is exactly what we predicted for *Homo sapiens* before it starts to branch out and diversify, before it started to develop racial features."

Not only are these specimens undoubtedly anatomically modern humans, they also had indisputably human cultural features. For example, mortuary practices, butchery of large mammals, and what evolutionists describe as "an interesting combination of Middle Stone Age and late Acheulean technology."[58]

The age range is regarded as "very secure" using a form of radiometric dating involving argon isotopes called the $^{40}Ar/^{39}Ar$ method. As shown in chapter 12, these dating methods are unreliable, but the problem is that Ross accepts them. And that puts still more undoubtedly modern humans well before his arbitary 60,000 date for Adam.

Ross argues that all pre-60,000 B.P. remains were merely *apparently* human in both anatomy and culture, and were actually spiritless "pre-Adamites." But this is clearly clutching at straws, and engaging in arbitrary, imaginative speculation.

Mitochondrial Eve

Let us now consider molecular biology and the alleged single-pair ancestry of modern humans. Hugh Ross labors under the following common misconception about the mitochondrial-DNA evidence (GQ:111–112):

> The recent date eliminates the possibility that modern humans evolved from another bipedal primate species (meaning that humans must be specially created).

It does no such thing. Since Ross so favors the opinions of scientists, he needs to be informed that no conventional scientist would accept the mitochondrial-DNA data as proof of a literal creation of some Adam and Eve a few tens of thousands of years ago, even if such scientists were open to divine intervention in the past. "African Eve" and "Y-chromosome Adam" only show that all *extant* humans are descended from one lineage. They do not, in the slightest, prevent the existence of other contemporary lineages of humans, which have since died out.[59]

Neandertal Man

This is the most famous "ape-man." The name comes from Germany's Neander Valley (*tal* is the German for valley) where the first specimen was discovered in 1856. The valley was named after the 17th-century minister Joachim Neumann, who used to walk in it, but after his pseudonym, Neander, the Greek translation of his name,

---

58. See footnotes 55 and 56.
59. For a correct account of evolutionary thinking, as well as evidence that "mitochondrial Eve" was far more recent, see C. Wieland, "A Shrinking Date for 'Eve,' " *TJ* 12(1)1–3 (1998).

which means "new man." When it was first discovered, the old German spelling *thal* was in use, although pronounced "tal," but in 1904, German spelling was modernized to become more phonetic, so Neanderthal became Neandertal. This is why the official scientific name must still be *Homo sapiens neanderthalensis* (if regarded as a subspecies — simply meaning a particular group — of *Homo sapiens*, as I do), or *Homo neanderthalensis* (if regarded as a different species), because the spelling at the time of the naming must be retained.

Mitochondrial DNA (mtDNA)

This is DNA separate from the main DNA in the cell nucleus, instead residing in the cells' "power plants," the mitochondria (singular: mitochondrion). In general, we inherit only our mother's mtDNA, although this is not universal. Ross argues (GQ:113–114):

> Recently discovered Neandertal DNA confirms Schwartz and Tattersall's conclusion that the human race neither descended from nor bears any biological connection to the Neandertal species.

But the reference he gave contradicted what he said, since it referred to the Neandertal as an "extinct human" in the title![60] Undeterred, Ross then cited further research by a team led by the well-known paleogeneticist Svante Pääbo, publishing in the journal *Cell:*

> [C]onfirmation came when members of the same research team and others published their analysis on a different fragment of the same skeleton.[61] They got essentially the same results as the first research effort and concluded that their analysis gave "no support to the notion that Neandertals should have contributed mtDNA to the modern human gene pool."[62]

However, this mtDNA evidence he quotes has never been critically re-evaluated, and is of very questionable validity.[63] It is statistically dubious to base so much on only a single specimen, and the molecular biologist Dr. John Marcus made this observation about a graph in the Pääbo article:

> This graph might lead one to think that Neandertal sequences are somewhere between modern human and chimp sequences. This could then give the impression that Neandertal is a link between chimps and humans. On closer examination, however, this is not the case. As labelled, the graph shows the number of differences between human-human, human-Neandertal, and human-chimp pairs. Significantly, the authors do not show the distribution

---

60. P. Kuhn and A. Gibbons, "DNA from an Extinct Human," *Science* 277:176–178 (1997).

61. M. Krings, A. Stone, R.W. Schmitz, H. Krainitzki, M. Stoneking, and S. Pääbo, "Neandertal DNA Sequences and the Origin of Modern Humans," *Cell* 90:19–30 (1997).

62. Ibid., p. 5584.

63. M.L. Lubenow, "Recovery of Neandertal mtDNA: An Evaluation," *TJ* 12(1):87–97 (1998).

of Neandertal-chimp differences. The reason they do not show this last of four possible comparisons between the populations is not clear to me. What is clear, however, from the DNA distance comparisons that I performed, *is that the Neandertal sequence is actually further away from either of the two chimpanzee sequences than the modern human sequences are. My calculations show that every one of the human isolates that I used was "closer" to chimp than was the Neandertal.* The fact that Neandertal and modern human sequences are approximately equidistant from the chimpanzee outgroup seems to be a good indication that Neandertal and modern humans comprise one species. Clearly, the Neandertal is no more related to chimps than any of the humans. If anything, Neandertal is *less* related to chimps.[64]

Furthermore, Pääbo *himself* claims that his paper has been misinterpreted, and that his data could not possibly prove that there was no genetic relationship between Neandertals and modern humans.[65] For one thing, because it's mitochondrial DNA, at best it would prove that Neandertal mothers did not contribute mtDNA to the modern gene pool. But there is nothing to rule out Neandertal fathers contributing nuclear genes to the modern gene pool. For example, in war, conquering Neandertal males could have impregnated more "modern"-looking females. Also, migration would probably have mainly involved men.[66]

In addition, the evolutionary anthropologist Wolpoff concurs with the fact that the mtDNA attributed to Neandertal man falls within the range of variation seen within the current human race.[67] Besides, the range of variation in the mtDNA in modern humans is very low compared with that of other primates to begin with, and hence the inclusion of the Neandertal mtDNA only brings the variation in the human race up to normal levels.

Finally, the differences of Neandertal mtDNA and that of extant humans, compared to chimps, occur in the same base-pairs. This fact, according to Wolpoff, demonstrates that Neandertal man was not a species that was separate from modern humans.

Differences Due to Mutational Hot Spots

The biochemist and neuroscientist Dr. David DeWitt has researched Neandertal DNA, and found that the sites where Neandertals differ from modern humans tend to be at the mutational hot spot sites in the D-loop of mtDNA.[68] But the sites where chimpanzees differ from us are *not* at these hotspots. He wrote:

---

64. Ibid., citing J. Marcus communication to M. Lubenow, emphasis his.
65. S. Pääbo interview on television/video, *Neanderthals on Trial*, Nova, 2002.
66. See footnote 63.
67. M.H. Wolpoff, *Paleoanthropology*, 2nd edition (Boston, MA: McGraw-Hill, 1999), p. 759.
68. W. Skinner and D. DeWitt, "The Neandertal's Place in Human History," *Virginia Journal of Science* 51(2):83 (2000).
   D. DeWitt and W. Skinner, "Rate Heterogeneity and Site by Site Analysis of mtDNA Suggests Neanderthals and Modern Humans Share a Recent Common Ancestor," *Discontinuity* p. 31, 2001.

Most of the researchers arguing for Neandertals being phylogeneti-cally separate do so because of the large number of [mtDNA] differences between Neandertals and modern humans. However, since they have the same mutation hotspots, it argues for a closer relationship. Because some of the sites are invariant and others prone to mutation, it means that you can't rely simply on counting the number of differences. Just because a Neandertal:human comparison has a larger number of differences than human:human does not mean that the Neandertals were not human, nor geneticically contiguous with humans. Moreover, Gutierrez pointed out that there is population bias in previous studies such as Kring's. They used a very large number of Europeans, (very similar sequences) which forces a larger difference for Neandertals.

An additional point is that just because Neandertal mtDNA sequences do not show up in modern populations does not mean that they did not interbreed. For example, in the U.S., we know that some of the Native Americans have interbred with European immigrants. However, we would be hard pressed to find [the mitochondrial evidence].[69]

DeWitt was referring to an important recent paper by Gutierrez et al.[70] which showed that the "Neanderthal-Human and Human-Human pairwise distance distributions overlap more than previous studies suggest." They also say, "The separate phylogenetic position of Neanderthals is not supported when these (other) factors are considered [i.e., the high substitution rate variation at these hot spots]."

Neandertal-Human Hybrids

If Neandertals and modern-looking humans could hybridize, then they must be the same species. It has recently been concluded that Neandertals lived side by side with modern humans in the Middle East for 100,000 years of evolutionary time, and made virtually identical stone tools.[71] Hybrids of Neandertals and humans are known from a number of areas,[72] including a child's skeleton in Portugal[73] and an adult jawbone from a bear cave in Romania.[74] It is not difficult to conclude that

69. D. DeWitt, personal communication, May 19, 2003.

70. Gutierrez et al., "A Reanalysis of the Ancient Mitochondrial DNA Sequences Recovered from Neandertal Bones," *Mol. Biol. Evol.* 19:1359–1366 (2002).

71. B. Bower, "Neandertals and Humans Each Get a Grip," *Science News* 159(6):84 (2001).

72. E. Trinkaus and P. Shipman, *The Neandertals — Changing the Image of Mankind* (New York: Alfred A. Knopf, 1993), p. 391.

73. B. Bower, "Fossil May Expose Humanity's Hybrid Roots," *Science News* 155(19):295 (1999).

74. J. Amos, "Human Fossils Set European Record," *BBC News*, <http://news.bbc.co.uk/1/hi/sci/tech/3129654.stm>, September 22, 2003; based on E. Trinkaus et al., "Early Modern Human Cranial Remains from the Petera cu Oase, Romania," *Journal of Human Evolution,* 2003 (in press); E. Trinkaus et al., "An Early Modern Human from the Petera cu Oase, Romania," *Proceedings of the National Academy of Sciences USA,* 2003 (in press).

Neandertal man was totally human, and that modern humans and Neandertals likely amalgamated in Europe.

Skull Features

Ross claims that Neandertals had unique nasal specializations, so could not be related to modern people (GQ:113). However, these features occur in human beings as diverse as African Bushmen and Eskimos.[75] But this is in any case all moot: although Ross grasped at these initial claims as fact, they turn out to be based on invalid reconstructions, and can now be discounted.[76]

Based on a statistical analysis of dental-crown data,[77] it has been noted that the Krapina (Croatia) Neandertals, on average, differ more from modern human groups than do the modern human groups among themselves. Yet there is a significant degree of overlap. Neandertals are more similar to modern northeastern Siberians than the sub-Saharan Africans are to any other *modern* group of humans (except the Chinese).[78] Likewise, the Krapina-Neandertal/modern-Siberian-human differences are *less* than those that exist between the Aboriginal Australians and every other modern human group (except the Siberians). So if, following Ross, we reckon the Neandertals as "soulless non-Adamites," logically we should also consider the sub-Saharan Africans as well as the Australian Aborigines as soulless non-Adamites. Obviously, only a racist would accept such a conclusion, however it's the logical consequence of Ross's teaching, even though he would not agree with it himself.

The non-dental features of Neandertal man also contradict Ross's notions. Wolpoff lists 18 skeletal features which are uniquely found in Neandertals, or at least are rare in other Pleistocene populations.[79] Significantly, a large fraction of these traits are found in post-Neandertal European human populations. Some even persist in modern Europeans. This evidence decisively falsifies Ross's belief that modern humans and Neandertals are unrelated to each other, and are separate creations.

Manual Dexterity

Neandertal hands, being more muscular and with wider fingers, certainly would have *looked* different from "modern" hands. But they were equally, or even more, dextrous than are those of modern humans. This was recently shown by researchers at the Department of Anthropology, California State University, San Bernardino, California, and the Archaeology Technologies Lab, North Dakota State University, Fargo, North Dakota.[80] They generated a new three-dimensional computer simulation of the

75. M.H. Wolpoff, *Paleoanthropology*, 2nd edition (Boston, MA: McGraw-Hill, 1999), p. 755–756.
76. R.G. Franciscus, "Neandertal Nasal Structures and Upper Respiratory Tract 'Specialization,' " *Proceedings of the National Academy of Science (USA)* 96:1805–1809 (1999).
77. A.J. Tyrrell and A.T. Chamberlain, "Non-metric Trait Evidence for Modern Human Affinities and the Distinctiveness of Neanderthals," *Journal of Human Evolution* 34:549–554 (1998).
78. Ibid., p. 550.
79. M.H. Wolpoff, *Paleoanthropology*, 2nd edition (Boston, MA: McGraw-Hill, 1999), p. 756.
80. W.A. Niewoehner, A. Bergstrom, D. Eichele, M. Zuroff, and J.T. Clark, "Manual Dexterity in Neanderthals," *Nature* 422(6930):395 (March 27, 2003).

Neandertal thumb and forefinger based on their scanned images of the corresponding bones in fossils found in La Ferrassie, France. They converted these images into a full-motion model, much as the most-advanced cartoon animators can do.

They showed that the Neandertal thumb was easily able to touch the tip of the index finger. This *opposable thumb* is the distinguishing feature of human dexterity. In fact, the researchers chose very *conservative* estimates for the range of motion, so the Neandertals' hand was, if anything, even *more* dexterous than our typical hand:

> Given the open configuration of the Neanderthal trapezial-metacarpal-1 joint, all Neanderthal thumbs were probably more mobile than that of modern humans.

Cultural Evidence

Ross dismisses evidences (for example, music, tool use, art, and burial practices) for the genuine humanness of Neandertal man because of the fact that, according to Ross, animals engage in comparable behaviors (GQ:110). In actuality, the inferred behavior of Neandertals bears no resemblance to the rudimentary behavior of even the most intelligent animals. There is a wealth of evidence for complex, premeditated and goal-directed behavior among Neandertals.[81] This includes tools and stones bearing signs of ritualistic and aesthetic considerations, sophisticated burial chambers with a preplanned geometric interment of remains, procurement of ochres (for artwork) from considerable distances, a "high-tech superglue,"[82] etc.

Conclusion

Paleoanthropologists are by no means in agreement as to whether or not Neandertal man is sufficiently different from modern man to be considered a separate species. The COV (coefficient of variation) of the cranial capacities and body masses of all of the supposed species of *Homo*, **pooled together**, does not exceed that of modern *Homo sapiens*. This is recognized as evidence for the position that all of the "species" of *Homo* are simply variants within our own species.[83] This supports the later review of hominid morphology by Wood and Collard.[84]

Homo Erectus

Once more, this is another variety of human. This was shown by the morphological analysis of various traits (see page 309). Also, their cranial vault size overlapped

81. B. Hayden, "The Cultural Capacities of Neandertals: A Review and Re-evaluation," *Journal of Human Evolution* 24:113–146, (1993).

82. J. Viegas, "Neanderthals Made High-tech Superglue," *Discovery News* http://dsc.discovery.com/news/briefs/20020114/neanderthal.html (January 16, 2002); "Neanderthals 'Used Glue to Make Tools,' " <http://news.bbc.co.uk/1/hi/sci/tech/1766683.stm>.

83. M. Henneberg and J.F. Thackeray, "A Single-lineage Hypothesis of Hominid Evolution," *Evolutionary Theory* 11:31–38 (1995).

84. B. Wood and M. Collard, "The Human Genus," *Science* 284(5411):65–71 (1999).
    J. Woodmorappe, "The Non-transitions in 'Human Evolution' — on Evolutionists' Terms," *TJ* 13(2):10–13 (1999); <www.answersingenesis.org/non-transitions>.

with that of modern people.[85] Further, a new specimen from Java, where *Homo erectus* was first discovered, "disproves an [evolutionary] hypothesis about the development of the large brains of our own species."[86] It was shown to have a "strikingly modern feature,"[87] a strongly bent or "flexed" cranial base. The paleoanthropologist Dan Lieberman of Harvard University said:

> This is an important find because it is the first *H. erectus* find with a reasonably complete cranial base, and it looks modern.[88]

Of course, Lieberman would see *H. erectus* as a human ancestor, but this evidence is consistent with *H. erectus* being just a variant of the human created kind.

And as recently as January 12, 2001, Wolpoff et al. showed that the features of various human skulls indicated that there must have been interbreeding among modern-looking *Homo sapiens* and Neandertals and even *Homo erectus*.[89]

Their cultural abilities are also strong evidence of their humanity. They even had evidence of seafaring skills! This was shown by butchered elephant bones on a small Indonesian island, too small and resource-poor to sustain a settlement, with tools and dating that identify *"H. erectus"* as the only candidate (in evolutionists' minds) for the butcher, but the island had to be reached by boat over quite a stretch of deep water.[90] Thus, there must have been migration of *H. erectus* from island to island, across straits ranging in size from several kilometers to a few tens of kilometers, and quite deep water. The islands involved in this peregrination included Lombok, Bali, Sumbawa, and Flores.[91] Clearly, *H. erectus* must have crossed the straits that separate the islands, and this implies at least some seafaring ability. And according to conventional dates, which Ross accepts, this happened some 800,000 years ago. The original researchers say:

> Furthermore, they [our findings] indicate that, somewhere between 800,000 and 900,000 years ago, *Homo erectus* in this region had acquired the capacity to make water crossings.[92]

---

85. J. Woodmorappe,""How Different Is the Cranial Vault Thickness of *Homo erectus* from Modern Man?" *TJ* 14(1):10–13 (2000).

86. A. Gibbons, "Java Skull Offers New View of *Homo erectus*," *Science* 299(5611):1293 (February 28, 2003).

87. Ibid.

88. Ibid.

89. Wolpoff et al., "Modern Human Ancestry at the Peripheries: A Test of the Replacement Theory," *Science* 291(5502):293–297 (January 12, 2001); comment by E. Pennisi, "Skull Study Targets Africa-only Origins," p. 231.

90. Morwood et al., "Fission-track Ages of Stone Tools and Fossils on the East Indonesian Island of Flores," *Nature* 392(6672):173–176 (March 12, 1998).
   New Scientist 157(2125):6 (March 14, 1998); based on Morwood et al., (see previous reference). See also *Creation* 21(1):9 (December 1998–February 1999).

91. R.G. Bednarik, B. Hobman, and P. Rogers, "Nale Tasih 2: Journey of a Middle Palaeolithic Raft," *International Journal of Nautical Archaeology* 28(1)25–33 (1999).

92. Ibid.

The seafaring skills of *H. erectus* were also highlighted by the noted "multi-regional" advocate Wolpoff as support for his views. Interestingly, the ardent "out of Africa" advocate Chris Stringer said that these seafaring skills would be evidence that *H. erectus* "was more human, just like us."

But according to Ross, *H. erectus* was a soulless pre-Adamite. Yet this so-called pre-Adamite possessed a decidedly human capability — that of designing boats capable of crossing many kilometers of open ocean! This is further proof that Ross's division of anthropological remains into "Adam's descendants" and "soulless pre-Adamites" is completely arbitrary.

CONCLUSION

The biblical view of history is diametrically opposed to Ross's on a number of points. The most obvious is the time scale, since the biblical genealogies point to a far younger age for mankind than Ross's big-bang–derived chronology would allow.

This has other baneful consequences for biblical anthropology. One is a faulty view of the origin of races. Ross's teaching says that God intervened to make the apparent racial differences that are the source of so much prejudice — yet molecular biology now reveals that such notions as biological/genetic bases for "race" in people have no foundation. Another is the relegation of Neandertals to subhuman, even though they had many human characteristics. Ross instead blurs the distinction between humans and animals by dismissing these characteristics as uniquely human.

Finally, the upper limit of Ross's "date" range for Adam places him *after* "dates" of fully modern *Homo sapiens*. Worse, his range even allows for the possibility that the Australian Aborigines were in Australia before the time of Noah and even Adam. Therefore, Ross's theology allows for the possibility that they are not human. While Ross himself is not racist, it is the logical consequence of misguided trust in long-age dating methods over Scripture.

CHAPTER 10

"BIBLICAL" OLD-AGE ARGUMENTS

This chapter refutes fallacious exegetical and emotional arguments for billions of years. All the "long-age" words are perfectly compatible with thousands of years, which really is an extremely long period. In fact, absence of long-age words from Genesis 1 is further support for a 6,000-year time scale. Contrary to Ross's assertions, creationists historically have never been afraid that billions of years would make evolution possible.

While we are often called "young-earth creationists," this is *not* our primary focus. This is rather a *corollary* of the authority of Scripture, hence accepting its clear teaching that:

- The days were 24 hours long.

- The whole universe was created during creation week, the same length as our working week.

- Mankind was created on day 6, "from the beginning of creation."

- The genealogies imply that Adam was created about 6,000 years ago.

From these, it follows that the universe is also about 6,000 years old.

Conversely, Ross has this back to front. He starts with the premise that the big bang is true, therefore billions of years is a fact. Most of his other beliefs are corollaries of this, for example, long creation days, billions of years before Adam's creation, and local flood. His other doctrines, such as soulless pre-human hominids and fixity of species, are also consistent with and/or flow from his main premise of billions of years.

Therefore, while there is no need in this chapter to explain any further why the Bible teaches a young earth, it is necessary to address some of Ross's ostensibly biblical rationalizations for his belief in billions of years. This chapter will also address some of Ross's miscellaneous arguments.

Billions of Years Is a Better Illustration of God's Eternality?

Ross claims (C&T:52):

> The brief span of terrestrial history (in context of the wisdom literature) seems like an inadequate metaphor for God's eternality. The fact that the Bible does consider the antiquity of the earth as a suitable metaphor for God's eternality suggests the biblical view of a very ancient earth.

For his illustration to make any sense, Ross must lapse into the view of eternity as an infinite time period. But then why should *any* time period be any better than another when compared with infinite time? Even a billion years would be a speck of time compared to this.

But in any case, as Augustine pointed out, and Ross has also rightly accepted elsewhere, God created the universe not in time but with time. That is, time itself is a created entity. (This is why predictions about the future, which is after all time yet to come, are no problem for the One who is the Creator of time itself.) But this means that eternity is *not* infinite time but a time*less* state. So when eternity is understood correctly, as Ross does elsewhere, Ross's argument collapses as an incoherent metaphor.

It comes down to what "very ancient" means. I actually believe that the earth *is* old — *very old.* It is *thousands* of years old — as many as *six thousand*, in fact. (So even if I granted Ross's argument, the antiquity of the earth would be an excellent metaphor for God's eternity in a 6,000-year-old universe.)

This way of thinking may surprise many, but this is because most of us have been evolutionized into thinking that "old" means billions of years, and thousands of years is a "geological instant." But "old" and "young" are *relative* terms (as are words such as "long" — how long is a piece of string?). I presently think anyone over 50 is old, but someone over 80 might regard a 50 year old as a youngster.

Even a few years is a very long time for much geological change. That is why tourists are amazed at the "petrified waterwheel" in Western Australia: "It only took

Photo by Bev Lunt

60 years to cover this thing in solid rock?" But 60 years of water continually dripping onto an object, depositing part of its dissolved limestone, is actually an incredibly long time.

This means that anything substantially older than the average life span of a human

can well be described as "old" or "ancient." So an earth thousands of years old is something that can be considered "ancient," and it is in fact an unimaginably long time. Back 3,000 years ago, David was King of Israel and the Western nations were still millennia in the future. But we are often known as "young-earth creationists" because the "young" is relative to the billions of years claimed by evolutionists and followed by Ross.

These considerations must be borne in mind when analyzing Ross's arguments in the next section. Ross glibly points out passages that call the earth, or its features, "old," "ancient," etc., and uses them as "proof" of an old earth and disproof of a young earth. However, we must interpret these passages in terms of the author's intent, not by reading modern fashions into these words. In particular, since these terms are *relative*, we must interpret them by other passages that provide *unequivocal* terms, such as the days of creation and the years of the genealogies. But Ross uses these relative terms, interprets them according to modern uniformitarian/evolutionary conceptions, and uses them to twist the meanings of the unequivocal terms.

Biblical Old-Age Words

Ross cites some passages to support his old-age rationalizations (FoG:151):

> **In describing the eternity of God's existence, Bible writers compare it to the longevity of the mountains or of the "foundations of the earth."** The figures of speech used in Psalm 90:2–6, Proverbs 8:22–31, Ecclesiastes 1:3–11 and Micah 6:2 depict for us the immeasurable antiquity of God's presence and plans. If these literary devices are used appropriately and accurately (as they must be, for they were inspired by God), then the earth and its foundations must reach back at least a few orders of magnitude beyond the relatively brief spans of human history. Habakkuk 3:6 directly declares the mountains to be "ancient" and the hills to be "age-old," while 2 Peter 3:5 states that the heavens existed "long ago."

This is the best Ross can do, and, as we pointed out, these are all relative terms, which can be shown by analyzing the Hebrew words. In fact, it's clear that in every one of these examples, analyzed in the order Ross presents them, the words are compatible with being old relative to human life spans. So, if anything, they point more toward thousands of years than billions.

Psalm 90:2–6

Before the mountains were brought forth, or ever you had formed the earth and the world, even from everlasting to everlasting, you are God. You turn man to destruction; and say, Return, ye children of men. For a thousand years in your sight are but as yesterday when it is past, and as a watch in the night. You carried them away as with a flood; they are as a sleep: in the morning they are like grass which grows up. In the morning it flourishes, and grows up; in the evening it is cut down, and withers.

Nothing is proved there, because the phrase "from everlasting to everlasting" applies to God, and this was before the mountains were brought forth. The previous section shows the folly of trying to prove millions of years for the age of the mountains by comparing it with God's eternity.

Proverbs 8:22–23 (Referring to Wisdom Personified)

The LORD possessed me at the beginning of His way, before His works **of old**. I was set up **from everlasting**, from the beginning, **or ever** the earth was.

"**Of old**" is מֵאָז ('az with the preposition *me*), which literally means "from then." It means "before now, earlier," as in 2 Samuel 15:34, ". . . as I [David] have been your father's servant in **time past**. . . ." The very same word in this context clearly refers to an event in the *historical* past, thousands, not billions, of years ago. Therefore, this is actually an argument *in favor of* the YEC time scale.

The other words in bold prove nothing because wisdom pre-existed the creation, and many commentators believe this refers to the preincarnate Christ, the eternally begotten Logos, or second person of the Trinity.

Ross supporter Dr. James Dobson, founder of Focus on the Family, resorted to a similar superficial appeal to the English translation "of old," in a radio broadcast of April 1991. However, Dobson's example was Psalm 102:25, which says:

Of old you founded the earth, And the heavens are the work of your hands.

In this verse, the Hebrew phrase translated is לְפָנִים (*lephanim*) is found in 19 other verses.[1] In each of these verses, *lephanim* clearly refers to events *within human history* — thousands, not billions, of years. So once again, an OEC argument actually turns out to support the YEC timescale.

On July 9, 1991, Dr. Russell Humphreys wrote a letter to Dr. Dobson politely pointing out the biblical context of the phrase "of old," and the implications for the age of the world. No reply was ever received.

Ecclesiastes 1:3–11

One generation passes away, and another generation comes: but the earth abides *forever*. . . . Is there any thing of which it may be said, "See, this is new?" It hath been already *in olden times* which were before us.

"*Forever*" is עוֹלָם ('ôlām) or עֹלָם ('ōlām), with the basic meaning "long time, duration" (HALOT). Even Ross doesn't believe the earth is infinitely old, or will last an infinitely long time. The context makes it clear that it is a very long time *relative to human generations*.

---

1. Deut. 2:10, 12, 20; Josh. 11:10, 14:15, 15:15; Judg. 1:10, 11, 23, 3:2; Ruth 4:7; 1 Sam. 9:9; 1 Chron. 4:40, 9:20; 2 Chron. 9:11; Neh. 13:5; Job 17:6, 42:11; Jer 7:24.

"In olden times" is likewise *'ôlām*, and, in this context, clearly refers to a time when *humans* knew about an allegedly new thing. For more on this word, see page 327.

Micah 6:2

> Hear you, O mountains, the LORD's controversy, and you strong foundations of the earth; for the LORD has a controversy with His people, and He will plead with Israel.

I fail to see how this has the slightest bearing on the issue. Perhaps it's a typographical error, the author having actually intended to cite Micah 5:2, which reads:

> But you, Bethlehem Ephrathah, though you are little among the thousands of Judah, yet out of you shall come forth unto Me He that is to be ruler in Israel, whose goings forth have been from of old [קֶדֶם, *qedem*], from the days (*yôm*) of eternity [עוֹלָם *'ôlām*, the phrase "days of eternity is עוֹלָם מִימֵי, *mîmê 'ôlām*].

Here, the "long-age" words are applied to Jesus in the prophecy about His birthplace (cf. the fulfilment, Matthew 2:6 and John 7:42). They have nothing to do with billions of years for the earth, and everything to do with the Messiah's eternal pre-existence (John 1:1–3, 8:58), a doctrine Reasons to Believe accepts as well. Keil and Delitzsch sum it up well: ". . . both קדם and מימי עולם are used to denote hoary antiquity; for example in chapter 7:14 and 20, where it is used of the patriarchal age."

Habakkuk 3:6

> . . . the *ancient* mountains crumbled and the *age-old* hills collapsed. His ways are eternal.

"Ancient" is עַד (*'ad*), which has a variety of meanings. In this passage, HALOT translates it as follows, הררי עַד the everlasting mountains, Habakkuk 3:6. This gives a different nuance from "ancient," which is backward looking; rather it has more of a connotation of "endless," so cannot be used as proof of long ages in the past.

Furthermore, there are many examples of *'ad* elsewhere in the Bible that are clearly connected with events thousands, not billions, of years ago. For example, in Job 20:4, *'ad* is translated "of old":

> Do you know this from of old, from the establishing of man [Hebrew "Adam"] on the earth?

The beginning of mankind was thousands, not billions, of years ago, even according to Ross.

"Age-old" is once more *ôlām*. Even in Genesis 6:4 it is applied to humans, again showing that it's compatible with thousands of years:

> Those were the mighty men who were of old. . . .

2 Peter 3:5

But they deliberately forget that *long ago* by God's word the heavens existed and the earth was formed out of water and by water.

"Long ago" is the Greek εκπαλαι (*ekpalai*). It occurs only one other place in Scripture, in 2 Peter 2:3, "whose judgment of old is not idle" in reference to human false teachers. This doesn't say *how* long this judgment has been in force, so cannot be used as proof of billions of years.[2]

Also, *ekpalai* is derived from the prefix *ek* meaning "out of" or "from," added to the root word *palai,* meaning "old." This is, once again, a relative term; does Scripture give any indication of how old "old" is?

Palai occurs six times in the New Testament. One is Jude 4, which, like 2 Peter 2:3, refers to false teachers "who were foreordained *of old* for this condemnation," once again providing no data about how long ago their condemnation was ordained. But the other five clearly refer to events within human history:

- Matthew 11:21 — Woe to you, Chorazin! Woe to you, Bethsaida! For if the mighty works done in you had been done in Tyre and Sidon, they would have repented *long ago* in sackcloth and ashes.

- Mark 15:44 — referring to just after Jesus' death, "And Pilate wondered if he were already dead; and having called to him the centurion, he inquired of him if he had *long* died."

- Luke 10:13 — identical to Matthew 11:21.

- Hebrews 1:1 — "In many and various ways God spoke *of old* to our fathers by the prophets."

- 2 Peter 1:9 — ". . . has forgotten that he was cleansed from his *old* sins."

Why Weren't Vast-Age Words Used in Genesis 1?

Ross's ostensibly biblical arguments for vast ages also backfire against him in another way. He has no problem asserting that there were vast-age words used in other places, and using them to "prove" billions of years, even though the words were equivocal. But if so, why weren't any of them used in Genesis 1 to indicate creation over vast eras if that's what God really meant, instead of numbered days with evenings and mornings, which, everywhere else in Scripture, mean 24-hour days?

Indeed, Ross seems to forget his old-earth "proofs" when he argues (GQ:65), "In biblical Hebrew (as opposed to post-Mosaic and post-Davidic Hebrew), no other word besides *yôm* carries the meaning of a long period of time" and cites his own book (*Creation and Time*) and *Theological Wordbook of the Old Testament* (TWOT). Ross's earlier book C&T claimed (p. 47):

---

2. BDAG says: "εκπαλαι . . . 1. pert. to a point of time long before a current moment, *long ago* 2 Pet. 3:5. 2. pert. to a relatively long interval of time since a point of time in the past, *for a long time* 2 Pet. 2:3."

Young-earthers also hold the view that the Hebrew word *'ôlām* (as opposed to *yôm*) would have been used to indicate a long time period. However, Hebrew lexicons show that only in post-biblical writings did *'ôlām* only refer to a long age or epoch. In biblical times it meant "forever," "perpetual," "lasting," "always," "of olden times," or "the remote past, future, or both." But the range of uses did not include a set period of time.

עוֹלָם (*'ôlām*)

Again, Van Bebber and Taylor (VB&T:76–77) point out that *Ross's own source (TWOT) contradicts him*, stating that the Hebrew *'ôlām* and its Greek equivalent αιων (*aiōn*), from which we derive the word "eon," *often* mean "long age."

TWOT 2:673 states that the word ". . . is not confined to the future," but can be used to describe something that happened long ago "but rarely, if ever, points to a limitless past" and that the word does not, in itself, contain the idea of endlessness. This "is shown both by the fact that they sometimes refer to events or conditions that occurred at a definite point in the past and also by the fact that sometimes it is desirable to repeat the word, not merely saying 'forever,' but 'forever and ever.' "

The BDB lexicon agrees, giving the definitions "long duration, antiquity, futurity." HALOT also states that *'ôlām* means "long time, duration." It adds, "usually eternal, eternity, but not in a philosophical sense" (i.e., of a mathematically infinite duration of time).

In Psalm 139:24, David asks Yahweh, "lead me in the everlasting way (עוֹלָם דֶּרֶךְ *derek 'ôlām*)." The word *ôlām* is in the construct state, which often looks back in time. Verses 1–18 indicate that *'ôlām* refers to earlier in the Psalmist's life, thus not billions of years.[3]

There were plenty of other words that God could have used if He had wanted to teach long periods of time.[4] For example:

- יָמִים (*yāmîm*, plural of *yôm*) alone or with "evening and morning," would have meant "and it was days of evening and morning." This would have been the simplest way to teach that the creation events took place a long time in the past. It could have signified many days and so the possibility of a vast age.

- דֹּרֹדוֹר (*dôr/dōr*) means "generation" or "period," so would have been ideal for signifying a series of ages, if that's what God had really meant.

- עַד (*'ad*) is a word we have encountered before to mean "ancient" and even "forever," and when it is used, it occurs with prepositions. By analogy with Job 20:4, God could have informed Adam that the earth, sun, stars, animals, etc. were "from old," if He had intended to do so.

---

3. D. Graves, *Psalm 139*, paper for Old Testament, Trinity Evangelical Divinity School, 2001, p. 19. He also believes that there is an aspect of eschatological fulfilment.

4. R. Grigg, "How Long Were the Days in Genesis 1? What Did God Intend Us to Understand from the Words He Used?" *Creation* 19(1):23–25 (1996).

J. Stambaugh, "The Days of Creation: A Semantic Approach," *TJ* 5(1):70–76 (1991).

- קדם (*qedem*) or קדמה (*qedmah*) is sometimes translated "of old" or "ancient time."

- נצח (*netsach*) denotes "always," "everlasting" or "forever."

- תמיד (*tamîd*) means "continually" or "forever."

- ארך (*'orek*), when used with *yôm,* is translated "length of days."

- זמן (*z*mān*) denotes a "season" or "time."

- עת (*'et*), means "time" in general, and could have been used to leave the time ambiguous.

- מועד (*mô'ēd*), "time," which is also used for a "season."

God could also have used phrases like "*x* myriad myriad years ago" to teach ages of hundreds of millions of years. For a less precise indication of vast ages, God could have compared the years to the number of sand grains or stars. Yet God did not use any of these — rather, He emphasized literal days.

GOD IS A MASTER CRAFTSMAN SO WOULD HE TAKE A LONG TIME?

When all eisegesis fails, Ross resorts to a highly subjective argument (C&T:142):

> Observe skilled sculptors, painters, or poets, artisans of any kind, and see that they always spend much more time on their masterpieces than they do on their ordinary tasks. Observe the painstaking yet joyful labor poured into each masterpiece of their design. Observe how often the artist stops to appreciate and evaluate the work in progress.

It's hard to believe Ross is serious. The main reason for the long time by human artists is their *limitation*. But the Almighty Creator has no limits. It should stand to reason that more power and skill should mean less time needed, so a being of *infinite* power and skill needs NO time! This point is even stronger when we realize that God is the Creator of time itself.

It's notable that one feature of God's miracles is their *speed*, for example, instantaneous conversion of water into wine. Furthermore, by Ross's "craftsman" analogy, the future creation of the new heavens and new earth would also have to take billions of years, presumably with lots of death and suffering occurring as well.

In any case, Ross's premise is wrong. There are many examples of masterpieces being created very quickly, such as Handel's *Messiah*, composed in only three weeks (August 22 to September 14, 1741).

"FEAR OF THE MILLIONS"

Ross claims that a main motivation of those opposing billions of years is fear that it would make evolution possible, hence the above subheading on GQ:92. As usual, Ross's claim betrays a willing ignorance of creationist literature as well as ignorance of evolution/variation, as shown above. Many years before Ross wrote any of his books, leading creationists like Dr. Duane Gish made it very clear that they believed the earth was only thousands of years old, on both biblical and scientific grounds. But Gish also strongly pointed out that evolution would be impossible even if billions of years were granted. For example:

> Therefore, whether the earth is ten thousand, ten million, or ten billion years old, the fossil record does not support the general theory of evolution.[5]
>
> Considering an enzyme, then, of 100 amino acids, there would be no possibility whatever that a single molecule could have arisen by pure chance on earth in five billion years.[6]

Further, the information-losing processes that creationists have repeatedly shown to characterize the inherited changes in living things would make things worse for evolution, not better, if more time were available. The accumulation of mutational copying errors, and the culling of information by natural selection, leads populations ever closer to extinction, not to uphill evolution. So if we are promoting matters that logically imply that vast ages are the enemy of evolution, how can we be said to be afraid of billions of years because they aid evolution?

Conclusion

Ross errs by using words of "old age" which are actually *relative* terms. All of them are consistent with an age which is merely old in relation to human history, such as a few thousand years. Correct exegesis means that they therefore cannot be used to prove what Ross means by "old," but must be interpreted by the unambiguous teachings of Scripture, such as the numbered days, with evenings and mornings, of Genesis 1, and the genealogies with numbers of years. Ross does the opposite — he is determined to make old-earth "science" his authority, and use that to interpret old-age words by this concept, which was totally foreign to the authors and intended readers of Scripture.

The availability of old-age words does mean that there were ways that God *could* have communicated notions of vast ages before man — *if* that's what He had intended. But God used *none* of these in regard to the creation. Rather, He went out of His way to indicate that Adam was created on the sixth day of an ordinary-length week of creation. The complete lack of old-age words in Genesis 1 is further strong evidence against the day-age theory.

Ross's other arguments are purely subjective, or based on unfair reading of the motives of creationists.

---

5. D.T. Gish, *Evolution: The Fossils Say No!* 2nd edition (San Diego, CA: Creation-Life Publishers, 1973), p. 43. This book has been superseded by *Evolution: The Fossils STILL Say NO!* (El Cajon, CA: Institute for Creation Research, 1995), but the 1973 book shows that Ross's claim has no basis whatever.

6. D.T. Gish, "The Origin of Life: Theories on the Origin of Biological Order," ICR *Impact* 37:iii (1976).

CHAPTER 11

SCIENCE AND THE YOUNG EARTH

T he final authority, the Bible, shows that the earth cannot be billions of years old. Such a belief conflicts with the biblical data of creation in six ordinary days, recent creation of man on the sixth day, and death of humans and animals arising from Adam's sin. Science is limited in dealing with the past, so cannot be used to prove or disprove the Bible. But it's still useful to show that, even under evolutionists'/long-agers' own uniformitarian assumptions, there are many "age" indicators that point to an age far less than billions of years.

DETERMINING THE AGE OF SOMETHING

Biblical creationists believe that the only way to conclusively establish the earth's age is the testimony of the eyewitness account in Genesis. In a court of law, a reliable eyewitness that a suspect was absent from a crime scene overrules any circumstantial evidence, and there is no eyewitness more reliable than the all-knowing Creator. Creationists have also pointed out that "scientific" methods are limited in dealing with the past, because of many assumptions. Therefore, it would be folly to use any of this circumstantial evidence to overrule the plain meaning of the Bible. Sadly, many Christians do just that, such as the progressive creationists and theistic evolutionists, as shown in chapter 1.

Fighting the Opponent with His Own Weapons

However, creationists have published a number of articles about scientific evidence, and this chapter will provide a detailed and up-to-date presentation of many of them. The point of these articles is to overcome the enemy's belief system (see 2 Cor. 10:4–5) by turning its own axioms against it. This is a form of argument well-known to logicians called the *reductio ad absurdum*, that is, showing that a premise is false by demonstrating that it implies an absurd conclusion. It is a technique that Christians can use to great effect, and Jesus himself used this and many other types of logical arguments.[1] Many

---

1. For example, Jesus' response to the Pharisees in Matthew 12:27, "And if I drive out demons by Beelzebub, by whom do your people drive them out? So then, they will be your judges." He was showing that *if* His opponents were right in their own assumptions, it would rebound against themelves. See further discussion in J. Sarfati, "Loving God with All Your Mind: Logic and Creation," *TJ* 12(2)142–151 (1998); <www.answersingenesis.org/logic>.

statements by anti-Christians might appear reasonable on the surface, but when each of these statements is turned on itself, it refutes itself. For example:[2]

- "There is no truth" — this would mean that *this* sentence itself is not true.

- "We can never know anything for certain" — so how could we know *that* for certain?

- "A statement is only meaningful if it is either a necessary truth of logic or can be tested empirically" (the once-popular *verification criterion for meaning* of the "logical positivists") — this statement itself is neither a necessary truth of logic nor can it be tested empirically, so it is meaningless by its own criteria.

- "There are no moral absolutes, so we ought to be tolerant of other people's morals" — but "ought" implies a moral absolute that toleration is good.

- "Our thoughts are really the motions of atoms in the brain obeying the *fixed* laws of chemistry in the brain" — yet atheists claim to have arrived at this position *freely* by thinking through the evidence!

Evolutionists rely on a principle sometimes called *uniformitarianism*: "the present is the key to the past." This is precisely the characteristic of the "scoffers" prophesied in 2 Peter 3:4 "all things continue as *they were* from the beginning of the creation." Peter reveals the huge flaw of the uniformitarian scoffers: they are "willingly ignorant" of special creation by God and a cataclysmic globe-covering (and fossil-forming) Flood.

What the articles in this chapter show is that the evolutionists' *own axiom of uniformitarianism* leads to conclusions contrary to their billions-of-years beliefs. If they wish to deny the conclusion of these articles, they must abandon their own axiom to do so. This is the whole point.

Four Main Points

1. Atheists have no ultimate basis for believing in the general uniformity of nature that makes science possible. It is impossible to prove that the universe is orderly, because all possible proofs presuppose the very order they are trying to prove. Conversely, Christians have a basis in the Creator God of the Bible — since "Jesus Christ is the same yesterday and today and forever" (Heb. 13:8).[3]

2. Atheists certainly have no logical basis for believing in a rigid uniformity in the past, which doesn't even have the merit of being amenable to observation or repeatable tests.

---

2. See also G. Koukl, "Arguments That Commit Suicide, Stand to Reason," <www.str.org/free/solid_ground/SG0107.htm>, July/August 2001.

3. Their faith in uniformity is not unreasonable in light of repeated everyday experience, but philosophically this is an unsound basis. Leading 20th-century logician Bertrand Russell referred to a turkey facing Thanksgiving who could argue that since every day so far had passed without it getting its head chopped off, it was safe in presuming that this would never happen.

3. Since atheists have this belief, it is legitimate for Christians to show that it leads to conclusions that refute their long-age beliefs.

4. Christians should not try to reinterpret the Bible to fit in with essentially atheistic theories.

SOME EVIDENCE FOR A YOUNG WORLD

As said, we are not trying to prove the biblical age with science. Arguments of the sort presented below, whether offered in support of an "old" or "young" earth, are always subject to revision in the light of new data or different assumptions. Rather, we are showing that, even granting the long-agers' premises about uniformitarianism, the *science* is overwhelmingly in favor of an age far younger than billions of years.

But Ross has tried to "poison the well." In FoG:155 ff., Ross has a heading "Bogus evidences for a young universe," and accuses young-earth proponents of being "misguided" and "misguiding." He writes:

All of these "evidences" of youthfulness involve one or more of the following problems:

- Faulty assumptions
- Faulty data
- Misapplication of principles, laws, and equations
- Ignorance of mitigating evidence

This is a debate tactic known as "elephant hurling." This occurs when the critic puts up summary arguments about complex issues to give the impression of weighty evidence, but with an unstated presumption that a large complex of underlying ideas is true, and failing to consider opposing data, usually because they have uncritically accepted the arguments from their own side. But we should challenge elephant-hurlers to offer *specifics* and challenge their *underlying assumptions*.

The section above pointed out the fallacy of the underlying assumptions, and the sections to follow will instead present some specifics. The following are a few of the "age" indicators that are inconsistent with billions of years, first with summaries (in sans-serif italic font), then with much more detail. As shown, for the few arguments Ross addresses, he is the one guilty of one or more of the faults he accuses YECs of.

1. Earth's Magnetic Field Decay

The earth's magnetic field has been decaying[4] so fast that it couldn't be more than about 10,000 years old. Rapid reversals during the Flood year, and fluctuations shortly after, just caused the field energy to drop even faster.

---

4. J. Sarfati, "The Earth's Magnetic Field: Evidence That the Earth Is Young," *Creation* 20(2):15–19 (March–May 1998); <www.answersingenesis.org/magfield>.

Cause of the Earth's Magnetic Field

Materials like iron are composed of tiny *magnetic domains*, each of which behaves like a tiny magnet. The domains themselves are composed of even tinier atoms, which are themselves microscopic magnets, and are lined up within the domain. But most pieces of iron are not magnets, because normally the domains cancel each other out. However, in magnets, such as a compass needle, more of the domains are lined up in a certain direction, and so the material has an overall magnetic field.

Earth's core is mainly iron and nickel, so could its magnetic field be generated the same way as a compass needle's? No — above a temperature called the *Curie point*, the magnetic domains are disrupted. The earth's core, at its coolest region, is about 3,400–4,700°C (6,100–8,500°F),[5] much hotter than the Curie points of iron (750°C, 1,380°F)[6] and indeed, of all known substances.

But in 1820, Danish physicist H.C. Orsted discovered that a sustained electric current produces a magnetic field. Without this, there could be no electric motors, vital to modern technological society. So could an electric current be responsible for the earth's magnetic field? Electric motors have a power source, but electric currents normally decay almost instantly once the power source is switched off (except in superconductors).[7] So how could there be an electric current inside the earth, without a source?

The answer is the 1831 discovery by the great creationist physicist Michael Faraday that a changing magnetic field *induces* an electric voltage, the basis of electrical generators.[8] Imagine the earth soon after creation with a large electrical current in its core. This would produce a strong magnetic field. Without a power source, this current would decay. Thus, the magnetic field would decay, too. As decay is change, it would induce a current — lower than, but in the same direction as, the original one.[9] So we have a decaying current producing a decaying field, which generates a decaying current. . . . If the magnetic field is strong enough, the current would take a while to die out — which can be observed when some appliances are switched off. The decay rate can be accurately calculated.[10] (The electrical energy doesn't disappear — it is turned into heat, a process discovered by the creationist physicist James Joule in 1840.[11])

---

5. "The Earth: Its Properties, Composition, and Structure," *Encyclopædia Britannica* 17:600, 15th ed., 1992.

6. "Curie point," *Encyclopædia Britannica* 3:800, 15th ed., 1992, named after Pièrre Curie (1859–1906), who later won a Nobel prize with his wife, Marie, for their work on radioactivity.

7. This is due to electrical resistance — the electrons collide with atoms and are soon moving randomly, rather than in a current. In superconductors, there is zero resistance, so currents can persist indefinitely. But superconductivity is a low temperature phenomenon and has never been observed at temperatures anywhere near those of the extremely hot core.

8. See A. Lamont, *21 Great Scientists who Believed the Bible* (Australia: Creation Science Foundation, 1995), p. 88–97.

9. This is the result of Lenz's law (after H.F.E. Lenz 1804–1864), which states that the direction of an induced current is that which *opposes* the cause producing it. In this case, the cause is the decaying current, so the induced current is in the direction to *retard* decay.

10. The decay is *exponential*, and for a simple electric circuit at time t with initial current I, resistance R and inductance L, the current is given by $i = Ie^{-t/\tau}$, where t is the time constant L/R — the

Consequence of Decaying Current

In the 1970s, the late creationist physics professor Dr. Thomas Barnes noted that measurements since 1835 have shown that the main part[12] of the earth's magnetic field is decaying at 5 percent per century[13] (also, archeological measurements show that the field was 40 percent stronger in A.D. 1000 than today[14]). Barnes, the author of a well-regarded electro-magnetism textbook,[15] proposed that the earth's magnetic field was caused by a *freely decaying electric current* in the earth's metallic core. That is entirely consistent with observations on the rate of decay and experiments on likely core materials.[16] Barnes calculated that the current could not have been decaying for more than 10,000 years, or else its starting strength would have been large enough to melt the earth. So the earth must be younger than that.

Evolutionist Responses

The decaying current model is obviously incompatible with the billions of years needed by evolutionists. So their preferred model is a *self-sustaining dynamo* (electric generator). Earth's rotation and convection is supposed to circulate the molten iron/nickel of the outer core. Positive and negative charges in this liquid metal are supposed to circulate unevenly, which would produce an electric current, generating the magnetic field.

Scientists have not produced a workable *analytic* model, despite 40–50 years of research, and there are many problems.[17] Dr. Gary Glatzmeier formerly of Los Alamos National Laboratory and now on the faculty of the University of California,

time for the current to decay to $1/e$ (~37%) of its initial value. For a sphere of radius a, conductivity σ, and permeability μ, τ is given by $4\sigma\mu a^2\pi$.

11. A. Lamont, *21 Great Scientists who Believed the Bible* (Australia: Creation Science Foundation, 1995), p. 132–141.

12. More technically, the "main part" is the "dipole" (two poles, north and south) part of the field, comprising over 90 percent of the field observed. The strength of the source of the dipole part, called the "dipole moment" is what is decaying at 5 percent per century. For the other 10 percent of the field, see the section below entitled Multipole components of the field.

13. K.L. McDonald and R.H. Gunst, "An Analysis of the Earth's Magnetic Field from 1835 to 1965," *ESSA Technical Report, IER 46-IES 1*, U.S. Government Printing Office, Washington, 1967.

14. R.T. Merrill and M.W. McElhinney, *The Earth's Magnetic Field* (London: Academic Press, 1983), p. 101–106.

15. T.G. Barnes, *Foundations of Electricity and Magnetism*, 3rd edition (El Paso, TX: Barnes, 1977).

16. F.D. Stacey, "Electrical Resistivity of the Earth's Core," *Earth and Planetary Science Letters* 3:204–206 (1967).

17. Measurements of electrical currents in the sea floor pose difficulties for the most popular class of dynamo models — L.J. Lanzerotti et al., "Measurements of the Large-scale Direct-current Earth Potential and Possible Implications for the Geomagnetic Dynamo," *Science* 229:47–49 (July 5, 1986). Also, the measured rate of field decay is sufficient to generate the current needed to produce today's field strength, meaning that there is no evidence for a self-sustaining dynamo operating today, if one ever did.

has produced a numerical model of the geodynamo[18] that even displays reversal behavior.[19] However, it is based on computer simulation using a large, complex code, which can easily have hidden flaws that can take years to discover. And they also depend on the starting parameters. Glatzmaier's simulation has an unrealistically high toroidal (donut-shaped) component to the field of about 150 gauss, but measurements indicate that this component would be less than a tenth of that. Also, the simulation assumes that the molten metal in the outer core has a very high core conductivity, about 400,000–600,000 mhos per meter. But laboratory measurements of materials supposed to be in the core indicate only 30,000 mho/m.[20] This means that the current would decay more quickly, requiring more generation from the liquid dynamo. It's also not clear whether Glatzmaier's simulations deal with the energy of the field, and whether they may turn out to support Dr. Humphreys' model (see page 337).

But the major criticism of Barnes' young-earth argument is evidence that the magnetic field has *reversed* several times — that is, compasses would point south instead of north. When grains of the common magnetic mineral *magnetite* in volcanic lava or ash flows cool below its *Curie point* (see page 334) of 570°C (1,060°F), the magnetic domains partly align themselves in the direction of the earth's magnetic field *at that time*. Once the rock is fully cooled, the magnetite's alignment is fixed. Thus, we have a permanent record of the earth's field through time.

Although evolutionists have no good explanations for the reversals, they maintain that the straightforward decay assumed by Dr. Barnes is invalid. Also, their model requires at least thousands of years for a reversal. And with their dating assumptions, they believe that the reversals occur at intervals of millions of years, and point to an old earth.

Hugh Ross strangely claims, although knowing better, that field reversals are enough to refute this whole creationist argument:[21]

> The oversight in Argument B [the earth's magnetic field is decaying too rapidly for an old earth] is that the earth's magnetic field does not undergo steady decay but rather follows a "sinusoidal" pattern. That is, the field decays, builds up, decays, builds up, etc. The proof for this pattern lies in ancient geologic strata found throughout the world. The rocks reveal that the earth's field reverses its polarity about every half million years — the reversal process itself lasting roughly 10,000 years.

18. G.A. Glatzmaier and P.H. Roberts, "A Three-Dimensional Convective Dynamo Solution with Rotating and Finitely Conducting Inner Core and Mantle," *Phys. Earth Planet. Inter.* 91:63–75 (1995).

19. G.A. Glatzmaier and P.H. Roberts, "A Three-Dimensional Self-Consistent Computer Simulation of a Geomagnetic Field Reversal," *Nature* 377:203-209 (1995).

20. R. Humphreys, "Can Evolutionists Now Explain the Earth's Magnetic Field?" *CRSQ* 33(3):184–185 (December 1996).

21. FoG:156; repeated at H. Ross, "Biblical Evidence for Long Creation Days," <www.reasons.org/resources/apologetics/longdays.shtml?main>, December 2, 2002.

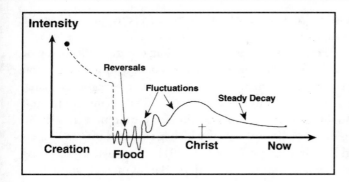

Creationist Counter-Response

The physicist Dr. Russell Humphreys believed that Dr. Barnes had the right idea, and he also accepted that the reversals were real. He modified Barnes' model to account for special effects of a liquid conductor, like the molten metal of the earth's outer core. If the liquid flowed upward (due to convection — hot fluids rise, cold fluids sink), this could sometimes make the field reverse quickly.[22] Geophysicist John Baum-gardner proposes that subducting tectonic plates were greatly involved in the Genesis flood.[23] Humphreys proposes that these plates would sharply cool the outer parts of the core, driving the convection.[24] This means that most of the reversals occurred in the Flood year, every week or two. And after the Flood, there would have been large fluctuations due to residual motion.

This is supported by the fact that archeological measurements on materials from about 1000 B.C. and A.D. 1000 show that the surface geomagnetic field *intensity* (B) slowly increased to a maximum at about the time of Christ, and then declined slowly, becoming approximately exponential about A.D. 1000 (see graph, above). But the reversals and fluctuations could not halt the loss of *energy* (E). This would decay even faster and has decayed monotonically throughout the whole period. Note that the field energy s is the volume integral of B^2, which is why the *intensity* could fluctuate up and down during and after the Flood, while the total field *energy* always decreased.

The Humphreys model also explains why the sun reverses its magnetic field every 11 years. The sun is a gigantic ball of hot, energetically moving, electrically conducting gas. Dynamo theorists had trouble explaining how the sun would not only reverse its field but also regenerate it and maintain its intensity over billions of years. But there is no problem if the sun is only thousands of years old. Dr. Humphreys also proposed a test for his model: magnetic reversals should be found in rocks known to have cooled in days or weeks. For example, he predicted that in a thin lava flow, the

22. R. Humphreys, "Reversals of the Earth's Magnetic Field During the Genesis Flood," in R.E. Walsh et al., editors, *Proceedings of the First International Conference on Creationism,* Creation Science Fellowship, Pittsburgh 2:113–126 (1986). The moving conductive liquid would carry magnetic flux lines with it, and this would generate new currents, producing new flux in the opposite direction. See also his interview in *Creation* 15(3):20–23 (1993).

23. J. Baumgardner, papers in "Forum on Catastrophic Plate Tectonics," *TJ* 16(1):57–85 (2002); <www.answersingenesis.org/cpt_forum>.

24. R. Humphreys, discussion of J. Baumgardner, "Numerical Simulation of the Large-scale Tectonic Changes Accompanying the Flood," in R.E. Walsh et al., editors, *Proceedings of the First International Conference on Creationism,* Creation Science Fellowship, Pittsburgh 2:29 (1986).

outside would cool first, and record earth's magnetic field in one direction; the inside would cool a short time later, and record the field in another direction.

Three years after this prediction appeared in print, leading researchers Robert Coe and Michel Prévot found a thin lava layer that must have cooled within 15 days, and had 90° of reversal recorded continuously in it.[25] And it was no fluke — eight years later, they reported an even faster reversal.[26] This was staggering news to them and the rest of the evolutionary community, but strong corroboration for Humphreys' model.

Humphreys sent a letter to Ross (June 9, 1991) which mentioned his ICC papers on magnetic reversals, and Ross in his reply (July 17, 1991) acknowledged receiving that information. Yet he continued after that to criticize Barnes' models and ignore Humphreys' refinements, over ten years later.

Response to Other Skeptical Arguments

As seen, Ross thinks (erroneously) that field reversals can counter this threat to his long-age faith, but there are other arguments that skeptics have used. So it's important to address these, too.

Exponential Decay?

Some skeptics, such as the Christadelphian heretic (i.e., who denies Christ's deity), Alan Hayward, whose book RTB stocks (and praises for "sound theology"), have claimed that an exponential decay curve is wrong, and a linear decay should have been plotted. Now, both exponential and linear decay curves have two fitted parameters:

- Exponential decay ($i = Ie^{-t/t}$) requires the parameters I and t.
- Linear decay of the general form $y = mx + c$ requires the gradient m and y-intercept c.

The fit is very similar for the limited range of data available, with no significant difference between the two. As the fit is equally good, there is no statistical reason to choose one over the other.

However, it is a well-accepted procedure in modeling of regression analysis to use *meaningful* equations to describe physical phenomena, where there is a sound theoretical basis for doing so. This is the case here. Currents in resistance/inductance circuits always decay *exponentially*, not linearly, after the power source is switched off.[27]

---

25. R.S. Coe and M. Prévot, "Evidence Suggesting Extremely Rapid Field Variation During a Geomagnetic Reversal," *Earth and Planetary Science* 92(3/4):292–298 (April 1989). See also the reports by Ph.D. geologist Andrew Snelling, *Creation* 13(3):46 50, 13(4):44–48 (1991).

26. R.S. Coe, M. Prévot, and P. Camps, "New Evidence for Extraordinarily Rapid Change of the Geomagnetic Field During a Reversal," *Nature* 374(6564):687–692 (1995); see also A. Snelling, *TJ* 9(2):138–139 (1995).

27. The decay is *exponential*, and for a simple electric circuit at time t with initial current I, resistance R and inductance L, the current is given by $i = Ie^{-t/\tau}$, where τ is the time constant L/R — the time for the current to decay to 1/e (~37%) of its initial value. For a sphere of radius a, conductivity σ, and permeability μ, τ is given by $4\sigma\mu a^2\pi$.

A linear decay might look good on paper, but it's physically absurd when dealing with the real world of electric circuits. In fact, linear decays of anything are rare in nature. Conversely, exponential decay is firmly rooted in electromagnetic theory.

Thomas Barnes, who first pointed out magnetic field decay as a problem for evolutionists, was a specialist in electromagnetism and, as indicated above, wrote some well-regarded textbooks on the subject. (He was Professor Emeritus of Physics at the University of Texas at El Paso.) Most of his critics are far less knowledgeable about electromagnetism.

Another important point is that even if we accept the skeptic's argument about a linear decay, it would still point to *an upper limit* of 90 million years, and this is far too young for evolution or Ross's big-bang theology.

A final point is that if the decay really were linear, we wouldn't have much time left before the earth's magnetic field were to disappear!

Multipole Components of the Field

Some skeptics have claimed:

> . . . only the dipole-field strength has been "decaying" for a century and a half . . . the strength of the nondipole field (about 15% of the total field) has increased over the same time span, so that the total field has remained almost constant. Barnes' assumption of a steady decrease in the field's strength throughout history is also irreconcilable, of course, with the paleomagnetic evidence of fluctuations and reversals [in the geomagnetic field].[28]

The "authority" turns out to be an anti-creationist *dictionary* compiled by an anti-Christian librarian with, as far as I'm aware, *no scientific training!* The reasoning may have been copied from the atheistic/agnostic geochronologist Brent Dalrymple, who has no qualifications in electromagnetic theory. Humphreys answered the "authority" in July 2001:

> Litany in the Church of Darwin: "The non-dipole part of the earth's magnetic field shall save us!" That is indeed an old and dismissive evolutionist argument. Tom Barnes discussed it in his papers during the 1970s. I discussed it near the end of my paper.[29]
>
> Over 90% of the field is dipolar (two poles, one north and one south), but the rest of it is non-dipolar, or multipolar, such as the quadrupole part (two north and two south poles), the octopole part (four north and four south poles), etc. Just imagine the fields from bar magnets tied together at various angles to one another.

---

28. R. Ecker, *Dictionary of Science and Creationism* (Buffalo, NY: Prometheus Books, 1990), p. 105.
29. R. Humphreys, "Physical Mechanism for Reversals of the Earth's Magnetic Field During the Flood," in R.E. Walsh and C.L. Brooks, editors, *Proceedings of the Second International Conference on Creationism,* Creation Science Fellowship, Pittsburgh 2:129–142 (1990).

In the 1970s, the evolutionists claimed that the very large energy (units are Joules or ergs) disappearing from the dipole part of the field is not really converted into heat, but is somehow being stored in the non-dipole part, later to be resurrected as a new dipole in the reverse direction. Some papers showed that the average *field intensity* (units are Teslas or Gauss) of some of the non-dipole parts is increasing slightly.[30]

But *field intensity* is not *energy*. To get the total energy in a component, one must square the intensity in a small volume around each point, multiply by the volume and a certain constant, and add up all the resulting energies throughout all space. The non-dipole intensities fall off (with increasing distance from the earth's center) much faster than the dipole intensity, so the non-dipole parts are not able to contribute nearly as much energy to the total as the dipole part. That means the small increase in some non-dipole *field intensities* does not appear to represent nearly enough energy to compensate for the enormous energy lost year by year from the dipole part.

I have my doubts that the paper referred to actually proves the point the evolutionists want to make, that "non-dipole energy gain compensates for dipole energy loss." Not only does my eyeball estimate above disagree, but the theory of reversals in my 1990 ICC paper disagrees [As shown below, Dr. Humphreys no longer has his doubts — he (and anyone who checks the numbers) now knows that the evolutionist claim is fallacious]. It says that some energy will go into non-dipole components, but not nearly enough to compensate for the energy loss from the dipole part. The reversal process I propose is not efficient; it dissipates a large amount of energy as heat. I discussed this, including non-dipole parts by implication, in the second-to-last section ("The Field's Energy Has Always Decreased") of my article "The Earth's Magnetic Field Is Young."[31]

As further evidence, I used the authoritative International Geomagnetic Reference Field data — more than 2,500 numbers representing the earth's magnetic field over the whole twentieth century. The bottom line is this:

In the most accurately recorded period, from 1970 to 2000, the total (dipole plus non-dipole) energy in the earth's magnetic field has steadily decreased by $1.41 \pm 0.16\%$. At that rate, the field would lose at least half its energy every 1,500 years, give or take a century or so. This supports the creationist model that the field has always been losing energy — even during magnetic polarity reversals during the Genesis flood — ever since God created it about 6,000 years ago.

30. Barraclough, *Geophy. J. Roy. Astr. Soc.* 43:645–659 (1975).
31. R. Humphreys, "The Earth's Magnetic Field Is Young," *Impact* 242 (August 1993); <http://www.icr.org/pubs/imp/imp-242.htm>.

The evolutionists, on the other hand, have no workable, mathematically analyzable theory of reversals. They are claiming that whatever process actually caused the reversals was 100% efficient — that the total energy in their hoped-for future dipole field will be equal to the total energy which was in the dipole field at its last peak (about the time of Christ). That is, their faith in a billion-year age for the field requires them to believe that each cycle is resurrected phoenix-like from the ashes of the previous cycle — with no losses.

Put another way, the Church of Darwin requires them to believe that the second law of thermodynamics — that all forms of energy devolve down to heat — does not apply to planetary magnetic fields. Sound familiar?

In 2002, Humphreys published an update[32] which explains the above and more in detail. The abstract reads:

This paper closes a loophole in the case for a young earth based on the loss of energy from various parts of the earth's magnetic field. Using ambiguous 1967 data, evolutionists had claimed that energy gains in minor ("nondipole") parts compensate for the energy loss from the main ("dipole") part. However, nobody seems to have checked that claim with newer, more accurate data. Using data from the International Geomagnetic Reference Field (IGRF) I show that from 1970 to 2000, the dipole part of the field steadily lost 235 ± 5 billion megajoules of energy, while the non-dipole part gained only 129 ± 8 billion megajoules. Over that 30-year period, the net loss of energy from all observable parts of the field was 1.41 ± 0.16%. At that rate, the field would lose half its energy every 1465 ± 166 years. Combined with my 1990 theory explaining reversals of polarity during the Genesis Flood and intensity fluctuations after that, these new data support the creationist model: the field has rapidly and continuously lost energy ever since God created it about 6,000 years ago.

2. Helium in the Rocks

Evolutionists assume that helium comes from alpha-decay of certain radioactive elements in the rocks. Helium atoms are very small and chemically unreactive so can quickly diffuse from rocks. Yet so much helium is still in some rocks that it couldn't have had time to escape — certainly not billions of years. This is strong evidence that nuclear decay rates were much faster at some time in the past.

Helium was first detected in light patterns in the sun (Greek ἥλιος *hēlios*) before it was detected on the earth. Helium in the sun is generally believed to be formed

32. R. Humphreys, "The Earth's Magnetic Field Is Still Losing Energy," *CRSQ* 39(1)1–11 (March 2002); <www.creationresearch.org/crsq/articles/39/39_1/GeoMag.htm>.

by *nuclear fusion*, most likely the sun's power source,[33] by converting mass into huge amounts of energy, as per Einstein's famous formula: $E = mc^2$.[34]

This is where atoms of hydrogen, the lightest element, combine to form helium, with huge amounts of energy released. On earth, helium is produced mainly by radioactive *alpha* (α)-decay. The great New Zealand physicist Ernest Rutherford (1871–1937) discovered that a-particles were really the nuclei of helium atoms. Radioactive elements in rocks — such as uranium, radium, and thorium — produce helium this way, and it leaks out into the air.

Scientists can measure the rate at which helium escapes from the rocks. This is faster in hotter rocks, and the deeper one goes into the earth, the hotter the rocks. The creationist physicist Robert Gentry was researching deep granite as a possible way of safely storing dangerous radioactive waste from nuclear power stations. Safe storage requires that the elements should not move too fast through the rock. Granite contains mineral crystals called *zircons*, which often contain radioactive elements. Thus, they produce helium, which should be escaping. But Gentry found that even the deep, hot zircons (197°C or 387°F) contained far too much helium — that is, if it had had billions of years to escape. But if there had really been only thousands of years for this helium to escape, then we shouldn't be surprised that there is so much left.[35]

Evidence of Accelerated Nuclear Decay

Humphreys has led a RATE (Radioisotopes and the Age of the Earth) project which explored this question further, and proposed that accelerated decay rates might explain the high helium retention.[36] This was from several observations about zircons ($ZrSiO_4$ crystals):

---

33. Hermann von Helmholtz (1821–1894) proposed gravitational collapse as the sun's power source, which wouldn't last anywhere near the proposed billions of years. However, standard physics shows that the sun's core is hot enough for fusion, and this produces neutrinos that we have detected. But there was a shortfall, so it was plausible to propose that 2/3 of the sun's energy could have been produced by gravitational collapse. This seemed likely when the standard models of particle physics postulated zero rest-mass for neutrinos, so forbade neutrino oscillation. However, there seems to be conclusive proof that neutrinos can oscillate, so the standard particle models are wrong. See R. Newton, "Missing Neutrinos Found! No Longer an 'Age' Indicator," *TJ* 16(3):123–125 (2002).

34. Four hydrogen atoms (mass = 1.008) convert to helium (mass 4.0039) losing 0.0281 atomic mass units (1 AMU = 1.66 x 10^{-27} kg), releasing 4.2 x 10^{-12} joules of energy.

35. R.V. Gentry, G.L. Glish, and E.H. McBay, "Differential Helium Retention in Zircons: Implications for Nuclear Waste Containment," *Geophysical Research Letters* 9(10):1129–30 (October 1982). See also Gentry's book: *Creation's Tiny Mystery*, 3rd edition (Knoxville TN: Earth Science Associates, 1992), p. 169–170, 263–264.

36. R. Humphreys, "Nuclear Decay: Evidence for a Young World," *Impact* 352 (October 2002); <www.icr.org/pubs/imp/imp-352.htm>.

   D.R. Humphreys, S.A. Austin, J.R. Baumgardner, and A.A. Snelling, "Helium Diffusion Rates Support Accelerated Nuclear Decay, in R.L. Ivey Jr., editor, *Fifth International Conference on Creationism*, p. 175–196, Creation Science Fellowship, Pittsburgh, Pennsylvania (August, 2003); <www.icr.org/research/icc03/pdf/Helium_ICC_7-22-03.pdf>.

- There must have been 1.5 billion years worth of decay — at current decay rates.

- Large amounts, up to 58 percent, of the helium are still there.

- Yet, as the new RATE experiments (confirmed by new published data from other laboratories) show, helium diffuses so rapidly out of zircon that it should have all but disappeared after about 100,000 years. In fact, the rate of helium leakage dates "billion-year-old" zircons at 5,680 ± 2,000 years.

Therefore, the decay that produced the helium must have occurred within that time frame. But then how could so much helium have been produced and accumulated in so little time? The best answer seems to be an episode of accelerated nuclear decay, during creation week or the Flood year, or more likely both.

Of course, if nuclear decay had been accelerated in the past, that falsifies one key assumption of radiometric dating, that is, that the decay rate has been constant. This is far from the only evidence for accelerated nuclear decay, as shown in chapter 12.

Ross's Failed Counterattack

On a radio broadcast in September 2003,[37] Ross and some colleagues tried to counteract the RATE project. Clearly, Ross had not even read some of the reports, and his "outside expert," Roger Wiens, had to rebuke RTB staffers several times for not understanding the work. But even Wiens had not read some of the papers either.

In attempting to escape the implications of the helium still in the zircons, Ross claimed that helium was too "slippery" to keep track of, that it would escape from minerals too fast. However, he overlooked the fact that most of the radiogenic helium is *still in the zircons*, despite escaping as fast as he agrees. To avoid the implication that the zircons are young, Ross illegitimately postulated that the zircons started out with over 100,000 times more helium (generated by the big bang, not radioactivity) than the large amount of helium in them even now, so that the rapid losses could still take place over billions of years. How zircons on the earth could incorporate a big-bang–generated slippery gas is not explained. And Ross ignored the RATE evidence that the large amounts of helium are not in the surrounding mineral. Lastly, he contradicted himself by suggesting that helium was somehow diffusing into the zircons *from outside*, that is, the *opposite direction of diffusion* to the big bang explanation. However, Humphreys et al. clearly demonstrated that helium diffuses from inside the zircon outward to the surrounding materials. This is consistent with the fundamental diffusion law that substances diffuse from regions of higher concentration to lower.[38]

---

37. RTB Critique of RATE project, Reasons to Believe radio broadcast, September 18, 2003, 6 to 8 p.m. Pacific time. Moderator: Krista Bontrager; studio participants: Hugh Ross, Fazale Rana, and Marg Harmon; telephone participant: Roger Wiens. Archived at: <www.oneplace.com/ministries/creation_update/Archives.asp>.

38. See also L. Vardiman, "Ross Criticizes RATE without Doing His Homework," <www.icr.org/headlines/rate-hughross.html>, October 4, 2003.

3. Salt in the Sea

Salt is pouring into the sea[39] much faster than it is escaping. The sea is not nearly salty enough for this to have been happening for billions of years. Even granting generous assumptions to evolutionists, the seas could not be more than 62 million years old — far younger than the billions of years believed by evolutionists. Again, this indicates a maximum age, not the actual age.

The ocean is essential for life on earth, and also helps make the climate fairly moderate. However, although the ocean contains 1,370 million cubic kilometers (334 million cubic miles) of water, humans can't survive by drinking from it — it is too salty.

To a chemist, "salt" refers to a wide range of chemicals where a metal is combined with a non-metal. Ordinary common salt is a compound formed when the metal sodium combines with the non-metal chlorine — sodium chloride. This contains electrically charged atoms, called ions, which attract each other, resulting in a fairly hard crystal. When salt dissolves, these ions separate. Sodium and chloride ions are the main ions in seawater, but not the only ones. The salty seas benefit man, because the ocean provides many useful minerals for our industries.

How Old Is the Sea?

Many processes (see below) bring salts into the sea, while these salts don't leave the sea easily. So the saltiness is increasing steadily. We can work out how much salt is in the sea, as well as the rates that salts go into and out of the sea. Then, assuming how these rates varied in the past and how much salt was in the sea originally, we can calculate a maximum age for the sea.

In fact, this method was first proposed by Sir Isaac Newton's colleague Sir Edmond Halley (1656–1742), of comet fame.[40] More recently, the geologist, physicist, and pioneer of radiation therapy, John Joly (1857–1933), estimated that the oceans were 80–90 million years old at the most.[41] But this was far too young for evolutionists, who believe that life evolved in the ocean billions of years ago. (And, of course, whatever age is assigned by them is adhered to by Ross and his followers.)

---

39. J. Sarfati, "Salty Seas: Evidence for a Young Earth," *Creation* 21(1):16–17 (December 1998–February 1999); <www.answersingenesis.org/salty>.

40. E. Halley, "A Short Account of the Cause of the Saltness [*sic*] of the Ocean, and of the Several Lakes That Emit No Rivers; with a Proposal, by Help Thereof, to Discover the Age of the World," *Philosophical Transactions of the Royal Society of London* 29:296–300 (1715); cited in S.A. Austin and D.R. Humphreys, "The Sea's Missing Salt: A Dilemma for Evolutionists," in R.E. Walsh and C.L. Brooks, editors, *Proceedings of the Second International Conference on Creationism*, Vol. II, p. 17–33 (1990).

41. J. Joly, "An Estimate of the Geological Age of the Earth," *Scientific Transactions of the Royal Dublin Society*, New Series, 7(3) (1899); reprinted in *Annual Report of the Smithsonian Institution* (June 30, 1899), p. 247–288; cited in S.A. Austin and D.R. Humphreys, "The Sea's Missing Salt: A Dilemma for Evolutionists," in R.E. Walsh and C.L. Brooks, editors, *Proceedings of the Second International Conference on Creationism*, Vol. II, p. 17–33 (1990).

More recently, the geologist Dr. Steve Austin and physicist Dr. Russell Humphreys analyzed figures from secular geoscience sources for the quantity of sodium ion (Na^+) in the ocean, and its input and output rates.[42] The slower the input and faster the output, the older the calculated age of the ocean would be.

Every kilogram of seawater contains about 10.8 grams of dissolved Na^+. This means that there is a total of 1.47×10^{16} (14,700 million million) tons of Na^+ in the ocean.

Sodium Input

Water on the land can dissolve salt outcrops, and can weather many minerals, especially clays and feldspars, and leach the sodium out of them. This sodium is carried into the ocean by rivers. Some salt is supplied by water through the ground directly to the sea — called submarine groundwater discharge (SGWD). Such water often has a high mineral concentration. Ocean floor sediments release much sodium, as do hot springs on the ocean floor (hydrothermal vents). Volcanic dust also contributes some sodium.

Austin and Humphreys calculated that about 457 million tons of sodium now enter the sea every year. The minimum possible amount in the past, even if the most generous assumptions about inflow rates are granted to evolutionists, is 356 million tons/year.

(Actually, a more recent study shows that salt is entering the oceans even faster than Austin and Humphreys thought, which means that the maximum possible age of the ocean is even lower than they calculated.[43] Previously, the amount of SGWD was thought to be a small fraction [0.01–10 percent] of the water from surface runoff, mainly rivers. But this new study, measuring the radioactivity of radium in coastal water, shows that the amount of SGWD is as much as 40 percent of the river flow.[44])

Sodium Output

People who live near the sea often have problems with rust in cars. This is due to salt spray — small droplets of seawater which escape from the ocean; the water evaporates, leaving behind tiny salt crystals. This is a major process that removes sodium from the sea. Another major process is called ion exchange — clays can absorb sodium ions and exchange them for calcium ions, which are released into the ocean. Some sodium is lost from the ocean when water is trapped in pores in sediments on the ocean floor. Certain minerals with large cavities in their crystal structure, called zeolites, can absorb sodium from the ocean.

---

42. S.A. Austin and D.R. Humphreys, "The Sea's Missing Salt: A Dilemma for Evolutionists," in R.E. Walsh and C.L. Brooks, editors, *Proceedings of the Second International Conference on Creationism*, Vol. II, p. 17–33 (1990). This paper should be consulted for more detail than is possible here.

43. W.S. Moore,"Large Groundwater Inputs to Coastal Waters Revealed by ^{226}Ra Enrichments," *Nature* 380(6575):612–614 (April 18, 1996); perspective by T.M. Church, "An Underground Route for the Water Cycle," same issue, p. 579–580.

44. Ibid., p. 580. Church comments, "The conclusion that large quantities of SGWD are entering the coastal ocean has the potential to radically alter our understanding of oceanic chemical mass balance."

However, the rate of sodium output is far less than the input. Austin and Humphreys calculated that about 122 million tons of sodium leave the sea every year today. The maximum possible amount, even if the most generous assumptions about sodium loss rate are granted to evolutionists, is 206 million tons/year.

Estimating the Age of the Ocean

Granting the most generous assumptions to evolutionists, Austin and Humphreys calculated that the ocean must be *less* than 62 million years old. It's important to stress that this is *not* the *actual* age, but a *maximum* age. That is, this evidence is consistent with any age up to 62 million years, including the biblical age of about 6,000 years.

The Austin and Humphreys calculation assumes the lowest plausible input rates and fastest plausible output rates, sustained throughout geologic time. Another assumption favorable to long-agers is that there was no dissolved salt to start with. If we assume more realistic conditions in the past, the calculated maximum age is much less.

For one thing, God probably created the oceans with some saltiness, so that saltwater fish could live comfortably in it. Noah's flood would have dissolved large amounts of sodium from land rocks. This would have found its way into the oceans when the floodwaters retreated. Finally, the larger-than-expected SGWD would further reduce the maximum age.

4. Missing "Old" Supernova Remnants

A supernova is an explosion of a massive star — the explosion is so bright that it briefly outshines the rest of the galaxy. The supernova remnants (SNRs) should keep expanding for hundreds of thousands of years, according to the physical equations. Yet there are no very old, widely expanded (Stage 3) SNRs, and few moderately old (Stage 2) ones in our galaxy, the Milky Way, or in its satellite galaxies, the Magellanic Clouds.[45] This is just what we would expect if these galaxies had not existed long enough for wide SNR expansion.

A *supernova*,[46] or violently exploding star, is one of the most brilliant and powerful objects in God's vast cosmos. On average, a galaxy like our own, the *Milky Way*, should produce one supernova every 25 years. An ordinary star is a gigantic ball of gas, about a million times more massive than the earth. It is potentially stable for a long time, because the energy produced by the core produces an enormous outward pressure, which balances the inward force of gravity acting on its huge mass.

However, when a star's nuclear fuel runs out, there is no longer any force to balance its gravity. If the star is very massive, much more so than our sun, most of

---

45. From J. Sarfati, "Exploding Stars Point to a Young Universe: Where Are All the Supernova Remnants?" *Creation* 19(3):46–48 (June–August 1997); <www.answersingenesis.org/SNR>. This is based on a paper by K. Davies, "Distribution of Supernova Remnants in the Galaxy," in R.E. Walsh, editor, *Proceedings of the Third International Conference on Creationism* (1994): p. 175–184.

46. See the article "Supernova," *Encyclopædia Britannica*, 11:401, 5th edition (1992).

it collapses very quickly — in about two seconds. This releases a huge amount of energy — one supernova will briefly out-shine all the billions of stars in its galaxy. The collapse is so violent that the electrons and nuclei are crushed together and produce a core of neutrons. This core is so dense that a teaspoonful would weigh 50 thousand million tons on earth. It cannot be compressed any further, so the incoming material from the rest of the star meets a solid wall. This material bounces off the core, rushes outward and shines very brightly. The remaining core, only about 20 km in diameter, is called a neutron star. Because it is spinning very fast, and has a strong magnetic field, it produces powerful radio beams. These sweep across earth's observatories once per pulsar rotation, so we observe regular radio pulses; thus the object is called a *pulsar*.

This huge expanding cloud of stellar debris is called a *SuperNova Remnant* (SNR). A well-known example is the Crab Nebula in the constellation of Taurus, produced by a supernova so bright that it could be seen during daytime for a few weeks in 1054. By applying physical laws (and using powerful computers), astronomers can predict what should happen to this cloud.

According to their model, the SNR should reach a diameter of about 100 parsecs (one parsec = 3.26 light-years = 31 million million km = 19 million million miles) after 120,000 years. So if the universe were billions of years old, we should be able to observe *many* SNRs this size. But if the universe is about 6,000 years old, no SNRs would have had time to reach this size. So the number of observed SNRs of a particular size is an excellent test of whether the universe is old or young. As we will see from the calculations which follow, the observed number of pulsars is consistent with a universe thousands of years old, but is a huge puzzle if the universe has existed for billions of years. Those readers who wish to spare themselves the task of wading through the calculations may wish to go straight to the supernova remnant table on page 349 and consider its implications.

A widely accepted model of super-nova expansion predicts three stages (see diagram on page 348).

1) The first stage starts with debris hurtling outwards at 7,000 kilometers per second. After the material has expanded for about 300 years, a blast wave forms, ending the first stage. By this time it reaches a diameter of about seven parsecs. This is an immense object — about 25,000 times larger than our solar system, which is "only" about eight light-hours across (about 8,600 million km or 5,400 million miles).

Since the first stage should last about 300 years and one SNR should occur every 25 years, there should now be 300/25 first-stage SNRs in our galaxy, or about 12. We should not expect to see them all — astronomers calculate that only about 19 percent of SNRs should be visible,[47] that is about 2 of the 12. It makes no difference whether the universe is thousands of years old as the Bible indicates, or billions of years old

---

47. K. Davies, "Distribution of Supernova Remnants in the Galaxy," in R.E. Walsh, editor, *Proceedings of the Third International Conference on Creationism* (1994) has detailed observational limitation formulae.

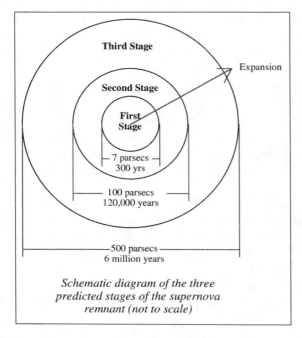

Third Stage

Expansion

Second Stage

First Stage

7 parsecs
300 yrs

100 parsecs
120,000 years

500 parsecs
6 million years

*Schematic diagram of the three
predicted stages of the supernova
remnant (not to scale)*

as evolutionary theory asserts. Actually, we see five first-stage SNRs, which is good agreement within the uncertainty range of the calculation.

2) The second stage SNR, known as the adiabatic[48] or Sedov stage, is a very powerful emitter of radio waves. This is predicted to expand for about 120,000 years and reach a diameter of about 100 parsecs. After this, it starts to lose thermal (heat) energy and begin the third stage. Now, if the universe were billions of years old, we would predict (remember, one supernova every 25 years, and taking into account SNRs in the 300-year first stage) that in our galaxy there would be about (120,000-300)/25 second-stage SNRs, or about 4,800. But if the universe has only existed for about 7,000 years, then there would be only enough time for (7,000-300)/25, or about 270. Astronomers calculate that 47 percent should be visible, so evolutionary/uniformitarian theory predicts about 2,260 second-stage SNRs, while the biblical creation theory predicts about 125. The actual observed number of second-stage SNRs is a good test of which theory best fits the facts.

There are actually 200 second-stage SNRs, with a diameter range from 6–106 parsecs observed in our galaxy! *This is in the right ball park for biblical creation, but is totally different from evolutionary predictions.* Evolutionists recognize this "problem" of the missing supernova remnants and have no answer.

3) The third, or isothermal,[49] stage is theorized to emit mainly heat energy. This stage would theoretically only start after 120,000 years, and would last about one million to six million years. The SNR would end its career when it either collided with similar SNRs at a diameter of about 420 parsecs or became so dispersed that it would be indistinguishable from the "vacuum" of space at a diameter of about 560 parsecs.

One calculation makes the generous (to evolutionary theory) assumption that the third stage starts at about 120,000 years and a diameter of about 100 parsecs, and lasts to an age of one million years and 200 parsecs. Thus, if the universe was

---

48. "Adiabatic" means "not transferring heat to or from its surroundings." During the second stage, the SNR loses very little thermal energy.

49. "Isothermal" means "staying at the same temperature." During the third stage the SNR should stay at about the same temperature and radiate excess thermal (heat) energy.

billions of years old, there should be (1,000,000-120,000)/25 third-stage SNRs in our galaxy, or about 35,000. Of these, about 14 percent should be observable, or about 5,000. However, if the universe is only about 7,000 years old, no SNR should be old enough to have reached the third stage, so there should be absolutely none, under currently accepted models. This is another test of the two theories; an old versus a young universe.

There are actually no third-stage SNRs with a range of 100–200 parsecs observed in our galaxy! Again, the observations fit the biblical model but contradict the evolutionary one!

Conclusion

Supernova remnant Stage	Number of observed SNRs predicted if our galaxy was:		Number of SNRs actually observed
	billions of years old	7,000 years old	
First	2	2	5
Second	2,260	125	200
Third	5,000	0	0

As shown in the above table, a young universe model fits the data of the low number of observed SNRs. If the universe were really billions of years old, we would have to conclude that more than 97 percent of the SNRs that should be in our galaxy are missing — more than 7,000 altogether. Some evolutionary astronomers, in the context of trying to find solutions to the shortfall, have commented on this as follows, "These two anomalies require explanation. Why have the large number of expected remnants not been detected? Is it reasonable that E_0/n[50] should differ so greatly from our estimates for the galaxy?" And they refer to "The mystery of the missing remnants."[51] They go on to claim:

> Both anomalies are removed if we *assume* that the N(D)-D[52] has been incorrectly estimated, owing to the small number (4) of remnants used. . . .
>
> It appears that, with the above explanation, there is no need to postulate values of E_0/n differing greatly from those in the Galaxy, and the mystery of the missing remnants is solved. It is, however, necessary to *postulate* that the excess (~3) of small-diameter Magellanic Cloud remnants is merely a statistical fluctuation; on current evidence this seems the most plausible explanation.

---

50. Ratio of supernova explosion energy to the number of hydrogen atoms in the interstellar medium.
51. D.H. Clark and J.L. Caswell, "A Study of Galactic Supernova Remnants, Based on Molonglo–Parkes Observational Data," *Monthly Notices of the Royal Astronomical Society* 174:267–306 (1976).
52. D = SNR diameter, N(D) = number of SNRs with diameter <D.

So their solutions are conjectural and assume flaws in previous estimates. But there should be no mystery — the low number of their remnants is a pointer to God's recent creation of the heavens and earth.[53]

5. Comets

Comets[54] lose so much mass every time they pass near the sun in their orbit that they should have evaporated after billions of years. Instead, evolutionists have proposed ad hoc sources to replenish the comet supply. But observations of the region of the proposed Kuiper Belt fail to confirm it as a cometary source. And there is a total absence of observational evidence for the Oort Cloud, among other scientific difficulties for both notions. Ross's published explanation that comets have an interstellar origin was discredited by secular astronomers long ago.

What Are Comets?

Comets are "dirty snowballs" (or "dirty icebergs"[55]) that revolve around the sun in highly elliptical orbits. They are usually a few kilometers across, but Halley's is about 10 km and Hale-Bopp, seen in 1997, is about 40 km and one of the largest comets known. They contain dust and "ice," which is not just frozen water but also frozen ammonia, methane, and carbon dioxide.

How Comets Shine — Problem for Long-agers

When comets pass close to the sun, some of the ice evaporates, and forms a coma about 10,000–100,000 km wide. Also, the solar wind (charged particles radiating from the sun) pushes a tail of ions (electrically charged atoms) directly away from the sun. Solar radiation pushes away dust particles to generate a second tail that curves gently away from the sun and backwards. The coma and tails have a very low density — even the best vacuums produced in laboratories are denser. The earth passed through a tail of Halley's Comet in 1910, and it was hardly noticeable. But they reflect the sun's light very strongly, which can make comets spectacular when they are close to both the sun and the earth. Their appearance like a hairy star is responsible for the term "comet," from the Greek κομητη *comētē* (long-haired).

This loss of material means that the comet is gradually being destroyed every time it comes close to the sun. In fact, many comets have been observed to become much dimmer in later passes. Even Halley's Comet was brighter in the past. However, the pathetic appearance at its last visit in 1986 was more due to unfortunate viewing

---

53. This is compatible with Russell Humphreys' white hole cosmology discussed in chapter 5, as he explains at <www.answersingenesis.org/spiral>.

54. J. Sarfati, "Comets: Portents of Doom or Indicators of Youth?" *Creation* 25(3):36–40 (June–August 2003).

55. Frank Whipple's model, for example, F.L. Whipple, "Background of Modern Comet Theory," *Nature* 263:15 (September 2, 1976). He expressed it more formally as a "dirty ice comet nucleus."

    G. Kuiper, "Present Status of the Icy Conglomerate Model," in J. Klinger, D. Benest, A. Dollfus, and R. Smoluchowski, editors, *Ices in the Solar System* (Dordrecht, Holland: D. Reidel Publishing, 1984), p. 343–366.

conditions. That is, when it was at its brightest, at perihelion (closest approach to the sun), the earth was on the other side of the sun, which therefore blocked it from view. And even when it emerged from behind the sun, it was far from the earth.

Also, comets are in danger of being captured by planets, like Comet Shoemaker-Levy crashing into Jupiter in 1994, or else being ejected from the solar system. A direct hit on earth is unlikely, but could be disastrous because of the comet's huge kinetic (motion) energy. Some evolutionists believe they have caused mass extinctions. The mysterious aerial explosion in Tunguska, Siberia, in 1908, which flattened over 800 sq. miles (2,100 km²) of forest, has been attributed to a comet, but no people were killed because the area was unpopulated.

The problem for evolutionists is that, given the observed rate of loss and maximum periods, comets could not have been orbiting the sun for billions of years since the solar system allegedly formed.[56]

Two Groups of Comets

Comets are divided into two groups: short-period (less than 200 years) comets, such as Halley's (76 years); and long-period (more than 200 years) comets. But the comets from the two groups seem essentially the same in size and composition. Short-period ones normally orbit in the same direction as the planets (prograde) and in almost the same plane (the ecliptic); long-period comets can orbit in almost any plane and in both directions. One exception is the short-period Halley, which has retrograde motion and a highly inclined orbit. Some astronomers suggest that it was once a long-period comet, and strong gravity from a planet dramatically shrank its orbit, and thus the period. So long-period and Halley-type comets are grouped together and called "nearly isotropic comets" (NICs).

The longest period that could be envisaged for a stable orbit would be about 4 million years if the maximum possible aphelion (farthest distance of an orbiting satellite from the sun) were 50,000 AU (AU = astronomical unit, the mean distance from the earth to the sun, 150 million km (93 million miles). This is a conservative estimate, because this is 20 percent of the distance to the nearest star, so there's a fair chance other stars could release the comet from the sun's grip.[57] However, even with an orbit this long, such a comet would still have had time to make 1,200 trips around the sun if the solar system were 4.6 billion years old. But it would have taken far fewer trips around the sun to extinguish the comet, which cannot therefore be anywhere near as old as this. The problem is much more acute with short-period comets.

Empty Evolutionist Explanations

The only solution for evolutionists is hypothetical sources to replenish the supply of comets.

56. C. Wieland, "Halley's Comet: Beacon of Creation," *Creation* 8(2):6–10 (March 1986); <www.answersingenesis.org/halley>. The most thorough article is D. Faulkner, "Comets and the Age of the Solar System," *TJ* 11(3):264–273 (1997); <www.answersingenesis.org/comet>.

57. This comes from Kepler's 3rd law of planetary motion, $a^3 = p^2$, where a is the semi-major axis in AU, and p is the period in years.

Oort Cloud

The best-known hypothetical source is the Oort Cloud, after the Dutch astronomer Jan Hendrik Oort (1900–1992), who proposed it in 1950. This is allegedly a spherical cloud of comets extending as far as three light-years from the sun. It is proposed as a source of long-period comets. Passing stars, gas clouds, and galactic tides are supposed to be able to knock comets from the Oort Cloud into orbits that enter the inner solar system. But there are several problems:

- **No observational support.**[58] Therefore, it's doubtful that the Oort Cloud should be considered a scientific theory. It is really an *ad hoc* device to explain away the existence of long-period comets, given the dogma of billions of years.

- **Collisions would have destroyed most comets.** The classical Oort Cloud is supposed to comprise comet nuclei left over from the evolutionary (nebular hypothesis) origin of the solar system, with a total comet mass of about 40 earths. But a newer study showed that collisions would have destroyed most of these, leaving a combined mass of comets of only about one earth, or at most 3.5 earths with some doubtful assumptions.[59]

- **The "fading problem."** The models predict about 100 times more NICs than are actually observed. So evolutionary astronomers postulate an "arbitrary fading function."[60] A recent proposal is that the comets must disrupt before we get a chance to see them.[61] It seems desperate to propose an unobserved source to keep comets supplied for the alleged billions of years, then make excuses for why this hypothetical source doesn't feed in comets nearly as fast as it should.

Kuiper Belt

The Kuiper Belt is supposed to be a doughnut-shaped reservoir of comets located at about 30–50 AU (beyond Neptune's orbit), postulated as a source of short-period comets. It is named after Dutch astronomer Gerald Kuiper (1905–1973), sometimes considered the father of modern planetary science, who proposed it in 1951.

To remove the evolutionary dilemma, there must be *billions* of comet nuclei in the Kuiper Belt. But astronomers have found nowhere near this many — only 651 as of January 2003.[62] Furthermore, the Kuiper Belt Objects discovered so far are much larger than comets. While the diameter of the nucleus of a typical comet is around

58. C. Sagan and A. Druyan, *Comets* (London: Michael Joseph, 1985), p. 175.

59. S.A. Stern and P.R. Weissman, "Rapid Collisional Evolution of Comets During the Formation of the Oort Cloud," *Nature* 409(6820):589–591 (2001).
   D. Faulkner, "More Problems for the "Oort Comet Cloud," *TJ* 15(2):11 (2001); <www.answersingenesis.org/oort>.

60. M.E. Bailey, "Where Have All the Comets Gone?" *Science* 296(5576):2251–2253 (June 21, 2002), perspective on Levison, following footnote.

61. H.F. Levison et al., "The Mass Disruption of Oort Cloud Comets," *Science* 296(5576):2212–2215 (June 21, 2002).

62. J.M. Parker, editor, *Distant EKOs: The Kuiper Belt Electronic Newsletter* 27 (January 2003); <www.boulder.swri.edu/ekonews/issues/past/n027/html/index.html>.

10 km, the recently discovered KBOs are estimated to have diameters above 100 km. The largest so far discovered is "Quaoar" (2002 LM60), which has a diameter of 1,300 km (800 miles), and orbits the sun in an almost circular orbit.[63] Note that a KBO with a diameter only 10 times that of a comet has about 1,000 times the mass. So in fact there has been no discovery of comets *per se* in the region of the hypothetical Kuiper Belt — thus it is, so far, a non-answer.[64] Therefore, many astronomers refer to the bodies as Trans-Neptunian Objects, which objectively describes their position beyond Neptune without any *assumptions* that they are related to a comet source as Kuiper wanted.

Ross's View: Interstellar Origin

Ross tries to solve the problem by claiming that comets have an interstellar origin (C&T:116–117). But this was amazingly outdated, even at the time he wrote. This is especially surprising for someone who always proclaims what a knowledgeable astronomer he is, and how Christians should accept the consensus view of astronomers, and let it override the grammatical-historical interpretation of Scripture. Almost no astronomer accepts this view today, because the comets would have hyperbolic orbits and speeds exceeding the solar escape velocity. But such are not observed, despite Ross's claim to the contrary (C&T:116). Therefore, while this answer was proposed in the past, virtually no astronomers accept it today. Otherwise, why would there be any need for the Oort Cloud or Kuiper Belt hypotheses, which Ross failed to mention at all in his book? Creationist astronomer Dr. Danny Faulkner rightly regarded this as one of a number of Ross's "blunders that call into question his competence."[65]

6. Lunar Recession

The moon is slowly receding[66] from earth at about 4 cm (12 inches) per year, and the rate would have been greater in the past. But even if the moon had started receding from being in contact with the earth, it would have taken only 1.37 billion years to reach its present distance. This gives a maximum possible age of the moon — not the actual age. This is far too young for evolution (and much younger than the radiometric "dates" assigned to moon rocks).

---

63. The name "Quaoar" (pronounced kwah-o-wahr) comes from the creation mythology of the Tongva people (the San Gabrielino Native Americans). Quaoar was discovered by Chad Trujillo and Mike Brown of Caltech in Pasadena in June 2002.

64. R. Newton, "The Short-period Comets 'Problem' (for Evolutionists): Have Recent 'Kuiper Belt' Discoveries Solved the Evolutionary/Long-age Dilemma?" *TJ* 16(2):15–17 (2002); <www.answersingenesis.org/kuiper>.

65. D. Faulkner, "The Dubious Apologetics of Hugh Ross," *TJ* 13(2):52–60 (1999). But a few years after Dr. Faulkner wrote, Ross interviewed him on his radio show, and the notes on Ross's website cite some papers on the Oort Cloud and Kuiper Belt.

66. D. DeYoung, "The Earth-Moon System," in R.E. Walsh and C.L. Brooks, editors, *Proceedings of the Second International Conference on Creationism* 2:79–84 (1990); J. Sarfati, "The Moon: The Light That Rules the Night," *Creation* 20(4):36–39 (September–November 1998); <www.answersingenesis.org/moon>.

Friction by the tides is slowing the earth's rotation, so the length of a day is increasing by 0.002 seconds per century. This means that the earth is losing *angular momentum*.[67] The *law of conservation of angular momentum* says that the angular momentum the earth loses must be gained by the moon. Thus, the moon is slowly receding from the earth at about 12 inches (4 cm) per year. Also, the rate would have been greater in the past because it is a steep function of the earth-moon distance (inverse sixth power).[68] The moon could never have been closer than 11,500 miles (18,400 km), known as the *Roche limit*, because earth's tidal forces acting on the moon (that is, the result of different gravitational forces on different parts of the moon) would have shattered it.

But even if the moon had started receding from being in contact with the earth, it would have taken only 1.37 billion years to reach its present distance.[69] Note that, once again, this is the *maximum* possible age — far too young for evolution (and much younger than the radiometric "dates" assigned to moon rocks) — not the actual age.

Some have explained this away by postulating that the current rate of tidal interaction is exceptionally large today. If, in more "normal" times, the rate of interaction was less, then we have underestimated the age by having an unusually high rate today. Since the tidal interaction is largely dependent on friction, it depends on the surface contact between oceans and ocean bottoms. So one hope for evolutionists is that a different continental arrangement would have had less surface contact in the past, therefore lower tidal interaction rates.

But the only thing approaching a direct measurement of lunar recession are features such as tidallites, or tidal rhythmites, comprising "layers of finely grained mud beds alternating with sandier, coarser-grained layers, as the tides move in and out on a daily and monthly cycle."[70] This, of course, assumes the evolutionary time scale and interpretation of rhythmites, so once again this is an example of using their assumptions against them. The data have high uncertainties, but they give every indication that today's tidal recession rate is typical, not unusually high. Varves spanning the past 900 Ma (according to evolutionary dating) present strong evidence that the

---

67. Angular momentum = mvr, the product of mass, velocity and distance, and is always conserved (constant) in an isolated system.

68. This is because tidal forces are inversely proportional to the cube of the distance. So the recession rate $dR/dt = k/R^6$, where k is a constant = (present speed: 0.04 m/year) x (present distance: 384,400,000 m)^6 = 1.29×10^{50} m^7/year.

69. Integrating the differential equation in the previous reference gives the time to move from R_i to R_f as $t = \frac{1}{7k}(R_f^7 - R_i^7)$. For R_f = the present distance and R_i = the Roche Limit, t = 1.37 x 10^9 years. There is no significant difference if R_i = 0, i.e., the earth and moon touching, because of the high recession rate (caused by enormous tides) if the moon is close.

70. K.J. Krelove, *The Earth-Moon Tidal System*, Marine Geology honors paper, Pennsylvania State University, May 2000; <www.personal.psu.edu/users/k/j/kjk176/Earth-Moon.htm>, December 12, 2002.

average rate of lunar recession over that interval closely matches the current rate.[71] As one researcher says:

> They can also provide constraints in the fact that tidal amplitudes have remained relatively constant over the time period sampled by tidalites. This is an important consideration, because it forces us to re-examine some of the data derived from early biological time scales and from predictions made based on modern observations of lunar recession. If the tidal amplitudes remained relatively constant or showed only a small increase over 900 million years, we are forced to conclude that a close approach of the Moon to the Earth could not possibly have taken place either within that time span, or close prior to the beginning of that time span, because of the drastic changes in tidal amplitude and duration which would occur in that case. Such "megatides" simply have not occurred in the last 1 billion years, at least, and any model which calls for or even hints at this must be reexamined. . . .

> It can also be concluded on the basis of the record that the moon has been present at least since the Proterozoic and that tides have not changed significantly (have not changed past our ability to reasonably interpret them according to modern patterns) in that time.[72]

However, she accepts the evolutionary age of the earth and concludes that the data demand:

> . . . a Moon formation of not less than about 3.5 billion years ago and much more likely about 4.5 billion years ago, making the age of the Moon on par with the age of the Earth.[73]

However, the data can be interpreted better as showing that the tidal recession we observe today is quite typical of the rates up to 900 Ma (according to evolutionary dating methods). This is almost to the time when the recession curve "steepens" markedly, as she seems to have overlooked. So the moon recession data do seem to seem to be a sound argument against the 4.5 Ga "age."

7. Dinosaur Blood Cells and Hemoglobin

Red blood cells and hemoglobin have been found in some (unfossilized!) dinosaur bone.[74] This was shown by the red globules under the microscope, and also by the chemical signatures of hemoglobin. But these could not last more than a few thousand years — certainly not for 65 million years, the "date" for the extinction of the last dinosaurs.

---

71. C.P. Sonett, E.P. Kvale, A. Zakharian, M.A. Chan, and T.M. Demko, "Late Proterozoic and Paleozoic Tides, Retreat of the Moon, and Rotation of the Earth," *Science* 273:100–104 (1996).

72. See footnote 70.

73. Ibid.

74. C. Wieland, "Sensational Dinosaur Blood Report!" *Creation* 19(4):42–43 (September–November 1997); <www.answersingenesis.org/dino_blood>, based on research by M. Schweitzer and T. Staedter, "The Real Jurassic Park," *Earth* (June 1997): p. 55–57.

Mary Schweitzer, a student of the famous paleontologist "Dinosaur" Jack Horner, was studying thin sections of *T. rex* bones under the microscope at Montana State University. Then, as she describes it:

> The lab filled with murmurs of amazement, for I had focused on something inside the vessels that none of us had ever noticed before: tiny round objects, translucent red with a dark center. Then a colleague took one look at them and shouted, "You've got red blood cells. You've got red blood cells!"[75]

Schweitzer's reaction was a perfect illustration of how one's bias determines the interpretation of the evidence:

> It was exactly like looking at a slice of modern bone. But of course, I couldn't believe it. I said to the lab technician: "The bones are, after all, 65 million years old. How could blood cells survive that long?"[76]

She showed the samples to Horner, who asked, "So you think these are red blood cells?" She replied, "No," and Horner said, "Well, prove that they're not." Schweitzer admitted, "So far, we haven't been able to."[77]

To make sure this was not simply a superficial resemblance, Schweitzer and some chemists from her own university and Wyoming State University analyzed these objects for hemoglobin, the red protein in the blood that carries the oxygen. The active component is known as a heme unit, comprising an iron atom bound to a porphyrin ring — it is the iron atom that loosely bonds to the oxygen molecule. This heme unit has a characteristic absorption spectrum (absorbing light at certain wavelengths) and Raman spectrum (due to molecular vibrational patterns when stimulated by laser light), as well as a particular behavior in a magnetic field (nuclear magnetic resonance and electron spin resonance).[78] The samples displayed these patterns, so Schweitzer said, "We felt fairly comfortable claiming that these dinosaur tissues contained heme."

However, hemoglobin is more than just heme — there are four peptide chains as well. And other proteins contain heme units, for example, cytochromes, which are found in all living organisms including microbes. So to rule out contamination, Schweitzer sent samples to an expert immunologist, who injected extract from the *T. rex* bones into rats. The rats' immune system generated antibodies, which showed that it was homing in on some protein fragments. Heme itself is too small to produce an immune response. Then the rats' blood was filtered to leave only the antibodies, forming an antiserum. This was shown to bond to hemoglobin from modern

75. M. Schweitzer and T. Staedter, "The Real Jurassic Park," *Earth* (June 1997): p. 55–57.

76. M. Schweitzer, Montana State University Museum of the Rockies, cited on p. 160 of V. Morell, "Dino DNA: The Hunt and the Hype," *Science* 261(5118):160–162 (July 9, 1993).

77. See footnote 75.

78. H.M. Schweitzer et al., "Heme Compounds in Dinosaur Trabecular Bone," *PNAS* 94:6291–6296 (June 1997); <www.pnas.org/cgi/reprint/94/12/6291.pdf>.

SCIENCE AND THE YOUNG EARTH · 357

creatures, including birds, crocodiles, and mammals. A control sample, that is, rat serum extracted from before they were injected with *T. rex* substances, did not bond to the modern hemoglobins.

This means that there is enough of the hemoglobin protein in the *T. rex* structures for the rats' immune systems to develop antibodies specific to hemoglobin. Such a specific response shows that there must have been a substantial amount of the hemoglobin protein remaining in the *T. rex* bones.

Heme survival for 65 Ma would be most unlikely, but hemoglobin itself is even more fragile. Schweitzer concluded:

> So far, we think that all of this evidence supports the notion that our slices of *T. rex* bone contain preserved heme and hemoglobin fragments. But more work needs to be done before we are confident enough to come right out and say, "Yes, this *T. rex* bone has blood."

Schweitzer has since claimed:

> We believe that there were possibly 3–4 amino acids from the original protein [which consisted of many hundreds of amino acids] attached to the heme, and that was what may have spiked the immune response.[79]

However, this is outside her field. But AiG's Dr. Pierre Jerlström, a molecular biologist whose Ph.D. thesis included identifying proteins using monoclonal antibodies, is an expert. He is most skeptical of the claim that only 3–4 amino acids, even with the heme, is enough of the protein to be recognized by hemoglobin-sensitive antibodies.[80]

Hemoglobin would not be the only well-preserved protein from dinosaur fossils or fossils of the same assumed age. The protein osteocalcin has been identified in hadrosaur (duck-billed dinosaur) bones from Alberta, Canada.[81] This is a protein specific to bones, so cannot be due to contamination from outside microbes.

And ligaments have been found in fossils "dated" to the same evolutionary "age" as the dinosaurs. Mud springs on the edge of the "market town" of Wootton Bassett, near Swindon, Wiltshire, England, are "pumping up" fossils that are supposed to be 165 million years old.[82] Dr. Neville Hollingworth, paleontologist with the Natural Environment Research Council in Swindon, noted:

> There are the shells of bivalves which still have their original organic ligaments and yet they are millions of years old![83]

79. M. Schweitzer letter to J. DeBaum, 2002.
80. C. Wieland, "Evolutionist Questions AiG Report [Ref. 75]: Have Red Blood Cells Really Been Found in *T. rex* Fossils?" <www.answersingenesis.org/RBC> (March 25, 2002).
81. Muyzer et al., *Geology* 20:871–874 (1992).
82. A. Snelling, "A '165 Million Year' Surprise," *Creation* 19(2):14–17 (March–May 1997); <www.answersingenesis.org/165>.
83. M. Nuttall, "Mud Springs a Surprise after 165 Million Years," *Times*, London, p. 7 (May 2, 1996).

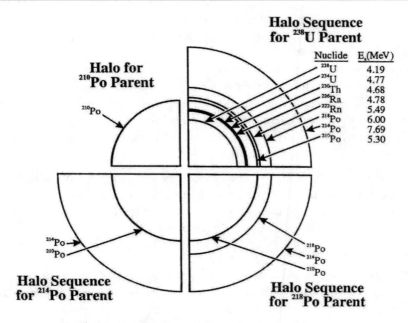

**Characteristic ring configurations for
different parent elements.**

In conclusion, an alternative to Schweitzer's skeptical question about how blood cells could possibly survive for 65 million years is, "I can see the blood cells and detect the chemical and magnetic signatures — in the present! Also, protein and DNA can be seen to break down so fast that they couldn't survive for more than a few tens of thousands of years. So how could they possibly be 65 million years old?"

8. Radiohalos

Polonium radiohalos in granitic rocks provide strong evidence for their rapid formation, and mature uranium radiohalos are good evidence for accelerated radioactive decay. Dual spherical/elliptical polonium halos in coalified wood are indications that much wood was catastrophically uprooted and compressed, and by the same catastrophic flood, although the layers are "dated" at millions of years apart. Also, uranium radiohalo centers in the same wood have so much uranium that they undermine the "established" millions of years of the layers they are in. Ross has tried to address only the rapid formation argument, but merely cites an amateur geologist publishing in a humanist journal, and by dogmatically proclaiming an alternative way of formation that the original researchers admitted was speculative.

Radiohalos are microscopic spheres, typically a few tens of microns across, in certain mineral crystals (one micron [μm] is a millionth of a meter). A good source is the mica mineral biotite, a component of granite, although some halos have been

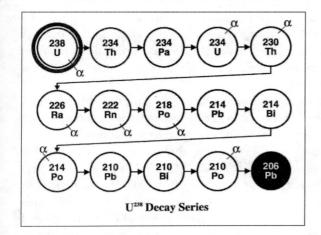

U²³⁸ Decay Series

found in a diamond.[84] Radiohalos are caused by a tiny speck, called the radiocenter, containing one or more radioactive isotopes that emit alpha (α) particles. They stream out from the speck in all directions, and discolor the mineral. This discoloration is most intense at the end of the journey, when the α-particles steal two electrons from any atom in the mineral.

Each particular isotope emits an a of a definite energy, and this means it will travel a definite distance in the mineral. So this will produce a sphere of discoloration of a radius that is characteristic for that element. Also, some isotopes have a decay chain, and some of the isotopes in the chain are also α-emitters. Therefore, a number of concentric spheres will form. In cross section, these spherical halos will be a series of concentric circles.

For example, ^{238}U has 15 isotopes in its "decay chain" (above), including eight that emit a-particles when they decay (including ^{238}U itself), forming eight rings. Of the polonium isotopes, ^{218}Po forms three rings, ^{214}Po forms two, and ^{210}Po forms only one. See schematic diagram of four different types of halos (above).[85]

Rapid Formation

The world's foremost radiohalo researcher for many years was the physicist Dr. Robert Gentry. A large portion of his career was spent at the prestigious Oak Ridge National Laboratories in Tennessee, and he published many papers in leading scientific journals.[86] He pointed out that there were a number of halos from polonium isotopes which have very short half-lives: ^{218}Po (3.1 minutes), ^{214}Po (164 microseconds) and ^{210}Po (138 days). They are "orphan" radiohalos, lacking the small-diameter rings of any ^{238}U "parent."

Since after 10 half-lives, there is only about a thousandth of the original material left, and after 20 there is only about a millionth (2^{10} and 2^{20} respectively), it means that these halos must form within about 20 half-lives, which is a very short

84. M. Armitage, "Internal Radiohalos in a Diamond, *TJ* 9(1):93–101 (1995).

85. R.V. Gentry, *Creation's Tiny Mystery* (Knoxville, TN: Earth Science Associates, 1988), p. 278.

86. R.V. Gentry, "Radioactive Halos," *Annual Review of Nuclear Science* 23:347–362 (1973).

R.V. Gentry, "Spectacle Halos," *Nature* 258:269–270 (1975).

R.V. Gentry, "Radiohalos in a Radiochronological and Cosmological Perspective," *Science* 184:62–66 (1974).

R.V. Gentry et al., "Radiohalos in Coalified Wood: New Evidence Relating to the Time of Uranium Introduction and Coalification," *Science* 194:315–318 (1976).

time scale for these isotopes. Also, they must form in a solid, because in a liquid the tiny spheres would simply dissipate. However, the dilemma is that once a rock has solidified, the polonium can no longer get to the radiocenter, especially in the time taken to decay. Gentry examined the halos for cracks that would allow minerals to get to the radiocenter, but ruled them out.

But then Gentry made the mistake of stating the implications too bluntly: that is, that the halos are *prima facie* evidence of rapid creation of basement granite rocks. After that, publishing avenues were blocked and his contract was ended.[87]

There were a number of criticisms, but hardly any had any merit. Naturally, Ross tries to discount Gentry's evidence (C&T:108–110). For example, Ross cites "geologist" Jeffrey Richard Wakefield as an authority (C&T:109). But he fails to mention that Wakefield is only an amateur geologist and a fireman, and Ross quotes him only in the endnotes of his book, making it less obvious that one of Wakefield's articles was not in the scientific literature but in the atheist-founded anti-creationist *Creation/Evolution* journal.[88] Ross also neglects Gentry's detailed response.[89]

Ross also claims:

> Two more geologists, Leroy Odom and William Rink, recently published an independent response to Gentry's polonium decay hypothesis.[90] They begin by pointing out that there are three classes of unexplained radio halos. In the case of one class, the giant halos, Odom and Rink explained them by another geological process called hole diffusion. (I hesitate to bring it up, because it, too, is far too complicated to explain in a few words to those who are not geologists or solid-state physicists. I would ask you to confirm this research with other geologists or solid-state physicists.)

There is a lot of scientific bluff and bluster in this paragraph. Okay, I have post-graduate training in solid-state physics (unlike Ross), and have asked geologically trained colleagues, and we disagree with Ross! He continues:

> Growth of halos by hole diffusion is an ultraslow process that would argue for an old earth rather than for instantaneous creation. The authors infer that since one of the three "mysterious" classes of radio halos has now been explained in terms of normal (old-earth), known physical processes, it is reasonable to conclude that the same will eventually be accomplished for the two remaining classes, including Gentry's polonium 218 halos.

87. R.V. Gentry, *Creation's Tiny Mystery* (Knoxville, TN: Earth Science Associates, 1988).
88. J.R. Wakefield, "Gentry's Tiny Mystery — Unsupported by Geology," *Creation/Evolution* XXII:13–33 (1988).
89. See footnote 87.
90. A.L. Odom and W.J. Rink, "Giant Radiation-induced Color Halos in Quartz: Solution to a Riddle," *Science* 246:107–109 (1989).

Also, the authors he cites don't agree that they have disproved Gentry, despite Ross's dogmatic claims. Odom wrote to Gentry personally (bold added):

> The *Science* paper was the result of an accidental finding; it is not something we are really working on. **As is obvious in the paper, we have proven nothing** — simply offered an alternative explanation. We had included a question mark at the end of our title of the paper, but it was removed apparently by the editor.

Ross also fails to inform his readers that, at best, Odom expained only one type of halo — one that Gentry doesn't use as evidence! It has no relevance to the polonium halos which are the basis of Gentry's key arguments.

Evidence for Rapid Decay

Some criticisms of the radiohalo argument for rapid *creation* of granite seem cogent. A major one would be radiohalos found in non-basement rocks, for example, the Stone Mountain granite near Atlanta, Georgia,[91] which would mean that they are not the result of the initial creation. However, as will be seen, they are still evidence for rapid *formation,* although not rapid creation.

Also, it seems that the halos from short-lived isotopes are only from those within the ^{238}U decay chain, and none from ^{235}U or ^{232}Th chains, so it could be asked why God didn't create halos directly from the short-lived isotopes within the latter chains. Of course, this is an argument from silence, but it is also consistent with some natural process involving only the ^{238}U chain.

However, this doesn't mean there is no longer any "tiny mystery" for the evolutionists — far from it! The RATE (Radioisotopes and the Age of The Earth) group of creationist geologists and physicists have analyzed halos in granites that they identify as Flood rocks.[92] For example, the Stone Mountain granite and the Cooma granodiorite and four other granitic bodies in southeastern Australia. They could not be creation-week rocks because they have clearly been formed by melting of Flood-deposited fossil-bearing sedimentary rocks, and have intruded into other Flood-deposited rocks.

These rocks all have biotite grains with lots of radiohalos. The main ones are ^{210}Po radiohalos — often 4–10 times the numbers of ^{214}Po or ^{238}U radiohalos — while ^{218}Po radiohalos are very rare. But the Cooma granodiorite and the four other granites of southeastern Australia contain more ^{238}U radiohalos than any of the Po radiohalos, while in two of these granites there are as many ^{214}Po radiohalos as ^{210}Po radiohalos. The Cooma granodiorite also contains many dark, fully formed Th radiohalos.

---

91. M. Armitage, "New Record of Polonium Radiohalos, Stone Mountain Granite, Georgia," *TJ* 15(1):82–84 (2001).

    T. Walker, "New Radiohalo Find Challenges Primordial Granite Claim," *TJ* 15(1):14–16 (2001) [perspective on Armitage, previous footnote].

92. A. Snelling, "Radiohalos — Significant and Exciting Research Results," ICR *Impact* 353 (November 2002); <www.icr.org/pubs/imp/imp-353.htm>.

U and Th have extremely long half-lives — 4.51 billion and 14.1 billion years, respectively. Therefore, the large number of dark, fully formed U and Th radiohalos implies that at least 100 million years worth of radioactive decay at today's rates must have occurred in these granitic rocks since they formed. But these rocks also show rapid formation only recently during the Flood year, so this implies that at least 100 million years worth of radioactive decay at today's rates must have occurred during the Flood year, when geologic processes were operating at catastrophic rates. However, such dark halos are absent in rocks that formed later, although under the uniformitarian dating there should still have been plenty of time. But this is explained if the rocks are really not old enough to have had time for the required amount of decay.

The observed halos in Flood rocks are consistent with a pulse of accelerated radioactive decay during the Flood year. This seriously undermines radiometric dating (see also next chapter). Furthermore, such accelerated radioactive decay would have generated a large pulse of heat during the Flood. This, in turn, would have helped to initiate and drive the global tectonic processes that operated during the Flood year, and to accomplish, catastrophically, much geologic work, including the regional metamorphism of sedimentary strata and the melting of crustal and mantle rocks to produce granitic and other magmas.

Po Halos *Still* Point to Rapid Formation!

While these radiohalos cannot have been primordial, they still must have formed quickly due to the short half-lives. Indeed, the Po must have been separated from its parent U, then transported and concentrated into the radiocenters before it decayed. It's likely that hydrothermal (hot water) processes transported Po and its immediate precursors tiny distances after they formed from U decay in nearby zircons. The radiocenters resulted from ions in lattice defects selectively concentrating Po isotopes, which then decayed and formed the halos. Because hydrothermal liquids are generated as the granitic magmas crystallize, the crystallization must also have been very rapid, a matter of only days, because the water would have carried away the heat quickly.[93]

Radiohalos in Coalified Wood Point to Recent Catastrophe

Gentry analyzed partially coalified logs recovered from uranium mines on the Colorado Plateau.[94] They were found in uranium-rich sedimentary rocks from three different geological formations, assigned radiometric "dates" of 35 to 245 million years. Since these are already granted to be non-primordial, the argument in this section is invulnerable to the criticism advanced against Gentry's other work (which actually requires only modification, not abandonment of his thesis, as shown above).

93. A. Snelling, "Radiohalos — Significant and Exciting Research Results," ICR *Impact* 353 (November 2002); <www.icr.org/pubs/imp/imp-353.htm>.

94. A recent popular-level article is S. Taylor, A. McIntosh, and T. Walker, "The Collapse of 'Geologic Time': Tiny Halos in Coalified Wood Tell a Story That Demolishes 'Long Ages,' " *Creation* 23(4):30–34 (September–November 2001); <www.answersingenesis.org/radiohalo>.

R.V. Gentry et al., "Radiohalos in Coalified Wood: New Evidence Relating to the Time of Uranium Introduction and Coalification," *Science* 194:315–318 (1976).

The main type of halo found here is due to ^{210}Po, with only one ring. The wood had been saturated in uranium-rich solutions, and tiny centers preferentially attracted polonium atoms, which then decayed to form the halos.

This shows what happens when there is a uranium-rich environment and easy percolation — still only the ^{210}Po halos form. The other Po halos do not form, because they decay even more rapidly, so they have no time to diffuse through the coal. This enables us to deduce the time for infiltration: were it to take much more than a year, ^{210}Po would decay before it was concentrated in the radiocenters; but it must have been more than an hour, otherwise ^{218}Po halos would have formed. So this is support for an *especially* rapid formation of the other Po halos in granite.

Dual Spherical and Elliptical ^{210}Po Halos Point to Rapid Compression

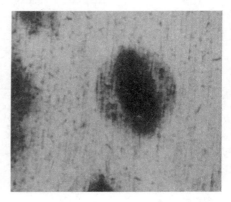

Many of the halos are elliptical, which means that after they had formed they were then compressed in one direction. Even more remarkable are some halos (right) that have a concentric sphere *and* ellipse. This means that after the compression, there was still polonium around to form a second halo. In other words, there could be only a few years between the infiltration and compression. Even if we grant that some was formed by decay of ^{210}Pb via ^{210}Bi, this would still only allow 22 years at most between these events.

These dual halos point to a catastrophic flood, which uprooted large trees over a wide area and deposited them so they were soaked in uranium-rich water. Then they were buried by huge amounts of sediment which squashed the halos quickly.

Furthermore, these dual halos were found in three different formations allegedly spanning 200 million years. But the evidence of an identical sequence of events points to their being deposited by the *same* catastrophe, followed by the same earth movement causing deformation — this is consistent with the global Flood recorded in the Bible.

^{238}U in Radiohalos Should Have Had No Time to Decay

Gentry also analyzed the radiocenters of ^{238}U radiohalos in these coalified wood specimens with the state-of-the-art technique called the ion microprobe. This revealed lots of uranium but hardly any lead — up to 64,000 times as much ^{238}U as the decay-chain–terminating isotope ^{206}Pb. If the decay rate had been constant, it would indicate that the uranium has been around for only a few thousand years, otherwise far more would have decayed to lead. Note that this argument uses the same assumptions as ordinary radiometric dating, but to falsify millions of years — again shooting the evolutionists' arguments down using their own weapons. All three geological formations gave similar results, indicating that they are really the same age, not over 200 million years apart.

Table 11.1 — Erosion Rates of Some Major Rivers of the World

Average lowering of the land surface within the drainage basin in mm (inches) per 1,000 years.[96]

River	Surface lowering/ mm (inches) per millennium
Wei-Ho	1,350 (53)
Hwang-Ho	900 (35)
Ganges	560 (22)
Alpine Rhine and Rhone	340 (13)
San Juan (USA)	340 (13)
Irrawaddy	280 (11)
Tigris	260 (10)
Isere	240 (9.4)
Tiber	190 (7.5)
Indus	180 (7.1)
Yangtse	170 (6.7)
Po	120 (4.7)
Garonne and Colorado	100 (3.9)
Amazon	71 (2.8)
Adige	65 (2.6)
Savannah	33 (1.3)
Potomac	15 (0.59)
Nile	13 (0.51)
Seine	7 (0.28)
Connecticut	1 (0.04)

9. Erosion of Continents

Continents are being eroded so rapidly[95] that they should have been worn away completely over billions of years. The problem is more acute in mountainous regions, and there are huge plains with hardly any erosion. Ross tries to address the continental wearing problem by positing that uplift balances the erosion. But this fails to explain the existence of erosion surfaces that are "dated" as very ancient.

Water is constantly eroding the continents, by dissolving many minerals, loosening soil and rock from the landscape, and transporting them to the ocean. The rate can be estimated by sampling the mouth of the river and measuring the volume of water discharged from the basin and the amount of sediment it carries. There is also "bed load," or sediment rolled or pushed along the bottom of the river, which is harder to measure. The erosion rate must be even greater because of rare catastrophic events.

All the same, sedimentologists have calculated the rate of land disappearance from their river sediment measurements. They show some rivers are excavating their basins by more than 39 inches (1,000 mm) of height in 1,000 years, while others move only 0.04 inches (1 mm) in 1,000 years. The average height reduction for all the

95. T. Walker, "Eroding Ages," *Creation* 22(2):18–21 (March–May 2000); <www.answersingenesis. org/erosion>.

96. From Ariel Roth, *Origins: Linking Science and Scripture* (Hagerstown, MD: Review and Herald Publishing, 1998), p. 264,.

continents of the world is about 2.4 inches (60 mm) per 1,000 years (Table 11.1), and this is from the estimated 24 million tons of sediment per year disappearing into the oceans.

Why Are the Continents Still Here?

The rates quoted in the previous section don't sound like much, but they add up to huge amounts over the alleged billions of years. A height of 93 miles (150 kilometers) of continent would have eroded in 2.5 billion years. Therefore, if erosion had been going on for billions of years, no continents would remain on the earth. For example, North America should have been leveled in 10 million years if erosion has continued at the average rate.[97] Note that this is once more an upper limit, not an actual age, but it is far shorter than the supposed 2.5-billion-year age for the continents.

This is a conservative estimate, because many rivers erode the height of their basins much faster than average (Table 11.1). Even at the slowest rate of 0.04 inches (1 mm) reduction in height per 1,000 years, the continents, with an average height of 2,000 feet (623 meters), should have vanished long ago. Furthermore, if anything, the climate was wetter in the past, which would mean that the erosion rate we measure now is slower than it was back then.

Mountains

The problem for evolutionists is even more acute with ancient mountains. In general, mountainous regions with their steep slopes and deep valleys are eroded fastest. Erosion rates of 39-inch (1,000-mm) height reduction per 1,000 years are typical for the mountainous regions of Papua, New Guinea, Mexico, and the Himalayas.[98] The rates have been as high as 750 inches (19,000 mm) per 1,000 years from a volcano in Papua, New Guinea.[99]

Plains

An opposite problem exists for allegedly ancient plains, which can stretch over huge areas but look pristine. It stretches credulity that areas could have lasted for millions of years with hardly any signs of erosion or having had any other layers on them. For example, Kangaroo Island in southern Australia is about 87 miles (140 km) long and 37 miles (60 km) wide and is extremely flat. But it is "dated" at over 160 million years old, based on the fossil content and radiometric dating.[100] One would expect that exposure to 160 million years of rain would result in some sort of channelization of the landscape, but there is very little.

---

97. Ariel Roth, *Origins: Linking Science and Scripture* (Hagerstown, MD: Review and Herald Publishing, 1998), p. 271, quotes Dott and Batten, *Evolution of the Earth* (New York: McGraw-Hill, 1988), p. 155, and a number of others.

98. Ariel Roth, *Origins: Linking Science and Scripture* (Hagerstown, MD: Review and Herald Publishing, 1998), p. 266.

99. C.D. Ollier and M.J.F. Brown, "Erosion of a Young Volcano in New Guinea, *Zeitschrift für Geomorphologie* 15:12–28 (1971), cited by Ariel Roth, *Origins: Linking Science and Scripture* (Hagerstown, MD: Review and Herald Publishing, 1998), p. 272.

100. See footnote 98.

Ross's Response

Ross tries to address the argument, but only touches on the erosion of the continents without addressing the additional problems of mountains and plains. He writes (C&T:104):

> This argument looks at one side of the equation only. The fallacy lies in its failure to acknowledge that lava flows, delta and continental shelf buildup (from eroded material), coral reef buildup, and uplift from colliding tectonic plates occur at rates roughly equivalent to, and in many cases, far exceeding the erosion rate. The Himalayas, for example, as a result of tectonic uplift, are rising at a rate of 9 millimeters per year. Lava flows have increased the land area of the state of Hawaii by several square miles since its admission into the United States in 1959.

However, this overlooks the fact that uplift balancing the erosion would mean that the mountains would have been eroded and replaced many times over in 2.5 billion years. If that were so, we would therefore not expect to find any old sediment in mountainous areas if they had been eroded and replaced many times. Yet, surprisingly, sediments of all ages from young to old (by evolutionary dating methods) are preserved in mountainous regions. The alleged antiquity of erosion surfaces is indeed a huge problem for conventional dating methods, although old-earth geologists cling to the dates in the face of "common sense." The renowned geomorphologist C. Rowl Twidale writes:

> If some facets of the contemporary landscape are indeed as old as is suggested by the field evidence they not only constitute a denial of commonsense and everyday observations but they also carry considerable implications for general theory.[101]

Creationist meteorologist Michael Oard wrote a response to Twidale's paper and sent it to the same journal, but of course it was rejected simply on the grounds that it challenged the long-age/evolution paradigm.[102]

Summary

This chapter was not trying to "prove" the Bible's time scale with science. And all scientific arguments on the age of things can only ever be tentative, anyway. Rather, it showed that there are many physical processes that point to a "young age," even granting uniformitarian assumptions. Therefore, this turns the evolutionists' weapons against them. Where Ross tries to counter these "young-earth" arguments, he ignores the most detailed and up-to-date formulations of them or otherwise misrepresents them.

---

102. C.R. Twidale, "Antiquity of Landforms: An 'Extremely Unlikely' Concept Vindicated," *Australian Journal of Earth Sciences* 45:657–668 (1998).

103. M. Oard, "Antiquity of Landforms: Objective Evidence That Dating Methods Are Wrong," *TJ* 14(1):35–39 (2000).

CHAPTER 12

REFUTING OLD-EARTH ARGUMENTS

The final authority, the Bible, shows that the earth cannot be billions of years old. Old-earth beliefs conflict with the biblical data of creation in six ordinary days, recent creation of man on the sixth day, and death of humans and animals arising from Adam's sin. Science cannot override Scripture, especially when science is limited in dealing with the past. But it is still useful to provide answers to many of the usual, supposedly scientific, arguments for age put forward by Ross and his fellow travelers.

This chapter refutes some of the most common old-earth arguments from geology, showing how the evidence fits best with a global Flood. For example, several observationally verified mechanisms have produced fine layers very quickly, while no one has actually observed them forming over many thousands of years, and the latter explanation fails to explain preservation of highly unstable fish coprolites within the layers.

A major argument for long ages is radiometric dating. The second half of this chapter explains how this works and the assumptions behind it. It also shows how recent findings of (short-lived) radiocarbon in "old" samples, including a diamond, fatally undermines millions of years.

VARVES

A common argument against the Bible involves varves — finely laminated rock formations with alternating fine layers or *laminae* (singular *lamina*). Each varve consists of two distinct layers of sediment, a lower layer of light-colored silty or sandy material and an upper layer of darker silt or clay. Annual changes are *assumed* to cause the light layers to be deposited in summer and the dark layers in winter. Varves are observed to form today in lakes fed by glacial meltwater. However, it is claimed that some ancient rock formations contain hundreds of thousands of varves, "proving" that the earth is much older than the Bible says.[1]

Note that the observational evidence in these rocks in the *present* is merely for laminæ. The term "varve" already carries *interpretive baggage* about how they are

---

1. A. Hayward, *Creation and Evolution: The Facts and Fallacies* (London: Triangle, 1985), p. 87–88.

supposed to have been formed in the unobservable *past*. Indeed, not all layered rocks are *varvites*, containing annual couplet layers. Some layered sediments are known to be the result of cyclical changes, such as waves or tides, and are called *rhythmites*. If the laminæ are not regular, the rock is called a *laminite*.

As will be shown below, the scientific evidence from the laboratory and the field show that violent events like the Flood described in Genesis and post-flood catastrophes could have deposited such layered formations quickly.

Laboratory Simulations

The French sedimentologist Guy Berthault studied sedimentation in the laboratory, including experiments at the Colorado State University.[2] He discovered that fine bands form automatically as the moving water transports the different-sized particles sideways into position.[3] Surprisingly, the thickness of each band was found to depend on the relative particle sizes, rather than the flow conditions.[4] The evolutionary journal *Nature* published a cover story about the fact that multiple laminæ can form rapidly.[5]

In one of Berthault's experiments, finely layered sandstone and diatomite rocks were broken into their constituent particles, and allowed to settle under running water at various speeds. It was found that the same layer thicknesses were reproduced, regardless of flow rate. This suggests that the original rock was produced by a similar self-sorting mechanism, followed by cementing of the particles

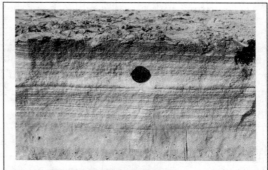

Figure 12:1: Top picture shows rapid layering in beach sand, with a lens cap for scale. The bottom picture shows detail of some of the layering.

2. <http://geology.ref.ac/berthault/>.

3. P. Julien, Y. Lan, and G. Berthault, "Experiments on Stratification of Heterogeneous Sand Mixtures, *TJ* 8(1):37–50 (1994); <www.answersingenesis.org/sandstrat>.

4. G. Berthault, "Experiments on Lamination of Sediments," *TJ* 3:25–29 (1988); <www.answersingenesis.org/sedexp>.

5. H.A. Makse, S. Havlin, P.R. King, and H.E. Stanley, "Spontaneous Stratification in Granular Mixtures, *Nature* 386(6623):379–382 (March 27, 1997).

   A. Snelling, "Nature Finally Catches Up," *TJ* 11(2):125–126 (1997); <www.answersingenesis.org/sednature>.

together.[6] Laminations can also be produced in the laboratory, in air, and even in a vacuum. The laboratory simulations show that all that's required are differently sized particles and some component of horizontal flow.

On a beach in Queensland, Australia, a sand slurry (30 percent sand and 70 percent water) was pumped at a rate of 400,000 liters (100,000 gallons, equivalent to 10 private swimming pools) per minute. This deposited about a meter (3–4 feet) of fine layers on a beach over an area the size of a football field in one hour (see picture).[7] This would be explained by Berthault's sedimentological observations.

Mount St. Helens

Recent catastrophes have been observed to deposit banded rock formations very quickly. For example, the Mount St. Helens eruption in Washington state on June 12, 1980, produced a significant thickness of finely layered sediment (see photo on page 370) in less than five hours![8] Thus, the claim that laminæ *require* a year to form each one is wrong.

The Mount St. Helens laminae were produced by a pyroclastic flow, which is hot ash and gas, surging at hurricane speeds. So some critics argue that this process is inapplicable to laminæ formed under water. But the *principle* is the same — as long as there are particles of mixed size and horizontal flow, laminæ can be formed. Thus, it is proper to use this example to show that laminæ need not take many years to form.

Ross manages to misconstrue the creationist argument about Mount St. Helens (C&T:110–112). We do not claim it is *proof* of a young earth; rather, we point out that this shows that many features, such as thick layers, fine laminæ, and canyons, *need not* take a long time to form. Further, creationists have *observational* evidence that these features can form rapidly, while the uniformitarians have *no observations* of these features forming over millions of years.

Turbidity Currents

In the field, an underwater landslide or turbidity current can even transport fine clay and silt to the bottom of a lake. Once the current dissipates, there will be a cloud of clay particles suspended above the deposited silt or sand. While clay particles might take years to settle in a quiet lake, with a turbidity current there is far less distance for them to settle so it could happen quickly. This results in a varve-like couplet. And the turbidity currents produce the same thickness of light and dark sediment. So this process will produce a "varve" couplet very quickly. There are a number of examples in the field where a number of varve-like layers were produced very quickly.[9] This is a different mechanism from Berthault's.

---

6. See footnote 4.
7. D. Batten, "Sandy Stripes: Do Many Layers Mean Many Years?" *Creation* 19(1):39–40 (1997); <www.answersingenesis.org/sandy>.
8. K. Ham, "I Got Excited at Mount St. Helens!" *Creation* 15(3):14–19 (1993).
   S. Austin, editor, *Grand Canyon: Monument to Catastrophe* (Santee, CA: ICR, 1994), p. 37–38.

Photo by Steve Austin

Figure 12.2: Fine layering was produced within hours on June 12, 1980, by a flow of hot ash and gas surging at hurricane speeds from the crater of Mount St. Helens volcano in Washington. The layered deposit dwarfs the person in the picture, and is exposed in the middle of the cliff. It is over debris from the May 18, 1980, eruption and under a mudflow from the March 19, 1982, eruption.

Green River Formation

Long-agers often make much of the Green River laminæ.[10] However, these bands cannot possibly be annual deposits, because well-preserved fish and birds are found all through the sediments. It is unthinkable that these dead animals could have rested on the bottom of the lake for decades, being slowly covered by sediment. Their presence indicates catastrophic burial.

It is often claimed that the fish and birds remained in prime condition at the bottom of the lake because the water was highly alkaline and this preserved their carcasses. Yet highly alkaline water causes organic material to disintegrate, which is why alkaline powder is used in dishwashers! Also, scientists from the Chicago Natural History Museum have shown that fish carcasses lowered onto the muddy bottom of a marsh decay quite rapidly, even in oxygen-poor conditions. In these experiments, fish

9. M.J. Oard, "Varves — The First 'Absolute' Chronology. Part I — Historical Development and the Question of Annual Deposition," *CRSQ* 29(2):72–80 (1992).

M.J. Oard, "Varves — The First 'Absolute' Chronology. Part II — Varve Correlation and the Post-glacial Timescale," *CRSQ* 29(3):120–125 (1992).

10. See refutation by P. Garner, "Green River Blues," *Creation* 19(3):18–19 (1997).

were placed in wire cages to protect them from scavengers, yet after only six-and-a-half days all the flesh had decayed and even the bones had become disconnected.[11]

Many of the Green River formation's fish fossils show evidence of *tetany* (extreme muscle spasms), which evidently squeezed out the intestinal contents, explaining the observed *coprolites* (fossil dung). Experiments on modern fish feces show that they must be buried in less than 24 hours if they are to be preserved as coprolites in the fossil record.[12] This is strong evidence that the Green River formation layers were formed catastrophically, because if the laminae were semi-annual, the dung would not be fossilized.

Another problem for the varve explanation is that the number of bands is not consistent across the Green River formation as it should be if they were annual deposits. Rather, the number of shale layers between two ash bed "horizons" (which each supposedly formed from a single volcanic event, and thus represent a point in time) varied from 1,160 to 1,568. That means that the number of "years" allegedly recorded between these two events increases by 35 percent from the basin center to the basin margin![13]

"EVAPORITES"

Similar bands in some huge deposits of calcium carbonate and calcium sulphate in Texas are also used to argue the case for long ages.[14] One explanation says the deposits were formed when the sun evaporated seawater — hence, the term "evaporite deposits." Naturally, it would take a long time to evaporate the volume of water needed, considering the size of the deposit. However, the high chemical purity of the deposits shows they were not exposed to a dry, dusty climate for thousands of years. Rather, a better scientific explanation is that they formed rapidly from the interaction between hot and cold seawater during undersea volcanic activity — a hydrothermal deposit.[15]

TOO MANY FOSSILS?

Another claim of biblioskeptics is that there are "too many fossils."[16] If all those animals could be resurrected, it is said, they would cover the entire planet to a depth of at least 0.5 meters. So they could not have come from a single generation of

---

11. R. Zangerl and E.S. Richardson, "The Paleoecological History of Two Pennsylvanian Black Shales," *Fieldiana: Geology Memoirs* 4 (1963).

12. D. Woolley, "Fish Preservation, Fish Coprolites and the Green River Formation," *TJ* 15(1):105–11 (2001).

13. H.P. Buchheim and R. Biaggi, "Laminae Counts within a Synchronous Oil Shale Unit: A Challenge to the 'Varve' Concept," *Geological Society of America Abstracts with Programs* 20:A317 (1988).

14. A. Hayward, *Creation and Evolution: The Facts and Fallacies* (London: Triangle, 1985), p. 89–91.

15. E. Williams, "Origin of Bedded Salt Deposits," *Creation Research Society Quarterly* 26(1):15–16 (1989).

16. A. Hayward, *Creation and Evolution: The Facts and Fallacies* (London: Triangle, 1985), p. 125–126.

living creatures buried by the Flood.[17] Like all criticisms of the Bible, the substance disappears when the detail is examined. The number of fossils is calculated from an abnormal situation — the Karroo formation in South Africa. In this formation the fossils comprise a "fossil graveyard" — the accumulation of animal remains in a local "sedimentary basin."[18] It is certainly improper to apply this abnormally high population density to the whole earth.

The calculation also uses incorrect information on today's animal population densities and takes no account of the different conditions that likely applied before the Flood. In fact, although critics claim that the reptile population densities are impossible, they actually exist on the earth today. John Woodmorappe shows that a population density of 800 animals per hectare results if the supposed 800 billion Karroo vertebrates are evenly spread over Africa south of the equator (10 million km^2). But studies of present habitats over wide areas show that iguanid lizards can live at 889 animals per hectare, anoles up to 110,000, Manchuria island pit viper 10,000, Colorado rattlesnakes 1,235.[19]

BIODEPOSITS

Unfortunately, Ross also dusts off some old arguments which allege the impossibility of the earth's biodeposits to have come from the global Flood (GQ:156–159, 208).

Too Much Coal?

Like biblioskeptics, Ross claims that there is too much coal in the earth's crust for it to have been formed in the Flood (GQ:156–158). Even worse, as "evidence," he cites some calculations from a *TJ* paper, "Too Much Coal for a Young Earth?"[20] However, the whole point of this paper was to *solve* that problem, by showing evidence that much coal had formed from large floating ecosystems comprising arboreal lycopods (club mosses), which had been catastrophically buried by water.

The fossil roots found in these layers are called *stigmariae.* Attached to these, we often still find the secondary roots, or *appendices.* These were arranged in life as shown in Fig. 12.3, coming out like spokes from a central hub. This is possible only if the roots were in water rather than soil.[21]

In the first edition of GQ, Ross also *omitted the question mark* when citing the title, thus further conveying to his readers the *diametrically opposite meaning* to the paper's intention.

---

17. Creationists accept that some fossils formed post-Flood, but the number of these is relatively small and does not alter the argument.
18. Carl Froede, "The Karroo and Other Fossil Graveyards," *Creation Research Society Quarterly* 32(4), p. 199–201 (1996).
19. John Woodmorappe, "The Antediluvian Biosphere and Its Capability of Supplying the Entire Fossil Record," in R.E. Walsh, editor, *Proceedings of the First International Conference on Creationism,* Creation Science Fellowship, Pittsburgh, II:205–218 (1986).
20. G. Schönknecht and S. Scherer, "Too Much Coal for a Young Earth?" *TJ* 11(3)278–282 (1997).
21. C. Wieland, "Forests That Grew on Water," *Creation* 18(1): 20–24 (December 1995–February 1996);<www.answersingenesis.org/forest>.

In the second edition of GQ, p. 227, Ross at least corrects the title by adding a question mark, and admits that they were trying to solve the problem. But Ross claims:

> While claiming to solve the problem of too much coal (by appealing to impossibly high conversion rates of solar energy to coal), the authors admit no solution exists when all the fossil fuel deposits (coal, oil, gas, peat, and kerogen) are considered.

Figure 12.3 Model and diagram (inset) of the central stigmarian root with radial appendices. Such a pattern is found in floating, not land, plants. Both the root and the appendices were hollow (air-filled).

And of course, their problems are exacerbated when one adds the remainder of biodeposits, namely top soil, limestone, marble, coral reefs, etc. to the fossil fuel deposits.

First, Ross misses the point of the paper, that is, the extra carbon source of floating ecosystems, not any "impossibly high conversion rates," for which we have only Ross's word. Second, the authors admitted nothing of the kind — not having a solution completely worked out is hardly the same as "no solution exists."

Third, the last part is just "elephant hurling," a tactic discussed earlier.

It's worth noting that Woodmorappe had shown long ago that vegetation living at the start of the Flood was not the only source of carbonaceous material which was eventually transformed into coal. There were about 1,600 years between the creation and Flood, enabling much peat to form, which could have been buried by the Flood and easily transformed into coal since.[22] It turns out that, contrary to the imaginations of critics, plant productivity during the antediluvian era is more than sufficient to account for all of the organic carbon stored in the earth's crust.

Even today, farmers in the U.S. Midwest commonly get yields of 10 tons/hectare of corn per year. This represents 10^4 kg/10^4 m^2 or 1 kg/m^2 per year. If we assume 1,500 years of such productivity before the Flood, this is 1500 kg/m^2 which corresponds to the equivalent of a meter-thick layer of coal. If we multiply by the area of the earth, 5×10^{14} m^2, we get 7.5×10^{17} kg or 750,000 gigatons of hydrocarbon. This easily accounts for all the biomass represented in the coal, oil, oil shale, and fossiliferous limestone in the geological record.

---

22. See footnote 19. Recently reprinted in J. Woodmorappe, *Studies in Flood Geology*, second edition (El Cajon, CA: Institute for Creation Research, 1999), p. 15–20.

Photo by J. Scheven

Kerogen

Kerogen is fossilized material in shale and other sedimentary rock that yields oil upon heating. Ross uses this as a long-age indicator. But Ross has again misled his readers. He insists that, based on carbon-isotope signatures, kerogens are of organic origin (GQ:158). However, the authors of the study which Ross cites have subsequently acknowledged that their original computations were in error.[23] While still preferring an organic origin for isotopically light carbon, they acknowledge that the new calculations cannot rule out an inorganic origin for such carbon. This would occur, for instance, if the metamorphic temperatures were high enough, and if the metamorphic conditions were unusually oxidizing. In fact, Naraoka et al. have shown that the distribution of the isotopically light carbon deposits shows a trend consistent with a two-component mixing model,[24] and this suggests an inorganic, instead of biogenic, origin of the isotopically light carbon which Ross cites.

Fossil Forests

The petrified forests of Yellowstone National Park have often been used to argue against Bible chronology.[25] These were once interpreted as buried and petrified in place — as many as 50 successive times, with a brand new forest growing upon the debris of the previous one. Naturally, such an interpretation would require hundreds of thousands of years to deposit the whole sequence, and is inconsistent with the biblical time scale. But this interpretation is also inconsistent with the fact that the tree trunks and stumps have been broken off just below ground level and do not have proper root systems. Furthermore, Dr. Michael Arct analyzed cross-sections of 14 trees in different levels spanning 23 feet (7 meters). He found that they all shared the same distinctive signature, and that four of them had died only seven, four, three, and two years before the other ten. These ten had apparently perished together, and the evidence was consistent with them all having been uprooted and transported by successive mud flows.[26]

Rather than 50 successive forests, the geological evidence is more consistent with the trees having been uprooted from another place, and carried into position by catastrophic, volcanic, mudflows — similar to what happened during the Mount St. Helens eruption in 1980.[27]

23. J.M. Eiler et al., "Carbon Isotope Evidence for Early Life," *Nature* 386:665 (1997).

24. H. Naraoka et al., "Non-biogenic Graphite in 3.8-Ga Metamorphic Rocks from the Isua District, Greenland," *Chemical Geology* 133:251–260 (1996).

25. A. Hayward, *Creation and Evolution: The Facts and Fallacies* (London: Triangle, 1985), p. 128–130.

26. M.J. Arct, "Dendroecology in the Fossil Forests of the Specimen Creek Area, Yellowstone National Park," *Ph.D. Dissertation*, Loma Linda University, 1991; *Dissertation Abstracts International* 53–06B:2759, 1987–1991.

27. H.G. Coffin, "Mount St. Helens and Spirit Lake," *Origins*, Geoscience Research Institute, 10(1):9–17 (1983).

H.G. Coffin, "The Yellowstone Petrified Forests, *Origins*, Geoscience Research Institute, 24(1): Special Edition (1992).

J. Sarfati, "The Yellowstone Petrified Forests," *Creation* 21(2):18–21 (1999).

J. Morris, *The Young Earth* (Green Forest, AR: Master Books, Inc., 1994), p. 112–117.

Noah's Mud-Bath?

Some attempts to discredit the Bible are wildly absurd — like the idea that there is too much sedimentary rock in the world for it to have been deposited by the one-year Flood. It is claimed that the ark would have floated on an ocean of "earthy soup" and no fish could have survived.[28] This argument takes no account of how water actually carries sediment. The claim naively assumes that all the sediment was evenly mixed in all the water throughout the Flood year, as if thoroughly stirred in a "garden fishpond." Sedimentation does not occur like this. Instead, moving water transports sediment into a "basin" and, once deposited, it is isolated from the system.[29] The same volume of water can pick up more sediment as it is driven across the continents — for example, by earth movements during the Flood.

Other Old-Earth Arguments

- Some modern coral reefs are extremely thick and must have taken millions of years to grow.[30] [Actually, what was thought to be coral "reef" turns out to be thick carbonate platforms, most probably deposited during the Flood.[31] The reef is only a very thin layer on top.]

- Fossil reefs are found within the geological layers and must have taken longer than a year to form, hence the layers could not all have been formed during the Flood. [In all cases studied to date, it seems that the "reef" is not a reef. It did not grow in place from coral but was transported there by water.[32]]

- Chalk deposits need millions of years to accumulate.[33] [Chalk accumulation is not steady state but highly episodic. Under cataclysmic flood conditions explosive blooms could produce the chalk beds in a short space of time.[34]

- Granites need millions of years to cool.[35] [Not when the cooling effects of circulating water are allowed for.[36] Furthermore, slow cooling is not necessary to form large crystals such as in granite. Large crystals can be produced when

28. A. Hayward, *Creation and Evolution: The Facts and Fallacies* (London: Triangle, 1985), p. 122.
29. P. Julien, Y. Lan, and G. Berthault, "Experiments on Stratification of Heterogeneous Sand Mixtures, *TJ* 8(1):37–50 (1994); <www.answersingenesis.org/sandstrat>.
30. See footnote 28, p. 84–87.
31. M.J. Oard, "The Paradox of Pacific Guyots and a Possible Solution for the Thick "Reefal" Limestone on Eniwetok Island," *TJ* 13(1):1–2 (1999).
32. A.A. Roth, "Fossil Reefs and Time," *Origins* 22(2):86–104 (1995).
33. A. Hayward, *Creation and Evolution: The Facts and Fallacies* (London: Triangle, 1985), p. 91–92.
34. A.A. Snelling, "Can Flood Geology Explain Thick Chalk Beds? *TJ* 8(1):11–15 (1994).
35. A. Hayward, *Creation and Evolution: The Facts and Fallacies* (London: Triangle, 1985), p. 93.
36. A. Snelling and J. Woodmorappe, "Granites — They Didn't Need Millions of Years of Cooling," *Creation* 21(1):42–44 (1998).

the nucleation rate is low and the rate of growth is high, which would occur if physico-chemical conditions changed rapidly.[37]]

- Metamorphic rocks need million of years to form.[38] [Metamorphic reactions happen quickly when there is plenty of water. During the Flood there was lots of water, and actually it is the slow-and-gradual, "long-age" geologists who have a problem.[39]]

- Sediment cover kilometers thick over metamorphic rocks took millions of years to erode.[40] [Only at the erosion rates observed today. There is no problem eroding kilometers of sediment quickly with large volumes of fast-moving water during the Flood.][41]

RADIOMETRIC DATING

Probably, the favorite "proof" of "deep time" is radiometric dating. Ross even published a major article[42] in his newsletter and his website defending this process, and this was claimed to be "faith building." But in reality, this paper simply regurgitates the basic theory about how radioactive dating should work. It looks impressive because he goes into so much detail. However, he does not address any problems in practice with the methods, nor does he discuss the sources of error or examples of errors. And while it was called "A Christian Perspective," it was indistinguishable from an atheist's perspective, citing many overtly atheistic anti-creationist sources.

How Radiometric Dating Works

Each chemical element usually has several different forms, or *isotopes*, which have different masses. Some isotopes, such as carbon-14, potassium-40 and all those of uranium, undergo radioactive decay to produce "daughter" isotopes of a different element. By measuring the quantities of radioactive isotopes and their daughter isotopes, secular geologists claim they can determine how much time has elapsed since a specific time in the past, such as when the rock cooled and crystallized from an initially molten state.

---

37. S. Swanson, "Relation of Nucleation and Crystal Growth Rate to the Development of Granitic Textures," *American Mineralogist* 62:966–978 (1977).

T. Walker, "Granite Grain Size: Not a Problem for Rapid Cooling of Plutons," *TJ* 17(2):31–37 (2003).

38. See footnote 33.

39. A.A. Snelling, "Towards a Creationist Explanation of Regional Metamorphism," *TJ* 8(1):51–77 (1994); <www.answersingenesis.org/regmet>. See also K. Wise, "How Fast Do Rocks Form?" in R.E. Walsh et al., editors, *Proceedings of the First International Conference on Creationism* (Pittsburgh, PA: Creation Science Fellowship, 1986), p. 197–204.

40. A. Hayward, *Creation and Evolution: The Facts and Fallacies* (London: Triangle, 1985)

41. Many of these answers to skeptics were based on T. Walker, "Geology and the Young Earth: Answering Those 'Bible-believing' Bibliosceptics," *Creation* 21(4):16–20 (September–November 1999); <www.answersingenesis.org/geol_ye>.

42. R.C. Wiens, "Radiometric Dating: A Christian Perspective," <www.reasons.org/resources/apologetics/radiometricdating/index.shtml?main>, July 24, 2003.

Half-lives, Decay Constants, and Dating Methods

The time t since radioactive decay commenced can be given by $N/N_0 = e^{-\lambda t}$, where N is the number of atoms measured in the present; N_0 is the initial number; λ, the decay constant, which is related to the half-life $t_{1/2}$ by $\lambda = \ln2/t_{1/2}$.

The half-life is the time taken for an isotope to decay to half its initial amount. After 2 half-lives, a quarter is left; after 3 half-lives, only an eighth; after 10 half-lives, less than a thousandth is left.

Atoms can decay by:

- Alpha (α) decay, mainly for heavier isotopes, where the nucleus emits a helium nucleus (two protons and two neutrons).

- Beta (β) decay, where a nucleus has too many neutrons, so one turns into a proton and emits an electron and anti-neutrino.

- Positron emission or β decay, where a nucleus has too many protons, so one turns into a neutron and emits a positron (anti-electron) and neutrino.

- Electron capture, where the nucleus captures one of the atom's electrons, which turns a proton into a neutron and emits a neutrino.

Some radiometric dating methods include:

- ^{14}C (carbon-14) which beta-decays into ^{14}N (nitrogen-14), but the ratio $^{14}C/^{12}C$ is measured; $t_{1/2} = 5,700$ years. This is normally used for objects that contain matter derived from living creatures, since they contain carbon and the starting condition is well defined (time of death).

- ^{40}K-^{40}Ar 11% of the alkali metal potassium decays into the inert gas argon by electron capture; $t_{1/2} = 1.25$ Ga. The remainder beta decays into ^{40}Ca. This is the most popular method for dating rocks, because of the abundance of potassium in rocks and because a gas like argon should easily escape from liquid magma and not be present originally.

- $^{238}U/^{206}Pb$, $^{235}U/^{207}Pb$ and $^{232}Th/^{208}Pb$ — specific isotopes of uranium and thorium turning into specific isotope forms of lead, via a series of intermediates involving both alpha and beta decay. Half-lives are 4.47, 0.704 and 14.1 Ga.

- ^{207}Pb-^{206}Pb — the ratio of these lead isotopes changes with time — ^{207}Pb forms faster because it comes from the faster decaying ^{235}U.

- ^{87}Rb-^{87}Sr — the alkali metal rubidium beta decays into the alkaline earth strontium; $t_{1/2} = 48.8$ Ga.

- ^{147}Sm-^{143}Nd — involves two lanthanide or rare earth elements, where a samarium isotope alpha decays into a neodymium isotope; $t_{1/2} = 106$ Ga, the longest half-life of any of the elements commonly used in radiometric dating.

However, the actual scientific data are isotope ratios; the deep time "determination" is an *interpretation*. There are other possible interpretations, depending on the assumptions. This can be illustrated with an hourglass, which represents the solid rock containing the radioactive isotopes. Consider that the sand in the top container represents the parent isotope, the sand in the bottom container represents the daughter isotope, and the sand flow between the two represents radioactive decay.

Figure 12.4: The hourglasses represent radiometric dating. It is assumed that we know the amount of parent and daughter elements in the original sample, the rate of decay is constant, and no parent or daughter material has been added or removed.

When the hourglass is up-ended, sand flows from the top container to the bottom one at a rate that can be measured. If we observe an hourglass with the sand still flowing, we can determine how long ago it was up-ended from the quantities of sand in both containers and the flow rate. Or can we? Unless we have actually observed the hourglass since it was upended, we must first assume three things which we can never know for sure are true:

1. We know the quantities of sand in both containers at the start. Normally, an hourglass is up-ended when the top container is empty. But if the top container was not empty, then it would take less time for the sand to fill the new bottom container to a particular level. Similarly, radiometric dating must assume the initial quantities of both parent and daughter elements.

2. The flow rate has stayed constant. For example, if the sand had become damp recently, it would flow more slowly now than in the past. If the flow were greater in the past, it would take less time for the sand to reach a certain level than it would if the sand had always flowed at the present rate. Radiometric dating must assume constant decay rate.

3. The system has remained closed. That is, no sand has been added or removed from either container. However, suppose that, without your knowledge, sand

had been added to the top container, or removed from the bottom container. Then if you calculated the time since the last up-ending by measuring the sand in both containers, it would be shorter than the actual time. If the reverse happened, that is, sand was added to the bottom container or taken from the top one, then the calculated time would be longer than the real time. Radiometric dating must assume that no "parent" or "daughter" elements entered or left the system.[43]

Let's look at each of these in turn.

Assumption 1: Initial Conditions:

This is questionable. Dr. Snelling shows that the composition of an igneous rock often depends on which reservoir in the mantle the magma came from, as opposed to being the result of decay in the hardened rock. In fact, isotope ratios are often used to identify the source reservoir.[44] With ^{14}C, there are several factors that would lower the initial ratio of this radioactive isotope to the stable isotope ^{12}C, which would result in higher ^{14}C "dates":

- More ^{12}C in the pre-Flood biosphere (more biomass, higher atmospheric CO_2), while the Flood would have buried lots of ^{12}C, making the post-Flood $^{14}C/^{12}C$ ratio higher.
- Less ^{14}C production due to a stronger magnetic field deflecting cosmic rays better (see page 334).
- ^{14}C starts building up at creation, so it would only have had 1,600 years to build up, nowhere near equilibrium.
- Volcanoes emit carbon dioxide with no ^{14}C, and plants can absorb this.[45]

Isochrons

This technique is alleged to eliminate the need to assume initial values for the parent and daughter isotope. But this is impossible, as we will see. Each isochron "age" is based on a number of samples and initial values still need to be assumed for each sample. In this case, it is assumed that the initial ratio of daughter to parent in each sample is the same as in all the other samples. It is also assumed that all samples formed (closed) at the same time.

In "whole rock" isochons, samples of different rocks are assumed to have come from the same geological unit and formed at the same time. This is called a *cogenetic*

43. L. Vardiman, A.A. Snelling, and E.F. Chaffin, *Radioisotopes and the Age of the Earth* (El Cajon, CA: Institute for Creation Research, and St. Joseph, MO: Creation Research Society, 2000).

44. A. Snelling, "Geochemical Processes in Mantle and Crust," in L. Vardiman, A.A. Snelling, and E.F. Chaffin, *Radioisotopes and the Age of the Earth* (El Cajon, CA: Institute for Creation Research, and St. Joseph, MO: Creation Research Society, 2000), chapter 5.

45. J. Woodmorappe, "Much-inflated Carbon-14 Dates from Subfossil Trees: A New Mechanism," *TJ* 15(3):43–44 (2001).

suite of rocks. However, in cases where it is clear from the field evidence that the suite is cogenetic, the different samples of rock are usually so similar in composition that the results cluster about a single point and do not form a well-defined line. Where rock samples are sufficiently different in composition that their results form a nice line, it becomes debatable whether the suite is indeed cogenetic. Another type of dating is the mineral isochron method. Here, different mineral samples from the same rock are analyzed.

In the isochron method, another isotope of the daughter element is measured for comparison. The point of this is that when the rock formed, it is *assumed* that the ratio of the two isotopes of the same element was constant throughout the rock (that is, it is assumed that the entire body of magma was isotopically well mixed). For example, rubidium-strontium dating measures the ratio of ^{87}Rb to its daughter ^{87}Sr. In the isochron, the isotope ^{86}Sr is also measured. So while the initial ^{87}Rb/^{87}Sr ratio may vary widely, the initial ^{87}Sr/^{86}Sr ratio (that is, using the third isotope) is assumed to be the same in all samples initially. In the isochron plot, ^{87}Sr/^{86}Sr is plotted against ^{87}Rb/^{86}Sr, and the slope (m) of the line gives the age (t) by:

$$t = \frac{1}{\lambda} \ln(m+1).^{46}$$

However, even this method does not eliminate the need to make assumptions about the isotopic composition of the rock in the past, and it also has a number of other problems. Geologist Dr. Steve Austin found that sometimes the mineral isochron is "*older*" than the whole rock isochron.[47] Geologist Dr. Andrew Snelling worked on "dating" the Koongarra uranium deposits in the Northern Territory of Australia. He found that even highly weathered soil samples from the area, which are definitely not closed systems, gave apparently valid "isochron" lines with "ages" of up to 1445 Ma.[48]

Dr. Tas Walker analyzed isotope ratios from the Somerset Dam igneous complex in southeast Queensland, Australia, including those for the Sm/Nd and Rb/Sr dating methods. He plotted the usual ratio of the daughter elements, ^{143}Nd/^{144}/Nd and ^{87}Sr/^{86}Sr, against the appropriate parent ratios, ^{147}Sm/^{144}Nd and ^{87}Rb/^{86}Sr, to obtain isochron "ages." However, he found that the daughter element isotopic ratios gave far better correlation when plotted against other isotopes that have nothing to do with the decay! I.e. ^{143}Nd/^{144}/Nd had a far higher correlation with the concentrations of K, Be and Co, than with radioactive decay of ^{147}Sm. And ^{87}Sr/^{86}Sr was far

46. D. DeYoung, "Radioisotope Dating Review," in L. Vardiman, A.A. Snelling, and E.F. Chaffin, *Radioisotopes and the Age of the Earth* (El Cajon, CA: Institute for Creation Research, and St. Joseph, MO: Creation Research Society, 2000), p. 39–43.

47. S. Austin, "Mineral Isochron Method Applied as a Test," in L. Vardiman, A.A. Snelling, and E.F. Chaffin, *Radioisotopes and the Age of the Earth* (El Cajon, CA: Institute for Creation Research, and St. Joseph, MO: Creation Research Society, 2000), chapter 4.

48. A. Snelling, "The Failure of U-Th-Pb 'Dating' at Koongarra, Australia," *TJ* 9(1):71–92 (1995).

more influenced by K/Ca, Nb/Co, Nb/Ca, Nb/Sr and Y/Sr than by radioactive decay of ^{87}Rb.[49]

This shows that the daughter element ratios are *not* primarily caused by radioactive decay. Evidently some other processes are causing the isotope fractionation in the daughter isotopes, and these processes are also affecting other element distributions. Such "false isochrons" are so common that a whole terminology has grown up to describe them, such as apparent isochron, mantle isochron, pseudoisochron, secondary isochron, inherited isochron, erupted isochron, mixing line and mixing isochron. Zheng wrote:

> . . . some of the basic assumptions of the conventional Rb-Sr [rubidium-strontium] isochron method have to be modified and an observed isochron does not certainly define valid age information for a geological system, even if a goodness of fit of the experimental results is obtained in plotting ^{87}Sr/^{86}Sr against ^{87}Rb/^{86}Sr. This problem cannot be overlooked, especially in evaluating the numerical time scale. Similar questions can also arise in applying Sm-Nd and U-Pb isochron methods.[50]

Austin provides several possible explanations for such linear plots, for example, inheriting isotope ratios from "aged" source rocks, mixing or contamination (e.g., from the country rock), partial melting, selective diffusion, and accelerated decay.[51] This shows that obtaining an age from an isochron plot is an *interpretation*. In fact, the results from such calculations are only accepted if they agree with what is already considered to be reasonable.

Some isochron plots of different elements in the same formation can give different "ages." This is explained by differently accelerated decay rates (see following information).

Assumption 2: Constancy of Decay Rate

We agree that radioactive decay is not significantly influenced by such factors as temperature and pressure. However, decay rates have been tested for only about 100 years, so we can't be sure they were constant over the alleged billions of years. Recent laboratory research has demonstrated that the beta (β) decay rate was sped up a *billion times* when atoms were stripped of their electrons.[52]

49. T. Walker, "The Somerset Dam Igneous Complex, Southeast Queensland," Honours thesis [1st class Honours or *Summa cum laude* awarded], Department of Earth Sciences, University of Queensland, 1998.

50. Y.F. Zheng, "Influence of the Nature of Initial Rb-Sr System on Isochron Validity," *Chemical Geology* 80:1–16 (1989); quote on p. 14.

51. See footnote 47.

52. F. Bosch et al., "Observation of Bound-state β-decay of Fully Ionized ^{187}Re," *Physical Review Letters* 77(26)5190–5193 (1996); J. Woodmorappe, "Billion-fold Acceleration of Radioactivity Demonstrated in Laboratory," *TJ* 15(2):4–6 (2001).

Also, the Ph.D. physicists and geologists who contributed to the RATE book have adduced several lines of evidence that decay has been faster in the past.[53] They propose a pulse of accelerated decay rate during creation week, and possibly a smaller pulse during the Flood year. Among the evidence is:

- ^{14}C data showing the earth itself is only thousands of years old, so the billions of years of decay at present rates of the long half-life isotopes must have occurred at much higher rates to fit within this short time span. See page 385.

- The presence of helium atoms still within the rock where they were apparently formed by nuclear α-decay. The diffusion rate of helium through minerals would suggest that it would have escaped if the rocks were really billions of years old. See also the section on helium diffusion, page 341.

- High correlation of heat flow at the earth's surface with concentration of radioactive isotopes. This is consistent with a pulse of accelerated decay during the Flood year to produce heat that hasn't had time to dissipate. This explains a correlation that had been a mystery to geophysicists.[54]

What Would Cause Accelerated Decay, and How Would It Affect Different Isotopes?

According to the nuclear physicist Dr. Eugene Chaffin, there are theoretical means of producing accelerated decay, for example, a small change in fundamental constants or the shape of the nuclear potential well can have a large effect on the decay rate (but little effect on radiohalo diameter). Alpha decay rates are extremely sensitive to the nuclear potential energy well.[55]

If God weakened the strong nuclear force (greatly speeding up alpha decay[56]), the nucleus would increase in size and restructure itself. The lower the decay constant (that is, the higher the half-life), the more the decay rate would be accelerated.

The restructuring would also speed up beta decay and electron capture, more for the forbidden decays and less for the allowed decays. The long half-life isotopes

53. L. Vardiman, A.A. Snelling, and E.F. Chaffin, *Radioisotopes and the Age of the Earth* (El Cajon, CA: Institute for Creation Research, and St. Joseph, MO: Creation Research Society, 2000), mainly chapters 6 and 7.

54. J. Baumgardner, "Distribution of Radioactive Isotopes in the Earth," in L. Vardiman, A.A. Snelling, and E.F. Chaffin, *Radioisotopes and the Age of the Earth* (El Cajon, CA: Institute for Creation Research, and St. Joseph, MO: Creation Research Society, 2000), chapter 3.

55. E. Chaffin, "Accelerated Decay: Theoretical Models," in R.L. Ivey Jr., editor, *Fifth International Conference on Creationism*, Creation Science Fellowship, Pittsburgh, Pennsylvania (August 2003): p. 3–15; <www.icr.org/research/icc03/pdf/RATE_ICC_Chaffin.pdf>.

56. L. Vardiman, A.A. Snelling, and E.F. Chaffin, *Radioisotopes and the Age of the Earth* (El Cajon, CA: Institute for Creation Research, and St. Joseph, MO: Creation Research Society, 2000), p. 358, Fig. 8.

(^{87}Rb and ^{40}K) involve "forbidden" decay,[57] while the beta decay from ^{14}C to ^{14}N is "allowed."[58] The more forbidden a decay is, the more sensitive it is to small changes in nuclear structure. ^{14}C would not be accelerated nearly as much as ^{40}K.

Drs. Snelling, Austin, and Hoesch were able to test this in the RATE project that analyzed radioisotope decay in the Precambrian sill in the Grand Canyon.[59] Evolutionists had previously used the Rb/Sr whole rock isochron method (see page 379) to obtain a "date" of 1070±30 Ma.[60] But the RATE research found that isochrons with different elements gave different "ages," although the individual plots gave excellent straight line fits:

- ^{40}K/^{40}Ar v ^{36}Ar/^{40}Ar — 840.4 ± 140 Ma

- ^{87}Rb/^{86}Sr v ^{87}Sr/^{86}Sr whole rock isochron — 1055 ± 46 Ma

- ^{206}Pb/^{204}Pb v ^{207}Pb/^{204}Pb whole rock isochron — 1249 ± 140 Ma

- ^{147}Sm/^{144}Nd v. ^{143}Nd/^{144}Nd mineral isochron — 1375 ± 170 Ma

These decay patterns come from the same geological formation, which must be the same *true* age. The different apparent ages are really the result of the isotopes decaying faster than they do now. The greater the apparent age, the greater the acceleration of decay. And the different accelerations match the theoretical predictions. All the alpha-emitters (^{238}U and 2^{35}U for the Pb isochron; and Sm) gave isochron "ages" that were greater than those where the decay involved the weak nuclear force (Rb and K), meaning that alpha decay was accelerated more than beta decay or electron capture (both involve the weak nuclear force). Also, within a single decay type, the longer lived the isotope, the greater the "age," so the greater the acceleration.

Assumption 3: System Closure

This is a huge assumption. Geologist Dr. Andrew Snelling has shown that nearly all parent/daughter ratios used in radiometric "dating" can be altered by a number of geological processes, including leaching by hydrothermal and ground waters, diffusion through minerals, and metamorphism. Uranium is especially prone to leaching,

57. In standard nuclear physics terminology, this means there is a spin or parity change of more than one. For example, ^{40}K to ^{40}Ar requires a spin change of four and is therefore a "triply forbidden" decay.

58. In standard nuclear physics terminology, this means that spin or parity change is one, so it decays fast.

59. A. Snelling, S. Austin, and Hoesch, "Radioisotopes in the Diabase Sill (Upper Precambrian) in Bass Rapids, Grand Canyon, Arizona: An Application and Test of the Isochron Dating Method," in R.L. Ivey Jr., editor, *Fifth International Conference on Creationism*, Creation Science Fellowship, Pittsburgh, Pennsylvania (August 2003): p. 269–284; <www.icr.org/research/icc03/pdf/IC-CBassRapidsSill_2-%20AAS_SA_and_WH.pdf>.

60. D.P. Elston and E.H. McKee, "Age and Correlation of the Late Proterozoic Grand Canyon Disturbance, Northern Arizona," *Geological Society of America Bulletin* 93:681–699 (1982).

lead atoms diffuse easily, and argon, a gas, moves very readily.[61] Secular geologists regularly attribute unacceptable dating results to open system behavior.

INTERPRETING THE DATA

As I pointed out on page 384, the real science involves measuring the isotope ratios with great precision. No one is questioning these observations, but rather their *interpretation*. According to the Bible's chronology, great age cannot be the true cause of the observed isotope ratios, and this will be supported in the next section on anomalies. However, we are not yet sure of the true cause in all cases. But a group of creationist Ph.D. geologists and physicists are working on this topic, and have already published a detailed technical book on the conclusions of their preliminary work.[62] Their aim is to find out the precise geochemical and/or geophysical causes of the observed isotope ratios, and their work addresses the three assumptions above.

Anomalies

"Excess" Argon

There are many examples where the dating methods give "dates" that are wrong for rocks of *known* historical age. One example is rock from a new dacite lava dome at Mount St. Helens volcano. Although we know the rock was formed in 1986, the rock was "dated" by the potassium-argon (K-Ar) method as 0.35 ± 0.05 million years old. And dates on mineral concentrates from the rock samples gave "dates" as old as 2.8 Ma.[63] Another example is K-Ar "dating" of five andesite lava flows from Mount Ngauruhoe in New Zealand. The "dates" ranged from <0.27–3.5 million years — but one lava flow occurred in 1949, three in 1954, and one in 1975!

What happened was that "excess" argon from the magma (molten rock) was retained in the rock when it solidified. The retained argon is symbolized $^{40}Ar^*$, as opposed to radiogenic argon produced by the potassium in the rock, ^{40}Ar, but there is no way of telling these apart. The secular scientific literature also lists many examples of $^{40}Ar^*$ causing "dates" of millions of years in rocks of known historical age. This excess appears to have come from the upper mantle, below the earth's crust. This is consistent with a young world — the argon has had too little time to escape.[64]

61. A. Snelling, "Geochemical Processes in Mantle and Crust," in L. Vardiman, A.A. Snelling, and E.F. Chaffin, *Radioisotopes and the Age of the Earth* (El Cajon, CA: Institute for Creation Research, and St. Joseph, MO: Creation Research Society, 2000), chapter 5.

62. L. Vardiman, A.A. Snelling, and E.F. Chaffin, *Radioisotopes and the Age of the Earth* (El Cajon, CA: Institute for Creation Research, and St. Joseph, MO: Creation Research Society, 2000).

63. S.A. Austin, "Excess Argon within Mineral Concentrates from the New Dacite Lava Dome at Mount St. Helens Volcano," *TJ* 10(3):335–343 (1996); K. Swenson, "Radio-dating in Rubble," *Creation* 23(3)23–25, a simpler account which refutes many of Dr. Austin's critics.

64. A.A. Snelling, "The Cause of Anomalous Potassium-argon 'Ages' for Recent Andesite Flows at Mount Ngauruhoe, New Zealand, and the Implications for Potassium-argon 'Dating,' " in R.E. Walsh, editor, *Proceedings of the Fourth International Conference on Creationism,* Creation Science Fellowship, Pittsburgh, p. 503–525 (1998). This paper documents many examples: six were reported by D. Krummenacher, "Isotopic Composition of Argon in Modern Surface

If excess ^{40}Ar can cause exaggerated dates for rocks of *known* age, then why should it not have exaggerated the ages of rocks of *unknown* age?

Conflicting Results

Another problem is the conflicting dates between different methods. If two methods disagree, then at least one of them must be wrong. For example, in Australia, some wood was buried by a basalt lava flow, as can be seen from the charring. The wood was "dated" by radiocarbon (^{14}C) analysis at about 45,000 years old, but the basalt was "dated" by the K-Ar method at c. 45 million years old![65]

Contamination was ruled out by a method known as the $\delta^{13}C_{PDB}$ test. This measures the amount of another stable carbon isotope, ^{13}C, which is about 1 percent of all carbon.[66]

John Woodmorappe has also published a well-documented book demonstrating many fallacies of radiometric "dating" and many discordant "dates."[67]

Absence of Short-lived Radionuclides (SLRNs)

Ross repeats another common old-earth argument (C&T:94–95):

> ... the universe cannot be very young because most radioactive elements no longer exist at all. The radioactive elements with half-lives of millions of years (except the byproducts of other radioactive elements with longer half-lives and the products of local or cosmic radiation) are completely gone. Enough time has elapsed for every bit of these elements to decay away. Therefore, the universe and earth must be at least a billion years old.

However, this commits the fallacy of arguing from silence. Ross's argument presupposes that God had created these short-lived isotopes in the first place! However, there are good reasons for denying this. The main one would be that short-lived isotopes, by definition, emit radiation more often. Also, the shorter the half-life, the higher the energy of decay in general, and definitely so with alpha decay. So would God create lots of isotopes with higher energy radiation and more of it, when this would be hazardous to life? This is an even greater problem when most of these isotopes form very soluble compounds, so they could be leached into dangerous hot spots.

Rocks," *Earth and Planetary Science Letters* 8:109–117 (1970); five were reported by G.B. Dalrymple, "^{40}Ar/^{36}Ar Analysis of Historic Lava Flows," *Earth and Planetary Science Letters* 6:47–55 (1969). Also, a large excess was reported in D.E. Fisher, "Excess Rare Gases in a Subaerial Basalt from Nigeria," *Nature* 232:60–61 (1970).

65. A.A. Snelling, "Conflicting 'Ages' of Tertiary Basalt and Contained Fossilised Wood, Crinum, Central Queensland, Australia," *TJ* 14(2):94–122 (2000).

66. The $\delta^{13}C_{PDB}$ test compares the measured difference of the ratio of ^{13}C/^{12}C in the sample to the PDB (Pee Dee Belemnite) standard — a fossil belemnite from the Cretaceous Pee Dee Formation in South Carolina. The units used are parts per thousand, written as ‰ or per mil (compared with parts per hundred, written as % or percent). Organic carbon from the different varieties of life gives different characteristic $\delta^{13}C_{PDB}$ values.

67. J. Woodmorappe, *The Mythology of Modern Dating Methods* (El Cajon, CA: Institute for Creation Research, 1999).

Another possible answer invokes accelerated decay rates (page 378). So it's possible that God created these isotopes, but any created SLNRs have decayed.

Furthermore, even Ross's caveat about some isotopes being regenerated is itself sometimes an assumption to preserve old-earth dogma. For example, in the Anarkardo basin formation, the ^{129}I ($t_{\frac{1}{2}}$ = 15.7 million years) present is *assumed* to have been produced by fission because the rock is said to be over 300 million years old.[68]

Carbon-14: A Short-lived Isotope That's the Undoing of Millions of Years

Many people have the impression that ^{14}C (aka carbon-14, radiocarbon) proves billions of years. For example, the "Rev." Barry Lynn, leader of the anti-Christian group Americans United for the Separation of Church and State, proclaimed in a nationally televised debate a few years ago, ". . . carbon dating, that shows the earth is *billions* of years old!"[69]

But this merely showed his crass ignorance of science. ^{14}C's half-life is only 5,730 years, so there is no way there could be any detectable ^{14}C in a sample if it were only one million years old. One gram of carbon contains about 5×10^{22} atoms of carbon, and only about one in a trillion of these atoms is ^{14}C, or about 6×10^{10}. After 36 half-lives, there should be no atom of ^{14}C left, and that means about 200,000 years.

Yet it has long been known that fossils allegedly much older than that show detectable ^{14}C activity, even after allowing for possible contamination. Unlike Ross's argument from *absence* of certain isotopes, refuted in the previous section, this argument is based on the *presence* of ^{14}C in rocks "dated" as millions of years old, although if Ross's old-earth dogma were right, it should be absent.

For example, fossil wood from Upper Permian rock layers has been found with ^{14}C still present. Detectable ^{14}C would have all disintegrated if the wood were really as old as the 250 million years that evolutionists assign to these Upper Permian rock layers.[70]

Paul Giem studied 42 papers from secular refereed journals such as *Radiocarbon, Science, Nuclear Geophysics,* and *Nature,* which documented ^{14}C activity in samples that are traditionally said to be far older than 200,000 years.[71] Giem also analyzes the most common explanations for the anomalies, for example, nuclear synthesis of ^{14}C *in situ,* contamination *in situ,* and contamination during sample processing. He finds them insufficient, and the evolutionary ^{14}C experts realize there are problems as well.

---

68. J. Woodmorappe, *The Mythology of Modern Dating Methods* (El Cajon, CA: Institute for Creation Research, 1999), p. 26.

69. B. Lynn, during the debate, "Resolved: The Evolutionists Should Acknowledge Creation," *Firing Line,* with William F. Buckley, Phillip Johnson, Michael Behe, and David Berlinsky advocating intelligent design against Barry Lynn, Eugenie Scott, Kenneth Miller, and Michael Ruse defending evolutionism, PBS, December 19, 1997. Lynn's blunder is about 1 hour and 25 minutes from the beginning.

70. A.A. Snelling, "Stumping Old-age Dogma," *Creation* 20(4):48–50 (September–November 1998).

71. P. Giem, "Carbon-14 Content of Fossil Carbon," *Origins* 51:6–30 (2001); <www.grisda.org/origins/51006.htm>.

More recently, creationist geophysicist Dr. John Baumgardner has selected ten coal samples comprising three Eocene, three Cretaceous, and four Pennsylvanian, that is, all "dated" at many millions of years old.[72] These were analyzed with very precise accelerator mass spectroscopy (AMS), which can detect ¹⁴C atoms

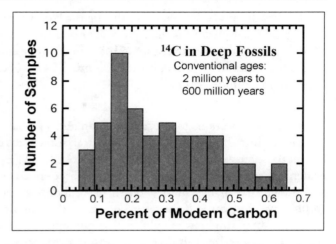

individually. By contrast, the original method of scintillation counting detected the radiation from a decaying ¹⁴C atom, that is, it directly counted only the small fraction of ¹⁴C atoms that decayed, not the actual number.

But all these samples consistently display ¹⁴C levels that are far above the AMS machine threshold, reliably reproducible, and typically in the range of 0.1–0.5 pmc (percent modern carbon — see histogram above). The narrow range suggests that these organisms died at about the same time. This is consistent with being buried in the same global cataclysm, only thousands of years ago, not millions.[73]

Baumgardner's most recent result was ¹⁴C in a diamond sample from Precambrian strata, evolutionarily dated at more than 600 Ma.[74] The level of ¹⁴C in the diamond was about 100 times the instrument detection threshold and consistent with other Precambrian inorganic samples reported in the radiocarbon literature. This South African diamond was formed some 200 km deep in the mantle, and because of the great strength of the bonds in diamond, the hardest substance known, contamination is simply not a possibility. The diamond's carbon-dated "age" of less than 58,000 years is thus an upper limit for the age of the whole earth. And this age is brought down still further now that the helium diffusion results have so strongly affirmed dramatic past acceleration of radioactive decay. Thus, it is powerful evidence the physical earth itself is only thousands, as opposed to billions, of years old. And this finding has since been confirmed by reputable laboratories on a further four diamonds.[75]

---

72. J. Baumgardner, A. Snelling, R. Humphreys, and A. Austin, "Measurable ¹⁴C in Fossilized Organic Materials: Confirming the Young Earth Creation-flood Model," in R.L. Ivey Jr., editor, *Fifth International Conference on Creationism*, Creation Science Fellowship, Pittsburgh, Pennsylvania (August, 2003): p. 175–196; <www.icr.org/research/icc03/pdf/RATE_ICC_Baumgardner.pdf>. R. Humphreys, "Carbon 14 Is Now the Creationist's Friend," *C-14 Newsletter* (2003).

73. See Baumgardner, Snelling, Humphreys, and Austin info in footnote 72.

74. J. Baumgardner, presentation at the *5th International Conference on Creationism*, 2003.

75. J. Baumgardner, personal communication, December 2003.

So why didn't accelerated decay during the Flood eliminate all ^{14}C? As explained on page 382, the greater the half-life, the greater the acceleration. More specifically, ^{14}C decay is an "allowed" transition, explaining its very short half-life. Therefore, the acceleration should not affect it nearly as much as isotopes with half-lives about six orders of magnitude greater.

CONCLUSION

All these objections to a recent creation and a global Flood have been touted as "unanswerable." If this book had been written some years earlier, we would not have had all those answers. In particular, the work of the RATE group has provided strong evidence that there was at least one episode of accelerated radioactive decay. They have also shown that many samples "dated" at millions of years old contain ^{14}C, which would have all decayed if they were any more than about 200,000 years old.

There may still be some old-earth arguments for which we haven't yet worked out a full answer, but this does not mean that the answers don't exist, just that we haven't come up with them yet. Biblical opponents may also try to come up with new arguments, or excuses to reject the answers already given. And when these are answered, there might be new ones again. This goes to show that science is tentative, so should never be used to overturn the plain Word of God.

Conclusion and Summary

Belief in a creation period of six 24-hour days and about 6,000 years ago has been the teaching of the Church for most of its history. This belief is not essential to be a Christian, so we are not saying that that those who do not hold the 6-day position are necessarily unsaved. But it is essential for *consistency* in doctrine and apologetics. The denial of this belief is foundationally the result of imposing outside ideas upon the Bible. Thus, it has baneful consequences which don't just stop with Genesis, but affect many areas, as is shown with Ross's teachings.

1. Authority

The Reformation recovered the biblical teaching that the Bible was both sufficient and clear — *Sola Scriptura* (Scripture alone). The contrary view was that Scripture needed to be supplemented by church tradition which had equal authority, and that the Bible could not be understood without the Magisterium. But, in practice, the latter view placed tradition and magisterial authority in a greater position than Scripture.

Now, long-age ideas also say that Scripture is insufficient — nature is now a 67th book of the Bible, as Ross puts it. And we allegedly need "science" to help us understand biblical history. In practice, where there is a perceived conflict with the scientific consensus and the Bible, it is always Scripture which is made to give way. This places "science" in a greater authority over Scripture, so instead of *Sola Scriptura*, it becomes *Scriptura sub scientia* (Scripture below science).

This is amply shown by the admissions of many evangelical theologians who believe in long ages. They admit that a plain understanding of Genesis would teach six 24-hour days and a creation about 6,000 years ago, but they can't accept that because of "science."

But this misunderstands the difference between Scripture and nature. The Bible is the infallible propositional revelation from God, that is, facts about things. Therefore, its teachings can be understood from its grammatical and historical context by the laws of hermeneutics, and are supremely authoritative. Nature is *not* propositional, and therefore the data of nature must be interpreted within a framework. But the alleged long-age consensus comes from interpreting the data in a framework that deliberately ignores God's special acts of creation and the Flood. Also, the current creation is cursed. So the correct procedure is to interpret nature in a framework based on the infallible history revealed in the Bible. That is, if there is a conflict, then reinterpret the "science," not Scripture.

2. Days of Creation

In Genesis 1:5, the creation days are defined as 24 hours long. The whole chapter has the word "day" (Hebrew *yôm*) in the context of *both* a number *and* the phrase "evening and morning." Everywhere else in the Bible where "day" is associated with either of these, it always means an ordinary day. But in Genesis, both these markers are present, a clear indication that the author intended to teach that they were ordinary days.

Also, the peculiar pattern associated with the Genesis days — the presence and absence of definite articles, and the pattern of ordinals and cardinals — is further strong evidence they were ordinary days. The Fourth Commandment of Exodus 20:8–11 makes no sense unless the days of the working week were the same as those of creation week.

Ross's rationalizations for non-literal days do not hold water. In particular, there is no need to postulate a long time for the activities of day 6. Ross is mistaken that the seventh day is still continuing — only God's rest is said to be continuing, not the day, which was the same length as the Israelite Sabbath.

3. History of Interpretation

Ross has often mentioned early commentators on Genesis, and claims they support his ideas of long creation days. But checking the commentators themselves, it's clear that Ross has been misleading his readers. Nearly all the ones he cited *explicitly* taught 24-hour creation days, and not one taught they were ages. Even the ones who did not teach literal days taught that the earth was only thousands of years old.

Ross may have been confused by some of the church fathers, who taught that the six creation days corresponded to — but were not equal to — six thousand-year periods of earth history, and that after 6,000 years this age would come to an end. In fact, these authors explicitly say that the 6,000 years was not yet up because the earth wasn't that old! So these writers don't just fail to support Ross's view, but contradict it.

The 24-hour day view continued through the Reformation and beyond. It's striking that the first hints of long-age views of Genesis came only when conservative exegetes became intimidated by long-age teachings of geology. This was the origin of the common compromise views such as the day-age, gap theory, and framework hypothesis. The absence of these views for most of church history is strong indication that they are not derived from the Hebrew text, but from outside sources.

4. Order of Creation

Some people naïvely believe that the order of secular astronomy and paleontology matches the sequence of Genesis. But the match breaks in a number of places. For example, secular "science" says the sun preceded the earth, while Genesis says the sun was created three days later. Secular "science" says that birds and whales came after land creatures, the opposite of Genesis.

Ross tries to twist the Scriptures to escape the contradiction. But these attempts had already been tried by former day-ager Davis Young, and he eventually abandoned the position as biblically untenable.

The correct solution is to regard the paleontological order not as a sequence of ages, but a sequence of burial by a global Flood and its aftermath.

5. Big Bang and Astronomy

The big bang is a keystone of Ross's apologetics. He made up his mind as a teenager that the big bang was a fact. And then he decided that the creation days could not have been 24 hours long. Now, as an astronomer, the big bang is a crux of his apologetics.

However, the big bang is actually based on non-biblical assumptions, in particular, that there is no special location or direction in the universe. It also has many scientific difficulties that Ross glosses over. For example, there is no adequate explanation for the absence of antimatter, the formation of galaxies, or how gas clouds could collapse into stars without pre-existing stars. The supposed evidence for the big bang is not really evidence at all. Rather, the big bang is a hypothetical model that is tuned to match certain observations, which are then turned around and claimed to be predictions of the big bang. This is circular reasoning!

The evolutionary theories of the origin of the solar system and the planets and moon have a number of problems, too. For example, the sun has most of the mass while the planets have most of the angular momentum. Also, the sun should become hotter as it ages, yet there is no proof in earth's record of a much cooler sun those alleged billions of years ago. There are also many vexing problems with accretion of the inner rocky planets and the outer ice giants. No satisfactory theory for the origin of the moon yet exists, and Ross managed to misunderstand the evolutionary collision model which he advocates. It proposes a glancing collision, not a "nearly head-on hit" as Ross claimed.

Ross also uses faulty apologetics based on the big bang as an evidence for a cause of the universe. First, this is not the way leading big-bang cosmologists picture it — most of them regard it as an atheistic theory. Second, arguments from a beginning to a cause go back at least to the 13th century, so do *not* need the big bang for validation. I have outlined a first-cause argument that is more effective for apologetics, because it is faithful to Scripture.

The argument that distant starlight proves billions of years has a fatal flaw — *the big bangers have their own light-travel–time difficulty*, called the horizon problem. If both sides have an unsolved problem in one area, this area cannot be used as evidence against only one of the models. Big bangers have a number of *ad hoc* solutions to their problem, none of which are adequate. Creationists have proposed some promising solutions for their distant starlight problem.

Ross's foray into string theory is misplaced since it is speculative. His ideas of an extradimensional deity have caused much concern, even to his supporters, such as the philosopher/theologian William Lane Craig. There are more biblical ways of using concepts of other dimensions.

6. Sin and Death

A major problem with all compromise views is the explanation of how a good God could allow death and suffering. The straightforward biblical view is that these are intruders into a very good creation because of sin. But Ross must believe they already existed long before Adam.

However, this contradicts the clear teaching that creation was "very good," and that death is the "last enemy." Ross claims that the death of Adam was just spiritual death, but that contradicts the Curse of Genesis 3:19. He also claims that there is nothing in the curse resulting in animal deaths, but this contradicts the biblical teaching that animals were created vegetarian, and will one day be vegetarian again in the Restoration. This is vital for theodicy, since notable anti-Christians such as Charles Darwin and Charles Templeton used human and animal death as an argument against God. And because of long-age teaching, they believed that any god must have created things this way. But apologist and Ross-supporter Norman Geisler pointed out the biblical teaching of original vegetarianism, without realizing that this is incompatible with his long-age beliefs.

The origin of carnivory and disease also has rational explanations in a biblical framework. Either some pre-Fall features were corrupted into harmful uses or God switched on latent genetic information at the Fall, which He foreknew.

7. Created Kinds

To understand the biblical creation model, it is important to understand the created kinds. God created a number of distinct kinds with an enormous amount of genetic variation. With genetic drift and natural selection, these kinds split into varieties by separating out this genetic information. Sometimes a variety would be unable to interbreed with its parent population, so a new biological species would be formed. There are also ways in which a loss of genetic information can produce a new variety.

Evolutionists love to play bait 'n' switch in calling all change "evolution." But goo-to-you evolution requires changes where the genetic information is *increased*. This they have yet to observe, yet it should be ubiquitous if evolution were true.

Creationists actually believe that variation and speciation should be much faster than most evolutionists predict. This is because the varieties of land vertebrates we see today derived from the ark passengers.

Ross is so keen to attack creationists that he copies evolutionary arguments that this variation and speciation is "hyper-evolution." But no new information is generated by this process. Ross goes further and declares that there is no speciation occurring, because we are still in the seventh day, so God is still resting. But this is refuted by the fact that there are numerous examples of new species observed, that is, specimens that can't breed back with the parent population.

8. The Global Flood

The Bible emphasizes, for instance by the repeated use of "all," that the Flood was global (for example, Gen. 7). Otherwise, building an ark would be pointless. However, a global flood would nullify the alleged evidence for billions of years in geology. So Ross relegates it to a local flood in Mesopotamia.

However, this has major problems. Mesopotamia is only a half bowl, so the postulated gigantic wall of water would flow out toward the south, and carry the ark with it. Also, the postulated Rossian flood would be far more catastrophic than the Spokane flood that carved the Channeled Scablands, yet Ross claims it left no trace.

Creationists at least from the time of the scriptural geologists right up to modern creationists have adduced much scientific support for a single global catastrophe. This includes the huge extent of thick rock layers and the smooth transitions between them in many cases, with no evidence of time gaps for erosion. Features such as polystrate fossils demand rapid burial.

Modern creationists have provided a plausible mechanism for the global Flood, in catastrophic plate tectonics. This not only explains the observations that the continents have moved apart from a single land mass (as Gen. 1:9 indicates), but explains features that are a puzzle for uniformitarian plate tectonics.

Ross also misrepresents the ark's cargo under a global Flood scenario, imitating skeptical attacks on the Bible. For example, he piles on about a billion species, although the biblical account clearly says that only land vertebrate kinds were on board. Ross also exaggerates the fossil numbers by orders of magnitude. But a proper analysis shows that only 16,000 animals at the very most needed to be on board. Over half of these were smaller than a rat, and even representatives of the largest dinosaurs could have been put on board before they went through a rapid growth spurt (for which there is recently discovered evidence).

Ross's geological arguments against a global Flood are shown to be fallacious, for example, his nonsensical claim that the earth would still be ringing.

9. History of Mankind

The genealogies in Genesis 5 and 11 have no gaps, so mankind has been around for only about 6,000 years, as most early church writers taught. Jesus himself taught that humans were around "from the beginning of creation." A biblical framework also explains cavemen, Neandertals, and *Homo erectus* as post-Babel descendants of Noah.

But Ross "dates" Adam far older than 6,000 years. He also relegates the Neandertals to sub-human, and explains away their very human characteristics. In effect, Ross goes down the evolutionary track of blurring the distinction between humans and animals.

Ross's ignorance of genetic variation leads him to a blunder on the origin of races. He posits supernatural intervention to create varieties to encourage separation.

Ross's erroneous dating of Adam has baneful effects concerning the Australian Aborigines, too. Accepted secular dates for Aborigines suggest they are at least 40,000 years old, by ^{14}C methods, which Ross accepts. But Ross "dates" Adam from 60,000 to 10,000 years old. So Ross leaves open the possibility that, if Adam dated from 10,000 years ago, the Australian Aborigines are not descended from Adam. If so, then they can't be human, even by Ross's own theology. This is not what Ross really believes, but he was very careless in allowing this possibility. He should have used the "established" date as a *terminus ad quem* for Noah, and therefore Adam, so the range, given Ross's faulty time scale, should have been 60,000 to 40,000 years old. (This is a somewhat more uncomfortable set of numbers for evangelical circles to accept as a "conservative, literal" approach to the Bible's genealogies.)

10. Alleged Old-Age Teachings in Scripture

Ross appeals to a number of old-age words in the Bible. But when every one of these examples is analyzed, they say nothing about billions of years. Rather, they were general old-age terms, and of course, "old" and "ancient" are relative terms! Indeed, they are all used of human history.

In fact, this backfires on Ross. Old-age terms could easily have been used in the Genesis creation account to teach millions or billions of years — if that's what God had intended to teach. But there is not the slightest hint of them.

11. Science and the Young Earth

I have explained how science is limited when dating the past, because we can't observe it. Therefore, it makes more sense to trust an eyewitness account. But secular scientists analyze processes in the present, and extrapolate to the past, given certain *assumptions*.

There are actually many processes, even given the same sorts of assumptions, that point to an age far younger than billions of years. This chapter has gone through a number of these, first with a summary outline, then with technical detail and refuting counter-arguments. Some well-known creationist arguments are featured, and updated where possible with new data. For example, measured helium diffusion rates in zircons indicates that they couldn't be older than about 6,000 years, otherwise the large observed amounts of helium would have escaped.

Ross has tried to counter these arguments, but has made blunders in doing so. For example, the decay of comets is a huge problem for billions of years, but Ross argued an idea, discredited by secular astronomers long before, of comets having an interstellar origin.

12. Refuting Old-earth Arguments

Geology has historically been used as an old-earth weapon against the Bible, and Ross has enthusiastically taken up the same approach to attack young-earth proponents. But these old-earth arguments were first based on an *a priori* assumption that there was no global Flood. Later ones were based on ignorance about what the Flood could do. In particular, field and laboratory work has shown that catastrophic conditions can produce many fine layers quickly.

Another major old-earth weapon is radiometric dating. But this has a number of assumptions, which are all open to question. Also, there are many examples where the methods fail on rocks of known age, or give conflicting results. When this happens, old-earth geochronologists claim that one or more of the assumptions were invalid in this case. But then it should be acceptable to question these assumptions whenever a "date" contradicts the biblical time scale.

Also, one form of radiometric dating is good evidence against millions of years. That is the best known of all, ^{14}C. This has a half-life of only 5,700 years, so if any activity is remaining in a sample, it can't possibly be more than about 200,000 years old. Yet, in one of many examples, ^{14}C activity has been detected in wood from rock "dated" at 230 million years old, and many other samples, including a diamond.

In summary, therefore, there is every reason that we should trust the Bible as written as the final authority about earth history. None of the "scientific" arguments against the biblical time scale holds up under scrutiny. With a firm foundation in Genesis, Christians should be able to stand strong in their faith and be better equipped to carry out the Great Commission of Matthew 28:16–20.

Subject Index

apoptosis, 210–211, 273, 300–301
ark, 18, 66, 89, 137, 205, 213, 233–236,
239, 241, 243, 250, 252, 255–257,
262–263, 267–276, 278, 281–282,
284, 287, 294, 300, 310, 375, 392–393
ark
cargo, 18, 272, 275–276, 393
dinosaurs, 14, 17, 68, 141, 281–282,
298, 304–306, 355, 357, 393
size, 152, 159, 165, 173, 175, 184,
191, 222, 227, 235, 238, 243, 253,
271, 275, 281, 309, 318–319, 347,
351, 369, 371, 376, 382
strength, 89, 260, 270, 272, 335, 339,
387
big bang, 17, 142, 147, 153, 181, 186
big-bang theory:
assumptions, cosmological principle,
147–149, 152, 190–192
carbon-14, 305, 367, 376–377, 379,
382–383, 385–388, 394–395
carbon-14
found in "ancient" samples, 386
carnivory, origin of, 34, 195, 207–209,
211, 214, 392
census in Luke, "all the world," 251–252
challenge/riposte paradigm, 22
Charisma magazine, 13, 23, 27
Chicago Statement on Biblical Inerrancy,
29, 37–38, 41, 47, 49–50, 56–57, 124,
150, 181, 296–298, 311, 370
church fathers, patristic writers, 72, 81,
88, 107–110, 114, 121, 135, 139,
243–244, 290, 390
comets, age, 350–353, 394
date of creation, *Anno Mundi*, 127, 289
days of creation, 15, 17, 23, 27, 31, 47,
57–58, 67–70, 72–74, 76, 78, 81–87,
96, 101, 107–117, 121, 123, 126, 139,
145, 245, 251, 292, 321, 323, 327,
331, 336, 367, 390–391

days of creation
literal, 13–14, 17, 27, 32–34, 38, 57,
67–71, 73–77, 79, 81–82, 84–87,
105, 110, 114–115, 118, 120–123,
125, 135, 139, 142, 144, 209, 219,
245–246, 256, 295, 297, 313, 328,
390, 394
day-age, 14, 17, 28–30, 56, 58, 61,
68, 80, 93, 101, 105, 107, 110,
113–114, 133, 135–136, 139, 142,
144–146, 242, 270, 329, 390
types for millennia, 114
death, 10, 15–16, 18, 26–27, 32–34, 36,
46, 57, 66, 71–72, 102, 112, 116,
124, 130, 136, 141, 181, 195–205,
207–212, 214–216, 218–223, 287,
291–292, 294, 297, 299–301, 326,
328, 331, 367, 377, 392
Fall, the, 16, 18, 23, 26, 30, 37, 44, 46, 57,
64, 68, 71, 102–103, 129–130, 135,
178, 195–198, 200–207, 209, 211–
215, 220–221, 223, 226, 235, 250,
261, 267, 270, 276, 299, 308, 340, 392
Flood, the, 15, 18, 26, 33, 35–36, 43, 50,
57–58, 62, 64, 66, 102, 104, 110, 118,
130, 133, 136–137, 173–174, 178,
196, 205, 207, 226, 233, 235–236,
238–246, 248–270, 272, 274–275,
277–280, 282–284, 287, 289–291,
293–295, 300–302, 304–305, 308,
321, 323, 332–333, 337, 339–341,
343, 346, 358, 361–363, 367–368,
372–373, 375–376, 379, 382, 388,
390–391, 393, 395
flood
global, 18, 26, 33, 35–36, 50, 102, 156,
233, 236, 241–248, 250–251, 253,
255–257, 261, 263–264, 269–270,
274, 277–280, 283–284, 362–363,
367, 372, 387–388, 391, 393, 395
local, 15, 18, 50, 136, 241–245, 250–
252, 255–257, 263–264, 266–270,
274, 284, 304–305, 308, 321, 372,
385, 393

Mesopotamian, 15, 18, 241–243, 245, 248, 251, 253, 255, 268–269, 393
Spokane/Lake Missoula, 266–269, 393
fossils, 15, 18–19, 33, 57, 101, 132–133, 142, 195, 208, 218–219, 221–222, 248–250, 257, 259, 279–281, 308–312, 316, 318–319, 329, 357, 365, 371–375, 385–386, 393
fossils: numbers, 10, 38, 71, 74–76, 78, 112, 118, 125, 180, 196, 222, 239, 244, 276, 279–280, 282, 302, 329, 340, 361, 393–394
galaxies, 65, 143, 149, 151–152, 156, 160–163, 188, 193, 346, 391
genealogies, 10, 18, 128, 137, 287–289, 292–295, 320–321, 323, 329, 393–394
genealogies: gaps, 18, 34, 40, 289, 291–292, 294–295, 303, 393
Haak Bible, 125–126
Hebrew: Ross's ignorance of, 14, 254
Ice Age, 234, 267, 283–284
inerrancy, biblical, 37–38, 50, 56–57, 78, 89, 137, 139, 240, 297
inerrancy, biblical: applies to original autographs, 37, 295, 297
Inerrancy, Biblical, Chicago Statement of, 29, 37–38, 41, 47, 49–50, 56–57, 124, 150, 181, 296–298, 311, 370
inflation model, 158–159, 181–182
information, genetic, 15, 18, 30, 40–41, 46, 59, 61, 64, 120, 134, 154, 166, 212–213, 225, 227–230, 233–240, 252, 273, 291–292, 300, 303, 329, 338, 372, 381, 392
interpretation, facts versus, 41
interpretation (biblical) hermeneutics, 37–38, 41, 47, 50, 61, 68, 78, 89, 101, 135, 209, 240, 389
interpretation (biblical), hermeneutics grammatical historical method, 40, 389
figurative, 68, 70, 121, 136
isochron dating, 379–381, 383
Kalām cosmological argument, 179, 183
kinds, created, 350, 352–353
Kuiper Belt, 350, 352–353

lamination, 368–369, 375
light travel time problems, 65–66, 158
light travel time problems
distant starlight, 39, 189–190, 391–392
light created in transit fallacy, 189
horizon problem, same problem for big-bangers, 157–159, 186, 391
long-age words, absence in Genesis, 9–10, 17–18, 35, 55–56, 64, 94, 107, 132–133, 136, 138–139, 141, 204, 208, 218–219, 222, 308, 320–321, 325, 333, 338, 353, 366, 374, 376, 389–390, 392
mankind
Adam, antiquity of, 10, 15, 18–19, 26, 30, 34, 44, 57, 66, 71–72, 83, 88–90, 93, 98, 101, 116–117, 119–120, 122, 127, 171, 190, 195, 197–205, 207–208, 213–219, 222–223, 248, 252–253, 281, 287, 289–292, 294, 296–299, 303–306, 308, 311, 313, 320–321, 325, 327, 329, 331, 367, 392–394
Australopithecines, 309–310
Homo erectus, 15, 19, 34, 306, 308–311, 318–320, 393
Homo sapiens, 306, 308, 310–314, 318–320
Homo sapiens idàltu, 311
Neandertals, 15, 19, 34, 305–307, 310–320, 393
Mercury, 171–172, 178, 208
moon, 64, 71, 84–86, 95–96, 111, 143–144, 175–178, 249, 353–355, 391
moon
origin, 18, 25–26, 28, 33, 43, 47, 50, 58, 64–66, 86, 97, 118, 120, 127, 147, 151, 154, 158–159, 162, 164–165, 168–169, 174–176, 178, 186, 195, 218, 228, 239–240, 256, 272–273, 301–303, 307–308, 310–311, 314, 320, 329, 350, 352–353, 371, 374, 390–392, 394

age, 9–10, 19, 42, 47, 66, 68–69, 79,
102, 109–110, 112–115, 121–122,
133, 135, 138–139, 160, 162–163,
170–171, 174, 192, 196, 218, 221,
234, 236, 238, 267, 282–284,
290–292, 295, 297, 301, 306,
312–313, 320, 324–325, 327, 329,
331, 333, 341–342, 344–346, 348,
351, 353–355, 357, 361, 364–367,
379–385, 387, 390, 394–395
nebular hypothesis, 147, 168–169, 172,
352
Neptune, 151, 171, 174, 352–353
Nicene Creed, 25, 108, 114
Oort cloud, 350, 352–353
pathogens and creation, 212
radiohalos, 358–359, 361–363, 382
radiometric dating, 19, 171, 177, 305, 313,
343, 353–354, 362–363, 365, 367,
376–379, 383, 385, 395
radiometric dating
accelerated decay, 381
anomalies, 384
assumptions, 157, 379
types of dating methods, 377
reformers, 23, 35, 37, 124, 139
ringing from a global flood? 278–279, 393
Rivers of Eden, 255, 364
scriptural geologists, 130, 132–133, 245,
247, 393
speciation, 18, 30, 225, 229, 232–233,
235–240, 274, 392–393
species definition, 51, 225, 230–232, 234,
239, 281, 392
stars, 13, 15, 23, 27, 31, 65, 84–86, 95–96,
111, 141–144, 149, 155–156, 158,
162–170, 178, 188, 190, 192, 327–
328, 346–347, 351–352, 391
stars
stellar evolution, 34, 164, 166–167
origin, 164–165

sun
axial tilt, 171
age, faint young sun paradox, 169–170
T-Tauri phase, 169, 178
thermodynamics not beginning at the Fall,
213
thermodynamics and "heat death," proof of
beginning of universe, 181
Uranus, 150, 171, 174
vapor canopy, 278, 280
varves, 19, 354, 367, 370
vegetarianism, 18, 31–32, 66, 195,
206–209, 212, 287, 392
vegetarianism
animals and humans created vegetarian,
206
humans vegetarian until after the Flood,
36, 55, 62, 71, 83, 94, 98–99, 101,
103, 105, 107, 109–110, 121–123,
141, 196, 200, 202, 204–205, 207,
215–216, 242, 244, 256, 269,
294–295, 298, 300, 390, 392
vegetarian animals in Restoration, 208
Venus, 171–173, 188
wayyiqtol (waw consecutive), 92, 100, 103
Westminster Confession, 125–126
yôm (Hebrew for "day"), 58, 67–71, 73–74,
76–79, 81–82, 102, 105, 116, 134,
145, 215, 325–328, 390

Name Index

Ambrose of Milan, 108, 113–114, 121
Ankerberg, John, 16, 24–25, 71, 73, 82, 143–144, 222, 235
Archer, Gleason, 23–24, 29, 57, 61, 73, 81–82, 89–90, 137, 143–144, 242, 288
Augustine of Hippo, 108–110, 113, 117–122, 180, 185, 197–198, 223, 244, 256, 322
Barr, James, 69, 81, 137, 289–290, 292
Basil of Caesarea, 86, 88–89, 97, 108–109, 112–113, 121
Batten, Don, 5, 28, 48, 113, 130, 232, 271, 283, 302, 369
Baumgardner, John, 5, 259–263, 337, 342, 382, 387
Berthault, Guy, 368–369, 375
Blocher, Henri, 58, 136
Blyth, Edward, 226
Boice, James Montgomery, 37, 57
Bonaventure, 179–180
Bontrager, Krista, 16, 46, 195–197, 201, 203, 207, 209, 212, 214–215, 221, 223, 343
Bretz, J Harlen, 267
Butcher, 13, 23, 27, 319
Calvin, John, 81, 84, 124–126, 198–199, 204–205, 244, 301
Chaffin, Eugene, 379–380, 382, 384
Copernicus, Nicolaus, 52–54, 124
Copleston, F.C., 179–180
Craig, William Lane, 49, 179, 181, 183, 185, 392
Davies, Paul, 159, 182–183, 346–347
Dobson, James, 24, 167, 248, 324
Draper, John William, 53, 55, 120
Ehrlich, Paul and Anne, 235, 279
Elbert, Paul, 81
Ellis, George, 148–149
Fairholme, George, 132, 257
Faulkner, Danny, 5, 14, 31, 51, 165, 170, 173–174, 178, 184, 351–353
Fields, Weston, 101
Fouts, David, 82

Fruchtenbaum, Arnold, 40, 216–217, 294–295
Galilei, Galileo, 53–55, 173, 177
Gamow, George, 154–155
Geisler, Norman, 37, 64, 220–221, 296, 392
Gould, Stephen Jay, 129, 226, 246–247, 258, 265, 267
Graham, Billy, 26, 219
Graves, David, 5, 327
Grigg, Russell, 5, 27, 55, 62, 68, 84–85, 90, 101, 186, 219, 228, 327
Guth, Alan, 158–159, 181–182
Hagopian, David, 23–24, 61, 110, 242
Halley, Edmond, 344, 350–351
Ham, Kenneth, 24, 26–28, 33, 45, 65–66, 98, 141, 218–219, 228, 245, 264, 294, 369
Harmon, Marg, 16, 343
Hartwig-Scherer, Sigrid, 310–311
Hasel, Gerhardt, 289, 292–294
Hawking, Stephen, 148, 162
Hayward, Alan, 75–76, 120, 123–124, 338, 367, 371, 374–376
Helweg, Otto, 82
Hovind, Kent, 16, 24, 71, 143, 222, 235
Hoyle, Fred, 52, 153, 186
Hubble, Edwin, 148, 151–152, 156, 167, 192
Hume, David, (18th-century biologist), 180
Hume, David (21st-century biologist), 210–211
Humphreys, Russell, 5, 28, 39, 156–157, 163, 173–174, 190–193, 324, 336–346, 350, 387
Hutton, James, 136, 226–227, 245–248
Irenaeus, 108, 116, 121–122
Josephus, Flavius, 108–112, 117, 121, 131, 244, 291–292, 296, 301
Kant, Immanuel, 168, 183
Kelly, Douglas, 5, 11, 28, 83, 135
Kepler, Johann, 53, 124, 129–131, 351

Kline, Meredith, 57–58, 95–96, 98–100, 136, 144

Kuhn, Thomas, 41, 150, 314

Kuiper, Gerald, 350, 352–353

Kulikovsky, Andrew, 23, 61, 68, 83–84, 90, 101, 110, 114

Lactantius, 108, 115, 121

Lakatos, 150–151

Laplace, Pièrre-Simon, 168

Leupold, H.C., 29, 81, 93, 102, 133, 135, 200, 241, 302

Luther, Martin, 23, 49, 81, 85, 123–125, 131, 216, 255

Lynn, Barry, 386

Malina, Bruce, 21–22, 40

Maniguet, Miche, 62, 83, 254

Marsh, Frank, 230–232

Martyr, Justin, 108, 116–117, 121, 244

Mayr, Ernst, 237–239

McKellar, Andrew, 155

Morris, Henry, 209, 244, 269, 278

Morris, John, 250, 374

Mortenson, Terry, 5, 56, 110, 130, 132, 245

Murray, John, 132–133

Nahigian, Kenneth, 48, 184

Newton, Isaac, 23, 53, 65, 129–130, 136, 150–151, 158, 170–171, 179, 342, 344, 353

Newton, Robert, 23, 53, 65, 129–130, 136, 150–151, 158, 170–171, 179, 342, 344, 353

Neyrey, Jerome, 22

Oort, Jan, 350, 352–353

Origen, 108, 117–118, 121–122

Pierce, Larry, 127–128, 247, 271

Popper, Sir Karl, 150–151

Pun, Pattle, 18, 57, 79

Rana, Fazale (Fuz), 16, 46, 195–197, 201, 203, 207, 209, 212, 214–215, 221, 223, 229–230, 232, 237, 273, 343

Rhind, William, 132–133

Rohrbaugh, Richard, 21–22, 40

Ross, Hugh, 13–20, 22–35, 37, 39–44, 46–48, 50–51, 56, 58–65, 67–73, 75–78, 81–83, 87–91, 93, 101, 105, 107–115, 117–119, 122, 126–130, 133, 135, 138–139, 141–145, 147–149, 158, 163, 167, 169–170, 175–176, 179, 181, 183–185, 189–190, 192, 195–198, 201–204, 207–210, 212, 214–216, 219–223, 225–226, 229–232, 235–237, 239–245, 248–257, 260, 263–280, 282–285, 287, 292–293, 295, 297–311, 313–314, 317–329, 333, 336, 338–339, 343–344, 350, 353, 358, 360–361, 364, 366–367, 369, 372–374, 376, 385–386, 389–394

Russell, Jeffrey Burton, 55, 120

Samples, Kenneth, 16, 46, 195–197, 201–203, 207, 209, 212, 214–216, 221, 223

Sarfati, Jonathan, 9–11, 13–14, 23–24, 26–30, 39, 45, 48–49, 71, 84, 124, 127, 143, 149–150, 153, 159, 165, 171, 179, 182, 217–218, 222–223, 235, 244, 264, 295, 309, 331, 333, 344, 346, 350, 353, 374

Scherer, Siegfried, 231, 234, 372

Shackelford, David, 82

Smith, John Pye, 245, 248, 269

Snelling, Andrew, 250, 258, 338, 342, 357, 361–362, 368, 375–376, 379–380, 382–387

Steinmann, Andrew, 77–78, 113

Strobel, Lee, 219–221

Swedenborg, Emanuel, 168

Tegmark, Max, 156–157, 187, 189

Templeton, Charles, 26, 195, 218–220, 392

Ussher, Archbishop James, 23, 127–131, 290

Vardiman, Larry, 343, 379–380, 382, 384

Walker, Tas, 5, 50, 131, 259, 272, 361–362, 364, 376, 380–381

Weeks, Noel, 46–47, 95, 97, 99
Wesley, John, 85, 130, 199, 204–206
Whitcomb, John, 71, 209, 244, 252, 269, 278
White, Andrew Dickson, 28, 53, 55, 120, 123, 163–164, 166, 168, 190–192, 244–245, 312, 350
Wieland, Carl, 5, 28, 45, 159, 162–163, 213, 218, 228–229, 231, 233, 237–238, 245, 265, 267, 273, 284, 300, 310, 313, 351, 355, 357, 372

Wiens, Roger, 16, 343, 376
Wilder-Smith, Arthur E., 186
Woodmorappe, John, 5, 236, 239, 243, 249–250, 270–272, 274–275, 278, 309, 318–319, 372–373, 375, 379, 381, 385–386
Young, Davis, 17, 110, 113–114, 144–146, 290–291, 391
Young, George, 132

Scripture Index

Genesis

1:1 101
1:1–2 135
1:2 ....101, 103
1:3 84
1:3–2:3 103
1:5 ....68, 69, 74, 77, 125, 126,
                                          133, 390
1:6–8 96
1:9 ....143, 393
1:10 96
1:11, 12, 21, 24, 25 225
1:12 100
1:14 ....69, 84, 96,190
1:14–19 ....96, 143
1:16 143
1:20 211
1:20–25 232
1:22 96
1:24 89
1:25 142
1:26–27 ....143, 232
1:27 ....101, 298
1:28 ....63, 90, 103, 197, 203, 253
1:29 ....207, 208
1:29–30 ....32, 66, 206, 208, 209,
                                          220, 287
1:31 ....102, 195, 198–200, 299
2:1–3 ....63, 83, 211
2:2 83
2:3 78
2:4 ....70, 71, 79, 91, 100
2:5 ....98, 99, 100
2:7 ....51, 142, 211
2:9 ....31, 88
2:10 255
2:13 255
2:14 255
2:15 89
2:17 ....71, 72, 116, 205
2:18 90
2:19 ....89, 91–93, 144
2:20 89

2:21 199
2:24 101
2:25 298
3:5 71
3:7 215
3:9–13 200
3:14–19 ....66, 200
3:15 ....62, 216
3:16 204
3:17–19 ....44, 203, 205, 207
3:19 ....201, 202, 205
3:21 215
3:22 202
3:22, 24 31
4:1 217
4:3–5 ....215, 217
4:23–24 95
4:25 ....294, 299
4:26 217
5:1 ....71, 72, 91
5:2 71
5:3 299
5:4, 7, 10 293
5:24 62
5:29 294
5:32 293
6–9 ....241, 252
6:3 ....271, 300
6:4 325
6:9 ....91, 196
6:18–22 257
6:19–20 275
6:20 282
7–8 243
7:11 261
7:12 261
7:19 ....241, 252
7:19–20 ....253, 254
7:20 243
7:21–22 252
7:22 275
7:23 257
8:1 257

GENESIS (cont.)

8:2.................................252, 261
8:4.................................262
8:4–5...............................255
8:5.................................125, 127
8:7.................................267
8:9–12..............................267
9:3.................................66, 207
9:6.................................209
9:11–16.............................243
9:21................................196
10:1................................91
10:19...............................98
10:25...............................301
11:1................................302
11:9................................20, 302
11:10...............................91, 294
11:11, 13, 17.......................293
11:12...............................295
11:26...............................292, 293
11:27...............................91
11:31...............................294
11:32...............................290
12:4................................290
12–50...............................100
14:19, 22...........................102
18:32...............................91
19:24...............................40
21:8................................71
24:16...............................196
25:12...............................91
25:19...............................91
26:1................................91
26:33...............................97
29:34–35............................88
30:30...............................88
30:36...............................74
32:32...............................97
37:2................................91
41:56...............................251
41:57...............................243
42:17–18............................80
46:30...............................88

EXODUS

4:11–12, 18.........................92
6:28................................72
9:25................................243
10:15...............................243
10:24–11:8..........................92
10:28...............................72
11:1................................92
11:1–3..............................92
12:29...............................126
16:12–13............................126
20:4................................307
20:8–11............31, 66, 72, 73, 87, 94,
                                  102, 287
20:25...............................307
21:28–29............................253
31:17...............................72
32:34...............................72
33:5................................118

LEVITICUS

17:11...............................211, 215
20:15–16............................253
23:15...............................127
23:32...............................127
25:3–4..............................73
25:43...............................203

NUMBERS

1:47–49.............................92
3:13................................126
7:10–84.............................71
8:17................................126
9:15................................81
14:7................................196
16:21...............................118
16:45...............................118
29:1................................125, 127
29:17, 20, 23, 26, 29, 32, 35.......77

DEUTERONOMY

2:10, 12, 20........................324
2:25................................243
6:4–9...............................37

16:4................................81
25:4................................36
29:5...............................214

Joshua
8:19, 28.........................253
10:12..............................124
11:10..............................324
11:11..............................253
14:15..............................324
15:15..............................324

Judges
1:10, 11, 23....................324
3:2.................................324
6:39................................90
11:1...............................294
15:3................................88
16:23...............................92
18:9...............................196

Ruth
2:3.................................92
4:7................................324

1 Samuel
9:9.................................324
18:11...............................92
30:12...............................80

2 Samuel
11:2...............................196
15:34..............................324

1 Kings
1:6................................196
2:11................................87
2:37................................72
4:24–25...........................203
10:24........................243, 251
18:27...............................20
20:29...............................80

2 Kings
19:15..............................102

1 Chronicles
1:34...............................294
1–9................................216
3:10–12............................292
4:40...............................324
5:37...............................294
6:11...............................294
8:9................................294
9:20...............................324
14:3...............................294

2 Chronicles
9:11...............................324
11:21..............................294
13:21..............................294
24:3...............................294

Ezra
9:8................................118

Nehemiah
13:5...............................324

Job
5:19................................75
7–19................................61
10:8–14.............................59
12:7................................59
17:6...............................324
19:25–27............................62
20:4..........................325, 327
23:12...............................61
34:14–15............................59
35:10–12............................59
37:5–7..............................59
37:10..............................283
38:22..............................283
38:39–41...........................209
38:4................................65
38–41...........................59, 62
39:27–30...........................209
40:15...............................16
40:17...............................16
42:11..............................324

PSALMS

16:8	52
19	60
19:1	163
19:1–2	94
19:1–4	59
19:7	60
24:3–4	94
46:5	81
51:5	50, 198
63:6	87
90:2–6	323
90:4	86, 87, 114, 115
93:1	52
102:25	324
104:7	95
104:11	95
104:21	209
119:148	87
121:2	102
139:1–18	327
139:24	327

PROVERBS

6:16	75
8:22–23	324
8:22–31	323
28:1	94
28:7	94
30:15	75
30:18	75

ECCLESIASTES

1:3–11	323, 324
1:5	51
2:16	62
4:1	62
7:15	62
9:5	62
12:13	62

ISAIAH

5:20	126
7:14	216
11:6–9	31, 32, 208

37:18–20	97
45:7	197
45:12–20	97
48:16	40
53:6	215
55:9	87
57:15	180
59:20	215
65:25	31, 32, 208

JEREMIAH

4:23	103
7:24	324
17:9	44, 198
17:9–10	208
22:15	92
24:2–3	196

EZEKIEL

28:11–19	197

DANIEL

4:23	79
7:25	79
8:1–14	82
8:26	81, 82
12:7	79

HOSEA

6:2	75
13:8	209

JOEL

2:32	26

AMOS

1:3	75

MICAH

5:2	325
6:2	323, 325
7:19	203

HABAKKUK
1:13 197
3:6 .... 323, 325

ZECHARIAH
14:1–6 74
14:7 74

MATTHEW
1:1–17 293
1:8–9 292
1:17 292
2:6 325
5:44 22
11:21 326
11:25 138
12:5 22
12:27 331
12:40 79
16:20 27
19:3–6 .... 101, 298
20:3, 6 126
21:23–27 21
22:15–22 21
23:27 20
24:37–39 243
27:63–64 80
28:1 127
28:16–20 395
28:18 251
29:1 125

MARK
9:48 288
10:6 .... 18, 36, 66, 287, 296
10:6–9 .... 101, 298
11:27–33 21
12:13–17 21
13:19 299
13:25 288
15:44 326
16:9 80

LUKE
2:1 .... 251, 252
3 101
3:1–2 77
3:35–38 296
8 101
8:10 101
10:7 36
10:13 326
11:50–51 299
13:1–4 218
17:26–27 .... 36, 66, 287
18:12 127
20:1–8 21
20:20–26 21
23:54 80
24:7 80

JOHN
1:1 40
1:1–3 325
1:1–14 .... 75, 298
1:1–18 40
1:12 40
1:14 40
1:17 40
1:18 40
1:3 40
2 99
2:24–25 251
3:12 36
3:16 36
4:20–21 289
5:17 83
5:18 75
7:14, 20 325
7:42 325
8:58 325
9 218
11:35 201
20:1 127

ACTS
3:21 31
3:21–22 208

ACTS (cont.)

5:38–39 25
15:6 27
17:10–11 37
17:11 ....19, 38, 288
17:26 214
20:27 22

ROMANS

1 ....60, 61
1:18 219
1:18–22 265
1:19–20 59
1:20 ....31, 265, 299
1:21 44
3:23 251
5:12 ....198, 201, 205
5:12–19 ....66, 200, 201, 287
7:15–25 198
8:20–22 ....44, 66 205, 208, 214,
                                      253, 287
10:9–13 26
10:13 61
16:17 22

1 CORINTHIANS

2:14 37
10:19–20 97
15 202
15:1–4 26
15:4 80
15:21 202
15:21–22, 45 26
15:21–22 ....36, 66, 200, 201,
                                      205, 287
15:21–23 201
15:22 204
15:26 201
15:45 ....120, 214
15:52 75
16:2 ....125, 127

2 CORINTHIANS

5:17 31
5:21 215
10:4–5 ....20, 331

GALATIANS

2:11 20

EPHESIANS

2:8 26
2:8–9 215
6:4 37

COLOSSIANS

1:15–17 63
1:16–17 203
1:17 214
2:16-17 73

1 THESSALONIANS

4:13 75

1 TIMOTHY

2:5 ....38, 214
2:11–14 101
2:13–14 198
5:18 36
6:16 202

2 TIMOTHY

3:15 39
3:15–17 ....27, 36, 44, 87
4:2 20

TITUS

2:13 75

HEBREWS

1:1 326
2:11–18 214
4:1–11 83
7:27 215
8:5 73
9:21 215

9:22..215
9:28..215
10:4..215
11..101, 217
11:1–2..216
11:6..46
13:8..332

2 PETER

1:9...326
2:3...326
3..251
3:3–6..265
3:3–7.............................66, 243, 287
3:4...298, 331
3:5...323, 326
3:8...114, 115
3:8–9..86
3:15–16..36
3:16..39

1 JOHN

1:5...197
2:19...219

JUDE

4..326
14..294

REVELATION

2:7...31
12:4...197
12:9...197
21:1...31
21:4...201
21:23..84
22:2...202
22:2,14,19..31
22:3...201
22:5..31, 199
22:18..59

For a free catalog of material supporting biblical creation, or for more information about what the Bible teaches, contact one of the Answers in Genesis Ministries below. Answers in Genesis Ministries are evangelical, Christ-centered, non-denominational, and non-profit.

Answers in Genesis
P.O. Box 6330
Florence, KY 41022
USA

Answers in Genesis
P.O. Box 6302
Acacia Ridge DC
QLD 4110
Australia

Answers in Genesis
5-420 Erb St. West
Suite 213
Waterloo, Ontario
N2L 6K6 Canada

Answers in Genesis
P.O. Box 39005
Howick 1730, Auckland
New Zealand

Answers in Geneis
P.O. Box 3349
Durbanville (Cape Town)
South Africa

Answers in Genesis
P.O. Box 5262
Leicester LE2 3XU
United Kingdom

website: <www.AnswersInGenesis.org>

In addition, you may contact:

Institute for Creation Research
P.O. Box 2667
El Cajon, CA 92021

ABOUT THE AUTHOR

J onathan D. Sarfati, Ph.D., F.M. was born in Ararat, Australia, in 1964. He moved to New Zealand as a child, where he later studied mathematics, geology, physics, and chemistry at Victoria University in Wellington. He obtained honors level in physical and inorganic chemistry, as well as in condensed matter physics and nuclear physics.

He received his Ph.D. in physical chemistry from the same institution in 1995 on the topic of spectroscopy, especially vibrational. He has co-authored various technical papers on such things as high temperature superconductors and sulfur and selenium-containing ring and cage molecules.

As well as being very interested in formal logic and philosophy, Dr. Sarfati is a keen chess player. He represented New Zealand in three Chess Olympiads and is a former New Zealand national chess champion. In 1988, F.I.D.E., the International Chess Federation, awarded him the title of F.I.D.E. Master (F.M.).

A Christian since 1984, he was for some years on the editorial committee of *Apologia*, the journal of the Wellington Christian Apologetics Society, of which he was a co-founder.

Dr. Sarfati currently works full time for Answers in Genesis in Brisbane, Australia, a non-profit ministry, as a research scientist and editorial consultant for *Creation Ex Nihilo* family magazine and the associated *Technical Journal*, and has written many articles for both. He also contributes to the Answers in Genesis Internet website. He is the author of *Refuting Evolution* and *Refuting Evolution 2*.